CW00498053

KEATING

— THE INSIDE STORY —

For Deborah

KEATING

THE INSIDE STORY

JOHN EDWARDS

VIKING

Penguin Books Australia Ltd
487 Maroondah Highway, PO Box 257
Ringwood, Victoria 3134, Australia
Penguin Books Ltd
Harmondsworth, Middlesex, England
Viking Penguin, A Division of Penguin Books USA Inc.
375 Hudson Street, New York, New York 10014, USA
Penguin Books Canada Limited
10 Alcorn Avenue, Toronto, Ontario, Canada M4V 3B2
Penguin Books (NZ) Ltd
182–190 Wairau Road, Auckland 10, New Zealand

First published by Penguin Books Australia 1996

10 9 8 7 6 5 4 3 2 1

Typeset in 13/15 pt Centaur by Post Typesetters, Brisbane, Qld
Made and printed in Australia by Australian Print Group,
Maryborough, Victoria

National Library of Australia
Cataloguing-in-Publication data:

Edwards, John (John Ker).
    Keating: the inside story.

    Includes index.
    ISBN 0 670 82028 8.

    1. Keating, Paul, 1944– . 2. Australia Labor Party – History
    – 20th century. 3. Politicians – Australia – Biography.
    4. Prime ministers – Australia – Biography. 5. Australia –
    Politics and government – 1976–1990. 6. Australia – Politics
    and government – 1990– . I. Title.

    994.063092

Every effort has been made to trace copyright holders of
photographs. The publishers would like to hear from any
copyright holder not acknowledged.

CONTENTS

ACKNOWLEDGMENTS

Without Paul Keating's invitation to collect material for this book while working as an economic adviser on his staff, it could not have been written. To this decision it owes its uniqueness as a narrative built on the documentary record, his own recollections, and my experience in his office.

Other than Keating himself, I am also indebted to the kindness of a great many individuals who in one way or another participated in or observed the events described, and who generously offered me their views or comments. In many instances these discussions or interviews are indicated in the text.

Professor Graeme Snooks of the Economic History Department of the ANU's Research School of Social Sciences provided both a temporary home for the Keating files, and an office for me. Over the course of researching and writing, I found the congenial atmosphere of the school and the interest of my colleagues sustaining and encouraging. Graeme's counsel was always wise, and the example he set as a scholar and writer has been inspiring.

Under the vigorous guidance of Publishing Director Robert Sessions, Penguin assigned a relay race of editors to this project, which was not without its problems. Meredith Rose and then Linda Ristow suggested many improvements to early drafts. Kerry Biram carried it through the difficult detailed work from a near final draft to published book. Cathryn Game meticulously proofed the galleys.

To all of them I am indebted for their professional skills and commitment.

I am grateful indeed for the work of the librarian of the Horrie Brown Library in Economic History in the RSSS, Barry Howarth, who detected and corrected many errors in earlier drafts of the manuscript, and compiled the index for the book. Throughout the project he was an unfailing source of encouragement.

Rod Cavalier, Bob Hope and John Nethercote were kind enough to read drafts at various stages and make extensive comments. The finished book is very greatly improved by their comments and corrections, and I am deeply grateful to each of them.

The warmth and welcome of my ANU office owed a great deal to the staff of the department – Barbara Trewin, Anne Howarth and Jeannie Haxell – who encouraged me to believe that the tasks would one day be finished and the book written. Wayne Naughton, also located in Economic History, kindly solved a number of software problems and kept the computer and printer working.

Writing in Sydney during 1994 and 1995 I found the interest shown by colleagues at Macquarie Bank, where I was working part of my time, sustained my own interest long after it might otherwise have failed. I wish to thank David Clark, Mark Johnson and Alan Moss for a number of interesting conversations about the 1980s and financial markets, which in one way or another influenced my thinking about the period.

Apart from the two years of writing there were many years of preparation for the book, during which a number of friends helped me sort out ideas. At different times Tony Abbot, Malcolm Johnston, Ian Marsh and Stephen Vaughan each gave me the confidence to keep going.

For all my colleagues in the Treasurer's Office in 1991 and the Prime Minister's Office from 1992 to 1994 I retain the highest regard and goodwill. Few of us, I think, will again share such exciting experiences in pursuit of a good cause.

My understanding of the policy processes in Canberra developed very greatly as a result of working daily with officials of the Treasury and then the Department of Prime Minister and Cabinet. I found the quality of officers in these departments to be of the highest order.

Much of the writing of the book took place at the ANU's University House – an environment so well designed and so well staffed it seems to improve the quality of any work.

Jill Hickson was an excellent agent for the book, and offered good counsel when the need arose.

Most of the burden of my absences and preoccupation fell on my wife, Deborah Hope, and sons Alex and Harry. To them, no sufficient acknowledgment is possible.

PREFACE

At 12.40 a.m. on the morning of Friday 10 November 1990, Treasurer Paul Keating called me in my Canberra hotel room. I was in the city seeking an interview with him for a book I was writing about his career. He was quite happy to talk to me, he said, but what was the point? In the time available, how much could he really tell me about the last eight years, of the great policy debates, the Cabinet battles, the key decisions, the struggles to shape Australia's destiny? In any one interview how much could he convey about how it all worked, how he related to Cabinet and the Prime Minister, the 'official family' of the Treasury and the Reserve Bank, and his own office? If I really wanted to know how it all worked, he said, I should come and work for him. That was the way to do it. He knew I had recently completed a doctorate in economics, and that I would soon be returning to Australia from Washington. Why not come and see how the text books related to the real world? I could write what I liked, but at least I would know how it actually worked.

Accepting the offer, I began early in 1991. I found him as good as his word. I did see what I wanted and hear what I pleased. The whole treasure trove of documents of the 1980s was opened to me. I was also writing speeches, interpreting statistics, sitting down with his other staff members on the lounges in his office on afternoons before Question Time, going through the possible questions, and joining them again for his re-enactments of the debates when he returned, exhausted and excited, from Cabinet. Keating asked me to take an interest in wages policy, which took me to the heart of the government because it formed the intersection of his relationship with ACTU Secretary Bill Kelty and with the Prime Minister, Bob Hawke.

He was right, of course. It was the way to see it, to understand it, to get some idea of what the man I had known slightly for twenty years had now become, of how he worked and how the Australian Government worked. As the months went by Keating himself became more and more interesting to me. He was charming, funny, intelligent, alive; and he communicated clearly whatever he was at any time.

Within a few months of my starting work with him, it became apparent that he was determined to challenge Hawke for the leadership before the August 1991 Budget. When he and his staff left the Treasurer's office following his defeat in June, I took the entire collection of his personal office files, covering eight years, over to the Australian National University's Research School of Social Sciences. It comprised ten four-drawer filing cabinets and a Compactus file – some thousands of documents, which together filled the back room of the Horrie Brown Library in the Economic History Department. Accepting a kind offer from Professor Graeme Snooks of a visiting fellowship in the department, I commenced seven months of intensive research into the records.

When Keating returned to office as Prime Minister, he invited me to rejoin him as an economic adviser. Though I was endlessly busy with One Nation and then a succession of other economic statements, with the battle against the alternative vision of John Hewson, with the trade aspects of APEC and with the Accord and industrial relations, I also found time to continue to fill notebooks and computer disks with records of his style, method and key decisions. At no point did he express anything other than interest in and enthusiasm for what he clearly regarded as a useful project. At no point then or later did he seek any right to excise material. He did not even ask to review the material before it was published, though I was very glad and grateful that he ultimately found time to read it in manuscript and make many valuable suggestions for its improvement.

What emerges, for all the shortcomings and omissions inevitable in producing a timely account of so vast a subject as Paul Keating's entire career, is a contemporary account of how Australia is actually governed that has been written with access to the official record, with personal experience and observation from the inside of all the main actors and many of the main episodes, and from the unparalleled viewpoint of both the Treasurer's office and the Prime Minister's office – the two most influential posts in Australia.

Though he has in every way most generously facilitated the writing of this account and made himself available for the hours of interview and conversation that inform the narrative, it would be quite wrong to place on Keating any responsibility for its content. There are many conclusions with which he disagrees, exchanges and episodes involving others that he believes might better have been left unrecorded, and judgments that he disputes. Ultimately, I hope, he will tell his own story in his own way.

PART I

THE MAKING OF
A POLITICIAN

WHERE IT
ALL BEGAN

JIMMY WARNER DROVE PAUL AND ANNITA on that bright September morning in 1993, the tyres softly thudding on the road from the Lodge to Fairbairn Air Force Base and Jimmy mildly making fun of them as he had since Paul had been appointed Treasurer of the Commonwealth of Australia and Jimmy his driver for more than a decade before. Still sometimes called Chookie Warner in his home town of Queanbeyan where his parents had run a chicken farm, Jimmy had become almost a more familiar figure and constant presence to the Keating girls than their own father – sufficiently so at least to sometimes brush Katherine's hair or to sign Caroline into Brownie camp and feel a parental pang as she trotted happily off. A kindly, sardonic, irreverent man who loved golf and horses, Jimmy would comment, when it was observed to him that Queanbeyan was really very pleasant compared to other towns, that he wouldn't know, since he had never lived in any other.

Now in his sixties, with fierce eyebrows and the spreading belly and humped shoulders of the lifelong driver, Jimmy had sat patiently night after night, year after year around the cramped Treasurer's office in the old Parliament House, and later in the bigger, grander office of the Treasurer and Deputy Prime Minister just across the Japanese courtyard from the Prime Minister's in the new Parliament House. He had driven out for pizzas and chicken curries during the long sessions when the Budget statements were drafted and redrafted, sitting watching the television, a pencilled racing guide lying under one large, flat palm, while the office buzzed around him and the smell of oil and garlic on cardboard and of curry settled over the filing cabinets and papers. He had waited until finally, around two or three in the morning, Paul would finish up and the Most Secret Budget papers, hatched across with almost unreadable revisions and outraged exclamations, would be dumped back in the bottom tray of a combination safe and Jimmy would walk out with him to the car and climb behind the wheel, Paul sitting beside him, already talking.

They would drive off, talking of the speed and handling of different cars or of the following day's schedule with the kids and Annita, or crossly disputing Paul's new and suddenly insistent idea of a quicker way to get home, until Jimmy might finally and gruffly say, with an edge of real irritation, that since he was driving the fucking car, mate, he would decide how to fucking get there, his employer then perhaps perfunctorily surrendering and turning almost without break to a rapid and indignant account of the low and ungrateful way he had been treated that day by the press gallery upstairs or by him across the courtyard, despite all he had done to enlighten them or help him, on this and all other days, so much so you could nearly weep, you had to wonder, what was the point, Jimmy not really listening now, thinking about something else entirely but occasionally punctuating yes . . . yes, mate . . . yes.

Driving him for more than a decade during which the country and its Treasurer had been through a long boom and a long bust and now a slow recovery. It was a time of which Keating claimed that he, personally, by the decisions he took and persuaded his often reluctant colleagues and then the country to accept, had changed Australia in important and perhaps enduring ways. More than a decade, during which he had not only delivered eighteen major Budget statements and uncountable speeches and press conferences but also participated in four national election victories and finally, only six months before, won one himself against all prediction including (very often) his own. And in that whole time only six months when he had been relieved – and not as his preferred choice – of the public celebrity and private tedium, the busyness, of high ministerial office, and then only to spend his time (not enough to please his supporters, who were astonished and perturbed by his pleasure in being out of office) tearing down the Prime Minister he would replace.

It was a decade in which Australia changed from a high inflation to a low inflation country, from what Paul called an industrial museum to one in which many manufactured products were competitive with those of other nations. A country in which labour strikes were becoming unusual, where tariffs were low and falling. A country above all where people were beginning to feel that change was ordinary. A decade in which living standards did not improve much, in which foreign debt and unemployment both rose, raising the question of whether the good outweighed the bad, whether in fact the good and bad were inseparable parts of the same change. And whether they were or they weren't there was anyway a question of whether they would have happened at much the same time in much the same way whether or not Keating had been Treasurer, either because they were inevitable under any government, or because Bob Hawke and other ministers would have done them if Keating had not, or because Bob Hawke and other ministers actually did them despite Keating's objection. These were questions to which Paul had clear and definite answers – the good vastly outweighed the bad, it was his doing, and wouldn't have happened without him – and on which his place in the brief history of the Australian Commonwealth would depend.

A decade in which the baby boomers reached middle age, in which a million Australians died and two and half million were born, in which governments came and went in other countries, in which people changed jobs or spouses or cities, completed or abandoned long projects, in which so much changed. Through it all Keating had remained as Treasurer and then as Prime Minister, through four heads of Treasury, two governors of the Reserve Bank, five heads of his own office, innumerable changes among his ministerial colleagues and his staff, and four changes in the leadership of the Opposition so far and pretty clearly more to come, as well as one Prime Minister.

A decade that developed in the strangest and most unpredictable ways so that he was always learning, always, as Don Russell said, trying to stay on his board although the immense and quirky wave on which he rode towered over and seemed at any number of moments about to toss him into the foam, always tottering and then regaining his balance by changing in subtle but cumulative ways the story he told about himself, about Australia, about why things were as they were, about what had been and what would be.

What began in 1983 as three or — conceivably — six years in high office had stretched out as middle age itself stretched out to become ten and now eleven and thirteen by the next election after which, win or lose, he could finally quit, draw his superannuation, pay off his debts, and begin something new. Thirteen years of the highest or the second highest public office in the country, almost exactly half of what by the time of the next election would be twenty-six years as a paid politician.

Although of course he had been changing too, from the slim confident bright man not yet 40 with three children under 8 when Jimmy first picked him up on the Senate side of the old Parliament House in March 1983, to the perplexed and fatigued veteran running on habit and will, substituting experience and guile for energy, now with two teenagers and two younger children. Although still owning the same huge half-renovated and unliveable terrace home in Sydney, with the tiny new kitchen, the new courtyard, reception rooms partly restored and redecorated in detail to his design, but all stopped and closed up years ago when the scale of the things proved just too immense and the piggery sucked up all his cash, suspended with some of it done grandly and the rest of it not much changed from the rooming house it had been; and now as then the same clocks, the same Empire statues and cabinets, the same old Mercedes coupé, the cufflinks he had not yet lost.

Cabinet in 1983 had followed fourteen years of apprenticeship in federal parliament and another half dozen before that in the Labor Party in Sydney, so that, although he was not yet 50, he already had thirty years of political experience behind him, experience that formed

habits and responses now so automatic and complex that not even
he could trace their origins. He had been in it so long he had seen
the same issues recur, the arguments, the judgements – even the people and their views come round again and again, although the detail
of their faces and names changed from year to year. As Neville Wran
remarked over coffee on the verandah at Kirribilli, with the authority and ease of an older man who had lasted as long as Premier of
New South Wales as Paul had as Treasurer and now Prime Minister, the worst thing about being what you might call a success in politics over a long period was that after a while the same fucking issues
were always coming up in the same fucking way. A remark that amused
Paul in his slightly clumsy way, looking at Neville while he was laughing to check it was a joke and that he was laughing at the right bit,
because somehow his sense of humour, fine as it was at a point, did
not run quite the full range.

A career so long and including so many of the key episodes of
Australia's recent political history that his story was not only part of
the story of his own generation, the generation born in the last years
of or just after World War II, but also part of Australia's story, of
a country's transformation so rapid and far-reaching that Australians
who had left and lived overseas for some years came back to find the
country not hostile but puzzlingly different, the tales they told overseas no longer fitting, their expectations no longer quite met, their
own clothes and manner and modes of address, their sense of what
Australia was all about, now a little quaint and off centre, reminding their listeners of Australia as it had once been, when they were
younger. Keating had been formed by this change, by the mushrooming
growth of the outer suburbs of the cities, by his father's business
struggles, by the battles with the Left of the Labor Party at a time
when Communism and Catholicism were real issues, by the Vietnam
War, the OPEC oil price increases, the collapse of the Whitlam Government, the aimlessness of the Fraser years. He had been formed
by it as a child and a young man, and then he himself had influenced
it with the float of the dollar, the deregulation of Australian finance,
the substantial end of tariff protection and the tilt to Asia, so that

now in his fiftieth year he embodied a good bit of the country's history.

It had been long enough for most of Jimmy's contemporaries to take redundancy or early retirement to brick villas on the coast, with a boat and a local golf course and a club. Long enough for the whole Commonwealth car fleet to shrink under the pressure of spending cuts, so that now Jimmy was one of the elders of the service, resisting with gruffness and subterfuge the new requirements that a driver should not only be able to keep in motorcade formation and drive coolly at high speeds, to control the car in skids and be courteous and discreet, at least when necessary, but also deal deftly with terrorists in unarmed combat, a test Jimmy was reluctant to take, he said offhandedly, because it would likely be bad for his back.

Jimmy had worked for Paul even when he (briefly) wasn't working for him, during the six months after the first, unsuccessful challenge to Hawke when Paul was a backbencher. Driving other Labor backbenchers he would with certain of them chuckle and nod and lead the conversation along until he could ask, in the most offhand tone, how the backbencher intended to vote when Hawke was once again challenged by Keating, a query that – coming from whom it came, and particularly in the casual chuckling manner in which it was posed – would have triggered a terrible alarm in the mind of the backbencher, who would respond, in the same casual and chuckling manner, with whatever he wanted Paul Keating to hear on his phone that night in the television room of his rented house in Beagle Street, Red Hill, sitting on the worn divan that Annita had long wanted to replace, amid the piled jumble of kids' videos.

More than a decade with this man whom he admired and whose company he enjoyed and for whom he felt affection and loyalty, but who puzzled him as he had eleven years before. Puzzling that a man with so much authority and speed of decision, so much knowledge and charm and influence, could also contain such a bewildering collection of interests and prejudices. Puzzling that the man who could confidently draw the big picture for his former leader and Prime Minister, and who would within a few days draw the big picture for the President of the United States, would also (for a time, until he wearied of it) have a glass of dark and strange Chinese herbal medicine served to him in the early evening by Guy, the butler and Jimmy's friend. Puzzling that he would talk about 'kidney energy', frequently visit a herbalist in Canberra, and read his own pulse with tender interest. More puzzling still that he had once set up a trampoline (for a time, until he also wearied of that) in the back garden of the Beagle Street house, not only because the girls wanted to jump on it but also because he himself wished to jump and believed – quite seriously believed, and would explain so in the calmest tones, as if explaining the world's roundness – that the few moments of perfect stillness at the apex of a jump, those few moments when you had risen as high as you would but not yet begun to fall, when your blood, bones and organs were suspended momentarily in space, were the moments when any cancer cells in your body would be annihilated.

Jimmy was often beguiled by the variety and unexpectedness of life. As if conferring on his son a reasonable, easy attitude to life, Jimmy's father had sent his mother by train to Sydney for the birth, and himself come up with the horse and sulky, stopping off to hunt and fish at Paddy's River and arriving finally at the Crown Street hospital to find Jimmy a happy healthy child, already a week old. Jimmy had been a star in the first grade of the Queanbeyan Whites football team and acquired an easy banter. For the first fifteen years of his working life he had held the Queanbeyan garbage contract. Seated on the dray behind his horse, he observed, pondered. These days he was a member of a golfing trio in which his partners were a clergyman of Calvinist leanings and the retired proprietor of a two-up school, and they would often ponder life's ironies while refreshing themselves after a game. In a full and varied life Jimmy had come to know many of life's unusual aspects, but Paul was something else entirely.

Jimmy found it interesting that a man could be so successful with so many unusual and chronic maladies. He knew that Paul rarely had a waking moment when he was not aware of ringing in his ears, an inescapable affliction all the more tormenting because it could not be seen or heard by anyone else or remedied by any medicine, Western or Oriental. Jimmy knew that since a boyhood disease the tear ducts in Paul's eyes had not worked properly, so that after a short spell of reading his eyes were sore and irritated, a problem he still sometimes palliated by licking his fingers and wetting his eyelid with saliva.

Then there was his back, which would go suddenly and without warning, as for example when he was out in Laurie Brereton's motorboat in Sydney Harbour in January of that year, 1993. Laurie had been standing in front gunning the boat at full throttle, the Prime Minister on a seat behind, and the boat had smacked into the wash of a passing ship with such violence that Keating was driven down onto his bench and up off it again, wrenching the bones of his back into the surrounding nerves and muscles with a sudden pain so disabling that, now white and speechless with agony, he could only lean sideways to incline his lolling head with aghast eyes and gasping mouth into the rush of air at the side of the boat, Laurie still watching ahead and laughing with excitement as the wash of another ship rippled towards them.

His back would go and each time it would be put back in place and soothed by the acupuncturist who was now nearly as close to the Keating family as Laurie Brereton himself, and for a few days afterwards the Prime Minister would either sit uncomfortably through his meetings on a straight-backed chair, or roam around the room with one hand tucked into the small of his back and one eye on the television news while his guests sat formally and made their pitch as best they could.

Then there was the angle of the lighting, which was never quite right for his eyes and which his staff were now accustomed to agree was, yes, shining right into their eyes, the Prime Minister groaning as he held a hand over his eyes in the Cabinet room as though he were gazing east into the morning sun off the Far North Queensland coast. There was the air conditioning, which was not quite warm enough or quite cool enough or which set up mysterious draughts and which his assistants had also become accustomed to agree was, yes, very hot indeed, or, yes, much too cool, or yes, very draughty, depending on the sudden and intense conviction of the Prime Minister at any point in a meeting, the staff knowing that only through prompt and sympathetic agreement could they minimise the necessary discussion of the peculiarities of light and temperature and air movement and their effect on the health and well-being of the Prime Minister and bring his attention back to essential points on which his guidance or imprimatur were required and on which their own well-being and comfort for the following week would depend.

Jimmy found it puzzling that Paul could combine so many strengths with such unexpected weaknesses, such free fall moments of political terror when, more often than not through his own doing, the ground would open up and he would plunge in headlong. Jimmy still recalled the day Paul mentioned off-handedly that he had a problem in relation to his tax return, the problem being that he hadn't actually lodged it a year after the due date and the letter from the Tax Office drawing this to his attention was in the hands of the Opposition Treasury spokesman Jim Carlton, whom Keating had teased and mocked as 'Rosie' Carlton till the good man's kindliness was almost exhausted. It was a disclosure to which Jimmy had heartily responded by saying with a laugh that too right Paul had a fucking problem, marvelling again that this connoisseur of political trade craft, no one's fool, and the one man in the entire country apart perhaps from the Commissioner himself who could have been expected to be wary enough at least to get this right, at least to file his own return, at least get his own money back, had let it slip month by month, because the Treasurer of the Commonwealth of Australia, like everyone else, found it a pain to add up his income and his deductions and put them down on a piece of paper.

Other politicians Jimmy knew were interested in golf, their gardens, or in race horses or in wines, on all of which Jimmy was well informed and could offer commentary and opinion. But Paul's interests were quite another thing, and Jimmy was still unsure, after eleven years, that he yet understood their full range. He shared with Paul an interest in classical music, particularly in the composers Mozart, Strauss, Beethoven and Liszt. He had introduced Paul to study of the bird life of Canberra, and now listened with pride as Paul explained to visiting dignitaries the names and habits of the brightly coloured parrots they saw flying by the road. He could talk about cars, of course, at least affect an interest in the grace and cleverness of the Mercedes Benz ball-bearings, of the classic engineering of the car itself, though even Jimmy's range and depth and understanding of motor vehicles did not match Paul's, who could and did take a Mercedes or E-type Jaguar engine to pieces and rebuild it as a diversion from his duties as Treasurer. He now knew a little about Empire clocks and ormolu statues and antique polished timber cabinets, if only because Paul talked about them so familiarly and with such nagging concern as to their safety from thieves, playing children, and careless cleaners. He even knew about the vases that Paul was trying to persuade the Australian National Gallery to purchase – wonderful acquisitions, he said, which could never be made by curators because curators liked being in the zoo and were never willing, as he was, to hunt in the jungle.

But that was only the beginning. There was the former convent in his own home town of Queanbeyan that Keating had persuaded his friend, the pianist Geoffrey Tozer, to buy as a residence and music school, arranging the finance and directing its renovation as a nineteenth-century brick building with high spacious rooms and long wide corridors, choosing the wonderful shades of green and pink in which it was painted, and arguing on the telephone in precise and detailed terms with carpenters and painters ('. . . no mate, no blue, *no* blue, I said *no* blue . . .') while the assistants gathered in his room glanced at each other and wondered whether he would be able to get across the remaining new issues in the few minutes still left before Question Time. A wonderful although perhaps impractically large house, one worthy, Paul said, of Tozer's talents, although Jimmy wondered quite how a celebrated music school might go in his native town and was not completely surprised, certainly not as baffled as his employer, when the pianist, soon after being presented with this building, sold it, green and pink rooms, long wide corridors, mortgage, and all.

There was architecture and decoration, there were cars and antiques and buildings and music now, and behind that, he knew, a long

succession of interests from budgerigars to sailing to flying to rock
music to real estate – not counting politics in which, as a matter a
fact, his interest had long since peaked.

His interests were unusual, and so were his friends. Other politicians talked to other politicians. When they became important they
talked to other important people. But the people Jimmy took Paul to
visit in Canberra, or whom Paul told him about, were often not politicians and often not important. There was Tozer, who seemed almost
a reluctant beneficiary of the Prime Minister's enthusiasm, almost as
if he preferred the obscurity of his quiet failure before Keating redis-
covered him, the pianist who had been such a prodigy in his youth,
as his son Patrick's music teacher, to the responsibility of having the
Treasurer of the Commonwealth of Australia driving down to persuade the chief executives of Chandos in London to make a CD of
Tozer's rendition of the Russian composer Nicholas Medtner as he
had once persuaded EMI in Australia to record some songs by the
Ramrods, and then attempting to create for him the school and residence that would cherish his talents and place him in a beautiful setting for music, the kind of setting that Paul himself imagined would
be appropriate were he himself to have become a musician, a possibility never explored in his youth. There was Ross Gengos, the owner
of a classical music store in Canberra, who would on a Sunday morning play for Paul five different versions of the first movement of Mahler's
Eighth, for example, to illustrate the qualities of different conductors and orchestras and recording engineers. For a long time his closest friend was the builder and developer Warren Anderson, a man with
Keating's intelligence and ambition but in a different field, a quite fear-
less larrikin who could knock down a quarrelsome contractor and himself take control of a huge dozer clearing scrub on his Central Australian
beef property. Paul liked to recall the time Anderson had bought a
Regency table in London, and the dealer called to apologise because
it had now been requested by Buckingham Palace for Charles and Diana
and regrettably the sale to Anderson was now cancelled, to which Anderson responded with a famously trenchant solicitor's letter, which secured
him the table. It was a perfect match. He was sometimes a dope – why

he wanted to import a herd of elephants for his beef property, for example, was hard to fathom — but never dull. Like Keating, he was interested in houses and antiques and prints, in clear old things, readily understood. The relationship flourished because, like Holmes à Court, Anderson pursued similar interests but in a larger way. Keating wasn't interested in his gun collection, but he did envy the Gould print plates, the noble house in Sydney's eastern suburbs, the rural retreats, so that when Anderson's property projects began to sour Keating was concerned and sympathetic, although the developer must sometimes have wondered at the value of this sympathy and concern from Keating the friend while Keating the Treasurer continued, month by month, to tighten the interest rate screws that were tearing apart just such developers as Warren Anderson. (Because while Anderson was building on borrowed money Paul was walking from the Reserve Bank Building into Sydney's Martin Place, cheerfully telling his adviser Don Russell, tall and wryly smiling, that together they had done more that day, with another interest rate increase, to de-spiv Australia than any two people since Federation.)

Whatever else Warren Anderson was, he was not an establishment figure, not part of a network of directors and chief executive officers of banks and big corporations. Before Anderson there had been in the 1970s Larry Hartnett, the former chief of General Motors-Holden (General Motors had sacked him, an episode that still rankled when Keating met him decades later), the perennially unsuccessful but unvanquished developer Sid Londish, then in a more conventional period the big miners and industrialists Jim Foots and Ian McLennan, then Packer, Murdoch and Holmes à Court during a period when he was pulling strings all over the country, then Warren and of course Leo Schofield and friends from the antiques trade, and then nobody very special except, say, the acupuncturist, and an old mate from the cement game who had done well. But never really the obvious and expected crowd and never, for very long, anyone who wanted to know him simply because he was Treasurer and then Prime Minister.

In Canberra, the Keatings had run out of interesting possibilities long ago. For a while, Bob and Hazel Hawke and Annita and

Paul had almost haunted each other, so great was the conjunction of their mutual needs and interests, but that had faded a long while before it became outright hostility and dislike. And of course they had kids. These days Ros Kelly and David Morgan came over every couple of Saturdays for a swim and an early dinner with the children around the pool. There were some family visits, occasionally Bill Kelty might come to dinner, or Laurie Brereton, or perhaps another minister or a difficult backbencher. Sometimes there would be business people, and the staff from his office would often visit with papers and problems, but Keating was by no means gregarious. Other than his family, he was closest to his staff, but only occasionally would he find a staff member sufficiently different from himself and sufficiently talented in areas in which he was not to be of real interest, and he couldn't really be good friends with one staff member without upsetting the rest.

(It was quite difficult, for that matter, to have friends at all without upsetting the rest. Only the day before his closest political friend for more than a quarter of a century, Industrial Relations Minister Laurie Brereton, had been negotiating with the Prime Minister's single most important and unwaveringly loyal political ally, ACTU Secretary Bill Kelty. They were in what had become an unpleasantly public dispute over the monopoly of the trade unions to conduct enterprise bargains, and this difficult meeting between his two closest political associates had concluded with Kelty asking Brereton, in that low and insistent tone, a ragged whine, echoed for emphasis, in which Kelty expressed his most lethal remarks, whether he was a fool or an habitual liar, because he must be one or the other, a choice that Brereton coolly declined to make and which left the minister all the more convinced that Kelty was unreasonable and strange beyond even his extensive experience of unusual negotiating techniques, and Kelty all the more convinced that Brereton was perhaps strong but certainly not smart. Paul liked and admired Kelty, but he went so far back with Brereton he could remember the two of them driving to Newcastle in a derelict car with no windscreen and otherwise so open and ramshackle that a snake Laurie had for some reason caught somehow wrapped itself around the neck of Brereton, who was driving; and remember too the occasion more than a quarter of a century ago when Laurie had ridden off on his motorcycle at 2 a.m. to rouse the returning officer in a vote dispute during Keating's closely contested pre-selection for the seat of Blaxland, a pre-selection that was the foundation of his political career.)

Jimmy would never say so, but Paul's habits were as unusual as were his friends. Most ministers Jimmy had known came to the office at nine or earlier and spent most of the day signing things. They ate in Parliament House and waited to be driven back to their hotel or apartment after Parliament rose late at night. Paul was different. Bill Kelty, visiting him at the Lodge at 9 a.m., might find him still in his pyjamas. On an exceptional day, perhaps when a foreign leader was visiting, he might arrive at eight or nine, but it was more usual for him to call Jimmy between ten and eleven, say, have a couple of meetings and then prepare for Question Time while having lunch in his room. There would be more meetings after Question Time and then, often, during the middle of the week, long Cabinet sessions, beginning with a meeting with a couple of advisers in his office, then perhaps with a couple of ministers, again in his office, then the full Cabinet for arduous and protracted sessions that as often as not would extend far into the night and sometimes into the following morning, the notetakers relaying in and out and the secretaries in the Cabinet room recording decisions and printing off amendments and quibbling over details, until Cabinet would finally rise perhaps to resume again the following afternoon for sessions that would leave Paul at week's end, as he said, brain dead.

For years Jimmy had tried to reconcile what he knew of the man sitting beside him in the car on the way out to Fairbairn Air Force Base with the man he read about in the papers. Years ago he had just given up. There was such a gap. 'I hear you drive Keating,' he would sometimes be asked by a new acquaintance at the Quean- beyan Leagues Club. 'What's the arrogant prick like?' It was always either that reaction or the scarcely more welcome response of the Prime Minister's fans, who would press Jimmy against the bar while extolling his employer's qualities and prevent him getting on with his drinking. Neither type knew the Keating Jimmy knew. Almost every story that Jimmy had ever read about him told of his ruthlessness, his lust for power. That was the premise of the stories, one he knew Paul enjoyed and promoted. But it just didn't square. The man next to him had a quite easy and modest charm. He did not dominate conversations except when pressed or required to perform, he sought and indeed insisted upon eliciting the opinions of others, he claimed expertise in a few areas like Georgian silver and furniture, the recent history of the Commonwealth Government, but was otherwise always a student of others and often perhaps too deferential to their opinion and too simple in his conviction that there would always be someone out there who was wiser than he and could explain things. In conversation he rarely expressed a strong view about political tactics and strategy. He listened and judged, marking each person's views in the light of their customary degree of optimism or pessimism. He worried about light, germs, cancers, draughts. He thought mobile phones emitted harmful rays. He drank mysterious potions and performed silly exercises. He resented attempts to determine his schedule, he grew weary of people quickly, he got to bed too late and got up too late, he was evasive and dishonest in small ways rather than surrender his freedom or hurt other people's feelings. He was above all a performer with the performer's ability to rise to the occasion and to drop into languor and weariness afterward. He was also extremely level-headed. Out of power, he barely missed it. He adjusted to ordinary life as easily as he adjusted to being Treasurer. (Although certainly he would sometimes insist on the dignity of his office. Now that Paul was Prime Minister, Jimmy missed the years of conflict with the RAAF guards at Fairbairn, where the Prime Minister and the Governor-General were entitled to be driven across the tarmac to the stairs of their waiting VIP aircraft, but the Treasurer was entitled only to walk across it. It was a ruling that Jimmy blandly ignored week after week, year after year, mildly responding to the shock and fury of the security detachment as he drove away by saying 'Don't tell me, mate. See that bloke going up the stairs? Tell him.')

So many wonderful qualities, but such a striking discord between what Jimmy knew him to be and the way he was imagined by those who did not know him. Not that it was entirely untrue, this personality tendered at second, third and fourth hand through the newspapers or television reports, but it was not actually the personality of the man riding beside Jimmy. It was an artefact, something created, a personality on the whole unpleasant and unlovely, which was sometimes useful and sometimes not, but so pervasive and strong that once Paul got out of the car even people like Jimmy himself, who of course knew better, could begin to believe the false personality, the artefact, against the real one.

Jimmy drove them out that bright September morning, the Prime Minister sitting beside him in a dark light-weight double-breasted suit ('No, no, feel it, feel the weight of it,' he would tell friends, 'put it on, feel it. It's that light!') concealing under it a slight pot belly and narrow shoulders, wearing, of course, the gold heads of Napoleon at his cuff and light black slip-on shoes and a colourful silk tie, the skin of his face only now beginning to sag around his chin, a little pasty beneath the olive sheen; just now beginning, as he approached 50 and in the second year of the ceaseless effort of being Prime Minister, to show a little age and physical weariness. Looking out the window with an abstracted severity not only because it was still quite early on a Sunday morning, when he would usually still be asleep, but also because immediately behind him lay two of the worst weeks (so far – there would be worse to come) of his time as Prime Minister, and in a day or so he would have his first meeting with the new President of the United States.

Bumped from the President's schedule by a Middle East peace celebration, Keating lunched with Bill Clinton on Tuesday 14 September. The two leaders began their conversation by talking about Jefferson's home of Monticello, from where Clinton had begun his inaugural the year before, his guest just sufficiently subdued by the novelty and immensity of the occasion to refrain from taking the President through the details of the structure and Palladian character of Monticello as he had taken the housekeeper at Blair House (the President's guest house) through a discussion of its treasures the day before, or even to offer his summary judgement that Monticello exemplified the rule that Georgian houses looked best when one storey only, with the brilliant exception of Monticello, which was two storeys but designed to look like one.

A President of the United States had in fact been almost his first visitor in those crowded days after he had been elected Prime Minister in a second ballot a few days before Christmas in 1991. With barely a week before Bush was scheduled to arrive, Keating had celebrated his victory, selected his ministry, recruited most of his staff, commenced work on One Nation, and then begun to prepare himself for the President's visit with briefings from public servants, academics and his advisers, refining an argument that the US must remain engaged in Asia, must look to East Asia for its renewal as Australia already was, and must cement the connection through the fledgling Asia-Pacific Economic Cooperation process, or APEC.

He knew it so well and was so eager to communicate it by the time Bush arrived that the President, in their first sessions together, was mostly mute with perplexity, his genial and easy expectation of deference puzzlingly ignored or somehow not even registered, not apprehended, apparently, by the Australian with his untiring flow of words and ideas; his aide, General Scowcroft, old, small and bright eyed, silenced with bland and polite wonder at the Australian's fluent eagerness, not realising that it was almost impossible for Keating to conduct a conversation of any real importance that was not directed at enlightening, improving, persuading and inspiring his interlocutor – President of the United States, Air Force general and elder statesman, whomever.

Keating had liked Bush, but seen his weariness, his adaptation by passivity to the unceasing activity of his job. He detected the complaint against circumstance, the press and human understanding that marked him as a political leader already defeated. Clinton was different. On the White House steps to greet the Prime Minister he was unexpectedly big and unexpectedly young, a tall man in a big blue suit, his hair puffed, with beautiful brown hairless hands. He was warm and relaxed and funny, as one professional and lifelong politician to another. Like Keating, Clinton had been in politics as a very young man and, like Keating, he was intelligent enough to be as interested in policies, in the machinery and matter of government, as he was in the contest for office.

His campaign rhetoric, the story he told, was about how America needed to trade more successfully, to be more competitive in the world, and that this ought to be more important in its foreign policy and economic policy. This was a story very like the one Keating told, so that it would be easy to make the point to Clinton that these goals could best be realised for the United States as for Australia by looking to East Asia – that was where the fastest growing markets were, the strongest competition, the greatest problems, the future.

Over lunch of Creole seafood gumbo the President asked the Prime Minister what was the biggest challenge he faced, was it Mabo perhaps, to which Keating responded that the biggest current challenge was indeed native title and reconciliation, but that the biggest challenge for Australia was to find its sense of self and at the same time its sense of identity in the region to which it belonged, a response that then allowed him to touch briefly on all the themes he had mentioned to the President in their formal talks a few minutes before and to reiterate the importance of the APEC and of the first summit of APEC leaders, which the President had recently agreed to convene.

A few days later he was in London, meeting in his hotel suite with the then British Labour Party leader John Smith. They sat in a circle of chairs talking politics. Smith was encouraged by Keating's win, opening an opportunity for the Prime Minister to explain how it was done. He went back to his leadership struggle with Hawke, which preceded the electoral victory and was the first requirement for it. 'I was doing most of the work and thinking for them,' he said. 'I was chief cook and bottle washer. They only gave me the job because it was hopeless. There was no one there to cook and wash bottles.' As he talked Paul, who had been groggy with fatigue, livened up, his hands flying and slapping, fingers raised, talking quickly – telling and retelling the story he had told. He talked about the election win six months before. 'We decided we could not do it just on the economic record,' he said. 'We ran on key social democratic themes – we never did in the 1980s. Then they were all economic. We came at them over the Thatcherite agenda.' Smith had heard Hewson's proposed 15 per cent goods and services tax had been important in the outcome. 'No,' said Keating firmly. 'It was symbolic. We didn't win the election on that.'

'The thing is,' Keating summed up, 'low inflation, growth, inclusiveness, a bit of the action for everyone.'

'What I call old-fashioned right-wing policy,' Smith agreed.

'Yes,' said Keating, 'the problem with the right wing is it got shouted down by the left.'

'It's not the particular policy propositions, is it?' Smith remarked. 'It's the story.'

After Britain came Ireland and, one early evening towards the end of September, to the dais of the community hall of the Galway village of Tynagh, the platform from which he would shortly deliver one of his most heartfelt speeches, unrehearsed and unscripted. Behind him local Irish politicians and the Catholic priest, the mayors and community leaders were seated in rows, their damp clothes steaming pleasantly in the press of bodies and warmth of fuel heaters.

That morning the Prime Minister and his party had left Dublin in helicopters for Thurles, Tipperary, from where the grandfather of Labor Prime Minister Ben Chifley had emigrated to Australia. 'No country in the world is more like Ireland than Australia,' he had told the assembled schoolchildren and townspeople in the town square of Thurles. 'And no place in Ireland has had a bigger impact on Australian than Tipperary.' His energy was waning. Dublin had come after Balmoral, Balmoral after London, London after New York, New

York after Washington, Washington after Honolulu. The Prime Minister's party was beginning to lose track of time and country and purpose as they followed him through dinner after dinner with the effortlessly fluent Irish, sleeping now on alcohol and Normison, recalling with weary anxiety that there was still Drumoland Castle and Villers-Bretonneux and Monaco to go before they could get back on the now familiar plane to their now familiar seats, swallow more pills and begin their flight back to Canberra.

It was only a few days before coming to Tynagh that Paul had exchanged thoughts with the Irish Prime Minister, the Taoiseach, in a light and modest room in Dublin decorated with high glass mirrors, grey cotton curtains and a large grey rug with a green border. Germany had been reunited and the Soviet Union had ceased to exist, he and Albert Reynolds observed with wonder, two events that neither would have expected in their lifetimes and which were so recent that the destruction of the Berlin Wall (now regretted, on iconographic and heritage grounds) had been contemporary with the tightening of monetary policy in Australia and the first serious moves to push Hawke out of his job. There was the Middle East peace as well as the end of the Cold War and now the release of Nelson Mandela from Robben Island. The world was bereft of trouble spots. As Reynolds said, of the great issues of the 1960s and 1970s only the civil war in Northern Ireland remained, and there were signs that with his support even that stubborn dispute might soon be better managed. They nodded vigorously – the world had changed with wondrous rapidity, and what seemed to have remained and grown, they benevolently agreed, were the various peaceful, commercial unions in which Ireland and Australia, respectively, were involved: the European Union and APEC. A world of trade and commerce in which both Ireland and Australia were now equipped to do quite well. Minor to middle players in the great game, certainly, but with wisdom and experience and reasonable information their leaders could read the significance of events as well as they were read in Washington, Bonn, or Tokyo – better, sometimes.

The Dublin program completed, he had flown by helicopter over the white and grey suburbs of the city, across green fields cut by hedgerows to Thurles, then to the coast, and now to Tynagh. It had been raining when Paul and Annita arrived, but the Keatings were all there, lining the steps from the cemetery of Keating graves to the village below. There were Patricks and Michaels and Pauls and Matthews, Katherines and Marys and Annes, Keating after Keating and Larkin after Larkin with pale red skin and black or grey hair, thick bodies and big open faces, and here he was, shaking hands with one after another, taller, thinner and olive-skinned, five generations gone from the village where John Keating, the son of a Matthew as Paul was the son of a Matthew, had married Mary Larkin in 1834, and twenty years later (surviving the potato famine, but determined not to endure another) emigrated to the colony of New South Wales aboard the ship *Mangerton*, arriving in Sydney on 29 July 1855 and duly recorded on entry as Roman Catholics who could read and write.

The graves of Keatings and Larkins filled the cemetery. There was a plot of land on the village outskirts that John Keating and Mary Keating née Larkin might perhaps have owned. There was the register in the parish records of the Catholic church, of the marriage of John and Mary 159 years before. They talked with Jim Keating, who could trace his line back to the same Keatings, which included the original Matthew, but who had remained in Ireland rather than emigrating. The streets of the village were crowded now despite the rain, and there were cars parked along it, but otherwise the village was not perhaps much changed in 159 years: still a farming village, still dominated by cemetery, church, school, pub, and tiny stores selling groceries.

John and Mary Keating had left in the middle of the nineteenth century, taking with them their 16-year-old son Matthew, on the same ship that brought to New South Wales nine-year-old Catherine Byrne and her parents from County Roscommon, the two children perhaps hardly noticing each other on the *Mangerton*, although fifteen years later they would marry in their new home town of Sydney. Matthew and Catherine Keating had a son William in 1874, who was 31 when he married Annie Harrington, another child of Irish emigrants whose parents came from Tipperary. Their son Matthew was to be the father of Paul.

The line of descent of the male Keatings thus ran from Matthew Keating, who was living in Tynagh at around the time the First Fleet anchored in Sydney Cove, to his son John and John's son Matthew, who emigrated to New South Wales in the middle of the nineteenth century. In the new country it then runs from Matthew to his son William and to William's son the next Matthew, who was the father of Paul. Counting them up, there are only six Keating fathers from the First Fleet to the Keating who became the twenty-fourth Prime Minister of Australia and who kept in a desk at the Lodge an old wooden pencil case incised with the words 'Matthew Keating 1847'.

But if there are six generations from that Matthew, then simple arithmetic tells us that if every child has two parents this first Matthew and his bride Mary Donellan were only two of sixty-four contemporary progenitors, all of whom have an equal chance of contributing to the gene pool embodied in Paul. Of the remaining sixty-two who stamped their design upon Paul, who ordained his height and weight, who formed the shape of his nose, the colour of his hair and the colour of his skin, the way in which he grew and aged, whose intelligence or cunning or fluency contributed to his, we know nothing at all – whether African, English, French or Russian, whether Catholic, Jewish, Muslim or atheist. For all we know Paul's chromosomal inheritance is more English than Irish, more Jewish than Catholic. Of his biological inheritance we know at six generations back only two parts of sixty-four – a little more than three per cent known, a little less than ninety-seven per cent unknown. Only two parts in sixty-four from the Matthew who was the father of John, but two parts that mattered, not so much because the Keating name was passed from father to son, or even that property was acquired and used and its remainder passed along this line of inheritance, but that ideas about values and meaning, about life and society, which were believed and accepted in Tynagh through the agency of the Catholic Church in Ireland were, at the end of this long trail of ancestry, passed along to the child Paul, a weight of inheritance much on his mind as he was finally invited in his turn to address the villagers in the crowded Parish Hall in Tynagh.

'We always, I suppose, all of us wonder where we are from, what part of the world we belong to, those of us who have come from other societies,' he said, thinking out loud and finding his way gradually as he sometimes does in unscripted speeches, speaking not from notes but from the sequence of thoughts and reflections as they link together, the new and old, in his mind. 'As Australia is a multicultural country, Australians have come from all over the world,' he continued. 'Now for you in Ireland, of course, you don't have to wonder about this. You know where you're from and you can turn up your parish records and find out exactly where you're from. But because so many of you took that fateful decision to cross the world and go to other places, you changed the lives of many other people. And not all of us have known exactly. While we've become sons and daughters of our native country, in terms of our ancestry you always wonder where you are from. And with a very good hard look, I found, to my great happiness, I'm from Tynagh and Galway.'

As he spoke Keating held the lectern with both arms, sometimes waving a hand in a little circle and then offering his hand palm upward to the audience, a gesture intended to punctuate or to underline the conclusion of a train of thought, those thoughts themselves building with clauses and then subclauses, small asides and associated suggestions; Keating all the time speaking a little wearily but with the haggard animation, the shadow of grey underneath the olive disclosing how much he now got by on willpower rather than energy or a strong constitution.

'I was so touched by the welcome, that so many of you have come out on this – a weekday – to greet Annita and I, so many members of the Keating family. And I was absolutely delighted to meet Jim Keating, my relative, my nearest relative from the great, proud clan of the Keatings. And seeing him here today, and the Larkins and the Molloys, and the other strains that run through our family – and there are a few others of course on my grandmother's side, the Harringtons, who are from Roscommon. There are not so many of them here today I'm sure but, nevertheless, on my father's side, as Father Kevin said, there was Matthew and then another Matthew and the Matthew, the son of John Keating, who left these shores. So the connexions are there.

'And I was particularly touched in visiting the school, by the children. By the singing and dancing, and by one song in particular and one very nice little speech made to me down there. And to see the sort of parish centre with the school and the old church, knowing that one's forebears had been down that road, had gone to Sunday Mass, had left the house and trundled down there and sent their children to school there. It's looking back, in a way, back into one's past, that one was never able to do. And then to be shown this block of land, this plot that my family had worked, in this town of Tynagh. And it's still there, just as it was, today . . . to know exactly where you're from, this is where the long journey began.'

Keating reads speeches badly and speaks from the heart well. What he was saying now was so arresting that even his staff, who had heard more Keating speeches, written — for that matter — more Keating speeches, than they cared to remember, were as moved as the audience. Stephen Brady, the trip organiser, who had been tapping his foot with impatience as the extempore remarks of the local greeters punished the schedule, was entranced. Linda Craige, the Prime Minister's personal secretary, was crying.

'I think it is a salute to the Irish,' he said towards the end, 'to their great strength and tenacity that they could take such a decision and leave this country knowing they'd never see each other again. The day they walked out of the village, one part of the family, husband, wife or son and daughter-in-law or daughter and son-in-law, and children, never to be seen again. And they all knew in their heart of hearts they would never see each other again. The population of Ireland dropped from something like eight million to five million in the middle to late nineteenth century, many families were broken and so many left, never to return, only to correspond by letter until basically they expired and dissipated. When John Keating and Mary Larkin left, and wished to come back, they couldn't have thought that all those many years later that someone would come back. But the truth is, the fact is, the pleasure is, that I was the one that came back.'

1

IRISHTOWN

EVERY TWENTY MINUTES OR SO a train clatters west from Sydney's Central. It stops first at Redfern, where the Keatings settled when they arrived on the *Mangerton* in 1855, and then Erskineville, St Peters, Sydenham and Marrickville. By then it has left the terraces of the central city, and the cottages on either side are old brick, with red tiled roofs and small gardens. It clatters on through Dulwich Hill, Hurlstone Park, Canterbury, Campsie, Belmore, Lakemba, Wiley Park and Punchbowl, the houses becoming newer, the gardens bigger, until it reaches the hub of the line, Bankstown. Once known as Irishtown, and in those days the furthest and wildest frontier of Sydney's westward spread, Bankstown is where the boilermaker Matt Keating and his wife Min, like thousands of other low-income people leaving the crowded terraces of the inner city, moved after they married during World War II.

For a decade the line between Bankstown and the city was the axis of their first child Paul's life. As a young man it took him to the Labor Party offices opposite Museum Station in Elizabeth Street, where he made his first contacts with the group that ran the party in New South Wales. It took him to Labor Party Youth Council meetings, where he achieved his first political successes. It took him to his job as a pay clerk at the County Council. It took him to Repins coffee shop where he and Laurie Brereton and Bob Carr and a dozen other young men and women talked about the Labor Party and how they would change it. Alighting at Town Hall, the train took him into the city to the annual conferences of the New South Wales branch of the Labor Party. He first discussed a political alliance with Laurie Brereton on the train between Town Hall and Central, and he first cajoled his ally Ron Dyer into not running for the presidency of Youth Council while walking towards St James station. And at night the train took him back to the fibro cottage at 3 Marshall Street and later back to the new big house at 8 Gerard Avenue, in what is still locally known as Top Bankstown.

Later he would fill his house at 12 Gerard Avenue, Bankstown, with antiques so there was, he told a reporter in 1977, 'more good taste in this room than in most establishment homes', he would find a wife from Holland and later still he would live in Canberra and begin to restore a town house in Elizabeth Bay, he would collect Mercedes cars and clocks and silver and settle for the dead chic of the Empire ('it never goes off')[1] but Keating would always nonetheless be Bankstown, a Sydney western suburbs boy, to his blood and bones. 'I am a Westie,' he declared as Prime Minister.[2] His opponents would always be harlots, sleezebags, frauds, cheats, blackguards, pigs, mugs, clowns, criminal intellects, boxheads, criminals, friends of tax cheats, brain damaged, loopey crims, stupid foul-mouthed grubs, pieces of criminal garbage, clots, fops, gigolos, hillbillies, ninnies, scumbags, thugs, dimwits, and gutless spivs. He would always dress self-consciously well and always fret that people, when he was younger, would sometimes not see how much smarter and quicker he was than other, more widely applauded people who were really phonies and jokes, and however far he made it into the world of Sydney money he would always insist on a phrase or a mannerism that defined his background as, when he had left an eastern suburbs Sunday lunch, the host giggled that Keating was coming along very well, very well indeed, if only he would stop cleaning his teeth with his fingernail.

Sprawling between the George's River and the Liverpool Road, Bankstown is now a suburb of single houses with garages and gardens, although, only two lifetimes before Paul Keating's, it was still the home of clans of Australian Aboriginals living along the river.[3]

Their remains are still found – a stone axe, 3000 years old, was found above the George's River, cave drawings and carvings of goannas and human hands were found near the riverbank in 1971 in the rubble of a demolition. Thousands and thousands of years for which we have some evidence; perhaps thirty or forty thousand years further back in which we can only guess at different peoples and different clans living on fish and shellfish and roots. Generations succeeding generations, unknown thousands of years of this culture until in April 1770 Captain James Cook sailed the *Endeavour* into Botany Bay, where the George's River enters the sea. He filled casks with water and cleaned the boat. His men caught fish in a net, including two stingrays weighing 600 pounds total, so that each man had six pounds of fish in the morning and five in the evening. Many were sick. He went ashore, and when threatened by natives he fired bird shot to wound them. The botanist Joseph Banks collected plants. Seaman Forby Sutherland died of tuberculosis and was buried ashore. The English sailors saw trees with a hard wood, which exuded a kind of red gum. After a few days Cook sailed away.[4]

Eighteen years later the British came back to Botany Bay, this time commanded by Captain Arthur Phillip with a fleet transporting soldiers and convicts into exile. Phillip stayed only long enough to conclude that Botany Bay was a poor site for a colony before sailing a few hours north to what he believed was the finest harbour in the world, at Port Jackson. The Europeans settled there, but sometimes they came back to Botany Bay for food. The convict McEntire, ordered to hunt kangaroo at Botany Bay, was killed with a spear. Phillip ordered a party of forty marines under Lieutenant Tench to capture two natives and kill ten, cut off their heads and bring them back to Port Jackson, hatchets and bags furnished for the purpose. Tench persuaded Phillip that only six should be shot, or only two hung if they could be captured. The tribe, however, had vanished.[5] Soon all the coastal tribes close to the settlement would vanish, killed by new diseases.

In late spring 1795, when the settlement at Port Jackson was already seven years old, George Bass and his friend Matthew Flinders sailed a boat into Botany Bay and across to the river that flowed into it. They sailed and rowed up the river for twenty miles, passing huge stands of blackbutt, clouds of parrots and cockatoos. They surprised wild ducks, pelicans and swans. They fished and shot birds, but were wary of the Aborigines they knew were watching from the bush. They sailed as far as the junction of the river with a smaller one, today known as Prospect Creek. Governor Hunter was well pleased with their report of the fertile lands along the river. He retraced their voyage himself two years later. The area upriver was named Banks Town, after the botanist who briefly visited Botany Bay with Cook, and who in London remained a patron of the colony of New South Wales.[6]

Hunter granted land to marines, little farms of 100 acres, English-sized plots. They planted wheat and grew sheep, but the George's River flooded and drowned their crops. The river was their only path to the European settlement. To the riverbank were tall stringy bark and blackbutt forests and scrub so thick that Governor Macquarie himself was lost in them one day in 1810, blindly cutting through the bush with no hut, no road, no track and no map until at last and by sheer luck he came out on the banks of the George's River and was able to work out where he was and where he now had to go.

Formally named Bankstown, it was universally known as Irish-town. Many of the marines to whom land was granted on the bank of the George's River were Irish, and the freed convicts were often Irish. By 1814, when the road from Sydney to Liverpool went through and opened up the back of Bankstown away from the river, there were three clumps of primitive farms and bark huts known as Irishtowns One, Two and Three.

Twelve miles from Sydney Cove, Bankstown grew slowly. In 1832 there were 48 houses and 252 people. By the 1860s, after the gold rush and after the rail line to Liverpool had left Bankstown a backwater, four miles from the track, there were only a thousand people, mostly market gardeners and timber cutters, though now with the Catholic church of St Felix de Valois and a Catholic school up near the Liverpool Road. The nearest villages were Liverpool, Burwood and Enfield. The rail did not come to Bankstown itself until the new

century, in 1909, but even then it remained bush. Soldiers were settled on poultry and pig farms after World War I. Even in 1922, however, the population was only 10 000 people. During the depression
people camped in cloth tents and corrugated iron shacks on the
George's River at the Vale of Ah, where Aboriginal tribes had watched
George Bass sail by a hundred and thirty years before. It was not until
World War II, when the hill near Bankstown aerodrome was honey-
combed with concrete bunkers, the bomb-proof headquarters of an
air defence command, that the town began to grow.

Even when Paul Keating was born in 1944 Bankstown was still
paspalum and poultry farms, still on the scrubby periphery of the
city. But it was just about to boom. People began leaving the inner-
city suburbs for the cheaper land of Bankstown. Immigration swelled
the flood of returning soldiers, and the government located a big
migrant reception centre in nearby Villawood. With good rail transport, plentiful labour and cheap land Bankstown attracted industry. The market gardens gave way to white fibro houses with red
tile roofs; there were swimming pools, libraries and more schools.
Between 1947 and 1965 the population quadrupled. By the early
1970s it was the most populous municipality in Australia, before
beginning to decline as that tremendous swell of the baby boom era
grew up and moved out to be replaced, though in lesser numbers, by
Vietnamese, Lebanese and Melanesians.

Successive generations of Keatings had lived for hundreds of years
in Ireland in a culture as unvarying as that of Australian Aborigines.
Then life speeded up. The length of time from Aboriginal tribes
watching Bass navigate the George's River to the municipality of
171 000 people housed in fibro cottages with red roofs, with churches
and schools, cars and television sets, spanned only three lifetimes.
There were people around when Paul was growing up, parishioners
at the church, elderly people in Marshall Street, who were old enough
to have known and to have memories of people who were alive early
in the nineteenth century, who in turn would have known the first
generation of Europeans to settle Australia and make their homes
there. Jack Lang, for example, who was still trying to hang on to

the remnants of power in the nearby suburb in Auburn when Paul was born, was himself born in 1876 and would later describe for Paul the Federation rallies of the 1890s. There were people – Mary McHugh, for example, who was born in 1876, educated at St Felix school, which Paul would later attend, and who died as Mrs Con O'Connell in 1967, when Paul was already running for office – who were old enough to have seen and known as children men and women who were young when Governor Lachlan Macquarie first entertained freed convicts at Government House, outraging the pretensions of the colony's tiny upper class.

Paul John Keating was born 18 January 1944 at St Margaret's Hospital, Darlinghurst. He was the first of the four children of Matthew and Min Keating, and he would afterwards attribute the boldness and confidence that were his lifelong characteristics to being the first in the nest. He was adored and encouraged.

Paul's father, Matt Keating, was born in 1918, and grew up in the inner-city suburb of Annandale. His father William was the son of Matthew, who emigrated with his father John Keating on the *Mangerton*. His mother, Paul's grandmother, was Annie Harrington before marrying William. Matt's brother Bill, a prisoner of the Japanese during World War II, would die on the Sandakan death march. Paul's uncle Jack was still living in the Trafalgar Street, Annandale, house in 1995, when Paul was Prime Minister. Though a manual worker, Paul's grandfather owned several properties and a car. In the Annandale house he displayed a studio portrait of his father, the immigrant Matthew, which would later come to Paul. The great grandfather had a long lean face, with strong cheekbones and a full white beard.[7]

Matt served his apprenticeship as a boilermaker. He worked first at the Everleigh Railway Workshops in Redfern and then in the Railway Workshops in the western Sydney suburb of Chullora. He married a Redfern girl, Min Chapman, and in 1942 they bought their own house in the raw but now rapidly growing suburb of Bankstown. Cheap but solid, the house at 3 Marshall Street had brick foundations, fibro walls on a timber frame, and a tiled roof. The front door opened on to a small brick porch, with a set of steps and a wrought iron railing down to the concrete front path. With children, parents and relatives there had been ten people in the Annandale house in which Matt grew up. Now he and Min had a place of their own. There was room for a car, although it was many years before the Keatings could buy one. The standard design of the house would later pain their older son, but in the early 1940s, and after lives spent in exactly the kind of inner-city terraces to which their son's generation would eagerly return, the space, the newness of it, the setting in this suburb of bush and small farms, would have been a delightful expansion of their lives.

Shorter than his son would grow up to be, thicker in body and broader in his shoulders, Matt stood correctly with his hard hands curled and his thumbs along the seams of his pants. When he was young his face was very like Paul's would be at the same age. His eyes were alert and watchful, gazing out through solid glasses framed in thick black plastic. In middle age he had a strong, square heavily lined face and black hair brushed straight back from his temples. Matt remained at the railway workshops, climbing the ranks from boilermaker to welding inspector. He rode a bicycle to work for years, although by the mid 1950s the family was doing well enough to buy a car. In his late thirties, however, Matt moved on. He accepted a job as the manager of a refrigeration plant, and not long after was offered an opportunity to buy into a small engineering business, then based at Silverwater. Then called Martin & Blake after its two partners, it was small and looking to grow. Spurred by immigration and the postwar baby boom, the construction industry was building hundreds of thousands of new dwellings. The firm made the revolving metal cylinders, as well as other metal equipment, for the ready-mixed concrete industry. Matt sold the car and borrowed on his house to buy his share. With a third partner, it was renamed Marlak Engineering.[8]

A supplier to two of the flourishing concrete businesses, Readymix and Pioneer Concrete, Marlak Engineering did quite well. It survived the 1961 recession and the tremors of the early 1970s, but it was limited by its capital base and by the age and ambitions of its founders. Matt had angina and needed to watch his health carefully. He was supposed to stop smoking, but found it hard. He would sit on the verandah, concealing the cigarette from Min. Paul would later develop a horror of cigarette smoke. The owners sold the business to John Leard's ANI in 1973 for $376 000 in cash and shares.[9] Marlak had provided a reasonable living, but not wealth. His father had also set up a business making ready-mixed concrete. It was sold separately, for more. Close to his father, Paul picked up an understanding of the concrete mixer business. He first visited the Snowy Mountains Hydroelectric Scheme, the greatest single national development project constructed during his childhood, on Marlak business with his father. He thought about going into the firm, and might well have done so if he had not succeeded early in politics. More than twenty years after Marlak was sold he could still explain the distinctions between different kinds of cement mixers and describe the technical advances in Marlak products.

Matt was a vigorous supporter of the Catholic opposition to communists and left-wingers within the unions and the Labor Party in the critical years leading to and following the great split within the party in 1955. He was an assistant secretary and then secretary of the Chullora branch of the Boilermakers Union in the early 1950s and remained an active unionist until he transferred to staff and was obliged to resign from the union. He was a member and later president of the Central Bankstown Branch of the Australian Labor Party, where he inducted his oldest son some weeks before his fifteenth birthday. Matt would hand out how-to-vote tickets at the Labor Party booth during elections. Sometimes, Paul recalled, boilermakers from Marlak would pass by and Matt would offer them a ticket. 'No thanks, Matty,' some would tell him, passing to the Liberal Party table further along. Matt was said to be an admirer of Jack Lang, although he did not know Lang, and by the 1950s conflicts over Lang had long been overtaken by others.

Doug McNally, Matt's friend and fellow party member, who was himself associated with B. A. Santamaria's Catholic Social Studies

Movement ('the Movement'), hints that Matt was also a member of the clandestine and highly effective organisation of lay Catholics fighting communists and left-wingers for control of the unions and the Labor Party.[10] Certainly Matt was a member of the Industrial Groups, formed by the Movement and by other anti-communists within the ALP to contest control of trade unions by communists and their left-wing allies.[11] Until they were abandoned and proscribed by the Labor Party in the mid 1950s, membership of the Groups was common in the right and moderate ranks of the party, and members and allies of the Groups controlled the New South Wales state executive of the party. The discussions Matt took part in on the steps of the church after Mass on Sunday, where the Movement's *News Weekly* was sold, were often about Labor politics both in the unions and the local branches. By the time membership of the National Civic Council, the Movement and the associated but more open Industrial Groups was banned by the Labor Party Matt would have left active union politics. While the Movement hardliners split off in New South Wales and other states to form what became the Democratic Labor Party, Matt remained loyal to the Labor Party. 'He couldn't abide the DLP,' recalls Paul.

While the Movement was banned in New South Wales as in other states, the enduring strength of the Right in New South Wales Labor politics and ultimately in national politics resulted from the decision of the majority of Movement members and the Groups to obey proscription and fight within the party rather than split off to form a new party, as they did in substantial numbers in Queensland, Victoria and Tasmania. Paul's early success, and therefore his subsequent career, for example, would have been impossible without the base of right-wing Catholic support on which he relied for pre-selection.

The importance of Matt in Paul's career is hard to overestimate. 'I shouldn't be here!' Paul would laugh, glancing around the lounge room of the Lodge in December 1995. 'I mean, I shouldn't be here at all! A lot of it was because of my father.' Michael Hatton, a friend of the family since childhood who later worked for Paul, says that Paul's social conscience and compassion, the idea of working in the community for those less well off, comes from his father.[12] Doug McNally agrees. Matt Keating was a hard worker, a churchgoer, and a lifelong supporter of Labor. Hatton recalls Matt as compassionate, placid and reserved, with a good sense of humour. He was a good organiser and an active Catholic. He worked for the Catholic charity, the St Vincent de Paul Society, and might have been a member of the Catholic lay men's group, the Knights of the Southern Cross. According to McNally, who knew him well, Matt was a 'single-minded fellow – not a quitter. He would go at something until he got it.' Father Michael McCarthy, assistant priest at the Keatings' church from 1965, says that Matt was 'a man of extremely strong principles, which he applied totally. He came from a strong Catholic background himself.' In support of the church, Matt was 'most obliging'.[13] Paul remembers also that 'my old man did clever things – he was technically clever', a gift that impressed the boy.

Michael McCarthy believes that the 'essential quality that comes through Paul from Matt is directness of approach, a clear line on what is right and wrong'. Matt transmitted his right-wing Catholic political preferences. When it came to finding a seat and organising the numbers to do it, Matt was effectively Paul's campaign manager. Matt himself was sufficiently involved in politics and had enough of the characteristics of a professional politician to have become one himself had his interests not turned towards business. He transferred his ambitions to his son. As McNally says, 'Matt quite deliberately prepared Paul for political life and then helped him to get into it.' He was the most important influence in his son's entry into politics, but another influence later discerned by his son was equally important. Matt showed Paul how an interest in business and markets could fit quite well with support for the Labor Party and for trade unions. It would remain a central idea in Paul's life in politics.

Paul would later recall, 'The family business background showed me that business and Labor could go together. I knew from my father that business people didn't have two heads.' There were particular things he would never forget. 'We got a contract to build three tin dredges for Malaysia,' he recalled in 1991, soon after resigning from the Hawke Government, 'but the bank wouldn't lend the money against a government guaranteed contract. They would only lend against sixty per cent of the value of the land and buildings. So I remember that about banks. Also about Division 7 tax – you couldn't keep any money in a private company. I noted the thing in my mind – you could not save.' As Treasurer Paul abolished Division 7 of the tax legislation, which taxed profits retained in private companies at the highest marginal rate. He introduced dividend imputation to minimise the double taxation of dividends, once in the hands of the company and again in the hands of the shareholder. Throughout his political career he has been sceptical of the established major commercial banks and, though he deregulated finance to allow them greater freedom, he also licensed sixteen new foreign banks to compete with them.

These were particular things but there was also a basic understanding of markets and prices, which is the most important insight taught by formal economics courses. Paul Keating has never done such a course in his life but he understood the basic idea. People running small businesses know all about money coming in and money going out, about price and profit, the cost of labour, the suddenness of market changes, the need to be quick and flexible, the need to specialise, the need to find a competitive spot and to work on it to stay competitive. He understood the key idea of market economics, which is that the myriad of daily decisions taken by employees and employers, consumers and investors and so forth are made consistent through the market and through prices, without the intervention of a planning authority or a government to bring it all together. This is the economic insight of Adam Smith, and remains the basic insight of modern economics. For many years, however, Paul modified Adam Smith with the older Catholic economic doctrine of distributive justice. It would be decades before the conflict between the two was resolved in his mind, and when it was the ageing B. A. Santamaria, the modern exponent of the medieval doctrine, would lament the new economic world that Paul Keating introduced.

From Matt Paul acquired a set of political views and a set of political allies. He learned enterprise and markets. He learned the employer's point of view and how it could be reconciled with the employee's point of view. His father contributed ideas, but there is not much about Paul's personality that fits with accounts we have of his father's. Paul when inspired is a relentless worker, but he is not consistently careful, diligent and methodical. He is charming rather than kind, generous rather than charitable. He is sometimes secretive but not reserved. He is an excellent listener when appropriate but could not be described as quiet. He was intermittently a good organiser in the days when he had to organise things himself, but he does not enjoy routine. And while Paul has an imperturbably enduring plainness and sincerity of manner, and likes to think of himself as a humble person, he has aspirations to various kinds of exclusive and select knowledge that set him apart from others. Paul recalls his father as 'a sweet sort of character: he always wanted a non-conflict model for everything', a description that does not fit the son.[14]

Father McCarthy believes Paul's personality exhibits his mother's qualities of energy and gregariousness. Min Keating doted on her older son, although she was a not a foolishly indulgent mother. Paul recalled that, 'My mother had views about how everyone should behave and if you didn't behave that way she'd give you a clip over the ear, simple as that. The place ticked over.'[15] One side of Min's family came from Ireland, but the other from England – she was perhaps conscious of the nuance of difference. Min is sometimes described as having a fox terrier manner, of relentlessly pressing her will and her views on those around her. Bob Carr says that Paul's mother 'is very strong willed',[16] and even in his forties he would say it with almost a tremor. Others who went to the Keating home as young men and who are now battle-hardened and callous adults slip into the same respectful tone of voice – slower, unconsciously lowering their voice as if she might still hear them from the kitchen. They almost whisper – Min was *very* strong willed. Of the two parents she had higher social aspirations and more easily fell in with the general upward climb of Catholics within Australian society. Min, for example, encouraged the children to consider post-secondary education, which

Matt thought a waste of time. She was devoted to Paul. At his wedding she stood with the erect posture of women of her generation, hands folded in front, handbag hanging from one wrist, eyebrows sharply stencilled, lips clearly defined, wearing a fur and dark gloves. Her expression was one of cheerless desolation.

It was a close-knit family. Paul was followed by a sister, Lyn, then another sister, Anne, and finally a younger brother, Greg. Lyn would later marry, and her husband Tony King would become secretary of the Australian Jockey Club, in Sydney. The younger brother, Greg, would become a partner in the Sydney law firm McClellands. Anne, ten years younger than Paul, would remain closest to their mother, but in other ways ignored the expectations of her Catholic suburban childhood. She became a senior executive with United Airlines and an independent businesswoman. Attractive, intelligent and energetic, she declined marriage and motherhood.

Paul would later recall that five or six of their neighbours in tiny Marshall Street were Irish. The Irish were strong in Bankstown, and so was their faith. St Felix de Valois church and school near the junction of Liverpool and Rookwood Roads was the closest church for the Keating family until the early 1950s, when part of that congregation was split off to form a new parish around St Brendan's on Northam Street, nearer the Keatings' home on Marshall Street. Matt and Min were two of the hardest working members of the new church. The church itself is a long low red building with yellow windows, fronted with a sandstone porch and a neon illuminated cross, now rusting. It was built up around a shell provided by a prefabricated shearing shed, with the local Catholic community helping in the construction.

Being a Catholic of Irish descent was a far more important distinction in the 1950s than it became a few decades later. The community still felt isolated from the rest of Australian society and its members still interacted more with each other than with other Australians. 'In those days,' says Hatton, 'it was an enclave, a very close, small, Irish Catholic community.' And not so very small. 'In Bankstown,' Father McCarthy recalled, 'we would have had three or four thousand people to deal with every Sunday. It is impossible for non-Catholics to imagine. It tends to make Catholics believe they belong to a large team.'

Through his childhood, adolescence and early manhood Paul's Catholic community in Bankstown was hostile to the political philosophy of the Commonwealth Government and to its leader, Robert Menzies. Paul was five when Menzies brought the Liberal-Country Party coalition back to power in Canberra in December 1949. He would remain Prime Minister until Paul was 22 and already working on his own political career. Intelligent, fluent, complacent, and sentimentally attached to the United Kingdom, Menzies also welcomed and cultivated Australia's growing orientation towards the United States. He drew on the tradition of Victorian liberalism defined by Alfred Deakin in the first years of the new century. He favoured high tariffs on manufactured imports. He favoured the rapid growth of Commonwealth power over the states, acquiring Commonwealth control over university education. And he was a superb political strategist. He created the Liberal Party from a rabble of conservative factions. He saw that the split between the Left and the Right in Labor in the 1950s would entrench the coalition in power. He encouraged the drift of Catholics away from the Labor Party by overturning all the principles and prejudices of his own party to introduce Commonwealth financial assistance for private schools in 1964. But if Paul's community was hostile to the Prime Minister, it did not care for his opponent, Bert Evatt. An intelligent, energetic and egotistical Sydney barrister and judge who had been foreign minister in the Curtin and Chifley governments, Dr Herbert Vere Evatt had at first encouraged the Catholic opposition to the Left in the Labor Party, and then joined forces with the Left to drive it out.

Despite the Allied victory in World War II and the UN victory in Korea, the world was still a threatening place. The Russians blockaded Berlin when Paul was 4. In Malaya British, Australian and New Zealand troops fought to put down what was said to be a communist rebellion, which began in 1948 and would last twelve years. Communists took over China in October 1949. They would soon replace Japan as a threat to rich, European and lightly populated Australia. The Korean War broke out when Paul was 7 and Australia sent forces. The Russians and the Chinese were behind the North Koreans, and the Russians now had both the atom bomb and the hydrogen bomb. Indonesia had won its independence in 1949 and Australia had cheered on the nationalists, but their leader Dr Sukarno was unpredictable and sometimes hostile to the West.

The world was threatening but Australia was prospering. Manufacturing continued to expand behind high tariff walls, and rural industries were enjoying strong world markets. At the same time important social changes were underway – a swollen cohort of children, the baby boomers, was being born and housed and would soon need to be educated. Women had entered the workforce in large numbers during the war, and while they would give way to the returning servicemen in the immediate aftermath of war, the proportion of women working would continue to climb steadily. The Chifley Government had initiated a major immigration program, which over several decades would diversify Australia's population. The link with Britain had also been weakened by the war in the Pacific. Australia had fought the last three years of the war mainly as an ally of the United States rather than the United Kingdom, and after the war Washington slowly but irresistibly replaced London as the principal focus of Australia's foreign diplomacy. Slowly, the new reality drifted away from the older generation's perception of Australia.

When Father Michael McCarthy was assigned to the Keatings' church, St Brendan's, in 1965, a block of land in Bankstown could still be bought for a thousand pounds. 'Bankstown then was new or at least there were still large new developments. It was the pits in a sense. I thought: distance, deprivation, concrete. But I found it a wonderful experience. They were hardworking people who knew what it was to go without. They worked to get their school and church going at St Brendan's. There was a strong cooperative spirit. No one had any notions of grandeur. Top Bankstown was the older area and they did have little tickets on themselves up there.'

Apart from the river and the hill upon which St Felix was built,

Bankstown was flat fields and housing estates. The only architectural distinctions were the beautiful Lansdowne bridge and a few old houses. But in the 1950s it was a wonderful place to grow up – there was space, safety, freedom, and the companionship of other children. To an adult, Bankstown was block upon block of new red-tiled fibro houses, but to the children it was a most mysterious and evocative place. Near Bankstown aerodrome were the remains of the Air Defence Headquarters for the south-west Pacific, a complex of underground concrete bunkers and tunnels safe from air attack. As children Paul and his friends ignored the warning signs and crawled under the barbed wire to explore the tunnels and bunkers, or play in the age-ing bombers and fighters on the margin of the airfield. To the east through crowded suburbs was Botany Bay. To the south were beach-side villages and then the steel-making city of Wollongong, and between them and the outer limits of Sydney were thousands of hectares of national park from the sea beaches to the foothills of the Great Dividing Range, a wilderness in which wallabies and kanga-roos could usually be seen and in which the kookaburras and cur-rawongs sang. Sometimes Paul and his friends rode to Wollongong, 70 kilometres away, on their bikes. Returning, Paul would catch hold of the tail railing of a semi-trailer crawling up the steep Bulli Pass, and then push off and glide free down the other side of the hill.[17]

To the north-east was the central business district and Sydney Harbour. To the west, through mostly open fields and raw housing estates, Paul and his friends could cycle to Wallacia and then to the banks of Lake Burragorang. Riding through the gums and wattles by the side of this inland sea bounded by sandstone cliffs slowly ris-ing to the Blue Mountains, this silent and uninhabited space, they would see white swamp eagles hunting ducks, islands of cormorants, egrets and nesting swans in the marshes, black swans and pelicans, and eels and trout in the water.

When he was older, Paul went with his friends in the Catholic Youth Organisation to picnics and dances. Travelling north-east by car or train and bus, he would go to Sydney's harbourside eastern suburbs and from there by ferry to Clark Island, a state park in Sydney

Harbour. Across to the north was the native bush of Bradley's Head
and Middle Head, to the west the Harbour Bridge, and, when he was
15, the beginning of work on the Opera House.

Paul first attended Bankstown Public School in Restwell Street
and St Jerome's at Punchbowl, but he was sent to St Brendan's school
on nearby Northam Street when it opened in 1952. He joined at
third class. In the early days the church was a single hall. Classes three,
four, five and six were taught in the hall during the week. On Sundays
the desks were put aside to allow Mass to be celebrated. Father
McCarthy recalled that, 'It was a disciplined Catholic formation.
Sister Ainese would have been the principal at St Brendan's, and
she ran a very tight ship. That was true of all Catholic schools then.
You didn't speak in class unless you were spoken to. You didn't have
the sort of general discussion that is now apparent from year one. In
those days the teacher spoke and you listened.' The nuns remembered
Paul as a 'docile little chap'.[18]

From St Brendan's Paul went to secondary school at the De La
Salle College attached to St Felix de Valois. 'Brother Michael Johnston
would have been the principal,' McCarthy recalled. 'In those days the
schools would have been staffed mainly by members of religious
orders. It's a big difference today when the staff are mostly lay people.' Morality was described in black and white. 'The whole basis of
a Catholic formation would be to give people a strong sense of why
they are here, the fact that they are created by God and destined for
heaven,' McCarthy said. 'It also carries through with strong moral
teaching. Acceptable and unacceptable behaviour would have been
strictly dealt out.'

Paul was always towards the bottom of the top third in class –
doing just enough, he later said, to stay there in the top third, and
no more.[19] He did not do particularly well at school and as an adult
prefers speaking and listening to writing and reading. He is also very
suspicious of conventional medicine and inclined to fanciful cures
for ailments. His world holds terrors of disease that people with only
a fraction of his boldness or courage do not even notice. These
characteristics are perhaps related to a serious disease he had as an

adolescent. He now believes he had undiagnosed peritonitis at school. During the Intermediate Certificate, for example, he had carbuncles on his arms and body, and big blisters or boils around his eyes. The disease left him with no lower eyelashes, and his eyes do not lubricate properly.

His secondary schooling was anyway quite brief, leaving after third year (now year 9) in November 1958, three months before he turned 15. He obtained his Intermediate Certificate. It was not at all uncommon then to leave at age 15 and start work. The majority of Australian children did so through to the mid 1960s, and it was not until the early 1980s that school retention rates climbed dramatically. Of Paul's contemporaries only one child in five completed secondary school and went on to higher education; one in ten left at 15 and obtained an apprenticeship to become skilled in a trade. Most of the rest expected to and did find plenty of jobs that required nothing more than the Intermediate Certificate. There were junior wages for these young employees who learned their vocational skills on the job. It was easy then to get a white-collar job in a career occupation. In the year Paul left school it was seriously asked in a research project whether the advantages of providing more education for adolescents, who otherwise left school at 15, would offset the economic consequences of their withdrawal from the labour market.[20] It was not until the 1970s, when the unemployment level in Australia doubled and then tripled, that young people found it impossible or extremely difficult to get a job with only an Intermediate Certificate. As Father McCarthy said, 'it was perfectly normal' for Paul to have left school at 15 in 1958.

But it is perhaps unusual that a child who would later display a quick intelligence and a strong memory should so lightly abandon school. It is true that his father denigrated university education. Paul's brother Greg, thirteen years his junior, didn't go to university either. 'My father was never real keen on university graduates,' Greg recalls. 'There was never any great pressure to go to university. Mum was a bit different. She thought it would be a good thing to do. But certainly not from Dad's point of view — he used to describe university graduates as bums. I did the Solicitors Admission Board – it was a compromise. I got a job and that kept Dad happy, and I did the course at night and that kept Mum happy.'[21] It is also true that St Felix school did not go through to the Leaving Certificate then and that Paul would have had to travel to another school to continue. But it is nonetheless telling for Paul that he left, and perhaps the realisation of his error might later have given him the energy and will to contest a difficult pre-selection battle. His parents certainly had enough money for him to stay at school. Bob Carr's father was a train driver and the family lived in a rented fibro home in Matraville – yet Carr went to university. Paul has sometimes said he just wasn't interested, but people have reasons not to be interested. Possibly his difficulty in reading, which is essentially what study and success in exams depends upon, handicapped him too greatly.

Paul not only left as soon as he could but also subsequently paid little attention to his Leaving Certificate studies at night at Belmore Tech. Paul himself recalls: 'I passed in four subjects, which was enough – I think.' (Four was indeed enough for the certificate.) He would soon demonstrate himself to be a tireless and highly focused worker when pursuing an objective that was important to him, but there is a gap there from the age of 15 when he started work to the age of 21 or 22 when he became deeply involved in Labor Party work. Paul, as a very young man, was taking it easy.

Immediately after his fifteenth birthday, he began working full time as a clerk with the Labor Party-controlled Sydney County Council, which bought electricity and distributed it to all of Sydney. He worked for a year in the then decaying and tattered Queen Victoria Building. The following year he moved to the SCC building in Pyrmont, working in the transformer handling department.[23]

A quick, interesting young man, Paul fastened on to teachers. Working on substations and reticulation cables in the Sydney County Council, he got to know a Russian mathematician, a fellow employee, who calculated electricity loads. He was fascinated by the algebra and eagerly absorbed the new knowledge. In his mind, what he learned directly in this way substituted for formal courses. He couldn't see the point of formal courses. At best he would qualify for a job as an engineer in the SCC, and that was a career he didn't want. 'Don't do courses,' the mathematician told him. 'Just find out what you want to know. Get the essence and move on.' He had a huge appetite to learn and developed an ability to seize and hold large amounts of information. Then and later he wanted to put things together, but he thought he could do it without formal study. He could see that he had different abilities from his companions. He found he was already becoming a better judge of people than his companions were.

He had part-time jobs as well. He took photographs of diners at the Metropole Hotel. He worked in David Jones' Bankstown store as a sales assistant for three hours on Saturday mornings. In 1994 a Sydney newspaper quoted what purported to be a personnel file from David Jones on Keating, which noted that he had the wrong attitude and should not be rehired. If true the report is scarcely surprising. He also worked in sales for one of the rapidly growing project home builders of the 1960s, Gavin & Shallala.

He remained at the SCC for six years from 1959 to 1965 and acquired the colloquialisms that he used to great effect throughout his adult life. Before politics crowded all else out, he looked about. He joined a wheat sharecropping syndicate, which leased a property in the Riverina, at Urana, north of Corowa. Sharecropping was interesting, but not for long. Thirty years later he would pounce on Kim Beazley in a Cabinet dispute over Western Australian wheat farmers, telling his colleagues that he knew what it was like to sit in the truck all night in line for the silo, an intervention calculated to unsettle Beazley, who had two post-graduate degrees and could always be disconcerted by a colleague's claim to hard hands and honest toil, even such a claim by the pale and finely boned Treasurer.

The rock music industry attracted him. In the early 1960s he used to go a pub in Enfield to hear an Australian group, the Ramrods, who played black American blues rock. He offered to be their manager. Band member Barry Connors recalled, 'He wasn't even in it for the girls, like most of the blokes who were in rock then. In fact, his morals were as high as anybody I've ever known. He abstained from all that stuff, he was too busy learning how to make things happen. I think he just liked music and wanted to get close to it.' He succeeded in arranging a record contract with EMI, but there were no big hits. Keating believed the problem was that they did not write their own songs. As politics became more demanding, he drifted away.[24] Recalling the period he said, 'I'd like to say there was some sense of order but I just went where life took me. It wasn't all planned back then. If you wanted to take an interest in music, you did. There was a great circle of us, and we'd go away in buses or hire a ferry every few weeks for parties. We'd stop at Clark Island or Shark Island, sometimes spend the night. I was always singing in those days. I didn't have a strong voice and could never have made it professionally, but I'd have a go at anything – Beatles songs, current hits, even Frankie Lane songs like "3.10 to Yuma", plus I would sing with the Ramrods. I loved it when performers were breaking new ground – people like Chuck Berry, Little Richard, Sam Cook, Otis Redding, the Beatles and the Tamla Motown crowd.'[25]

Thinking of a business career, he left the SCC in 1965 for a Hong Kong trading company, Wheelock Marden, where he worked for eighteen months with a couple of accounts, including lead battery plates and cordial from Tasmania's Huon Valley. When the company was reorganised and the Sydney staff sacked, Paul moved on, but he would ever after take a very dim view of the British traders of Hong Kong and the British role in what was then called the Far East. He went next to the Electricity Commission of New South Wales for a year and finally the Federated Municipal and Shire Council Employees Union in 1968, when he was 24 and already well on his way to winning pre-selection for a federal seat.

As a young man Paul looked like his son Patrick at the same age, Trish Kavanagh, who married Paul's friend Laurie Brereton, would sometimes say – the same olive skin, the same embarrassed, adolescent beauty. But in photographs Paul looks a thinner boy than Patrick, so thin and tall as to be slightly concave most of the time. Paul was never much interested in team sports and, for the competitive person he was to become, he was not interested in competitive sports. His press releases as Prime Minister describe him as supporter of Canterbury-Bankstown Rugby League Club 'since early childhood', but while he might have been an occasional fan he was not a player. Bankstown had an excellent Olympic pool and Paul became a good swimmer. For a time he seriously trained for competitive swimming under Olympic swimming coach Don Talbot. 'I was certainly in the state championship area. I never pulled it off but I was within a hair's breadth.'[26] Somewhere along the line he also became a reasonable tennis player. Later he would dabble in sailing and flying, but his most absorbing hobbies were ones that involved machines, like cars, clocks and aeroplanes. As in other activities in his life, in his pursuits and friendships, in his intellectual interests, he liked to move from one to the other, coming back when his interest was refreshed by diversity. He kept budgerigars. He loved powered model boats, and Annita was surprised to find he had them still at age 30, when they married.

He discovered he had a ready sensitivity to beautiful things. His eyes and ears opened to aesthetic pleasures. At 15 he was interested in the mechanism of timepieces, then in their appearance. He learned about the famous French watchmaker Breguet, and bought a few timepieces made by members of his school. At lunchtimes he stared into the window of Stanley Lipscome's antiques shop in Bathurst Street, Sydney. Soon he was going in, and learning about the Empire period in France and the Regency period in England, the period of classical revival in art, architecture and decoration. He learned about Palladian architecture and the connection between the admiration of the aesthetic ideals of Greece, the French Revolution, and the American Declaration of Independence. Order, reason, progress – they were political ideals, represented in art. Napoleon and Jefferson fascinated him. He read about Thomas Hope, the founder of the Regency style in England. He admired the civic virtues, the stoicism that the style evoked, and the elegant simplicity of its forms. Later he would become a world-class expert on the period 1790 to 1814 in decoration, and particularly on the Retour d'Egypte period of French decoration. He would possess some of the greatest examples of the period, and his views on provenance and authenticity would be sought by dealers and curators in England and the United States. He would know as much about the silver of the period as anyone on earth and possess a well-chosen collection. As a young man he found he was charmed by beauty. Throughout his political career he would find, he later reflected, that music, painting, decoration and architecture 'filled the bottle up' and restored the vivacity drained by the cares and conflicts of political office.

He also had a passion for design. He thought the E-type Jaguar the cleverest car of its time and as a young man bought one. Engineering and design would remain lifelong interests.

Neither of his parents read books, listened to music or visited art galleries. But it is surprising how little difference this makes to a child's interests if there are council libraries and radios. As a young teenager he rode his bike to visit a friend in a nearby suburb. His friend's father happened to be playing Richard Addinsell's 1941 'Warsaw Concerto', a popular piece composed for the film *Dangerous Moonlight*. Listening on the verandah to the record being played in the lounge-room, Paul was entranced. It was his introduction to music in the classical style. He listened to recordings of Tchaikovsky, Rachmaninov, and Mendelssohn. Widening his interests, he went by train and bus to the Opera House building site to hear Paul Robeson sing in a visit arranged by the Communist Party. He heard one classical concerto, and a little later he heard a record of the same concerto conducted by Klemperer and was alerted to the importance of musical interpretation. He bought more records – Beethoven now, as well as Brahms. Then along came the Beatles and Paul gave up classical music. He would not take it up again until his mid twenties, during the long pre-selection battle for Blaxland upon which his whole future career depended. After a day and a long evening soliciting votes, visiting the homes of party members and sharing tea, organising his supporters, talking and planning, the 24-year-old would return home and put on the headphones, Chopin's Barcarolle or a Beethoven symphony spilling into his ears and evoking glory in his heart, while Matt and Min, Lyn, Anne and Greg slept peacefully on in the otherwise silent house.

He visited Bankstown library. When he was 17 he read Alan Bullock's *Hitler: A Study in Tyranny* and Hugh Trevor-Roper's *Last Days of Hitler*. To Bullock, Hitler was a calculating, clever politician; to Trevor-Roper, a fanatic – two of the many aspects leaders could present. Those two books about a man still alive when Paul was born, whose actions would still influence the conduct of nations and the map of the world when Paul became Prime Minister, vividly demonstrated to the growing boy the seriousness and consequence of political struggle. Politics in Canberra when he was an adolescent might be about ten shillings on the basic wage or two shillings on the pension, but politics could also be about the lives and deaths of millions. It showed him that it was political leaders who ran things, not generals or civil servants. It taught him what the Holocaust had meant in Europe. 'If I was a four by two [a Jew],' he would say, more than thirty years later, 'I wouldn't even have given them a trial – just bang, bang, bang.' As a young man he read Churchill's World War I history, *The World Crisis*. Later his reading was more focused. He read Teddy White's *Making of the President, 1960* so thoroughly that Bob Carr, when he first met him, believed it was the only book he had ever read. He read about Roosevelt, whom he found the most humane and big personality, and Churchill, who was the most exciting. Matt was showing him how the local politics worked, these books showed him the wider world.

Politics, he thought, was an arena, 'where one would have a great influence on events, where the canvas was broader and all that I ever read convinced me this was true.'[29] Never a reader of novels, he enjoyed Labor Party history, all political histories, and biography – particularly biography. He liked to see the pattern of great lives, their successes and failures and points of decision. As a young clerk in downtown Sydney, he haunted Berkelouw's secondhand bookshop in King Street. He bought Billy Hughes' *The Case for Labor* and the *Labor Daily Yearbooks*, which inventoried social welfare and industrial achievements throughout Australia. But he enjoyed listening and talking as well – he wanted to apprehend reality in a way impossible through a book, and he had a gift for communicating his need and his enthusiasm.

His work life to age 24, a total of nearly a decade, hardly fitted him for the kind of country Australia was becoming. He did not have sufficient schooling to allow him to enter university or to make any further formal study easy. He did not have enough experience of private enterprise to encourage him into his own business. Unlike his father, he did not have a readily saleable skill or one that could form the basis of an independent business. He did not have a skill like accountancy that would allow him to rise in clerical work. He has sometimes said that he would have gone on to become an engineer if he had failed pre-selection, but even by the late 1960s he would have needed a university degree in engineering to compete against thousands of others in the same field. To Paul the most obvious alternative work was the concrete business. He had persuaded his father to make ready-mixed concrete, as well as manufacture the mixers. The new business proved more profitable than the old. But he knew the concrete business well enough to know exactly how his life would be shaped. Taking the orders in the morning, despatching the trucks, checking the accounts, negotiating with the suppliers. He would have a nice house and a nice car. For a boy who read avidly of Churchill directing the British fleets in World War I, or promising blood sweat and tears in World War II, and who thought about Roosevelt pulling the world out of the Great Depression, running the concrete business was simply impossible. It was useful, necessary and important – but it was not grand, romantic, or noble. 'I'd have been very comfortable,' he recalled, 'but what was the point?' Compared to public life, Paul thought, these alternatives open to him were 'nowhere'. Churchill was 'one of the reasons I am in public life. I thought everything else paled into insignificance.' But other politicians from poorer homes – John Hewson, John Howard and Bob Carr are examples – made more of their first twenty years than Paul.

It was characteristic of Australia of the times with steady growth, high tariffs, low unemployment and the assurance that clerical jobs in government organisations were secure and available. This ordinariness was not merely a misleading prelude to an exceptional career. It was and remained an essential part of Paul Keating. It was the hard rock upon which his plain manner and colourful vernacular speech would be built. His ordinariness would in time become one of his greatest strengths, one of the sources of his charm and the most beguiling element of his complexity.

The most important characteristic of Paul's childhood, its most revelatory fact, the attribute he would take from it that would determine his most secret and his most obvious being, was its complete absence of emotional trauma. It was such a normal upbringing, in the sense in which Father McCarthy would use the word, that it cannot even be called normal because to be that close to the ideal is abnormal. The secret of Keating's exceptional, even brilliant, political skills is that they are built on a core of inviolate and impregnable personal security so complete that is not noticeable. His childhood was one in which he was automatically pre-eminent among his siblings, in which none of these siblings died or vanished and all were more or less equally normal, in which his parents did not go broke or become wealthy or separate or divorce or go mad or suffer fantastic delusions or badly misperceive the world. In which his father worked diligently and seized such opportunities as came his way and in which his mother was fully employed keeping the house and raising the four children. In which the children were encouraged but not driven and in which no unreasonable ambitions were entertained for their future success and in which the Catholic church provided at least a temporary explanation of and method for dealing with both the rational and the irrational forces of life: sex, ambition, hatred, envy, love, why are we here and what should we do. It was an upbringing in which there was sufficient but not excess, in which there was a council pool for swimming and cheap local Catholic schools for learning, and acres of space for playing.

He got on reasonably well with and was well accepted by other boys, but he was not then a leader. He was not a troublemaker or a rebel in school. He accepted without any real question or examination the principal beliefs of the Catholic church, though he did not then or later exhibit the slightest zealotry. There was no spiritual or philosophical crisis to shiver his certainties. His knowledge of the world outside Bankstown, St Brendan's, St Felix de Valois and the Catholic Youth Organisation was quite slender. He had not yet travelled much within, let alone outside, Australia. He had not experienced poverty or wealth, hardship or luxury, despair or delight. He was not sad, not lonely, not strange, not challenged. He was a round peg in a round hole.

Paul lived in the same modest house with the same family members for the first twenty-two years of his life, moved only when they moved and to the same house they moved to, and ultimately left his parents' home only when he married at age 30 and only then to move next door but one, an arrangement that seemed sensible to him, although it could not have been entirely satisfactory to his wife. The result is that Paul does not seem to have gloomy periods of self-doubt, he does not need or crave or even allow himself to be much influenced by the approval of others and recognises this independence as a great source of strength. Despite a quite sensitive and emotional personality, he is almost invariably sensible and sober in his judgements of situations and people, something you cannot be if you are not yourself perfectly self-possessed as well as deeply experienced. The only negatives he seems to have carried away from this childhood are those characteristics of a child confident to an unusual degree of his mother's love and his family's devotion – the assumption that his charm will forgive him his discourtesies, the conviction that what he does is always right or at least justifiable. He was sometimes a bit of skite.

2

THE PARTY

KEATING'S ORDINARINESS in his late adolescence was real but also misleading, because there was one element in his life that utterly changed its course and which would lift him high above the path he appeared to be following. That element was the Australian Labor Party. It was the Labor Party that provided him with the theatre to discover and then develop the peculiar set of talents which were to make him such a formidable politician. It would also provide him with a career.

Paul had been born when John Curtin was Prime Minister. He was 5 when Menzies swept Labor from power in 1949. He was only 10 in 1954 when Dr Evatt and the federal parliamentary Labor Party won just over half of the vote but just under half the seats in the House of Representatives.

From the time Paul was 11 he was helping his father hand out how-to-vote cards in the Labor Party booths around Bankstown. He would have been on the booths in 1955, when Menzies obtained a dissolution of both the House and Senate following the split within the Victorian Labor Party. More than 15 per cent of the Labor vote in that state went to the Democratic Labor Party. He was 14 by the 1958 election for the House and half of the Senate. The split had spread to Queensland, and branches of the DLP had been formed in other states to raise its total vote to nearly 10 per cent. The Labor Party won just under 43 per cent of the vote. Even in New South

Wales, the Democratic Labor Party won nearly six per cent of the vote, and the hostility around the polling booths in Bankstown, where fellow churchgoers were on opposite booths, was intense.

Paul was 17 when Arthur Calwell led the Labor Party to within two seats of victory in 1961. In the next federal election two years later Labor lost a couple of percentage points in its overall vote but ten seats in the House and with them any expectation that it would soon return to office. An entire generation of able politicians was wasting its talents and growing old in Opposition, and a new generation was already lining up for their seats. By 1966, when Menzies' successor Harold Holt annihilated Labor in an election fought on Vietnam, Paul was already seeking a career in the party, positioning himself to run for Labor pre-selection in the next House election. When the next election came round he was the Labor Party candidate for one of the safest Labor Party seats in Australia.

Out of power in Canberra, Labor remained in office in New South Wales all through Paul's childhood. William McKell was Premier when Paul was born, then Jim McGirr, Joe Cahill and Bob Heffron before Jack Renshaw lost to the Liberals' Bob Askin in May 1965, when Paul was 21.

Matt took him along to join the Central Bankstown Branch of the Labor Party in 1958. The members were mostly 'blokes in their fifties and sixties', he later recalled, and for many years Paul remained the youngest member by several decades. They passed resolutions calling for the State Government to install more traffic lights on the Hume Highway, which divided North Bankstown from Central Bankstown. They debated whether Dr Evatt should go.[1]

Labor Party branches meet monthly. The secretary tables the minutes of the previous meeting, reads correspondence, and makes any necessary announcements. There is a general business session during which members propose resolutions in favour of this or against that, instructing the government to do this thing or the other, or expressing the outrage of the branch on an issue. Following or preceding general business there is often a talk from a visitor who is generally the local federal or state member or a senator who has been allocated the district in his party responsibilities. As well as debating resolutions, the branch elects delegates to a state electorate council, which includes all the branches in the state electorate, and to a federal electorate council, which includes all the branches in the federal electorate. These councils function as campaign committees during elections and are also the bodies from which delegates are drawn for the state conferences.

Paul joined the party at a time when it was still reeling from the aftershock of the split and the wounds were fresh enough to hurt. The Catholic hierarchy had already withdrawn support for the Movement, but the right-wing Catholics who formed the overwhelming majority of the Bankstown branch were troubled by the split with their co-religionists in the Democratic Labor Party. Those who left often regarded those who remained as either communists or fellow travellers compliant with or hoodwinked by the communists and their allies. Accused by the Left of being sympathetic to the National Civic Council, which Santamaria formed in December 1957 to continue his work outside the Catholic hierarchy, right-wing Catholic Labor Party members in New South Wales were also treated as traitors by NCC members, by the new Democratic Labor Party, and by important members of the Catholic church hierarchy. Later Paul would find that Catholics interstate regarded New South Wales Catholics who stayed with the Labor Party as traitors. Evatt had first dallied with the Industrial Groups, then led the fight against them, so right-wing Catholics remaining in the party were often hostile to his leadership. 'In our branch,' Keating recalled, 'it was unspeakable what people thought in those days about Evatt.'[2]

Because it retained the Industrial Groups and the Catholic Right, the Labor Party in New South Wales remained broad and powerful but the war continued within it. Right-wing union officials dominated the New South Wales Labor Council and elected its officers. They commanded a majority on the floor of the State Labor Conference and elected the party officials. As Paul became active in the party he was drawn into a network of sympathetic Catholics carrying on the work of the Movement and guided from the offices of the

Paulian Association in Sydney. Aspiring young politicians like Paul would present themselves for inspection if they wanted a word in the right quarters. The dominance of the Right was contested by the Left Wing Steering Committee, representing left-wing unions and their allies in the Labor Party branches. Organised by Labor Party state branch officers, right-wing Catholics and their allies fought the Left for control of most branches and unions in the state, and nowhere was the struggle more intense or harder fought than in Sydney's western suburbs, where the prizes were Labor pre-selection for safe federal and state parliamentary seats. In neighbouring electorates the Left was powerful, the more so as the children of working-class parents began entering universities in large numbers and were radicalised by the conscription issue and Australian support for US military intervention in Vietnam. Paul's truculent style in political combat was born in that harsh battle between the Left and the Right of the Labor Party.

Paul was, however, very far from being a conventional Catholic right-winger in the mould of so many of his contemporaries. He mined an older Labor tradition. While working in the city he began regularly visiting former New South Wales Premier Jack Lang, who would become, after his father, the first of several older mentors on whom he drew for experience. Paul's attraction to the political generations preceding his own, together with his lack of formal education, marked him as a political oddity even within his own faction.

Paul visited Lang for years. 'I was in the Youth Council in 1965 and I knew him before that so it was probably 1964 when I met him. I went there weekly and twice-weekly for years and years. I got him back into the party in 1971 and I was still seeing him just before he died in 1973 or '74. When I was in the Municipal Employees Union the secretary Reg Triggs used to say, "Going off to see Lang, are you?" because Reg had been in the Colbourne–Chifley group and they hated Lang. I used to pick him up at his home at Schofields near Windsor and take him to schools where he gave speeches.'

Paul was 20, becoming prominent in Youth Council, and Lang

was a strong, deaf 89. Lang published his newspaper *Century* out of an office opposite the southern end of Hyde Park near the ALP offices on Elizabeth Street in Sydney. The old man and the young clerk fell into a pattern of having lunch once or twice a week, Paul taking his sandwiches up to the *Century* office, and presenting to the fierce, deaf old man a list of things he wanted Lang to talk about.

Born in poverty in 1876 in the inner-city slums of Sydney, Lang had picked up skills as an accountant before becoming a wealthy and successful real estate agent in the developing western suburb of Auburn, just north of Bankstown. A big man, John Thomas Lang was nearly two metres tall and weighed just over 100 kilos. In 1913 he had become a Labor member of the New South Wales Legislative Assembly, in 1920 Treasurer in a Labor government, and in 1925 and again in 1930 Premier of New South Wales. Though fiscally orthodox as Treasurer ('our duty is to balance accounts,' he said in his 1920 budget speech) and, as his biographer Bede Nairn remarks, 'by no means a social reformer',[3] he had a combative demagogic style, which aroused fierce loyalties and antagonisms. Responding to the depression-induced fiscal crisis in New South Wales, in 1931 he repudiated interest payments on overseas loans, an action that led the Governor of New South Wales, Sir Philip Game, to dismiss him from office the following year. Failing to win government back in the subsequent election, Lang's career declined. William McKell wrested the leadership of the New South Wales parliamentary Labor Party from him in 1939. Forming a short-lived Anti-Communist Labor Party in 1940, he was expelled from the ALP in 1943 after sustained attacks on the party in *Century*. As a candidate of Lang Labor, he won the seat of Reid in federal parliament in 1946 but was defeated at the next election in 1949. Lang spent the next twenty-six years, until his death, defending his reputation and attacking his old enemies within the party, who included John Curtin, Ben Chifley, Ted Theodore and, earlier, William Holman.

There were many points of resemblance between Lang and the politician Paul was to become. Both were Catholics (although Lang only nominally), both were from Sydney's western suburbs, and Keating was later able to switch into the kind of populist rhetoric that was Lang's bread and butter. Both had roots in small private business, and both opposed and fought the Left in their own party while themselves exploiting resentment against the rich and the established. Both were natty dressers. But there the similarities ended. Lang was champion of states rights, Paul became a champion of Commonwealth power. Lang never left Australia, was xenophobic and opposed to Asian immigration, and deeply suspicious of 'Jewish finance' and foreign banks. Lang came from a childhood of real poverty, in which his father was too sick to work and the family lived in the meanest of rented accommodation; Paul's parents owned their own house and their own business and provided a home so secure, loving and comfortable that Paul did not leave it until marriage. Lang hated people who were cleverer or more assured than he was; Paul admired them and sought to emulate the qualities he valued. Lang was unsure, abrasive and gauche; Paul was charming, secure and at ease.

They could scarcely have been more different in personality, but Keating kept going up there, week after week and year after year, with his sandwiches and his list, sometimes with a friend but usually alone, sitting in an uncarpeted office across a timber desk from the huge old man with well-polished shoes and gold cufflinks whose pants were hitched half-way up his chest and who scowled more than he smiled, sometimes using his thumb to push back a loose cap on his front tooth, and so deaf that he addressed the solitary Keating as if he was at a public meeting. Talking with point and pattern for the precise interval between Keating's scheduled arrival at midday and the old man's abrupt declaration that the discussion was over one hour later, then rising, taking his fob watch off the desk in front of him, clearing his sandwich bag, pulling up his braces, attaching his collar, putting on his coat and hat, and walking down the steps to his barber for a haircut and shave.[4]

Paul's views at this time would have been drawn from his father, Catholic social teaching as communicated by the parochial authorities,

Labor Party right-wing attitudes, and Lang. All of these strands of thought were hostile to expanding foreign investment in Australia, to the idea that the free play of markets would produce the most socially desirable outcomes and to the idea that society should be tolerant of homosexuality, promiscuity, independent and assertive women, or abortion as means of birth control. Paul did not need Lang to be suspicious of markets and big business. Lang might have communicated some crank ideas in economics, but a very important and permanent contribution to Keating's approach to politics was to identify the economy as the battleground and the subject on which a politician would have to win support and take decisions.

What drew Paul to the weekly sandwich lunch was not Lang's views but his memories. 'The policy was not useful,' he says, 'it was the history.' Lang described John Latham, Eddie McTiernan, William Holman and Billy Hughes. He was able to recreate past times for Paul. Lang had been at Henry Parkes' rallies to support Federation of the Australian colonies. He had lived through the conscription split in Labor in 1916 and supported the expulsion of Holman from the party. He had been Treasurer and Premier of New South Wales at the time when being Premier of New South Wales was a bigger job and more highly regarded than being Prime Minister of Australia – before the Commonwealth had obtained control of a preponderant share of revenues and when Australia's defence and foreign policies were still subsidiary to the defence and foreign policies of the United Kingdom. He had been through the depression. He had raised his scissors to cut the ribbon on the Sydney Harbour Bridge when de Groot rode up and slashed it with his sword. He had been dismissed by the Governor and addressed huge rallies in the Domain. He had known, and hated, Curtin, Chifley, Ted Theodore. Bert Evatt and Arthur Calwell, towering figures to Paul, were newcomers and novices to Lang. In his memories Lang covered the whole of the recent past that was of interest and of use to Paul, although from a peculiar perspective that Paul for a time acquired.

Paul's friend Bob Carr would later talk of the excitement of reading Fin Crisp's *Ben Chifley* and other texts of Labor history. Keating read the books, but his Labor history was re-enacted in the memories of Lang. He acquired Lang's interest in finances, in the play of international markets and influences, in government spending and taxing. He acquired a focus that was primarily economic. In his early twenties Keating revered Lang as 'the greatest living Australian.'[5] Speaking to reporter Joe Glascott in 1969[6] Paul said, 'My political mentor is Jack Lang.' By his late forties Paul was sensitive on the subject of Lang, not least because Prime Minister Bob Hawke had associated Keating's failure to properly revere Curtin (or Hawke, or anyone else) in a speech to the National Press Club at the end of 1990 with the lingering influence of Lang. Keating told one interviewer that: 'Lang wasn't an inspiration to me. My inspiration came from other people, Churchill and Roosevelt. But [meeting Lang] gave me a sense of a round of history, and he was a very strong, huge, gigantic personality. Oh, you couldn't meet him and not see it, all the views and the power, huge power . . . I had a much better mind's eye picture of the party's background going back from the 1960s, 1950s, 1940s, 1930s, 1920s, – you know? So not only did I have a big contemporary operation, but I had all these bits and pieces filled in, pen sketches of personalities or whatever.'[7]

Throughout his life the stories and maxims of Lang would form part of Keating's patter, of his own collection of frequently retold anecdotes that constituted his story. 'There is only one reliable friend you have in the world, son,' Lang would say, 'and he is sitting right here in front of me now.' He would say he had met someone who admired Paul greatly and that in the end would be the only person Paul could trust. When Paul asked who it was, he said 'you'. He would say, 'Always put your money on self-interest, son, it's the best horse in the race. It's always a trier.' On budgets, 'As the New South Wales railways go, so goes New South Wales', or 'as New South Wales goes, so goes the Commonwealth.' In respect of flashy and meretricious early successes in politics, 'They are the sky rockets of politics – a shower of sparks and then a burnt stick falls to earth', a saying Paul would still be repeating thirty years later because he found after arriving in Parliament that he had to wait until he was nearly 40 before he could get a chance to show his real talents. 'Lang was a kindly man,' he recalled to former federal minister Clyde Cameron in 1993, 'you couldn't get him to talk about the past.' To others Paul said emphatically, 'Here he was at 90, and he would never *never* talk about the past – unless you asked him. Never. He never looked back.' One thing stuck: 'I think the thing I learned about him was the hardness of his judgment about people, how to judge people, how to be a hard judge of other people.'[8]

At the same time as he was visiting Lang and becoming a more assured and prominent member of his Labor Party branch in Bankstown, Paul was being drawn into the party's Youth Council. It met in the evening at least once a month in a room of the party offices in Elizabeth Street, Sydney. For some years it was acrimoniously split between the far Right and the far Left.

The meeting room was quite small for the crowd of between seventy and a hundred young people, and the atmosphere was often highly charged. The delegates sat on wooden fold-up seats facing a table at which the secretary, president and assistant secretary sat. Behind them was a small frosted-glass partition where the officers of the council could caucus during the frequently heated clashes between the factions.

Every meeting was a brawl, and every meeting made the party look bad. In 1966 Labor Party State Secretary Bill Colbourne had a solution. 'Jack,' he asked his assistant secretary John Armitage, 'why don't you ask the Organising Committee to abolish Youth Council?' Armitage thought there might be a less drastic remedy, and that night the committee gave him the brief to produce a new leadership at Youth Council. The officers wanted to remain in control, but they wanted more guile and deftness in handling their opponents.[9]

John Armitage got to work to devise a new right-wing leadership for Youth Council. In the first year the leader was Peter Gould but then Gould got married and began a family, and Armitage had to find some new recruits. One group was out at the University of New

South Wales, and his son introduced him to a young member of the Labor Club, Bob Carr. Another was Laurie Brereton, already active in the eastern suburbs, and another, one he met at Repins coffee shop one evening in the company of Brereton, was Paul Keating.

Keating had already attended a few Youth Council meetings and was on the list of reliable people brought in as delegates to support the new leadership of Gould. Laurie Brereton recalls that he had first met Keating at a Youth Council right-wing caucus in 1965 when Paul would have been 21. Soon after this meeting, during a conversation on a train between Town Hall and Central, Keating proposed that he and Brereton take over Youth Council themselves – Keating as President, Brereton as Secretary.[10] One of Gould's supporters, Ron Dyer, had a claim on the President's job, so one night, walking in Hyde Park, Keating told him he wanted the job and asked if Dyer would postpone his own run. He needed the Youth Council presidency to strengthen his campaign for pre-selection. Dyer agreed.[11] Laurie Brereton worked the eastern suburbs delegates, Paul the western suburbs, John Armitage supplied the list of names of people to contact. Elected President and Secretary respectively in 1967, Paul and Brereton ran the Youth Council until they resigned in 1969.

By the mid 1960s the temperature of the factional division at Youth Council had been raised by conscription and the war in Vietnam. The Left now included radical students while the right faction remained solidly based on the network of the Catholic Youth Organisation, of which Paul was a member. The typical left-winger at Youth Council was a student, the typical right-winger was already working. While the Right's religious basis can easily be overdrawn, there is no doubt it was an important element. Keating's successor as Youth Council President, Leo McLeay, remembered, 'What they really used to ask you was, what school did you go to? Because the sort of line was always "Catholics versus Protestants".'[12] Carr says that it was basically seen as 'Catholics versus Comms', although he and Ron Dyer were not Catholics.[13] Graham Richardson, later to become state secretary, said that the Right 'was fundamentally CYO based' while the Left was 'Vietnam based'. When the CYOs died in the early 1970s, the Right lost Youth Council leadership.[14]

The Vietnam War was a difficult issue for Paul's faction. There were certainly some members of the Right who were in favour of sending American and Australian soldiers to support the government of South Vietnam. Prime Minister Ngo Dinh Diem was a Catholic, supported generally by the international hierarchy. He was fighting communists. The Irish Catholic Right traditionally disliked the UK but liked the US. John Kennedy was a Catholic of Irish descent. His successor, Lyndon Johnson, was also a liberal Democrat. The opponents of Australian and American involvement, some of them actual supporters of the North Vietnamese (or the NLF, as they preferred to think), included traditional enemies of the Right – communists, Trotskyists, revolutionary socialists of all kinds who did not accept or support parliamentary government. These were all reasons to support the South, but there were also many to oppose Australian policy. The Australian Government had initiated and pursued the involvement, and the Australian Government was Liberal. It had introduced conscription, which, because it was first proposed in World War I in support of the British Empire, was still anathema to many Catholics. Labor's federal leader Arthur Calwell had promptly and forthrightly opposed the sending of Australian troops in 1965, although the party remained ambivalent about America's commitment. As the war dragged on unsuccessfully for the Americans and the Australians the Labor Right became disenchanted, because, as a pragmatic group, it hated any sort of failure.

Paul was one year ahead of the conscription ballot age, which began with those born in 1945. His views on Vietnam were, he later realised, 'somewhat confused. Sceptical about getting into a land war in Asia; uncertain about the real portents flowing from the Viet Cong. I don't think I argued in favour of Australian involvement. I came to the conclusion that we were better out of the Vietnam War – probably later than some people.'[15]

Paul was climbing in the Labor Party at a time when it was dispirited, deeply divided, and unsuccessful. It lost in New South Wales after twenty-four years of government, and the government that lost was sad and elderly, not the kind of government that people then in their twenties admired. It would be more than a decade before it returned to government. In Canberra, with Arthur Calwell as leader, the party's fortunes had never been so low. For young people then entering the party, people like Keating, Carr and Brereton, it was not at all obvious how it would recover. The Left dominated the party in Western Australia and Victoria, and it could usually count on allies in South Australia and Queensland. Closed door meetings of the Federal Executive and the Federal Conference, which still excluded the party leaders in parliament, presumed to dictate policy to the party in parliament. The policies, on issues like the American alliance, the North West Cape and Vietnam, were ones on which Labor could not hope to win. There was only one hope federally, Keating, Carr and Brereton agreed, and that was Calwell's deputy, Gough Whitlam.

Carr recalls, 'We had imbibed Labor history from our parents and from Fin Crisp's book on Chifley and the Lang books and all the rest. The question was always how Labor might be revived, since this was the period of its greatest decline. It was a ramshackle joke. It had Calwell as national leader. It had lost in New South Wales. There was no vitality in the party except in South Australia, and even there they had lost after one term. The one hope on the horizon was Whitlam. But Whitlam had precious little support in the party outside New South Wales. So all our conversation in the coffee shops after Youth Council was about how you could revive the party, get back into power in New South Wales and federally, how you could combat the Left, which was then easily demonised with Joe Chamberlain and Bill Hartley who had very significant influence and opposed Whitlam's reforms. That was the climate.'[16]

The issue animated Youth Council and the branches. Gough Whitlam was all that Calwell was not – relatively young, a successful professional, articulate on new issues, clever, well educated, handsome and imposing. As Labor leaders always do when under threat (Whitlam in his turn, then Hayden and Hawke in theirs) Calwell turned to the Left for support against Whitlam. Paul's faction was strongly in favour of Whitlam replacing Calwell. To Keating Whitlam 'was a hero'.[17] Whitlam was from New South Wales, he was an opponent of the Left, and his criticisms of the war in Vietnam deliberately echoed those of US congressional doves rather than the European Left or the Communist bloc. But it was also significant that Whitlam was a university graduate and by upbringing a Protestant, two characteristics that undermined and finally destroyed the social solidarity of Keating's political associations and forced him to rethink and rework his position. Its ambiguity over the war in Vietnam hurt the Right with the new generation of Labor-oriented students; its support for Whitlam helped it with the same group.

Youth Council was a useful blooding. Paul later recalled a couple of hundred people banging their feet up and down. 'That what it is all about, developing that authority – and handling difficult situations. I had an idea about where I was going, but you still have to try yourself out on all these things. You've always got to come out on top, you can't ever let them get on top of you.'[18] His success at Youth Council introduced Paul to the core of party officials, leaders of right-wing unions, labour lawyers and key parliamentary politicians who controlled the party and constituted its governing milieu. It was, as Brereton said, an opportunity to meet the heavies. The party head office group was important, although limited. In the New South Wales Labor Party at the end of the 1960s party pre-selection for electorates was in both theory and practice determined by a general ballot of party members living within the electorate. The head office was powerful, but Paul's career chances actually depended on the branches in his electorate. No patron could arrange things for him or for a competitor. Keating later explained that there is, in the New South Wales Labor Party, a head office life and separate boondocks life, because of rank and file pre-selection. 'One lives in two camps,' he said, and the Youth Council was 'a way of jumping from this one to that one,' because 'it was always in orbit around the power apparatus.'[19]

While working in the party's youth wing, he also climbed within the main party organisation, and a few years after joining the

Bankstown Central branch he was an electorate delegate to the State Conference, which met each Queen's Birthday weekend in Sydney Town Hall. After the intimacy and the familiarity of meetings of the Central Bankstown Branch, the annual state conferences of the New South Wales branch of the Australian Labor Party were exciting and momentous events. Paul went to his first around 1962. The conference would run over three days with nearly a thousand delegates from branches, trade unions and parliaments. The federal leader of the party would usually address the delegates, as would the state leader. The conflicts between the Left and Right were great bitter clashes, upon which depended not only ideas and symbols and party policies but also trade union and party jobs and selection for parliament.

Laurie Brereton had been immediately drawn to Paul by his energy, single-mindedness and good humour. It was a common response to Paul in those days – whatever else, he was fun to be with. Carr, then a university student, recalls first meeting with Keating in John Armitage's office. 'Paul was very well dressed and that is one of the most remarkable things out of those years. My contemporaries and I were all shabby and here was Paul in very smart suits and even when he wore a pullover under his winter-weight suits, the colours were perfect. I remember him saying on one occasion, "I can't resist a bit of good tweed." [20] They talked politics, and they enjoyed themselves. 'Keating had an infectious sense of fun,' says Carr. He liked all types of music – Ginger Rogers and Fred Astaire records, classical music. Carr once called him at home and heard music over the phone, 'I'm soaking up Tchaikovsky,' said Keating. Later he told Carr that he used to listen to Mozart all the time, but he'd 'gone off it now.' He brought battered old clocks home, pulled them apart and restored them, so they became beautiful things. Later, Keating's interests seemed to multiply depending on the number of interviews he gave. He was just about to take his flying licence.

Keating had hobbies and jobs, and he took courses, but he was more and more preoccupied with winning a seat and becoming a professional politician. Carr recalls visiting him at the union, taking down a Youth Council leaflet to be duplicated. Keating would come out and take the sheet, ignoring the union members waiting around the enquiry counter, and disappear back inside. Youth Council had lost its interest for him. 'Listen,' he told Carr in 1968, as he pressed him to take over the leadership of Youth Council, 'I don't have time to worry about this shit.'

Paul had decided that he would prefer a political career to the other alternatives available to him. It was an easy decision to make. His choices were to continue working as a clerk, to finish his matriculation and begin serious university study, to begin working in his father's business, or to try his chances at becoming a federal politician and potentially a leader of his country. For a young man discovering that he had more energy and intelligence than most of the people he came in contact with, and discovering also that he could excite, enthuse and amuse people so that they sought his views and his company, politics was the natural theatre for his talents. Certainly he believed in Labor policies and rejected those of the Liberal Party. But politics as a career also had higher status, paid more and offered many more opportunities than any other alternative he had open to him. It was also the career Matt Keating had nudged him towards from his earliest years. However, it was one thing to want a career in politics and quite another to have one. 'You can't decide on a career in politics,' he said later, 'because you've got to find a seat in Parliament, and they are not easy to come by.'[21]

He had got to know Eric Costa, federal member for Banks since 1949, the seat that covered the Labor Party branches in the Bankstown area where Paul and his father were best known. 'Costa said to me privately that he would not stand again,' Paul remembered, 'so I knew before the 1966 election that it would be his last. That's when I decided to go for it, when I knew he was going. I would never have opposed him; it would have been dumb.'[22]

The decision made, 'By the time I was 21 I was flat out, working flat out on my pre-selection every night of the week. I went for it because federal seats were one-in-twenty-years jobs. I knew it would come up and if I didn't get it, that was it. So it was now or never. I thought it's going to take me at least four or five years, I've got to start now.' But it was a risk. 'Four years – virtually every night of the week for four years – I could have lost the lot. What would I have done then? But it was a four-year investment, longer than that – a ten-year investment. Four years at absolute fever pace. I pursued it like a hungry dog, I never let it go. I hung onto the bone.'[23]

Eric Costa was an anomaly in Banks. He was a right-winger in an area where the branches were predominantly left-wing. Matt and his allies in the Catholic Labor Right called it 'the red belt', a wide stretch of the western suburbs reaching from the bend of the George's River near Bankstown airport north to Parramatta. Costa had won his seat in 1949, and the Left let him alone. When he retired, they meant to have their own candidate to succeed him.

To win Banks Paul would need to build up the branches with his own supporters. His campaign generals were Matt and a tax office official then in his forties, Vince Martin. He had been a friend of Matt's since they had met in the Industrial Groups and together fought the Left in the East Hills state electorate council.[24] Other key supporters were Wal Adnum and Vic Beavis. Their main stronghold was the Bankstown Central branch in which Paul's supporters were predominantly drawn from the St Brendan's crowd. The branch met in the Bankstown Sports Club, a more attractive venue than the tin-roofed school change shed in which the nearby Condell Park branch met. This branch remained under the control of left-winger Murt O'Brien, a metal union official. 'Paul was more mature than those of us who were students,' recalls Carr, 'because he realised quite early that the route to power in the ALP was pre-selection.' Keating needed to win pre-selection for a safe Labor seat and to do that he needed to bring in enough new Labor Party members who would be committed to him to overwhelm other potential candidates.

Keating had to get the numbers, and he got them where he could. 'He had to get out there night after night to persuade people to join an ALP branch. You had to talk to friends of friends. You get familiar with problems like what happens when you get a new branch member and you get his girlfriend, and then they break up. Can you still get the former girlfriend to take out a ticket?' recalled Carr, who had had much the same experience himself. 'The best people to recruit are little old ladies. Lang had told Keating that and he was right. I was to discover this myself when I got serious about lining up the numbers for Maroubra in the early 1980s. Little old ladies who were in the Labor Party with their husbands. They will back you through thick and thin. It is one of the eternal laws of rank-and-file pre-selections. There is a Left mythology that he just got Catholics into the party. He told me once that wasn't the case – you got them where you could find them. Friends of friends, people from clubs. That's how it works.'

To join the party a potential member needed to attend one meeting to be proposed and seconded, and then another to be admitted. Keating had to make sure the member came to the first, and then not only came to the second but also came with the money to buy his or her ticket. 'It's the hardest task in the world, Robbie,' he later told Carr. 'Of course in a third of cases you get them to their first meeting and then they are not able to come to the second,' says Carr, 'so that means you have to get them to come along to the one after that or you lose them. Then you have to make sure they sign the attendance book, and have their money to take the ticket out and sign the roll book. Then you have to make sure you get them to come back for another two meetings within twelve months to be eligible to vote in the pre-selection ballot.' Ron Dyer, later a minister in Carr's government in New South Wales, recalls visiting the Keating home in Gerard Avenue in those days and seeing on the wall of Paul's bedroom the cardboard chart that had his supporters' names down the left-hand column and dates of meetings across the top, so he could tell at a glance who would have to be dragged along to a meeting to maintain their eligibility to vote.

Not only did eligible voters have to attend a minimum number of meetings, but they also had to have been a member of the party for one year prior to the announcement of the timing of the pre-selection ballot. This meant that all the requirements for voting had to be completed one year before the vote. Under party rules, new members were required to join the closest branch in their state electorate. These rules were central to the dispute that developed over the legitimacy of Paul's pre-selection.

Paul's votes were not all Catholics, but the network of the Church and the CYO was the most important single source of support. For Bankstown Central, his strongest branch, the congregation of St Brendan's was the key. Michael Hatton was one of more than forty who joined the Bankstown Central branch one night to vote for Keating. Michael's grandmother also joined. So did his uncle, a couple of aunts, his brother and sister-in-law and his mother.

Keating accumulated the numbers during 1967 while putting in appearances at the union office and running Youth Council, slowly accumulating numbers for the seat of Banks until, in the electoral redistribution in early 1968, the part of Banks that included his strongest branch, Central Bankstown, was shifted to the seat of Blaxland. The electoral boundary shifted from Marion Street south to Milperra Road. 'Redistributions are fucking awful things,' he told Carr. The seat of Blaxland included his strongest branches but excluded others he had painstakingly stacked. It also brought with it a sitting member, Eli (Jim) Harrison. In his younger days Harrison had been a force within the ALP, a protégé of Chifley and the man who had defeated Lang for his seat in federal parliament. Never a smart or energetic man, Harrison had declined over the years and now spent a good deal of his time living in a Melbourne hotel. Harrison was certainly vulnerable, not least because, although the seat of Blaxland had the same name, it was otherwise quite altered from the old seat of Blaxland. Of fifteen or so Labor branches in the electorate, only a few had been in Harrison's former electorate and could be expected to support him. Several of the biggest branches, including Chester Hill and Bass Hill, had been formerly in Tom Uren's electorate of Reid and were firmly left-wing. The numbers had dramatically altered and Keating was suddenly looking – at age 25, with minimal formal education and a modest clerical job – at the possibility that his four-year bet might be lost and that he, like countless other smart young people who wanted to get into parliament but couldn't, might spend his life on the periphery of power.

Keating could choose between running for Banks or running for Blaxland. On the numbers at the time Blaxland seemed like a safer seat for Labor. (Banks, time would reveal, was also quite safe.) It would probably be harder, however, for a right-winger to win pre-selection in Blaxland. Keating knew he would not face such strong left-wing opposition in Banks, but he would not have the backing of Bankstown Central, which was now in Blaxland. 'In the end,' he recalled, 'you have to follow your people. Tommy Uren had to go where his people went, and I had to go where my people went. I decided I would rather lose in Blaxland and try again than be an orphan in Banks.' His lieutenant Vince Martin, in his late forties and bored with his career as a tax official, was delighted and astonished to find himself the inheritor of Paul's majority in Banks. Paul faced a knock-down drag-out fight with the Left in Blaxland.

Paul Keating and Vince Martin were two unknowns but their fortunes were closely watched in Canberra. Gough Whitlam believed he must reform the party if it was to win government. When Tasmanian delegate Brian Harradine was excluded from the Federal Executive of the party in April 1968 after his inflammatory warning that 'friends of the Communists' would try to silence him at the meeting, Whitlam resigned from leadership of the party to seek a vote of confidence. He won 38 votes. His opponents, Victorian left-winger Jim Cairns, who in February 1967 had won only 15 votes in the election that followed Calwell's resignation, this time won 32. Two more votes for the Right would help Whitlam; two more votes for the Left would bring it closer to the leadership of the party.

From the Chester Hill branch, the Left produced the kind of candidate who could give Keating the most trouble. Bill Junor was already a teaching fellow in economics at the University of New South Wales, the kind of young and well-educated economist the party obviously needed, the kind of person who might make a good Treasurer in ten or fifteen years, who could and did talk about the aims of the party and what it should stand for. He was pleasant, a Catholic and a moderate Leftist, energetic and controlled. An adroit choice. He was backed by the Steering Committee, but he himself had not attended a Steering Committee meeting and did not regard himself as a member of it. (When he did attend his first Steering Committee meeting, after the pre-selection ballot, he opposed a resolution to condemn federal intervention in the Victorian party.) He was strongly opposed to the US and Australian military action in Vietnam but, unlike orthodox left-wingers, he was strongly in favour of government aid to poor private schools – effectively, to the Catholic parochial system in which he himself had been educated. He thought of himself as a left-winger, but his supporters reached beyond the Left.

Complicating Keating's chances were three other candidates who could draw votes from the Right. One, of course, was Harrison, another was the man who would later became Lord Mayor of Sydney before being dismissed by his own party, Doug Sutherland, and the third was the man who very nearly ended Paul Keating's career as it was beginning, right-winger Jack Stewart.

Matt and Paul had built Bankstown Central into a formidable political machine based on the St Brendan's parishioners. It was the biggest single force in the pre-selection. But its appearance of strength concealed a flaw, which the Left detected well before the ballot. Many of its members were drawn not from the Bankstown state electorate, which included the branch, but from the Bass Hill state electorate, which included Condell Park, the neighbouring branch. Under party rules, members should join the closest branch in their state rather than federal electorates. The Keatings had enrolled these supporters in Bankstown Central, which met at the Bankstown Sports Club, for tactical reasons. For a while it concealed from the Left the extent to which the Keatings were organising the numbers. The Bankstown branch met in far more pleasant circumstances than the Condell Park branch, so it was easier to get people to attend meetings. In the looming contest it would be safer to have people in a branch where the Keatings kept the attendance books and issued party tickets than in a branch that the Left controlled.

The Keatings had good tactical reasons to bring new members

into Bankstown Central, but they were joining the wrong branch under party rules. Their votes could be challenged. Members of branches in the electorate began getting anonymous letters pointing out that many new members of Bankstown Central should have joined Condell Park. Recognising the danger, the Keating forces moved quickly. They began transferring members from Bankstown Central to Condell Park. Eventually Matt, Min, Lyn and Anne would also join Condell Park and take over the leadership positions. The Keatings also appear to have unsuccessfully sought Central Executive approval to create a new branch or to transfer the area from which their supporters were drawn from the Condell Park branch to the Bankstown Central branch. As the Keating majority became apparent, disputes erupted at meetings. The Left challenged the right of the new members to transfer. The Keating supporters doggedly insisted. Many of the transfers, however, were occurring during the one year prior to the announcement of the ballot, which meant that the eligibility of these members to vote in the pre-selection depended on their membership of Bankstown Central.

Paul and Vince Martin did the footwork and much of the organising, but Matt made many of the strategic decisions. It was he, for example, who decided to take over the Condell Park branch. During the four-year campaign the Keating family moved to 8 Gerard Avenue in Condell Park. Paul purchased 3 Marshall Street from his parents and used it mainly to garage his cars, but the family nominally resided there to retain membership in and control of Bankstown Central.

Both Matt and Paul saw the contest in simple terms. The left-wingers were communists. Catholics should support Paul. Matt indignantly censured Jack Stewart, a Catholic right-winger whom he mistakenly believed had agreed on an exchange of preferences with Bill Junor. He was appalled by Junor. 'How can you as a Catholic work with Communists?' he asked him.[25]

The candidates worked hard. Armed with lists of members, they canvassed at night and on weekends. When branches met they would come along to speak. There were serious issues, Junor recalls. They spoke about Vietnam, conscription, and the future of the Labor Party. Paul advocated price control; Junor opposed it.

On the evening of 26 October 1968 the ballots were counted for the six candidates for the safe Labor seat of Blaxland, effectively giving to one of them a life-time career as a politician, followed by a well-paid retirement. A few weeks before, the returning officer, Murt O'Brien, had overseen the credentialling of voters, examining attendance books and party tickets to confirm adherence to the voting requirements. At this meeting the Left disputed the credentials of Keating supporters in the Condell Park branch, arguing that some of them had originally joined the wrong branch. The Keating forces raised an objection to votes from the Bass Hill branch. They claimed the books had not been properly kept, and that the only valid votes were those of three Keating supporters who had recently transferred to Bass Hill as part of the general movement out of Bankstown branch. This dispute went to the relevant New South Wales Party committee, which ruled that the Condell Park members were eligible to vote but accepted the Keatings' objections to votes from the Bass Hill branch. (It was generally conceded that the Bass Hill books had not been properly kept.) But on 26 October, the night of the count, Junor's campaign managers gave O'Brien a copy of a letter to the ALP Federal Secretary, repeating the charges that had been dismissed by the New South Wales Branch. If these people voted and their votes were counted, it would be impossible in the secret ballot to separate valid votes from invalid votes later.

Refusing to concede the Keating supporters' argument that the credentialling issue had already been decided according to party rules, and accepting the argument that the challenged votes should be sequestered to allow later resolution, O'Brien put them aside and counted the remainder.

As the votes were taken from the box, O'Brien announced them. Junor had polled 88 votes, Keating 81 and 63 votes went to other candidates. Because he had sequestered votes O'Brien did not declare a result, but the scrutineers for the candidates calculated preferences and saw that the outcome on the night was: Junor 124, Keating 108, with 49 votes challenged and uncounted. It was a startling result for Keating. Stewart's unexpectedly strong vote cut into Keating's, and many of Stewart's preferences flowed on to Junor. The Keating people – Matt, Min, Ron Dyer, and the chief scrutineer for Keating, Laurie Brereton, were aghast, not only by the result but also by O'Brien's determination to take the counted and uncounted ballots home for safekeeping. They knew, as did the Left, that the disputed ballots would give the pre-selection to Keating. But since the ballots were unopened, they were concerned that false ballots could be substituted. 'Murt did not accept the credentialling by the party,' a still-indignant Keating recounted twenty-eight years later. 'He had his own credentialling. He excluded people who transferred from Bankstown Central to Condell Park. Then he wanted to take the ballot boxes home! He did his own list, declared Junor the winner, then wanted to take the ballot boxes home!' After a hurried consultation, Brereton left the building, a Scout hall in Weigand Avenue, hopped on his motorbike and roared off to call Lindsay North, the New South Wales Branch returning officer. When North refused to come out to the hall, Brereton telephoned and woke the federal leader Gough Whitlam in the nearby electorate of Werriwa. Whitlam knew what one caucus vote might mean, and he called North and peremptorily ordered him out of bed. North turned up at 2 a.m. in Bankstown, his pyjamas showing over the tops of his clothes. Six days later he declared the result of the ballot. Keating 145. Junor 125. Following the earlier party decision, the challenged votes for Keating were accepted. Keating was the Labor candidate for Blaxland.

Later portrayed as the candidate of the party officers' machine, Keating received little help from it. Six months after he had won pre-selection the Labor Party Secretary Bill Colbourne told John Armitage, 'If I had been here, he never would have won it.'[26] Colbourne hated Lang and he thought young Keating was an upstart who should wait his turn. Of the inner group at the time, Armitage says he did not oppose Keating's run in Blaxland, and John Ducker, who was then a party vice-president and just about to take over and completely transform the party in New South Wales, supported Keating. 'Ducker was then I think vice-president,' Ducker himself later said, speaking as he sometimes did in a disconcerting third person. 'You must appreciate there were some generational aspects to the officers at that time. Personality differences, so there was not coherence among the officers. I was supporting Keating. I don't know that some of the others were. I think there was a feeling on the part of some that he was young and brash and a bit smart alecky – and not controlled. And Bill Colbourne of course had very definite views about Jack Lang.'[27]

Keating would later say that only party President Charlie Oliver was kind and helpful and encouraging, but Oliver was completely preoccupied by an internal revolt in the Australian Workers Union in New South Wales, which threatened to depose him as secretary. With Colbourne away during a critical time in the pre-selection battle, with Armitage neutral and tied up with an electoral redistribution in New South Wales and then winning pre-selection for his own seat at Chifley, there was no one to stop Keating. There was no one to lend a helping hand to Barney French, a party vice-president and secretary of the Rubber Workers Union, who had been active in the area for years and wanted the seat for himself. Oliver told Keating not to worry about French – Oliver would look after him. He was later made a member of the New South Wales Legislative Council.

If it didn't help him win the pre-selection, the party machine did make sure he kept it. In any other year the result would have been final and unquestioned. Armitage says of Keating, 'I made sure when the ballot was being disputed that some of the silly things he was doing at the time didn't count against him or against the party and particularly the state Labor Party.' Certainly Keating needed head office help to effect the smooth transfer of members from Bankstown Central to Condell Park, and then head office help to refuse objections to the validity of their vote. Had the party upheld both the Left objections to disputed Keating votes and the Keating objections to the disputed Junor votes, Junor would have been the member for Blaxland and not Keating.

Once the New South Wales party had ruled that would, ordinarily, have been the end of the dispute. But times were changing. To win government in Canberra Whitlam needed to destroy the left-wing branch in Victoria. To destroy Victoria with the support of Queensland and South Australia, he would have to accept that the equally monolithic, equally narrow but right-wing branch of New South Wales would also need to be opened up. One result of this was the 1970 Federal Executive meeting in Broken Hill, at which the New South Wales Labor vice-president, John Ducker, prevented intervention in New South Wales by agreeing to increase the voice for the Left. At the meeting the Left strongly criticised pre-selection procedures in New South Wales — especially in Blaxland. Keating was grateful to Ducker for a trenchant defence of the new member's interest.

Another outcome of the Broken Hill meeting was the secret Burns report, which among other things looked at pre-selections in New South Wales. Tom Burns was a Queensland left-winger. In subsequent years the nature of the Burns report became clouded. But Burns was quite firm about what he thought, and he thought that Keating's pre-selection had been a rort. After detailing the final result of the ballot Burns went on to write:

> The action of the New South Wales Executive secured the result by allowing supporters who had joined the party outside the expressed party rules to participate. Twenty-seven supporters of Mr Keating who were allowed a vote were admitted into Central Bankstown Branch, yet they not only lived in the Condell Park area but also in joining Central Bankstown branch were outside their State Electorate and their Federal Electorate subdivision.
>
> Rule 43 (b) provides that an applicant for membership shall, subject to Clause c of this rule, attend an ordinary meeting of the Branch in the area in which he resides. These persons did not live more than three miles from the Condell Park Branch.
>
> In the case of the Bass Hill Branch, twelve long-standing members were denied a vote because it was alleged the Branch had lost its charter. I understand that it was because the Branch Secretary failed to carry out his duties, yet whilst the Branch did not have a charter, three members who were supporters of Mr Keating, and who incorrectly joined the Central Bankstown

Branch, were transferred to the Bass Hill Branch and ruled by the Executive on 18. 10. 1968 – Officers Report B68/266, to be the only ones eligible to vote.

So we have three members of a Branch without a charter, or, in other words, a non-existent Branch, voting, whilst the members of that Branch are unable to vote.

I believe the decisions made by the Executive were slanted to support Mr Keating, and were inconsistent with decisions made in respect of the Chifley pre-selection contained in the Credentials Committee Report 68/265 dated 18. 10. 1968.

Burns then examined a set of allegations about the Banks pre-selection and concluded:

These allegations, along with many others, indicate a feeling that is rife throughout the Party that if you stand in a pre-selection ballot against the officers 'pea' the chances of winning are nil, and the chances of having any appeals upheld are also nil. The obvious stacking of branches and sacking of branches appears to have been carried out deliberately, intending to ensure certain people gain pre-selection.

As some of these people are now federal members of Parliament, these actions must assume importance in the eyes of the Federal Executive. I strongly disapprove of the actions of the New South Wales officers in these pre-selection ballots.

Again throughout my discussions and throughout the submissions you will note that there is evidence of a growing feeling in the party in New South Wales of an indifferent and arrogant group of officers who are prepared to manipulate the rules and grant preferential treatment to their friends.

Arbitrary decisions have destroyed the Executive's creditability amongst its own members. Complete restructuring in New South Wales is the only way to overcome this disturbing situation.

It was a tough report, designed to support the case for a 'complete restructuring' of the New South Wales party. But its criticisms of Keating's pre-selections were technical rather than substantive. Certainly he had stacked branches, but both sides did so, had always done so, and were expected to do so – party membership grew because of it. The major criticism was that 27 Keating voters had joined Bankstown Central when they should have joined Condell Park. Both branches, however, were within the new boundaries of Blaxland and both had been within the old boundaries of Banks. On the scale of crooked ballot charges in Australia or elsewhere, they were trivial. There were no allegations or instances of violence, of bribery, or even of libel and slander. And while the Left had its suspicions, it was not able to demonstrate any falsity in the attendance records of the Keating supporters.

It had been a four-year struggle, and Paul was still only 24 when he won pre-selection in 1968. 'You have to get out of bed very bloody early to do that,' he said.[28] Nothing he would ever do again would be as difficult, as time-consuming and as uncertain of outcome as putting together the 146 votes he needed for pre-selection. It hadn't been easy, it was very nearly calamitous, and even twenty years later, as Treasurer pushing to be Prime Minister, the means by which he won would continue to be raised by his opponents on the Left and Right. He would later say that the most brutal phase of a political career was 'the mezzanine phase, before you have got to the first floor. That is where all the sorting is brought on in earnest. Once you are at the first floor, it's a bit like coming to the top of a mountain. As you get near the apex there are fewer places to go, fewer places to hide and it is all more obvious. So the selection becomes more automatic if you have what it takes. But down at the base it is harder.'[29]

The election that would make Paul a salaried politician was almost exactly a year away, but he did not wait around. A reporter covering the 1969 campaign found the 25-year-old candidate wearing a slim-line navy blue suit and a $300 gold fob watch. He visited the clubs and pubs. 'I like this work,' he told the *Sydney Morning Herald*'s Joe Glascott. 'Hotel canvassing is like the confessional – you get to hear all the life stories.' The electorate was hung with 300 3 × 2 foot placards, featuring a circular photograph of the candidate and announcing his name in yellow lettering on a blue background. 'The poster is straight from John Kennedy's campaign,' he explained to the bemused veteran reporter, 'only the party name and the photo have been changed.' He bought a bus for $1800, painted it white and put his name on the side and 'Next Stop Canberra' on the back. He explained to Glascott, 'John Kennedy supporters used a white bus for campaigning in one of the southern states. It sure stops the crowds.' A pamphlet went out to the 27 000 electors urging them to 'Put Paul Keating to work for Blaxland'. 'That's from Robert Kennedy's New York campaign,' he explained to Glascott.[30] Later he would claim that the bus and the placards were 'the start of modern campaigning.' [31]

His opinions on the eve of becoming, at 25, the youngest member of the House of Representatives were solidly working-class Catholic. He was not yet thinking for himself, and it would be years before his experience was sufficiently diverse for him to do so. He said one of the main problems facing Australia was 'the erosion of the family.' He told Glascott, 'Too many young married women are being forced out to work because of the high cost of living in this country and families are missing out. The divorce rate is too high, and large families have become unfashionable. I am also concerned about the growing overseas ownership of Australian industry. This will be tragic for Australia in the 1980s and 1990s, and it requires a strong government to stop the trend.'

Paul was socially conservative. Father McCarthy says, 'It would have been a normal belief at the time, especially among Catholics, that women should not go out to work. My father would have been horrified, as I am sure Matt would have been, at the thought of Mother going out to work. During the war women got used to working, but I remember people would still speak of going to help a friend or of going to a business. They would never admit they were working. The norm would have been for the husband to believe he was the breadwinner, and for the wife to work diminished him. That was perfectly common and Paul would have subscribed to that.'

The young politician interviewed by the *Sydney Morning Herald*'s

Margaret Jones in October 1969, just after the election, had a long road to travel. She found him to be 'tall, slim, apparently self-possessed, and far from flamboyant. He is a sharp dresser within a completely orthodox framework and his hairstyle is standard Bankstown. He has a modest manner and is not to be lured into talk of any future ambitions within the party.' He wanted a referendum to give the Federal Government powers for 'rigid price control', and he wanted federal control over business other than in the federal territories, since 'this would help the government to block overseas exploitation of Australian resources, and to encourage domestic development particularly in oil and minerals.' He wanted stronger powers for the Commonwealth, although curiously she reported, 'He is, he says, a federalist and not a centralist. He admits that the states have created a monster and that the monster is eating them up.' But he also wanted, as she pointed out, federal control over all business. Mr Keating, she wrote, is very strong on the social ownership of key industries and on control of prices, which he regards as essential to the stability of family life in Australia. 'For a young man brought up in an era of working wives,' she wrote, 'he takes an unusually traditional view of young mothers going out to work, seeing this as a tragedy which erodes the whole family structure. His remedy: prices geared to the family's wage packet so that women would no longer have to go out to work.' A penetrating and successful reporter with assignments in Washington and London already behind her, Jones must have wondered how long it would take this young man to grow up.[32]

Election day was 25 October 1969. Paul won 61.67 per cent of the vote. This was a rise of nearly 6 per cent on Jim Harrison's 1966 result, though the redistribution made any comparison dubious. Matt and Min threw a party at home for two hundred. Sam, the family black kelpie, ate too many sausage rolls and vomited.[33] Paul bought two new pairs of shoes. He was 'in' and now 'part of the game.'[34] Whitlam had brought the party within striking distance of victory in the next election.

Keating had been elected to Parliament in October. The month before, an ACTU research officer, Bob Hawke, had won a difficult, close contest with ACTU secretary Harold Souter for the presidency of the union's peak council. Hawke was the candidate of the Left. His generals included Ray Gietzelt, federal secretary of the Miscellaneous Workers' Union and the sustaining force behind the Left Wing Steering Committee, which had backed Junor in Blaxland. While Keating prepared to attend Parliament for the first time in the new year, John Hewson and his first wife Margaret were moving from a small Canadian college to take up a doctoral scholarship in economics at Johns Hopkins in Baltimore. Another future leader of the Liberal Party, John Howard, was still an obscure suburban solicitor in Sydney. He would not enter Parliament until 1974. Andrew Peacock was about to be appointed Minister for the Army after four years in Parliament.

3

THE NEW
MEMBER

'I WAS NEVER ONE OF DUCKER'S BOYS,' Keating would later say. 'Never.'
He was never, like Graham Richardson, a protégé of Ducker's. But
he was, he thought, 'very much part of the Ducker apparatus'.

Whatever it was that drove John Ducker, it began early, drove
him hard, and then quite suddenly vanished at the end of the 1970s,
a decade in which he contributed profoundly to the electoral success
of a Labor government in his own state, and to the potential for success of the Hawke Government, which would win office years after
Ducker himself had withdrawn from Labor politics.

A solidly built immigrant from the Yorkshire seaport of Hull,
Ducker had a wide round face, thick turned-out lips that seemed
thoughtfully pursed when not actually moving, and a permanent shadow
of black beard. His manner was calm, considerate and thoughtful, three
words he frequently used, and at the same time definite and implacable – another two of his favourite words. He could flatter people
and charm them, and he could be cruelly and credibly threatening. His
Yorkshire accent, combined with a little trick of speech that might have
originated as an impediment but became his signature, was so pervasive and irresistible, so much a part of him, that for many years in
the New South Wales Labor Party it was impossible to say certain
words – a word like 'moderate', for example, which would invariably
be included in any of his speeches – without hearing Ducker say it in
one's mind – 'Mood-er-it' – said slowly and painstakingly, to emphasise

how very mood-er-it he was. He was nicknamed Bruvver Ducker to imitate that characteristic trick of speech, which turned 'apparatchik' into 'aparchic' and the financial journalist and Keating biographer Edna Carew, a difficult one for him, into 'Adna Canoo'. Outwardly avuncular, Ducker was frequently said by his intimates to 'live on his nerves'. He sometimes drank too much, and over the years some of his colleagues were puzzled by the complexity of his style. They believed, Ducker later thought, that: 'I was a funny bugger, inward, suspicious, stressed, didn't pick up vibes, I didn't convey thoughts in a way to gain agreement, I was an enigma.' As he saw it, at least, he was the moderate, and his colleagues – certainly including Keating and Labor Council organiser Barrie Unsworth in the first half of the 1970s – were the hard Right, the unforgiving take-no-prisoners enemies of the Left. They saw it quite the other way. More importantly, they did not care for Ducker's protégé, Labor Party state Secretary Geoff Cahill.

Ducker was a man of interesting complexity. Although widely regarded as an Irish Catholic stronghold and certainly including many of Irish Catholic descent, like Bill Colbourne and Keating, the controlling groups in New South Wales had a more peculiar relationship with the church. Colbourne was a devout man, for example, whose two sons became priests, but Oliver was not a Catholic, nor devout. John Ducker, Barrie Unsworth and Unsworth's successor as Labor Council secretary, John MacBean, were all Catholics, but all converts and all influenced in their religious views by Johnno Johnson, a union official who later became president of the Legislative Council.

Ducker was a man of great charm, though, as he himself said, in his early days inclined more to battle. He began as a labourer in an ironworks, took an interest in the Federated Ironworkers Association and became a protégé of the union's federal secretary, a remarkable though relatively discreet force in the Labor Party for thirty years, Laurie Short. He was a member of the Industrial Groups fighting the Left and the communists in the unions until the Groups were proscribed by the Labor Party in the mid 1950s, and thereafter merely a member of the equally solid, equally determined Labor Right, which happened to share a very similar membership.

From the Ironworkers he moved to the Labor Council as an organiser, and from organiser to assistant secretary. By the later 1960s he was assistant secretary to the now elderly and unmotivated Ralph Marsh as Secretary, and a vice-president of the New South Wales ALP, working under those older figures, Bill Colbourne and Charlie Oliver. They had once been the new Right, the new Right of the Groups that had overturned the old Right in the 1952. Now Ducker would be the new Right, with his close ally Labor Council organiser Barrie Unsworth and Labor Council compensation officer Geoff Cahill.

From his Labor Council base Ducker, as he says, began to 'assert' himself within the Labor Party in 1969 and 1970. It was in 1969 that Bill Colbourne retired and John Armitage went back into federal parliament, leaving the key job of secretary of the ALP open. John Ducker named Colbourne's successors — former federal secretary Cyril Wyndham, then later former political science lecturer Peter Westerway, still later his Labor Council colleague Geoff Cahill, and finally and most successfully — his predecessors all one way or another proving unsatisfactory — his young protégé Graham Richardson. It was in 1970 that a rebel AWU member, Lew MacKay, won control of the New South Wales branch of the union and temporarily succeeded in isolating Charlie Oliver, a defeat that allowed John Ducker to take his place as president of the Labor Party in New South Wales and restore the party to its close and subordinate relationship to the union majority that controlled the Labor Council. It was in 1969 that Ducker fought in his first national political campaign, this one to attempt to stop ACTU research officer Bob Hawke from winning the presidency of the union council. Ducker and Unsworth were the two generals for the rival bid of ACTU secretary Harold Souter. At the 1969 ACTU Conference, Ducker and Unsworth later claimed, they whittled Hawke's majority down by half. It would be many years before Ducker became a Hawke ally.

So began Ducker's decade of control. While he was asserting himself in New South Wales, Gough Whitlam had won eighteen more seats in the House of Representatives in the 1969 election that brought Paul to Parliament, positioning the party for victory when the Liberal

Government next held a House election. The war in Vietnam was going badly for the US and its South Vietnamese allies, and within a few years Nixon would make an opening to China, which would strengthen Whitlam's foreign policy prestige and make the Liberal Government appear foolishly outdated. The Australian economy was entering a slowdown, which would also undermine the Liberal Country Party coalition.

Before Labor could be certain of federal victory it needed to win more seats in Victoria, which became an argument for replacing the left-wing Victorian Labor Party branch with an electorally more appealing group. At the crucial Federal Executive meeting in Broken Hill, Ducker was officially an alternate delegate for New South Wales, but in practice, it soon emerged, the principal tactician for the Right. The Right in New South Wales had previously prevented intervention in Victoria because the price of South Australian and Queensland support for intervention was intervention also in New South Wales, a price that would later ruffle Keating with the Burns report. But on this occasion Ducker ended the alliance with Victoria. 'I asked the president of the Victorian Branch, Bill Brown, if there was a knock-for-knock agreement,' Ducker recalled in 1987, 'because if there is, I told him, I want to respect it. He said you are on your own. There is no deal. I said thank you, I wanted to make sure because New South Wales keeps its word.' Ducker, his conscience crystal-clear, then helped to destroy Brown, accepting as his part of a good bargain the appointment of a left-winger as assistant state secretary in New South Wales and minority representation for the Left on state party committees.

With these changes Ducker brought the New South Wales branch into the 1970s, but while he was seen as all-powerful and was in fact extremely influential, there was frequent dissent in the councils of the Right.

Keating had not begun as a member of the New South Wales machine. Had Colbourne not left the country after the June conference of 1968, Keating might not have won pre-selection for Blaxland. Had Armitage not been preoccupied he might have been enlisted to stop the brash young man from Bankstown. Paul thought Oliver was helpful in encouraging him and in giving him some protection from Colbourne but not in delivering a single vote. When Keating fought and won pre-selection he hardly knew the emerging new force, Ducker. He was not then part of the ruling group of the party, and in practice in 1968 and 1969 the party officers' machine was ceasing to exist and was about to be replaced.

With Ducker's ascendancy in New South Wales, Paul's relationship with the party centre would change. Within twelve months Keating the outsider would become one of the new insiders, attending the Thursday night meetings of the ruling faction before the Labor Council meeting, and in Canberra seeking (not always successfully, and not always with Ducker's approval) to manipulate federal parliamentarians with more party experience than he. When Ducker unexpectedly left in 1979, Keating took over one of the many jobs that Ducker had filled, President of the Labor Party in New South Wales.

The years of Ducker's supremacy were also Keating's formative years in the federal parliament, when his status as a new member was elevated by his access to Ducker and his membership of the Thursday committee. It was at those meetings that the faction leaders decided on how to handle the Left, how to handle the maverick John Woods of the Liquor and Allied Industries Employees Union, how to handle Barry Egan of the Shop Assistants and Warehouse Employees Federation, how to handle the disputed pre-selection for the federal electorate of Shortland. A nominally senior figure like Armitage did not come to these meetings. Nor did a senior federal parliamentarian from the New South Wales Right, Lionel Bowen. But, until he himself fell out with Ducker, Keating did, as did his equally junior state colleague Laurie Brereton, until he too fell out. His growing repute within the party depended quite as much on his position within the faction as it did on his growing knowledge of public policy issues in Canberra. Like few other politicians, Keating combined success at machine politics with a deepening interest in government policies.

At age 25 Paul was a member of parliament, one of the members of a confident, strong Opposition as the Liberal leadership decayed.

A celebrity among his friends in Bankstown and in the Labor Party Youth Council meetings, in Canberra Paul was the youngest and most junior member of caucus. Like many other members he stayed in the Kurrajong Hotel. Ben Chifley had gossiped there after parliament rose each evening, he had peed in the wash basin of his room when he was caught short, and eighteen years before Paul arrived he had died there, on the narrow single bed of his small and simply furnished room, the last Labor leader who had been Prime Minister. Generations of parliamentarians had complained of the small rooms and poor food and minimal service. They were grateful, however, that the Kurrajong was cheap. Generations had sat talking into the small hours in the downstairs lobby at this bachelor dormitory. There were new members of caucus in 1969 and there would be more still in 1972 – a whole cohort of young teachers, public servants, a few union officials, from the outer suburbs of Melbourne and Sydney – but most of Paul's new colleagues had been in Opposition for decades. He met famous names – great men whose reputations for power, wit, guile, deadliness in combat and intellectual acuity had stirred and encouraged him in the long obscure battle to win pre-selection. In the House he now met Clyde Cameron from South Australia, Kim Beazley (senior) from Western Australia, Fred Daly from New South Wales, Frank Crean from Victoria. In the Senate he met Lionel Murphy from New South Wales, John Wheeldon from Western Australia and Justin O'Byrne from Tasmania. Some he knew were bad, dangerous men – but to the new member they were pleasant enough.

Paul stayed at the Kurrajong from 1969 to 1978, when he bought a house in the Canberra suburb of Curtin. Even a quarter of a century later, recalling her over dinner in Seattle on the eve of the first summit meeting of Asia–Pacific leaders, Paul still referred to the Kurrajong's director as *Miss* Jackson, a woman who stood no nonsense. He ate his breakfast in the same place at the same table at the same time each morning, or missed out. One senator, he recalled, would invariably be breakfasting there, always in the same seat, assumed to be a guest, though he slept in his Senate room and saved the allowance. Other members continued to piss in the sink rather than rent a room with a shower and toilet. 'A lot of people around here, you know, save their lunch money,' Paul would say. He was never stingy.

The old Parliament House is a low white-stuccoed building at the base of the rise known as Capital Hill. It is constructed in straight, clean lines, with three floors of offices including a basement set, and another set of offices above for the media. The floors are dark polished parquetry timber. In some corridors there is thick linoleum – green for the House side, and red for the Senate side. Inside as well as outside the building is painted white. Parliament usually met Tuesdays, Wednesdays and Thursdays in two or more sessions each year. The only appearances Keating was absolutely required to make were at Question Time when parliament began after lunch, during a vote or division, and at certain set-piece debates lead by Whitlam.

Paul's maiden speech in the House four months after his election was the speech of a young man with very little idea of the world in which he actually lived, and certainly very little of where it was going.[1] It was composed without any staff help, after careful thought and reflection. It represented the most authentic expression of his mind at that point of his development. As he acquired experience his speeches became more like those of his colleagues. Like most maiden speeches it was delivered to a quiet but almost empty chamber, where even those members who preferred to lounge there rather than in the members' bar or the library were not, at 10. 26 in the evening of 17 March 1970, at their brightest and most attentive.

He spoke first about Blaxland. 'I would like to be able to describe my electorate as a scenic district, as something of beauty,' he said, 'but unfortunately I cannot. The suburbs within the Blaxland electorate would serve as some of the best examples of chaotic development that can be seen. Unsealed roads, gutterless streets, filthy sewers and lack of adequate sanitation are reminders of the shortcomings of government generally in this country.' The financial burden on local government was becoming intolerable. The Labor Party took the view that local government should be recognised as an equal partner in the structure of Australian government. 'The leader of the Labor Party,' he said, 'has often been criticised for sounding like a municipal mayor or shire president, but he believes that Australians cannot enjoy a high standard of living while they have to live in a substandard environment.'

That was contemporary enough and very much an echo of Whitlam's approach, but his next theme showed how far he had yet to come, even when compared to Whitlam who was himself impatient of economic constraints. Keating said there had been several explanations of inflation offered but 'the real explanation for the problem of inflation is that prices have outdistanced wages,' a statement that confused a possible effect of inflation with its cause. 'It's a well-known fact,' he went on, 'that a high proportion of Australian families live at or below the breadline. It is true that we are experiencing full employment but this does not mean that our families are enjoying a standard of living which the wealth of this country should allow. The real challenge which the government must face is how to control inflation. There is only one effective answer – control over prices and services.' It was, he said, the only way to a regulated economy. He wanted the Commonwealth to set up a statutory authority to include consumers and producers that would 'fix prices for all goods and services used by Australian people'. It should, he said, 'inquire into an average family's needs in respect of clothing, food, recreation, entertainment, housing and health. From all this information it should recommend a wage adequate to provide a standard of living determined by the authority. This wage would be set by an act of parliament and varied from time to time.'

The only hint of the Treasurer to come fourteen years later was his conviction, often to be repeated in later years, that unchanged income tax scales now caught workers into higher tax brackets. 'If we cannot keep wages at reasonable levels and yet maintain adequate purchasing power we will be priced out of every secondary export market in the world', the same argument for the wage–tax trade-offs in the Hawke Government, which would be justified by the same appeal to international competition. 'Secondary export markets' meant manufacturing exports – another permanent interest.

The other basic social ill facing the country, he said, was the problem of workers having two jobs. 'It is bad enough,' he said, 'for the working man to be dragged away from his home at night when he should be with his wife and family, but it is even worse when he has to send his wife out to work to make ends meet . . . husbands have been forced to send their wives to work in order to provide the necessaries of life. Young mothers have been forced out of their homes by economic pressure.' He believed that 'family life is the very basis of our nationhood. In the last couple of years the government has boasted about the increasing number of women in the workforce. Rather than something to be proud of, I feel that this is something of which we should be ashamed.' Was the government doing anything, he asked 'to put the working wife back in her home?' He said it would be better to spend money on child endowment than on immigration. He attacked the Country Party for neglecting the small farmer. He attacked the government for its FI11 program and for neglecting Australian defence. He applauded Sweden for building its own fighters.

He sat way at the back of the House chamber, on the Opposition benches to the left of the Speaker. Over his leader's head at the table he could see the handsome, squashed face of the Prime Minister, John Gorton, and behind him on the government front bench the members of his despondent and factious government, including Foreign Minister Bill McMahon, who would succeed him, and Defence Minister Malcolm Fraser, who had helped Gorton win the leadership and would soon help to take it away.

Keating was placed next to the aged Arthur Calwell, the Labor leader Whitlam had replaced, a Victorian who four years before had led the party to one of its greatest and most glorious defeats when he went into an election against Harold Holt promising to end conscription and withdraw Australian troops from Vietnam. Earlier that year, 1966, Calwell had been shot at through the shut window of his Commonwealth car by a temporarily mad young man. He immediately forgave his assailant who later became a considerable poet and playwright. It would take two elections to recover from the losses of 1966, but Labor had won the allegiance of a new generation.

The slim, dark Paul Keating lounged on the remotest back bench next to the aged warrior, hard of hearing and with every line of his face chiselled in rock, still with the firm and outward thrusting jaw and the harsh grating voice, the rasping whisper of his rousing speeches, now with certain tiny scars in his face where the impact of the .22 bullet on the window had impregnated that jaw with glass fragments. Struggling to catch the Speaker's eye, Keating was startled to feel Calwell's gnarled, arthritic and harsh claw drop onto his knee, and hear that rasping voice whispering to him, 'If you want to ask a question, sonny, this is what you do . . . ' Hurriedly writing speech notes, he saw again that arthritic hand closing over his own, taking the pencil with which he was writing, and writing over Paul's reference to medical practitioners, *medical brigands*, rasping, 'That'll put the kettle on tomorrow, sonny.' Twenty-five years later the Prime Minister would be asked a question without notice by the new Liberal member for Canberra, a still astonished young public servant, Brendan Smyth. Declining the bait, Keating responded by saying he had sat almost exactly where Mr Smyth now sat when he first came into Parliament, and from it asked a question of the then Prime Minister, John Gorton.

Paul was surprised to find some very clever people in parliament. 'There's a lot of good minds,' he found, 'and it pulls you back a bit'.[2] He discovered that backbenchers are idle most of the time and there were always people to join for tea or coffee in the dining room. Warned of its perils, he mostly avoided the bar. At the Kurrajong there were at least sixty members of Parliament, and every night after the adjournment there would be a big group in the lounge. There was nothing to do but it was fun. The Labor Party was by now good at Opposition, he later said, and he enjoyed it. It was not as solemn a place as he feared. Older members cultivated their eccentricities. Calwell would come to the adjournment debate at 10.30 wearing a gaberdine coat and an Akubra hat. It was important to wear a hat in the chamber, he gravely told the younger members. Although rejected as a leader, Calwell was loved. Whitlam invited caucus to drinks, at cost. 'Before my elongated successor,' Calwell wrote over the invitation on the caucus notice board, 'the leader paid.'

Paul impressed his elders. He was candid, ambitious and funny. Clyde Cameron found him 'always well dressed. He looked to have pride in himself. He showed very early that he was a man of great intelligence.' Cameron was close to Paul's New South Wales colleague Lionel Bowen, and got to know his young friend. The more he got to know him, the more he liked him. 'He had a sense of humour,' Cameron remembered, 'a very attractive personality. He was cunning, crafty, able to grasp details quickly. He was good company. He has a nice smile when he gives someone a serve. He almost chortles as he turns the knife. I found it attractive because he was a bit like I would like to be – tough and shrewd. These qualities endeared him to Bowen'.[3]

Paul thought himself gregarious and endearing. 'As for getting around the place and getting to know people, oh, I was good at that. The people business – that's where I come from,' he remembered.[4] But others remember him as solitary, distant and silent. Lionel Bowen said, 'He was keen to get on, I remember, but we didn't mix a lot. He didn't mix much with anyone.' Barry Cohen said the same. 'He wasn't the sort of person you just went and had a yarn with. He was pretty aloof. The only time you took any notice of Paul was when there was a ballot on because he always seemed to be running it, or trying to.'[5] Throughout his career Paul would be charming when he wanted to be; distant when he didn't. As Ducker said, 'He drifted in and out with people.'

Paul was eager for experience, and for sucking up the experience of others. He preferred talking to reading. He remembered, 'I was trying to truncate experience. Compress into a fewer number of years as much experience as I could get. There's only so much experience you can get yourself, so you've got to get someone else's, you understand, try to suck some experiences from someone else.'[6] Someone with experience was Lionel Bowen.

As a new member Keating was asked by the whip Gil Duthie to share an office on the lower level, L96. It was a tiny room with two desks and two telephones. His room-mate was the member for the New South Wales seat of Kingsford Smith, Lionel Bowen. Keating's relationship with him would be one of the most important friendships of his first years in Parliament. Though nearly twice Keating's age, Bowen was also new to federal Parliament. Born in 1922 to a poor family in Sydney's inner city, Bowen had been brought up by his mother after her divorce from his father. They had no money, and moved from one rented house in Redfern to another. The boy went first to a state primary school and then to a Marist Brothers secondary school, which he left with his Intermediate Certificate. He completed his Leaving Certificate at night school. Following army service during World War II, Bowen used an ex-service scholarship to study law at Sydney University. He was admitted as a solicitor in 1948 and set up practice in the Adams Chambers in Sydney. At the same time he pursued a political career. He joined the Labor Party in 1941, after the war became an alderman and then mayor of his home suburb of Randwick, and in 1962 the local member of state parliament. While Keating was fighting pre-selection in Blaxland, Bowen was fighting from his state seat for pre-selection for Kingsford Smith. He won and entered the House of Representatives after the same election as Keating.

They had much in common. Bowen was a Catholic; his parents were manual workers. Both voted with the Right, although neither had won his seat because of support by the officers' group in the party, and both were to assert their independence of the head office. Both admired Jack Lang – Bowen perhaps more than Keating. Bowen was from the same part of Sydney as Laurie Brereton and Bob Carr, so that he was also a source of support and something of an early mentor to the two contemporaries closest to Keating in the New South Wales party. In some ways he was a model for all three young politicians.

Allowing for the difference in their ages and the fact that Bowen had been in the army in World War II, he and Keating came from similar worlds. Bowen had been a member of the Sydney County Council from 1957 to 1962, so he was at the top when Paul had joined as junior clerk in 1958. (Bowen had placed the young Laurie Brereton there as an apprentice electrician at around the same time Paul had joined as a clerk.) In the party machine his one 'great mate', as he would later say, was the former party president Charlie Oliver, whom Keating would also claim as his main supporter in the party offices. Both Keating and Bowen claimed a link with Oliver, distinguishing them from those brought to prominence by Ducker.

As a model for Keating, Bowen demonstrated that it was quite possible to be a Labor member of Parliament and at the same time build up wealth through business. By 1978, Bowen would be a partner in a business that owned apartment blocks, an interest in a shopping centre at Mt Gravatt in Brisbane, and a beef cattle property at Orange in New South Wales. He also demonstrated that it was possible to be independent of the machine in New South Wales yet at the same time succeed in the federal Labor Party caucus. Ducker would later describe him as 'the most under-estimated man in federal politics' and as 'the leader of the moderate New South Wales group in caucus'. But Bowen stayed at arm's length from Ducker, and if he led the New South Wales Right in caucus, it was very quietly indeed.

Unlike Keating, Bowen was not very interested in discussing economic issues. As time went on his grasp of them appeared poorer and poorer by contrast with the growing sophistication of his younger colleague. Bowen was a protectionist in 1969; he remained one when he retired twenty-one years later as the longest serving Labor minister in the history of federal Parliament. One monument to that long service was an extremely ugly telecommunications tower with a restaurant on top of Canberra's Black Mountain, dominating the city. Bowen had bulldozed it through Cabinet and caucus over Canberra protests when he was Postmaster General in the Whitlam Government. He was a determined and literal-minded minister in the service of a conservative and literal-minded department. He was an unqualified supporter of uranium exports. As Attorney-General in the Hawke Government he came good with the patient negotiation and then the creation of the Australian Securities Commission as the sole and national regulator of corporate financial disclosure.

He was modest, funny, laconic, down-to-earth, and zealous in maintaining his electoral base and his private business interests. But at 47 his attitudes were not very different from his attitudes at 37, and at 67 they would not be very different from those he had had twenty years before. Bowen did not grow as Keating grew. Keating would share Bowen's views on tariffs for some years, until the experience of the Whitlam Government, his work with the mining industry and his exposure to standard economic thinking fundamentally altered his views. Bowen was later to be strongly in favour of developing a domestic uranium mining industry, right through to waste product disposal through a synthetic rock proprietary process developed at the ANU known as Synroc. Bowen recalls Keating in 1969 as being very much in favour of the development of a uranium industry, but by the 1970s Keating had become cautious. Part of his strength and skill is that he has mostly known how far to go and when to stop.

Paul liked Bowen. He was laconic and humble, 'but not to the point where he didn't understand what his own value was to the system'. He remembered, 'I learned lots from Lionel. He was a great assessor of people, he was a people studier. He could always read their personalities very well. And I could not do it quite so well. I couldn't read them so well. He'd say things about people, make observations – I couldn't see it, you know? Some of it I could see. But a couple of years after I was in there, I could see it clearly.' Paul believed that Bowen read behavioural give-aways – the way people treated dining-room staff, whether they kept agreements. Keating developed his own 'model' over the years, a term Keating has borrowed from economists and uses to mean 'framework' or 'analytic structure'.[7] He needed the model 'because in politics every personality is a problem. Everyone who's in front of you, you've got to assess them quickly. And mostly be right, otherwise they may give you a problem.'[8]

Bowen contributed to Keating's store of wisdom. Twenty-five years later, when he himself was 50, and two years older than Bowen was when he first met him, Paul remembered that Bowen said to him, 'I'll tell you this, champ. When you get to my age you end up concentrating more on the end of your life than the beginning of it.'

At 25, who cared? But at 50, Paul thought, 'that's probably right. When you're young all the future is there and it gives you that Peter Pan quality, but I think later you can't delude yourself.'

Paul was outgrowing father figures; in any case Bowen preferred a more equal relationship. Cameron remembered, 'Keating was not seen as a protégé of Bowen and they were very often on opposite sides. Bowen's attitude to Keating was one of amused liking. If someone amuses you it is very hard to dislike them.'

Older than Paul, with a family of his own, and with both men inclined to keep their own counsel, the relationship did not run very deep. Even a quarter-century later Bowen would say of Keating, 'I'm a friend of his but we don't see each other. That's been the case all the way through. Our friendship goes back to L96 because that's where we sort of lived together. But I've never visited his home and I think he might have dropped in on mine once. So we're good friends but we never meet, you follow me? I mean, I've been in the Labor Party since 1941. We're different age groups, different generations. I could talk to him any time, I would think, but we don't have much to discuss, put it that way.'[9]

For several years Bowen would influence or at least reinforce some of Paul's views, but as a model Bowen was mostly a dead end because his policy views were increasingly at odds with the trend of events. His enmities and rivalries, especially with Ducker and Whitlam, did the young Keating no good, while his presence as a friend, colleague and senior rival complicated several of Keating's subsequent attempts to climb up the ladder.

When Gough Whitlam tapped Arthur Calwell on the shoulder after the 1966 election, Paul Keating was one of thousands of branch members who cheered on the Deputy Leader. He had been delighted in February 1967 when Whitlam beat left-wing leader Jim Cairns in the ballot to succeed Calwell. He now came into Parliament a little in awe of his leader. He found, however, that a highly educated middle-class Protestant like Whitlam had a less flattering assessment of

Keating's talents than the new member did himself. Whitlam's strongest faith was in education. He thought Keating should improve himself, as Bill Hayden was doing. He should matriculate and study at night for a degree. 'He was the big figure of the day,' Keating remembered, 'but he's an intellectual snob. He used to see how many degrees you had and if you didn't have any he didn't think too much of you.'[10] He found Bowen much more congenial, but the competing models they presented had subtleties and possibilities that would play out in unexpected ways.

Keating realised later: 'Gough was a process man: reform, the Constitution, the federal structure, and those sorts of things. He was also into social, foreign and other areas of policy, whereas my interests were . . . it was a different view of the world. My job was to try and see what made the structure of the country, what held the structure together, what made it tick, and how it could tick better. It takes you quite a long time to form views about those subjects, but I did form them on observation and thinking about it.'[11]

Whitlam was a lawyer whose father had been a lawyer and Canberra public servant who had become Crown Solicitor. He thought in terms of laws and what was written in laws, both in Australia and in world bodies. Paul was the child of a tradesman who later ran a business. His own experience was as a clerk in a huge electricity company. His mind was untrained. He thought by flashes, intuition, by discarding everything that was not big and essential. Compared to Whitlam, Keating was more interested in the whole than the analysis of the parts, more interested in being able to grab something intuitively through practical experience over a number of years, in the manner of someone not trained in formal analysis. He found that his strength was to grasp the main point and to hold on to it – others could work out the process, refine the arguments for and against, put things into laws. It would not be until he had been Treasurer for several years that he began to achieve the degree of understanding that he had sought from his late teens. Treasury was his school. Paul remembered, 'I had some particular interests but I am more a generalist. General interests are always the hardest to get into, of course.

General interests, meaning the structure of society and the economy, our place in the world, those sorts of things.'[12] Whitlam had a structure of ideas but he was never as curious as Keating, never as driven to find out how it all worked and how all the pieces fitted together. He had *programs*, policies and programs, while Keating hardly ever in his career had a program or a policy laid out in advance that could compare in detail with a Whitlam program, although this was perhaps partly because he was never Opposition Leader. Keating's strength was in understanding circumstances and in responding to them, in making them go in his direction where possible, and keeping upright and apparently in control when not. Keating would always have a much keener nose for changes and responding to change – a quality Whitlam displayed on party matters, and perhaps in picking up the great sentiment for change from the swelling low-income outer suburbs, which he evoked in 1972, but which he could not accurately sense in government. Paul would prove to be better at the big picture than Whitlam, who thought little could be done without the right laws.

Their minds worked differently, but they had much in common. The distinctive quality of both was courage. Both knew that sometimes the essence of political leadership was in disregarding sensible advice. If the leader was really a leader, he knew that his position allowed him to see things, his experience allowed him to feel things, that others could not see or feel so clearly. Whitlam took on the Left in the party and won. So, in his turn, would Keating. Whitlam was surer of himself in some ways and higher minded. He could be catty, but soon forgot grievances. Keating nursed them. Both forced their predecessor aside – but there was nothing unique in that.

Paul claims not to have been influenced by Whitlam's low opinion. He said, 'He always had a lot of presence and style and a lot of go; you can never take that off him, and I wouldn't want to try. He always had a lot of style and a lot of panache. Why would I want more recognition? I knew I had basically more to offer than he had, so why would I want his recognition?'[13] He was, anyway, the least of caucus. Between Paul and the Leader well on his way to becoming Prime Minister, there was only passing contact.

In his mid twenties and after a decade of low-paid clerical employment, Keating had a substantial income. He was still single, still living at home. He could travel free anywhere in Australia, first class. He had an allowance to employ an electoral secretary. By the standards of his friends, he was rich. More importantly, he was free to use his time as it suited him. As a potentially powerful politician, he was cultivated.

Two years after his election he was invited by the US State Department to join a group of young leaders from other countries on a tour of the United States. It was his first visit to another country. Richard Nixon was in the White House, and the following year he would win re-election in a landslide against the Democrat George McGovern. At the US State Department the group met the Under Secretary of State, U. Alexis Johnson, and George Bush, Nixon's ambassador to the United Nations. Bush was charming, though that evening the UN had defeated the US and its allies by voting to admit China. As Prime Minister of Australia twenty-one years later Paul would meet Bush as President of the United States.

Touring the US, Paul's companions entertained hookers in their motel rooms in most towns, leaving the shocked young man much in the company of the tour guide, a black American. Hitching up his pants cuff, the guide showed Paul a pistol strapped to his leg. Together they listened to Aretha Franklin, one of Paul's heroes, in an Atlanta nightclub and Paul asked her for a song. Visiting Manhattan, he and the guide were followed at midnight by a car full of toughs in midtown, near the Roosevelt Hotel. The guide pushed him into a doorway and brandished his gun from behind a set of trash cans. Paul was impressed. America was a violent, exciting place – just like the movies.

Paul visited New Guinea in 1971, as part of a caucus delegation. With forty hours flying training, he persuaded the pilot to take the dual control and let him land the DC3 at Rabaul. Paul was elated and told the Leader. 'You bastard!' said Whitlam, with a tone that

Keating could not quite pick. 'You could have killed us all.' Travel broadened his mind. He was shown over the Canadian Parliament by Paul Martin, a former Foreign Minister. 'See that man over there,' said his guide, pointing out a dignified gentleman. 'That's Diefenbaker. He's full of shit.' Somehow he swung a visit to Japan, where he charmed the elderly chairman of Nippon Steel, Mr Inayama, and began to cultivate relationships he would keep over the years.

At age 25 Keating's ideas of what Labor should do in government were very different from those he would discover himself to possess as a reforming Treasurer fourteen years later. As he later said, 'If you come here at 25 you are narrow. It's a fact of life. It's a consequence of your age, your experience. But I think I always wished to see things in a framework. I was always working on the big canvas.'[14] His ideas about the economy, and most particularly about the regulation of prices and wages, were derived one way or another from Thomist ideas of a system of economic justice rather than the Smithian idea, which he would later adopt, of a self-regulating mechanism that would usually produce the best outcomes automatically.

Keating was interested in policies, which distinguished him from most machine politicians, but they were of an unusual kind. Carr recalls him putting his head into a Youth Council foreign affairs committee meeting one day and saying mysteriously of the pact forming the European Economic Community, 'The Treaty of Rome. Look at the Treaty of Rome!' 'It was pure Lang,' says Carr, 'though of course, as it turned out in our world today of great trading blocs, it was a very important treaty.' Ron Dyer recalls Keating being interested in 'unusual economic issues' of which one example, which seemed at that time to be much on Keating's mind, was roll-on roll-off cargo handling. Long before Keating became a disciple of Rex Connor, he was an admirer of Charlie Court, the Western Australian Minister for Development and then Premier. Somehow, and quite early, Keating thought of the economy as some sort of giant national enterprise that politicians ran at the centre, a vision similar to that of Rex Connor and not uncommon among young politicians who talked expansively about 'national development', which at that time was just about all politicians.

Building his understanding of the Australian economy, he met Larry Hartnett, a former managing director of General Motors-Holden's who had left the company after sharp differences with its Detroit headquarters. Forgotten, obscure and in his early seventies, Hartnett was still indignant, still believing in the possibility of an independent Australian manufacturing industry. Hartnett was a far more influential figure than most Paul met in Canberra. He was a maker of things, like Matt Keating. He knew about machines. But the car industry had protection from imports, and perhaps would not survive without it.

Paul did not get very far with flying lessons (he held a restricted licence before politics claimed all his attention), but he was still interested in planes. Even as Prime Minister he could still identify different models of the 747 and discuss their history. He had grown up near Bankstown Aerodrome, the biggest centre for private and amateur flying in New South Wales. He visited the Government Aircraft Factory, where planes were built during the war. He thought Australia should continue to build planes, but that industry, too, would need protection. He developed ideas about what Australia could do in manufacturing. Becoming interested in secondary industry generally, he met Sir Ian McClennan, who was the managing director of the company that dominated Australia's iron and steel industry, BHP. He would later recall that he learnt a lot from Ian McClennan and Hartnett. His new experience resonated with and built on his father's experience running a metals manufacturing business in Sydney.

Some themes would remain important. By 1970 he was demanding a national policy to exploit uranium resources, enforced by government control over exports.[15] The issue would later bedevil him as shadow Minister for Minerals and Energy. And as early as 8 April of that year and again on 28 August he had advocated that the ownership of TV and newspapers should be separated in Australia. He would pursue this separation for a quarter of a century before achieving it.[16]

In his first year or so in Parliament he often spoke on defence issues, perhaps because those concrete warrens he had played in as a

child had stimulated his interest but also because he had many soldiers in his electorate. 'Our defence forces are vastly inadequate,' he
told Parliament in October 1970.[17] Earlier in the month he had
colourfully speculated: 'I have a sneaking suspicion that with the
non-ratification of the treaty on non-proliferation of nuclear weapons
this government is keeping its options open for the construction of
nuclear weapons.'[18] (Australia did sign the treaty and had been one of
its strongest proponents – although Gorton liked nuclear power.) By
June 1971 he was telling a reporter that Australia needed an aircraft
industry, and that his two major interests in Canberra were defence
and national development.[19] Later that year he told Parliament that
Australia needed a firm industrial base to 'be able to supply our troops
with Australian-manufactured equipment. We should not depend
on the resources of other nations.' Whatever the ambiguity of his earlier views, he had now reached a firm view about Vietnam. He complained that the government in Vietnam was not democratic, and that
'the guilty men opposite have sent 500 Australian boys to their death.'
He also said that the National Service Act 'was a response to political pressure from the United States and it is an Act which destroys
the government's credibility in the eyes of the Australian people'.[20]
Throughout his career defence issues popped back to his mind every
now and then. As Prime Minister he arranged for the Defence Department to buy an auction lot of cheap FI I Is, still packed in grease. Like
many Keating decisions, it appeared to come from nowhere only because
its antecedents had been lost in the long course of his career. It brought
together his interest in aeroplanes, his eye for a bargain, and his conviction that Australian views were received more seriously in Asia if
its Prime Minister was known to believe in a strong defence force.

With greater experience his views on the economy began to modify. Within a few years of coming to Canberra, Keating was haunting the small press gallery office of the *Australian Financial Review*, which
almost alone consistently called for lower tariffs and more competition. The paper, through its political correspondent Max Walsh and
indirectly through its editor Vic Carroll, had perhaps more influence
on the way Paul's thinking developed (as distinct from his opinions

at the time) than most of his caucus colleagues. But it would not be until after the catastrophe of the Whitlam Government that he began to radically alter his views on the economy – and even then it would not be until after he became Treasurer that he changed the bedrock. And some social views, his personal preference for women staying at home and taking care of the kids, for example, never really changed, although as Prime Minister he would improve national child-care programs.

4

THE WHITLAM GOVERNMENT

FOR PAUL THE ELECTION of the Whitlam Labor Government on 2 December 1972 was a thrilling affirmation of his political beliefs and predictions. The party he had joined at the age of 14 and which he now represented in parliament was not a permanent minority – it was now the Government of Australia. It would clear away the accumulated debris of a decade of poor leadership. Australia would swiftly recognise China, introduce universal medical insurance, extend financial help to government schools and greatly expand spending generally on hospitals, education and income security. It would extend equal pay to women, cut tariffs, strengthen competition laws. It would do it all in a rush – not least because many ministers and staff members had allowed themselves to be convinced that the Liberal–Country Party coalition was the natural federal government of Australia. They should do what they could before returning to the Opposition benches.

Paul was certainly in a hurry. At 28 he now had three years' parliamentary experience behind him. Being a government backbencher was, if anything, worse than being an Opposition backbencher. At least an Opposition backbencher was more or less the equal of his colleagues. At least he could attack the government. At least he could propose new policies. He might be widely regarded as a junior member of caucus, but if the Labor Party was in government, Paul wanted to be in government.

He had a chance, but his circumstances were not ideal. Whitlam regarded him as no more than a promising young pug who could perhaps, over time, improve himself by undertaking part-time study. There was room for a few new faces on the front bench, but the Leader had in mind two others – former diplomat Bill Morrison and the member for Riverina, Al Grassby, who, though neither a migrant nor a farmer, was sufficiently mutable to be good for both the rural vote and the migrant vote. The ministry was elected by caucus so Whitlam's opinion would not particularly matter if Keating had strong support elsewhere, but he did not. He was not gregarious or widely known. The faction system was primitive compared to its later development, and in any case the New South Wales Right included many parliamentarians senior to Keating. His closest colleague in the federal parliament was Lionel Bowen, who was himself new to Canberra and commanded no great support within caucus. There were few spots likely to be available to newcomers. Most would be claimed by the lions of decades of Opposition, all of them thirsting for government – people like Clyde Cameron, Frank Crean, Jim Cairns and Fred Daly.

Anticipating Whitlam's win and the subsequent ballot, Keating had been unusually pleasant to the Left. To the outside world and especially to the Left, the 'New South Wales Right' was usually an implacable united force. Within, it was divided into shifting alliances of such bewildering complexity that even the participants later had difficulty remembering them. After losing his state seat in a redistribution in early 1971, Paul's friend Laurie Brereton pursued a path that was entirely his own. In the early 1970s he allied with a powerful group within the Right arranged around the secretary of the Shop, Distributive and Allied Employees Association, Barry Egan. Beginning as a protégé of Ducker and an ally of the NCC-dominated federal office of his union, Egan hosted a right-wing push to destroy Ray Gietzelt's left-wing control of the Miscellaneous Workers Union. Under Brereton's influence he shifted steadily to a more independent course.

Both Brereton and Keating, for different reasons, put feelers out to the Left. Keating persuaded a fellow right-winger not to fight

Tom Uren for the 1971 pre-selection for Uren's federal electorate of Reid. In return, Keating did not have a Left challenger in Blaxland. 'The thing was, I would have won and he would have won, so why drive each other mad?' Keating later explained. Convincing Egan that supporting a rebellion against the leadership of the Miscellaneous Workers Union would not be in his long-term interests, Brereton arranged a peace meeting with Ray Gietzelt, his brother Senator Arthur Gietzelt, Keating and Egan at a Sydney restaurant. They agreed they would cease conspiring against each other's union base (or, in the terminology of the day, cease to 'interfere in a union's internal affairs').[1] Keating wanted a détente with the Left, which could help him in the ballot for ministerial positions when Labor came to office federally. The shadowy and unacknowledged accommodation with the Left would remain important to Keating. Throughout the decade Keating was portrayed as the hard man of the New South Wales Right, while often quietly negotiating with the Left to support his own ambitions.

Keating and Arthur Gietzelt were both members of the 'Tuesday Club', a group of members who lunched regularly together when parliament was in session. It included Keating, Gietzelt, Lionel Bowen, Gordon Bryant, Les Johnson, and Moss Cass. With the exception of Keating and Bowen, they were from the Left or leaning that way.[2] Led by Keating and Gietzelt, the most practised ballot technicians, the Tuesday Club offered a list of candidates, a ticket, for the ministerial ballot.

The ticket included both Keating and Gietzelt, as well as other members of the club. Unlike later factional tickets that emerged from negotiations within the factions themselves, this list of candidates was more an attempt to attach Keating and Gietzelt on to the end of a predictable line-up of senior caucus members – to pick the winners and add two more to their coat tails. It purported to have the character of a consensus vote guide rather than a factional alliance.

Keating thought that such a ticket could be effective because the ballot was preferential, success depending partly on primary votes and partly on the distribution of preferences from candidates progressively excluded in the course of the counting. While individuals could organise their own primary votes, the ticket could guide the allocation of the secondary preferences, which determined the result. In practice, however, in the first ministerial ballot those with the most primary votes with one exception also picked up secondary votes in the same order.[3]

The caucus met in the government party room on 18 December 1972. There were twenty-seven positions available in the Cabinet, which, in the Whitlam Government, included all members of the ministry. The four party leaders, two in the House and two in the Senate, were first re-elected unopposed. Balloting then began for the election of ten members of the House and four senators to be elected in simultaneous ballots. Keating entered the House ballot and won 23 primary votes, putting him fifteenth.

The final ballot was for the remaining nine members of the ministry, with 31 nominations from both Houses. In this ballot Keating came tenth (Geitzelt was fifteenth). Immediately ahead of him, the last elected member of the Whitlam ministry, was Bill Morrison. The third on the list of ten elected was Al Grassby, also from the Right in New South Wales. Although they were older than Keating and for different reasons better known, they were also new to Parliament.

After the presidency of Youth Council and the pre-selection for Blaxland, it was his third big contest and his first big defeat. Inexperienced in failure, he did not take it well. He did not forgive, forget and move on. He did not think that the best men won. He responded as he would often subsequently respond to failure – by threatening to leave the game and by nursing a grievance against those he believed had failed him.

Considering his youth and lack of experience, Keating was quite exorbitantly outraged by his loss. He claimed that both Ducker and the New South Wales Party Secretary, Peter Westerway, had promised him support while actually steering those votes they could influence towards Grassby and Morrison. Even a couple of decades later Keating was still annoyed that, at the age of 28 and after three years in parliament, he was not elected to the first Whitlam ministry. Lang had told him, 'You are a young man and when you get to Canberra they will all tell you you have plenty of time. But the truth is you haven't a second to lose'. Paul told one interviewer, 'I got ratted on by a couple of people in head office. I never got the support that I expected or that I was entitled to. I think they probably thought I was a bit young and could wait, and when I look back that is probably a view that I can understand better now than then. But I was very unforgiving at the time.'[4] Ducker and Westerway felt Whitlam deserved their support, and Whitlam wanted Grassby and Morrison. At the head office of the Labor Party and Labor Council Keating's pretensions to the ministry and his indignation at the result were treated lightheartedly. 'He did well to win a Cabinet vacancy in 1975, let alone 1972,' Barrie Unsworth said later, his eyes smiling in his blank face.[5]

Miffed by the ministerial ballot, Keating thought of himself as the 'senior backbencher'. To come tenth in a ballot for nine positions was not a bad showing for a 28-year-old with one term of parliamentary experience, although the following years repeatedly disappointed his implied claim to the next vacancy. Meanwhile, Paul's only role was to vote in the House for the government when required. Twenty-seven of his former Opposition colleagues now had Commonwealth cars and drivers, offices and staff. They made decisions, which public servants dutifully wrote down. They were interviewed and quoted in the newspapers. He saw Al Grassby and Bill Morrison giving interviews on television at night. The ministerial corridors were crowded with busy, important young people hired as advisers or press secretaries. To them, government backbenchers were nuisances. Within Parliament House there was a hierarchy, and he was near the bottom. At the top were ministers who participated in decisions and had access to the information flow of Cabinet submissions and decisions. Then there were advisers and press secretaries, who could influence their minister's decisions, and who also had access to the information flow. There were reporters, whose goodwill and acquaintance were cultivated by ministers and advisers. Beneath all these, beneath also the Opposition shadow Cabinet, were the government backbenchers. They did not take part in decisions of consequence. They did not have easy access to the government information flow. Paul's party had won but, for a backbencher, Opposition was perhaps more fun than government.

He claimed to gain control of the New South Wales Right in the federal caucus and was certainly an active organiser. 'After 1972 when Frank Stewart stopped doing the numbers, I took over,' he says. 'Of course, it wasn't like a Federal Electorate Council. These were people who had won a seat. They were all somebodies.' Organising was sometimes an unexpectedly selfless role. 'If you do the numbers you can't win yourself,' Keating told New South Wales left-wing leader Rod Cavalier. Reporters credited Keating with an authority over New South Wales right-wingers he did not possess and membership of a united leadership group, which was in fact divided by personal tensions. Never trusting, the relationship between Ducker and Keating became brittle. Ducker was annoyed by the appearance of a factional alliance with Gietzelt and the production of a ticket that did not include two candidates he preferred. The young parliamentarian did not accept Ducker's claim to control the New South Wales Right in federal caucus. He did not respect Ducker's protégé, Geoff Cahill, who replaced Westerway as party secretary in 1974. He refused to accept Cahill's direction. 'I wouldn't put up my hand when Geoff wanted,' he recalled. For the moment Keating remained within the inner council, but he would soon find himself in the cold.

Ducker's lieutenants shared with each other confidences about their leader's shortcomings. Some of his internal opponents arranged themselves around his Labor Council deputy, Barrie Unsworth. These included Keating and Bob Carr, who was then working for the Labor Council with the title of education officer. Ducker thought of them as hard-liners, who disapproved of his friendliness towards ACTU President Bob Hawke. But the fault lines of dissent were by no means clear. Within the leadership group the main tension was between Ducker and Unsworth, a difference that perhaps arose mainly from the difference between Unsworth's blunt, direct, but more limited, intelligence and Ducker's additional layers of wiliness and complexity. It also arose from a difference in their roles. Ducker dealt frequently with Hawke as a member of the ACTU executive, and he was soon brought under the influence of Hawke's charm and goodwill while, as organiser and then as assistant Labor Council secretary, Unsworth's job was to keep their own troops happy and disciplined, to keep the faith.

Ducker saw himself as a moderate concerned with results in a hard-line leadership group concerned with symbols and with the enjoyment of battle. His high and deep policy intrigued and offended some of his colleagues. Ducker acknowledges that there was tension with Unsworth. It was 'never to the point of no return, but there were different views. I was always for the main game and what was necessary to achieve it. Sometimes some of my colleagues became enthusiastic about particular persons or issues to the exclusion of the total situation. But whenever there were sizeable jobs to be done, Ducker, Unsworth and Keating would be as one. Implacably and effectively so.'

Ducker sponsored the independent-minded John Morris, who had overthrown the communist leadership of the liquor workers union. Unsworth found Morris would not do as he was told. 'Not everyone saw John Morris with a rosy glow,' recalled Ducker. 'I saw him with a lot of delegates. Not everyone believed it was necessary to have a reasonable cooperation with the Left. Not everyone was an enthusiast for Neville Wran.' (Unsworth and Wran somehow did not quite hit it off. Wran felt the demands of the union movement on the New South Wales Government were limitless, its gratitude negligible.) Ducker liked to portray himself as friend of reason; his colleagues wondered where it would all lead. He believed that: 'Sometimes my desire to compromise and to calm in difficult factional situations was seen as weak and giving unnecessary opportunities to the Left.' Keating had dallied with the Left, and his friend Brereton was playing a complicated game with it. Keating resented Ducker's dominance and drifted closer to Unsworth. 'Paul tried to look at the main players,' Ducker said, 'and conclude which he agreed with on specific issues, bearing in mind his pad was the federal parliamentary party. His desire for moderation there dictated his attitude to other things. He had good relations with Unsworth.'

The relationship between Unsworth and Ducker was one of the

mysteries of the faction, as mysterious to the two men, perhaps, as to their colleagues. Ducker and Unsworth could have their differences, but by the beginning of the 1970s they had already been close friends for a decade, bonded by innumerable battles. Unsworth first met Paul in 1968. By then he had known Ducker for eight years. They had known each other before either married and it was Unsworth who organised Ducker's bucks' night.

Unsworth had a gift for friendship, for being direct and straight and manly and so intimidating that people sought his friendship, and Ducker too placed a high value, although a less instinctive one, on friendship. With Ducker friendship was policy too, friendships like those he formed in his 'picnic club' of fellow right-wing officials, friendships on a 'family basis' formed at the Labor Council's holiday cottages at the beachside union holiday village of Currawong, where there would be the wife and kids and a barbecue, sack races and the inevitable keg.

'There was never any falling out between Ducker and me,' Unsworth believed, but there were nuances and differences. Ducker was moving closer to Hawke, partly as a result of intervention in Victoria and partly in response to Hawke's move to include the Right in the central consensus on the ACTU. By 1974 Ducker was supporting Hawke for the presidency of the ALP, despite the qualms of his faction and in particular the opposition of Keating. 'I was calling the shots and I called them for Hawke,' recalled Ducker. Keating went along. As Ducker said, 'People did not do otherwise.' Ducker's drift to Hawke, and the even stronger move in that direction by Ducker's protégé Geoff Cahill, alarmed Unsworth. He was concerned with the loyalty of right-wing trade union officials in New South Wales, who, in the end, were the base of the party officers' support.

Following the 1968 invasion of Czechoslovakia by the Soviet Union, the Communist Party in Australia had split. The majority condemned the Soviet Union; a minority continued to support Soviet policy and split off to form the Socialist Party of Australia. Through trade union links and historical associations, the Labor Left soon reflected the same split. While the majority remained within the

Steering Committee, a hardline minority split off to form the Socialist Objective Committee after a dispute over the Left ticket for the Legislative Council in 1972.

Seizing his opportunity to split his opponents permanently, John Ducker cultivated the Socialist Objective faction and at the June 1973 state conference supported one of its members, John Benson, to replace Arthur Gietzelt as the second of the two New South Wales delegates to the national executive of the party. Barry Egan supported Gietzelt, as did Brereton and Keating. Gietzelt was narrowly re-elected when the Building Workers Industrial Union delegation swung behind him.

Paul was a member of the Administrative Committee of the party, which ruled it between conferences, but disputed Ducker's control and Cahill's directions. Paul was so deeply offside with Ducker and Cahill by 1974 that he later believed and often repeated that he had been dropped by his faction from the party's Administrative Committee in 1974. In fact he was a member continuously through the 1970s, though Brereton was excluded for one term. The Gietzelts, Brereton, Keating, Barry Egan and Charlie Oliver drifted into an understanding of sorts, in which they were arrayed against Ducker and his new Socialist Objective allies.

By June 1975 there would be a new and strange grouping on the floor of conference. 'Those who were left out started to come together,' Keating remembered. It included an amalgamation of the shop assistants and the Australian Workers Union, run by Charlie Oliver and Barry Egan. It also included Keating, Brereton, Tom Uren and Arthur Gietzelt. Voting together, and in this instance with the support of many conventional right-wing delegates and the independent Liquor Workers, they defeated a proposal by Geoff Cahill to change State Conference from 1000 delegates every year to 400 delegates every two years. It signalled the beginning of the end for Cahill.

Idle, unencumbered by office, offside with John Ducker, Paul was becoming ready for one of the transforming experiences of his life. As a young man he had had many romantic relationships of varying degrees of seriousness and longevity. The only one that endured was with a girl from the nearby suburb of Kingsgrove, a relationship that settled down into the comfortable, familiar association of people with similar backgrounds and experience, in which she got to know his family and he hers. They were often together, he at her house or she at his. They were already planning marriage when, within six months of Whitlam's victory, Paul fell in love with another woman.

Flying to Europe on a parliamentary visit with a colleague, he was dazzled by a hostess in the first-class cabin of an Alitalia flight to Bangkok. Annita Van Iersal was tall, with a figure that twenty years later would remain near perfect. She had dark, wild hair and olive skin. She had large white even teeth, big eyes, and a mole under her left eye. In her mid twenties she was gorgeous, although remote. Paul was wearing cream leather shoes, pale blue slacks and a paisley shirt. 'He was so skinny,' she remembers, 'and very quiet. He was studying me most of the time. He didn't eat much. He thought I was a poor little Italian girl.' She thought he would look fantastic in an Italian suit.[6]

Departing the flight in Bangkok, Paul left his companion and ran back, claiming to have left something behind. He gave his card to the hostess. Some time later she telephoned him during a stopover in Australia, where her brother lived. Temporarily based in Melbourne with the airline, she visited Canberra with her mother during a parliamentary session, and they had dinner together. They met again in Sydney that year and Paul took her to a Sydney beach. She had a way of tucking in her chin, smiling slowly and looking upward at him. She didn't have the frank and direct smile of Australian girls. There was something, perhaps, about the angle of her head, the slow and contemplative gaze of her eyes, the dazzle of her teeth, that charmed him, that was enough for him to feel he was seeing a new world suddenly opening, a world neither Bankstown nor Kingsgrove, not Irish and not the Labor Party, not even Roman Catholic as he knew it. A world that had something to do with lovely old furniture, simple, well-designed homes, older civilisations.

They had a lot to talk about. She knew little about Australia, and nothing about the Labor Party, Australian society, the excitement of politics and what a political career meant. Paul had ideas about how the world worked, economics, the purpose and design of things that were entirely new to her. He was a sharp dresser and alive to music and painting. He was intelligent and amusing. He was already a member of Parliament and at 28 had an exciting and perhaps lofty career ahead. She had taste, style and assurance that was completely new to him. She knew materials, cuts, trends and places to shop that he didn't know even existed. He would not then or later even try a foreign language; she could speak with reasonable fluency four languages other than Dutch. She knew Europe as casually and as familiarly as he knew Bankstown.

They were an unlikely pair, but behind their differences they had much in common. Like most Australians, he was a city child, and cities all over the world have their common patterns. Neither had been to university, both their fathers ran small businesses – Paul's in engineering and metals fabrication, Annita's in leather. Both were Catholics. They believed the same things. Both came from small stable families, which they intended to replicate in their own lives. And if Annita was sophisticated and glamorous to Paul, he in turn was new, interesting and challenging to her. Both found the other familiar, yet exotic.

Breaking off his planned marriage was difficult and unpleasant. Hurt and shocked, his former fiancée sued for breach of promise. Paul did not talk about it, then or later. When it was raised in Parliament more than a decade later by Liberal backbencher Wilson Tuckey, he was white with anger and distress. For Paul that decision was the most important turning point in his life outside politics. Instead of reinforcing his background and upbringing by marriage with a woman of similar background and upbringing, he joined his life with someone quite different.

The courtship lasted three and a half difficult years. He was working in Canberra, she was living in Rome and flying across the world. Paul travelled the world in pursuit of her. They were more often apart

than together, and sometimes apart for as long as six months. At one
time he was visiting London almost weekly. He met her in Buenos
Aires, and attempted to demonstrate in the hotel swimming pool that
he was a more elegant and faster swimmer than one of his rivals. He
met her mother Anni and father Jan in Holland. They married in January 1975 in Annita's home town, the village of Oisterwijk. Paul wore
a grey top hat, morning coat and gloves. Annita wore white, with a
veil and a pill box hat. She carried a bunch of white flowers.

They honeymooned at the Austrian ski resort of Kitzbühel.
Annita was a superb skier. Paul could not ski or speak German. He
fretted for a more familiar world. Returning to Sydney, they moved
into their new house at 12 Gerard Avenue, next door but one to Min
and Matt. Paul was in Canberra during parliamentary sessions and
often travelling, leaving Annita to explore Bankstown. Min stopped
by to see that things were all in order. Still in her mid twenties, Annita
wondered where she would find friends in this vast city of single-
storey brick homes, each with its patch of grass and paling fence.

Paul was in love, excited, agitated and uplifted by romance for
the entire term of the Whitlam Government. The period that, for
the Whitlam Cabinet, was a sequence of ever larger disasters, of losing control, of feeling helpless and inadequate to the mysterious
forces at work in the world, was to Paul the period in which he enjoyed
the love affair of his life. Furious and vengeful at missing out in
the first ballot, he was oddly calm about the subsequent sequence of
losses, although he did talk about resignation. He actually missed
one ballot, while getting married, and seemed almost unconcerned.
'They all did me a favour by not putting me in,' he would say, when
it no longer mattered. 'I just had more time to float around and see
the world, and I met my wife during that period . . . The other thing,
I missed out on the silly part of the Whitlam Government, I came
in when it was actually improving, and that was good.'[7]

During the Whitlam Government the people most influencing Paul
were still a generation older than him. They were inclined to regulation,

to protecting Australia from the world, rather than to encouraging markets confidently and Australia's engagement with the rest of the world. Lionel Bowen was one of these influences, and his steadfast certainties allowed no room for greens, women, gays, free trade or free investment. He was successful in his own way in his own world, but his insularity was so strong a characteristic that he was distant even from his own faction. Paul could learn only so much from him because Bowen did not change. Paul saw less of him now that Bowen was a minister, but he remained Paul's most important link to the inner circle of power in Cabinet. A more powerful and, for a time, a consuming influence was Rex Connor, the Minister for Minerals and Energy. Like Bowen, Connor had come from the New South Wales Parliament and was elected to the tail end of the ministry on the final ballot. With a detailed knowledge of Australia's mineral and energy resources and of the history of their discovery and development, Connor believed in Australian ownership and government regulation. He had no more confidence in the market than he had in the talents of mine owners and managers.

Coming to office as the impact of the first oil price increase of February 1971 and the second, much greater increase of December 1973 made themselves felt in inflation and unemployment in the global economy, Connor found himself unexpectedly in the forefront of public policy. Mineral discoveries and exploitation in the 1960s had dramatically changed the pattern of Australia's trade, with minerals replacing agricultural products as the major export. Now the doubling and tripling of oil prices globally pushed up the prices of other energy sources like gas and steaming coal, which Australia had in abundance. Interest in Australian resources increased but Connor was determined to prevent non-Australians increasing their share of ownership. At the same time he directed his department to intervene in negotiations between Australian suppliers of minerals and energy products and their customers to force up prices. The opposition to Connor from Australian and foreign miners was intense, which did not trouble him at all. But the whole approach did run into two serious problems. The first was that the OPEC price rises caused both unemployment and inflation in the industrial countries, which reduced the demand for Australian minerals and energy. The second was that Australia did not have sufficient capital to develop major mining projects rapidly without foreign money, let alone the ports, highways and roads upon which the success of mines depended.

Connor's response to both problems was a bad idea, typically grand in scope and quaintly zany in execution. The intent was for the Australian Government to borrow a very large amount of money to build roads, railways and ports on a huge scale. It would also develop mines through a government authority. Connor was in the market for at least $8 billion by late 1974. Distrustful of Treasury, which he correctly expected would oppose the whole scheme once it became aware of it, he chose to work through the head of his own department, Sir Lenox Hewitt, and through a Pakistani intermediary of no substantial repute in international finance, Tirath Khemlani. The minister authorised Khemlani to raise money on a generous commission.

In every respect the venture was a failure. 'Would not a decision to proceed on the basis of presently available information expose the government to grave charges of imprudence?' Treasury official John Stone queried in a note, after pointing out that the proposed contracts were with unnamed and unidentified principals, ostensibly prepared to lend immense sums at well below market interest rates through little-known agents who were demanding high commissions to be paid before the loans were received.

Despite the generous terms and the attractiveness of the borrower, Khemlani was not actually able to raise money. Ignoring a Cabinet decision to terminate the search for a lender, Connor continued. And despite his secrecy the Opposition were informed and were handed an irresistible opportunity to bring down not only Connor but the government as well. The information for the Opposition in all likelihood came from Treasury, but the government's failure was due not to the leak but to the inexperience of the minister.

All of this was clear in retrospect, but at the time Connor was fighting Labor's most bitter enemies – international capital, the mining industry owners, Treasury, and the Opposition, and he fought with the loyal support of his young admirer, Paul Keating. 'We were made for each other,' Paul had said of Connor in 1979. 'We were both frustrated technocrats, keen about development issues. Connor would talk to me all night. He'd say, "Have you got the story on the direct reduction process in iron?" You'd say, "No, Rex." You'd then get a brilliant lecture on different blast furnace feeds and why parts of the Pilbara should be developed before others. Connor has left a legacy. Medibank has gone. But not offshore sovereignty, proper pricing for exports, coal as an energy bridge, the issues of ownership and control.'[8] Even a decade later he was still gentle on Connor's memory. 'He never quite understood private business and how it felt and operated. I mean, I suppose that's where I've got the jump on a lot of guys in this place – I always have, by and large.'[9]

Reflection on the experience of the Whitlam Government would change Keating but during it his views remained orthodox. Like many members of caucus, he had little respect for Whitlam's political judgement or grasp of economic policy and had no hesitation in dissenting. In the early 1970s people thought quite differently; they still lived in the glow of the 1960s, when unemployment was low, growth high and persistent. They did not foresee the consequences of the oil price rises in pushing up inflation, at the same time pushing down growth worldwide. They did not foresee the extent to which the effects of rapidly rising wages and rapidly rising government spending within Australia would soften the impact on employment but amplify the impact on inflation of the doubling and tripling of global oil prices. As Keating later realised, 'No one knew the growth was finished,' that the golden years were over.

If the government was generally thought to be too radical in economic policy, to Paul it was not radical enough. Like many Labor politicians unfamiliar with office and observing a public service leadership that had become accustomed to Liberal governments, he believed the public service was thwarting Labor's plans. In April 1973 he moved successfully in caucus for a special enquiry into the public service and in particular the role of Treasury. Subsequently, although not as a direct result, the Coombs Royal Commission on Australian Government Administration was appointed.

As Keating himself would do nearly twenty years later, the inner leadership of the Whitlam Government dramatically tightened monetary policy on the advice of the Reserve Bank and Treasury. The circumstances were somewhat different, but one of the motivating forces in each was speculative rises in house prices. On Sunday 9 September 1973, in a decision that had quite as much to do with the subsequent electoral rejection of the government as the antics of Rex Connor, the Prime Minister, his deputy and the Treasurer agreed to an increase in interest rates and an increase in the exchange value of the Australian dollar. Home loans rose a then-dramatic 1 per cent. In a special caucus meeting held the following Thursday, Keating moved that government should direct trading banks to exempt home mortgages. He also wanted to extend lending controls to cover finance companies, which he said would reduce speculation in house prices. Whitlam successfully moved that it be referred to the economic committee. In the event the government did limit the rise to 1 per cent. When Keating himself pursued the same policy lines at the end of the 1980s, it would be Graham Richardson, in pleas to Prime Minister Bob Hawke, who would attempt unsuccessfully to protect mortgages from the interest rate increases.

Paul was a regulator and remained a protectionist. In October 1974, six months after the Whitlam Government was re-elected, Keating was opposing what he described in Parliament as the 'defeatist' car protection plan proposed by the government. 'Australians will continue to purchase small comfortable Japanese cars at a growing rate,' he said, 'and therefore their cars ought to be manufactured here rather than imported.' He continued to favour tax indexation. In April 1975 he told Max Hollingworth of the *Australian* that, 'if we leave the situation as it is, we will end up with everybody on the maximum rate of tax about fifteen years from now.'

On moral issues, he remained a son of his church but with a liberal position. In the Family Law Bill debate on 19 May 1975 he wanted no-fault divorces available only after two years separation rather than one. He accepted one year where both parties consented or where there was fault such as cruelty.[10]

By the middle of 1975 Keating thought the Whitlam Government was on the mend. He strongly supported Treasurer Bill Hayden's budget in that year, moving its adoption and arguing it through a hostile caucus. 'That crazy caucus was an affront to my sense of order,' he recalled. Paul was being married in Ostewijk when caucus balloted for a ministerial vacancy caused by the departure of Lionel Murphy to the High Court. But he was back in October when Rex Connor resigned when it was revealed that he had continued seeking an international loan after he had been directed to stop. Running against South Australian Mick Young, Paul won the ballot, and on 21 October 1975 the Governor-General, Sir John Kerr, swore him in as Minister for Northern Australia. The Opposition had decided to block supply five days before. The constitutional crisis had already absorbed the energies of the government, and in less than four weeks Kerr would sack the entire ministry. At Paul's first Cabinet meeting only one of the twenty-seven chairs crowded around the table was empty. It was, of course, Rex Connor's. Reflecting Connor's seniority, the chair was close to the Prime Minister's. When Keating sat down on it Whitlam said, 'Don't sit there, you pushy bastard!' He asked Lionel Bowen to move up and Keating to move down. But it was good-humoured. Cabinet and caucus were united in their determination to stare down the Opposition in the Senate.

'Once you've been a minister,' he had told Bob Carr as both young men talked over their ambitions, 'you've been a minister,' neither needing to say more. Cabinet was where the decisions were made, the sanctum so secret that notes of the discussion were at least in theory concealed from all members except the Prime Minister and kept secret for decades. Between 21 October and 11 November 1975, however,

Keating was able to attend only two Cabinet meetings. At the first one the Prime Minister terminated an exposition by the Attorney-General, Kep Enderby, by asking, 'When are you going to shut up, you garrulous bastard?' 'I thought, is this the Cabinet of the Government of Australia?' Paul later told Clyde Cameron, both men feigning shock.[11]

Paul hardly had time to arrange his new desk as each day the government came closer to a crisis in which it would not be able to pay the bills. Whitlam relied on his old friend, the Governor-General. He would know his constitutional responsibility to listen to the advice of his Prime Minister. Paul went out to Government House with Whitlam, forming, with Kerr, an Executive Council meeting to formally approve some appointments in Paul's portfolio. Whitlam and Kerr were genial, close. 'Look at this leonine mane!' said Whitlam to Keating, admiring the Governor-General's silver hair. Driving back to Parliament, Paul expressed anxiety about Kerr. 'You can rely on him,' said Whitlam, settling into a catnap, 'he is a very proper person.' Five days later Paul flew down with a Liberal senator from Sydney. The Senator said, 'This can't go on — we have done the wrong thing. It's bound to fail.' Later that day, Kerr, without warning, dismissed Whitlam and appointed Fraser as Prime Minister pending an election. Paul thought then, and later, that Kerr acted wrongly. The government had enough money to run for a few more days, he believed, and the Senate Liberals were about to crack. The Governor-General did not, as he should, take the Prime Minister into his confidence. Keating was convinced that Whitlam would not have sacked Kerr.

Later, the story was often told of Whitlam coming back to Parliament House after his dismissal, furious and bewildered, and passing his newest minister on his way in. 'You're sacked,' he told Keating, striding by. 'Me?' Keating replied, wheeling around after him. 'What did I do?' The incident never occurred.

On 14 December 1975 Malcolm Fraser and his Coalition won the election with the largest majority in Australian history. There could be no doubt about the public's judgment of the Whitlam Government. Only at the beginning and the end had it succeeded. In between times it made poor policy decisions and poor political decisions. Cairns and Connor had been sacked, Cameron and Crean had been forced from their first offices, but the most striking mis-judgments – on economic policy, on seeking overseas loans, and finally on the reliability of John Kerr – had been made or endorsed by the Prime Minister himself.

For Keating's whole generation, the World War II baby boomers who throughout his life would determine the political priorities of government, from the provision of schools when they were young to superannuation schemes when they were old, the dismissal of the Whitlam Government and its subsequent repudiation by the elec-torate coloured both their understanding of the past and their con-duct in the future. There had been twenty-three years of Liberal and Country Party coalition government, tailing away with a succession of second-rate leaders and a commitment to a war that many of Keat-ing's generation vehemently opposed. To them, good and truth had triumphed in 1972 with the election of a Labor Prime Minister clearly superior to McMahon, Gorton and Holt, who had first reformed his own party and then, as Prime Minister, promptly set about clearing the debris his Liberal predecessors had accumulated. Now, only three years later, Whitlam himself had been shown to be capable of great misjudgments. People experienced in politics knew that he could never win again.

Later calamities would make Australia's economic performance under the Whitlam Government look reasonable. Measured from year to year, there was no economic contraction. But inflation did increase substantially, and when Labor lost office in 1975, unem-ployment, at 5.3 per cent, was twice as high as it had been three years before. It would take Australians more than a decade to get used to higher unemployment and higher inflation. As important as the fact of higher inflation and unemployment was the widespread belief that the government was puzzled, confused and divided. Whitlam had been shown to lack understanding of how to manage his ministers, the economy, and the presentation of economic policy. Not only was Whitlam repudiated but also so was much that Keating's generation had believed or at least accepted. The world had changed abruptly. Inflation was now a serious problem. Unemployment was persistently high. The old solutions were discredited. To win back office, Keating knew, Labor had to renovate both its leadership and its policies.

The experience of the Whitlam Government was the beginning of a slow but decisive change in Keating's political attitudes. He had never regarded Whitlam as an ally or patron. He had always felt that Whitlam foolishly underestimated him because he had not been to a university, and he had long scorned Whitlam's political judgment. The change was deeper than his opposition to Whitlam as political leader. He was confirmed in his conviction that economic management was the key to successful government and that the appearance, as well as the reality, of control was the key to successful economic management. There were also lessons in selling. 'We moved too fast before,' he would say. 'We have to learn how to package our policies, sell them to the electorate: you have to be with the consensus, not ahead of it. The electorate is conservative, basically; you've got to market things carefully.'[12] The party's leaders remembered other problems. Cabinet was too big. Ministers were not obliged to be loyal to its decisions. When Labor returned to office these problems would be addressed.

Rejecting Whitlam's leadership, Keating adopted many of his positions. Whitlam recognised that tariff protection was in the long run bad for the Australian economy. The only significant tariff cut in the thirty-three years between 1945 and 1988 was made by Whitlam in 1973 (against the advice of Treasury). He was unable to prevent it, but Whitlam certainly knew, and told his ministers and their advisers, that a government could not accept both rapidly increasing budget spending and rapidly increasing wages. As a backbencher Keating had been a nuisance. He attempted to prevent interest rate increases for housing mortgages; he was in favour of tariffs; he supported Connor's insistence on undiluted Australian ownership of minerals and energy developments. In coming years all these positions would change, first to catch up with those of Whitlam, and then to move well beyond them.

He also acquired from Whitlam (or at least had in common with him) certain elements that would reappear when Keating himself was Prime Minister. Whitlam himself was delighted when Keating's One Nation statement in February 1992 completed the standard gauge rail links between Brisbane and Perth. After the Fraser and then the Hawke years it was Keating who returned to Whitlam's highly visible support for arts funding, Australian identity and urban design. One of Keating's most potent weapons against Hawke was his complete commitment to Commonwealth dominance in taxation, a commitment that cheered Whitlam. He always queried Whitlam's style and especially Whitlam's fussiness with detail and his obsession with legal instruments, treaties, clauses, articles and statutes. But Keating was far more like Whitlam than Hawke.

5

THE HARD YEARS

THE ELECTION HAD LEFT AUSTRALIA sharply divided. The trade union leadership and the Labor Party did not accept the legitimacy of Fraser's victory, so that it was never possible for him to appeal plausibly for a national, common purpose. It was hard slog all the way. But the Labor Party was also divided, more over leadership than policy. Three brief years of government were followed by seven long years of opposition and recurrent struggles over leadership.

While Whitlam would influence Keating more than the young politician cared to admit, Fraser's victory convinced Keating that Labor needed to change its leader before it had any chance of returning to power. Personal and factional ties as well as common policy views bound him to Lionel Bowen, who, in most important ways, represented a throwback to the party of the 1960s. Repudiating Whitlam, he could not repudiate the much less able, much more conservative Bowen. The hard young man was also a sentimentalist.

Whitlam called the shattered party together in the Opposition caucus room on 27 January 1976. On 11 December there had been ninety-two members. Now there were sixty-three. On election night Whitlam had been sufficiently distraught to want the former Treasurer Bill Hayden to take the leadership. Hayden had refused. Now Whitlam decided to recontest the leadership. Lionel Bowen stood against him, more to make the point of his opposition and to stake a claim than in any real expectation of winning. He was not supported by the New

South Wales machine, which remained loyal to Whitlam and anyway did not much care for Bowen. Whitlam won handsomely. Bowen was well liked, careful, and busy. Only the candidate thought of himself as a Labor Party leader. Keating supported Bowen, grateful that on this occasion Bowen had stood for the leadership and not for the deputy's job, which Keating eyed for himself. 'I thought then that Bowen had more savvy about where things were going in a public sense, so I thought he might be able to do a better job. He was not of them, but he came from the New South Wales tradition of Pat Hills and Reg Downing, and he was electorally sure-footed,' he later explained. But Keating seemed half-hearted about Bowen. Earlier he had tried to persuade Hayden to run. Hayden insisted that he wanted to do a law degree and refused not only the leadership but also a shadow ministry.

Keating's new standing was demonstrated in the deputy leader's ballot. The candidates included the Left's Tom Uren and South Australian centrist Mick Young, as well as a field of five others. Keating and Young had marked each other in the Whitlam Government. They regarded each other as rivals for the eventual leadership of the party. Keating had defeated him for the ministerial vacancy in 1975. Now Young was supported both by Whitlam and by some of Whitlam's party enemies, including former Labor minister Clyde Cameron. On primary votes Uren was 15 against Keating and Young, who were both on 13. After preferences Uren was 33, Keating 30 — Uren won by only three votes in sixty-three cast. A vote for the veteran Uren was a vote for balance within the party; a vote for Keating was a vote for Whitlam's successor.

Cameron told Uren, 'Keating's problem is that he is too young. Almost every member of caucus sees himself as a future minister and a large number fondle the idea of becoming a Prime Minister. Once a young man like Keating gets on the pillion seat everyone knows it won't be long before he is riding the motorbike. And at his age that will tie up the job for another thirty years. The ambitious ones don't like that. It's not only the older ones who take this view but the younger ones as well. In caucus ballots one will always find young candidates throwing away their preferences to older candidates, especially if that candidate's life expectancy does not appear particularly bright.'[1] Cameron hated Whitlam but he did not want Keating on the pillion seat.

A few months after the ballot it was revealed that Whitlam and the party Federal Secretary David Combe had been willing to accept a large campaign donation from the ruthless junta that controlled the government of Iraq. Astonished by the revelations, Keating seized the chance to attempt again to evict Whitlam. On 7 March the party's federal executive condemned Whitlam, Combe and left-winger Bill Hartley for trying to raise Iraqi funds. Ten days later caucus discussed a National Executive report on what were known as the Iraqi Funds Allegations. When left-winger Ted Innes moved that caucus merely note the report, Keating strongly opposed the resolution. It was not sufficient to thank the executive for their report, he said; Whitlam's conduct (in introducing a contact of the Iraqis to Combe) would have compromised the party if it had been elected to office. 'It should cause the leader to examine his future role,' he said without subtlety.[2]

Cameron noted in his diary, 'Keating said there was no doubt at all that Whitlam thought we would be getting money and that if we had we would have been totally compromised. The Governor-General could have dismissed us with honour, and the Senate could have refused us supply with honour. The credibility of the leadership is being questioned in the electorate. Whitlam should seriously consider tendering his resignation.' Cameron was avid for stories of fights with Whitlam. That night he wrote, 'Paul Keating has cooked his goose with Whitlam, who was livid over Keating's speech in caucus this morning. When he passed him in the corridor tonight he ground his teeth and hissed, "You sneaky little cunt." Keating just grinned, I'm told. He is a tough little customer.' Later Paul told Cameron that Whitlam had brilliance but not judgment.[3] But Gough was a big man who forgot quarrels. Among some members of caucus, Keating was acquiring a repute for smallness and inveteracy, like Cameron.

Paul returned to the new parliament on the front bench, to the left of the Speaker. It was his seventh year in parliament, almost all of which he had spent as a backbencher. Now he was on the front bench, but in Opposition.

The fall of the government had accelerated change at the top of the party. Even before the government fell former ministers Lionel Murphy and Lance Barnard had left. Many other lions of the 1960s and early 1970s could not reasonably hope to be ministers in a future Labor government. In the new caucus Keating was suddenly a senior figure, a former minister who was young enough not only to be a minister in a new Labor government but also perhaps one day a Labor leader. Certainly he thought so.

Narrowly losing the deputy leadership, he was temporarily assigned to agriculture and was given minerals and energy when Whitlam finalised the shadow Cabinet appointments. He was senior but on the second rung of public recognition. He did not have a leadership position. But given the diversity and political complications of the job, the minerals and energy slot was an acknowledgment of Paul's new seniority. He was to remain minerals and energy spokesman for seven years, making it by far the most important formative policy experience before he became a minister once again in the Hawke Government. His work there would fundamentally change his views about Australia and the Australian economy in a way that prepared him to be a reforming Treasurer in the next decade.

Shadowed by failure, rent by old enmities between men who would never again enjoy power, the federal parliamentary Labor Party was a small, unhappy group. Pushed aside, the older members watched. Pursuing his vendetta against Whitlam, Clyde Cameron incidentally kept track of Keating. He noted on 18 March 1976, 'Paul Keating didn't handle his first assignment as shadow minister this afternoon too well when, after an amendment to the second reading of the States Grants (Fruit Canneries) Bill, he permitted the second and third to go through without calling for a division. [That is, Keating moved amendments and then did not ask for a vote on them.] It is not the kind of thing he is likely to do again. One has to take into account that he was a minister for only six weeks [sic], and has been in this job for only a few weeks. After all, the procedures of the House must be confusing to someone who hasn't much experience of them.' Clyde was in earshot when the leader corrected his shadow minister. Cameron recorded, 'Gough was in no mood for charity and, no doubt remembering the serve that Keating gave him in caucus yesterday, turned on him, grinding his teeth and glaring with hatred. He said to him, "You fucking smart bastard, you talk about corruption – you and your mates in New South Wales, Brereton and Cahill, and now you've gone and fucked up this bill." '[4] Cameron was fond of the image of Whitlam grinding his teeth.

Paul suspected that years of Opposition lay in front of him, years of speaking and planning but not of exercising power. Whitlam and Uren, the Leader and Deputy Leader, were yesterday's men to him and to his generation. He was now 33. His income had been cut back again to a backbencher's salary. But in other ways his life was more varied and interesting. In 1977 he and Annita would have their first child, Patrick, and he now had more time to interest himself in antiques and architecture. There were things to learn, things to see, people to cultivate and influence. A good shadow portfolio, with free travel and the liberty to arrange things as he wished, was not so bad for a curious mind that thrived on new understanding.

Since the 1960s mining had been acquiring a renewed importance in the Australian economy and now accounted for more than half of its export income. The industry was predominantly foreign-owned, and Connor had outraged it by creating instrumentalities through which government could own and develop mines, and by insisting on complete Australian ownership of new private mining or energy projects. When Paul took the job at the beginning of 1976 it remained party policy that energy projects had to be 100 per cent Australian-owned and all other mining projects at least 50 per cent Australian-owned. That would need to be changed before Labor could devise policies that fitted the realities of the industry. Unlike farming, manufacturing or the service industries, mining was a global industry, dependent on large amounts of equity or risk capital, with global ownership, global markets, global technology and often global management. Opposed to tariffs and in favour of a low Australian dollar, the mining industry was international in scope. It introduced Paul to the long trails of international commerce and capital. He had learned about manufacturing from Matt Keating, from Larry Hartnett and Australian National Industries' John Leard; about property development from Sid Londish. Now he began to learn more about mining from the leaders of the industry – men like Mount Isa Mines chief Sir James Foots, BHP chief Sir Ian McLennan and CRA's Frank Espie. The more he learned, the more he questioned the views he had brought to parliament and the views he had acquired from Rex Connor.

Uranium would never be an important export for Australia but it aroused passions. Were nuclear power plants safe? Was technology being developed to store nuclear wastes permanently and safely? Could nuclear fuel be diverted into weapons production? If the answer to all these questions was uncertain, should Australia export uranium? These were difficult issues. A committee of inquiry headed by Mr Justice Fox had been appointed to examine them. Like Vietnam, the issue separated the young and the old. Lionel Bowen saw no problems. Nor did Rex Connor (who also wanted sand mining on Fraser Island). Bob Hawke seemed to have few qualms. But the Left was outraged, and in opposition the Left were generally more important than they were when Labor was in government. Paul was cautious. At a caucus meeting on 3 November 1976 Paul told his colleagues that he had not yet formed a definite view on uranium exporting, but his own tendency was to oppose uranium exports, while recognising there were existing legal contractual commitments. On 17 November he supported honouring existing contracts, with a warning that new contracts would not be binding on a future ALP government.[5]

Keating successfully fought against a left-wing proposal to ban uranium exports totally, and later he supported a compromise policy that would allow the opening of a new mine in South Australia. But both Bill Hayden and Bob Hawke were more prominent in pressing for Labor acceptance of uranium mining. Uren later wrote that that he 'never had problems' with Keating while he was deputy leader, and Keating did not confront him on uranium. 'I don't think he thought it was a matter of great significance.'[6] Paul was not really interested in debates that were more about symbols than substance. He did not wish to alienate the Left on an issue he thought of little true consequence. He later recalled that:

> My position on the uranium debate was that there was a world glut, so why cut ourselves to ribbons over it? We couldn't sell it anyway. I didn't want to do anything about policy, except we could not leave the South Australian party permanently offside by vetoing the Roxby Downs development. Bob Hogg and Bill Hayden got together and got that lifted. We were happy with that.

For the next seven years Labor would be defined as much by its opponent as by its own actions. Tall and forbidding, Malcolm Fraser had come to political leadership with surprising suddenness. When elected to parliament for the formerly Labor Victorian provincial seat of Wannon in 1955, Fraser was 25, the same age as Keating when elected for Blaxland fourteen years later. Like Keating, he had had no other career than politics and, like Keating, part of his mental furniture was the solitary and heroic opposition by Winston Churchill to the appeasers of the pre-war Conservative governments of Stanley Baldwin and Neville Chamberlain. Fraser's maiden speech in parliament contained passages Keating could have spoken. He was in favour of faster development of Australia, of the Ord and Fitzroy River irrigation schemes, of a national communications plan, of a population of 25 million by the year 2000. There were also similarities in their upbringing. Both were adored sons of reasonably happily married parents and enjoyed the strength and resilience of a secure childhood. There the similarities ended.

Fraser's parents were wealthy graziers, who had moved to Victoria's Western District when he was a child. His grandfather was the reactionary businessman and politician, Sir Simon Fraser, who had been a Minister without Portfolio in the Victorian Government, a participant in the constitutional conventions, and a senator from Victoria to the new Federal Parliament. Educated at Melbourne Grammar and Oxford, Fraser had returned to Victoria without scholastic distinction or professional qualification, his mind now burdened with the results of an Oxford tutorial system that focused on great books. It gave him Toynbee and Keynes but not the analytic apparatus to deal with them. He did have, however, an early and well-formed ambition to win for the Liberals the Western District seat of Wannon, then held by Labor.

Fraser had spent a decade on the backbenches before Holt appointed him Minister for the Army in 1966. It was not just his youth and the long line of deserving backbenchers in front of him that kept him off the front bench. He had an independent mind and had disagreed with Menzies' opposition to Britain joining the European Common Market, and he was sharply critical of apartheid in South Africa when Menzies was trying to keep South Africa in the British Commonwealth. When Harold Holt drowned off Portsea in 1967, Fraser was the key member of a small group that managed John Gorton's campaign for the leadership of the party against Paul Hasluck, Leslie Bury and Billy Snedden. When Gorton became Prime Minister, Fraser was rewarded with the Cabinet post of Education and Science, and later the key post of Defence Minister in 1969. Fraser was strongly in favour of Australia's commitment to Vietnam, but dissatisfied with the control exercised by the Department of Defence over the services and by the minister over the Department of Defence. Brought into conflict with the army commander-in-chief as the culmination of a series of disagreements with the Prime Minister, Fraser believed that Gorton was not supporting him and resigned from Cabinet. His resignation and subsequent attack on Gorton in his resignation speech in the House helped to bring down the Prime Minister, but Fraser was not preferred by Bill McMahon when he replaced Gorton as Prime Minister in March 1971. Nor was he or generally liked by his colleagues. It was August 1971 before he was returned to Cabinet, again to the post of Minister for Education and Science.

After McMahon's defeat and resignation in 1972 Fraser ran for the leadership in a ballot that included Billy Snedden and Andrew Peacock. He won only a handful of votes. In his first experience on the Speaker's left in his seventeen years in Parliament, Fraser was competent but undistinguished. His strength, invisible to others, was that he was not frightened of Gough Whitlam. In 1973 very few people would have imagined Fraser as Leader of the Opposition, let alone Prime Minister. Yet within two years he had taken advantage of Snedden's failing performance to rally the Right of the party and its Victorian base to win the leadership, and a year later he had used the Opposition's strength in the Senate to block finance bills and force an election on a reluctant, failing government.

Fraser became Prime Minister flying the colours of smaller government, lower taxes, adamant opposition to union power, and a stern foreign policy. In office, he proved himself to be more conservative than radical. Government spending fell compared to the level it reached in the economic downturn of 1974 and 1975, but it did not come close to returning to the levels of the 1960s. As a young backbencher Fraser had been critical of Australia's high tariff levels but, as Prime Minister, far from allowing the market free play, Fraser raised tariffs and attempted a general wage freeze by government order. He assented to the appointment of the Campbell Committee to review financial regulation, but refused to implement its far-reaching reform proposals. He was strongly critical of unions but did very little to change the system of wage arbitration upon which part of their power depended. He made stern speeches about the Soviet Union, but in foreign policy devoted much time to cultivating alliances with left-leaning governments of the Third World, including supporting a UN-sponsored fund to increase prices in commodity markets.

Keating learned from the experiences of the Whitlam Government and so did Fraser, but the lessons were quite different. Fraser came from the paternalistic tradition of conservatism and followed an opportunistic approach in office, so that the new ideology of markets, a minimal role for government, and all the consequences of deregulation and lower taxes were not seriously proposed or implemented while he was Prime Minister. He was not of the same mould as Reagan or Thatcher, but rather Prime Minister Robert Muldoon across the Tasman in New Zealand, or Edward Heath in Britain, who also sought to resist globalisation and to control the economy by command.[7]

Paul claimed leadership of the New South Wales Right in Federal Parliament but there were problems. Portrayed as united and clever, the public solidarity of the New South Wales Right machine concealed complicated conflicts. The internal story was of the seizure and assertion of authority by John Ducker and then its slow but consistent repudiation by his younger associates – at first Barrie Unsworth, Paul Keating and Laurie Brereton, and then Bob Carr at the tail end of Ducker's control. As Paul was to recall in November 1991, 'It wasn't really a happy family,' and the unhappiest part of it until 1979, when Ducker resigned his positions, was the tension between Paul Keating and the Sydney alliance of Ducker and his protégé as party Secretary, Geoff Cahill.

Keating did not care for Cahill's pretensions to direct the New South Wales right wing in the federal parliamentary Labor Party. By 1976 Cahill was losing other allies. He was said to be urging Bob Hawke to enter Parliament, though Hawke was potentially a rival of Keating and still a union enemy of Ducker's Labor Council deputy, Barrie Unsworth. Ducker encouraged Cahill's relationship with Hawke, but Cahill was also said to have known of and perhaps even participated in a deal in which Queenslander Bart Lourigan defeated Ducker as senior vice-president of the Labor Party. There were also troubling misjudgments. In 1975 Cahill had been heavy-handed in withdrawing Labor Party endorsement of Botany aldermen who refused a request from their local member, Laurie Brereton, to oppose the rezoning of a property belonging to Rupert Murdoch's News Limited. During the 1975 New South Wales State Conference Cahill had a lost a vote on the future form of the conference itself.

Ducker and Cahill were close friends as well as close colleagues. Their wives worked together in the offices of the Paulian Association. By the 1976 June conference, however, Cahill was already marked for execution. As early as 16 May Clyde Cameron had privately asked John Ducker about reports that he was proposing to depose Geoff Cahill. According to Cameron, Ducker denied the reports, saying he had the fullest confidence in Cahill and that he had done a 'magnificent' job in the state election of 1976, which brought Neville Wran to power in New South Wales. Ducker was not an unreasonably candid man.

Convinced finally that Cahill was jeopardising the faction's control, Ducker agreed with Unsworth, Keating and their allies to force Cahill's resignation on his return from an August 1976 jaunt to the United States. Keating suggested that Unsworth and not Ducker should be sent out to meet Cahill at the airport and accompany him home. Ducker, he said, wouldn't be able to resist the charm of Cahill's little children. Cahill would then be brought to the Labor Party offices.

Cahill arrived with Unsworth at the tenth-floor Labor Council offices in the Labor Council building in Sussex Street, still in the trench coat he had worn from the airport. Those in the room included Peter McMahon, Barney French, John McBean, Unsworth and Keating. Ducker did not attend the whole meeting. He was too distressed by the sad, though necessary, execution of his friend and colleague. Cahill's successor, Graham Richardson, was at the Labor Party offices on the ninth floor. He telephoned upstairs every now and then to find out how the meeting was going.

The meeting was silent when Cahill walked in. The hard men of the Right were reluctant to strike the blow. 'I've lost the support of my mates, have I?' Cahill asked, looking around the stony faces. 'Yes, you have, Geoffrey,' Paul genially replied, breaking an embarrassed silence. He proceeded to list the accusations of misjudgments that had threatened the Right's control. 'But we will take care of you, Geoffrey,' he concluded. 'We always bury our dead.' Cahill assented to a press release announcing that he was going on to seek further challenges in his career, and a short time later he received a government appointment. Graham Richardson, whose political abilities Paul respected, was appointed Cahill's successor.

These shifting struggles were of the greatest importance to Keating. Ultimately they would determine the support of the New South Wales Right for alternative candidates for the federal party leadership. Bob Hawke was contesting the leadership of the federal parliamentary Labor Party almost from the time the Whitlam Government began to fail in 1974, and became an active though undeclared challenger as soon as Whitlam lost the election. It would be another five years before he was in Parliament, but Hawke did not deviate from this aim until he attained it. Hawke was the favourite son of the Right in Victoria. But there were other candidates in the wings. Premier Neville Wran scraped to a first victory in New South Wales in 1976 and won by a landslide when he went back to the polls in 1978. By 1980 he too was looking at the federal leadership. Ducker quite liked Hawke; Wran, however, was blood. Some day Keating wanted the leadership himself and in some ways the shadow candidacy of Neville Wran was more of a complication for him than the shadow candidacy of Bob Hawke. 'I told Neville I would support him if he came,' Paul recalled, but he could scarcely have been excited by the idea.

Whitlam had been re-elected leader in January 1976, but everyone knew the leadership was unresolved. As Keating would later say, 'Losers have to be dispensed with, it's as simple as that.'[8] Caucus provided that another leadership ballot would be held in eighteen months. Recognising that Uren was an electoral liability and a dead-end for the party succession, Whitlam attempted in the following months to draw Hayden into a new ballot for the deputy leader's position. With Hayden as deputy, the line of succession would be clear, and at the same time Whitlam would be better able to choose the time for graceful resignation. There would even be a possibility, Whitlam may have imagined, that he could be returned to government. But if Keating stood again for deputy and divided the Left and Centre, Uren would have a good chance of holding the job.

Towards the end of 1976 Whitlam's ally, Senator Jim McClelland, a former solicitor, was assigned by the Leader to persuade Keating to stay out of any new deputy leadership contest and to help persuade Hayden to enter it. The choice of McClelland as his emissary demonstrated Whitlam's failing touch. Keating enjoyed McClelland's sour wit but had no more regard for his political acumen than for Whitlam's. Formerly a close friend of Sir John Kerr, McClelland had reassured Whitlam's Cabinet that the Governor-General would do the right thing. Witty and urbane, he remained lightweight.

Keating had other ideas about the appropriate role for Bill Hayden. To him a more sensible and convenient outcome would be for Hayden to contest the leadership against Whitlam and win, and for Keating to contest the deputy leadership against Uren and win. Labor would then have a plausible and youthful leadership that had ministerial experience but was not held responsible for the shortcomings of the Whitlam Government.

Keating and Hayden dined together in Canberra just before the February 1977 session of Parliament.[9] He did his utmost to persuade Hayden to run for the leadership, with himself as deputy. Hayden's thoughts were turning towards the leadership anyway. After a year of light responsibilities and part-time work on a law degree, after the calamity of the Iraq loan proposal, Hayden had decided he would run against Whitlam, but he had a gift for thwarting himself. He disapproved of the New South Wales Right. He thought they were thugs who could not be trusted, and he felt obligated to Mick Young, whom he wanted as deputy. An alliance with Keating was impossible. Hayden let slip the chance for an alliance with Keating and the New South Wales Right that Hawke would attempt to seize three years later.

Hayden announced that he would contest a ballot against Whitlam. The mid-term leadership ballot was scheduled for a caucus meeting on 31 May 1977. Whitlam had once wanted to give the leadership to Hayden; now he did not want to surrender it. Once again, a Canberra leadership ballot forced a division between Keating and Ducker, just as it had in 1973. Whitlam met with John Ducker at the Parramatta Travelodge. 'Gough, we've never let you down,' Ducker told him.[10] Forcing Whitlam out now while the Murdoch press was still campaigning against him on the Iraq loans issue, Ducker and Richardson argued, would alienate party workers and Labor loyalists. Whitlam also picked up the Left, which cherished the legend of the Whitlam Government. Ducker and Richardson had another motive in supporting Whitlam against Hayden. Bob Hawke was already actively campaigning for the leadership, arguing that neither Whitlam nor Hayden were capable of leading the party to victory. Richardson was an admirer and ally of Hawke, and Ducker had been moving closer to the ACTU leader year by year. Keating had encouraged Hayden to run; now Keating's factional boss was promising to support Whitlam. It was unpleasant. He later remembered: 'Ducker told me we had to support the leader – but he also knew Whitlam was finished. I said, if he is finished, why back him?'

Paul planned to nominate for the deputy leadership. An interview he gave to Craig McGregor for the *National Times*[11] temporarily upset his strategy. Cameron heard about it indirectly, from Bowen. 'Paul Keating is quite distressed by an interview he gave today to the *National Times*,' Cameron recorded in his diary. 'He appears to have attacked Hawke and made other statements which, according to Bowen, are more likely to do him harm than good. He told me Keating threw his hands in the air and told him he was going to get out of politics altogether – you can't win in this game, he said. It will be interesting to see what the *National Times* publishes. Paul says he will try to persuade them to edit some. I doubt he will succeed.'

McGregor had found Paul Keating hard but chatty. 'He's ambitious, he's ruthless, he's a master player of the numbers game – and he's young.' Unlike some of his colleagues, McGregor reported, Keating did not have sexual affairs. He was reputed to have said, 'If you want to be in power, you can't afford to fuck around.' Talking to people who knew him, McGregor reported, 'Most of them say quite bluntly they don't like him – but they respect him.' McGregor thought Keating would be leader some day, and quoted sources predicting that he would be Prime Minister. Bob Carr was one source. He told

McGregor, 'The future is about manufacturing industry and resources diplomacy. I can see Australia, led by Keating, developing into an important resources power. If Australian politics in the 1980s is going to be about industry policy, and exports, and tax strategy, then Keating's the man.'

Keating himself spoke with unusual prescience. What he had to say quite remarkably foreshadowed the views he would have and the positions he would take as Treasurer six years later or as Prime Minister fourteen years later: 'Minerals, wool and wheat – that's our long suit. And we have to make secondary industry competitive.' McGregor added: 'He doesn't think Australia has a future as a little European enclave in the Pacific; it has to trade its way into the South-East Asian community.' Though Paul was running for the deputy leadership he seemed to be talking about the leadership itself. Speaking of Whitlam, he told McGregor, 'Someone's got to put the Labor Party back together again – the party and the industrial movement. I'd like to give the labour movement a sense of unity after the aberration of the Whitlam years. I'd like to make it broader, make people feel more involved.' He also said, 'I'd like to steer the ALP into a consensus position, on the economy, employment, what kind of future agriculture has, minerals, will our resources keep growing, whether we can afford certain reforms . . . the welfare bag of policies has finished.' McGregor reported, 'He hasn't got much time for Bob Hawke either, but that is his ambition showing through.'

Then, as later Keating told himself, as much as others, politics was not his only option. 'I'm not on some huge mental kick like the Big Bloke's on,' he said. 'If it gets too tough they can ram it. I could move into business.' No plodder, no pocketer of his lunch money, Keating admired large lives, on the scale of Lang, Curtin and Theodore. But politics is a 'solitary game', and 'what a politician needs is shrewdness, cynicism, cunning – and a lot of nerve.'

'The article has certainly done Keating a lot of damage,' Cameron noted in his diary on Monday 28 March. 'Keating was so disturbed by the article that he announced to the Parliamentary Executive that he would not be a candidate for the deputy leadership. But actually it is his blunt candour that warms him to so many of his friends. Keating has overreacted.' In politics things are rarely as bad as they appear to the person directly involved.

The leadership ballot was not held for another two months; Whitlam won by 32 votes to 30. Paul then nominated for the deputy leadership. The other candidates included Tom Uren and Chris Hurford. Keating could only be viewed as Whitlam's successor, a fact that bothered his rivals within caucus. Hurford won 12 votes, Keating a respectable 22, but Uren a solid 28. Hurford's preferences went half each way, leaving Keating on 28 and Uren on 34. Keating thanked his supporters and pledged to support both leaders. But it was a disappointing outcome. The year before he had lost to Uren by only three votes.

If one caucus member had switched from Whitlam to Hayden the result would have been a tie and Whitlam's position would have been impossible. Torn between his opposition to Whitlam and the stern directive of his faction, Keating told different people different stories about how he voted. He told some Hayden supporters he voted for Hayden, but they were inclined to think he voted for Whitlam. Certainly it would have complicated his position with his faction, whose votes he needed for the deputy contest, if he had openly confessed to breaking the faction line. His duplicity did him no good. The New South Wales machine believe he had voted for Hayden, and Hayden's supporters believe he had voted for Whitlam. Graham Richardson, for example, believed Keating voted for Hayden.[12] Tom Uren believed he voted for Whitlam.[13] Cameron was still hunting him down months after the ballot. 'I am convinced Keating did not vote for Hayden,' he recorded on 16 August 1977. Ten days later Cameron was recording a remark by Joan Taggart, who was Rex Connor's assistant, that Keating had told Connor that he had voted for Whitlam. Cameron himself recorded on 26 August that Keating had said to him at the Federal Conference in Perth, ' "Clyde, don't ever tell anyone about this conversation. I had to play along with my mates in New South Wales because I needed their votes, but I was playing along with you for a long time and you didn't know it." He [Keating] had to let

his mates in New South Wales know he was voting for Whitlam.'
Cameron commented, 'Treachery.' In 1996 Paul recalled clearly that
he voted for Hayden in the May 1977 ballot.

Seizing his opportunity while Whitlam remained leader, Fraser called
an early election for 10 December 1977 to coincide with periodi-
cal elections for half the Senate. After the great loss of 1975 Labor
won a swing back of only 1.1 per cent. Given that unemployment
and inflation were still high, it was a poor result. As the returns came
in, Whitlam decided to resign the leadership. Hayden and Bowen
declared they would run. Paul announced on 20 December 1977 he
would run for the deputy leadership. Other contestants were expected
to be Tom Uren and Mick Young. In the ballot held on 22 December
Hayden defeated Bowen by 36 votes to 28. Keating supported Bowen.
Keating told Hayden that, despite supporting him in the previous
ballot, he felt he could not let Bowen down. This did not help Keating
with Hayden, but he was even worse off when Bowen then stood
against and defeated Uren for the deputy position. Bowen would hold
the deputy's job from 1977 to 1990, when Keating succeeded him.
Keating had very little choice, but were it not for Bowen he would
have been on better terms with Hayden and perhaps been deputy
leader of the party a decade earlier. Often presented as Keating's
kindly patron, Bowen more often than not got in his way. Hayden
would be party leader for just over five years.

Keating's experience of the mining industry was changing him. 'I went
to the Mining Industry Council, all around the mining areas of
Australia and talked to the business groups. I went down just about
every mine in the country, I knew all about it, I knew most of the
companies, the personalities. I liked the mining industry because it
was a successful, internationally competitive export industry. It
wasn't laying down in a sort of rut of tariffs and protection, it was
out there doing something.'

Bits of the pattern were starting to come together in Keating's mind. Fraser was having as many problems with the economy as Whitlam. There was evidently something deeper at work than a temporary interruption to the steady growth, low inflation and low unemployment of the 1960s. Recalling it in his Sydney office in May 1995, Keating said that some time in the late 1970s the understanding of the world he had been seeking since adolescence finally snapped into focus. It was a view that would inform his conduct in office for the following decade. 'I can remember well how I formed my view about the exchange rate. I was visiting Mount Isa mines. A wonderful mine. You could eat your lunch off the floor. I was talking to Jim Foots in the manager's cottage. I knew the mine was well run, the US dollar prices for metals were okay, labour costs not too bad but the mine did not earn well. Why? I realised it had to be that the exchange rate was overvalued, making us substantially uncompetitive. From then I was on the trail. You could look back and see the OPEC oil price rises, the wage increases of 1973–74, the budget spending increases, and it started to make sense.'

Paul's father and his partners had sold Marlak in 1973. Matt had angina, he was still active in the church and interested in his son's career, but his health was declining. In 1976 he had a stroke from which he recovered, but his heart still troubled him. One Saturday afternoon in August 1978 he walked past Paul's house on his way to put on a bet at the TAB, exchanging remarks with Paul in the front garden. He then walked on out of Paul's sight, sat down on the kerbside and died of a heart attack. Alerted by neighbours, Paul reached him a few minutes later. Paul was devastated. 'I never got over it. Never have,' he says. Matt was only 60. Part of Paul's urgency later in life was his fear that he too would die relatively young. He might not have time to wait his turn.

Ducker resigned from his party and union jobs in August 1979 following a heart attack. With Ducker leaving, the faction rearranged itself. Keating was elevated. In September 1979 he was elected President of the New South Wales party, one of seven party and union jobs that Ducker was vacating. He was a reluctant candidate for the job. He needed the Left to win leadership in Canberra, but he could succeed as President of the New South Wales party only by savaging it at the annual conference. Unsworth had to come to Canberra to persuade him to take the job. 'He said he could run the industrial wing but he couldn't also run the party.' Keating nominated at the last moment but he was vexed. 'I mean, they tipped me off the Administrative Committee and then they told me I had to be President!' He was appointed to the post by the Administrative Committee, beating left-wing candidate Robert Tickner 14 to 8. The following year he won 61 per cent of the vote at state conference.

He had long ago lost interest in organisational and factional issues, and the duties of ensuring numbers had no charm. State Secretary Graham Richardson was expected to take care of securing the faction's base, which in the 1979 June conference had once again been seriously threatened by a coalition of the Left and dissident right-wing unions. Keating changed the faction's name from Right to Centre Unity. He remained a star turn at the June conference and portrayed himself as creating a policy program for the new Centre Unity faction – a program emphasising economic growth rather than redistribution. Now augmented by Greens and by members of the young tertiary-educated middle class who had moved to the inner-city suburbs, the Left challenged the Right in its traditional bastions. In a widely reported speech in late 1981 Keating said his Left opponents, 'Believe in wider nature strips, more trees, and let's go back to making wicker baskets in Balmain. That is their policy.'[14] But he also recognised that the old tricks in the inner suburban right-wing fiefdoms were bringing discredit on the party. Sharing their influence on councils and contracting, some right-wing power brokers worked with criminals. They used rough tactics to preserve their patches. Keating was outraged when left-winger Peter Baldwin was bashed, presumably by criminals associated with the inner-city

Right. 'I got rid of crook behaviour,' Keating later claimed. 'All the Left fights were over tickets, books and attendances. Once we got that cleaned up they dropped off. We never looked back after that.'

The presidency of the party in New South Wales brought some extras. He was made chairman of a Labor-Party-owned radio station, 2HD Newcastle, and the party gave him a car. 'His Mercs got dirt on them when he drove them,' Unsworth later explained, in his flat nugatory way, 'so we fixed a car up for him.'

By the end of the 1970s and the beginning of the 1980s the Keatings were becoming prosperous. Their first child, Patrick, was now a toddler. Caroline had been born in 1979. There were two more daughters to come. Paul had become well informed about the Directoire, Consulat and Empire periods of architecture, painting and decoration. 'It's the smart vivacious Roman and Egyptian style of this great thirty-year classical period that interests me – Percier and Fontaine producing under the tutelage of Napoleon,' he told his chronicler of the period, Bob Carr.[15] He was interested in Napoleon as a statesman and a brilliant general who regularly beat the odds.

Now in his mid thirties, Paul was buying and selling properties and antiques. He had bought the old Marshall Street home from his parents and then bought a house in Gerard Avenue as a home for himself and Annita. In 1978 he bought a house in the Canberra suburb of Curtin, which he shared with a parliamentary colleague. It was common and within the rules for members of Parliament to use their travelling allowance to pay off a Canberra mortgage rather than pay hotel bills. He was also a partner with antiques dealer Paul Kenny in a small but valuable Paddington retail property, and he was eyeing other properties around Sydney. He astonished new acquaintances with his knowledge of the prices, owners and recent sales of Sydney waterfront houses. Within a few years he and Annita would decide to buy a big terrace house at 25 Roslyn Gardens, Elizabeth Bay. One of the row had been the Sydney home of cattle baron Sir Sidney Kidman, but when Paul bought their terrace, it was a backpackers' hostel. Contracts were exchanged in November 1982, with a price of around $250 000. It has a Victorian stucco exterior. He was reported as saying grandly that the interior of the house reflected his 'continuing interest in the neo-Grecian period.' It was a huge, dark terrace in a drab street. Despite great expense and years of renovation, the Keatings would never live in it.

Later the range and quality of Keating's assets would raise questions. Where had the money come from? The answer was not complicated. His father had run a successful business. He himself had been working since the age of 15. At a time when university graduates were looking for their first job, Paul had already been earning money and saving for six or seven years. By the time his contemporaries were in their mid twenties and on the lower rungs of professional or business life, Paul was a member of parliament with a salary equivalent to a very senior public servant, a travelling allowance, electoral allowance and free travel. He didn't smoke, didn't drink to excess, and lived with his parents until his early thirties. Later he would share in his father's bequests. The Canberra property was offset by his Canberra travelling allowance, and the Paddington property could have been negatively geared and reduced his tax. At around the time he bought in Elizabeth Bay he sold both Paddington and Gerard Avenue. The Paddington property would have fetched around $350 000. The Curtin house was also sold in the early 1980s.

As the turbulent decade drew to a close, Keating took pleasure from his increasing command of the minerals and energy shadow portfolio. He had visited Washington and Tokyo several times in the year of Opposition, gathering ideas and meeting industry leaders. Even in 1979, three years into the job, his diary listed meetings with the Japanese Chamber of Commerce, the Australian Institute of Energy, the chairman and board of ANI, the chairman and board of BHP. He had visited the Bowen Basin, Kalgoorlie, the Pilbara, the Cooper Basin, Kambalda and the North West Shelf. Overseas he had met David Rockefeller of Chase Manhattan Bank and Sir Mark Turner of RTZ. He had visited the US Department of Energy, Britain's National Oil Corp and the UK National Coal Board.[16]

In his policy declarations he supported a profits-related resources tax rather than crude oil levy. He wanted to lower petrol prices by breaking the nexus with import parity. He wanted a government-owned Australian hydrocarbons corporation to explore, trade, refine and distribute oil, as did Petro-Canada and Britain's National Oil Corp. Carr wrote, 'His reservations about nuclear power now run deep and he lives happily with Labor's moratorium on mining.' Keating said, 'The nuclear industry is languishing. It's a buyers' market. Serious research into waste disposal is still proceeding – we can afford to wait. Anyway, one major accident and the industry is dead.'

In the battle of developers versus conservationists, Paul picked his way carefully. His instincts were for development – but some proposed developments were silly. On 28 February 1979, Tasmanian Senator Ken Wreidt moved in caucus for Labor to support a Senate enquiry into drilling on the Barrier Reef. To Paul there was no need for an enquiry. 'We assert,' he told caucus, 'that on environmental grounds there should be no drilling on the Reef at all.' The motion was lost.

Paul was also developing his interest in the media. Kerry Packer thought Australia should have a domestic commercial satellite. He spoke to many politicians, including Keating. They had lunch in June 1979; this was the beginning of a relationship that would remain warm and reliable for more than a decade.

In Australia the 1970s ended with the promise of a boom. Driven by inflation as well as economic growth, commodity prices had rapidly increased, and Australia's exports were mostly commodities. Increasing world demand for energy and minerals prompted big investment plans for Australian resource developments. Fraser would win the 1980 election on the promise of the investment boom. The government published a fat book listing resource projects about to be developed. Largely unnoticed by Australians, however, the United States was about to arrest the slowly increasing inflation.

Meeting in Washington DC in October 1979, the Open Market Committee of the US Federal Reserve System adopted a radical new policy proposed to it by the chairman of the Federal Reserve Board of Governors, Paul Volcker. The US central bank would fight and break inflation, not by small incremental increases in interest rates, but by adopting firm targets for the growth of the money supply. Instead of controlling the price of money – interest rates – the system would control the quantity – money growth. The strategy was designed by Volcker and his officials to allow much bigger increases in interest rates than had been possible previously. Within weeks of the decision, interest rates were rapidly rising, with long-term rates responding just as rapidly as short-term rates to the collision of rapid inflation, rapid economic growth, and falling money supply. By the middle of 1980 the US economy was contracting. After a brief return to growth the US economy entered a protracted recession from which it did not begin to emerge until it felt the impact of President Ronald Reagan's tax cuts and increased defence spending in 1982. Inflation rapidly collapsed, forming the foundation for the seven years of growth that would follow.

In one form or another most countries felt some impact from the changes in the US. In Australia the effect was delayed but powerful. With falling inflation and growth, commodity prices fell globally. Resource projects in Australia were cancelled and investment spending fell, but not before the trade deficit had swelled with capital equipment imports. Wages had rapidly increased on the promise of the boom to come. By 1982 the Australian economy was in deep recession, and the defeat of the Fraser Government at the next election was confidently expected by both the Prime Minister's opponents and his supporters.

Hayden's first three years as Opposition leader had been strong enough to confirm his grip on the leadership as Malcolm Fraser manoeuvred towards an election in 1980. Hayden had successfully beaten off the Left on public ownership questions at the 1979 Adelaide conference and successfully intervened to restructure the party in Queensland in 1980. But he had little impact on the electorate. The 1980 election would bring Bob Hawke into Parliament.

Hawke had always said that if he went into Parliament he would want the party leadership, and believed that an alliance with Keating would help them both. Months before he came into Parliament, Hawke met with Keating and proposed an alliance. The meetings were arranged by Barrie Unsworth, and took place at Sydney's Boulevard Hotel. In 1996 Paul recalled, 'Barrie was dead stuck on Hawke. He changed right around. Graham had always been keen on him, but I hadn't had a substantial discussion with him before the meeting Barrie arranged in 1980. He asked for my support. I said, "It all depends on how you go in Parliament." He said, "Well, you know how I'll go – you've seen me perform." I said, "I don't – it's a different place altogether." Bob said he needed my support, that he couldn't win without my support. "I only want it [the leadership] for five years; that's enough for me. Then you can have a go." According to Keating, Hawke mentioned a specific period for his tenure in the leadership: 1983 to 1988. This would have involved some big assumption – that Hayden would not win the election expected later that year, that Hawke would then take the leadership, and that Fraser would call the next election exactly three years later. Keating also told Hawke, 'The first Labor leader I tear down will be the one I replace.' This, he says, was in response to a question of whether he would assist Hawke by helping to eject Hayden, and he said: 'Of course I would not.'

As Hawke saw it, he was strong in the Victorian branch of the party, Keating in New South Wales. Hawke knew about the trade union movement; Keating knew about the parliamentary party. They were both practical people who believed in sensible policies that could win elections. Above all, Hawke was 50 and Keating was still only 36. There would be plenty of time for Hawke to lead the party for a reasonable time, and Keating would still be relatively young when he, in his turn, took over.

Hawke came away from the meeting believing he had Keating's understanding and goodwill. By chance I was Hawke's host on a visit he paid to Washington, where I was then living, soon after the meeting with Keating in Sydney. Driving into Washington from Dulles Airport, he explained the new alliance to me. At some point he would replace Hayden as leader, with Keating's support. When I asked why Keating would help him into a job he no doubt wanted for himself, Hawke said that Keating recognised that he was still young. At some point Hawke would step aside, and Keating would take over. Hawke did not mention five years, but he was clear that he had suggested to Paul that he would be his successor after a reasonable time.

Keating recalls that Hawke called him later in 1980, just before nominations closed for the federal poll. 'I was in Gerard Avenue sitting on the laundry steps. He said he was ringing to be certain of my commitment. I said, "You can't ask me for an assurance of commitment; I might be an opponent of yours. You can't ask me to make your decision for you; you have to make up your own mind."'

Whatever reservations Keating might have expressed to Hawke, the trade union leader knew that Keating's faction now supported him. Ducker had been supporting his leadership ambitions for years. Geoff Cahill had supported him, and Cahill's successor Graham Richardson was an even stronger, more loyal and certainly more effective ally. After years of hostility Barrie Unsworth, now running the New South Wales Labor Council, was a supporter. Of the inner group of the leadership, only Keating was still resisting Hawke.

Paul was annoyed by Hawke's drive for the leadership. 'I would have followed Hayden. I would have got it if Hayden left; probably unopposed. Maybe Mick [Young] would have stood, but I would have got it. Arthur Gietzelt and Tommy Uren would have voted for me against Hawke, because they hated Hawke for giving the Left away. But I was then only 36 — you just can't *wrest* the leadership at 36.' Had it not been for Hawke's entry to Parliament in 1980 and his challenge to Hayden, Paul believed, he only had to wait for the leadership to come his way. And he didn't share his colleagues' admiration for Hawke. He thought a series of ABC Boyer lectures given by Hawke in 1979 were devoid of anything useful or substantial. Of the 1980 meetings he told Carr, 'He hasn't got much idea, Bob. I had to give him the broad picture, put it together for him. He is very naive.'

Paul had deepened and enriched both his political views and his personal interests in those otherwise arid years of Opposition. Profiled by the *Sydney Morning Herald*'s Jenni Hewett[17] at the end of 1981, Keating was cool and 'so sharp it hurts'. But he chewed his fingernails. 'Bundle of nerves,' he explained, 'like all politicians.' He 'scoffed' at big spending programs. 'For him it's the efficient market place that is the real guarantee of long-term social reform, of making everyone a middle-class success story.' He acknowledged he was hard. 'You have to make harsh judgments about people. If you want to get to the top, the place hardens you. It knocks a lot of the humour out of you or makes it pretty rarefied. It's an unfunny business.' While praising Lang, he had now picked up the theme that William McKell (who defeated Lang in the New South Wales party) embodied a mainstream Labor tradition that Keating inherited and the Left (despite its claims to represent the Labor heartland) did not. 'The continuity here is as clear as day. The powers have been handed down from one generation to the next. These people are trying to make my party into something other than it is. I'm in the mainstream of my party. A lot of others are not. They're appendages.'

His thinking about the economy was developing, but it was still in the Labor mainstream of the 1970s. During a Sydney Chamber of Commerce lunch in October 1981 he criticised 'the drones of the Australian banking industry'. He told the group that he supported any moves by the Campbell Inquiry to put more competition into the banking industry, which was a bold position within his party. But he was much more of a regulator then than he would be two years later. He wanted controls on short-term and speculative capital inflow, claiming that more than two-thirds of the capital inflow in the last year had been of a speculative nature. He said, 'This sort of investment does nothing to increase Australia's productive capacity but merely increases the profit flow overseas and decreases the level of Australian ownership of industry.' He wanted a 'national fuel and energy commission' and with it a 'national investment strategy to co-ordinate public investment and determine public investment priorities.' He claimed, 'Australia is the only industrial country in the world in which no form of medium to long-term economic forecasting or integrated coordination takes place.'[18] The following month he called for 'a limit on debt raising by foreign companies in Australia.' He also opposed foreign purchase of Australian real estate.[19]

'Commitment to economic growth is the starting point of Paul Keating's philosophy,' Carr reported early in 1982.[20] Keating told Carr, 'Growth is the sole avenue for raising living standards while maintaining a healthy level of investment' – not higher taxes and not redistribution of the existing pie.

Keating would later reflect that his thinking had changed most radically during the 1970s. He recalled, 'I was always very sympathetic to manufacturing because my father was a manufacturer, and I was very interested in well-made, engineered things. Just after I arrived in Parliament, for example, I took up an interest in the aviation industry. I visited the Government Aircraft Factories in Melbourne. We saw that manufacturing got massacred in the 1970s. The Left was arguing you should not have new mines. Willis was somewhat attracted by that too.

'I had also come to the view that industry would not thrive behind high tariffs. I fought the Gregory thesis, which basically said primary exporting industries would prevent successful manufacturing exports. [Treasury Secretary John] Stone did not help by saying we needed more imports to keep the exchange rate down – he seemed to be agreeing that it was a case of one or the other – you couldn't have both. The Left adopted it, because they didn't like coal mines or aluminium smelters or uranium.

'That was what my speech on the basket weavers of Balmain was all about. Someone later told me the political Left lost the industrial Left with that speech – it was directed at Tommy Uren and Moss Cass. I said they were in favour of wider nature strips, but what about the people who couldn't afford to drink good wine at lunch in Balmain? Were they better off if you didn't have uranium, or coal or aluminium smelting? I thought we should not stop the creation of wealth through commodity exports.'

He knew a lot about minerals and energy. He also learned a lot about art and decoration. At 38 he had settled on what Julie Flynn of the *National Times* described as 'neoclassical purism' – the architecture and furnishings of the French First Empire, a stylistic period running from 1780 roughly to 1820, with its focus on the eleven years between 1804 and 1815. 'There is an agelessness about ancient Greek architecture and decoration,' he told her. 'Its great appeal is the finality of elegance. It is perfection, at once absolute and forever.' The First Empire was the culmination of three decades of refinement on the themes of ancient Greece. 'It's dead chic. It never goes off.' After classicism he liked art deco. 'After art deco, there's only fag packets and bottle tops.' He now knew as much about his period, he said, 'as any museum curator in the country.' He was down on the new rich. 'They put all their money on the outside of their homes in big flashy cars and motor cruisers, while the insides are full of discount store furniture.'

He was becoming more interested in city design and the urban environment. He thought Australian cities poorly designed. 'In architectural terms Paris is the centre of the world. It shows what can be done to improve the quality of life for everyone.' He wanted to return Garden Island to the public. He listed his priorities in life as 'my family, politics and neoclassicism.'[21]

Neoclassicism did not put him off his political stride. He remained a rough and formidable fighter. Named (i.e. directed to leave the chamber) by speaker Sir Billy Snedden after a particularly vituperative attack on the government on 6 May 1982, he at first refused. 'You name me to protect this stinking corrupt government,' he told the Speaker. As the bells rang for a division on a vote to eject him, he agreed to leave. 'This place is being run like a banana republic,' he said in leaving, adding that he left the House out of respect for it, not respect for the Speaker, the Prime Minister, or 'the crooked government behind him.'

By the beginning of the 1980s Keating was feeling the tedium of Opposition and the futility of three successive election defeats. In his 1980 meetings with Hawke he told him he would get out if Labor did not win in 1983. 'I would have been there fourteen years and I didn't want to become like the generation that was there when I came.' His fortieth birthday was now only a few years away, he had a growing family, and he had now spent more than five years in the same role as spokesman on minerals and energy. By the beginning of 1983 he had bought the house at Elizabeth Bay – the base, perhaps, for a new life in Sydney, but not in politics. History, however, was about to tap him on the shoulder.

Hayden had performed well in the 1980 election, though falling short of victory. He dithered long enough with a possible capital gains tax to give Fraser an easy opening, which he exploited. Keating thought, 'He would have won but for that.' Hawke was now in Parliament, and he began building his challenge to Hayden.

Keating remained distant from Hawke, but the course of events favoured the challenger from Victoria. One such event was the formation of an alliance between the New South Wales and Victorian Rights. At the 1981 ACTU Conference in Sydney the industrial Right were shocked by the strength of the Left following Hawke's departure. 'After the 1981 ACTU Congress in Sydney we had a big meeting in Choy's Inn,' Barrie Unsworth recalled. 'There was Hawke, Crean, Keating, Richardson and me. Crean had got dudded at the Congress. The hegemony looked like falling apart. So those people got together and then went from strength to strength – it went beyond industrial strength. It was Labor Unity in Victoria and Centre Unity in New South Wales.' If there was a national Right, New South Wales could no longer make its own decisions – it had to take into account the view of the Victorian Right, which was solidly supporting Hawke's challenge to Hayden.

Once an implacable opponent, Unsworth had been charmed by Hawke. He recalled, 'Rapprochement was effected between myself and Hawke by 1978–79. When he went into Parliament in late 1980 we were the only state Labor Council that put on a decent testimonial dinner for him. I organised it. I was closer to Hawke than to Hayden, who wasn't all that helpful on the Federal Executive of the party. Richardson, of course, was a Hawke man all through that period.' But Paul Keating was not.

Hawke was helped by Hayden's suspicion of the New South Wales right-wing members of caucus. He did not exploit the differences between the party officers in Sydney and the parliamentary members in Canberra. 'The real reason Hayden lost the leadership,' Keating thought later, 'was because after the 1980 election he did not support [right-wing New South Wales Senator] Doug McClelland becoming deputy leader of the party in the Senate. Richo and Doug arranged it with him, because the deputy leadership came with a slot on the national executive [of the ALP], which was very important to New South Wales because of intervention. But then Hayden supported [Senator] Don Grimes. That was the stone end of it with Doug, with Kerry Sibraa, with Graham, our senators. He had me but he lost them. If Hayden had given Doug McClelland the deputy leadership of the Senate, he would have been Prime Minister of Australia.'

By July 1982 Hawke was ready to strike. There were no policy disputes of substance between Hawke and Hayden. Hawke's simple claim was that he was more popular in the electorate and therefore more likely to win the next election. Keating did not like the challenge at all. He told Tom Uren at the July ALP conference that he was still in Hayden's camp. According to Tom Uren, he and Keating discussed the leadership in January 1981 at a party at the home of journalist Max Walsh. They agreed that if Hayden was not to be the ultimate leader, it should be Keating and not Hawke.[22] But by the middle of 1982 Uren was shifting. To his colleagues he defended his change of line with the unusual reasoning that, while Hawke was totally opposed to the party's three mines uranium policy, he would support it in government, but Hayden – who was far more sympathetic to Uren on the uranium issue in general – might not.

Attempting to burst Hawke's bubble, Hayden scheduled a ballot for the leadership. Keating did not support Hawke, but Richardson and Unsworth did. So did the Victorian Right. In a series of meetings in Sydney, Keating was isolated and then overwhelmed by the members of his own faction. On 14 July 1982, after a joint meeting of the Victorian and New South Wales rightwing leaders, he announced that the New South Wales Right would support Hawke. The announcement had been written by Gareth Evans.

The ballot was held on 16 July. Hayden won, 42 to 37. Hayden had survived, but Hawke's vote was high enough to make another challenge highly likely. The ACTU leadership helped Hawke in November and December by its reluctance to agree upon the terms of a prices and incomes arrangement with Hayden and its apparent willingness to discuss a wages pause with Prime Minister Malcolm Fraser. Hayden campaigned in a by-election in the Melbourne outer-suburban electorate of Flinders. The poll on 4 December showed a 3 per cent swing to Labor, 2. 5 per cent short of the swing necessary to win the seat. In a rapidly deteriorating economy, a 3 per cent swing to Hayden in a by-election was interpreted as a very poor outcome for the Opposition leader.

Scrambling to defend himself against Hawke and at the same time strengthen his team against Fraser, Hayden made a decision that would give Keating his place in Australian history. He shifted Ralph Willis to a new position in charge of a 'national reconstruction program' and appointed Paul shadow Treasurer on the evening of Thursday 13 January 1983. Keating and Willis agreed that taxation, Commonwealth–state financial relations and the prices and incomes accord would stay with Willis. The reconstruction of the shadow Cabinet was announced the next day. 'You're the only one who is tough enough to handle [Treasury Secretary John] Stone,' Hayden told Keating.

Keating went to some trouble to demonstrate reluctance to accept the portfolio. Unlike Willis, he had no economics training, and the

issues in the portfolio were serious, difficult and sometimes technical. It was the second most important job in both Opposition and
in government. His opponent would not now be a quite ordinary
coalition minister but the Prime Minister and his Treasurer, John
Howard. Before accepting it he discussed the proposal with John
Ducker (now at the New South Wales Public Service Board) and
Barrie Unsworth. He also discussed it with antiques dealer Bill
Bradshaw and with speechwriter Graham Freudenberg, who happened
by Bradshaw's Paddington shop while walking his dog. Friends could
see that it was a good move by Hayden because it put Keating offside with Willis, who was close to Hawke, and made Keating dependent on Hayden to keep the job. If Keating was good at it, Hayden
was helped. If he failed, the New South Wales Right lost some of its
shine.

For all its problems, however, Keating's reluctance to take the job
was more feigned than genuine. He had earlier suggested to Hayden
that he give it to him and had been disappointed when Hayden refused.
He was already in an economic portfolio, so the transition would not
be as difficult as it might have been. Willis was keeping some of
the most technical aspects of the job, and, while that would not work
in the long term, Paul would not have to field questions about
Commonwealth–state finances or taxation arrangements for the next
few months. His principal assistant, Barbara Ward, was an economist
by training, and together they could work their way into an understanding of the job.

To reporters, Keating was quite conservative where he would soon
be quite radical. He said of foreign banks, 'I don't think we should
let them in,' and said he would review the terms and conditions under
which licences were issued. He was critical of the fluctuations of the
world banking system and said, 'This is the worst possible time to
expose ourselves to the vagaries of that system.' He believed, 'There
will be increasing difficulty in maintaining stable economic management. Interest rates, the money supply and the exchange rate could
all become more unstable, and we have fairly decent controls over the
money supply and exchange rate at present.' The *Australian Financial*

Review's Anne Summers reported him saying (as a criticism) that foreign bank entry to Australia 'would inevitably force the Australian banks
to push for total deregulation of the banking system because they would
have to suffer the penalties of having to cater for small business.'[23]

There was very little chance, however, to work his way into the
job. Fraser was racing towards an election as fast as Hawke and his
allies were shaking Hayden out of his job. Given the state of the
economy, Fraser's best, and perhaps only, chance was to run while
Hayden was still leader but visibly under threat by Hawke. No election could be called while Australians were on holiday in January, but
by early February Fraser was about to move. Before he could complete his plans, Victorian Senator John Button, who was personally
and politically close to Hayden, defected to Hawke and made Hayden's
position untenable. At a parliamentary party executive meeting in
Brisbane on 3 February he resigned his position in Hawke's favour,
at the same time as Fraser was preparing to leave for Government
House to seek an election. By the evening of that day Labor had a
new leader, and an election for the House of Representatives and the
whole Senate was scheduled for 5 March.

When the election was called Paul had been Shadow Treasurer
for a little more than two weeks. He had inherited a party economic
document principally devised by Willis and a staffer, John Langmore.
Keating had no hesitation in adopting the goal of more rapid growth
– it was entirely his way of thinking. 'We've got to go for growth,'
he repeated during the campaign, like a mantra. The policy also
promised a prices and incomes accord with the trade unions to
restrain wage increases and inflation while the economy grew. Keating
was not so sure of that – he was suspicious of the ACTU's ability to control its members. The New South Wales Labor Council,
which was the union body he knew best, had always resisted the
ACTU's claims to control the union movement. During the election campaign Keating met ACTU secretary Bill Kelty for the first
time in a meeting called to discuss the proposed agreement. Paul
was not deeply troubled about the document. As Kelty would tell
it later, Keating cheerfully told the union leaders he believed the

agreement was for the election, nothing more. His commitment was so transparently superficial that he got the party into the only serious trouble of the campaign. Asked whether it would work, he told a morning radio program, 'I'm not sure we can make it work, but we are going to give it a good shot.' The storm died down after a day or so.

The election result was a crushing defeat for the coalition. Already linked by a vague pact of succession, personally distant but sharing the same supporters, the same attitudes and the same philosophy within the Labor Party, Bob Hawke and Paul Keating found themselves catapulted into the two most influential public offices in Australia: Prime Minister and Treasurer.

PART II

TREASURER

THE EIGHTIES

DECADES ARE ARBITRARY PERIODS, BUT the 1980s can be fairly claimed to have been a time of exceptional transformation. Australia changed during them, in ways that were often important, surprising and irreversible.

Certainly much of the change had little to do with the then Federal Government. Many changes were external to Australia, ones to which we might respond but did not initiate or influence. The Cold War ended, the Soviet Union collapsed, Germany reunified, South Africa progressed towards majority rule. In our own region, China adopted a market economy and boomed, growth in South-East Asia was consistent and widespread, yen appreciation forced Japanese industry offshore, Vietnam opened its economy. Global trade swelled in a long expansion.

Other changes arose simply because time passed. Two and half million Australians were born; a million died. People moved houses. Streets, suburbs and towns changed character. The baby boomers reached middle age, with children, mortgages, second marriages. Their parents retired, reached old age, died. Their children found it harder to get into university or technical college, though there were many more places. They found it harder to get a job, though many more people had jobs. The fastest growing population group, though still small, was Asian.

The culture changed. But some of the most interesting change

was in ways that could be influenced by Federal Government decisions – in people's working lives, in their wealth and prospects, in
what they bought and sold and did for a living. There were more
than six million people with jobs at the beginning of the decade,
nearly eight million by the 1990s. More were in part-time work.
More of those with jobs were women. More than one in ten people
in the workforce was looking for a job by 1983, and the same
number again soon after the end of the decade; only at the beginning of the decade and very briefly towards the end did
unemployment fall below 6 per cent. By the early 1990s the
economy produced a seventh more for each Australian than it had
a decade before, but income distribution had changed. The very
poor had come up, high-income people had done very well, but
the rest had felt little real improvement in their standard of living.
Wealth increased more rapidly than incomes. Housing prices in
most cities doubled, sometimes tripled. From trough to peak, share
prices had risen five-fold, and even at the end of the 1980s they
were still four times higher than they had been at the beginning
of the decade.

The way the economy worked changed. Bracketed between the
Federal Reserve Open Market Committee decision to bust inflation
at the end of the 1970s, and the global downturn at the end of the
1980s, Australia experienced an investment boom and a steep recession, and one of the longest post-war expansions in between. Inflation was cut from more than 10 per cent to less than 4 per cent, trade
doubled compared to GDP, and the current account deficit expanded
dramatically. The dollar was floated, exchange controls abolished,
banks deregulated, tariffs cut, compulsory arbitration of wages
restricted. At the end of the decade production was a third higher
than at the beginning and its pattern had altered. Exports substantially increased as a proportion of output, tourism expanded, some
manufacturing had become internationally competitive and some had
ceased to exist (though manufacturing output overall was up by a
sixth). In 1981 more than four million working days were lost in
industrial disputes. By 1991 it was well under half that level, though

the employed workforce had increased by a fifth. Beginning with very little, all employees by the end of the decade were covered by super-annuation plans and starting to accumulate assets that will, by the turn of the century, constitute a sea change in retirement funding and in the financial wealth of middle- and low-income people. At the beginning of the decade Telecom and OTC monopolised national and international telephone calls. Qantas, TAA and the Commonwealth Bank were all fully government owned. By the 1990s Telecom and OTC had merged and were competing with private providers of telephone services, Qantas and TAA had merged and been sold, and the Commonwealth Bank was being sold. What had once been thought to be abiding arrangements – high tariffs, com-pulsory arbitration, regulated finance – were fast fading or had already vanished.

Many of these changes in people's working lives were the out-come of millions of separate decisions taken by individuals and busi-nesses, intended to affect only their own lives or their own prosperity. But these decisions were themselves often influenced by the decisions of the Federal Government.

One of the peculiarities of the 1980s in Australia (though it was also true of the United States and the United Kingdom) was the continuity of the national government first elected in March 1983. It would prove to be the longest-lived federal Labor government in Australian political history – itself something of an unexpected change in the post-war political pattern. Not only did the Prime Minister and the Treasurer and many other important ministers remain in office through this whole turbulent period but so also did a number of their key advisers. Bernie Fraser, Ted Evans and Don Russell, to mention only three, were part of a group of advisers of similar outlook (and frequent disagreement) who were influential in several of the key pol-icy episodes of the period. There was also an unusual degree of una-nimity on the basic principles of policy. Hawke and Keating ultimately fought for the leadership of the party, but they almost never dis-agreed about policy. And despite the fireworks of political con-flict, on most important issues the unanimity extended to the press and to the Opposition. Without the latitude offered by the Opposition, many of the economic reforms of the period, especially tariff cuts, banking deregulation, and restricting compulsory arbitration, would have been much harder.

What follows is an account of Paul Keating's work as Treasurer in making some of these changes. The account draws on official records as well as interviews, press reports and books. Though he was not Prime Minister in the 1980s, more of the work of economic change fell to him as Treasurer than to any other single individual in government, including the Prime Minister.

In the Westminster system the executive of government – the Cabinet – has more authority over the legislative arm of government than does the President of the United States over Congress. But the US President has far more authority over his Cabinet members, all of whom he appoints and dismisses as executive assistants, than an Australian Prime Minister has over his Cabinet members. This is particularly true in the Labor Party, where ministers are elected by caucus rather than selected by the Prime Minister (although the Prime Minister does allocate portfolios and influences the choice of ministers by caucus). A strong minister with an independent support base can avoid, delay or obstruct the development in his portfolio of policies that he does not like, even if the Prime Minister supports them. He can encourage and sometimes advance into Cabinet policies to which the Prime Minister is opposed. The major arms of executive authority in economic policy – the Treasury and the Reserve Bank – both report to the Treasurer, a duty supported by the law as well as by usage. Only the Treasurer can bring forward a Cabinet submission on the Budget or on general economic policy, and by and large all decisions on spending, taxing, and legislative change must be made in or endorsed by Cabinet. A successful Treasurer needs the support or at worst the neutrality of the Prime Minister, whose authority in Cabinet is signified by his control over the listing of submissions and the agenda of the meeting. But no economic policy can be helped or hindered without the active cooperation of the Treasurer.

The story of economic change generated from the Federal Government through perhaps the most dramatic period of change in the twentieth century is largely, though certainly not entirely, the story of what Paul Keating did and did not do as Treasurer.

A HORRENDOUS BUDGET OUTLOOK

ELATED BY VICTORY, THE DECISIONS Keating would have to make as Treasurer did not wait until he was elected to the ministry by caucus, selected as Treasurer by the Prime Minister and sworn into office by the Governor-General. They did not even wait until his predecessor, John Howard, had packed his papers and left his office. The decisions began less than twenty-four hours after the election victory, at 2.30 on a drowsy Canberra Sunday afternoon, in the closed saloon bar of the Lakeside Hotel.

At that hour Treasury Secretary John Stone and a deputy, Dick Rye, came into the ground floor of the hotel through a back entrance, while Hawke, Keating and their advisers came down from Hawke's suite. There was no private room where they could meet, so the manager opened up the bar, still smelling of beer and cigarette smoke. The blinds were drawn, the bar gloomy. The politicians and their advisers were exhausted, though Hawke, as one participant recalled, was 'purring contentedly'. Also at the meeting were Barbara Ward, who had been with Keating as his principal assistant for four years, John Langmore, an economist who had joined him from Ralph Willis's staff in January, and Barry Hughes, an economist from Flinders University in Adelaide.

Though the press were later told the meeting had discussed the Accord, in reality it had a quite different agenda. Its purpose was to discuss a devaluation of the Australian dollar's international exchange rate, which was set by government decision. Devaluation had been advocated during the campaign in a private letter from Australian National University economist Ross Garnaut to Hawke. It had been widely expected by financial markets, and at this point would have been extremely difficult to resist, even if the incoming government had wished to.

Stone had fought earlier devaluations but he was prepared to accept this one — at least to the level of 5 per cent. In the first signal of policy differences that would deepen over the year, the Reserve Bank indicated it preferred a 10 per cent devaluation. Keating's own preference was for a bigger devaluation than the market expected, which would eliminate betting on a further devaluation.

Stone was in what some of the other people in that shuttered bar thought surprisingly good spirits. They did not know that the day before Stone had voted Labor for the second time in his life. Notwithstanding his cheerful contempt for Hawke's claims to intellectual distinction, he had held an uproarious dinner at his home later that evening in celebration of the defeat of Malcolm Fraser and John Howard. He had no sooner said goodbye to the last of his guests at 2 a.m. than he had gone to the national tally room to check the figures, to enjoy in its symbolically most vivid form the way in which Australian democracy could send great men packing and perhaps also to make absolutely sure that Fraser had indeed lost office and would not be back there on Monday. Stone had not returned home till daybreak after celebrating with the Labor politicians and now, only hours later, he was advising the Prime Minister and Treasurer-elect. The Prime Minister still thought he had the option of not appointing Keating Treasurer, but he was about to find he did not.

There was little dispute, and the devaluation decision was agreed in principle that afternoon, though it would not be announced until Tuesday morning. In the intervening day Hawke and Keating consulted other Labor frontbenchers, Victorian economist Peter Sheehan, and the Reserve Bank, all of whom favoured or accepted devaluation.

During the Lakeside meeting Stone had given both Hawke and

Keating a copy of a document outlining the revenue and spending sums for the current and the next financial year, the 'Budget numbers'. Neither Hawke nor Keating had time to examine the document. Within a few days it would create deep division within the government and become the basis on which Hawke and Keating overturned the economic strategy upon which they were elected.

Between the decision to devalue on Sunday afternoon and its announcement on Tuesday morning, Hawke and Keating flew to Sydney for dinner at the Prime Minister's Sydney harbourside residence, Kirribilli House. For the first time they travelled in the Prime Minister's motorcade with police escort from Sydney Airport, dashing through the inner industrial suburbs into the city, over the grey Harbour Bridge, then picking their way through the narrow streets of Kirribilli before driving through the gates to the colonial-style stone house, with its lawn sweeping down to the harbour and the great city opposite – a trophy of government they had not been able to enjoy since Gough and Margaret Whitlam left eight years before.

It was from Kirribilli House that evening that Keating made his first contact with the official who would in many ways have the greatest influence on him during the coming year, Reserve Bank Governor Bob Johnston.

At dinner that night Bob and Hazel Hawke were the hosts. Their guests were Keating, John Langmore, speechwriter Graham Freudenberg, and two of Hawke's assistants, Jean Sinclair and Jill Saunders. After a pleasant meal, Freudenberg rose and offered a toast. Hawke was the third federal Labor leader he had worked for in a speechwriting career that began with Arthur Calwell and had its headiest moments in the Whitlam Government. 'To Mrs Hawke', he said, with gallant emphasis on the 'Mrs'. 'Thank you for including us in your first meal in this place.' He then turned to the Prime Minister.'Bob,' he said, 'you have been elected by the people of Australia to the highest office to which an Australian can aspire. It is a great honour and a great responsibility.' The honour, the responsibility and the harbourside house to which Freudenberg was once again welcome after so long an absence reminded him of the words of Pope Leo X, which he commended to the party: 'God has given us the Papacy. Now let us enjoy it.'[1]

For the moment there was little to enjoy. Fraser had been defeated by recession; Labor was elected to bring back prosperity. It was, as Bob Hawke said, the worst downturn since the depression. When Labor won government, unemployment was 10 per cent and increasing; in March alone the economy lost 30 000 jobs. There were nearly 700 000 looking for work. In the three months to the end of March, production fell nearly 3 per cent but inflation was running at more than 11 per cent.

High inflation and high unemployment now went together. During the 1970s most economies had experienced rising unemployment and rising inflation. In Australia average earnings increased by 17. 5 per cent in 1973–74 and 30 per cent in 1974–75. In the three years to 1982–83 average earnings rose by more than 13 per cent a year. The governments of Gough Whitlam and then Malcolm Fraser had responded by raising interest rates and slowing the economy, accepting the resulting unemployment as the inevitable price of preventing inflation increasing further.

The Fraser Government had compounded the problem by loudly cheering on a resources boom in the early 1980s, encouraging a rash of wage claims on the promised prosperity. Clashing with a global downturn, the prosperity vanished, but the wage increases remained. When Labor won, profits were too low to fund investment and wages too high to allow unemployment to be rapidly reduced.

If wages and profits were one problem, the exchange rate was another. One technique used by the Fraser Government to control the consequences of the inflationary boom was to encourage a high Australian dollar to make imports cheaper and increase competition in Australian markets. Combined with an investment spike and a simultaneous wage push, the high exchange rate encouraged a flood of imports and demolished large sections of Australian manufacturing. In 1981–82 the trade deficit – the excess of imports over exports – reached levels that it would not reach, even at its worst, under Labor.[2]

In the two years to June 1983 manufacturing production fell a tenth. Not until 1986 would it regain its former level and begin to move well beyond. In June 1981 there were 1 300 000 employees in Australian manufacturing; when Labor took office there were 150 000 fewer and jobs were still being lost. It would be towards the end of the decade before there were as many jobs in manufacturing as there had been in 1981. Investment had also crashed. By 1983–84 it had fallen by a fifth from its peak in 1981–82.

Some industries were in crisis. Australia's largest private corporation, BHP, was threatening to close down steel production. The motor vehicle industry said it could not compete against imports. Dockyards and heavy engineering claimed special problems. All demanded urgent assistance.

As serious as they were, unemployment and economic contraction were problems that would be automatically remedied as the economy began to grow again. There were many other more intractable problems that influenced the pace and the way the economy would grow, the number of jobs that would be created during growth, and Australia's ability to compete with other countries in the years to come. Tariff protection of Australian industry had been increasing for a decade: shoes, cars, clothes and a vast number of manufactured goods were more expensive in Australia than they needed to be because of import tariffs. The industries making them employed skilled workers and capital that could have been diverted to industries in which Australia was more efficient and competitive. At the same time the northern Asian economies were rapidly growing, and the South-East Asian economies would soon become major exporters. There was a chance for a bold government to rebase Australia's trade and lock into the growth of eastern Asia. There were problems, too, with inefficient government businesses like Qantas, the post office, and Telecom.

Although there were problems, Hawke and Keating had some important advantages in March 1983, some of which were not then apparent.

During the election campaign Hawke and the ACTU had announced an Accord on incomes and prices, which promised no wage claims outside the decisions of the Conciliation and Arbitration Commission so long as the real value of wages was maintained by 'indexing' wages for general price increases. But the Fraser Government had already put in place a wages pause in December 1982. This meant that the issue was not the difficult one of how to stop the growth of wages but the way in which wages growth would be restarted. The Fraser Government's wages pause would probably not have held against determined opposition by strong unions, but it certainly created a good platform to negotiate the terms, principles and timing of subsequent wage increases. Without drawing attention to it, the government and the ACTU left the pause in place until the first indexation decision of the commission became effective a year after the pause began.

Another advantage discovered by Hawke and Keating was that an economic recovery of some sort was in the making. From a peak of more than 17 per cent in April 1982 the Fraser Government had brought the short-term interest rate down to 10 per cent by the time it lost office. It had greatly increased public spending and won a breather from wage increases. The depth of the downturn had been increased by drought – the strength of the upturn would be enhanced by rain.

The world was also lending a hand. In the United States and much of Europe inflation had fallen away with the recession of the early 1980s. By 1983 the Reagan administration's policy of cutting taxes and increasing defence spending was beginning to make itself apparent in a US turnaround and increased world trade. Much of the globe was entering a seven-year upswing – the longest and strongest for decades. For Australia the pattern of world growth was to be particularly important; a lot of it was to be in the nearby markets of northern and South-East Asia.

Above all, Hawke and Keating began their work at a time when Australians were recognising that the old ways no longer worked. After two explosions of wages and then unemployment within a decade, most union officials and their members recognised that there had to be a change in the way industrial relations worked. The top marginal income tax rate was 60 cents – and wage inflation meant it cut in at a lower real income level than before. That had to change. In his far-reaching 1981 report, Sir Keith Campbell had laid the foundations for financial deregulation. Malcolm Fraser would not implement it, but the ground had been prepared in the media and the business community. And within the Liberal Party the dry faction was newly assertive with Fraser's failure and resignation. In the years to come the Opposition's support for tariff cuts, financial deregulation and industrial relations reform would give the government room to do what the Fraser Government had not attempted.

Twenty-four hours after the decision to devalue, Keating made another decision of greater significance. On Monday morning he visited the Treasury building near Parliament House, alone. It was to be his first meeting with his new department, and he decided not to take John Langmore with him. He believed his success as Treasurer, certainly at first, would depend on having behind him a strong and loyal Treasury. Although Hawke and Ross Garnaut, the economist he would that day ask to be his office adviser, both thought Stone should be promptly sacked as Treasury head, Keating had already decided to keep him on. In Keating's view the incoming government should, as he said, 'wipe the slate clean' with Stone and offer him the chance to demonstrate his usefulness. Memories of the Whitlam Government, of its efforts to raise billions through small-time brokers and chance contacts, were still fresh enough in the memories of the international financial community to make Keating hesitant to sack immediately the one Treasury figure internationally known for fiscal rectitude. He wanted Stone to stay, and he wanted Treasury's support to carry him over the learning period and strengthen his arm for the Cabinet struggles to come. To take Langmore on his first visit might suggest to Treasury that Langmore's views were Keating's, and that Langmore would filter Treasury advice to the new Treasurer. That was an impression Keating did not wish to create. Nor was Keating at all convinced that he needed Langmore or wanted him to remain.

An economist who had worked in New Guinea, Langmore had joined the staff of the Labor Opposition, assigned to frontbencher Ralph Willis. He had worked on developing the prices and incomes policy and was Willis's principal assistant when he was shadow Treasurer. Langmore was a gentle Christian and an unwearying advocate of a set of gently Christian views about economic policy. He was and remained an advocate of bigger deficits – bigger, generally, than whatever they happened to be – because he believed they would increase output and employment. He was opposed to financial deregulation and deeply distrusted the idea that free markets produced the best outcomes. He was happiest when the choice was clearest, when he could be for the weak against the strong, for the unemployed against the Fraser Government, for the hungry of the Third World against the rich and selfish of the first, for intervention and against markets. He thought there were people in the world who did wrong because they had bad beliefs, and quite a few of those were in the Commonwealth Department of the Treasury. The worst of them, he believed, was John Stone. His own ambitions were modest enough, but definite. He wanted to be principal private secretary to the Treasurer of a Labor government, an intention that elicited the response, when he communicated it to Keating, that he might well be one day, old son, but not for this Treasurer.

Alert to the currents of challenge and response in personal relationships, Keating did not want Langmore's sense of triumph interfering with his own objective of winning Treasury over to the willing service of the new Treasurer. So he went alone, across from Parliament House to the Treasury building, to meet Stone, Rye, and their colleagues Ted Evans, Des Moore and David Morgan.

Though Malcolm Fraser had carved away some of its powers, and John Howard was so deeply at odds with its officials that he had as little to do with them as possible, Treasury remained the pre-eminent economic policy department in Canberra. In a country where economic policy was more important than any other, it was the most powerful bureaucracy. When Fraser created the Department of Finance he had removed from Treasury its close control over each and every spending program of each and every Commonwealth department and instrumentality. But Treasury was still responsible for preparing submissions on the spending totals in the Budget, it retained control over tax policy, and it still drew up the spending totals, the revenue projections, and the economic scenario, which together constituted the annual budget of the government of Australia. When Labor took office the official (though secret) quarterly forecasts of output, inflation and unemployment were still controlled almost entirely within Treasury. Through his chairmanship of a four-member committee that instructed the Reserve Bank foreign exchange desk, the Secretary of the Treasury controlled exchange rate policy for Australia. Treasury also controlled monetary policy, through its control over the funding of government operations and thus, by a little-noticed extension, the buying and selling of government debt by the Reserve Bank. It was the principal and unavoidable source of advice to the government on interest rate changes, taxes and spending – among the most important and electorally pertinent decisions the government makes.

In all the great financial operations of Australia, Treasury had a hand. It controlled the payment of grants and loans to the states of Australia and the loan programs of Australia overseas for both the Commonwealth Government and for the states. In New York, London and Tokyo, it was Treasury officers who dealt with the great investment and commercial banks. In New York, for example, Treasury dealt always with one leading investment bank, Morgan Stanley, which handled all of Australia's borrowings in the United States markets. In the New York offices of Morgan Stanley, the Secretary of the Australian Treasury was a frequent, honoured and highly valued guest, and on his behalf Morgan Stanley would arrange meetings with the leaders of American finance and industry.

In the long years of Australia's post-war expansion behind tariff walls that created a strong but internationally uncompetitive industry, and which injured the creation of an industry that could be competitive on world markets, Treasury was often the solitary refuge of economic rationality in Canberra. Presiding over this still-powerful but deeply troubled institution was the Treasury Secretary, John Stone, with whom Keating would battle for control over economic policy in the first year of government.

As Treasury Secretary, Stone typically wore spectacles framed in black plastic, a grey suit and a patterned navy tie, but there was nothing ordinary or dull about John Stone. He was the bright son of a small West Australian wheat farmer who had, at the age of 11, won a scholarship to the intellectually rigorous Perth Modern high school. He had been good at academic work and at hockey, striving and competitive partly because it was in his nature to excel and partly because, as he later realised, his parents' divorce in those pre-war days had made him feel a little different. From Perth Modern he had gone to the University of Western Australia to excel with a first-class honours degree in mathematical physics and to play hockey for Western Australia and for Australia. From there he had gone to Oxford as Western Australia's Rhodes Scholar, two years before his classmate Hawke, who had been, as Stone would often point out, a contestant also for the Rhodes in 1950 and who was then known more as a sporting man. 'I'd have to say,' he later said, 'that Bob was rather unrecognised in the intellectual stakes. I think the thing that offends me about Hawke in this area is his pretensions and the continual harping on things like the Rhodes scholarship, three honorary doctorates and goodness knows what. I didn't know him very well; I didn't think he was a very nice boy. He wasn't my type. He was a bit of a lair, loudmouthed, cocky and full of himself even then.'

At Oxford he decided that life as a mathematical physicist was not quite what he wanted and switched to the course in politics, philosophy and economics, a decision that left him, as he said, with the clear conviction that economics was not a social science but one of the humanities, and though he had a lot of maths — a great deal more than the usual run of mathematically adept economists — equations did not appear in his economic analysis. He joined Treasury in London in 1954, but it was not until 1956, when he was 27, that he found himself for the first time in Canberra, settling as a junior officer into the Treasury building, and establishing a reputation for incisiveness and quaintly academic sarcasm, which would become his customary form of communication not only with bureaucratic colleagues but also with international bankers, treasurers and prime ministers. Tactfully exiled to Washington as a director of the International Monetary Fund and of the World Bank from 1967 to 1970, he was still remembered there, a decade later, as one of the first and only directors of what were really puppet boards to actually read his briefing materials, ask difficult questions, and treat the World Bank and IMF bureaucrats as fallible men and women like others.

Now aged 54, Stone had been head of Treasury through four difficult years, rising to the post after years as the deputy secretary in charge of macroeconomic policies. He had been at the heart of economic policy-making in the declining years of the post-war Liberal–Country Party Governments, in the three short but dramatic years of Whitlam's Labor Government, and in the seven years of Malcolm Fraser's government. None of the ministers in the new government, none of their advisers, had even a fraction of his experience as a policy-maker. He had seen Treasury blamed by John Gorton for his defeat in the party room in 1971, he had seen Treasury being blamed by Gorton's successor, Bill McMahon, for the 1971 Budget and for its defeat by Whitlam in 1972. In that year Stone himself had voted Labor for the first time in his life, less, he said later, out of any confidence in Whitlam than out of contempt for McMahon. He had welcomed Labor, and in the first few months some of what Labor wanted to do coincided with what Treasury thought ought to be done. Stone was on a committee that recommended deep cuts in subsidies for farmers and rural town dwellers. He was pleased when Whitlam, on Treasury advice, twice increased the exchange value of the Australian dollar – a decision that McMahon had attempted, and which the Country Party had refused to permit. But thereafter the Whitlam Government and John Stone fell out. Stone objected even to a 25 per cent tariff cut announced by the government, less because he didn't like tariff cuts than because he was not involved in the decision to make them, a conflict between right policies and the prerogatives of Treasury and John Stone that would recur in the Hawke Government.

Keating knew Stone from Labor demonology, and from late night drinks at the annual dinners of the Australian Mining Industry Council, but he did not know him well. He began to realise, in the shuttered bar of the Lakeside, that Stone was a man of interesting complexity. 'This is the nefarious Mr Rye, who sometimes goes to Paris,' Stone had said to the Treasurer-elect as he introduced one of his officials, Dick Rye, who had been publicly accused of persuading the OECD to alter a report on Australia to produce a conclusion more favourable to the Fraser Government. Rye's mild and inoffensive demeanour suggested nothing nefarious. Physically rugged, intellectually formidable and direct, Stone spoke in a flat monotone varied with falsetto changes of amplitude and pitch. A weary monotone when speaking sometimes; at others, and in conversation, he varied the speed, overrode interruptions, seemed almost to fade away into a mumble and then start again loudly and quickly, smiling and laughing at his own sarcasms.

The decision to keep Stone was the most important Paul himself would make in the first days of government. Hawke and Garnaut wanted Stone sacked. Both Barry Hughes and John Langmore were also hostile to Stone, but Paul wasn't listening to them either. As a result of his decision to keep Stone as Treasury Secretary, Keating was easily portrayed, in the first year of office, as a figurehead in the Treasury job, with the real power exercised by John Stone. It was an image to which the Prime Minister's advisers did not mind contributing. Cartoonists depicted Keating in canine pose, paws forward, while Stone offered him bones, or as a ventriloquist's dummy used by Stone. Later the game would change.

Paul later would reflect with wonder on the transformation of his circumstances in those few short weeks of 1983. At 39, he had been a professional politician for fourteen years, but in all that time he had spent only three weeks in a position of real government authority, and that in a junior ministry at the tail end of a failing government. He had married, and now he had three children: Patrick, seven, Caroline, four, and Katherine, who was still an infant.

Paul was Treasurer in everything now except the formality of his re-election by caucus and his swearing in by Sir Ninian Stephen at Yarralumla, though he had not been to an economics class in his life. He was being presented with facts, terms, concepts, statements and numbers for which he did not have organising principles. He did not have in his head what he would later come to call a framework, a model. He would have to rely on advice, but he did not yet know enough to be able confidently to choose which advisers to rely upon, and which to jolly along or freeze out. He had ideas about economics and economic policy, about what made the place tick, but that did not mean he knew the conceptual structure of John Stone's or Barry Hughes' minds. He did not know how they fitted things together; he could not tell from their language which were basic and uncontested ideas and which were merely arguments or precarious interpretations presented with authority that made them seem like facts.

He had learned from Lang and Bowen something about judging people, about the importance and the method of interpreting their hidden motives from outward but unintended signals, of the need in politics to judge what people said in the light of their customary degree of optimism or pessimism, with appropriate weights for their characteristic clarity or confusion, intelligence or stupidity, to make allowances for the usual way in which egotism or insecurity would affect a person's views, the myriad ways in which partialities of various kinds – love, political partisanship, ambition, pride, self-hatred – might create small or large errors of assessment. He had learned many of these skills in politics, but economics had a language of its own, employed by a group of people new to him, a group of people he had not yet been able to handicap.

He was not yet sure which of them were bright and discerning and disinterested, which of them were stupid and partisan, and in which ways and in what circumstances they would be bright and discerning and in which stupid and partisan. He couldn't yet read them. He was not sure of the exact or special meaning of terms they used, like 'terms of trade' or 'net income deficit', certainly not with the confidence he needed to undergo examination by an economics reporter who did know. He was not sure of what he would come to call the 'weights and balances', such as, for example, whether foreign opinion mattered and how it mattered, and which foreign opinion mattered in which ways. He had some feel for the political weight of things, for the impact of tax increases, for example, or interest rate cuts or inflation or depreciation. But to know these things made it all the more alarming for him that he was not completely sure of the connections between, say, a decision to devalue and some subsequent decision that might have to be made to reduce wages, or between a decision to change a tax rate in one area and its impact on others.

Some of these things would come in time and the rest he learned to ignore as being beyond useful calculation. However, in early March 1983 the task of coming to grips with understanding it seemed to him so great as to be much bigger than anything he had ever undertaken. He had to understand it sufficiently well to be able to choose confidently among options presented by John Stone or to ask for other options or to insist on a completely different option, to be able to give an interview confidently to a knowledgeable reporter, quite apart from the difficulty of arguing a controversial submission in Cabinet against the persistent queries of a well-informed critic like Ralph Willis. It could not in the end be solved to the point of quiet confidence, of course, because the more he progressed the more he discovered the truth that most of what he was told as fact was contingent and interpretive, something that would probably work but might not and quite often didn't. Ultimately therefore he found success in combining a public assurance that all was under control and well understood with a private and increasing scepticism in relation to any proposition put to him with the same force and confidence as he himself would put to it a roomful of economic reporters.

It was a moment in his life perhaps as important as running for Blaxland or later in running against Hawke, and all the more so because he had nothing much to go on – nothing to assure him, really, that he would behave in a way that inspired confidence, and that he would at the end, if not master the brief, at least have some conviction that he was no more confused than anyone else. Always he would operate, in this respect, on several levels: he would assert, for example, that he could see all the connections from April 1983 onward – which perhaps meant merely that from that time he knew enough of the terminology to be as glib as the reporters.

Those with him then would remember his insecurity in those first months – that first year – his hesitancy and his readiness to follow Treasury advice. Those who hated Stone would sometimes say that Keating's insecurity gave Treasury a pre-eminence that it had been denied under the Fraser Government, and the result was the triumph of what they called 'economic rationalism' and 'market economics'. It was an account that proved not to fit because John Stone and Treasury opposed the single most important market reform sought by the government, and the opening up of Australian industry to more competition and market pressure occurred only long after Stone had gone. While Stone was there the government adopted many policies Stone opposed, but it was true that Keating had a very sensible and tonic humility in the face of the daunting task of acquiring the level of economic knowledge he would need to acquit himself well and to take control as distinct from ticking the decisions of his officials. Insecurity of this kind is inseparably part of the learning process, and the more rapid the learning, the greater the insecurity. Ralph Willis, by contrast, was quite secure, quite sure, and quite wrong. It would take him several more years to drop his orthodoxy, and only to acquire a new one.

The difficulty was all the greater because understanding the way economists thought was only part of it. When it came to making decisions in economic policy there might be a half dozen different possible solutions, all within the conventional canon of economics and all pressed somewhere within the bureaucracy or the Cabinet or around Parliament House. There might be minor differences between two policies – between, say, a deficit one billion more or one billion less, or an interest rate one per cent more or one per cent less – which could and did become flash points of epic struggles within the government and the bureaucracy. In time he would find the breadth of thinking within the conventional canon of economics useful to him, providing a plausible defence of one line at one time and a totally different line at another time.

Many solutions were possible, but it was often hard to be certain of the problem. Most of the decisions he would be asked to make now would affect the economy later. Interest rate changes, budget spending or taxing changes were intended to change the way the economy would perform in six months or a year, and the case for or against the decisions often depended on just what you believed the economy would be like in six months or a year, with and without the proposed change. You had to decide where the thing was going, knowing that you didn't really know and that the only quite certain thing about any prediction was that it would, to a greater or lesser degree, be wrong.

A forecast for the economy would imply a certain policy response, so arguments about the right policy often became arguments over the plausibility of forecasts. And it was not only that you didn't really know where you were going – whether unemployment, for example, would be 8 per cent or 10 per cent in a year's time, whether the economy would keep getting stronger and stronger or weaker and weaker or was already swinging back the other way – you also did not know where you were. It would not be until June 1983 that the government would be told by the statistician where the economy had been in March 1983, when they were elected. They did not know where they were going or where they were, and they very often did not know where they had come from. It was not until the end of March 1983, three weeks after the government had been elected, that the statistician could say what had happened to the economy in the three months to the end of December 1982, when Malcolm Fraser and John Howard were still running things. Even when they found out where they thought they had come from, they might find out later they hadn't been there at all. The Whitlam Government recession, for example, was revised away by later and more accurate statistics.

It was important to know how far forecasts could be trusted, and at first Keating had no experience on which to base his assessment. He had no feel. As time went on he learned, through repeated and grave errors in forecasts. The forecasts, for example, for the entire 1988 Budget scenario, the size of the current account deficit in 1989, the likelihood of recession in 1990, the strength of recovery in 1991, the fiscal deficit in 1992 – all of them were wildly, hilariously wrong, though mostly quite sensible at the time they were made. The best one could expect was to get the general direction of policy right, and he would discount those forecasts that contradicted his own sense of how things were going.

He would discover, too, that while Treasury and Reserve Bank economists spent a lot of time working up their forecasts, most of the important things that happened were not in them. Anything that happened unexpectedly was by definition excluded from a forecast – and the unexpected included exchange rate movements, share price changes, oil price increases, and most decisions of other governments. Things excluded could and often did change outcomes more than things included. And while the effect of interest rate increases or spending cuts was the subject of a detailed forecast, policy changes of much greater significance were not – the float, tariff cuts, or banking deregulation, for example. Changes like these altered the structure of the economy in ways that were often not expected.

Paul sometimes liked to say that economic policy was levers and pulleys, manipulated at various times over the various instruments of economic policy with, as he said, due regard to the leads and lags of their effects. He became fond of whiteboards and coloured pens and charts. As his experience accumulated he became more wary and would instead say that monetary policy, for example, was more art than science and you just had to have a feel for it. Budgets didn't turn out as predicted. Sometimes the numbers for something – the current account or growth – turned out more or less as predicted, but not for the reasons predicted, because one huge error one way was cancelled out by a huge error the other way. As Paul become more practised and familiar he learned to trust some parts of a forecast but not others. He learned to be wary of whiteboards, vividly coloured charts and confident briefings. You could expect total budget spending, for example, to be more or less as predicted so long as the number of unemployed and the number of jobs was more or less correctly predicted, though often they were not. But estimates of revenue could vary wildly and for reasons that had nothing to do with the economy or perhaps for no reason. Forecasts of consumer spending might be reasonable, but forecasts of investment spending and of exports and imports were almost always wrong. Later he would say that forecasts were all bullshit anyway, and he relied ultimately on the opinion of a few people in business or government whose experience was long enough, and whom Paul had known long enough to be able to interpret accurately.

Knowing Australia was to know only part of the puzzle, because there was also the rest of the world. A change in interest rates decided in a meeting of the Federal Reserve's Open Market Committee in a building on Constitution Avenue, Washington DC, could, and often did, change interest rates in Australia, or it could affect the inflow of money into Australia or the exchange rate. It would affect the prices for the commodities Australia sold and the terms on which people were prepared to invest. So Japan also mattered and Germany mattered and, later in the government's long life, China and South-East Asia and Korea mattered.

Being Treasurer in Australia was always the second most important job in the Federal Government. In some ways at some times in some hands it was *the* most important job. There were almost fifteen and a half million Australians when Paul became Treasurer, more than a third of them in jobs. They would produce more than $180 billion of goods and services measured in 1983 dollars, of which about $22 billion was sent abroad. Whether or not people had jobs, whether or not people felt they were becoming better off or worse off, whether prices in the shops were rising or stable, were all responsibilities of the Treasurer – all things that he or she was supposed to be in charge of, on which success or failure would be reckoned, even if he or she could do little about them. These things, and whether the distribution of wealth was fair, whether exports were rising with imports, whether taxes were fair – the list was endless.

For the first time in his career Paul's job was the focus of sustained and intense media interest. Economic policy was made under the glare of public scrutiny. Even if reporters did not follow it all, his ministerial colleagues and their departments, state governments, lobbyists, business economists, and the Opposition did. There was not a decision he could make that would not sooner or later come to light. The record of successes and failures were in the statistics published month by month and quarter to quarter, available to everyone else at the time they were available to him. Policy was generally made in secret, but its effects were usually immediately apparent and the results public. As never before, Paul was in the public eye.

He read everything. He read the submissions proposed for the Treasurer, the briefing papers explaining inflation or employment numbers, the forecasts, the analyses and the ceaseless flow of minutes. The amount of paper coming over to his office was staggering. Hundreds and hundreds of letters to review and sign on tax issues and foreign investment applications. Minutes and requests for decisions and guidance for Treasury in its work across the government. Advice and submissions on each of hundreds of Cabinet decisions. Forecasts, comment and opinion, records of meetings with officials of foreign governments and state governments. A Treasurer could spend almost his entire time sitting at his desk signing paper – indeed some had, and the Treasury had been very happy that they did so.

At first, and for some years, Keating would annotate the papers, seek further opinions from other officials or advisers. But he soon realised that a Treasurer who did all the paperwork required of him by Treasury was not doing the job required of him by Cabinet. By 1991 it had changed. The kaleidoscope of the economy might change, but its essential issues, the basic orientation of his advisers, the limits on what economists really could know of the world, did not.

Eventually he only needed to glance at a paper's title to know what was in it, from the first to the last numbered point. The papers accumulated unread on his desk until his secretary, Linda Craige, returned them, unmarked, to whomever had provided them. Later it was hard even to feign interest when an assistant or an official briefed him on an issue, the official or adviser a little puzzled perhaps by the apparent unresponsiveness of the Treasurer, realising only after some time that he or she was the fifth, sixth or seventh adviser or official to sit in much the same spot making many of the same points, only the face and the inflection of voice changing, only the particular combination of a set of facts varying. The smart adviser soon acquired the knack of merely updating the Treasurer, merely summarising in ten or fifteen words what he or she discerned to be the important new piece of information to add to the existing stock in the Treasurer's mind.

The job was intellectually and practically immense, but in the first few weeks of government his first task was to organise his staff, his office, and his family. Barbara Ward remained with him in government. Economist John Langmore was attached to his staff, but there was no intellectual empathy between the two. A university economist, Barry Hughes was a welcome addition as a part-time consultant with a particular interest in labor market issues and then economic forecasting. Searching for a principal private secretary, preferably from Treasury, Keating was guided to a Treasury officer then travelling in Europe, Tony Cole. John Stone warmly commended the choice and set about tracking Cole down. Within a short while Cole had the office humming. His energy, capacity for work and loyalty to his new boss created a lasting reputation for the Treasurer's office as one of the best run in Parliament House.

The Keatings decided to move to Canberra. On a ministerial salary plus a travelling allowance for working days in Canberra they could afford it. Former Treasurer John Howard supported Paul's decision – he knew the difficulties. A Treasurer needed to spend long hours on the job with his staff and officials, so if he was to see his family at all other than on Saturday evenings after a Saturday afternoon flight from Canberra and before a Sunday night flight back, they needed to be together in Canberra. Coalition ministers had in the past claimed travelling allowance for working days in Canberra, even though their residence was Canberra rather than their electorate. In a few years Keating's travelling allowance claim would be a campaign issue.

Ministerial office meant higher pay and a car and driver on call. While awaiting his permanent driver from the car pool, Paul was assigned Jimmy Warner, whom he asked to seek out a house to rent without disclosing the tenant. Jimmy found one and showed it to Annita, who approved. It was to be the first of several houses to which the Keatings moved around Canberra, as their owners returned from overseas assignments. Canberra was a very small town after Sydney, but Annita would soon come to enjoy the clear air, cool nights, and her greater independence from Paul's Sydney friends and family.

In those early days of March 1983 he had views, of course, though it was only later that he could discern which of the views he had then were really influential and which were not – and the ones he remembered were naturally the influential ones, not the ones he sloughed off as his understanding grew. He looked back on this nine years later, sitting in Room 101 on the House of Representatives side, his backbencher's office in Parliament House. As it turned out, it was just a few days before he became Prime Minister. It was a room he rarely used and which had the tidy clutter of such a room, with invitations to speak stacked across tables and chairs, a few magazines, a small library shelf of books he intended to read but somehow hadn't found time to read, the usual green- and red-backed Hansards – again unread, unopened – and on the walls of the reception area, near where Linda Craige had her desk, two strikingly lovely Tasmanian landscape photographs.

Paul did not keep a detailed journal. He had an appointments diary, of course, and he had collections of notes passed back and forth. Once he made a detailed record of certain discussions with Hawke, and then for a time lost it among the myriad of papers passing through his office. He had access to detailed files, but his principal means of recalling events was a pile of press clippings, which he himself cut out at night and (to Annita's annoyance) stacked around the house, the piles yellowing as the years accumulated. He would glance at the clip and recall the associated events, the background, the sequence.

During the 1970s, he said that day in December 1991, recalling what had been in his mind in his first days in the Treasurer's office in the lower level of the old Parliament House, beneath the Prime Minister's office, he had come to the conclusion that the economy was not growing fast enough. He was interested in manufacturing and thought we could have more of it without having less mining. He also believed by the end of the 1970s and the beginning of the 1980s that industry would not thrive behind high tariff walls.

> I was not an economist; I didn't really understand it, but I came to the conclusion that the exchange rate was uncompetitive – that we had been ripping off the farmers and the miners for years. I also thought we had real wage overhang – that wages had got out of line in the Whitlam period. I didn't know what to do about the exchange rate. My solution to real wage overhang was to hit the unions on the head. Others had other ideas, like a wages accord and an incomes policy. But while people had been advocating these in the late 1970s, the Accord itself only came out of the 1982 recession. Of course, you have to remember that there was no economic policy debate in the 1970s – not like today.

Keating's attitude to incomes policies was similar to Hayden's – they did not think they could be relied on to control inflation. This had become an issue in the opposition to Hayden, and remained a point of keen sensitivity to the incoming government. In early 1983 Keating had a radically different view from that of Hawke, Willis and Langmore on the possibilities of the Accord.

He thought the exchange rate was too high but did not at this point know how to get it down. He thought real wages were too high and wanted to biff the unions, but he would discover this was both impossible and undesirable. In 1991 he couldn't recall any views he would have had about the stance of monetary policy – 'I didn't understand it well enough, to tell you the truth.' The fiscal policy announced by Hawke and to which he was committed during the campaign was to add $1. 5 billion to a deficit believed to be $4. 5 billion. That would soon be shown to be obsolete.

Keating had ideas and inclinations that he would in time develop, but in March 1983 he was a little awed by the immensity of it, by Hawke's confident claims to understand it all and by the prestige that now attached to Hawke as the actual Prime Minister, the man who had won the election and who now commanded the affection and respect of all of Paul's colleagues. Later Keating would separate himself, but in those first weeks and months he was subsidiary to Hawke – so much so that Hawke conducted much of the economic debate in the first few months.

During the campaign Labor had promised to boost spending to create jobs, to manage an accord with the unions to prevent another round of inflationary wage increases, while at the same time maintaining the value of wages after price increases. These commitments were seen by some of the party leaders, especially by reconstruction shadow minister Ralph Willis, and his adviser John Langmore, as the key to their central objective: to encourage economic growth by increasing government spending and the deficit, while at the same time holding down wage and inflation pressure through the price–income policy agreed with the ACTU. Wages would not rise, but employment would grow more rapidly. To them, the government's commitment to higher spending outlined in the campaign was its part of a bargain in which the ACTU would for its part accept lower wage increases. One went with the other. It had been their approach now for more than a year. It was strongly supported by Victorian Treasurer Rob Jolly, who claimed weight and experience in economic policy, and by the economic advisers to the Victorian Labor Government.

In his policy speech on 16 February 1983, Hawke had promised new programs, which he said would add $2.75 billion to the deficit, to be partly offset by cutting down on tax avoidance and falling unemployment benefit payments expected to result from increased growth. The net effect would be a deficit increase of $1.5 billion. There were to be income tax cuts, a cut in oil taxes, an accelerated public works program, a community works program, pension increases, increased spending on public housing, and a national health insurance scheme financed by a 1 per cent levy of taxable income. Far from its later concern about international competitiveness, the policy speech promised no reduction in existing protection levels. Hawke said he would 'review the need for additional short-term assistance in selected industries.' And, far from promising deregulation of banking, he said Labor would help housing by maintaining interest rate controls on bank mortgage interest rates and extend them to building societies. It would also require banks and building societies to set aside a proportion of their funds for housing. These protectionist, public expansionist themes were much more apparent in the National Recovery and Reconstruction Plan. Ostensibly the economic program Labor was elected to carry out, it appears today like the fossilised remnant of traditional post-war Labor.

Two abiding themes of the government were in the policy speech. One was consensus. The other, closely related, was the Accord. Both remained icons but in practice neither bore very much resemblance to their promised character.

That was the election program, but some Labor leaders privately now had entirely a different idea. They believed that the economy had probably bottomed and that the trajectory of increased spending already programmed by the Fraser Government in its last year was sufficient to stimulate recovery. If they were right, then it followed that more spending might have the effect of weakening rather than strengthening the prices and incomes accord by sooner or later placing too much pressure on prices and the rate of increase in employment. When Bob Hawke called Ross Garnaut to ask him to be his economic adviser, Garnaut told him that he would by happy to do so, but believed very strongly that both interest rate and budget policies had already changed enough, that the economy was turning round, and Hawke's campaign promise of higher spending should be modified. To his surprise, Hawke completely agreed. (Hawke also privately believed that wages would have to fall after inflation, not be maintained as he had said during the campaign.) This was also the adamant view of Treasury, though Treasury was typically less concerned with the issue of how long a recession might last than with how permanent and how deep might be the cut in inflation that accompanied it.

Keating himself leaned strongly to the position Hawke had already taken and which Treasury supported. Against it was a powerful coalition of Labor leaders and advisers. Peter Sheehan thought the economy needed more stimulus, and he was supported by the Victorian Labor Premier John Cain. John Langmore was also supporting higher spending.

The extraordinary document that John Stone had prepared for the incoming government and handed to Hawke and Keating at the Lakeside meeting changed the internal debate over the implementation of Labor's election commitments. Dated Sunday 6 March and headed 'Current Fiscal Situation and Outlook', its content would allow Stone to direct the new government's energies from increasing the deficit to cutting it. It would also set the pattern for Keating's budgets, which year after year would cut back public spending, which had expanded under Whitlam, and which Fraser had not been able to alter substantially. The document summarised the whole debate that would emerge in Cabinet between the election in March and the Budget in August. By bringing Hawke into alliance with Keating against Willis, it also confirmed Keating's hold on the Treasurer's job against his rival, and created an association between the Prime Minister and the Treasurer that was certainly not there on 6 March.

The report was startling. In August 1982 Treasurer John Howard had forecast a budget deficit of $1674 million for the year ending

30 June 1983. Based on the mid-year review carried out by the Department of Finance in January, the likely deficit would actually be $4345 million. Spending would increase by 7. 5 per cent after inflation – the highest after-inflation growth since the notorious Budget of 1974–75, written by Treasurer Jim Cairns and all but disavowed at the time by Treasury. The Public Sector Borrowing Requirement (PSBR) – which totalled state deficits and the Commonwealth deficit – would be $11 000 million and would be the highest public sector borrowing, in relation to the size of the economy, since World War II.

Stone had been asked about the 1982–83 Budget deficit but, 'because the prospective situation in that area for 1983–84, so far as we can foresee it at this time, is so truly alarming,' he wrote, 'I feel that I must also take this opportunity of informing you on that topic.' Some of the deficit increase was caused by recession, some by tax income falling and some by unemployment benefit payments increasing. But Stone argued that there were also 'structural' problems in the Budget, which would mean the deficit would continue even when tax income was up and unemployment benefits down. Stone told Hawke and Keating: '. . . the 1983–84 Budget outlook is far more serious than generally appreciated: it presents, by any standard, a truly alarming prospect.' With no policy changes the deficit would come in around $9. 6 billion. But the new government had promised new programs, which Treasury estimated would cost $1. 8 billion in 1983–84.

Stone then gave Hawke, Keating and their advisers their first exposure to his style of Treasury advice. 'On this admittedly very rough and ready figuring, the prospect is for a 1983–84 Budget deficit of almost $12 billion. Such a deficit would be equivalent to around 6½ per cent of GDP, the highest in Australian post-war history', with a Public Sector Borrowing Requirement of 11 per cent, a record for the post-war period by a margin of nearly 4 percentage points of GDP.

Stone wrote that a great deal of the deficit increase was not in unemployment benefits or falling tax revenue but in public debt interest, tax sharing grants to the states, pensions and benefits, and defence.

These sources of increased spending would not automatically be corrected as the economy recovered. He argued strongly against further deficit increases, the new government's promised 'stimulatory action'. Rather than increases, he believed it was imperative to cut the deficit, which might otherwise push up interest rates as a recovery took hold.

For Hawke and Keating it was at first a shocking document, then a welcome one. It meant that the fiscal expansion Labor believed would be necessary to pull out of recession was already occurring. It also meant that those promised spending programs could now be modified on the ground that the deficit was very much higher than Labor had been led to believe. And it wrecked the Liberal Government's claim to greater fiscal prudence than Labor. It was a gift to the new government, a gift backed by the full authority of John Stone as Treasury Secretary, and became a very powerful argument that John Stone should be kept on to reinforce Labor's credentials as responsible economic managers compared to their reckless predecessors.

During the election campaign Labor had warned that Australia was sliding more deeply into recession. The forecasts supplied in Stone's suggested that the worst was over. It also argued that the promised prices and incomes policy 'cannot work in an environment of inadequately supportive macroeconomic policies'. Wage restraint would not be successful if interest rates were too low or the budget deficit too high. According to Treasury, a mild but reasonable recovery would be underway in 1983–84. GDP would increase by 3 per cent compared to 1982–83. Non-farm employment would rise by 1. 7 per cent from June 1983 to June 1984. Inflation (the rise in the private consumption deflator) would be between 7 and 9 per cent over the same period. By inference, the government's principal policy problem was not the recession but the Budget deficit.

For a Cabinet meeting scheduled for 16 March, Treasury official Ted Evans set out for the Treasurer a set of spending and revenue figures that 'amply confirm an horrendous Budget outlook for 1983–84.' Within ten days of winning government, therefore, the Treasurer and the Minister for Finance were renouncing the promises on which they were elected – and with good reason.

Thirteen days later, on 29 March, Keating and Finance Minister John Dawkins were presenting Cabinet with a joint submission very different in tone from what many of their supporters, and current staff members, had expected only three weeks before. In the sixteenth submission seen by the new Cabinet, '83/84 Budget – Economic Policy Considerations', the two ministers formally laid down the framework that they urged other ministers to accept. They also proposed the deficit number, already agreed between the Treasurer and the Prime Minister, which ignited controversy within the government. The submission claimed there were signs of a pick-up and so profit margins should be increasing. The US appeared to be recovering, and, of course, there was fiscal stimulus from the Commonwealth and from the states. The result would be 'a change from decline to expansion of economic activity with some acceleration through the course of 1983–84.' But: 'We are of the view that there is a need to substantially reduce the prospective budget deficit in 1983–84.'

The deficit could of course be reduced by tax increases, but there the ministers – in one of the key policy choices for the government – firmly opted for spending cuts.

The submission declared of the deficit cut, 'Were we to approach that task, even in part, by way of tax increases which directly and significantly affected the lower income earner,' the ministers warned their colleagues, 'we would be putting at risk the possibility of significant success from the Prices and Incomes Accord. That is not to say that tax measures have no role. We will move in on the more obvious tax abuses, and we may have to consider measures beyond that. It does however emphasise the inevitability of giving prime consideration to reducing government outlays.'

With this submission, Keating and Dawkins firmly linked the success of the Accord to minimising tax increases. The argument had become that a successful prices and incomes accord required no income tax increases (and no sales tax increases – these would increase prices). It also required 'adequate support' from macroeconomic policies – which effectively meant reducing the projected deficit and a 'non-accommodating' monetary policy. In this context, 'non-accommodating' meant that interest rates would go up if wages increased beyond the agreed level. This would be a continuing theme for the remainder of the decade. The Treasurer had also quite promptly caught an argument that 'supportive' policies were needed for the Accord, including a lower budget deficit and a monetary policy that would not accommodate an increase in nominal GDP beyond that envisaged by the Accord assumptions.

The ministers recommended a budget deficit of $8. 5 billion for the financial year beginning 1 July 1983.[4] It would be a 'reasonable compromise' between providing sufficient stimulus to the economy but 'not so large as to imperil the ongoing success of the Prices and Incomes Accord'. The new target implied a $1 billion cut from the deficit, which would have occurred with no change of policies, and a cut of nearly $4 billion from what it would be if Labor's policies had been added on to the existing projected deficit. Since Keating was also ruling out tax increases, most of the saving had to be in spending cuts. The only substantial new program the government would have room to adopt was the universal health insurance scheme, Medicare.[5]

The new deficit target ignited controversy within Cabinet and caucus. The Left was strongly opposed to the lower deficit, as was Ralph Willis. It was argued that the economy was weaker than Treasury thought and that a lower deficit would lose the ACTU cooperation upon which wage restraint depended.

While Keating had been working on the Budget in preparation for a statement in May, John Langmore and the Department of the Prime Minister and Cabinet had been arranging an economic summit, to be held in the House of Representatives' chamber in early April. The idea of the summit was Hawke's rather than Keating's, and the style of consensus politics was also Hawke's rather than Keating's. The

Treasurer was and remained for some time sceptical of the value of agreements with the ACTU on wages growth. The New South Wales Labor Council was nominally the state branch of the ACTU. In practice it was, and remained, hostile to the Melbourne-based leadership of the ACTU and to the whole trend towards stronger federal branches and weaker state branches of individual unions as the movement of employees from state to federal industrial awards continued. Paul was influenced by the state view, which was not offset by any personal knowledge of the key ACTU officials.

The Summit, however, was not only about wages. By breaking the convention restraining the Senate from refusing money bills and forcing the Whitlam Government to the polls, Fraser had forfeited the chance to reach a national consensus on Australia's economic problems. Elected in the midst of recession, with poor profits and falling output as well as rising unemployment, Hawke saw the opportunity to use his personal popularity and pragmatic politics to create the consensus that had eluded Fraser. Wage restraint was part of that, but so was a deficit target pitched between too much and not enough. As the Department of Prime Minister and Cabinet and Treasury became more deeply involved in Summit preparations, the emphasis quietly shifted towards agreement on a deficit target. Three scenarios were drawn up by officials: a big deficit, which would increase interest rates and deter investment; a small deficit, which would cut spending and growth; or a medium deficit, which was just right.

Keating's Summit speech in the chamber was his first major public address on economic issues. He was still nervous and insecure in the job, and still searching for the right balance of stimulus and restraint, of Labor orthodoxy and Treasury orthodoxy. Barry Hughes wrote a first draft of the speech, which Keating rejected. It was too polemical, he thought. It did not have that dull, authoritative Treasury thud. David Morgan went to Sydney and spent a weekend working through a new version, which Paul polished for the Summit.

The Summit served to publicise and win general acceptance for a 1983–84 deficit that was higher than the year before but lower than it would be without cutting spending, for a monetary policy that would allow reasonable growth without inflation, and for an objective of reasonably rapid growth and job creation so long as trade union restraint contained wage increases.

The Accord with the ACTU was, in these early months of government, handled by the Prime Minister and by the Minister for Employment and Industrial Relations, Ralph Willis, and it was based on joint arguments that would be presented to the Conciliation and Arbitration Commission. Together the government and the ACTU would seek to preserve but not increase the real value of wages by asking the commission to award a single national increase of wages for inflation. How frequently that increase should occur, and with what delay, was argued within Cabinet.

Later the Accord would become a central part of Keating's thinking, to the point where he took it over and became its principal negotiator for the government. During 1983, however, he remained sceptical of its value and waited to see whether unions and their factory shop committees would adhere to the 'no extra claims' provision of the single central increases. In the meantime, Treasury pulled him one way and Hawke and Barry Hughes the other. In those first months of government Keating frequently went to Hawke's office after dinner, and the two men would sit talking late into the night. Hawke told him that ACTU Secretary Bill Kelty was 'solid gold'. His word could be relied upon. Back in his own office, Barry Hughes would argue the centrality of an agreement with the ACTU to Labor's economic policy. Without it, wages would take off when growth resumed, inflation would rise, and the government would have to cut it off with high interest rates. To Stone and Treasury, the idea that unions would adhere to a single quarterly or six-monthly wage increase, and no other, was quite unlikely. The first increase was not until the end of 1983. The first evidence of adherence to it was not until well into the following year. Slowly the evidence would bring Keating round.

Paul thought he was fine from the Summit on, that he had mastered the brief and could reproduce the expected patter. He might not have been completely on top of his brief, but he was certainly more fluent, persuasive and confident. He delighted Treasury. Ted Evans watched him persuading a suspicious and reluctant caucus that the deficit had to be cut rather than increased, and that some Fraser Government programs would go. He had mastered the lines from a set of Treasury dot points. Labor had inherited an unexpectedly big deficit. The Accord would be put under pressure by interest rate increases and later by tax increases unless spending cuts could be found. Labor needed spending cuts to find room for its programs, especially Medicare. The economic recovery would be choked off by higher interest rates and a rising dollar unless the Budget was controlled – point by point down the page, but really meaning it, really believing it, saying it with a passion that took the dot points right off the page and made them his own in a way Evans had never heard, and slowly bringing over to him a hundred or so Labor parliamentarians whose party had seen three brief years of government in thirty-five years.

He delivered his first major economic statement on 19 May barely three months after Hawke's policy speech. A great deal had happened since then, including the discovery, a happy one, of a larger-than-expected deficit forecast for 1983–84. Where Hawke had promised another $2. 75 billion in spending, Keating announced new initiatives costing little more than $0. 5 billion. Where Hawke had promised $1.2 billion in spending cuts and increased revenues, Keating announced nearly $1 billion. Instead of increasing the deficit by 1.5 billion as Hawke has promised in his policy speech, Keating announced that it would be reduced by a little more than $400 million from the outcome if current Fraser Government programs continued unchanged.

Working closely together, Hawke and Keating prevailed. They established the principle that the deficit had a structural or long-term element, which must be gradually remedied by containing its expansion during downturns. The deficit should not be cut by tax increases but by spending cuts, on the grounds that the Accord prevented further cuts in take-home pay. The Accord also had to be supported by firm demand-management policy. These principles were opposed by the Left and by Ralph Willis, who led the push for a larger deficit. The agreement on these policy points between Hawke and Keating sealed their alliance and eliminated Willis's chances.

By the time Keating delivered his first Budget on 23 August its elements were not only already well known but also by now accepted by his colleagues. The Prime Minister, the Treasurer and Treasury had thus within a very short period of time formed an alliance around some propositions that were not then widely recognised within the government, but which would remain important parts of its policy foundation for years to come.

The numbers were only just beginning to show it, but the economy was turning. Labor had won government at the end of the trough; the contraction of the March quarter was the worst of the whole recession. In the following three months production increased and by September it would be growing strongly. Overall the production contracted by nearly 2 per cent in the financial year ended June, and bounced back to grow by more than 6 per cent in the following year. Unemployment continued to rise until September because there were fewer new jobs than people coming into the workforce. From May 1983, however, jobs were no longer being lost, and by the end of December 130 000 jobs had been created. Keating had come to office at the beginning of an expansion that was to continue to the beginning of the next decade. But it was to be also a time, as he came to call it, of thrills and spills. The economy would grow very rapidly through to 1985, when the dollar began to plummet and the trade balance rapidly deteriorated. With higher interest rates the economy slowed through 1985 and then 1986, before catching a second wind in 1987, experiencing an investment boom in 1988 and 1989, despite high and sustained interest rates, before crashing into the beginning of a deep recession in 1991.

7

THE FLOAT

HE WOULD REMEMBER IT LONG AFTERWARDS, the uncertainty he felt in those first months in the face of the easy assurance, the geniality, the almost affectionate patronage of John Stone. Always confident, always knowing, the Secretary was able to explain good humouredly to the new Treasurer why it was that things must continue to be done in the way they had hitherto been done and no other. Even eight years later, hurtling along the freeway to Tullamarine on a black, wet night, Keating would recall Stone's cheerful condescension in that first eighteen months. 'I would tell him we couldn't go on with the way the exchange rate system worked by money rushing in, and he would say, "Oh, no Treasurer, don't believe that bullshit." I had to appoint the Martin Committee to freshen up the Campbell recommendations myself, he didn't want it. "Rubbish, Treasurer, you're new and impressionable, Treasurer, you set this up and it can only lead one way and you will regret it." All said in his charming way, but *all the time, all the time!*'

From the beginning Stone and Keating differed over many issues, but one of the most fundamental was financial deregulation. Stone had opposed the appointment of Sir Keith Campbell's Committee of Inquiry into the Australian Financial System in 1979 (losing out then to the Treasurer's adviser, John Hewson), and when the committee reported in 1981 he opposed many of the recommendations. Alone with Hawke, Keating had cautiously welcomed the recommendations in caucus. Both had been defeated by Opposition Shadow Treasurer Ralph Willis, who argued that banking deregulation would serve the interests of banks at the expense of home buyers, small business and farmers.[1] Soon after being appointed Shadow Treasurer at the beginning of 1983, Keating had issued a press release opposing foreign bank entry, which he later said was prepared by John Langmore for Ralph Willis, and which Keating issued under his own name rather than create a fuss with his colleagues in the first days of the new job. But Keating had also publicly opposed foreign banks before he was Shadow Treasurer. Suspicious of the big commercial banks since childhood, he always wanted more competition. It took him a few more steps to favour *foreign* competition.

As Campbell and his colleagues saw it, Australian banks were crippled by regulation of the interest rates they could pay and charge, the amount they could borrow or lend, and the kinds of securities they could sell or debt they could issue. A host of smaller merchant banks and brokers were gobbling up traditional banking businesses, innovative new techniques were outrunning new ways of regulating, and because most developed countries were one way or another moving in the direction Sir Keith had advocated, Australia risked becoming a closed backwater in a global financial market. They believed that the Australian Government should stop trying to control the pattern of interest rates and the level of the exchange rate. Instead, these prices should be determined by the balance of supply and demand in the markets. Certainly the government could, and should, influence the supply or demand for loans or for dollars, but it should not directly attempt to fix the rate.

Slowly converted by his experience of the mining industry to market economics, Keating leaned towards the deregulation of financial markets. It was also part of his approach to government, part of the lesson of the Whitlam Government, that if he could, as Treasurer, make reforms that business wanted without deeply offending his own Labor constituency, he would do so. He would not adhere to a policy simply because Treasury preferred it, or because Stone warned him against change.

Sitting next to Campbell at a barbecue on the last day of the April 1983 Summit, he told him he would implement some of the report. Campbell had replied that even to implement a bit of it would make a big difference. The following day Campbell died suddenly. Keating thought Campbell was the most public-spirited businessman he had ever met. He had some of the same qualities possessed by Sir James Vernon, chairman of the famous Menzies era report, but a stronger intellect. Of the business people Paul knew, Campbell had the best and biggest idea of how it all fitted together, and he also had an idea of public service, of doing something for the country.

Advised by keen deregulators in the Department of Prime Minister and Cabinet and in his own office, and himself inclined to financial deregulation, Hawke warmly encouraged Keating down the path he was already taking. Within a few weeks of taking office Keating signalled that he intended to open up the financial system. In an interview with economics writer Ross Gittins published on 4 April 1983, Keating said that he did not want the Campbell Report to 'simply collect dust on the shelf. To that end what I will be putting to the Government fairly soon is that we establish a committee of review with a very short time to report – say, three or four months – to look across the Campbell recommendations'. Rather than taking the issue to Cabinet, he obtained from Hawke on 20 April a letter supporting the appointment of such a committee. In the same interview with Gittins Keating said the government would look at the entry of foreign banks into the Australian market in 'the not too distant future'. He would also look at issuing more bank licenses to Australians.[2] In late May Keating announced that the former chief of the Commercial Banking Company of Sydney, Vic Martin, would lead a committee to review the Campbell recommendations. There could only be one result from appointing such a group: to endorse in one form or another the objective of financial market deregulation.

'You have to understand that the Campbell Report was dead at that point,' Keating said in December 1991. He recalled that the committee was appointed at his suggestion, not Stone's. It was not suggested or pushed by any of his personal advisers. In appointing as its members Vic Martin, economics professor Keith Hancock, and Treasury official Richard Beetham, 'I did not even consult Hawke. It was set up without Cabinet approval.'

The Martin Review group was to report in 1984, but by that time the battle over the boldest of the Campbell recommendations – that the Australian Government end exchange controls and allow the exchange value of the dollar to be set by the market – had already been fought. It was a fight that pitted John Stone against the Prime Minister, the Treasurer, and Bob Johnston, Governor of the Reserve Bank.

Long an appendage to Treasury, Australia's central bank was beginning to emerge as an institution with its own power and province. Johnston would challenge and overcome the dominance John Stone and Treasury maintained over interest rates and exchange rates. In the new configuration of power in economic policy the Treasurer's position would be enhanced at the expense of his Cabinet colleagues, while Treasury's position would diminish.

Formally clothed with the power to create money and to fund the Commonwealth, the Reserve Bank influenced interest rates and the growth of money, maintained the agreed value of the Australian dollar in foreign exchange, and arranged borrowing for the Commonwealth. It was one of the least known and most important of Australia's official institutions, and Bob Johnston was nearly as insistent as his predecessors on the quaint discretion that it believed was necessary for it to function successfully. Even under this enlightened Governor, fighting for an open financial system, reporters entering the building were still asked to surrender tape recorders to one of the many uniformed attendants chatting amiably in the lobby, a practice defended with the preposterous rationale that, in this way, the Bank's security system could prevent listening devices being covertly left in the Bank's board room. A reporter asking for a copy of an old board report was told that it would not be possible, since papers seen by the board were permanently closed to public inspection.

The Reserve Bank operates under legislation that gives the government in Canberra the right to appoint its top executives and its board, and to instruct it if there is irreconcilable disagreement between the Bank and the government. There has never been such a formal disagreement because no government wants to tell parliament formally that it has instructed the Bank to act in a way which is against the best advice of the Bank, and no governor of the Bank wants to fall so far foul of government that he has to be told what to do. In practice the relationship between the Bank and any Treasurer is subtle. Every month or so the Governor and the Deputy Governor brief the Treasurer on the most recent board meeting and exchange views about monetary policy and the economy. It is often, though not always, then that monetary policy decisions already discussed in general by the board are given their final form and effect or perhaps changed. The Treasurer can and does also call the Governor at any time, and officials from his office are in frequent contact with the Bank, as are Treasury officials. At the beginning of 1983 Treasury and the Secretary of the Treasury were still the most influential forces on the Bank, though this was changing.

Bob Johnston had been appointed to the top job in the Bank in 1982 by the departing Treasurer, John Howard. His appointment had been unexpected because he was the head of the Secretary's Department at the Bank and junior in rank if not in age to the Deputy Governor, Don Sanders, and the appointment surprised both of them. Johnston had turned what was normally a dry clerical job in the Bank into a key policy post by taking on the responsibility for representing the Bank to the Campbell Inquiry. He prepared the Bank's views, he marshalled what evidence the Bank believed pertinent, and above all he encouraged the deregulatory views of the Inquiry, despite the hostility of Treasury and the qualms of the Bank. He welcomed the report's conclusions, and when Howard came to appoint another committee to consider the reports, Johnston was on it.

Johnston had been back in Australia only three years from a long posting in London, followed by a period with the World Bank in Washington. After the excitement of Washington, in the very year in which OPEC had again doubled oil prices and Paul Volcker at the Federal Reserve Board had cracked down on inflation, he found that the position at the Reserve Bank's unobtrusive and featureless building on the corner of Martin Place near Macquarie Street was rather a letdown. His eyes required surgery, so he felt his age and the lack of fulfilment of it. Researching the Bank archives in preparation for the Campbell Inquiry, he sometimes felt, he confided to friends, no more lively than one of the marble busts in its quiet library, a bust of one of the many figures of Australian finance and government who had contributed to the Bank and whose exact role and period of influence it was now difficult to recall. He could enjoy the wonderful collection of Australian paintings that the former Governor Dr H. Coombs had bought, the Dobells and Drysdales, and which were now hung here and there in the corridors, as though the Bank was reluctant to throw them out but not sure where to put them. He could enjoy the pleasures of working in the centre of Sydney and living on the North Shore, but his career appeared to be winding down. The particular annoyance of it was that it had once been so bright and engaged so much of his talents.

Reporters were generally surprised when he was appointed Governor, but the real surprise had been that he was not appointed Deputy Governor in 1975, instead of Don Sanders, and assured of succession many years before. Bob Johnston was, after all, a veteran of some important economic policy struggles of the early 1970s, struggles that would be extremely pertinent to the forthcoming ones within the Hawke Government in which Johnson's air of world-weary amateurism, his light irony, would be pitted against the intellectual ferocity – the heavy sarcasm – of Stone, and which Johnston would win. Johnston did not claim Stone's intellectual power. 'We may not be the smartest people in the world here,' he told a reporter writing a story about the Bank, a remark that Stone would never have passed about a Treasury Department that included himself. The six-year age difference between Johnston and Stone was important, because it was the difference between those whose adolescent years had been stamped by the discipline and camaraderie of wartime years in the military forces and those who had not. Johnston had left Essendon High in Melbourne in 1940 when he was 16 to join the Commonwealth Bank, but it was not long after that he was in the Royal Australian Air Force. Stone had been full time at the University at Western Australia and full time at Oxford, where he had had scholarships and played hockey for Australia. Johnston gained his commerce degree from Melbourne University at night, now a blooded RAAF veteran, and a Commonwealth Bank officer again by day, remaining so until he transferred to the still-new Reserve Bank of Australia in 1960. Stone spent the early 1960s in London. Johnston spent them learning his trade in Sydney. And while Stone was by the beginning of 1970s, coming into intellectual possession of economic policy in Treasury, Johnston was still just breaking through at 45 to be chief manager of the International Department at the Bank – someone Stone might occasionally deal with, but not as an equal.

The times and the trend of events, however, favoured Johnston in the coming contest, which would pit him against Stone and the Reserve Bank against Treasury. Johnston took over as chief manager of the International Department just as the Bretton Woods system collapsed, as Richard Nixon (and Paul Volcker) took the dollar off a fixed and redeemable value in gold and began the system of floating rates, which in time would become nearly universal. Johnston had already been influential in switching Australia from basing its currency value on sterling to basing it on the US dollar, and the Nixon devaluation now posed a political conundrum for the McMahon Government in Canberra. If Australia preserved its existing relationship with the dollar, it would mean it depreciated against other currencies like the pound and the yen. Imports priced in those currencies would probably become more expensive in Australia, which could be inflationary. It also made Australian assets relatively cheaper in those currencies and thus prompted people holding those currencies to buy them and to buy Australian exports. Guided by Treasury and the Reserve Bank, Prime Minister Bill McMahon wanted

to appreciate the currency. As a general rule the Treasury and the
Reserve Bank were almost always in favour of appreciation because
they worried most about inflation. But the Country Party was
resolutely opposed. Its constituency of farm exporters (and city manufacturers, too, who were worried about cheaper imports) lost most
when Australian dollars became more expensive. In a prolonged Cabinet crisis McMahon could do no more than partially move up against
the dollar, a vivid lesson to Johnston of the high desirability of taking this decision quite out of the Cabinet. Johnston had stayed on
at the International Department through the fall of the McMahon
Government, through the two revaluations urged by Treasury and the
Bank in the first term of the Whitlam Government, through the tightening of monetary policy in September 1973, which preceded the
downturn in 1974, and through the swift deterioration of the government thereafter. By 1976 Johnston was 51 and, in what might
perhaps have been the first move to sideline his career, he was sent as
the Bank's representative to London and then to Washington. When
he returned it was 1980 and the high point of Fraser's popularity
and command. He could, however, already see the ebullience of the
resources boom at home, the lushness of the rhetoric and the grandeur
of the lists of proposed mining projects compiled by government
officials, which made a very sorry and intriguing contrast with the
suddenness of the change of monetary policy in the United States.
This change was made and announced three blocks from his office
in the World Bank. He knew it would reach Australia quite soon and
garrotte the resources boom soon after the wage claims made upon
its promise had been cheerfully granted.

There was not much in Johnston's experience to commend the
wisdom of governments to him, and he had also acquired in London and Washington a strengthening conviction that the way of
the world was now towards financial deregulation, to the 'market', to
the mingled result of the clipped telephone bids and frantic hand
signals of hundreds of recent graduates, many who found a degree
quite unnecessary but could yet produce a better result for the Australian economy than the best efforts of aged and experienced

treasurers and their Cabinet colleagues, with and without the advice of John Stone. It was an astonishing and difficult concept, one that seemed to run against all logic, but Johnston thought it was probably right and Stone thought it was probably wrong, and though Stone was smarter and better trained and younger and had been in the centre of action now for more than a decade, it was Johnston who knew the way the world was moving and Stone who did not.

Johnston presented to the world a patina of gentle amused world-weariness, the wisdom acquired with age and experience, with disappointments and successes equally unexpected. At the gloomiest point of some barren discussion of the economy's prospects Johnston would remark that he supposed the sun would still rise tomorrow, and he would often say, satirising the style of bank economists, of Australia's emphatic style of economic commentary, 'Ah yes, we are often wrong – but never uncertain.' To reporters Johnston was accessible, illuminating, candid and charming; to politicians and ministers he was down to earth and clear. He was everything an Australian central banker ought to be and rarely had been, his predecessors being mostly shy and stuffy men, though curiously his staff within the Bank often found him lofty and remote, scathing to his subordinates – a bully. It was a peculiar thing. Stone, who was intellectually menacing and apparently always convinced that his course was the right one, was adored by his subordinates, even very junior economists, who enjoyed jousting with him because they could sometimes win and Stone was quite happy to acknowledge it, and in any case liked the fun of it. Johnston, who appeared to be world-weary and broadminded, did not care to be contradicted by his juniors, perhaps because he was simply not as intellectually lively as Stone, and perhaps also because, like so many in the leadership of the Bank, Johnston was by training actually a banker. His successors did not think of the Bank as a bank at all but as a monetary policy authority, which would sometimes, but certainly not exclusively or even mainly, conduct its policy through the instrument of commercial banks. He was the last of his generation, the last official to be important in Australian economic policy who had fought in World War II and also the last banker at the Bank. Johnston helped to create an economic revolution in Australia. He was arguably one of the most influential of its creators, and the revolution brought Australia into the modern economic world only just in time, but Johnston's credentials as an economist were quite as thin as Paul Volcker's, and only a little stronger than those of the Treasurer.

When Keating took over Treasury, Australia still had a fixed exchange rate. The Reserve Bank had to buy or sell dollars to keep the rate where it wanted, and these dollars taken into or out of the private banking system changed the money supply. The Reserve Bank could 'sterilise' the money supply increases it created by purchasing dollars in the market, but, to the extent it did so, it supported the level of interest rates that had attracted the speculators in the first place.

Day-to-day decisions about the exchange value of the dollar were made by a committee of four officials, acting on Cabinet's behalf. The members of the committee were the Secretary of the Treasury, the Secretary of the Department of Prime Minister and Cabinet, the Secretary of the Department of Finance, and the Governor of the Reserve Bank. Part of the speculators' thinking about the dollar was that this committee was inclined to support a stronger dollar, because that would lower import prices and therefore help to reduce inflation. If this was so, buying dollars following a major depreciation was a one-way bet. During 1983 the government was forced to raise the exchange rate gradually in response to increasing demand for the dollar, so that over a few months the 10 per cent devaluation of March was reversed.

In principle exchange controls should have prevented the big inflows of money. In practice they did not. A study of these capital movements by the Reserve Bank was one of the principal weapons in the debate over the exchange rate. Huge volumes of dollars were bought and sold during the middle of 1983, which caused, via the fixed rate, equivalent changes in the measured money supply. Johnston was able to show that 99 per cent of the tidal waves of capital had been perfectly proper transactions under the existing controls. Exchange rate controls might or might not increase the volatility of the dollar value in a float, but it didn't matter, because exchange rate controls were ineffective anyway in the kind of economy Australia had developed. Exchange rate controls were a nuisance for migrants wanting to send money to relatives abroad, and they were a nuisance for tourists, but for BHP or Westpac they were no problem at all.

Despite success with the Budget and the Accord, by the second half of 1983 Keating had three major policy problems arising from the exchange rate. One was that money kept coming in, putting the money growth targets under pressure. Another was that the dollar had to keep going up, which discouraged Australian exports. And the third problem was that speculators were successfully punting on successive small appreciations of the currency. They bought Australian dollars from the Reserve Bank at today's lower rate in terms of US dollars, and sold them back to the Reserve Bank at tomorrow's higher rate in terms of US dollars. Their profit was the gain in US dollars, and each dollar of profit for them was a dollar of loss for the Reserve Bank and for Australian taxpayers.

In some ways, though not perhaps as much as Keating and Hawke later claimed, the system for setting the exchange rate was the key to deregulation of the entire economy. But general arguments in favour of deregulation were not important at the time; the principal arguments within Treasury and the Reserve Bank were all in terms of control over the money supply.

While there was often argument about the process by which rates were set, the underlying debate was over the level at which it was set. Some of the most important players had radically different views on the value of the dollar. Paul Keating had long believed the Australian dollar was over-valued. Ross Garnaut, coming from the ANU economics school and with experience in New Guinea, also preferred a lower dollar. Both Keating and Garnaut emphasised the importance of exports. John Stone, by contrast, almost always preferred a stronger dollar, because it helped control inflation by making imports cheaper. Though there was not a necessary connection, most of the people who wanted a lower dollar, including Keating and Garnaut, also thought a lower dollar was likely if it was the balance of private demand and supply that set the value of the currency, rather than a committee dominated by Treasury. There was also another important strand of opinion, which included Ed Visbord in the Department of Prime Minister and Cabinet and a number of younger Treasury officials, who thought financial markets should set the dollar's value because they thought foreign exchange markets would in the longer run better attune the dollar to changing economic circumstances than would a government committee. They recognised, too, that if the government was no longer responsible for setting the exchange rate, it would have more freedom to adjust interest rates and greater control over the money supply.

Within the bureaucracy the Department of Prime Minister and Cabinet was strongly in favour of floating the dollar, which meant that the market would determine its value; Treasury was strongly opposed. This battle continued from the Fraser Government, when the Prime Minister's Department (allied with the Treasurer, John Howard, and his adviser, John Hewson) had fought for financial deregulation against Treasury. The coalition of Howard, Hewson and Visbord had created the Campbell inquiry into financial regulation in Australia, and the same coalition had fought Treasury to take the few steps down the path of deregulation that had been allowed not only against Treasury but also against the Prime Minister, Malcolm Fraser.

The float of the dollar later in 1983 has generated a deep and abiding controversy between Keating and Hawke over which of them deserved the most credit for the decision. Other than the leadership itself, it is the most enduring of their disagreements, and one way or another it colours most accounts of the decision. Hawke's version of the sequence of events leading to the float was published in his *Memoirs*.[3] In Hawke's account he himself is the prime mover in the decision, assisted by his office's economic adviser, Ross Garnaut, and a deputy secretary in the Department of Prime Minister and Cabinet, Ed Visbord. This is also the version that has been offered on and off the record by members of his office and by one of Keating's economic advisers, Barry Hughes. Keating is portrayed as a reluctant participant who was unduly concerned about the very strong objections posed to the float by the Secretary of the Treasury, John Stone. For his part, Keating portrays himself as the prime mover, while acknowledging that Hawke supported him and encouraged a float sooner rather than later. Keating's version is supported in its essential parts by his then private secretary, Tony Cole.

While there is no doubt that Hawke, Garnaut and Visbord supported floating the dollar, Hawke's account of it in his *Memoirs* is certainly quite wrong. In it Keating does not appear at all in the float decision until October of 1983, though at this point Keating had already been discussing the issue with Reserve Bank Governor Bob Johnston and with Hawke, and all three were agreed on the desirability of floating.

Prompted by my enquiry, in March 1996 Keating wrote his own version of the decision to float. It appears as the appendix to this book. Keating's account, however, does not include advice he received from the Reserve Bank and Treasury, which is crucial to understanding the sequence of events and which is presented in this chapter. Keating's version also places too little weight on Treasury's opposition to the float.

Keating's own preferences were for a float from quite early in the government. Even by the early 1980s he was inclined to prefer a cheaper dollar, a view he had acquired from the mining industry. In December 1991 (and in earlier interviews) Keating recalled that he first discussed the exchange rate system as early as April or May in the Reserve Bank Governor's Sydney office, with only the two of them in the room. These discussions followed their experience with the depreciation in the first days of office and Keating's annoyance that speculative inflows and outflows of capital were often successful bets against the Reserve Bank. Johnston 'said the crawling peg system had had it,' Keating remembers. 'I said we ought to consider going for a float. He jumped back!' Johnston confirms that a discussion of this kind took place quite early in the year. (The 'crawling peg' meant that the government fixed the exchange rate, but would change it depending on speculative pressures or the state of the economy.)

An influential figure with Hawke was his economic adviser Ross Garnaut, then 36, an economist who, like Stone and Hawke before him, had been at Perth Modern. He had then done his undergraduate degree and his doctorate at the Australian National University in Canberra. He had also, at some time in the 1960s when Hayden was rising within the party and also studying part-time for an economics degree at Queensland University, become friends with the future Labor leader. He had worked in the Department of Finance in newly independent New Guinea from 1975 to 1977. He had written speeches and papers for Hayden, and had met and impressed Hawke. When Graham Evans asked him to come over and see Hawke he had been delighted to accept, after some discussion, a job as economic adviser. In his two and a half years in his office, before the Prime Minister and the Minister for Foreign Affairs rewarded him with the job of Australian Ambassador to China, he remained influential with Hawke. Garnaut was a strong proponent of the float and urged it with Hawke, who was well disposed.

But while the Prime Minister, the Treasurer and the Governor of the Reserve Bank were all in favour of floating the dollar, the Secretary of the Treasury was not. By the second half of September, when there was another rush to buy dollars, the choice before the government was a higher dollar or a float. The Reserve Bank had sent Keating a memorandum arguing against the fixed rate system as early as 29 July. Even as late as 19 September, when the float was under active discussion, Treasury was still pressing for a higher fixed rate. In a submission to brief Cabinet on the condition of the economy it was asserted that: 'If we wish to limit domestic interest rate pressures, we must do what we can to ease the pressures on bond sales by restraining capital inflows, which may require, in the short term, an exchange rate higher than would otherwise be the case.' (Treasury was saying that bond sales – which tended to increase interest rates – were needed to offset money supply increases caused by capital inflow. If the dollar was higher, it was less attractive as a speculative asset, capital inflow would fall, and fewer bonds would need to be sold.)

A key document was drawn up within the Reserve Bank. On 20 September Johnston sent Keating a document entitled 'Interest rate volatility, the exchange rate and monetary policy'. Referring to the initial memorandum dated 29 July, he summed up subsequent work by the Bank. 'The main point emerging,' he wrote, 'is that much of the volatility in interest rates springs from the fact that while domestic financial markets are now virtually deregulated and very flexible, the exchange rate is relatively inflexible. Variability is therefore thrust onto the domestic money supply and interest rates.'

Johnston's document continued, 'We have been examining various options for dealing with this imbalance. The main candidates seem to be some technical adjustments to the exchange rate fixing arrangements or a move to a quantity-based (rather than price-based) foreign exchange intervention system. We see the first as perhaps the more immediately practicable but nevertheless as a palliative.'

At this point the Bank was not directly arguing for a free float of the dollar. Instead it preferred to talk of switching from fixing the price of foreign exchange to a 'quantity based intervention system'. The implied choice between fixing by price and fixing by quantity was quite obscure. The Bank appeared to have in mind a distinction between achieving a certain exchange rate by offering to buy and sell at that price, and achieving it by intervening in a free market to change the price.

The board would be meeting on 4 October to look at how alternative arrangements might work in practice. Johnston enclosed the working papers, which specified a number of options to reduce volatility of interest rates. According to the research, interest rate volatility in Australia was higher than in other OECD countries, and exchange rate volatility was correspondingly lower. The options for reform included everything from direct controls to a 'dirty float' in which there would be frequent intervention to maintain a target rate. The only option not included was that of a 'clean float', which was adopted two months later.

At this point in the development of the argument a clean float, in which the market alone would determine the rate, was apparently still considered too radical by Bank officials, though Keating says that he and Johnston had always favoured one. For a decision of such consequence the papers were extremely thin. There was no quantitative evidence of the propositions, no specific countries were mentioned in what purported to be international comparisons, and there were no dates. They concluded that a dirty float 'would provide a path to controlling the growth of monetary aggregates and would be helpful in the task of bringing down inflation.'

Within the government the discussions continued. On 16 October Treasury weighed in with a long minute on 'Exchange Rate Management Problems'. Addressed to the Treasurer, it was discussed by the Treasurer and the Prime Minister, and appears to have been left with the PM after a Lodge meeting.

A large part of the argument for a float was the suspicion within the Prime Minister's office and his department that Treasury was edging the rate up. A float would at least take it out of Treasury's control. Stone first addressed the argument that the rate was too high, saying that the rise in the trade-weighted index value of the Australian dollar since devaluation in March had done no more than 'reverse the politically inspired "run" on the $A' in the election period. 'Governments cannot long manage the rate in directions market forces would not have taken it,' he wrote, 'but can smooth peaks and valleys, and moderate trends.' In his view, the rate would actually have moved up further and faster in the past six months if left to the market. With this approach Stone minimised the difference between a free and a floating system, since both went in the direction of the market, and switched the argument to the causes of exchange rate movements. In this case, the underlying issue was the job of financing the deficit, which required higher interest rates and caused a capital inflow, which expanded the money supply unless it was cut off with a higher exchange rate. He underlined the conclusion. 'It is not the exchange rate system that has caused these problems.' The most basic remedy, therefore, was to get the deficit down. That could take time. Meanwhile, options included controls on short-term capital inflow, though he did not think that option should be pursued right then. Another approach might be the 'revolutionary' approach preferred by the Bank, about which Treasury, he said, had some reservations. He argued that a more volatile exchange rate would result, and this had costs. He also argued that, under a managed float, foreign exchange flows might be no less volatile than today, and if this were so then money supply and interest rates might not be more stable. The recommended change was therefore a 'leap in the dark', and he felt that 'evolution not revolution should be the order of the day.' Governments should only change policy on the basis of written advice and specific proposals. Apparently referring to the scanty Reserve Bank research, he wrote:

If the Bank is confident of the soundness of its case it should be able – and willing – to put it into writing and have it tested in a 'due process' manner. Mere conversational processes are not an appropriate basis for government decision-making, particularly on a matter of this order of importance.

He also wrote:

Given what might be called 'Treasury views' of the overwhelming importance of reining in inflation – views which, however, I believe you to share – it could be argued that the time has now come to tear down such fences as we have between us and the outside world and expose our own economy to the full force of those financial flood tides to which I have referred – this on the basis that such an approach would more effectively lock us into a more deflationary world which now prevails beyond our shores.

From one viewpoint I must say – as I have recently done – that there is some attraction in the course. Removal of the 'dead hand' of government from this area of policy ought, on those grounds, to be a plus for more rational economic management. If Treasury were made up of those latter-day

Machiavellians which the journalists continually paint it as being, we should be supporting the Bank's advocacy without demur.

Of course, the journalistic mythology is just that – mythology. As public servants it is, I believe, our job to alert you – and through you, the government – to the possible (and perhaps likely) dangers which we see in such advocacy for the government. We do think that there are such dangers for you and I believe we would be failing in our duty if we failed to bring them to your attention.

We would support the Reserve Bank to the extent of agreeing that some change in the system is warranted. But we believe that change in this area should be undertaken in stages. A complete and wholesale leap to a full market system overnight would be an act of faith to which the government has no need to commit itself at this time and the consequences of which cannot clearly be foreseen.

Stone nonetheless agreed to support setting the $A/$US rate later in the day than was then the case, which widened the permitted spread between buying and selling rates, and the whole or partial withdrawal of the Reserve Bank from the forward exchange market. The 'forward rate' is the exchange rate today for settlement later, and reflects the difference between the interest rates paid on deposits in the currencies over the period. With the withdrawal of the Reserve Bank from this market, traders would acquire pricing experience and be able, to a limited extent, to hold net positions in foreign exchange.

On 18 October Stone again minuted Keating on the exchange rate management system before meeting with him. He supplied details of the 'evolutionary steps' proposed two days before. The minutes make it clear that Treasury supported and in fact proposed – though of course as an alternative to a bigger change – the freeing of spot against forward, which had been proposed by the Reserve Bank a year before. (The spot rate is that exchange rate at the present time.) The attachment explained that the proposed changes were aimed at 'developing the market in foreign exchange' and 'loosening up the exchange rate'.

It noted that because the rate is set at 9.30 a.m., speculators can take foreign exchange positions during the day based on Asian market developments, which give a clue to the Reserve Bank of Australia's setting the following morning. It recommended that the exchange rate be set later in the day (12.30), that the spread be widened, and that the Bank be allowed to withdraw from the official forward market. It noted that 'floating the forward rate would increase pressures on the spot rate to be flexible, and it would be more difficult for the authorities to insulate that spot rate from swings in the market sentiment'.

Towards the end of October the principal players gathered together in the Reserve Bank building in Canberra. The meeting was chaired by Keating. Those present included Johnston, Phillips, Stone, Treasury officials Des Moore, Bob Whitelaw and Ted Evans, and Keating's private secretary Tony Cole. Garnaut came from Hawke's office, but the Prime Minister did not attend. According to Cole's recollection, Keating and Johnston were ready to decide on a float at that meeting, and Garnaut would presumably have advised of Hawke's support. Stone very strongly objected, however, and he was supported by Des Moore and Bob Whitelaw. Following his minute Stone argued that the case for a float had not been documented and that its consequences could include a dramatic increase in the value of the Australian dollar, which would harm export industries. He also argued that Australian foreign exchange traders needed more experience, and they would get it if the forward rate was floated while the spot rate remained under government control. Keating was not happy with the decision.

Keating recalled:

We were prepared to do it in October when we floated the forward rate, but Stone was dead lemony. He said it would tear the place apart, and the rate would be appreciated substantially. He would say we are just a small country and we will be bobbed around like a cork on the ocean. It's not so easy to do it and be assured of the outcome when the principal Treasury officer is saying that. He might let it be known what his attitude was, and you are in

trouble with the markets. This was at the RBA in Canberra. On the foot-
path outside I said to him, 'That's the last time you stand me up on this.
Between now and the next run you will have to get accommodated to the idea,
because we are going to float.' He said he wasn't sure there would be another
run, and we should wait and see how the current measures worked.

The decision to float the forward rate was then endorsed on 27 October in a meeting in Hawke's office, which included Keating and Stone
but not the Reserve Bank officials.[4] The following day, 28 October,
Hawke announced in a speech to the Merchant Bankers' Association
in Melbourne that the forward rate was now free and that exchange
positions would be settled only once, in the evening, so that the dollar price could be set by the market during the day. These two decisions put pressure on the fixed spot because they allowed the market
to lead and could in some circumstances compel the Bank to follow.

Stone's front within Treasury was collapsing. Keating went to a
Treasury meeting that included Stone, Ted Evans and other officials.
Keating said he knew they were all opposed to him on the float. This
was the kind of direct and flat preliminary to which his officials were
now only slowly becoming accustomed. Ted Evans was an official
with a quiet, almost whispering, voice and a calculatedly modest presence, and was not only a close friend of Stone's but also his ally in
a decade of difficult battles. He now remarked in that whispering
but absolutely distinct way, an unemphatic but quite final statement that arrested the meeting into sudden silence, 'I support you,
Treasurer.'

Stone enjoyed a joust within the department, but it was one thing
to joust within the department and quite another to break the solid
unity of the Treasury Line, to demonstrate before the Treasurer himself that his officials had different opinions. A demonstration like
this might encourage the Treasurer to persist with his own opinion,
and Stone rapidly said that that might be Ted's opinion, but it was
not Treasury opinion: Ted did not speak for Treasury. John Stone had
changed with the years; his tolerance had diminished, and in that
simple exchange he buried a decade of friendship and battles fought

together. At no time had it been suggested that Ted Evans' opinions were not also those of Treasury. Keating paused and went on. 'There would be nothing easier than to overrule you,' he told Stone, 'nothing easier than to tell you I want to float. But I want your support. I want you to come on board. I want to persuade you. I could roll you. Nothing easier than to roll you. But I don't want that. I want to take you with me. I want you to support it.'

He wanted to persuade him not least because Keating still believed in Stone's power. He still believed his was the voice that was listened to in Morgan Stanley and the Chase Manhattan Bank, and that these banks determined the views of the New York financial community. The New York financial community deeply influenced the level of foreign investment in Australia and the value of the Australian dollar.

Losing the float argument, Stone switched his focus to preserving exchange controls. Since exchange controls would allow the government to monitor and at times slow down or prevent large purchases and sales of Australian dollars, exchange controls would allow Reserve Bank intervention on the foreign exchange market to be far more effective than it would otherwise be. But the foreign exchange market would not be as deep or free as it could be without exchange controls, and companies could not be as confident about their ability to borrow or lend in foreign currencies. Companies that evaded exchange controls would continue to be rewarded. Those that went by the book would continue to be penalised.

Keating and Treasury expected that the capital inflow of November and early December would reverse itself, but instead it increased. The system survived through November, but by the beginning of December it was threatened by another great wash of money.

The crisis came on the evening of Thursday 8 December when the Reserve Bank was told by its New York office that another large inflow would be arriving the next day. Altogether $1.5 billion would arrive in the first nine days of the month, adding a full 2 per cent to the money growth rate, which was already above the 9 to 11 per cent target. Stone, Keating and Johnston were on the phone all afternoon. Stone said they should stare it down.

At a dinner meeting in Hawke's office, attended by Hawke, Keating, Visbord, Garnaut, and Hawke staffers Peter Barron and Graham Evans, there was unanimity that the government should float the dollar. To float, however, would mean closing the Australian foreign exchange markets on Friday and putting the new arrangements in place over the weekend. It was not until late in the evening that Keating was convinced in conversation with Johnston that the timing was right. At the same time he sounded out key ministers, including Bill Hayden and Ralph Willis, to test the response of Cabinet to a decision to float. According to Hawke and his advisers, Hawke's political adviser Peter Barron was sent down at midnight to tell Keating to call Johnston and close the exchange. Keating and Cole do not recall this visit, and Keating points out that it would have been very unusual and offensive to send an adviser to instruct a senior minister on a matter of great weight.

Keating called Johnston at 1.30 am and asked him to close the foreign exchange market on Friday and come to Canberra, bringing the black plastic folder, which was the 'War Book'. Keating recalled, 'I called Bob and I said, "Close it down. Call the banks and tell them you want square the positions tomorrow." He said, "You realise this means we have to float?" I said, "Yes, I do. I think you'll have to do Stone over again." '

He, Sanders and Phillips flew to Canberra early on Friday morning. With the exchange closed a float was unavoidable, but the issue of whether or not capital controls should be retained had not been determined.

Johnston saw Keating alone. He told him the Reserve Bank board had met on Wednesday, and it was greatly concerned about the flow of funds into Australia. The alternatives were tighter exchange controls or no exchange controls. Johnston said the board did not like the idea of tighter controls. Sanders and Phillips were then called in, and they supported Johnston.

By 10 a.m. they were all gathered together in Hawke's office. The meeting included Stone, Dick Rye, Garnaut, the Department of Prime Minister and Cabinet's economist Ed Visbord, Graham Evans, Keating, Tony Cole, Barry Hughes and Reserve Bank officials Bob Johnston, John Phillips and Don Sanders. While the decision to float had effectively been taken, the decision to drop capital controls had not necessarily been foreclosed. Certainly, Stone told the meeting, the decision on exchange controls could be postponed until Treasury could present written submissions. 'I didn't learn much as a public servant,' Stone would later say, 'but I did find out that ministers should know what they were doing. They didn't know what could happen on exchange controls. No papers went to them on the subject.'

To Stone the impending decision to drop capital controls resembled in every way by the Whitlam Government's decision in July 1973 to cut tariffs by 25 per cent, a decision that had also outraged him, not because he objected to tariff cuts but because it had not been taken with Treasury advice and Treasury support or with all the studies he believed necessary for decisions of such magnitude. The decision to float and drop capital controls, he told the group, would be far greater in its political impact that the tariff cut, which he did not need to remind Hawke or Keating had been one of the reasons Labor had lost Bass by a landslide in 1975, a loss that had encouraged the newly elected Opposition Leader Malcolm Fraser to force the government to a general election by refusing it finance in the Senate. But for Stone's audience it was as if the world had been turned on its head and the great defender of economic rationality was its strongest critic. There was no one now in that room other than Stone who complained about the 25 per cent tariff cut – it was, after all, the decision that accounted for almost all of the reduction in protection for Australian industry of the last fifteen years. They liked the 25 per cent cut. It was one of the few things they admired Whitlam for doing. Stone's mention of it reminded them that he had opposed that as he now opposed the float, and they were not at all bothered.

Stone argued that the Australian currency was a small proportion of the world's tradeable money supply, so a float would be subject to manipulation by a small number of dealers. He also predicted the currency would appreciate, and cause unemployment and hurt exports. He would be surprised, he said, if the dollar did not rise to 95 US cents. He argued that if exchange controls were to be abolished, the government should follow proper procedures, with Cabinet submissions in the normal way.

In reply, Johnston was scathing. In the last nine days the reins had been handed to Stone as Johnston had declined responsibility for a system they now thought unworkable. Alone, Stone had decided to stare down the inflow by actually lowering the rate. 'For the last nine days,' said Johnston, 'we have made asses of ourselves.' He argued that a float could not operate successfully with exchange controls, and that under present arrangements the Reserve Bank could not effectively carry out monetary policy. He said interest rates had been pushed lower to deter capital inflow, but they were unsustainably low. The current system was clearly not working so speculation would continue. He said that no one knew where the dollar would go after the float, but that any appreciation reached by the market after the float would be less than the appreciation the government would need to impose to deter further capital inflow. Phillips predicted that in time the dollar would depreciate. (Over the next few months the dollar rose to 93 US cents, then began to fall. Phillips was right.)

Hawke summarised. He thought the country should float and drop controls, and the economic committee of Cabinet would be called together for the final decision.

None of the participants making the decision to float had a clear idea of its consequences. There were no studies predicting its effect, and indeed its effect could not have been predicted except as a lucky guess – there were far too many variables in play. Stone's complaint that there were no high-quality studies of the issues was quite right – the quality of the papers provided by the Reserve Bank to Keating was very poor, and for its part Treasury contributed very little beyond a list of Stone's objections.

Keating would later say that he was aware of what the decision would come to mean for the government's wages policy and for the indexation formulas agreed by the government and the trade unions, but this does not seem credible since the wage agreements would only be powerfully affected by a major depreciation. A depreciation big enough to affect wages would also be one that would express itself, one way or another, without a float.

The float did, however, mean that currency depreciation, when it began thirteen months later, was resisted much less than it would have been under the old system. Using wage–tax trade-offs, Keating and the ACTU were able to keep wages growth low after the depreciation, allowing Australia's international competitiveness to increase dramatically.

The removal of exchange controls, which was part of the float and an essential element in removing official control over the rate, might well have been one of the factors assisting Australian corporations and banks to expand their overseas borrowings greatly later in the decade. Some of this borrowing financed the overseas expansion of Australian industry, which increased its global orientation. Some of it added to Australian savings to allow a higher level of domestic investment. The increased borrowing was represented by the higher current account deficit, which by the mid 1980s had become the most difficult issue for economic management.

But the most significant impact in the short term, the one immediately noticed and welcomed by commentators, was that the value of the Australian dollar could be immediately and dramatically influenced by the views of participants in the foreign exchange market. This essentially theatrical effect was to become one of the important influences on the pace of economic reform. Dollar depreciations and the threat of them were widely, though inaccurately, interpreted as signals of falling confidence in Australian economic management. The response of the foreign exchange market became an important discipline on the government spending of ministers and on the ACTU, a discipline that Keating welcomed and dramatised.

Prime Minister Keating would say that his biggest achievement in politics – the thing he was most proud of – was the internationalising of the Australian economy. Most of that – the entry of foreign banks, two sets of tariff cuts – was still to come, but the abolition of exchange controls and the float of the dollar were the decisions that sped it along.

Perhaps the most important long-term result of the float, one that Stone attempted to prevent, was that the Reserve Bank became increasingly independent of Treasury. Stone and his Canberra colleagues were no longer determining a rate that the Reserve Bank would implement. In a little more than a year money supply targets were also dropped, which took Treasury out of monetary policy formulation except as a junior partner to the Reserve Bank. Keating's relationship to the Bank became stronger and more direct as the Bank itself came out from under the Treasury wing. Though Keating was criticised later for influencing Bank decisions – and he certainly did, and believed he should – the float and the later dropping of money supply targets made the Reserve Bank a far more powerful and independent institution under Keating than it had been at any time in the past.

Within the Labor Caucus the float represented a bigger break with their expectations of a Labor government than the earlier decision to adopt a deficit target of $8.5 billion. The Left was particularly displeased. On 20 December Brian Howe, then Minister for Defence Support, wrote to all members of the Caucus Economic Committee stating that the decision was in direct conflict with the party platform. In terms almost identical to those of John Stone he complained of undue 'reliance on international market forces', which might 'exacerbate the trend towards foreign control of the Australian economy'. He believed the dollar would move up and that upward movements in the dollar would have serious implications for Australian manufacturing. He warned that the party would need to give careful consideration to implications of allowing foreign banks access to Australian financial system. He concluded:

> It is difficult not to see this recent decision is at least as risky as the 25 per cent cut in tariffs decision taken by the Whitlam Government. It would appear that on that occasion there was only minimal debate in the government.

Both Hawke and Keating have claimed principal credit for the float. There is no doubt that both supported it. Hawke presents the meeting in his office on 27 October and the meeting on 8 December as part of a story in which he continued to press a reluctant Keating towards the float. According to Tony Cole, who participated in many of the key meetings from early in the year, 'There were a series of meetings on the general topic which preceded the 28 October and 9 December announcements. I think it is fair to say that both the Treasurer and the Prime Minister had decided a float was on prior to 28 October – from then on it was only a matter of when the circumstances were right'. There is no doubt Keating and Hawke agreed, and also no doubt that it was not only Keating who was concerned about the opposition of Stone. Cole recalls:

> We tried for a float in October, but neither Keating nor Hawke wanted a float over the dead body of John Stone and Des Moore. We couldn't even get Bobbie Whitelaw to support it. In October when we floated the forward rate there was an acceptance that the float would have to occur. We had in mind December or January, when the markets would be quiet. The discussion was always over whether you could get Stone on board or do it without him.[4]

Hawke's account also ignores the role of the Reserve Bank, and particularly of Bob Johnston. Without Johnston's active encouragement it would have been extremely difficult to float. His version also omits to mention that Keating and Johnston had agreed on the desirability of a float quite early in 1983, and that they – and not the Prime Minister – bore the official responsibility for the management of the currency.

Keating discussed it with Johnston quite early and indicated he was in favour of changing the system. The Bank had supplied material bearing on this as early as July. There is no doubt that by October Keating was vigorously pushing for a float. Equally, however, there is no doubt that he was bothered by Stone's refusal to agree, took great pains to persuade him to agree, and allowed Stone's opposition to postpone the float when it was first proposed in October. As a result the float occurred six weeks later than it otherwise might have. The delay, however, was insignificant in the context of a decision of such magnitude.

The float was the big decision of 1983, symbolically if not actually the transforming decision of the Australian economy in the 1980s. Keating had opposed Stone's view, and events showed that Stone was wrong. He had been encouraged by Hawke but took public credit for the decision. Following the float Keating would be more independent of both Hawke and Stone.

8

RUNNING THE COUNTRY

KEATING WAS MORE COMFORTABLE in the job by the end of 1983, though by no means as confident as he would become a few years later. He was developing an easy relationship with Reserve Bank Governor Bob Johnston, but was beginning to suspect that John Stone's powerful intellect and readiness to entertain debate concealed a deep, stubborn and unreasoning conservatism. He was getting to know and enjoy the company of Ted Evans, David Morgan and other Treasury officials. He liked Treasury. He thought it was intellectually a very powerful department, which stimulated and entertained him, and from which he had much to learn.

For its part, Treasury warmed to their new minister. Because he liked it, because he was victorious in Cabinet and caucus, because he was energetic and got things done, because by and large he agreed with it, Treasury liked him more than they had liked either Phillip Lynch or John Howard, or perhaps even Bill Hayden. Stone evidently thought of him as a politician with real potential, if he were properly guided. There were, however, differences between them. Stone and Keating had agreed about the need for a lower deficit, but not how much lower. They were both pessimistic about the Accord, but Stone was much more pessimistic than Keating. 'Since the Government came to office,' he had written to the Treasurer in mid September 1983, 'the pressures on ministers, and on you particularly, have hardly slackened for a day. You have, so to speak, been running flat out the whole time. So, as you know, have we.'

Treasury had wanted a 'substantially lower' deficit, Stone reminded the Treasurer, and it was important now to resist any pressures to increase a deficit that was already too high. He told Keating he opposed indexation of wages, that it was quite out of place to be concerned that policies were too tight when the money supply target might not be achieved with current settings. Stone's view was that the Treasurer needed to resist pressures for a 'softer' exchange rate and instead conduct monetary policy to achieve the money supply target, for genuine recovery continued to depend on winding back the deficit. The broad elements of a medium-term strategy, he believed, should be reducing the structural budget deficit, keeping firm monetary conditions, an exchange rate policy 'not over-dominated by considerations of short-run "competitiveness"', and increased flexibility in the economy – for example, by reducing tariffs.

By the end of 1983 Keating was no longer too bothered by Stone's homilies. After fourteen years of backbench or opposition politics he was now, as he would say, running the country. Certainly the Prime Minister was the more dominant figure, but Keating was even then unquestionably the second most significant and influential person in the government. Only Hayden could dispute his claims, but Hayden agreed with him most of the time, and was in any case often travelling abroad.

Keating had learned a great deal in a short time. With the Prime Minister's strong support he had successfully persuaded his Cabinet colleagues and caucus to accept a deficit of around $8. 5 billion rather than $10 billion or $15 billion. His opponents had said the recession would be deepened or prolonged, but Keating was reasonably confident now that the economy was growing quite strongly and that the growth would continue. He had been less than warm to the Accord, but he was now finding that it had solid foundations. He had been in favour of floating the dollar and dropping exchange controls, despite the opposition of Treasury. He was now discovering that the float was widely welcomed and appeared to be successful. Stone had been wrong and he had been right.

Though the summit, the Budget, the Accord and the float had

increased the Treasurer's confidence and the regard of his Cabinet colleagues, he was still obliged then to consult his colleagues closely in most important actions. 'They didn't trust me,' he recalled in 1991. 'I was too pro-market.' He reported to the Economic Committee of Cabinet. He had to report to the caucus Economic Committee. He briefed meetings of the Economic Planning and Advisory Council (EPAC). 'We had a very formal system,' he said. 'I spent a lot of time on it. I consulted my head off.'

He was also beginning to find himself drifting further and further from the thought patterns of his factional base. Hawke still had much to teach him, and he continued to charm the Prime Minister. But other bright and contemporary spirits were in different factions, or none at all. They were forming a group within the ministry that would sustain economic reforms to come. He liked John Dawkins, who was in the Centre Left and who, as Finance Minister, was already Keating's reliable ally in disciplining the spending ministers. He liked Peter Walsh, a Cabinet member and Minister for Resources and Energy, and who was a good antidote to the fatuous conventionality of many of his other colleagues. He liked Bill Hayden, though he was wary of Hayden's brooding bitterness against Hawke. With some reservations he admired John Button, the Industry Minister. In a way, he later reflected, he had actually changed factions and was conceptually in his own faction, which now included Labor's industrial leader, ACTU Secretary Bill Kelty. He was in the Right only when it came to voting, which for the Right was all that really mattered. Graham Richardson was now in Canberra, and Keating was quite happy to leave all matters connected with organising the NSW Centre Unity faction to him. Graham, he thought, was basically a party general secretary type, a good comrade in the trenches but fundamentally a B-grader. For his part Keating was scaling mountains.

In January 1984 Keating turned 40. He was still a young man and looked young. In the photographs of the time Keating is still sharp-featured and angular. The pouches under his eyes were not pronounced. His son and oldest child, Patrick, was still a child. 'It ages you,' he marvelled, looking back eight years later. His family life was now easier. Annita and the children had come to live with him in Canberra. He did not enjoy the city very much, but it was quite good for young children, and at least they were together more often than they had been when he was flying home to Bankstown on Friday night or Saturday afternoon and returning to Canberra on Sunday night. Annita had not found life on Gerard Avenue sustaining or easy. She had not really enjoyed immersing her life in that of his family two doors distant. In Canberra they saw very few people. Paul did not enjoy mixing with other ministers on weekends, and it was hard to have private friendships with public servants, whose careers could be influenced by the access they enjoyed with a minister. He had always liked people who broke the mould. But they did not need dinner parties or barbeques. Paul was often working, often at unpredictable and unsociable hours. He preferred to keep weekends free, although not very successfully in those early years in the job. If he was free they could take the kids to Weston Park on the shore of Lake Burley Griffin, where they swung on the bars or rode on the little train. They could drive out to Tidbinbilla Nature Reserve, where the kids would watch the kangaroos and emus, and try to spy reclusive koalas high in the gum trees. Paul went shopping in the Fyshwick market on Saturday mornings, carrying the vegetables in a carton to the car. He browsed the record shops. He listened to music and read antiques catalogues. He travelled a lot, often on a VIP flight, and Annita could visit Sydney or Melbourne with the children if Canberra was too cheerless.

They did see the Hawkes from time to time. Annita and Hazel were now friends. Bob and Paul worked together closely, and were as close as perhaps it is possible to be in politics. 'As far as one can have a "good mates" relationship in politics I think Bob and I have it,' Keating told Michelle Grattan.[1] Speaking to Paul Kelly in mid December 1983 about his relationship with Hawke, he said, 'Fortunately we do see eye to eye on almost everything and, if any sense of kinship is important in this, then I think the Prime Minister would agree with me that we finished the year with a closer, stronger relationship than we started out.' Keating was close to Hawke, though he was also getting his measure. His relationship with Hawke was reasonably comfortable. Both men knew that Keating was young enough to spend many years at Treasury before succeeding Hawke, and that his work as Treasurer gave him a strong claim on the job. Keating thought then and later that the work he did as Treasurer was likely to be more important than the work he could or would do as Prime Minister.

His closest and most cheerful relationships after his family were with his office staff. In Tony Cole as his principal private secretary, Greg Smith as a tax adviser, Barbara Ward and Barry Hughes, he was discovering that he had a talented staff whom he could inspire with loyalty and affection. They were not friendships, because they could not really be equals. But they were easy relationships because they could not be rivals. Keating was charming to his staff, and he had a way of treating people equally and with complete conviction and sincerity. John Howard preferred to be addressed as 'Mister' (an instruction obeyed by everyone on his staff except Gerard Henderson, whom Howard did not care to correct.) In Keating's office they were all on first name terms. Some staff members called him 'mate'. He sought their views, listened intently and often did as they suggested. If they wrote a speech, he would correct it if necessary, but he would not think up silly quibbles just to show he was in charge. He encouraged his staff to assert themselves, to enlarge their interests and to exercise power. He celebrated their birthdays, their arrivals and departures. He made little speeches on all these formal occasions about the difficulties of working under such pressure as they did, and how he was grateful to them and depended on them, and that they were a team. He said he thought of himself as really just another member of the office, and he acted like it. His staff were soon reputed around the press gallery and other offices to be extremely loyal to their minister – something that was less common than one might expect. Inside the office people generally talked freely, and there were not many constraints on what one could see or read. But outside the office the staff did not gossip about the Treasurer or the office. There were fights, of course; there is no love lost among courtiers. Sometimes he would hear screams, shouts, howls of outrage. Paul would close the door and pretend not to notice. 'I just don't know,' he would say, as equable Matt might have said, 'I don't know what's going on out there.'

It was a good office. It hummed. In former years the private secretary provided by Treasury had been there to handle the paper flow. Old hands could remember how the minister's private secretary would wait on the Treasury Secretary, Sir Frederick Wheeler, on a Friday afternoon to give a complete account of all the minister had been up to that week. Tony Cole was Stone's recommendation, but soon his loyalty was to Keating. Barbara Ward was a smart and adroit adviser, completely familiar with the key ministers and their advisers and the way in which the Labor Party worked. For the first year Barry Hughes was a little out of things, but helpful in countering Treasury's criticisms of the Accord and of the ACTU and in slowly bringing Keating around to see the Accord as an important and distinctive tool of policy. In Greg Smith, a young, subdued adviser who came to the party in Opposition and stayed in Government, Keating found what he would later say was a genius. Smith's understanding of the complexities of tax issues, his ability to relate the accountancy approach of tax administration to economic policy and to political needs, and then to think up ways in which the whole could be rearranged, was quite astonishing. (Later in Treasury when Smith created Australia's tax imputation system, ordinarily dry colleagues would describe it simply as 'beautiful'.)

Reporters followed Keating closely. He talked cleverly and vividly. When he wanted to be, he was quite dazzlingly candid. He thought in terms of columns and news stories. One close contact in the gallery was Paul Kelly, then the political reporter for the *Sydney Morning Herald*. Reviewing the Treasurer's year towards the middle of December,[2] he recalled that in March Keating 'stood at the bottom of a very steep mountain that he had to climb quickly. Today . . . Keating can pause a fair distance up the incline having caught his second wind after hacking his own path to the top.' Willis had been Keating's chief opponent, wanting a bigger deficit than $8. 5 million and not liking the float, but Keating had 'carefully cultivated first Bob Hawke and then the senior ministers and easily won the approval of the Hawke cabinet.' He had won against Stone and against the ideology of the Labor Party. Kelly added percipiently, 'By floating the exchange rate, Keating has opened the window to international pressures on Australia and, when it comes to decision making, on the Hawke cabinet . . . the move to internationalise the economy makes the application of the expansionary policies of the Labor left both incongruous and more politically dangerous than ever.' Keating told Kelly that he had learned 'how the linkages operate'.

By the beginning of 1984 Keating claimed recovery from recession as his most important achievement. The recovery itself, however, would have happened anyway. As Treasury would say, the important thing was not recovery itself but the terms of the recovery. The way in which the economy recovered influenced to a great degree the quality of the subsequent expansion. The real achievement in economic recovery was that, with much lower wages growth, employment would increase faster than it otherwise would and inflation would be lower. With less damage done to the structure of the budget, revenues would recover more rapidly.

Things were going well and, in the opinion of Treasury, perhaps too well. Towards the end of 1983 and into 1984 officials were bothered by what they believed to be a relaxed monetary policy. Interest rates in the second half of the year fell by two percentage points, partly to counter an inflow of funds under the old exchange rate system. With the float the government had more options in setting interest rates. It was an abiding Treasury belief, one reiterated nine years later, that the most common mistake in a recovery was to loosen monetary policy too far and allow too rapid a recovery. (Statement 2 of the Budget would warn later that year, 'There is now general agreement that past errors of monetary laxity have been most damaging in the early stages of recovery.')

Just before Christmas, on 21 December 1983, Treasury minuted Keating on its worries over monetary policy. According to the minute, 'economic growth appears to have proceeded – and to be continuing – at rates rather higher than expected at Budget time,' and therefore ' . . . the risks that economic recovery could be aborted by an over-rapid pick-up are now somewhat greater than at budget time.' The money growth target should be kept, which meant 'a marked tightening of liquidity conditions in the near future.' Interest rates rose to March 1984, then reached a plateau until the following year.

Certainly the deficit should fall as the recovery proceeded. On 23 March Keating told Cabinet in a submission marking the beginning of the 1984 Budget cycle that the economic outlook was pretty good. By the end of the current year unemployment should have fallen back to 9 per cent. Consumer price inflation would be down to 6 per cent. Consumer spending was responding more strongly than forecast at Budget time, but a recovery in business investment was required if the expansion was to be sustained. The big threat was that the Budget deficit would push up interest rates and the exchange rate, discouraging investment. The goal, then, should be a deficit less than the $8. 5 billion expected for the year ending 30 June. It was 'imperative' that there be income tax cuts, which meant spending cuts. Ministers had agreed to a goal of cutting $1 billion off the forward estimates for programs in 1984–85.

Keating's forecasts of a stronger recovery were confirmed six days later on 29 March, when the national accounts data for the December quarter of 1983 were released. Keating told parliament that a 'stunning' turnaround had been achieved, laying the ground for a 'true recovery'.

Pleased by applause for the float, Keating steadily enhanced his control over economic policy. Inevitably this meant diminishing John Stone's control. The conflict between the two was quite well disguised, but certainly the greatest challenge to Keating's authority as Treasurer in his first two years of office came from Stone rather than

Hawke or Hawke's departmental or office advisers. Forecasts for the economy were often central to debates over policy decisions, but neither the Treasurer nor the government generally were able to participate in formulating them. They were drawn up by a committee of government officials, dominated by Treasury. To the extent that Treasury could without serious contest control the official government forecasts, it could control policy decisions. This was not only because the forecasts themselves often implied certain policy decisions or excluded other policy decisions, but also because the process of formulating forecasts gave Treasury officials a fluency and authority with economic data that other contestants in the policy game could not emulate. Keating's natural impulse was to break up this monopoly and increase the number of informed contestants within his own circle of authority. With a more open (but still internal) debate he would be likely to have more policy choices and more freedom to move.

His opportunity to move came early in 1984. On 9 March Ted Evans had reported to the Treasurer on the outcome of the National Income Forecasting Committee (NIFC) meeting of 17 February. The recovery was radically stronger than Treasury had expected. Evans wrote soberly, '. . . the outlook for activity and employment in 1983–84 is significantly more favourable than was expected at Budget time; the outlook for inflation is basically unchanged.' Non-farm growth in 1983–84 was now forecast at 4 per cent, twice the Budget-time estimate of 2 per cent. The farm sector was recovering too, so 'GDP is expected to grow by around 5½ per cent, about 2½ per cent above the Budget forecast.' The growth of employment through the course of 1983–84 could be 3 per cent, about twice what was expected at Budget time. Next year, however, the rapid rate of growth 'is likely to slow'. Still, non-farm product growth was likely to be 4½ per cent and GDP 4 per cent. Dwelling investment would slow, and private business investment was expected to remain flat.

The covering letter did not report on the current account, which did not attract policy interest at the beginning of 1984. The NIFC forecast a current account deficit of $6 billion, or 3 per cent of GDP, compared to $5.4 billion in 1983–84 (also 3 per cent) and 6.3 billion in 1982–83 (4 per cent of GDP).

The Treasury forecasts annoyed Barry Hughes. He argued that the NIFC appeared to predict the recovery petering out by the June quarter of 1985 as stockbuilding ceased and imports increased. Hughes wrote, '. . . while there are good grounds for expecting a pronounced slowdown in the rate of recovery during 1984–85, there is a strong suspicion that NIFC has overstated the relapse.' Hughes believed that imports would not grow as rapidly as NIFC suggested, so the net export contribution would be greater. Hughes called the value of the whole NIFC process into question, leading to the suggestion that, as the Treasurer's adviser, he himself should sit in on the meetings that produced the forecasts. This would provoke an important clash with Stone.

By the end of May the simmering dispute over the make-up of the NIFC boiled over into an exchange of terse minutes. Stone refused to invite Hughes to participate in the NIFC. Keating responded by insisting that the NIFC be reconstituted as a formal interdepartmental committee, with his office represented.

According to a note from Stone, Keating had raised the issue on 16 April, when Stone was on leave. He had since discussed it twice with Stone, once in Paris on the evening of 2 May. The most that Stone was prepared to do, in a note to Keating on 29 May, was to provide Hughes with 'all the relevant documentation'.

'As you know,' Stone wrote, 'we (and I in particular) have never had much faith in forecasting. Not infrequently, our forecasts turn out to be seriously wrong . . . We simply do the best we can, in as professional a manner as we can – and, if it is any consolation, no one seems to be able to do any better, at least over the long haul. We always emphasise the uncertainties that attach to the forecasts – but we cannot ensure that such qualifications are heeded, and plainly they often are not.'

On 13 June Keating replied in writing to Stone. He said that his difficulties with recent Treasury forecasts do not relate to 'their not being "appropriate" for example for publication, but to whether they are believable . . . '. He could not accept Treasury advice based on assessments with which he disagreed. The forward estimates had included a 9 per cent forecast for the deflator. Keating continued:

> While I have no intention of seeking publication of unrealistically optimistic forecasts, I am also not prepared to see the confidence this government has nursed back into the economy dashed by excessively pessimistic prognostications from Treasury.
>
> I should also make it clear that my difficulties with Treasury forecasts began prior to my receipt of the February 1984 forecasts. You might recall that at Budget time last year I (and the Prime Minister) expressed doubts about the employment, unemployment and benefit recipients numbers for 1983–84. My staff also queried the pessimistic discussion of the interest rate outlook contained in the drafts of Statement 2 and the very small increase projected for private investment in housing. While we did not make an issue of it, in November we also thought the downward reduction in forecast private consumption rather odd and did not believe the continued prediction of an increase in unemployment over the year. I think my rather more optimistic view of the overall progress of the recovery was made clear to the department during our disagreement over the revision of the M3 projection.

He added that Hughes should be there to contribute his expertise and to better prepare him to explain the forecasts to the Treasurer.

Keating said he was inclined to the fifth option presented by Stone: the NIFC to be replaced by an interdepartmental committee, with composition to be determined by the Treasurer. He wrote, 'It is a fact of life that governments today stand or fall on the strength of their economic management. Accordingly it seems somewhat anachronistic that the major government forecasting effort remains an informally organised Treasury department affair.'

Over Stone's continuing objections the National Income Forecasting Committee was reconstituted as a formal interdepartmental group including representatives from Treasury, Finance, Prime Minister and Cabinet and the Reserve Bank. An adviser from the Treasurer's office had the right to attend meetings.

Keating was developing an agenda of things he wanted to do in 1984 and 1985. The Martin Committee was soon to report on financial deregulation. Keating wanted to admit foreign banks and if possible increase the number of Australian banks. He wanted to remove the remaining controls on interest rates and loans. He had decided when he was Shadow Minerals and Energy Minister that tariffs were bad for Australian industry. At some time he wanted to do something about them. Since first coming into Parliament fourteen years before he had argued that the income tax rates were too high. He knew they could be lowered only by a dramatic cut in government spending, which he did not want, or by cutting out exemptions to income tax like capital gains and fringe benefits, or by increasing sales taxes. Major reform was required. Treasury continued to press for action to reduce 'structural flaws' that would make the high deficit persist in the recovery. Both he and Treasury agreed that inflation was too high. The introduction of Medicare produced a one-off reduction in the consumer price index, which now gave less weight to private medical costs. Wage indexation increases would accordingly be less, providing an opportunity for a sustained fall in inflation in 1984. Suddenly, the Accord appeared to be a means not only of managing inflation but also of obtaining a significant fall in it.

Now convinced of its value, Keating's economic strategy was increasingly based on exploiting the possibilities of the Accord with the ACTU. If the Accord always increased wages to compensate for price increases, high inflation would persist. But if the ACTU could be persuaded to accept income tax cuts as substitutes for wage increases, then costs would fall, and so should inflation. To pay for tax cuts Cabinet would have to keep spending under control, which would, over time, reduce the size of the government sector.

On 12 May 1984 Keating explained this approach to a meeting of the full ministry. There had been considerable success over the last year, he said. Inflation had fallen to 7.6 per cent in year to March 1984 compared to 11.5 per cent the year before. The 'underlying' rate, which excluded temporary influences, was under 5 per cent. Between April 1983 and May 1984 there had been a growth of 3.7 per cent in employment, a total of 234 000 jobs to date. Already Labor was half way to its three-year target of 500 000 additional jobs. The first year, he said, had been 'a startling performance'.

Inflation, employment and growth remained the objectives in which Labor must make progress. The first year's growth was based on temporary influences, including the fiscal stimulus, housing, the end of the drought, stock rebuilding, exports and higher consumption. These would need to be replaced by permanent influences. 'To sustain momentum and give us a good level of growth will require business investment to pick up,' he said. 'Our aim must be to convert the pick-up into a sustained economic recovery with spending and investment taking over the fiscal stimulus and other elements of this year.'

It was 'so far, so good,' but 'now comes Labor's historic opportunity.' There was an opportunity to break the back of inflation through the wage pause of the year before and the effect of Medicare in reducing the CPI in 1984. 'Our whole strategy now turns on maintaining the Medicare effect,' Keating emphasised. In turn this meant tax cuts in the next Budget to compensate for a real wage cut. 'No one can question the need for a tax cut,' he said. 'If we can keep inflation down we'll get spending and investment up.'

Two days later, on 16 May, in a statement on Economic Policy and the Accord, Keating outlined publicly a strategy he had outlined to the ministry. By using the Medicare effect and substituting tax cuts for some part of wage indexation increases, the Accord would become the principle instrument for reducing inflation.

The Treasurer shared responsibility for Accord negotiations with the Minister for Industrial Relations (Ralph Willis), but as time went on Keating's role became more and more dominant. This was partly because only the Treasurer could offer tax cuts or spending increases on social welfare, and partly because Kelty liked Keating more and more and Willis less and less. It was a question of personal sympathy. Keating and Kelty were large and imaginative; Willis, who had many good qualities, was cautious, prosaic and never enthusiastic.

The wage–tax tradeoff at the heart of the Accord negotiations was not a new idea. It had been put forward in the 1970s, and not for the first time. However, it was the degree of refinement attained by Keating and Kelty in its implementation that was novel. Over the years of the Accord negotiations the tax cuts purported to be offered in return for wage increases supposedly foregone were rarely more than the additional income tax flowing to the government as a result of past wage increases.

In the agreement reached at the time of the 1984 Budget, Keating was the primary player for the government. It was Keating who told Kelty in general terms how much would be available for tax cuts. The ACTU then put forward a proposal on how they should be distributed. This was interpreted by the press as 'The ACTU's $1.3 billion Tax Cut Package', which in a sense it was.[3] The agreement was reached when Keating, with Treasury officials Bernie Fraser, Tony Cole and Greg Smith, went down to discuss them with the ACTU in Melbourne on the night of Monday 23 July, running them through a tax model on the spot to find a distribution that matched the amount available. The result in this instance was a cut of $7.60 a week for wage-earners on incomes from $240 to $520 a week, at a cost of $1.3 billion.

The tax cuts were the key to the Budget delivered on the night of Tuesday 21 August. 'Tax cuts all round as Hawke gears up for an early election,' headlined the *Australian* the following morning, reporting the personal income tax cuts, extended investment allowance for business, pension increases and a big cut in the projected deficit to $6.74 billion (down $1.21 billion), all financed from an expected 23 per cent increase in tax revenue mainly from economic recovery.

Defeated on the float and the elimination of capital controls, unhappy with the centrality of the Accord and of wage indexation, and compelled to give up control of economic forecasting, Stone prepared to leave. The policy differences were now irreconcilable, and in their final clash Keating and Stone drew them out in a debate over the content of Statement 2.

In past years there had sometimes been tension between treasurers and the Treasury over the content of Statement 2 of the Budget papers, which offered an analysis of the economy over the past year and explained the forecasts for the coming year. Serious conflicts had occurred in the Whitlam Government and reappeared when John Howard was Treasurer. According to a telling but possibly apocryphal story told by Keating, when John Howard was Treasurer he once asked Stone how Statement 2 was shaping up. Stone had replied, 'Very well indeed, Treasurer. You'll be pleased.' By 1984 Keating was confident enough of his position to insist not only that Statement 2 reflected his own views rather than Stone's but also that it was carefully redrafted in his own office – especially in consideration of issues in the past year in which Stone and Keating had disagreed. 'It's got my name on the front, John,' Keating told the protesting Secretary. He would not allow the Secretary to rehash old disputes in the guise of commenting on the year past.

Stone had by now decided to leave and, before the Budget, went off on his last overseas tour as Secretary. On 15 August Keating would announce Stone's intended resignation, the same day that he received Stone's letter informing him of it. Considering its inherent difficulties, the relationship between the two men was surprisingly civil. The final dispute over Statement 2 was detailed in a meeting between the two, later minuted by Stone. In a difficult meeting Stone went through his proposed draft with Keating, instructing a Treasury officer accompanying him to note down all the changes insisted upon by the Treasurer. The bemused officer was Dr Don Russell, newly returned from the OECD in Paris, witnessing for the first time the unusual relationship between the rising Treasurer and the departing Secretary.

On 20 August Stone sent across a detailed minute headed, 'Statement No. 2 – Changes made at your direction'. The minute was by implication a catalogue of the policy differences between the Secretary and the Treasurer. 'The purpose of this minute,' he wrote, 'is to set down, for the record, those changes to Statement number 2 which have been made at your direction – the major ones which you conveyed personally, the lesser ones conveyed through your staff.'

The substance of the changes was virtually a list of the policy issues on which the Treasurer and his department head had disagreed over the past seventeen months. They reflected disagreements over the Accord and the float of the exchange rate, with Keating refusing to allow Stone to write Statement 2 as an implicit criticism of the government's past decisions on the float and the Accord.

Stone, for example, objected to the deletion of this paragraph from the overview section:

> The evident deterioration in the current account deficit of the balance of payments – from an already high base – is one cause for concern; another is the limited scope, within the framework of the present arrangements for wage determination, for preventing volatile exchange rate behaviour from being automatically reflected in the domestic cost structure.

He also objected to:

- cutting a reference to the removal of almost all exchange controls as 'perhaps even more important for the long run' than the float itself;
- cutting a reference to the pre-float regime as having the advantage of relieving the foreign exchange markets 'of the gyrations typical of floating exchange rates';
- cutting a statement that heavy flows across the exchanges in a managed regime happened (only) when the market held a different view from the authorities;
- the deletion of material hinting that superannuation was too expensive for employers; that there was a question whether wage rises post-pause might have been still less without the centralised increases; a criticism of the small scope for changing relativities in the Accord process;
- the deletion of the view that, 'As discussed in earlier years in this Statement, the long and variable lags with which monetary policy affects the economy suggest that monetary policy should be formulated in a medium-term context. While there is legitimate debate regarding the influence of monetary factors on the level of activity

and the rate of inflation in the short term, there is broad agreement that, over the medium term, growth of monetary aggregates is an important determinant of the rate of inflation . . . Moreover, there is now general agreement that past errors of monetary laxity have been most damaging in the early stages of recovery. That underlines the case for giving particular attention to this matter in Australia at this time';

- the deletion of the view that 'international experience testifies that foreign exchange markets can readily get out of kilter with the underlying competitive positions of economies. It follows that governments cannot completely ignore the exchange rate';

- the deletion of a statement that 'the concurrent (and in many respects more important) decision to remove virtually all exchange controls in December 1983 has locked the Australian economy more closely into the international financial system than ever before in the postwar period. The float has given the authorities much greater scope to influence domestic monetary developments, but it has also increased the need for settings of monetary policy to be – and be seen to be – appropriate. If policies are perceived to be inappropriate this will quickly be reflected in the exchange rate with potentially disruptive effects on domestic economic performance';

- deletion of a reference that the Joint Economic Forecasting Group (JEFG) be established 'at the direction of the Government';

- a deletion of a reference to JEFG assumptions not including the recent emergence of an ACTU claim for extension of superannuation schemes in 1985.

By the spring of 1984 the Treasurer could not have been more pleased. With an election likely by the end of 1984 the first phase of his job was ending. The economy had recovered. Unemployment was falling. Unions, employers and the Arbitration Commission were abiding by the terms of the Accord, to the surprise and delight of both the Treasurer and Treasury. As he had hoped, the 'Medicare effect' was helping to contain inflation. After a shaky start, the dollar was now successfully floating, and businesses were getting used to a more volatile exchange rate. John Stone had announced his intention to leave, and his successor would be much closer to Keating's way of thinking.

In the first year or so of government Keating had learned from Hawke and worked closely with him. Hawke had been much more strongly in favour of the summit and the Accord than Keating or Treasury. Keating now agreed with Hawke on the value of the Accord. Hawke and Keating had together settled on a lower deficit target in 1983 than the rest of the ministry expected. Hawke supported Keating's review of the Campbell Committee Report, which they expected would endorse its recommendations.

But in a Cabinet government of the kind that Australia has, a Prime Minister cannot lead a strong, intelligent Treasurer for very long. Key decisions need to be made or at least endorsed by Cabinet as a whole, which means that the Prime Minister cannot simply tell the Treasurer what to do. The Prime Minister has many other demands on his attention, so after a while the Treasurer has a much better grasp of the state of the economy, the agenda of policy and the attitudes of the various players in the policy game. The longer the Treasurer is in office, the stronger will be his command over economic policy. The Prime Minister, his staff and his department can talk directly to Treasury or Reserve Bank officials, but only by courtesy and only candidly when the Treasurer and the Prime Minister are not fighting. Malcolm Fraser had found it impossible to direct Treasury from the Prime Minister's Office, and by the time he left office, Treasury simply did not communicate with the Department of Prime Minister and Cabinet. When it came his turn eight years later, Keating found it quite as hard as Prime Minister to keep tabs on his treasurers as Hawke and Fraser had earlier.

Urged by his advisers and his department, Hawke sought such points of influence as he could. He continued to chair the Expenditure Review Committee, for example, which meant that his department and his office were essential to the annual budget cycle. They had to be informed of Treasury economic and budget forecasts, and their support had to be sought for or against particular programs. Presented as a way of preventing ministers from seeking to have ERC decisions overturned by Cabinet or by the Prime Minister, Hawke's role on the ERC buttressed his influence over the budget. But there were other areas where his influence was weak. Since the float, it was no longer necessary to present Cabinet with a report by the Exchange Rate Management Committee and seek a Cabinet view. More importantly, the Reserve Bank was gradually becoming more influential because its decisions on interest rates were not subsidiary to Treasury decisions on the exchange rate. Under the Fraser Government there had been a Monetary Policy Committee of Cabinet, which looked at interest rate decisions. Keating and Hawke did not continue this committee, and throughout the entire period of the Hawke and then the Keating governments there were virtually no Cabinet discussions of monetary policy. As time went on the decisions were made more and more by Keating and his officials, though Keating would always make a point of consulting Hawke about any significant decision and his staff would consult Hawke's staff. The Prime Minister sometimes queried Keating's proposed interest rate changes, but no one on his staff or in his department ever attended the Reserve Bank 'debriefings' or had access to Reserve Bank board papers. Formally and informally the Reserve Bank reported to the Treasurer. It was quite difficult for Hawke to dispute Keating's moves on monetary policy.

It had been difficult, but three or four years further on those first two years of government would seem simple, fruitful and even uncontroversial. Policy choices during a recession and recovery are relatively easy, particularly if the recession is not blamed on the government. Later in the upswing in Australia the current account deficit usually expands threateningly, there are greater inflation risks, the fiscal deficit must be brought under control, and interest rates always rise. Keating would experience all these problems for the first time during 1985, at the same time as he attempted more fundamental reforms of the structure of the economy. He wanted to tackle the task that had been too hard for the Fraser Government – taxation reform. At the same time he would find himself dealing with the first intimations of current account problems that would ultimately propel Australia back into recession.

With the Budget out of the way, the economy growing and employment increasing, Hawke was urged to call an election while the government was in a favourable position. A half-election for the Senate was due anyway. Without a simultaneous poll for the House, an election for the upper chamber could become a protest vote against the government. Keating had objected. He wanted to run the full three years, using 1985 to accomplish some of the changes that could not fit in the first eighteen months. Already, he privately complained, election pressure had prevented him forcing through a tougher Budget, with a lower deficit, than he had been able to win support for in June and July. Policy decisions including Medicare had added a net amount of $1. 2 billion to Keating's first Budget, and $0.6 billion to his second Budget. Hawke was convinced he should seek another three years while the opportunity offered, however, and on 8 October he announced an election for the House and half the Senate to be held on 1 December 1984.

The Prime Minister was a troubled man. The campaign was barely under way before it became apparent that his distress over his daughter's heroin addiction was uppermost in his mind. Distraught, unable to concentrate on a two-month campaign, which he had deliberately designed to be twice as long as usual, Hawke could not prevent Liberal leader Andrew Peacock improving on what began as a position of hopeless inferiority. Because the government had promised to reform the taxation system, Peacock had ample scope for a scare campaign, in particular on the prospect of a tax on income from capital gains.

Keating himself did not make major new economic commitments during the campaign, but the Prime Minister did. On 19 October he agreed with a Perth radio announcer that a meeting like the April Economic Summit might be a good way to handle the consideration of tax reform options. Before the day was out he found himself committed to a tax summit, an idea not previously discussed and which Keating very strongly opposed on the ground that it would rob the government of the option of decisively carrying out its reform, allowing the electorate to judge in a subsequent poll.

Stirred by Peacock's attacks, Hawke attempted to control the tax issue. He could not detail the reforms, but he could detail the criteria on which they would be selected – criteria like equity and efficiency, with no increase in the overall tax burden. On 31 October he announced nine of these principles to govern tax reform; a list composed, one participant recalled, in a hurried meeting in which seven principles were agreed before the Prime Minister's political adviser, Peter Barron, said he thought seven was a 'funny number' and insisted it be nine.

During the campaign Hawke also announced a 'trilogy' of fiscal commitments. Neither the deficit nor federal government taxation would increase as a proportion of total output, and spending would increase by less than the rate of general economic growth. The origin of these commitments was later hard to trace. The Department of Prime Minister and Cabinet had a hand in them; Graham Evans and Ross Garnaut are said to have tinkered with them; and Keating and Hawke discussed something along the lines of the later commitment at a Lodge meeting. Importantly, however, the initiative for them had not come from Treasury (which generally discourages firm and binding rules on its decisions) or from the Treasurer. The Prime Minister was asserting his authority, and in an election campaign he could not be queried. Reflecting a consensus among the economic policy-makers that the deficit should be wound back more rapidly now that the economy was strongly expanding, the budget tightening implied by the trilogy preceded evidence that the current account deficit would be a major problem in 1985 or that the currency was about to fall. By limiting tax increases the trilogy confirmed the policy that Hawke and Keating had adopted at the beginning of 1983 – Labor would not seek to close the deficit (or fund additional spending) through tax increases. This would be a consistent and powerful theme for a decade and one of the reasons Labor won elections.

Economic news during the campaign was excellent. On 25 October, for example, the September quarter CPI of 1. 3 per cent was the lowest for that quarter in five years. Over the year, as the *Financial Review* headlined the following day, inflation was at the lowest point for eleven years.

Applauding the industrial harmony and wage restraint of the Accord, and the free market approach represented by the float and a commitment to allow some foreign banks to enter the Australian market, the *Australian Financial Review*, the *Sydney Morning Herald* and the *Australian* all supported Labor. They referred approvingly to the Hawke–Keating dominance over the party. Even when the Liberals had governed in coalition it was not usual to refer to a Menzies–Fadden Government or a Holt–McEwen Government or a Fraser–Anthony Government. There had been a Whitlam–Barnard Government for a few weeks before caucus elected a ministry, but otherwise the Whitlam Government was the invariable reference. But now with no official sanction, and certainly with no encouragement from Hawke, the names of the Prime Minister and his Treasurer were automatically coupled.

The election was held on 1 December. The result was a setback for the government. There was a 1. 4 per cent swing to the Opposition on a two-party preferred basis. Labor had 75 of 125 seats in the old House, 82 of 148 in the new. Its majority was cut from 25 to 16. Peacock was jubilant. Publicly the poor result for Labor was attributed to Hawke's decision to have a long campaign and to debate Peacock. Privately it was put down to his depression and anxiety over his daughter. With a subdued and distracted Prime Minister, the Treasurer's control over economic policy and the shape of the government's strategy increased.

9

DEPRECIATION AND THE CONSUMPTION TAX

FIVE DAYS AFTER THE 1984 ELECTION KEATING, Hawke, their staff members and officials met in the Cabinet room to discuss the government's economic strategy for the coming year.[1] The second term of the Hawke Labor Government would be, they hoped, a period of rapid economic reform. In the first term the priority had been strengthening the expansion and reducing unemployment. The float was a major reform, but for the Prime Minister, the Treasurer and their advisers, it was only the beginning. The tax system had to be fixed. Spending had to be reduced and better managed if the deficit was going to keep coming down during the economic expansion. Now that the economy was growing well and the government had another three years, it was time to do difficult and unpopular things that could be achieved before the next poll.

The Prime Minister and Treasurer quickly agreed on the tasks for the first post-election Cabinet meeting. It would need to endorse the trilogy commitment. The commitment would be phased so that it should be achieved over three years of government – not necessarily in each and every year. Spending would be brought under control quickly. The Expenditure Review Committee process, which pruned ministers' spending proposals, would be speeded up to allow savings decisions to take effect from the beginning of the new financial year, 1 July. 'It should be made completely clear,' officials recorded, 'that there will be minimal scope for new policy initiatives involving additional outlays and that the focus of fiscal policy will be on the taxation side.' And tax reform was to be a high priority. There was 'a predisposition to hold the Taxation Summit in June, to be preceded by the issue of a draft White Paper.'

Though Keating and Hawke were guarded in public, in private the option of a consumption tax was well developed. The trick was to impose a consumption tax as soon as possible. Income tax cuts paid for by the new sales tax had to be in place well before the next election if the government was to have a hope of winning it. It was also important to pass through the Consumer Price Index price rises induced by the new tax. The price effect would take five quarters or fifteen months to pass through, so the planning within Treasury was already based on schedules indicating that various steps should take place 'no later than' a fixed date.

At the meeting on 6 December the ministers were advised that 'it might be possible to put in place a broad-based indirect tax twenty months after a decision to move in this direction was taken. On this basis, a decision in June or thereabouts would permit a new tax to be in place early in 1987, accompanied of course by a reduction in personal income tax.' Keating told the meeting he would bring forward proposals for new bank entrants in late February or early March.

At a meeting prior to the Cabinet room conference, Keating had discussed the issues with his Treasury officials. Treasury wanted an 'early start, leading to the preparation of a draft White Paper, a tax summit and the implementation of a substantial reform package twelve months before next election.' The minute noted, 'there would be a presumption that a more broadly based indirect tax system would figure prominently in the package, along with lower personal income taxes.'

Stone's successor as Secretary of the Treasury was Bernie Fraser, a tall, strongly built man whose suits, however expensive they later became, seemed always a little short in the sleeve and a little tight around the chest. Fraser had dark, steady and almost expressionless eyes and a distinct whispering voice. He smiled occasionally to acknowledge a joke but did not invite ease. Born in the New South

Wales country town of Junee in 1941, Fraser did well at Junee High and went on to study at the University of New England. Stone had done his degree at Oxford. Fraser's competitor for the top job in Treasury, Chris Higgins, did his PhD at the University of Pennsylvania. Fraser did a BA with a major in economics at New England and joined the Commonwealth Public Service at 20.

He did well in Treasury. He could get things done. He was calm and straightforward with ministers. There was no bullshit with Fraser. He found that the quality ministers seek is not a flash intelligence or political sympathy but weight, reliability, steadiness, reasonable judgement, and the quality of command. He found that experience counts in economic advice, that officials who have been through a recovery, an expansion, a boom and a bust will give better advice next time around, or will at least be able to assure the minister, by their weary demeanour, that the economic circumstances he then faces are no more perilous than they were four or five years before, or will be four or five years hence.

There was nothing remarkable in his history or his personality, but there was something remarkable indeed in Fraser's ideas about economic policy. Unusually for a Treasury official, Fraser was very wary of the power of interest rates. John Howard had been impressed by him, just as Keating was. He had been promoted out of Treasury in 1981, but at the beginning of 1984 he was brought back as a deputy secretary. When Stone resigned there were two strong candidates to succeed him, Fraser and Higgins. Keating asked them both to write essays for him on the Secretary's role and their policy views. Higgins was certainly a better-trained economist, but Keating thought Fraser the better adviser. At the Cabinet meeting that decided the succession to Stone, Keating was Fraser's only supporter. Other ministers wanted Higgins. After expressing his own preference for Higgins, Hawke supported Keating's choice. He was appointed Secretary in September 1984.

Keating wanted to move rapidly to change the tax system radically, but had to keep an eye on the economy as well. A few days before Christmas 1984, Higgins, now Acting Deputy Secretary (Economic), sent over to the Treasurer the latest JEFG report with a comment on the economic outlook to June 1986. With the recovery well under way, Treasury was worried about wages getting out of hand. Linking the forecasts with policy decisions for the coming year, Higgins wrote,

> . . . the exercise throws into sharp relief just how much hangs on the policies of this Government succeeding in changing the normal Australian historical pattern in which wage settlements get out of control in any strong upturn, bringing it to a premature end. What we need is optimism, but restrained and realistic, about our economic situation and potential. The fostering of a 'boom mentality' as has characterised past episodes in this country is to be strenuously avoided.

Higgins believed, '1985 is a year of transition,' in which a kick-started economy would get on to a self-sustaining path. He found the strength of response of business investment has been pleasantly surprising. It was only at the close of his note that Higgins picked up the issue that would soon dominate government thinking. He remarked that JEFG predicted the current account deficit would widen and remain relatively large. (The current account deficit is the difference between imports and exports, plus the difference between interest and dividends received from abroad and interest and dividends paid to foreigners.) He wrote, however,

> Large current account deficits of themselves are not subjects for particular concern provided they are the counterparts of savings being sustainably attracted from abroad into productive, profitable application in Australia. There are now faint glimmerings of doubt about that, providing yet another reason for the public sector to reduce its overall borrowing requirement.

The forecasters now predicted that the current account deficit would widen from $6.9 billion in 1983–84 to $9.25 billion in 1984–85 and $9.5 billion in 1985–86. 'If anything,' Higgins noted, 'there could be an upside risk to these forecasts', meaning they could be higher.

(The outcomes were $10.7 billion in 1984–85 and $14.6 billion in 1985–86.)

The risk of higher current account deficits soon became much greater. Early in the New Year sources within the Australian Government leaked news that Hawke had agreed to a US Administration request to use Australian facilities in tests of the MX intercontinental ballistic missile, a weapon designed to destroy Soviet missiles in their silos, command and control facilities and other targets requiring high accuracy and rapid attack. The Labor Party was outraged. While supporting the US on most issues, there was little sympathy in caucus for a nuclear weapon that could, in a crisis, shift the odds in both the United States and the Soviet Union in favour of shooting first. With little understanding of the significance of the weapon, Keating got on the phone from Brussels and urged Hawke to stare down the caucus opposition. Keating told Hawke he should never have made the commitment but, having made it, should stick to it. Better advised back in Australia, Hawke gave in to caucus protests. Suddenly the combined result of several changes spooked the foreign exchange markets: the Prime Minister's defeat on an issue concerning the Australian alliance with the US, a declining US dollar, an announcement that monetary targets would be dropped in favour of a checklist of influences on interest rate decisions, and a public service dispute that delayed the deposit of cheques into government coffers. The dropping of monetary targets had been forced because changes to the financial system were distorting the various measures of money. The dollar began rapidly depreciating in February and continued declining until April. From the end of January to late February the dollar declined nearly 14 per cent measured against a trade-weighted basket of currencies. Against the American dollar it fell nearly 16 per cent to 68.85 cents. It fell again in the first three weeks of April, with a record low on 22 April at 63.08 cents.

Behind the immediate causes for the decline there were good reasons for a lower dollar. The trade deficit widened as the economy recovered. Freed by the suspension of capital controls, Australian banks and businesses were supplementing borrowings in Australia by borrowing in foreign capital markets as well. As Higgins had explained to Keating, so long as the borrowings were wisely invested they would pay for themselves. But in the meantime, increased borrowings had to be reflected in increased imports, and increased imports in turn suggested to the foreign exchange market that the dollar should fall. Over time a cheaper dollar would mean higher exports and lower imports, narrowing the trade gap. But in the short run in Australia imports cost more in Australian dollars, so the trade gap would widen. This was the 'J curve', the textbook graph showing the response of the trade deficit to a depreciation – at first increasing, and then narrowing. From February Higgins was arguing that the trade account would be likely to follow this traditional pattern, which meant the current account deficit would get worse before it got better.

Despite great media excitement the government was at first unconcerned by the dollar drop. It was, in fact, exactly the result Keating and others had sought from the float in December 1983, and which had been delayed for so long. But a drop in the foreign exchange value of the dollar would not improve Australia's competitiveness for long if higher import prices were reflected in higher wages and then in a permanently higher price level. In that case there would be a 'nominal' depreciation but not a 'real' depreciation because, although the Australian dollar was worth less in terms of foreign currencies, it would also buy less within Australia. Treasury and Keating quickly focused on the fact that the basis of the Accord was that wages would be adjusted for price movements. If Australia's competitiveness was to be improved as a result of depreciation, that part of price increases due to higher import prices should be withheld or discounted from wage increases following on from general price increases. If they could be discounted in this way, competitiveness would improve, exports would increase, and employment would increase. Instead of being a problem, import price increases would become part of the solution.

The lower dollar could in these circumstances become a new and substantial stimulus to export growth – and, with a widening trade deficit, growth in exports was exactly the kind of growth Australia needed. Very quickly, Keating saw that the new goal of economic policy would be preserving the real depreciation by discounting wages, using the depreciation to propel growth even while the budget deficit was being rapidly reduced. Within a month or so of the 1984 election, the circumstances of the economy were suggesting a rapid reordering of economic policy priorities. The Accord would once again become central, just as it had with the Medicare effect and the tax cuts of 1984.

But while achieving a 'real' depreciation ultimately emerged as the focus of policy, there were a number of preliminary steps. At first Keating publicly said that the foreign exchange market was not the government's business any more. At the same time the Reserve Bank was actively 'smoothing' the market by buying Australian dollars to counteract what would otherwise be deeper and more sudden falls. Keating, Treasury and the Reserve Bank also began to resist the depreciation by increasing Australian interest rates. They argued that it was necessary to underpin the dollar with interest rate increases until fiscal policy could be tightened and wages discounting agreed. This meant that interest rate changes were recognised to be effective short-term instruments. Monetary policy was now 'swing' policy. As early as February the interest rate most closely affected by the Reserve Bank began to be increased, from 11 per cent to a peak of 17 per cent by the beginning of 1986. (Higher interest rates supported the dollar by making Australian dollar securities more attractive, compared to Japanese yen or American dollar securities.)

With interest rates now rising to stabilise the falling dollar, there was concern within the government about whether economic growth would continue. On 15 April Fraser provided the Treasurer, who had been talking up the Australian economy abroad, with some points for an oral briefing to Cabinet on monetary policy later that morning. As Fraser wrote, 'Welcome home!'

The minute implicitly acknowledged that monetary policy had

indeed tightened, an admission that Keating was still wary of making, but insisted that the tightening was now sufficient. (In fact policy rates would continue to climb for the rest of the year, except for a period around June and July.) Its main thrust was to use the depreciation to build support for reducing the budget deficit. It argued that the 'recent weakness of the $A reflects a multitude of factors, with doubts about the Government's ability to hold the line on wages and budget outlays occupying a prominent place. As soon as it is possible to get some runs on the board (actions not words) in these areas, in a sensible and sustainable way, that will be all to the good.'

On 17 April Keating met with Kelty to discuss the effect of depreciation on wage indexation. In a note to Hawke, Keating claimed that he 'Got Kelty OK to everything but timing', though the size of the discount, the compensatory tax cuts and the other commitments of what would become Accord Mark II were not agreed until September. The Expenditure Review Committee worked hard, and in his May statement Keating was able to announce $1.26 billion in savings.

Depreciation meant that all policies had to be tightened, compared to expectations of only a few months ago. The depreciation itself would have to power growth through increased exports. On 15 May Higgins brought the Treasurer up to date with the 10 May report of the Joint Economic Forecasting Group (JEFG). In a covering note Higgins commented on the dangers of a free fall in the exchange rate, however helpful it might be in the long run for exports. The report, he wrote,

confirms the view – with which you agreed – that a sharp and sustained devaluation as large as 20 per cent cannot be digested. Indigestion would show up first and worst as inflation with enormous consequential pressures on wage determination and the Accord. Bearing in mind that 1985–86 is the third year of recovery, and that a healthy growth rate was expected before the depreciation, there was already the prospect of pressures on wage determination. Indeed, evidence of wages drift during 1984 underlines that we are quickly arriving at the true testing period for the Accord. Assuming a sizeable depreciation is sustained, the external sector could add at least a percentage point to domestic demand in 1985–86, rather than subtract from it as was the case this financial year. Activity and employment would be stronger in 1985–86 than we were expecting around Christmas.

He concluded that monetary policy should be kept at least as tight as it was, and the 1985–86 deficit should be lower than the pre-depreciation starting point deficit of $6 billion. (The 'starting point' deficit is the number that results assuming no change in spending and revenue policies.) There should be credible wage restraint.

Keating had promised to reduce the regulatory constraints on banks. The Martin Review Group had reported in February 1984 and, as expected, it had ticked the Campbell Committee's advice to remove interest rate controls on borrowing and lending, and to allow foreign banks entry into the Australian market. The thrust of the recommendations was to remove restrictions on banks, to allow them to compete with non-banks. Keating took them through the Caucus Economic Committee to win party support. Nearly three months later, on Tuesday 19 June 1984, he had announced that forty new licences had been issued to deal in foreign exchange. At a Labor Party Federal Conference in Canberra in early July 1984 he had pressed for the party to allow the entry of foreign banks to Australia. Without more competition, he argued, the four major Australian trading banks would dominate the market completely and exploit households and businesses. Against Left opposition, Conference agreed to admit foreign banks.

Treasury and the Reserve Bank called for applications, which were considered over the following few months. The government was expected to proceed slowly, introducing competition by degrees. Perhaps four banks would be permitted, perhaps six, compared with the ten foreign entrants promised by John Howard in January 1983. In February 1985 Keating astonished the banking community by announcing that sixteen foreign banks would be licensed to operate in Australia, more than doubling the number of banks. 'And they said it couldn't be done,' Keating told a press conference.

With the decision to license the foreign banks in Australia, Keating completed a key step in deregulating the Australian financial system. John Howard had ended the practice of telling banks how much they could lend. He had partially removed interest rate ceilings on deposits. He had abolished the 'tap' system under which Treasury tried to control interest rates on government debt. Beyond those changes Malcolm Fraser would not permit his Treasurer to go. Together Hawke and Keating had floated the dollar and then expanded the foreign exchange market. Later Keating had removed term restrictions on interest-bearing deposits. Now he permitted a significant expansion of the Australian banking system, which would increase competition for the four major Australian banks.

Over the next five years the float of the dollar and the deregulation of Australian banking would together influence the economy for good and ill. Together they allowed corporations and households to borrow more than they had been able to in the 1970s. In the middle to late 1980s the amount of debt doubled compared to the GDP, though the increase had begun at the beginning of the 1980s. With the new foreign banks hunting for corporate borrowers, competition to lend was intense. Easy borrowing fuelled a rapid rise in the price of assets like houses and shares. From the trough in the early 1980s to the peak in October 1987 share prices rose 400 per cent. On average house prices more than doubled. At the end of it, debt remained at levels well below many other developed economies and the increase in asset prices was markedly less than in Scandinavia, Japan and the UK for the same period, but the conditions had been created for a financial crash. Because asset prices increased much faster than the income they generated, these assets often could not support the debt they carried. When interest rates increased, as they would in 1988 and 1989, companies with heavy borrowing would become vulnerable.

The expansion of debt in the 1980s contributed to the severity of the recession and the slowness of recovery in the early 1990s. It would be said later that these were 'transitional' effects, which is true. Bank management learned, companies went broke, state banks failed and were absorbed, and many – perhaps most – foreign banks lost money. By the 1990s the financial system was more efficient, more rational and better managed than it had been in the early 1980s. Deregulation was a necessary adaptation to changing technology as much as a reform inspired by belief in markets. Computers, telecommunications and deregulation had fundamentally altered the nature of financial systems everywhere else. Banks were cleverer at finding ways around regulation than the regulators were in thinking up new rules. Companies were taking offshore some transactions they would otherwise have completed in Australia.

In the later accounts of it there would almost always be an assumption of the inevitability of financial deregulation. It would be said that Australia could not have resisted the global reach of financial markets driven by cheap computers and cheap telecommunications; that under any government and any Treasurer the result would have been much the same at much the same time. But even a decade after the change was completed it was still opposed by the former Liberal Prime Minister, Malcolm Fraser, who had opposed it until his defeat in 1983 and who presumably would have continued to prevent it had he been re-elected. At the time Keating and Hawke deregulated the Australian financial system their work was against formal Labor Party policy and opposed by the Left of the party (and earlier by Shadow Treasurer Ralph Willis). It was also opposed by the former Secretary of the Treasury and some (though not all) of his senior subordinates. Perhaps it was inevitable some day, in some form, but there was nothing at all inevitable about the shape and timing of the swift and almost complete deregulation of interest rates and the exchange rate, and the increase in the number of banks, in Australia in 1983, 1984 and 1985. Had it not been for the persistence of the Treasurer, it would not have happened when it did or to the extent it did. In many countries with which Australia had close economic ties it had still not happened a decade later.

Keating's attempt to win agreement to a national 12. 5 per cent sales tax in the autumn and winter of 1985 would be the most concentrated

and exhausting campaign of his political life since winning preselection for Blaxland seventeen years before. Very often during the five
decisive months of March to July the Treasurer, his staff and key people in Treasury worked eighteen hours a day, seven days a week, assembling their package and trying to sell it to the Cabinet, the party, the
ACTU and the press.

From the late 1960s Keating had believed that the top marginal income tax rates paid by lower- and middle-income people were
too high. In 1985 the top rate was still 60 cents in the dollar. Nearly
half of all wage and salary earners were paying 50 cents on each dollar of overtime or their indexation increase. The Opposition was
promising tax cuts; Labor had to be prepared for its attack. Tax was
an issue in every election contest. There was no issue on which the
government would be more vulnerable.

In principle there were two major ways to reduce income tax for
middle- and lower-income earners without reducing government
revenues. One way was to extend the income tax to cover fringe benefits offered by businesses to their employees; the other was to extend
it to gains on the sale of assets. This was known as base broadening.
By taxing all income sources equally, it would level the field of choices.
It would reduce the incentive to buy too many assets like property
that had low income but potentially big capital gains, and to con-
sume too much of products like private school education or motor
vehicles that were provided as part of a fringe benefits package.

Extending income tax in this way would generate enough additional revenue to allow a cut in the income tax rates, but not by
very much. Treasury argued that if the government wanted a major
cut in tax rates without cutting tax revenue it would have to introduce a new sales tax, a broad-based consumption tax (or BBCT),
to replace part of income tax revenue. Then the income tax rate cuts
could be very large. Since Australia already had a wholesale sales tax,
which the BBCT would replace, the net increase would not be as great
as it would otherwise be. And since lower-income earners would pay
more sales tax on their purchases without benefiting much from
income tax cuts, they would have to be compensated in various ways

that would again reduce the additional revenue from the new tax. All up, if the government wanted to change income tax rates substantially the new tax would have to be at least 12. 5 per cent, applied to all goods and most services at the point of sale to its final consumer. Even so, Treasury argued, taxpayers generally would be better off because the new tax would bring into its net people who evaded income tax. It would also increase economic growth. These two last propositions were the keys to the whole idea of changing the tax mix, because it was only if they were true that honest taxpayers could be better off paying both a sales tax and income tax than paying income tax alone. In the event, neither proposition was plausible or convincingly demonstrated.

Because it would in the first instance increase prices to the consumer, a new sales tax would be reflected in the Consumer Price Index. If it was then awarded to employees through indexation increases, a once-only price increase would turn into inflation, and employees would be paid again in wage increases for what they had already been paid in income tax cuts. Under the Accord arrangements, before the tax could be introduced the ACTU would have to agree to discount from indexation the price increase caused by the new tax. From the outset this gave the ACTU an influence that approached an effective right of veto over the new tax, which was strengthened by Hawke's decision to hold a tax summit. The influence of the ACTU was all the greater following the depreciation, which began in February, since the ACTU was now being asked to accept and defend to its members a sizeable cut in cost of living adjustments to wages.

One way or another a general sales tax was not new in Australia. John Howard had wanted to do it, and Treasury had been pushing for one for years. Nor were the government's plans new. As early as March 1984 Max Walsh had written an extremely well-informed piece in the *Bulletin* mentioning David Morgan's appointment to the tax policy unit in Treasury. Walsh wrote that the government believed that tax changes had to be revolutionary and rapid, and that the main thrust would be to shift tax from direct to indirect or from incomes to retail sales. He also said fringe benefits would be taxed, as would capital gains in some form.[2] Keating would later point to a Melbourne *Age* interview in 1983 in which he had advocated the idea of a broad indirect tax to replace some of income tax. He also claimed to have first mentioned the issue to the ACTU in 1984. As we have seen, both the Treasurer and the Prime Minister were actively discussing the schedule for a consumption tax as early as 6 December 1984.

Treasury's work on the tax package was being directed by Ted Evans, then aged 44. Evans had a reddish complexion and ginger hair already turning grey. He spoke very softly, but while he did so he looked at you long and deep, as if satisfying himself on some point of your understanding, or as if implying something not apparent in the words themselves. Keating admired Evans and would very soon rank him second to Bernie Fraser in influence. Keating was drawn to Evans by his air of calm and strength and his delight in public obscurity, and also because Evans was not, like Stone above him or David Morgan beneath him, a man whose only experience of life had been as a public service economist.

Evans had begun his working life as a telephone linesman. He had been a telephone exchange technician for more than ten years, which was very nearly as long as he had been a Treasury officer. He knew the location and layout and wiring of telephone exchanges across thousands of miles of Queensland long before he began to learn about indifference curves and the equality of savings and investment in evening classes, and it was not until 1967, when he was already 26, that Evans won a full-time scholarship to do his final honours year of economics at the University of Queensland. It was a time when an industrious student would very soon know more economics than most of the staff. Evans had the books, however, and the craving to understand, and thrived on them.

A classmate then was Peter McCawley, who later worked for Bill Hayden, and Evans himself mostly worked around Hayden's electorate of Ipswich, so that he had seen more of the working of government when Hayden was Treasurer in 1975 than he had seen in his past six years in Treasury. He had researched for Hayden a study of Treasury advice before the 1961 recession, and satisfied both himself and the Treasurer that official advice was blameless (except in failing to predict the severity of the downturn). He had worked for Hayden but not been close enough to the Whitlam Government to be marked as a Labor sympathiser by the incoming Fraser Government.

His career had prospered. Evans brought to the department a somewhat different perspective from most of his colleagues. It had never left the back of his mind that to work in an office on a good salary, to employ his mind to the limit of its training and endowment, to work with others whose talents were also fully employed, and to influence the course of the Australian Government, were grand things and were for him already a great achievement and not merely a step to some more lucrative or celebrated enterprise.

He did what he did with good humour, and with a deep conviction of its high purpose. He thought formal economics training could reveal connections not apparent, but that otherwise economics was mostly common sense. He thought of an econometrician, the statisticians and model builders now recruited into Treasury, as a good mind wasted.

As head of the tax division Ted Evans and his deputy David Morgan were driving the Treasury work, which was based on previous work for John Howard. There was very little change in the approach of the officials, including in their approach to the White Paper, once the framework was organised. The idea was to present three options in increasing order of attractiveness. Option A simply broadened the income tax base. It did not require a new sales tax, but it did not provide sufficient for a major change in income tax scales. Option B was Option A with small sales tax, sufficient to pay out the existing wholesale sales tax. This was good economics, but again there was no major change in the income tax scales. Option C was a 12. 5 per cent broad-based consumption tax plus Option A. It allowed big changes in the rate scale, plus the replacement of the wholesale sales tax.

Other departments within government, however, had other ideas. At the Department of the Prime Minister and Cabinet, Ed Visbord explored the idea of retaining the existing wholesale sales tax and imposing a much smaller tax on final sales or perhaps only a tax on services. Officials within the Department of Finance liked variants of Option B. The possibilities were endless once the Treasury package was disassembled. Keating's strategy was to prevent this disassembly by making tax reform equivalent to Option C. In the recollection of the officers most involved, Keating was inclined to the Option C approach towards the end of 1984 but not truly committed. He became committed, however, quite early.

Whatever his subsequent decisions about the politics of the sales tax, Hawke was an early exponent of the need for one. At a 7 March meeting, for example, a Treasury official recorded that the Prime Minister said tax reform must be substantial and that the government cannot sufficiently broaden the income tax base to lower marginal tax rates significantly. 'A broad based consumption tax was therefore necessary,' the official noted of the PM's views, 'subject to the ability to ensure low income groups were not worse off'.

By the end of March Treasury was well down the road to writing its tax White Paper and Keating was getting across the complex issues involved. On Thursday 28 March, for example, Keating met with Simon Crean and Bill Kelty from 8 p.m. to midnight. Others there included Bernie Fraser, Ted Evans, Greg Smith and David Morgan, who later filed a note. The purpose of the meeting was to discuss the handling of the tax issue between the government and the ACTU in the lead-up to the summit scheduled for July.

The ACTU officials said they wanted a small negotiating group and emphasised that they would need to show a favourable bottom line to their membership. Following Keating's presentation of the issue, Morgan recorded:

Crean and Kelty agreed with the Treasurer's diagnosis and felt there was no other way to go than the broad-based consumption tax route. They said they were prepared to go out and sell hard a saleable package, including seeking an agreement on discounting. They agreed that the Treasurer's proposals provided the basis for such a package. They noted that they had fought hard to keep the options alive during the election, but their constituents were now starting to become a little restless, in part because of the lack of firm options on the table.

But there was a catch:

Kelty added that, notwithstanding the arguments noted in the prevision paragraph, on grounds of loyalty, if the Prime Minister asked him to provide the excuse to walk away from tax reform (e.g. by a statement that discounting would be impossible to deliver), Kelty would do so.

By 2 April Ted Evans was able to supply Keating a 'Packages Paper for Revenue Committee Meeting'. Used at Budget time as an inner Cabinet to review tax proposals, the Revenue Committee had been selected as a vehicle to manage Cabinet discussion of the emerging tax options. The paper supplied on 2 April contained three options, of which the third was a 12.5 per cent broad-based consumption tax, which would collect $6.1 billion net of increased outlays and allow income tax rates to drop 28 per cent.

Cabinet met in Canberra at 2 p.m. on Sunday 12 May to consider the draft White Paper. It continued on through the afternoon and evening to finish shortly before two. on Monday morning. Unusually for Cabinet, a number of officials and advisers were present for most of the meeting. Speaking from prepared notes, Keating introduced the paper by reminding his colleagues around the Cabinet table that the government had committed itself to tax reform right through 1984. It had given a reference on tax reform to EPAC in early 1984, and at the time of the national conference in Canberra ministers had spoken in terms of reform. He recalled that the government had published nine principles of tax reform when pressed by the Opposition on capital gains and wealth taxes, and that it had announced a national taxation summit. 'The political momentum of this issue is enormous,' he said, 'but the political momentum is basically driven by the economic issues of the tax debate'.

The 'politically salient fact' that first took the government on the path of reform, he said, was that 'the majority of wage and salary earners will be facing marginal tax rates of nearly 50 per cent during the life of this parliament – an unsustainable position.' This was an argument he had used when he first came to Parliament sixteen years before. 'So in both Bob's opinion and my own,' he said, 'tax reform is not optional, it is mandatory. If we were to squib it we hand Peacock the issue on a plate; we will have been seen to have lacked the courage – the follow through – with our own policy, or we'd be seen as being run by the unions.' Because of this, 'the PM and I have taken this more seriously, put more time into it, had more discussions over it than any other issue. And that includes economic policy in 1983, the float, or anything else. What you have before you in the White Paper is the most comprehensive and conscientious effort we are capable of presenting to you. We've worn ourselves out over it.'

Summarising the conclusions of the paper, he said that running repairs would not pass as reform, and that the income base was incapable of full repair. Both the consumption and income bases needed to be reformed, which basically meant broadening the base of each and lowering the marginal rates of income tax. Both bases were too narrow, and the high rates were causing both distortions and evasions. The White Paper, he said, concludes that both bases should be preferred, with 'some switch to consumption from income'. The wealth base is rejected, he said, primarily for political reasons. 'We are not asking you today to approve a tax package, in detail, for every dot and comma, but we are asking for a clear focus on this strategy of reform. Otherwise the debate will rattle on to the next election – without direction.'

A Treasury official reported on the detailed discussion. Keating had outlined the income tax broadening path. Cabinet was broadly satisfied that $1.6 billion was about as much as could be expected from this route by 1987–88. Cabinet had also agreed that fringe benefits tax ought to be imposed, whatever happened to the rest of the reform package. The Treasurer said that fringe benefits would probably be the hardest part of the package – presumably referring only to income tax base broadening. The Treasurer said, however, that the income tax base broadening measures would not on their own constitute a viable package and would have to be 'sweetened' with a broad-based consumption tax. He said that the alternative package proposed by Finance Minister Peter Walsh, which addressed the marginal rate difficulty with a revenue cost of around $2 billion, offered a rate scale that would be wholly unacceptable to the ACTU.

Keating then went on to present the case for reforming the consumption tax system, quite apart from the case for a change in the tax mix. According to Morgan, only Dawkins had reservations about the case for dropping the existing wholesale sales tax system. Dawkins wanted to retain the wholesale sales tax on an interim base and introduce a 5 per cent broad-based consumption tax across the board. This tax would then be raised when the wholesale sales tax was phased out. Keating's strongest opposing argument was that it would require two rounds of ACTU deals, and it would postpone a second stage of reform and leave 'a great deal of room for misrepresentation'.

Treasury Deputy Secretary Chris Higgins was asked to speak about the macroeconomic effects of the switch. He offered the judgement that 'there was unlikely to be any significant slowing of growth due either to the deferral/acceleration of consumption spending or to temporary increases in private savings ratios while taxpayers made decisions with respect to the disposition of their higher nominal pay packets.'

The Cabinet agreed that Keating could continue discussions with the ACTU and report back to Cabinet during the weekend of 18–19 May. It also agreed that the basic structure of the White Paper was fine, but it needed 'a more discreet tone. Government views should be expressed in terms of initial dispositions, inclinations, etc., rather than decisions.' According to Morgan's note, the idea was to amend the draft to suggest a logical sequence. First, there would be the income tax base broadening measures, concluding with an indication of the rate scale changes that these measures alone could finance. Then there would be a bit about a tax on services and its implications. This would be followed by a discussion of the implications of a 5 per cent across-the-board broad-based consumption tax in which some elements of the wholesale sales tax would be retained. Finally the White Paper would reach what Morgan called 'the preferred "Hawke–Keating" position'. Morgan noted, 'The Prime Minister did not want these presented as separate packages but rather as stages on the way to the preferred package. The government's disposition would be decided by Cabinet in the light of the Treasurer's discussions with the ACTU.' During the meeting Ralph Willis raised the possibility of increasing the broad-based consumption tax sufficiently to knock off state payroll taxes. This was the strategy eventually chosen by John Hewson but it found little support in Cabinet.

Keating briefed Morgan and others on the parts of the discussion from which officials had been excluded. Susan Ryan had supported the thrust of the bold central option. Willis was uneasy about the figuring, especially the 'magic pudding' said to arise from catching evaders, and increasing economic growth. Button wanted a less explicit tone. Hawke wanted a less dogmatic tone, with the preferred package emerging at the end of a logical progression. The strength of the preference should be 'fuzzed up a little'. Willis also felt the White Paper should not adopt a hard and fast position. Ted Evans said he had listened closely all day to the discussion 'and that no one had so far been able to put a substantial hole in the Treasurer's package.'

The bottom line of the meeting, Morgan recorded of the debriefing discussion, was that 'Cabinet gave the Treasurer authority for him to speak with the ACTU on a range of options and report back to Cabinet.'

The following month Keating was back with a restructured White Paper proposing as the government's preferred option a 12. 5 per cent broad-based consumption tax and a 30 per cent top marginal tax rate. Discussions with the ACTU remained promising but inconclusive. In four days of marathon Cabinet meetings, Keating day after day confounded objections, answered or at least repelled questions, confused and exhausted his opponents with numbers and more numbers while the clock ticked away minute by minute towards the deadline at which the paper had to reach the printers. Even after four days, the resistance was so strong that the equally exhausted, equally stubborn Stewart West could still say across the Cabinet table to Keating that he didn't think he had a Cabinet majority for Option C – the firm supporters included only Hawke, Kim Beazley, and Gareth Evans, with John Button and Don Grimes lukewarm – and Keating could only reply that he might not have a majority but that he had to leave right then to take the White Paper to the printer and West did not have a majority to stop him. He then gathered his papers in complete silence and walked out of the Cabinet room, Ted Evans stumbling out after him, the ordinarily imperturbable Treasury official astonished by the tension of a political duel as daring as he had seen in any Cabinet at any time.

Keating was able to claim Cabinet support for Option C, but it was only skin deep. Throughout the debate Hawke had drifted from one side to the other, sometimes convinced Keating was right and sometimes wondering whether it was worth pursuing a general retail sales tax in the face of strong opposition. Within his office, economic adviser Ross Garnaut, who was on the White Paper task force, opposed Option C and, when invited by Hawke, presented his arguments against it to Cabinet. He thought that the highest priority was to fix the income tax base – Option A. Hawke swung between Keating's advocacy and Garnaut's opposition.

Three weeks later the Tax Summit convened in Canberra. Keating had been out campaigning, but the appearance of widespread support for a 12. 5 per cent consumption tax was an illusion. Welfare groups were strongly opposed to the new sales tax. Business groups wanted the new sales tax and income tax cuts but not the capital gains tax or the fringe benefits tax. The ACTU leadership was prepared to go with a consensus for Option C, but there was no consensus to join. Kelty and Crean asked Keating privately to drop Option C. He refused. In a late Wednesday night meeting with the ACTU at Canberra's International Hotel, Hawke, without Keating's knowledge, agreed to dump Option C and instead examine an alternative proposal put forward by the ACTU to retain the wholesale sales tax with a new tax on services, together with the major elements of Option A.

Keating was not at the meeting. For the proponents of Option C it was a bewildering shock. David Morgan and Tony Cole heard the news with disbelief – they thought agreement to Option C was close. Keating was furious that Option C was dumped by Hawke during a summit that was, after all, Hawke's idea.

Ted Evans and Tony Cole thought then and later that the tax summit failed because the employer groups, especially the Business Council of Australia, would not support a tax on fringe benefits provided by companies as part of a salary package. Since the BCA did support a sales tax, its objection to the fringe benefits tax and to capital gains taxes was rightly interpreted by the ACTU as a narrow assessment of self-interest, which made it harder for trade union leaders to overcome objections to the new sales tax from their own colleagues and from welfare groups at the summit. According to Keating,[3] Kelty told him he would go along with Option C if the employers went along. But the ACTU's support for Option C had never run much beyond Kelty and Crean, and their support was often half-hearted. In the end the logic was inescapable – middle- and lower-income earners could only be better off or no worse off under the new tax package if it collected tax from people who evaded income tax, or if it allowed the economy to grow more rapidly. Neither proposition was convincing. Sales taxes could be evaded, just as income taxes were evaded, though by different groups in different ways. There was no evidence from the experience of consumption taxes in other countries that they encouraged saving (though this remained a deeply held conviction among the tax's business, and some academic, supporters). The sales tax didn't suit the ACTU, and Kelty knew that agreement at the summit would be just the beginning of his troubles as the tax was legislated and implemented. Ambivalent from the beginning, Hawke decided that the cost of dropping Option C was less than the cost of pursuing it. At the hotel Kelty exercised the option he had mentioned to Keating months ago. He gave Hawke the excuse to drop it.

The defeat of Option C in May 1985 was the bitterest blow of Keating's career. He had campaigned for the new tax for months. He had, as he said, chased every rabbit down its hole. Now it had collapsed. He had prepared for the setback, as he would for other risky challenges, by imagining a pleasant life outside politics. 'Life after politics for Paul Keating would be the silk road to Paris where he and his family would own a villa on the Avenue Victor Hugo. He would be seen at antique auctions at Sotheby's in London and Sotheby Parke Burnett in New York, only returning to Australia to consummate the odd business deal,' reported John Short after a plane trip with Keating.[4] Earlier Paul Kelly had reported Keating remarking of Option C: 'If this sort of proposal doesn't get up, one has to decide if there's much point in someone like me worrying about Australian institutional processes, and in Australian institutions, very much longer.'[5] Defeated, he stayed on. The tax cart had crossed the finishing line, he told a press conference on the last day of the summit, but with one wheel off – like the chariot in Ben Hur.

It was the greatest defeat of his career to that point, yet despite his own prediction, within a few weeks he regained his usual buoyancy and confidence and announced a budget in which policy decisions for the first time in the Hawke Government netted out to a spending cut and prepared the way for a new Accord and a new tax package the following month. At 41 the Treasurer could bounce back as if his defeats were victories.

In many ways it had been a quixotic adventure. Almost all the arguments he was later to make against John Hewson's version of the same tax were true of his own. His reforms to the income tax later in 1985 demonstrated that it was possible to lower marginal tax rates substantially by applying more discipline to government spending and broadening the income tax base. It was not possible for a change in the tax mix to improve significantly the way the Australian economy worked – to discourage imports, for example, or encourage exports, or contain inflation. His failure was more surprising to him, to his staff and to

Treasury than it was to other members of the political community. The real wonder is not that he lost but that he succeeded in taking the proposal for broad-based consumption tax as far as he did within the Labor Party. In the retelling the defeat would be as glorious as a victory, but it was an episode that snapped the collegial bond of trust between the Prime Minister and the Treasurer and put in its place a harder, more enduring, but wholly mercenary relationship of mutual advantage.

Keating was particularly annoyed with the business community, which supported the consumption tax but not the other elements – the fringe benefits and capital gains taxes – which alone could make it acceptable to the ACTU. The business community ratted on him, Keating thought, 'and they could get fucked'.

Keating also blamed Hawke for the defeat of Option C. Graham Richardson and Peter Barron had been critical of Keating during the tax debate. Garnaut had opposed Option C. Keating had been highly critical of Hawke. There was now more discussion in the press about Keating's ambition to be Prime Minister. When he appointed a New South Wales party official, Seamus Dawes, to his staff in October there were reports that Keating was counting caucus numbers.

Eight years later, with the election win against John Hewson only a week behind him, Keating went to Melbourne for a victory speech to the ACTU executive. Afterwards he sat chatting over a cup of tea with Bill Kelty and Martin Ferguson, the two elated enough at least on that day at that hour to share a space companionably. Kelty was in shirt and pants and black zippered boots, a short, broad man with grey hair now awry, who had been even more convinced than most of us that we were too far behind to win the election Paul had won the week before; he had thought, ever since the March 1991 industry statement, that the government was too far behind and it was only a matter of waiting. He giggled a little as he sipped his tea and said to Paul that there was one thing at least he could thank the ACTU for, one thing more important than all the work it had done in the election, all the money it had encouraged its members to contribute, all the Accords and all the protests against the elimination of awards.

That much more important thing was that the ACTU had in 1985 killed the goods and services tax.

By August 1985 it was apparent that there was a risk of serious difficulty for the Treasurer. A consumption tax had been ruled out. The dollar was dramatically lower. If higher import prices were captured by higher wage increases, inflation would increase and the competitive gains of the depreciation would be lost. The solution to both difficulties was to change the nature of tax reform radically. Now it would be mainly confined to reforming the income tax base by removing inequities and reducing the marginal rates – by broadening the base and lowering the rates. At the same time Keating would provide a major tax cut to compensate partly for a further discount off wage indexation.

Keating was approaching his third Budget. He had been the principal in the decision to float and to allow the entry of foreign banks. He had gone through recession, recovery and now a dollar depreciation and a monetary policy tightening. In the realm of economic policy, he was, after two years and half years, an old hand.

Life in Canberra was settling down. Patrick was nine, Caroline six and Katherine three. There was another on the way – a daughter, Alexandra, who would be born the week following the Budget. The Treasurer was congratulated by friends in the press gallery. 'Another little tax payer,' they said, kindly. He was present at the birth, as he had been for his other children.

His notes for the Budget speech showed the pattern of his thinking:[6]

Since government came to office produced extraordinary turnaround. 5–10 year task to get country back to full health. govt got to have sense of history; small part of the total job. devote speech to Labor Party, improved lot of the poorest people, for those who took the brunt, Labor traditionalist. Youth/pensions – sense of theme – got to deal with those who have missed out, those we have not yet come to. FAMILIES. (no resort to selfishness)

Keating delivered the Budget on Tuesday evening, 20 August. It was the first year of serious spending restraint. Outlays were to increase by 1.3 per cent in real terms, which meant they would fall as a proportion of GDP. It was the lowest real increase since 1979–80. The deficit was cut by $1.8 billion to $4.9 billion. Taxation revenues were expected to remain the same as a proportion of GDP. The trilogy commitments were therefore met. Budget Statement 2 explained: 'Exploiting the opportunities provided by depreciation while avoiding the potentially destabilising inflationary effects will be a major focus of policy in the short run.' Looking back on the year past, Keating could point to a 5 per cent increase in non-farm GDP, the largest since 1972–73. Inflation was 5.8 per cent, the lowest since 1970–71. But the current account deficit was nearly 5 per cent of GDP – not the forecast 4 per cent. The current account deficit was predicted to decline as a percentage of GDP over the coming year.[7]

With the consumption tax ruled out by the summit, Treasury had been working up an alternative tax package that would broaden the income tax base. Hawke had proposed looking at a services tax, but this was quickly ruled out as impractically difficult, given the huge number of relatively small tax points. The better options were those base-broadening measures for income tax already presented in the White Paper. It would extend income tax to capital gains and fringe benefits, two of the major leakages. Unlike the earlier package, however, the amended package would now include a tax cut to accommodate the deal with the ACTU, so it required an offsetting spending cut to maintain the trilogy commitments.

Keating drew up a proposal, and Hawke convened a full ministry meeting to examine them over the weekend of 14 and 15 September 1985. To Keating's extreme and unconcealed annoyance, Hawke then left for an official visit to New Guinea, leaving Keating to get the changes through against persistent, though muddled, opposition from left-wing ministers Arthur Gietzelt and Tom Uren. They objected to the fall in the top marginal rate of tax. Keating argued that this merely reflected the extension of the income tax to capital gains and fringe benefits, which would impact most heavily on the income groups benefiting from the lower top marginal rate. 'You couldn't sell ice-cream in the Gobi desert,' he told them disgustedly. Others opposed taxing parliamentary allowances. Keating remarked, 'If there was a PhD for greed you blokes would get first-class honours.' The discussions continued on Monday morning, before Keating won agreement for his package.

In the Budget Keating had foreshadowed discounting of wage indexation for the price impact of depreciation. It had been agreed in outline in April. The deal was concluded with the ACTU at the beginning of September. On 3 September in Melbourne, Keating and Willis offered tax cuts in return for a 2 per cent discount from full indexation. The government would support industry superannuation schemes. The government and the ACTU envisaged that the postponed case seeking a 3 per cent increase for increased productivity would now go ahead but with the unions asking that the 3 per cent be delivered as a superannuation contribution by employers. (The following year the commission decided that occupational superannuation schemes could go ahead from July 1986.) The cost to revenue was estimated to be around $2 billion, and the average wage-earner would get a tax cut of $5 a week. The deal was accepted by the ACTU Wages Committee subject to ratification by the ACTU Congress in Sydney the following week. Well informed, the press were pleased. The Accord was extended for a further two years.

Keating revealed the package in an elaborate media event on 19 September. The package included $2 billion in income tax cuts, fringe benefits tax, capital gains tax, dividend imputation, some wholesale sales tax 'simplification', a proposal for an 'Australia' identity card to reduce tax fraud, and a foreign tax credit system.

He had reconfigured the Accord to keep wage increases low in return for tax cuts. It worked well, and he would use it several times more. In aggregate the tax cuts did little more than return the increase in total income tax that occurred as wage increases pushed more income into higher marginal tax brackets, though tax as a proportion of GDP came down. Tax cuts of this order were already implied by the trilogy promise, though their construction to benefit low- and middle-income-earners was not. The strategy committed the ACTU to tax cuts, which necessarily meant government spending cuts – a logical connection so inexorable that after a few years the public service and teachers' unions begged the ACTU to refuse further wage–tax trade-offs. The discounts were extremely successful in restraining the growth of wages but not of inflation. In 1985 and 1986 the persistence of inflation could be attributed to increasing import prices. By 1987 it had become apparent that there had to be a deeper explanation. Profits were being 'restored' – handsomely. It would not be until the next recession that inflation fell, but the absence of a high floor of wage inflation meant it could fall very low.

Keating was exhausted but pleased. Hawke was still off his game. Keating was running the country. The tax package discussions followed immediately on the Budget Cabinet and wage–tax trade-off negotiations, which had followed the collapse of Option C in July. Before that, there had been the internal debate over depreciation and monetary policy and the endless hours of preparation of the White Paper. But he could tell a good story. He claimed 430 000 new jobs in two and half years, portable occupational superannuation, an expanding economy, single-digit inflation, repairs to the tax system, competition in the banking sector, and the float.

After two and half years hard running Keating seemed to think he was just about home. He told reporter Geoff Kitney, 'We are getting to the end of what I considered my agenda. That is the truth of it. I think I will never outstrip my achievements [as Treasurer], whatever job I might hold in the future.'[8] He acknowledged that he would like to be Prime Minister some time. 'I would like to enjoy the fruits of my work here, in this job,' he said. 'I would like to be able to sit back and look at the fabric of Australia in a broader sense; to say, "All right, well, we have made this much progress as a government; where else can we make it better?" – in social policy, defence policy, foreign policy, and whatever the other areas are. It would be nice to be able to pull the threads together.' Kitney reported that Keating's preference would be to succeed Hawke in the prime ministership, probably sometime after victory in the next election, 'when there is a natural vacancy'.

Paul Kelly reported the following month, 'For the first time since early 1983 there is serious talk now in Parliament lobbies about the leadership of the Labor Party.'[9] An election was then expected in 1987. Kelly reported that a contrast was drawn between Hawke's poor form and Keating's energy. Keating wanted Old Silver's job after the next election. But Hawke was then only 55, Keating only 41. Kelly warned that Hawke would not quietly disappear at 58 if he won the next election.

While Keating was publicly contending that the balance of payments and inflation constraints had been shattered, his Treasury officials were advising him more cautiously. The goal posts were about to move. Overnight interest rates were now 5 percentage points higher than they had been in March 1983, wages were to be discounted for depreciation, and the trilogy had been more than minimally met, but it might not be enough. If an adverse scenario developed, wages would have to fall again, interest rates would have to increase more, and spending would be cut more deeply. Writing to the Treasurer on 3 October on 'The Economic Situation: Some Contingency Thinking', Deputy Secretary Chris Higgins summed up 'economic policy-making at the present juncture' and suggested 'some lines for your thought about contingencies over the next six months or so'.

Higgins argued that policy changes prompted by depreciation 'are only just beginning to have their effects on the measured economic indicators'. There was a need to publicly develop the idea that it takes time to adjust the external imbalance. The present mix of policy he thought 'broadly appropriate', and 'we have no major changes to propose at this time'.

A forecaster by profession, Higgins knew too much about the

business to rely on JEFG's predictions. He instead offered alternative scenarios – one favourable, one unfavourable. In the favourable scenario the dollar rises in value and the current account deficit narrows. The outcome would be lower interest rates, though 'at present monetary policy is leaning on the firm side'. In this scenario authorities might not resist sustainable interest rate reductions occurring in the market.

The alternative was the adverse scenario, where the current account deficit increased, September and December quarter consumer price indexes were very high and there was renewed pressure on the Australian dollar. In those circumstances, Higgins believed, the rest of the world would be telling Australia that adjustment was 'inadequate, and that we needed to lift our game'. He added, 'You have already explicitly considered what would be the <u>major</u> policy response to this contingency, namely that the wage indexation arrangements agreed in the extension of the Accord would have to be reopened,' together with further tightening of monetary policy and an early announcement of budget goals. Without a better wage outcome, the policy would have to be 'draconian'.

Keating was overseas for the remainder of October and early November and returned to find a sterner note from Treasury Secretary Bernie Fraser, dated 7 November. 'During your absence overseas,' the Secretary wrote, 'there have been some unhelpful developments in the foreign exchange and bond markets.' The trade weighted value of the dollar had fallen from 64 in mid October to 59 that afternoon. It was now 13 per cent below the level assumed in the Budget. Bond yields had risen 1 per cent in same period. The sell-off had apparently been started by bigger-than-expected broad money figures, suggestions of continuing high imports, and concerns about the National Wage Case decision. Nothing in the recent JEFG forecast (which was based on a trade weighted index of 64) 'would lead us to recommend any significant change in policy at this stage'. Nonetheless, he warned, the decline in the exchange rate was moving them to the adverse scenario painted by Higgins in his earlier note.

Fraser thought that markets were probably overshooting in the exchange rate, but it was not too early to look at possible support actions. One possibility was intervention, but the Reserve Bank had spent $100m in the last two days, and there was scepticism over its likely effectiveness. There would be costs in raising interest rates further, especially if the effects of earlier tightening were yet to come through. Another option was to change the mix — to reopen wage negotiations now to seek additional discounting and further delays.

Fraser emphasised that he was explicitly opposed to policy-induced monetary tightening now because of its recessionary consequences. He would prefer wage discounting. Nonetheless, the policy rate was raised 2 percentage points to counter the currency weakness. Keating thought a sharp, dramatic increase would crush expectations of a falling dollar.

10

MY MOST
IMPORTANT
YEAR IN
POLITICAL LIFE

'UP TO 1986 WE CONTROLLED THE AGENDA,' he would reflect in the 1990s, twelve days before he became Prime Minister, 'and then we did not'. For three years he had been increasingly assured. 'We busted the balance of payments constraint with the dollar floats and we busted the wage restraint problem with the Accord. They are two things which have given us eighteen-month recoveries and eighteen-month troughs right through the seventies,' he had told a reporter in September 1985.[1] In 1986, however, he would discover that the Australian economy still had tricks up its sleeve.

The tax debate over and Keating now fluent in the language, numbers and concepts of economic policy, the Treasurer's office became more important, the Department of the Treasury less. He encouraged it. He had good staff, and he enjoyed watching them learning to duck and weave in the continuous warfare of politics and policy. Keating was developing a warm and affectionate relationship with former *Sydney Morning Herald* economics reporter Tom Mockridge, recruited as his press secretary in 1985. He had recruited a young New South Wales Labor Party official, Seamus Dawes, as a political adviser. He also found a new staff member who, over time, would accumulate a quite remarkable degree of influence over economic policy.

Succeeding Tony Cole as the senior private secretary in September 1985, Treasury official Don Russell was the son of a prominent South Australian economist. He won his doctorate at the London

School of Economics and worked in Treasury in economic policy and forecasting before being sent to Paris as one of Treasury's representatives to the OECD. While in Paris he had been instructed to buy Keating a suit of woollen underwear to protect the Treasurer from the cold during a state funeral in Moscow. Recommended by his Treasury superiors, Russell came to work for Keating wearing a blue Romanian suit he had bought in a Paris flea market.

He found the Treasurer's style dazzling. He had had few personal contacts with Keating. Russell had silently taken notes on John Stone's instruction as the Treasury Secretary went through the economic policy review in the 1984 Budget with the Treasurer, painstakingly detailing his objections to Keating's revisions of a document Stone had come to think of as his own. Russell found his new job with the Treasurer brought great prestige but also many enemies. His new enemies were not merely the staff of spending ministers and, for that matter, the spending ministers themselves, but also State premiers and treasurers, backbenchers, business leaders, pleaders and mendicants of all kinds, staff colleagues; they all required access to the Treasurer. Russell's opponents interpreted his shy diffidence as silent menace. He found his unpunctuality and apparent disorder no disgrace in the Office of the Treasurer; it was actually a good way of fending off the multitude of demands on his time. He intelligently adapted his unlikely personality to the job, relabelling it so that it was perceived in a quite new way. It was a technique that could also be applied to politics and policy and at which he would become so adept as to excel the Treasurer himself. (The companion skill was to change the product while keeping the label, so the difference was not noticed. They were good at that, too.)

Russell was tall with a shaved head. He was intelligent though apparently unread. He didn't attempt to keep up with economics articles. He read newspapers closely. His car radio was permanently tuned to high-volume rock music. At the London School of Economics he had perhaps breathed the air of Bloomsbury, of vague relationships and vague plans, of the value of intelligence and good humour. Raised to a pinnacle of real power by Keating, he lost his ambition to rise

in the ranks of the Commonwealth Public Service. He was funny
in a wry way. When David Morgan sent across an exculpatory note
headed, 'Don't Shoot the Messenger', Russell noted, 'I guess we didn't'.
Responding to the draft of a speech circulated in March 1991, which
concluded with the thought that the outlines of victory over inflation – over the current account – were becoming apparent, he annotated, 'Looks Good', adding as an afterthought, from the experience
then of five years, 'We are always just about there.'

Keating liked his eccentricity, his private acumen, the style of his
mind. Keating is a lively, nervous and excitable man, and he loved
Russell's sleepy grace. His most urgent state was placid. It might not
have been so at the beginning, but within a few years they thought
the same way, came up with the same solutions. If there was a fault
it was this: that he and Keating thought too much the same. Russell chiefly admired the Treasurer's courage, as well as his speed and
charm. Leaving the Treasurer's office, each wearing a white shirt, dark
tie, black shoes, each of similar height and weight, and each with the
same impassive, abstracted and intimidatory air of menace, Keating,
Russell and Mockridge would stride the corridors of Parliament
House with what Keating would call a rolling sort of swagger. Somehow, though, Russell would not quite fit the part. At the end of his
long, straight arms his hands were turned back, his fingers extended
and separated. His shirt-tail would often be out, his trousers slipping down. Paul called him Big Bird.

He would become Keating's closest collaborator in government, his
vizier and his co-conspirator. Wearing a dark, venerable double-breasted
suit, a white shirt with a wrinkled collar, which he credibly insisted he
himself had ironed only that morning, and cheerful cartoon socks, Russell sat amid piled paper with an ironic, shy and knowing smile. The
smile was his mask. Warm and sometimes affectionate, that smile sometimes did indeed suggest affection, but more often it signalled wariness,
caution, deferral, the vagueness and inability to act quickly, which was
his perpetual and most successful technique in accumulating power.
Russell manipulated the machinery of government by ambiguity, silence
and disguise. He remained, however, sweet at heart.

Russell missed most of the excitement of the tax debate in the Treasurer's office. He would first see the Treasurer at top form during the Banana Republic episode, the most acrobatic of Keating's policy switches. He and Keating would perform together, gripping hands as they swung through space from trapeze to trapeze.

By the beginning of 1986 Keating could look back on a reasonably satisfactory record of achievement. Employment had grown so rapidly that unemployment had now fallen 2 percentage points to just over 8 per cent. He had announced a reform of the tax system, broadening the income tax base and allowing lower marginal tax rates. On Bill Kelty's suggestion he had proposed the introduction of superannuation into all awards. Accord Mark II, announced on 4 September 1985, embodied a wage discount for the currency depreciation of early 1985, which meant the currency fall had been turned into a long-lasting competitive advantage, which ought to help exports and discourage imports. With the float and the decision to license foreign banks, he was able to point to a list of substantial changes that improved the way the economy worked, required political skills and had mostly not been expected from a Labor government.

Economic policy had been tightened, and tightened again. The 1985 Budget had cut spending from forward estimates by three-quarters of a billion dollars. Interest rates had been increased after the February depreciation, and then increased by a startling 2 percentage points to counter another round of currency weakness in October and November. By December the overnight rate was above 18 per cent – higher than it would be in 1989.

There were problems. Under the trilogy commitments, tax cuts implied spending cuts or revenue increases, and Keating was not sure where either would come from. The states had been promised a real increase in their tax-sharing grants. The wage discount meant that wages would not rise as fast, and tax collections would be lower than they would otherwise have been. Somehow cuts would have to be made.

Keating observed that world growth was faltering and commodity prices were falling. The rate of growth of Australia's exports would likely be less than in the past couple of years. Export prices would be flat, while import prices were being pushed up by the depreciation of 1985.

He was also concerned about interest rates. There were signs that the economy was slowing markedly. Though Keating did not then have the evidence, the economy in fact contracted in the December quarter of 1985 for the first time since March 1983. It was flat in the March quarter and contracted again in the June quarter of 1986.

Worried about growth and jobs, Keating pressed for interest rate cuts from around January 1986. Reserve Bank Governor Bob Johnston, his deputy Don Sanders and the Bank's research head, Peter Jonson, resisted, arguing that high rates were needed to reduce inflation and the current account deficit. 'I was on the phone every day,' Keating recalled. It was not until February that the Bank began to lower the policy rate sharply, from an average of 18.16 per cent in that month to 16.74 per cent in the following month, towards a low point of 12.31 per cent in May 1986, before rates began to rise again in response to a new crisis in the economy.

In pressing for lower interest rates Keating had an ally in his Treasury Secretary, Bernie Fraser, who consistently pushed for a tighter budget and lower wage increases as an alternative to higher interest rates. Writing to the Treasurer as Australia returned to work in early February, Fraser recalled that interest rate increases in the last months of 1985 were designed to 'buy time' for the current account deficit to improve as a result of earlier measures.[2] Now that exchange rate had strengthened, '. . . the risks of maintaining the present degree of monetary tightness until mid-year (particularly but not only in terms of effect on business investment) outweigh the risks inherent in modest and gradual and downward adjustments in official inspired rates which essentially track reductions in the market place.' He believed that 'while no one can be confident as to its timing, evidence of an improving trend in the current account can be expected to show up shortly.' He warned that 'if business investment dries up because of sustained very high real interest rates we might never see the improvement in the current account that we are all watching for.'

Then as later, Fraser wanted to 'lighten the relative load being borne by monetary policy'. Although 'the Government/ACTU wage agreement does not appear capable of being renegotiated to yield greater wage restraint, the government will need to squeeze every last drop of restraint out of the present agreement', and 'all this boils down to a very tough expenditure budget for the Commonwealth, and in its dealings with the States.'

The forecasters also reported at the beginning of February that the current account deficit forecast was up and economic growth down.[3] The 1985–86 current account deficit prediction was now $12.25 billion, up $1.5 billion on budget forecast. (The JEFG's prediction was still, however, $2.5 billion short of the actual deficit.) Growth would be lower, with non-farm product increasing 3.25 per cent compared with the earlier forecast of 4.5 per cent, because of higher rates.

With internal forecasts of both the current account and the budget deficit increasing, Fraser floated publicly the advice he had been providing the Treasurer privately. He told an audience in Perth that the government might have to renegotiate the Accord if the trade balance did not improve in 1986. Keating himself told reporters said that he expected a 'blowout' in the current account deficit, but it would fall significantly over the year.

As preparations for a May statement were put in place, Treasury emphasised the need for a big deficit reduction. In a minute of 21 February Higgins told the Treasurer the deficit objective should be of the order of $4.5 billion. He warned that 'much more' hung on expenditure restraint this time than last. The current account deficit was the difference between what Australia invested and what it saved. The Commonwealth Government could contribute to national saving by reducing the budget deficit. Reducing the budget deficit ought to reduce the current account deficit by the same amount – always providing private saving and investment did not change.

By May 1986 the dollar was holding up reasonably well, while the policy rate had been brought crashing down to 12.5 per cent, compared to nearly 18.5 per cent at the beginning of the year. Both the Treasurer and the Bank insisted that the government was in this instance only following market sentiment, but there was no doubt monetary policy was easing.

Keating was optimistic about the current account deficit, though the numbers were disappointing. It had fallen below $1 billion in seasonally adjusted terms in February, but in March it rose again. When the number was published in April, Keating was compelled to rethink the risks of lower interest rates. The April deficit was nearly $1.5 billion. Though it was a peak, which preceded a trend to lower numbers, the April deficit coming after the March record crystallised a dramatic public policy change.

Between the publication of the March current account deficit in April and the April current account deficit in May, Keating met on Sunday 4 May with Bob Johnston, Bernie Fraser and other officials to discuss the outlook. There were sharp disagreements. At the Bank, research chief Peter Jonson believed strongly that the current account deficit would get bigger and bigger as the economy and imports picked up in response to the interest rate cuts that Keating had demanded. The argument turned on whether and when the higher import prices and lower export prices brought about by depreciation would sufficiently modify the rule of thumb that imports increased three times as fast as national spending.

If, as the Bank argued, the trade balance would get very much worse, then the policy alternatives were not at all appealing. There would have to be more discounting, more spending cuts. Interest rates might have to go back up. Such a dramatic change of policy, however, could not be brought about without public evidence of a new crisis. After having invested so much energy in sustaining the depreciation and being in any case wary of the effects of interest rates on the economy, Keating was inclined to hope that the trade balance would improve without increasing interest rates.

According to the record of the meeting on 4 May,[4] Keating argued that if the depreciation were to go on encouraging import substitution, then the outlook for the current account deficit was quite different from that forecast by the Bank. It was not very difficult to generate stable current account deficits of 3.5 per cent of GDP, which contrasted with the Bank's 5 per cent and rising estimates.

Bernie Fraser was sceptical of the Bank's projections. He saw little value in projections that extended beyond the next financial year and in any case felt that the Reserve Bank had built a somewhat pessimistic set of assumptions into their numbers. There was a case, however, for further discounting at the next indexation hearing.

Peter Jonson defended the bank's calculations. He said there should be a period of austerity to rectify the current account and that a further fall in the exchange rate could be anticipated later that year on the basis of current policy settings. He wanted an early additional wage discount.

Chris Higgins was worried by growing debt and the erosion of competitiveness implied by likely wage and price movements relative to those overseas. Australia had to adjust to the large fall in terms of trade and, like Peter Johnson, he drew attention to the need to secure real wage adjustment and a cut in government expenditure. He also suggested that, on the basis of present policy settings and the outlook for the current account deficit, it was likely that the exchange rate would again come under downward pressure some time in the calendar year.

Bob Johnston's view was that it was very important to get a sensible budget for 1986–87. His main concern was how the authorities should react to the next bout of exchange rate weakness, which he felt could well occur later in 1986. He agreed with the Treasurer that the monetary policy response had already been played and there was little point in resisting a major shift in market sentiment. The question then would be to secure an appropriate policy response to ensure that the real value of any fall in the exchange rate was not dissipated.

The Treasurer agreed that the Bank should not just give in to any downward movement in the exchange rate and that any such tendency should be fully tested.

Bob Johnston said that, if only for his self-respect, he would not want it stated after the event that monetary policy had been conducted in an unwarrantedly easy manner. Keating questioned him on the future course of interest rates. The Governor did not see much scope for major falls in 90-day bills, which had averaged 16.15 per cent in April and 14.5 per cent in May. Keating said that bills rates in order of 13–14 per cent were necessary to enable business to function effectively. Johnston was non-committal but agreed that the objective was to achieve a level of rates compatible with growth in non-farm product of 3.5 per cent a year.

During the meeting Keating said that unfortunately a policy response of the magnitude being canvassed would be extremely difficult to implement before any fall in the exchange rate. It is apparent from the record of this meeting that at the beginning of May, despite the March current account figure, Keating thought there was room for rates to come down a little. He was also inclined to be more optimistic about the trend of the current account than was Peter Johnson. He thought that, even if Johnson were right, it would be difficult to find sufficient support for a change in policy without an exchange rate crisis. It is also apparent that, while a fall in the terms of trade was one factor in the widening current account deficit, it was not the only or even the most important factor. (The 'terms of trade' is the ratio of export prices to import prices. If export prices fall, perhaps because commodity prices fall, then the terms of trade fall. If import prices rise faster than export prices, perhaps because of a currency depreciation, then the terms of trade will also fall. Both factors were operating in the latter half of 1985.)

Keating had been optimistic in the face of Peter Johnson's pessimism on 4 May, but the disappointing April current account published on Tuesday 13 May and the adverse market reaction to it prompted him to change his position dramatically. At $1.4 billion, the deficit was $0.5 billion higher than the market expected. It disappointed expectations and threatened another panic round of dollar selling. Keating refused at first to comment on the numbers, but on Wednesday 14 May, while attending a fund-raising breakfast for

Victorian MHR Neil O'Keefe, he arranged to take a call in the kitchen of the function hall from Sydney radio interviewer John Laws. Annoyed by his intrusion into their work area, the cleaning staff seemed to be deliberately clashing cups and saucers as Keating spoke to Laws. Though their political views were far apart, Keating admired Laws' professionalism and respected the size of his audience.

Keating told Laws that Australia was 'living beyond our capacity to meet our obligations by $12 billion'. He said, 'we just can't let that continue'. He blamed policies in the 1970s and early 1980s, which he claimed had hurt manufacturing, as well as the currently low commodity prices. 'The world has given us a very swift kick in the pants,' he told Laws. There had been a dollar devaluation of about 30 per cent, which was working to correct the problem, but then there was a commodity price fall from October 1985.

'I have been saying lately that the economy has to slow,' he claimed. 'The government lifted interest rates in October.' Rates were high from October to February, yet 60 000 new jobs were created in April. 'There is one thing that is quite certain,' he now insisted, 'and that is Australia cannot afford to have 5 per cent economic growth this year, like last year. Because if we do, we will just suck in more imports and make the problem worse.' His solution was to get Australia exporting manufactures and to slow demand for imports. Previous governments had overvalued the exchange rate. He warned that the states need to take their share of cuts.

'Politics,' he told Laws, 'is the clearing house of pressures, and in the clearing house one has got to get the right policy through. That is what the job of being Treasurer or Prime Minister is all about. It's about delivery.' His theme was to cut the budget deficit and state spending rather than cut the private sector through higher interest rates. Low commodity prices have got 'nothing to do with the government'.

This was the 'Banana Republic' interview, but when Keating said, 'Then you have gone. You are a banana republic,' he was actually referring to the situation outlined by Laws in which high interest rates choked off demand for imports and induce a depression. He affirmed a commitment to growth of 'three plus'.

Keating was defining the task as tightening fiscal policy rather than raising interest rates – it would be higher interest rates, he said, that would risk creating a banana republic. The month of May, nonetheless, saw the trough in the policy rate. It would rise slowly through the year – though never to the level it reached in December 1985, after the November tightening. He had put the blame for the widening current account deficit on falling commodity prices. These had the convenience of not being the government's fault, but were only a part of the explanation of rising current account deficits.

On 14 May, the same day Keating was speaking to John Laws, Higgins sent over the May 1986 JEFG report. The group was now more pessimistic about the current account deficit outlook. With the dollar plummeting, Fraser summed up his thoughts on policy for the Treasurer. He believed that foreign exchange markets had overreacted but that 'nonetheless, the April numbers were a decidedly unwelcome kick in the head. The question now is what more can or should be done in the light of those numbers and the reactions to them.'[5]

A sustainable long-term strategy to turn the current account deficit and debt must include employment growth. 'By and large the strategy has been working well enough', and 'the tightening in monetary policy late last year was intended to be temporary and has now been unwound.' But the policy had always accepted that the government would need to demonstrate 'exceptional fiscal discipline' and 'squeeze the maximum degree of wage restraint out of the Accord'. Recent events 'serve mainly to spur all of us to redouble our efforts in these two areas; they could also help in achieving the necessary outcomes'.

Visiting north-east Asia, Hawke was caught unawares by the change of rhetoric. The dollar had plummeted after Keating's remarks, which were front-page news in every Australian newspaper. Reporters pressed a bewildered Hawke on whether there would still be tax cuts in September and if wages were to be further discounted. Hawke's adviser Peter Barron, travelling with him, told the Prime Minister that if he did not take the lead, Keating would. Annoyed and bewildered,

Hawke gave a background briefing critical of Keating. The two abused each other over the telephone. Hawke pointedly announced that Lionel Bowen would be in charge of arrangements for a 'mini summit' of employers and unions, which Keating and Industrial Relations Minister Ralph Willis had proposed. Later he announced he would be making a statement on the economy, effectively trumping Keating by declaring a national economic emergency requiring immediate action by the Prime Minister.

The National Accounts, released on 29 May, showed on preliminary figures negative growth for two quarters. At the beginning of the year Keating had been concerned about recession; now he pointed to evidence in the national accounts of declining terms of trade.

Treasury was not entirely happy with the sudden sense of crisis or with the Prime Minister taking over the drafting of the national economic statement. In a minute of 1 June, Bernie Fraser enclosed what he described as 'Mickey Mouse' papers 'allegedly' sought at the request of ministers on the ad hoc committee preparing the national economic statement. He wrote,

Like you, we are concerned about what this particular flurry of activity might signify and where it might lead. Apart from requiring time, it was always understood that the economic strategy embarked on last year would require a tightening of fiscal policy and, sooner or later, some action on the wages front as well . . . An air of slight crisis is all to the good if it helps to produce decisions resulting in cuts in government spending and borrowing, and a better wages outcome. But that is not the way things seem to be moving – as many of the papers in the folder testify, the season of the snake oil salesmen has now arrived. Your task of concentrating the minds of your colleagues on the fundamentals is not made any easier by exercises of this nature . . . Indeed, we cannot avoid an uneasy feeling of having seen this sort of exercise, for the worse, on a number of occasions in the past. Its hallmarks are an overdone air of crisis; an enormous volume of paper containing much that is irrelevant but some things which are potentially quite sensitive; compressed policy advising and decision making timetables; and results which might give the appearance of activity but touch only on the periphery (if that) of the real problems.

Paul in the House of Representatives at Question Time; 1993
Michael Jones, News Ltd

Paul with Annita at the Press Club, March 1993, towards the end of the
election campaign

Paul Keating, Mabo Press Conference; June 1993
Andrew Chapman

Paul with the Dalai Lama at the Parliament
House office; 1993

Paul with President Suharto; 1994

Paul Keating's farewell to politics. Election night, 2 March 1996 at Bankstown Sports Club.
Andrew Chapman

Paul and his sister Lynne

Paul at ALP Youth Council;
about 1964–65

The Blaxland campaign bus; 1969

Paul with Jack Lang; 1971

Selling the Consumption Tax; 1985

Keating with the official family: Bob Johnston (Governor of the Reserve Bank)
and Bernie Fraser (head of Treasury) at Reserve Bank of Australia, Sydney; 1985

With Prime Minister Bob Hawke, at the 1985 Tax Summit
at Old Parliament House

The Keating family at their home in Beagle St, Red Hill, 1989. From left: Caroline,
Alexandra, Annita, Paul, Katherine. Patrick was away at boarding school.

If Treasury was annoyed, the Treasurer was furious. The policy crisis he had created and dramatised, and which Hawke had at first queried, was now being manipulated by Hawke, not Keating. Tensions between the two men increased, with Keating publicly criticising the 'Manchu court' of the Prime Minister's advisers, who had 'never been elected to anything but they think they have.'

On 11 June Hawke announced a spending cut and a deferral of tax cuts planned under the Accord. Deferring tax cuts for three months reduced by a quarter their cost in revenue forgone in the coming budget. The government-encouraged crisis of May and June won major cuts, though the tenor of the changes was not at this point very different from the approach Keating had outlined in a leaked budget submission at the beginning of the year. The main changes were the postponement of the tax cuts for three months and the opportunity the crisis provided to reduce the promised general revenue grants to the states.

By June Keating was telling the ERC he wanted a deficit with a 'four in front of it'. At the beginning of the year it had been $5 billion. This was a change, but not a big one. There was, however, another round to come. Over May and June the dollar declined by less than 10 per cent on a trade weighted basis. In July and into August it would fall by more than ten per cent, providing the opportunity for Keating to cut spending further than Hawke had foreshadowed. Keating supported the currency, but not as rapidly or as much as he had in 1985. Interest rates were lifted by around 1 per cent in June, then another 2 per cent in July and August. But they were still lower than they had been at the start of the year.

Hawke and Keating had differences, but their partnership was working. At the end of June Keating presented a thoroughly alarming submission that informed Cabinet:

As we all know, this is a critical time for economic policy formulation. The Prime Minister has identified the nature of the problems before us and the broad strategy for tackling them. Those problems boil down to the need to close our unsustainably wide current account deficit; to maintain competitiveness; to lower interest rates; and to foster increased business investment.[6]

It said the government would seek a further discount at the next wage case. By a highly suspect calculation, applying old prices to new quantities, Australia was said to have lost 3 per cent of GDP through the decline in the terms of trade. It predicted a current account deficit in 1986–87 of 'as high as 5.25 per cent of GDP'. Publication of such a forecast in the Budget would put enormous pressure on the exchange rate, which could wreck inflation prospects. He wanted total growth in real budget spending limited to an increase of no more than 0.5 per cent, which, given the increase in national debt interest and other unavoidable spending, would mean real reductions of 0.8 per cent in budget payments to the states.

While Keating worked on the Budget, the markets remained nervous and the dollar began to slide. On Friday 25 July Higgins reported to Bernie Fraser a call from Nicolas Sargen, the Salomon Brothers Australia specialist in New York, to Treasury official John Fraser. 'Sargen said he was having difficulty maintaining his position of support for Australia. An increasing number of their clients are beginning to think of cutting their losses – now some 20 per cent,' John Fraser had recorded. Salomon's view was that what was needed was a tightening in monetary policy and a statement that the government was going to hold the rate. Higgins reported he had passed the information on to John Phillips at the Reserve Bank straight away.

Foreign holders of Australian dollar assets had been annoyed by Keating's 1 July decision to impose a 15 per cent tax on their interest and dividends payments before they were remitted abroad. It was a decision pushed hard by Treasury, which he already regretted. Over the weekend Keating and Fraser worked on a package to steady the currency. Treasury prepared for an announcement that the new withholding tax would be removed and that a rule confining foreign investors to holding a maximum half share in real estate developments would be relaxed.

After a busy weekend Keating arrived at his Parliament House office in mid-morning on Monday 28 July. He had not, he later remembered, listened to the morning news programs. Over a cup of tea, Don Russell serenely told him that the dollar was in trouble but that it was nothing to worry about. The Australian dollar was in fact plummeting. Beginning from 63 cents, that day it would touch its lowest value ever against the American dollar – 57.3 cents. Despite the tightening of 1985 and Hawke's economic statement, the dollar was weaker than it had ever been.

Keating called Bob Johnston and asked him what they should do. Keating recalls that Johnston replied, 'Frankly, Treasurer, I don't know what to do.' He asked Johnston to support the dollar with intervention and to increase the policy interest rate. 'Throw another billion' at the dollar, he told him. Later that day he announced the reversal of his 1 July decisions, together with some other incentives to increase the attraction of Australian dollar assets. The 15 per cent dividend withholding tax for profits repatriated overseas by resident companies was eliminated; certain securities that had been brought into the withholding tax net were again exempted; a 5 per cent branch profits tax was eliminated; and a minimum Australian half share in real estate developments was no longer required.

The ERC was in almost continuous session that day. Keating dramatised the weakening dollar by keeping a small Reuters screen in front of him. As the dollar dropped, his colleagues sought ways to cut the 0.5 per cent real growth in outlays to zero, allowing a deficit to come in under $4 billion. Later that week Bob Johnston was brought to Canberra to emphasise to the ERC and Cabinet the gravity of the crisis.

In the Budget, Keating was able to announce a deficit of $3.5 billion, well below expectations. Total outlays fell slightly in real terms. As Keating said, 'On only three occasions in the last thirty years has real growth in total outlays' been less than zero. Income tax cuts were now delayed for three months. He also announced that the government would seek a discount from wage increases.

Keating made less of it publicly but, at the same time as spending growth and the deficit were reduced, interest rates were sharply
increased. They would remain high right through to April of the following year. Thirty-day bank bills promptly rose from 15 per cent
to 18 per cent, well above the level which, at the beginning of the
year, Keating had thought too high for investment. The change of
rhetoric was more resounding than any change of policy. It was Keating who had been bringing interest rates down in the face of opposition from the Reserve Bank. If there were demand pressures now
he had added to them. But at the time he warned of growth of '5 per
cent plus', the economy was continuing to slow. In private meetings
both Keating and Fraser had been much more concerned about the
slowdown than about the dangers of too-rapid growth. Keating took
advantage of the higher-than-expected current account numbers to
force a further tightening in the Commonwealth Budget – including
payments to the states – and in wages.

A success, then the crisis of 1986 also sowed the seeds of later failure. The Banana Republic interview committed Keating to the idea
that the current account deficit was bad and foreign debt was bad.
The combination of currency depreciation, interest rate increases,
wage cuts and spending cuts helped to increase exports and slow
imports, demonstrating the successful application of policy to a problem that Keating had defined. Next time the current account deficit
would rise much more persistently, and the measures that worked
in 1986 to slow the economy and turn the current account around
would in 1989 touch off a sharp and protracted recession. The roots
of the recession of 1990 and 1991 lay in the successes of 1986.

The Budget announced, the dollar strengthened. The US economy
picked up speed after the slowdown of late 1985 and early 1986.
Exports picked up and the current account deficit began to narrow.
As we sat over dinner ten days or so after the 1986 Budget, the first

time I had talked with Keating at length for many years, I had found him unexpectedly relaxed, funny and obliging. He was also experiencing, and actually enjoying, a strange sort of mid-life crisis. He was unexpectedly discovering, he would say, that his whole pleasure in the exercise of power – the crushing victories and dismayed opponents, the television cameras, the secret knowledge of things other people wished to know, the enjoyment of watching people melt with barely concealed pleasure when he confided in them or sought their advice, the gratification of rising in the world so that people who were once hard to see directed at him the full force of their charm and fraternal ease – had diminished with familiarity and been replaced by the most irresistible of seductions: the enjoyment of beautiful things and the need for freedom.

In his mid forties he was discovering what most of his colleagues would never discover, what Bob Hawke, for example, would never discover, that politics, because of its vanity and transience, cannot nourish some instinct for growth and development that pressed within him. Of his colleagues, only Bill Hayden clearly had the same affliction. Keating could observe in Hayden's quirky, black bitter hilarity the consequence of inward growth withering in the aridity of politics.

The Treasurer had learned a lot about people and affairs over the last three years, but he had also begun to realise that there was a whole world of music before and after the Romantics, the whole world of painting and sculpture in all cultures other than European, and in European everything in sculpture and painting before Fragonard and after Ingres of which he knew next to nothing.

There were pleasures, gratifying triumphs of daring, but there was no rest in victory. He had discovered that he had to fight each time, not so much for victory as for his perception of reality so that he could define it through conflict. He had to fight each time for what he thought would work, and he had to fight hardest against his own desire for ease, his own desire to go along when everyone else wanted to go one way and he another, as he did over imposing an interest withholding tax, because once you start to give in, he discovered, you start to lose control.

There was also pain, not often the pain of defeat and ignominy, but frequently the pain of the banal and humdrum. He had moved from one rented house to another in Canberra and they were not – with his wife and four children – wonderful places to live. They were often small, ugly and badly decorated, so that the few well-wrought objects he brought with him, the Empire *objets d'art* and the paintings, were out of place, bizarre and pathetic, making the houses look even more dismal than they were. They were, he would say, shitheaps. There was no Number 11 Downing Street, an official home for the Treasurer, which made it all the more galling that the one official ministerial home in Canberra, the Lodge, was serenely occupied by Hawke, who apparently intended to have a very long stay.

The longer he continued as Treasurer, he said at dinner, the more he pondered a remark made to him by a man who was once a very close friend and mentor, of similarly powerful political intellect, the journalist Max Walsh. 'You are a conscript of history,' Walsh told him years before, when Keating was a restless backbencher haunting the tiny *Financial Review* office in the Parliament House press gallery, learning how all the bits connected and how economic policy lay at the heart of it all. 'You are a conscript of history,' Walsh had said in one of those arresting prophecies that had gained certainty and lost accuracy as Walsh himself acquired grandeur, 'and when the rest of us are enjoying our lives, you will be chained down here doing history's bidding'. Keating pondered that remark because it was turning out to be true and because it became part of the game he played with himself; a dangerous game, which could end his career more surely than any circumstance of the economy, and which he played out entirely in his own mind.

Keating at last understood things about money and power that had fascinated him when he visited the *Financial Review* office in the long vacant years of opposition and bachelor life in Canberra, and he had learned how to operate the levers and pulleys himself. Arriving at the centre, he said, he found it surprisingly simple. Half a dozen key people, three or four levers or pulleys or settings (he used the words interchangeably) over which he had some influence. The rest, he often said, was leads and lags, which is another way of saying that he expected a certain outcome but didn't know when.

That year he had seen one of his remarks drive the dollar down six cents, and another bring it up. He had learned how financial markets worked, how they responded to news, how they responded to political leadership, and he had seen how the financial centres of London and New York and the policy-making centre of Washington related to the things he did in Canberra. And all along he had been measuring himself and his world against the people he met and the other worlds he encountered. He learned and he judged. He realised in talking to former US budget director David Stockman that the problems of the US budget were just like the problems of the Australian budget, with some noughts added. He talked to former US Federal Reserve chairman Paul Volcker, unquestionably the most influential economic policy-maker of his time, and he realised that Volcker's mind and training were virtually identical to that of the Governor of the Reserve Bank of Australia, Bob Johnston, and that the problems they faced were much the same. Some of the great people Keating met were smarter than he; some – a great many whose brilliance he had once read about – were not as smart; and some were so hopeless that he automatically and instinctively took over, as he took over in an Australian Cabinet subcommittee.

There was no job in the world, he now concluded, that he could not creditably do, not because he was Australia's greatest son but because he had discovered how ordinary the occupants of most of these jobs really were. Keating now understood it, but in satisfying his curiosity he was also beginning to exhaust his interest. Now that he understood how all the bits fitted together, the knowledge of it had lost its fascination. Now that he had met the great of the world, they had lost their mystery. He asked himself, as people do around his age, whether this was all there was, and the implacable answer so far as politics was concerned was – yes, that was it. There was his wife and family, the source of his greatest joy; there was a tranquil pleasure in beautifully made things; there was satisfaction in renovating a large Sydney house to his idea of perfection – each room painstakingly designed as to colour and detail, then sketched in water-colour; and there was a pleasing sense of a recompensing gift in planning the museum of antiques he thought he might leave to the national estate; but as far as politics was concerned, it was as good now as it ever would be.

It was characteristic of his mood as a seasoned Treasurer that he should think as often of his Elizabeth Bay house as of the current account deficit. It may have been the simple pleasure of acquisition, the powerful impulse of our twenties and thirties, which took him into Consulat and Empire art, as it had taken him into Mercedes cars and real estate. But at the beginning of his forties it was the example of those clockmaker craftsmen, their obscurity and their pride in their craft, that chastened him as he retraced their work in meticulous restoration.

The Canberra house may be a shitheap, and Australia itself sometimes seemed to him crawling all over with buzzing blowfly journalists who never believed a word he said, who gave him no credit for the good things he did and who tried to destroy him. There were the frauds and phonies of all kinds who are forever rabbiting on as if they really knew what was what when they didn't know a thing and weren't bright enough to recognise it if they were told. There were dopey businessmen who continued to run him down and criticise him when he had broken his back for them and give them more in four years than the other mob had given them in forty years. He was buzzed by the lefties and maddies of all kinds, fortunately too witless to matter, and by the other mob, who were now just cannon fodder for himself and Bob to blow apart in the House.

And that was only just the beginning of his list of problems with this small inward-looking frightened little country, which ran down people who had a go, like his developer friend Warren Anderson, or his still wealthier friend Kerry Packer, and which was now, after the floating of the exchange rate and the great depreciation of the mid 1980s, finally changing and responding to the rest of the world with screams of rage and howls of pain and blaming the Treasurer for the inconvenience. It was a hell of a country in many ways, and the worst of it was that for a politician it was the only country he had.

So what was he to do? He played a game with himself, the chicken game or Russian roulette of mid life. He arranged the choices in his mind, in his friendships and his financial planning so that an alternative life was also attractive. He prepared for political defeat in this way, but he also increased the risks he could take, the grace with which he could act, and the good humour with which he could accept setbacks in his political career. He convinced himself, and sought to convince others, not only that he did not wish to lead the Opposition, to spend years of his life travelling to small political meetings, but also that he did not much care if he ceased to be Treasurer and never became Prime Minister. And his conviction, so far as it went, was quite genuine. As reporter Kerry O'Brien noticed in a television profile of the Treasurer, he had begun to use in politics concepts that were drawn from the lexicon of antique collecting. Not only had he begun to incorporate the language but he had also begun to incorporate its artistic values of integrity and authenticity into the rudimentary impulses of greed, conceit and contempt that inspired the New South Wales party machine and which remained another important part of his character.

This game had an obvious political purpose in creating a stronger bargaining stance with his colleagues, with the press and the electorate, but it also had a private purpose, which was directed by Paul Keating at Paul Keating. If it was intended to delude, then it was most of all intended to delude him. The mind has mountains; cliffs of fall. And perhaps he was deluding himself because the available alternatives – business, an international job, antique dealing – may not on closer scrutiny be attractive at all. Like Hayden after the 1975 election, he might struggle to free himself, to break loose of politics and obey some other impulse, fail, and remain to be Prime Minister, an unhappy Opposition leader, or a roving statesman and antique collector, the kept man of some more definite and limited leader. Or, like Neil Batt of Tasmania, he might actually get out, actually get a job in an international agency and then plead to be let back into the party, the accustomed society where he has prestige and a place where his skills are valued, when he discovers that what drives him away is not consoled by a change of location.

He didn't want money, or not a lot of money, he would say, though he did need enough the keep the family and buy antiques. He didn't understand the impulse of men like Rupert Murdoch, who continued to pile up assets long after they themselves were fantastically wealthy. 'Why do you want it?' he asked Murdoch once over dinner, when the publisher was acquiring another corporation, much bigger than the last. 'Why bother?' Murdoch had to pile up wealth; for him it was a necessity; Keating did not share that view. But he did want the freedom wealth gives, the freedom he observed longingly in Robert Holmes à Court, who happily described to him once how he would fly across to his London residence when he wanted, how he could buy this or that wonderful object when he wanted. He envied Warren Anderson's ability to buy the entire set of master engravings of John James Audubon, or Kerry Packer's ability to buy the finest silver collection, though he also thought he could do a lot with taste and persistence and information and that his house in Elizabeth Bay, his collection painstakingly built, put him at least in the same collecting league as these vastly wealthier men.

Keating knew that if he now went for great wealth he would have to spend his forties and fifties working singlemindedly to acquire it; that he had now irretrievably lost to politics his twenties and thirties, the decades in which wealth might be acquired to be enjoyed at his present age, and that he would have to pursue it without the accustomed redemption of working for the national interest. And even so he might still not be as wealthy as some other smart kids who also left school at 15 at the end of the 1950s and skipped thirty years of building loyalties, winning preselection, hanging around in opposition and finally taking care of the rest of us, who instead stumbled into making money in meat or trucks or real estate and these days wonder whether we might not have a go at politics. It would be dreary work for Keating, conducted among people who had not and never would rise out of the valley and see all the wonders that he had not only seen and commanded but also were now his habitual and accustomed landscape.

Maybe, he sometimes told himself and visitors with the boyish candour and egocentricity that was so marked a characteristic, he would trade in antiques, do something in business to keep afloat, and of course there was a generous parliamentary pension for which he was already eligible. He could live in Paris or London, he would say, or somewhere in the US for a while, and learn new things. He could do things that really gave him pleasure, like collecting beautiful objects, and escape the things that no longer gave him pleasure, like television interviews. But another part of him knew that this would be fun only for a while, and that it was very difficult to take a few years off in politics. That part of him knew that he had only one short life, and that it was already too late to do anything other than stride along the path already traced out for him, to remain history's conscript.

Following the alarm of the 1986 Budget Keating had predicted a long, slow period of good news leading up to the next election. Entering 1987 the government began to see it. Impelled by depreciation, strengthening exports and stronger investment, growth resumed an upward trend by the second half of 1986. The monthly current account deficits continued to narrow.

So good did the news become that it would later be said that the seeds of the 1988 boom were in the easy-going economic policies of 1987. But to the Treasurer and his colleagues in early 1987, policy did not seem easy going at all. Nor did they or other forecasters predict that the economy would grow as steadily as it did.

At the start of 1987 monetary and fiscal policies remained quite tight. At this stage the policy rate was still over 15 per cent. As late as March it was over 16 per cent, and 90-day bank bills were 16.25 per cent. Fiscal policy was much tighter than it had been. After a period of inflation, wages were falling. The current account was narrowing. Inflation in the March quarter was still running at an annual rate of 8 per cent or so, but the upsurge had been caused by higher import prices. As these worked through, inflation would fall back. Though employment continued to increase, unemployment remained over 9 per cent – higher than it had been in the middle of 1986. There was a strong case to lower interest rates, and in April 1987 the overnight rate was brought down by around 2 percentage points.

The officially forecast outlook was for slow growth. Neither the coming stock market crash nor the incipient boom were contemplated. Treasury's forecasters predicted in their JEFG review non-farm growth of 1.75 per cent in 1986–87 and 3 per cent in 1987–88. The current account deficit would be $14 billion in 1986–87 and $12 billion in 1987–88. Unemployment would remain at 8.5 per cent. The CPI would be nearly 9 per cent in 1986–87 and 7 per cent the following year. The forecasters did note that at this time last year the current account deficit for 1986–87 forecast was $9 billion, not the $14 billion now predicted – so there were uncertainties. (The actual current account deficit was $11.7 in 1986–87 and $10.2 billion in 1987–88.)

Nor was there evidence of the credit boom, which would contribute to the speed of the expansion in 1988 and 1989. Total lending to the private sector by all financial institutions grew more slowly in 1987 than it had in either of the two preceding years or the two following years. In 1987 there was very little evidence of the splurge to come.

Certainly there was evidence of dramatically increasing asset prices, but the assets involved were shares on the stock exchange. Between the low of the early 1980s and the market crash later in 1987 equities prices would increase fivefold. Since increased share prices ultimately meant more funds for income-producing assets like factories and offices there was little complaint or criticism.

In the course of 1987 fiscal policy on at least one measure became much tighter than it had been at any time in the Labor Government. Because the current account deficit is equal to the gap between domestic saving and domestic investment, Treasury argued that the government could reduce the current account deficit by reducing the federal budget deficit and thereby increasing government saving.[7] Responding to this advice, Keating pressed for and achieved spending cuts in 1987 deeper than those he had achieved in earlier years. The 1987 May statement made deeper cuts to projected spending than had the more dramatically announced Budget of 1986, and the May cuts were followed up in the 1987 Budget.

But the May 1987 statement did contribute to the problems of 1988 and 1989 in another sense: it confirmed Keating's commitment to reducing the current account deficit. Needing to press the spending cuts in a reluctant Cabinet, Keating invoked the threat of a widening current account deficit. If the government saved more, the current account deficit would fall. Don Russell firmly believed that the government's fortunes were tied to the current account deficit. Tom Mockridge told his colleagues and Treasury that there was a simple message to get across: foreign debt is bad.[8] In Treasury both Chris Higgins and David Morgan were firm and proponents of the 'twin deficits idea'. Bernie Fraser and Ted Evans supported spending cuts and were happy to go along with the message. The threat of debt was used to drive fiscal tightening. But the message was too simple. It omitted the fact that, while increased saving would lower the current account deficit, increased investment would increase it. And, unlike debt, investment was good.

With the May statement behind them, interest rates moderated and the current account deficit stabilised. At Keating's urging, Hawke decided to go to the polls. Hawke had argued that the government should run through to 1988 and take advantage of the good feelings engendered by the bicentenary. He publicly ruled out an election in 1987. Keating told him Australia would have a party on 26 January and that would be the end of the celebration. The election was announced on Wednesday 27 May for 11 July. Tax cuts were scheduled for 1 July, and a national wage case pay rise would become effective around the same time.

During the election campaign Keating dramatically exposed an arithmetical flaw in John Howard's proposed economic program. One commentator described it as 'the Paul Keating election', after Keating bagged Howard.[9] As for the government's record, Keating claimed complete success. The big macroeconomic issues of growth, employment, the trade imbalance and inflation had been solved. Now it was time to look at the more 'delicate' microeconomic issues. After speaking to the Treasurer, Michael Stuchbury of the *Financial Review* wrote: 'Optimistically claiming to have fixed the macroeconomic fundamentals, Treasurer Paul Keating has set the sights of a third term Labor government on micro-economic efficiency issues.'[10] He wanted increased public sector efficiency, some state government activities moved into the private sector, restrictive work practices negotiated away in a two-tier wage system, and industry unionism:

We are turning the current account around, we have brought consumption down, and we are seeing the growth come off net exports. It's not a light at the end of the tunnel – it's a huge arc lamp.

Keating also said,

This government has been so overwhelmed by the immediacy of its problem in 1983 – repairing the factor shares, dealing with competitiveness, the terms of trade collapse, rapid adjustments to fiscal and wages policy – that some of the more delicate issues in micro policy have been left to be dealt with another time. We have intellectually chosen the route of internationalisation. If you are going to internationalise it must be about being efficient in world terms, that is our only place in the future. And that means you must attend to the micro issues of efficiency.

The government won comfortably on 11 July. Keating told reporter Steve Burrell at midnight in Bankstown, 'You need that sort of result to restore your faith in what you are doing, to keep you going.'[11] He refused to be drawn on the deputy leadership, which would become vacant on the expected retirement of Bowen. Later, with his staff at the Café Jax in Kings Cross, he told Burrell, 'Mate, I've got the levers in my hands for another three years and I'm hanging on to them.'

Delayed by the election and a post-election break, Keating returned to Budget-making on 6 August. Fraser was now pressing for the deficit to be eliminated. Keating was thinking of a deficit of around $1.5 billion. He had mentioned publicly a goal of $1.7 billion.[12]

Claiming to have largely fixed Australia's macroeconomic policy, both Hawke and Keating believed microeconomic reform was the new priority of government. An awkward term, 'micro-reform' usually meant applying competitive market principles in government enterprises and in government rule-making for the private sector. Keating was very interested in tariff reform, telecommunications, aviation and the media. Treasury wanted the Treasurer to play an even bigger role, with an agenda that included industry and trade, vocational education and training, transport and communications, intergovernmental finances, the financial sector, foreign investment, occupational superannuation, and sales of government assets.

Keating delivered the Budget on 15 September. He described it to TV presenter Ray Martin as a '24 carat budget'. Not content with this, he added, 'This is the golden age of economic change.' According to Treasury figuring, the net effect of policy decisions was to save $3.5 billion off forward estimates of spending. The deficit was expected to be $27m – effectively zero. Spending declined 2.4 per cent after inflation, the largest real decline in thirty years. He reported that over the past year, 'adjustment had been proceeding without major disruption,' though the current account deficit 'remains unsustainably high'. The forecasts for the past year had not been too bad. The current account deficit outcome was 'lower than expected'. But the world economy was mispredicted – 'There are no conclusive signs of an early reversal of the growth slowdown.' There was a long triumphal and didactic account of government policy towards the current account deficit. The forecasts would be quite wrong.

Chuffed by the election win, Hawke was asserting himself. Reporters wanted to know if he planned to retire. He said publicly in late August that the party would be in very good hands if it decided to select

Keating as his successor, but Hawke was in no hurry to go, and there were other qualified contestants. Reporters wondered how long Keating would wait around and how soon Hawke would go. The *Age's* Michelle Grattan wrote that Keating's performance in the election campaign had been more impressive than Hawke's. The *Financial Review's* Greg Heywood wrote a story headlined 'Labor strategists plan for Keating's PM run'.[13] He claimed that Hawke would stay through to the next election, so what was planned was a three- to five-year transition. In the *Sydney Morning Herald* Alan Ramsey wrote that the real story of Australian politics over the next two years 'is going to be how successful Paul Keating is in matching reality with desire in his ambition to become Prime Minister in the life of this Parliament'.[14] Hawke was saying he would serve out this term and was equivocal about the next. Privately Hawke was saying he would go to a fourth election in 1990. Ramsey reported that earlier that year Keating had told Hawke, 'If you want to wear the belt you have to have the fights. And if you won't have the fights, you'll have to take the belt off.'

Concerns about the current account deficit continued, however, to dominate policy. Don Russell, for example, was worried about the surprising strength of the dollar. On 24 September in a note to Keating he wrote, 'I don't think that the Treasury fully appreciates what has happened to the exchange rate and how important it is to the strategy.'[15] He pointed out that, measured by the trade weighted index, the dollar was 10 per cent higher than a year ago. Against the American dollar it was 17 per cent higher. If the TWI stayed where it was many firms that invested in good faith would get burnt. (The trade weighted index is a measure of the dollar's value.) Also, the current account deficit was around 4 per cent of GDP. In Russell's view it should be a maximum of 2.5 per cent. Using a higher exchange rate to slow the economy down 'will get us nowhere'. Further reductions in the current account deficit would be increasingly dependent on the J-curve. He said the Reserve Bank should be told that it should reduce intervention, that the exchange rate should not go up and if anything should go down, and that cash rates should be adjusted by as much as necessary to accomplish this. Rates can come back again if necessary. There should be no public statement. A few days earlier Russell had told Keating the interest rate cut should be substantial – 2 per cent. He advised him, 'You should ring Bob Johnston today as he is leaving tonight . . . Assure him that rates can go up again if necessary . . . Tell him you want a big enough cut in rates to let the exchange rate float freely but at a TWI below 57.'

Russell's advice was attached to a note from Bernie Fraser on the domestic money market and the foreign exchange market. His advice was contrary to Russell's. Fraser wrote, 'The Governor sent you a timely message yesterday on policy options for addressing looming problems in these markets.' In Fraser's view the currency had not yet risen too high (to discourage exporters) or interest rates fallen too low (to engineer a boom), so there was no need for precipitate action. 'In particular, to engineer a dramatic decline in interest rates would be unwarranted, in my view'.[16]

He argued that interest rates would need a big drop to bring down the exchange rate, and it would later need to be reversed. He suggested letting markets determine the exchange rate and interest rate by ceasing intervention in the foreign exchange market. 'This could result in some upward movement in the short term,' he said, 'but would remove the one-way bet. They should also let cash rates come down with sizeable funds inflow. They should lower the rediscount rate and set a lower rate for the new Australian Savings Bond series.

This dispute between two close advisers was forgotten a little over a month later when equity markets crashed worldwide. Touched off by a falling US dollar and accelerated by new computer trading programs, which dumped millions of shares into markets, the boom in share prices came to an abrupt end. In Australia the impact was wildly overestimated. In the *Australian Financial Review* P. P. McGuiness wrote, ' . . . it is almost inevitably the harbinger of a world depression.' The US, he wrote, 'is likely to follow the same path as it did in 1930–31 when the Smoot–Hawley Act lifted US tariffs, evoked retaliatory action by other countries, and thereby caused a collapse of world trade'.[17]

Soon after, Bob Johnston wrote formally to the Treasurer.

My Dear Treasurer,

At its meeting last Tuesday, the Bank Board naturally enough was anxious to make some assessment of the implications of the stock market collapse for the economy and, hence, for policy settings.

It was readily agreed that it was too early to be certain as to how things will turn out; the restoration of a reasonable degree of market stability and confidence in Australia was the immediate task. Accordingly, the Board's decisions for the immediate future were that the Bank should:

- seek to maintain stability in financial conditions, whilst keeping a close watch on the adequacy of system liquidity; and
- in its foreign exchange operations, test sharp movements in the exchange rate without seeking to prevent well based rate movements in either direction.

From the point of view of monetary policy, looked at narrowly, the stock market reversal and the subsequent decline in the exchange rate have had some useful effects. They have removed some of the Board's recent worries about the possibility of demand overheating and the money and credit aggregates growing too strongly. The exchange rate has reached a more serviceable level. We can probably stand some further easing of interest rates if demand falls away subject, of course, to keeping an eye on foreign investment.

The big issues, however, are whether the US will make any worthwhile policy adjustment and, whatever the outcome, whether commodity prices are likely to receive a check. The Board had no particular insights into these issues but most members felt the odds were that commodity prices would fall; and moreover, that the improvement in our current account had stalled before the share price fall.

The fact that the downturn had hit us relatively harder than most countries came as a shock and has moved members to feel that our own efforts towards economic adjustment will have to be that much tougher. It was generally agreed that if there was a fall in commodity prices, there will be little option but to go back and review policies across the board. Some felt that this should be done now anyway but others felt it preferable to wait until the case was clearer.

If a severe downturn emerges, the Board could see that we may well be in the 'catch-22' situation of needing to press on with the necessary structural adjustments in the face of increased balance of payments problems. As to the latter, we would be starting from a higher level of debt and with investors more wary and less patient with us. We must assume that in those conditions the exchange rate also would likely be under downward pressure, reviving the spectre of depreciation-led inflation.

There might be less scope for monetary policy to help, since domestic conditions might well require continued relatively low interest rates. (One can't be sure about this in advance.) The balance of payments would, therefore, have to be addressed by other means.

Wages policy would be crucial. The desirable objective would be to absorb any fall in the rate of economic growth with least cost to employment. That would point to further efforts to rein in nominal incomes and to raise productivity. If real incomes were to be affected, as would seem inevitable, it would be better for this to reflect in lower nominal incomes than in higher inflation.

Fiscal policy would need rejigging if the gap between national expenditure and national savings seemed likely to widen. The role of the States' finances would become even more pressing.

I am sorry that these thoughts tend to be rather gloomy; events may well turn out to be much brighter. Personally, I think we can wait a little while before deciding on new courses of action but contingency planning now and, perhaps, some preparation of the community, would seem to be good insurance. However, we have to be alert to the speed with which conditions can deteriorate.

So far as monetary policy for the immediate future is concerned, we see no difficulty in continuing to sustain domestic liquidity whilst smoothing moderate further declines in the exchange rate if this occurs. A major slide in the exchange rate, of course, would be a different matter.[18]

Responding to the crash, interest rates were lowered. Keating urged calm and rejected claims that a world depression had commenced. Within a few months it became evident that the crash had been almost completely confined to share markets. Most economies continued growing, and some picked up speed.

It had been a hard year. On Christmas Eve 1987 Alan Ramsey found Keating still working in his Parliament House office, 'just knocking the last of the paper over'. With a chart and a board the Treasurer took Ramsey through 'the big picture . . . his game plan for the Australian economy: where he says he is, where he's been since 1983, where the economy is going if he gets his way in Cabinet, which he usually does. After another hard, long year, his authority remains immense.' Keating had set up an easel in his office with fifteen large pasteboard illustrations – coloured graphs of economic indicators. His message was that Australia was trading its way out of its current account problem. 'He turned two of the graphs to the wall,' reported Ramsey, 'propped them against the back of a settee, and began drawing furiously – figures, arrows, additions and subtractions, squiggles, bumps, curves, circled sweeps, hard underlines, his pen rarely pausing; the Van Gogh of Treasurers.' Keating talked for an hour, and then had a note delivered to Ramsey, 'just in case you balls it up.'[19]

11

SOUND OF A HARP

THE BOOM AND BUST OF THE LATE 1980s and early 1990s over-shadow Keating's record as Treasurer. The period continued to per-plex him long after it was over and he had ceased to be Treasurer. 'If there was a mistake,' he said, a weak brandy and dry in his hand and a plate of gristly beef before him as we flew back to Canberra from a campaign visit to Geelong in mid 1992, 'it was getting too concerned about the current account deficit, about the monthly import volumes, then, as it were, getting hoist with your own petard.'

But was it really just the current account, I wondered, mis-understanding then the extent to which Keating had linked his polit-ical fortunes to the current account deficit. Wasn't it also that he needed a crisis like the current account in 1988, as he had in 1985 and 1986, to force budget changes through a weary Cabinet?

'Perhaps,' he said, 'perhaps' – meaning no – 'but the thing is, Chris Higgins, you know, was really devoted to the twin deficits idea. He really believed if we got the budget deficit down we would get the cur-rent account deficit down. And of course if you were explaining what happened in 1988 and 1989, you had to remember the experience of 1986' – when he had also raised interest rates in the face of a widen-ing current account deficit – ' . . . then . . . ' – his hand sloping down an imagined graph in the air above his plate – 'the easy slowing of demand. It misled us. I think now the effect of interest rates is expo-nential. Quarter after quarter' – his hand going slowly up the graph as interest rates increase — 'quarter after quarter and then suddenly — bang! And their effect becomes exponential. Quarter after quarter, and then suddenly. I realised it in September 1989. I said to Don I could feel it. It wasn't there yet in the import volumes but I could feel it. But I knew I could not convince financial markets.

'I'll tell you what. This is all bullshit about the science of monetary policy. All bullshit. Every month for years we had papers on credit growth, the yield curve, etc., etc., the relation to GNE, and it was never any good at prediction. Never. You have to be able to feel what is happening.'

'Like the horses,' nodded press secretary John Miner, sitting opposite, 'you digest all the information, you have the experience, then after while you get a feel.'

'Yes, you need a framework, you need experience, you need judgment — one of these alone is not enough. We — Dawkins, Willis, me — haven't got the energy we once had, but we have experience. It's very important. We are cleverer. You get cleverer with age. Things are puzzling and confused; you see them all jumbled up, and then one day — it's like putting on a pair of glasses — they are suddenly clear and bright and you can see the arrangement, how all the bits fit.'

Beginning in March 1988 Keating would encourage and authorise — sometimes, in the face of objection, insist upon — a series of interest rate increases, which were the cause of the subsequent recession. This recession was in many respects the most severe Australia had encountered in half a century. But for the recession, half a million or more people might have been in jobs rather than unemployed. But for the recession, total production might have been $50 billion greater. How and why those interest rate increases were decided upon is a story of the intertwining of economics and politics, of conflict and uncertainty within the inner circle of advisers, and of the difficulties of economic prediction.

At the beginning of 1988 both the boom and the recession were very far from the Treasurer's mind. The year would, he thought,

be the time he could declare victory over the current account, inflation and budget deficits – the three challenges of the 1970s and
1980s. By February Keating was already discussing with the ACTU
a $4–$6 billion tax cut package, which could take the top off inflation by reducing wage growth. Although many commentators had
warned of world recession in the wake of the stock market crash,
Australia was now entering a second year of reasonably good growth
after the 1986 check, which itself had followed the two good years
of 1984 and 1985. Treasury forecasters had expected slowing
growth in 1987 and perhaps a downturn in the world economy.
Far from collapsing, the global boom was catching a second wind
in 1988.

The January JEFG report was the first to take account of both
a stronger economy than expected at Budget time and the stock
market crash.[1] The current account deficit the following year might
increase in nominal terms, even though the forecasters still expected
slowing world growth. It said, 'The key features of the outlook are
a stronger rate of non-farm and total GDP growth in 1987–88
than forecast at Budget time, but with product growth slowing in
1988–89 as the effects of the stock market crash and slower world
growth are felt.' Domestic demand was expected to be a good deal
stronger than forecast at Budget time. The current account was in
line with the forecast but likely to widen in 1988–89. The group
failed to predict the rapid output growth of 1988 and the still more
rapid growth of 1989. It forecast, 'On current assessments there
seems likely to be a marked slowing in the growth of domestic
demand in 1988–89, reflecting slower private consumption growth,
and falls in non-residential construction investment and public final
demand.' The current account deficit in 1988–89 would be $12
billion. (It was $17.9 billion. Domestic final demand grew at 5.5
per cent in 1988–89, compared with 4.23 per cent in 1987–88.)

The JEFG thought that the current account deficit would be a
problem, not because they predicted the rapid expansion that would
occur, but because they believed it would stop shrinking. An official
noted, 'The Group generally considered that the outlook for 1988–89

was not viable, largely because of the stalling of the balance of payments adjustment. If events unfolded as forecast, the Group felt that there would be upward pressure in domestic interest rates and/or downward pressure on the exchange rate.'[2] He concluded, 'Further tightening of policies would seem to be needed to avoid re-emergence of financial market pressures.'

Keating was independently coming to a more alarming view. Some of his business friends were developers and, with both a tourist boom and growing bank lending, developers were busy. Over January 1986 he was on holiday at the Queensland town of Noosa. The town, he recalls, was 'full of bulldozers'. He called Bob Johnston, urging the Reserve Bank to look at raising interest rates. Johnston was reluctant to move quickly. Still concerned about the effects of the stock market crash three months before on highly indebted Australian entrepreneurs like Robert Holmes à Court, Johnston was wary of a sharp and sudden move that might panic markets. Behind the struggling entrepreneurs stood the major commercial banks, and behind the commercial banks stood the Reserve Bank. Johnston's first concern was the stability of the financial system.

Throughout the year Treasury Secretary Bernie Fraser would be the most reluctant of Keating's senior advisers to support the push to higher interest rates. He believed the economy was quite strong, though, like everyone else, he underestimated the strength of the gathering investment boom. He was in favour of restraint but thought then and later that monetary policy was the least preferred tool for slowing demand, especially demand for imports. Higher interest rates would (and did) accelerate the rise in the dollar, which had then started to make imports cheaper. Privately within the policy-making community, Fraser held the same critical attitude to the emerging monetary policy strategy as many academic economists. His consistent position for most of 1988 was that, if wages and government spending could be restrained, then raising interest rates should not be necessary.

He told a CEDA conference on 2 February 1988 that he opposed an increase in interest rates.[3] The story reported him saying that, while imports had been strong last year, the government suspected there was an element of overordering, with many companies building up stocks. With import growth expected to ease in the first half of the year, there was no need to tighten monetary policy to stem demand. A tightening of monetary policy would be avoided as long as possible to maintain low interest rates and boost investment in import competing and export industries.

Following Fraser's reported remarks, Johnston wrote to Keating on 9 February, apparently leaning towards a tighter policy, but not yet explicitly recommending an interest rate increase.[4]

Fraser then wrote to Keating on 15 February on 'The Road Ahead'. Referring to the latest forecasts, which he enclosed, he wrote:

> The most worrying feature of the forecasts is that there is no reduction in the absolute size of the current account deficit in 1988–89 ($11.5b) . . . We will have to do better than that to keep the ship afloat and on course. Apart from the implication such a forecast would have for markets, the country is already in hock to the extent that net debt servicing costs are siphoning off almost $1 in every $5 we earn from the export of goods and services – and this burden is continuing to grow.

Fraser expected stronger world growth and better commodity prices than JEFG assumed in 1988, but a cyclical downturn occurred in the world economy in 1989. 'My own hunch,' he wrote, 'is that economic growth through 1988 will be stronger than is envisaged in the JEFG forecasts.'

In these respects Fraser was more discerning than JEFG. But he nonetheless opposed an increase in interest rates. He wrote:

> Suggestions are now emerging in various quarters that it would be appropriate to start tightening monetary policy, both because the need to maintain generous liquidity in the wake of the October share market fall is passing and because domestic demand needs to be checked for current account purposes. The Governor wrote to you on 9 February drawing attention to these considerations but he stopped short of advocating any real tightening of monetary conditions for the time being.

Monetary conditions obviously require careful watching, the more so if my hunch that domestic activity in the current half year turns out to be somewhat stronger than the JEFG forecasts. I would not advocate any significant tightening of monetary policy at this time, however. The outlook for business investment remains weak and higher interest rates would be unhelpful on that score. Tighter monetary conditions might also exert unwarranted upward pressure on the exchange rate. For these and other reasons the major macroeconomic policy adjustments should be made in the fiscal and wages areas, with monetary policy being held in reserve for use in the event of shortcomings in those areas.

Another reason for not raising rates was the strong recovery in housing. It would have adverse implications for business investment. Fraser mentioned the May statement, when fiscal policy would once again be tightened. At this point it was reasonable to expect a surplus of $1b for 1987–88 and again for 1988–89.

Within Treasury, differences of opinion that would become deeper over the course of the year were beginning to emerge. The official forecasts were prepared within the Economic Division. In October 1987 David Morgan had been appointed Deputy Secretary (Financial), giving him a responsibility to advise Keating on monetary policy. His own view about the economy differed from that of the forecasters. He thought the economy was somewhat stronger than the forecasters' consensus. He appeared to be leaning towards an interest rate increase. Morgan was quite tentative, however, and also underestimated the force of the investment boom.

In early March he wrote to Keating asking for a meeting with Reserve Bank officials the following afternoon.[5] He recalled that at the last meeting with the bank, on 2 December 1987, 'a good deal of uncertainty still existed about the fallout from the stock market decline'. Now that the storm had been weathered, 'it is desirable to refocus fully on the ongoing objectives for monetary policy. Above all, this means ensuring that rates of domestic demand growth and inflation are consistent with appropriate progress in further reducing the current account deficit.'

The Sydney property market, he noted, was returning to bullishness, and the world economy was more resilient than they had thought. He believed, 'The clear danger at present is that the slowdown may be less than assessed at the time the JEFG forecasts were prepared, raising the possibility of an even less satisfactory outlook for the adjustment process.

'In respect of domestic pressures it is worth noting explicitly the point which Dr Higgins reports from Mr Kelty: concern at holding the wages situation in a stronger economy.' (Higgins had apparently had a discussion along these lines with Kelty at a Reserve Bank board meeting.) Monetary policy had to make a contribution to restraint, particularly in the period immediately ahead. Dwelling investment seemed to have considerable momentum. Business investment in plant and equipment had less overall strength than they would like, although it was occurring in the right activities. While the exchange rate strengthened during February, it remained well below levels prior to the share market decline.

His arguments pointed that way, but Morgan stopped short of suggesting an interest rate increase. He concluded, 'Against that background the recent dampening of market expectations of further interest rate declines at the short end is to be welcomed. Given the current account outlook, and with the May statement still a few months away, we would be happy to see that situation persist for a time, and for the Bank to lean against any further downward pressure on interest rates, should it emerge.'

The bank evidently had the same point of view and said so publicly. I spoke to Reserve Bank officials John Phillips and Ian Macfarlane in March 1988. In an on-the-record interview, Macfarlane pointed out that US Federal Reserve chairman Alan Greenspan was now publicly worried about the economy overheating – not long before he had been worried about it being in recession. Phillips said that he was concerned about the growth of imports. 'At the moment,' he said, 'one would have hoped to see the growth of imports

into Australia being less.' He said, 'It's obvious that the bank is keeping the market tighter than it used to, and it's obvious it does not
want to see interest rates move lower.'

By the end of February, the bank was 'leaning against the wind' in
the money market. By late March, sentiment swung in favour of
increasing rates. But even by mid March there was no urgency. On
11 March, for example, Morgan mentioned, in the course of a note
enclosing an International Monetary Fund draft report on Australia,
that: 'The statement that it seems clear that the economy is growing too rapidly at this stage may be a little too categorical (although
we agree that all the recent data tends to point in that direction).' The
IMF preferred to see more action on spending. Excessive reliance on
monetary policy would have an adverse impact on investment and
exports, although undue ease would also jeopardise the adjustment
process. However, 'The seasonal drain on liquidity should be allowed
to affect interest rates, exchange market interventions should be dis-
continued . . . and any upward pressures on the exchange rate should
be accepted.'

Preparing for a meeting with Reserve Bank and Treasury officials
later that day, Morgan minuted Keating on 30 March, that: 'As you
are well aware, the primary objective of policy is to ensure that progress
in correcting our external imbalance on a sustainable basis pro-
ceeds as rapidly as practicable.' Morgan recalled, 'You indicated earlier this month that the pace of domestic demand in the first half of
1987–88 was too fast to be consistent with sustained improvement
in net exports.'[6]

Morgan now believed that there was a clear danger that domestic demand was running too strongly to ensure the desirable rate of
progress in adjusting the current account and moderating the accumulation of foreign debt. Implicitly contradicting Fraser, he argued
that there was limited scope for more changes in spending or wages.
As a result, 'We think the time has come for a marginal firming in
financial conditions to help ensure that demand growth does not

become excessive as we get into 1988–89 . . . the tightening we have in mind is marginal rather than a big hit: the sound of a harp rather than a blunderbuss.'

Keating had independently reached a stronger conclusion.

By custom the Governor of the Reserve Bank discusses the views of the board with the Treasurer soon after each board meeting. Known as 'debriefings', these discussions with Keating were designed to reach agreement between the Governor and the Treasurer on the next moves in monetary policy. Formally, the Treasurer could not tell Johnston what to do without also telling Parliament. Formally, Johnston could not implement policy if the Treasurer was unaware of what he was doing. In practice, each needed the general agreement of the other. Johnston and Keating often talked on the telephone and sometimes met privately, so that the debriefing sessions would sometimes record a consensus or note a disagreement of which both were already aware. Treasury officials also attended the debriefings, and it was sometimes one of their few opportunities to put an argument directly to the Treasurer and the Governor. Since the meetings were completely private and within the Treasurer's official 'family', the discussions were often of real substance, and real disagreements could be, and sometimes were, aired openly.

During the meeting with Johnston, Sanders and Phillips on 30 March, Keating recalls that he wanted a 2 per cent increase in the overnight rate.[7] Fraser was opposed, and so was Johnston. Keating's recollection, expressed in a letter later that year, was that the Bank officials were reluctant to agree and that the board in its earlier meeting had adopted a 'wait and see' attitude for April. Russell recalls that the Treasurer was handed a piece of paper by the Bank calling for a watching and waiting strategy. Keating believed they wanted to wait until they saw the context of a promised May statement – possibly the officials or the board believed that fiscal tightening would be sufficient.[8] John Phillips and board member Gordon Jackson were said to have been particularly reluctant to raise rates as that time – though my interview with Phillips around this time confirms that he was quite concerned about the strength of the economy. According to

Russell, they agreed to a 1 per cent increase. Keating's clear recollection is that the Bank did not want to agree to increase rates. Bank officials tell a somewhat different story. They agree that Keating was certainly pushing for an increase, though they do not recall 2 per cent as a specific number. In those days policy was often discussed as a 'tightening of monetary conditions' rather than specific numbers. While agreeing that Keating was pushing for an increase, they insist that Bank officials at the meeting also sought an increase. Finally, they say that Johnston was not clear what had been decided by the end of the meeting, though other Bank officials present believed an interest rate increase had been agreed. I suspect that one element in these conflicting accounts is that Keating pressed for a big increase and the Bank people present, while leaning towards some increase, did not want a formal decision in advance of a consensus on the board and among themselves. Bank officials were also reluctant to adopt explicit interest rate targets that minimised their discretion.

The difference between Keating and the Bank at this point was partly over the prospects for the economy, but also partly over the way in which monetary policy was conducted. Keating and Russell thought interest rate increases could have a rapid depressing influence on expectations. Once businesses and households had felt the shock, the increases could be wound back.[9] They had seen this work in 1985 and 1986. Keating thought rates should go up quickly and come down quickly. Partly because of its longer-term view of how monetary policy worked, and partly because of the more bureaucratic way it worked as an organisation, the Bank was slow to put rates up and slow to bring them down.

Keating expected the increases would be effected immediately or at least quite soon. But Johnston travelled overseas for two weeks after the meeting and postponed the increase until his return. Don Russell, meanwhile, was calling the Bank daily to find out what had happened to the increase, which did not begin until May. Over the course of that month the policy rate (the overnight rate in the official market) rose by 1.75 per cent. The change in monetary policy was not announced. It was alluded to in a speech by Keating to the Premiers'

Conference in June, but only in vague terms. In another of those controversies that were to dog this whole policy episode, Keating was later criticised for failing to declare publicly and forthrightly that interest rates were rising. Had he done so, the argument runs, the effect of the increases might have been magnified and accelerated, lessening the need for increases later. Keating himself asserts this argument quite strongly, and insists that it was the Reserve Bank that insisted upon this policy of lifting rates without declaration, a policy known as 'snugging'. Bank officials assert it was Keating who was reluctant to announce the new direction of policy. When I asked Keating in May 1996 why he had not announced the tightening of policy, if that is what he wished to do, he replied, 'I would never have publicly said something that was not agreed' at the debriefings. He reiterated that it was the Bank that resisted the announcement. Certainly monetary policy in that period was conducted very differently from the way it was later conducted. Traditional central bankers — and the careers of both Bob Johnston and the most assertive of his subordinates, John Phillips, spanned decades — were reluctant to announce monetary policy moves, or even to talk in terms of interest rates as opposed to vague expressions like 'monetary conditions'. It was not until Bernie Fraser became Governor that the Bank began to publicise its moves. If Keating had wanted to announce the change hard enough, however, I have no doubt he would have found a way to do it. He could not have pressed very hard, and for its part the Bank does not seem in this period to have pressed at all.

What began as the sound of a harp would be the first move in a change of policy that would take cash rates from a monthly average of just over 10 per cent in March 1988 to just under 18 per cent in November 1989, 90-day bills from nearly 11 per cent to over 18 per cent, and home loan rates from 13.5 per cent to 17 per cent. It would certainly be the immediate cause of the recession, which began in 1990 and which would leave Australia with a million unemployed.

There was nothing inevitable in the sequence. The 30 March

agreement on an increase did not contain within it an agreement on all or indeed any succeeding increases. On its own it was a sensible and ordinary decision. Commentators and Keating himself would later say the increase should have occurred sooner and should have been bigger. There is little doubt, however, that Keating was in front of the consensus in both the Bank and the Treasury in pressing for a sizeable increase. The context of the decision about the increase rates did not at this point suggest the sequence of increases to come. The October stock market crash had been not long before, and it had been widely expected to produce a check to growth, if not a recession. Growth in 1987 had been good but below the level of 1984 and 1985. There were few signs of increasing inflation. The 1987–88 Budget was the tightest Keating had yet delivered. Treasury forecasts had only just begun to suggest that growth might be higher than they had expected at Budget time 1987. There were grounds for a precautionary increase in interest rates at the beginning of 1988 (and Australia followed the US as the second OECD economy to increase rates after the crash), but there were no grounds for a very large, sustained, increase. Neither Keating nor his advisers predicted the boom to come. Nor could they. There was little evidence to suggest it.

Keating knew it almost by instinct, but Russell was perhaps the first adviser to realise how completely the float of 1983, the deregulation of banking in 1984 and the dropping of money supply targets at the beginning of 1985 had changed the economic policy game. Cabinet was no longer the centre of contest, as it had been in the Fraser Government and the first year of the Hawke Government. In those days the Treasurer had reported and sought approval for foreign exchange policy and, through the Economic Committee or the Monetary Policy Committee of Cabinet, for money supply targets and their implied interest rates trends. In 1983 Cabinet had continued at least formally to ponder exchange rate settings, and the Secretary of the Treasury had at least formally been joined in the daily determination of the rate by the Secretary of the Department of Finance and the Secretary of the Department of Prime Minister and Cabinet as well as by the Governor of the Reserve Bank. By late 1985 no monetary policy issues – not the exchange rate or interest rates or the money supply – were discussed in Cabinet except as part of the annual Budget economic framework submission. Formally, there were no exchange rate decisions or money supply target decisions to make. Only officials within the portfolio of the Treasurer had any formal authority to be informed of monetary policy issues, though informally the Department of Prime Minister and Cabinet stayed in touch. Once the top player, even Treasury's role was reduced. The Secretary of the Treasury could no long determine the exchange rate. Treasury officials could no longer draw up money supply formation tables so that certain Commonwealth deficits resulted, through a chain of tortured accounting identities and assumed outcomes for other variables, with certain money supply targets. They could no longer blandly describe the movement of interest rates as more or less automatic variations necessary to achieve the money supply outcome.

The Reserve Bank had been junior to the Treasury under the old arrangements. The issue of its independence was a fictitious one before the float, because it did not determine the monetary targets or the exchange rate policy. Interest rates offered by banks were often set by regulation. Under the new arrangements, so long as the Governor of the Reserve Bank could carry his board he could deal directly with the Treasurer. The Secretary of the Treasury remained a member of the Bank board, but one among others. The Governor and the Treasurer could talk, they could accommodate each other, and they could reach an agreement on where they wanted interest rates to go – all without involving Treasury except as a courtesy. After they found they could do these things, they did them more and more often.

The Treasurer acquired a greater degree of direct executive authority over the level of interest rates – and what power the Treasurer acquired, Russell shared. Together, as Keating would often later say, they made monetary policy in the late 1980s. Keating was always careful to discuss monetary policy changes with Hawke, and Russell with Hawke's economic adviser or principal adviser.[10] Hawke might have objected, but in practice, though he sometimes queried them, he endorsed all Keating's proposed monetary policy decisions. The Treasurer acquired more power over monetary policy – but at the expense of Treasury and of Cabinet, not the Reserve Bank.

As interest rates began to rise, the official forecasts began to change rapidly and dramatically. The JEFG report of April 1988 revised the predictions in the January report to forecast higher demand and activity, reflecting a stronger world economy and growing realisation that the October 1987 share market crash had no impact on growth. Domestic demand in 1987–88 was now expected to increase 4.25 per cent, compared with a January forecast of 3 per cent. The following year it was forecast to come back 4 per cent, compared with the 1.5 per cent previously forecast. Treasury official John Cosgrove noted, 'The much stronger than expected rise in commodity prices has not led to a more substantial decline in the current account deficit because of poorer outcomes likely for net export volumes.' Cosgrove thought, 'The recent marked improvement in Australia's terms of trade will be adding to domestic incomes and demand during the forecast period.' He advised more action on wages, more action on spending, and that 'some tightening of monetary policy will probably be required to buttress the effectiveness of other policies.'[11]

By 5 May 1988, when another meeting with the RBA was scheduled, Morgan at least wanted another increase and an explicit declaration that monetary policy had been tightened. Wages policy was considered 'very tight'. Keating had agreed to cut spending in the May statement by a quite sharp 1.5 per cent after inflation. Other than raising interest rates, the only way to slow the economy down more was via a tax increase.[12]

Morgan minuted Keating[13] that: 'It is generally accepted by officials, and I believe by you, that we are now seeing an unacceptably fast expansion in domestic demand that appears set to continue in 1988–89 . . . If you believe that the target of 1.5 per cent real decline in outlays is as good as can be achieved, action is needed to moderate private spending by tightening monetary policy (assuming, of course, that you do not wish to pursue discretionary revenue raising measures).'[12] Morgan asked that cash rates be lifted from the present 11.5 per cent to 12 or 12.5 per cent.

> Practical considerations involved in open market operations mean that adjustments to interest rates are not usually immediate. However, the Bank took the opportunity provided by the large tax payments during April to target official cash rates at around 11.5 per cent. With company tax and PAYE collections due early this month, the Bank could again take the opportunity offered by large cash withdrawals to increase official cash rates.
>
> The recent modest moves by the Bank to allow financial conditions to tighten during the seasonal liquidity rundown have not been acknowledged by the Government, nor by the Bank. If a further tightening was carried out over the next few weeks it could be referred to in the May statement as part of an integrated approach. That is a matter for your judgment, but if you agree to some further tightening an explicit recognition will be required before long.

Morgan acknowledged that the implications for the exchange rate are the 'major constraint' on monetary policy. It is apparent from his minutes and those of Cosgrove that the principal aim of interest rate increases was to slow domestic demand, and that the principal threat posed by increasing domestic demand was increasing imports and a higher current account deficit. But the higher rates also pulled up the dollar, which reduced Australia's competitiveness. Morgan wanted early action, but it was not until July that rates moved up again, this time by half a per cent.

If internationalising the economy was Labor's greatest economic policy achievement, the float of 1983 and the tariff cuts of 1988 and 1991 were the essential preconditions for it. From 1987 Keating spoke out strongly for faster micro-reform, including tariff cuts. Building towards a statement in 1988, he pushed hard and successfully for cuts deeper than those first offered by Industry Minister

Button. He and Don Russell went up to see Hawke again and again in the preparation of the statement, arguing that tariffs should be cut by a third from the top rather than smaller 20 per cent average cut offered by Button. Hawke ultimately agreed with Keating; Button told both they would regret it.[14] On 23 May in his 1988 Economic Statement Keating was able to announce the first major tariff cuts since Gough Whitlam's 25 per cent across-the-board cut of 1973.[15] It reduced the average effective rate of assistance for manufacturing from 19 per cent in 1986–87 to 14 per cent in 1992–93. Keating's role was important, but it would not have been possible without the support of Hawke and the cooperation of Button and without the years of advocacy that had preceded it. The case for lower import protection was well established by the time Keating became Treasurer. He himself had become a convert to it in the 1970s, and he shared these views with most of his senior colleagues including Hawke, Finance Minister Peter Walsh and (with some reservations) Employment Minister John Dawkins. Important as it was as a landmark in internationalising the Australian economy, the May statement was the beginning rather than the end of the tariff reform in the Hawke Government. In 1990 and early 1991 Keating again pressed for deep cuts, offering Button new self-assessment tax rules to please his constituency in the business community. Later, when Prime Minister himself, Keating would have to defend the cuts against the combined assault of Bill Kelty and the ACTU, many members of caucus – and John Button.

The May 1988 statement was well received, but the pressure of increased interest rates was insistent. By early June, cash rates had increased from 10.3 at the beginning of the year to just under 12 per cent. Treasury forecasters, however, were seeing more signs that the economy was strengthening. The day before a meeting with the Bank on 9 June Morgan minuted Keating, 'The central policy issue is whether enough restraint is now in the pipeline.'[16]

He argued that the latest national accounts highlighted the strong growth over the past six months. He believed, 'The recent tightening in monetary settings, together with the action on the fiscal side, will be helpful in restraining demand, but it may not be enough and the effects delayed.' On monetary policy he reported, ' . . . our judgment at this stage is that we may need to move further before too much longer. We cannot afford the risk of letting the economy overheat. There is a real possibility of that happening if recent measures do not have a fairly quick impact in moderating the recent strength in the economy.'

Treasury usually mentioned that monetary policy operated with a long lag – of between a year and eighteen months. It was not mentioned now. There was no mention of the medium term. Nor was there an estimate of the effects of past increases, or an analysis of the impact of increases on different segments of the economy, or on the economy via the exchange rate. Though aware of the strong growth of lending, there was no indication here that Treasury was thinking seriously about the impact of higher interest rates when companies were more highly geared than before.

As part of the Accord and of election planning, Keating envisaged a tax cut for the following year. A joint statement with the ACTU in July committed the government to tax cuts in 1989 in return for wage restraint. Keating believed the Accord restrained inflation more effectively than monetary policy, so it was worth preserving. To keep the Accord, Kelty had to show something in return for flat real wages, which meant tax cuts. In the event Keating was correct. When Labor had arrived in office in 1983 at the trough of the recession, inflation was still over 10 per cent. In contrast inflation did not markedly increase during the boom of the late 1980s and – unlike 1982 – rapidly fell away during the recession. The reason inflation was minimal after the 1991 recession was not because of the recession itself but because of very low wage increases during the boom. Morgan drew out this implication in a note preparing the Treasurer for a 12 July meeting with the Bank.

The official forecasters were catching up. Morgan wrote that the most recent JEFG report argued, 'On the basis of present policy settings, prospective domestic demand growth and inflationary pressures are much stronger than desirable and forecast net export performance less than desirable.'[17] He noted, 'You are contemplating a very major personal tax cut (perhaps of the order of up to 2 per cent of GDP) around mid 1989.' This meant, 'As you well appreciate, to deliver responsibly a personal tax cut of that order of magnitude around the middle of 1989 would require the economy to have a good deal less of a head of steam in it than the JEFG forecasts indicate.' It 'would risk pouring petrol on the flames.' Since policies operate with a lag, it was necessary to think at that point about action towards domestic demand as the economy approached a major tax cut towards the end of 1989. Morgan argued that the balance of risks were higher in leaving monetary policy unchanged, given a tax cut down the track. He presented it as another small adjustment

another small notch of tightening now – another stitch in time, as it were – would seem prudent. That is, we should be seeking to direct a little more of our large terms of trade gain in prospect this financial year out of expenditure and into saving.

Wages policy was 'in the locker', and it would be hard enough to keep spending to a cut of 1.5 per cent. Because of the terms of trade gain, commodity producers were 'not really disadvantaged' by a higher dollar. Signs of stronger investment suggested that higher interest rates were not hurting it. He recommended 'an early "snugging up" of unofficial cash rates, perhaps of the order of half a per cent or so.' Over July and August the policy rate increased by about 0.75 per cent, taking it above 12 per cent.

Keating believed he was using fiscal policy to slow the boom. His sixth Budget, on 23 August 1988, projected a surplus of $5.5 billion. Real outlays were expected to fall 1.8 per cent after falling in 1987–88. Policy decisions had taken more than half a billion off outlays – much less than the $3.5 billion in 1987–88, but that was because there was so much less room to cut. Revenue was up 2.1 per cent in real terms, the lowest increase in six years, but certainly 'contractionary'.

The forecasts were changing to reflect a stronger economy, but not changing fast enough. Budget Statement No. 2 reported that world developments 'were decidedly favourable' and that 'the stock market upheaval of October 1987 did little to check the pace of global economic expansion.' The current account deficit was $11.9 billion in 1987–88 compared to $13.2 billion in 1986–87. (The deficit had fallen as predicted but not in the manner predicted. Imports had risen far more than expected, but so had exports.) The statement argued:

> Resource rich economies such as Australia which are net borrowers from abroad need to use foreign savings to generate sufficient income to provide an adequate return to investors, including any risk premia that might be built in. So long as that condition is met, growth in external liabilities will be manageable and, indeed, beneficial.

However, policy 'must ensure that the recent rapid pace of demand in the Australian economy does not rekindle inflationary pressures'. The forecast for the current account would be way off this time. Overestimating the effect of a tighter fiscal and monetary policy, it predicted a deficit of $9.5 billion for 1988–89, a little more than half the actual number.[18]

The Budget was intended as a triumph – the final, stunning achievement in five years of economic reform, a triumph of policy intended to set the scene for a triumph of politics – because Keating wanted Hawke to go. He wanted his job, and he wanted it now. The government had already won three elections, and Keating believed it would be very lucky indeed to win a fourth. A fifth election win was almost impossible. He didn't care, he told friends, for the job of Opposition Leader – for three to six years, as he said, of staying at motels in Mt Isa or Bunbury while visiting the local party conferences and cheering on the candidates around the country. He wanted to be party leader while they were still in government. If Hawke left in 1988 he would have a year or two to make the job his own, then an election, then perhaps three years of being Prime Minister before the party was inevitably defeated.[19]

He thought he deserved it. He had been constantly in the

engineroom of the government for five years. He believed it was his work rather than Hawke's that had been behind financial deregulation, tax reform, budget reform and cutting tariffs. He recalled that Hawke had told him in the middle of 1980, when Hawke was looking for his support for a leadership contest against Bill Hayden, that Hawke would want to be Prime Minister for a couple of terms, perhaps, and then it would be over to Paul.

Within the party some colleagues encouraged him. Bill Hayden, who was about to be appointed Governor-General, had never forgiven Hawke. He encouraged Keating. John Dawkins had become an admirer of Keating. He encouraged him. John Button thought Keating should succeed Hawke. Outside parliament, Bill Kelty thought Keating was the heart and soul of the government.

But the numbers weren't there. Hawke and Keating both depended on the Centre Right faction. The Victorian chief of the faction, Robert Ray, disliked Keating intensely and said so. Keating thought Ray's policy views underdeveloped and said so. The New South Wales chief of the faction, Graham Richardson, supported Hawke and would continue to do so. Keating knew Richardson thought Premier Brian Burke of Western Australia was perhaps a better bet to succeed Hawke in the long term than Keating.

So long as Keating was a successful Treasurer his work helped Hawke. Caucus colleagues thought they were a good team. To have any chance of displacing Hawke, Keating must threaten to leave.

Hawke's response, the day after the Budget, was to publicly air the view that Keating was a very good Treasurer but he was not indispensable. Dawkins, for example, would also be a very good Treasurer. Keating was indignant. He saw Hawke and threatened war. Keating later recalled the episode: 'I spoke to him about it at the Lodge in February 1988, you know. I asked him what his intentions were. He said he would stay, so I said, "OK, well, I hope you change your mind but I will stay anyway." It wasn't till he bagged me after the 1988 Budget. I had been up to my arms in blood in that Budget, risking my health, and the day after the Budget he bags me! I went right round to see him. I said, "Is that what I get for thirty days in the ERC? Well, I tell you right now, mate, I'm not going to be another Charlie Fitzgibbon for you. I'm not going to be someone else you can walk over. When I decide to come at you, mate, I'll take your head right off!" [20]

Keating threatened to leave. After Richardson intervened, Hawke retracted on television. Leaving for a scheduled visit to Europe, Keating brooded. It was only after his return on 13 October, during Question Time on 17 November – and perhaps as much to his own surprise as to that of his staff and colleagues – that he mentioned in response to an Opposition probe that he would be remaining as Treasurer and loyally serving his leader.

Hawke offered another discussion of the leadership and succession. He saw that he could only satisfy his Treasurer and prevent a long-running and public battle by promising to resign some time after the next election. At a meeting in Kirribilli House on 25 November Peter Abeles and Bill Kelty witnessed the pact. Hawke said he would leave at some decent interval after the next election. In the meantime Keating was to come to Cabinet meetings on time and treat his Cabinet colleagues graciously. If Keating disclosed the deal, it was off.

Paul was willing now to take it on trust – there was, anyway, no alternative now but to wait until after the next election, and see. Tom Mockridge, Don Russell and economics adviser Ken Henry, all of whom soon knew about the deal, thought there was a chance Hawke would keep his promise. Only Annita was quite certain that he would not. She thought he now envied Paul, and for that reason would work against him. Keating took Hawke at his word. Unless the government won the next election, Keating could not anyway succeed Hawke as Prime Minister. They could not win without internal unity. The Kirribilli agreement allowed two years of peace. Hawke and Keating worked surprisingly well together through the rest of 1988, through 1989, and well into 1990.

While Keating tried to push Hawke out, the outlines of the investment boom became clearer and the economic strategy outlined in the Budget disintegrated. In an August Reserve Bank meeting Keating had lamented that, with the benefit of hindsight, the major macro-economic policy mistake in 1987–88 was that the decision to tighten monetary policy was delayed for too long. From the March quarter to 7 September – six months – unofficial cash rates rose 2.2 per cent to 13 per cent, bank bill rates 2.6 per cent to 13.6 per cent, and prime rates by 2.1 per cent to 15.5 per cent.

Tensions were increasing within the official family. Morgan's faction of hawks now comprised most of the senior policy-makers, including Chris Higgins and usually Ted Evans. Almost alone, Bernie Fraser continued to express doubts about the reliance on interest rate increases and where the economy might be heading. Keating remained with the hawks, as did the Prime Minister.

Tensions flared with a note to the Treasurer from David Morgan, in which he offered advice for the meeting with the Reserve Bank the following day, 8 September 1988.[21] As before, Morgan wrote,

> The key policy consideration remains whether there is enough overall restraint in the pipeline to meet medium term objectives, especially as they relate to reductions in the current account deficit and inflation . . . With fiscal and wages policy now essentially 'in the locker' for the time being, scope for adjusting the tightness of policy lies with monetary policy.

He believed,

> Over the last three years, there has been a tendency (within the 'official family' and more generally) to underestimate the strength of prospective domestic demand and inflation. If more could not have been done on the fiscal and wages fronts, it could be argued that monetary policy has been somewhat looser, on average, than appropriate.

If domestic demand had been as forecast, current account deficit would have been lower. 'As you observed at our last monthly meeting, with the benefit of hindsight, the major macroeconomic policy mistake in 1987–88 was that the decision to tighten monetary policy was delayed for too long.'

Rates had 'increased marginally' over the past month or so because of increases in overseas rates, market sentiment and some '"snugging up" of official rates'. The key question was whether the tightness was now enough. What data there was indicated continuing buoyancy and 'even if Budget forecasts were to be realised, the projected growth in GNE, import volumes, net exports, wages and foreign indebtedness raise a question as to whether the overall stance of policy is tight enough.'

He concluded: ' . . . we believe the balance of risks for 1988–89 is for stronger than forecast inflation and domestic demand and slower than forecast external adjustment. RBA forecasts, while generally similar to those outlined in the Budget papers, reflect such a view.' He argued that 'a further marginal tightening of monetary policy would be useful in minimising these upside risks, and as an insurance against any prospective slowing in world activity (and hence in demand for our exports) during 1989.' He also believed that tax cuts in 1989 'will almost certainly require adjustments elsewhere' unless the economy weakened unexpectedly. The minute had been prepared in consultation with Dr Higgins, who supported its conclusions. Morgan did not mention the Secretary.

Coming only a few weeks after a Budget in which a declining current account deficit had been forecast, Keating reacted angrily to the note. It was dangerous to be portrayed as a dove on monetary policy, and Keating may have thought Morgan's note allowed just such a presentation. He also objected to Morgan's evident opposition to the tax cuts in 1989. By September Keating was negotiating a major tax cut with Kelty, and was very sensitive to the political force of the argument that tax cuts meant interest rate increases. Most importantly he objected to the implication, so soon after its delivery, that a Budget with which Treasury had been delighted had been insufficiently tight.

He wrote back to Morgan in his own hand.

David
I find the tone and content of this note very annoying. For a start the whole message is unnecessary. The note is trying to prove a case in a strident way for a strategy that I am already publicly and privately committed to. I said in the

Budget speech that demand must be kept under watch and control and that monetary policy must play 'its vital balancing role'. I wrote those words myself knowing precisely what they mean.

I regard the line about inviting criticism that we have not done enough on fiscal policy as bizarre. 'Presentational difficulties' with a surplus of 1.7 per cent of GDP and negative outlays of 1.8 per cent with whom? – Des Moore?

. . . This means that Treasury is saying three weeks after the Budget that the forecasts were wrong and that the structure of policy is wrong.

Finally, you refer to my statement at an earlier meeting that monetary policy should have been tightened earlier this year with the inference that I was supporting a delay. You might recall that at the 30 March meeting between the Trsy and the RBA in Sydney I argued that the stockmarket crash was behind us and that rates should be tightened . . . and that we should not lose 8 weeks or so before the strength of activity was more evident in the data. The body of the group thought we should wait. We did and rates started to move only in May.

On the substantial point, let me restate that I believe monetary policy should play its appropriate role and if I judge the end point of the current tightening to be insufficient, I will have no hesitation in agreeing to tighten the game up further.[22]

In a note back to Keating, 'for the record', Morgan did his best to minimise the offence. He wrote:

. . . There was absolutely no inference intended that you were supporting a delay in tightening monetary policy early in 1988 and I apologise if the minute led you (or anyone else) to draw such an inference. Specifically I recall clearly on 30 March going to Sydney on a VIP plane with you and your support for a tightening of monetary policy. I also remember very clearly you arguing for a significant tightening at the meeting with Treasury and RBA officials later that same day in Sydney. The Treasury record of that meeting recorded your view as follows:

'. . . he was of the view that some tightening in monetary policy was required and that such a tightening could not wait until the content of the May statement was clearer'.[23]

Rates were raised to an average of 13.2 per cent through September. In mid October Higgins reported to the Treasurer that 'the monetary tightening of mid 1988 has now reached a magnitude and duration where it can be expected to influence spending decisions. But this shows up only with a lag and it will probably be into 1989 before the effects reach their maximum.'[24] Despite this analysis that interest rate increases would show up on demand only with a lag, they were raised another 0.5 per cent in November, another 1 per cent by March 1989, and another 1 per cent again before their peak. In all they would be raised 4 percentage points after Higgins' note compared with less than 3 percentage points before it.

Both Treasury and the Bank itself argued that the tax cuts likely in 1989 as a result of a proposed wage–tax tradeoff justified a tighter policy.[25] For Keating, however, achieving a cut in cost of living increases in wages in return for tax cuts remained a key economic and political strategy. It bore down on inflation, and it delivered tax cuts — usually in time for elections. Following discussions with the ACTU and decisions of the Industrial Relations Commission in 1987, the single national wage case had been replaced by a two-tier wage system in which flat dollar or percentage increases were granted to all wages, and a second increase could be available where unions were able to show or agree to changes in the award or in working practices that enhanced efficiency and productivity. Gradually and inevitably the wage system was heading back towards fragmentation and greater variation in wage changes. Under the influence of Kelty and Keating, the government and the ACTU would soon ask the commission to diminish its own involvement in cases in favour of direct negotiation between the parties to make enterprise bargains. But while centralised decisions still accounted for a large part of increases, there was room, Keating believed, for a few more wage–tax tradeoffs. In May 1987 Keating foreshadowed tax cuts, provided there was an agreed wage tradeoff in 1989–90.

In discussions with Kelty the outlines of the deal were becoming apparent, though it would not be until April 1989 that a new formal agreement between the ACTU and the government was reached. It contained a commitment to a substantial tax cut, an overall ceiling of 6.5 per cent growth in average weekly earnings, and increases linked to restructuring.

Through 1988 Keating had been pushing up interest rates against what his advisers thought was an economy unexpectedly strong after the stock market crisis, deep spending cuts, and falling or flat real wages. Treasury forecasters were inclined to attribute the economy's strength to stronger commodity prices. In the second half of 1988, however, a new element entered the picture, one that was for a long time unrecognised in the statistics and the Treasury analyses, and which transformed a fairly routine exercise in demand management into an almost personal contest between Keating and the Australian economy. That element was an investment boom – a sudden and unpredicted swelling of spending on plant and equipment as well as buildings – on a scale not seen in Australia for a decade. Far more than commodity prices, the terms of trade, rising asset prices or expanding lending (though all these were connected), it is the investment boom of the late 1980s that explains the peculiar nature of the policy problems with which Keating was groping.

By December the policy rate had increased 4 percentage points. The goal was to slow domestic demand pre-emptively and with it an increased current account deficit and higher inflation. The current account balance, however, had continued to deteriorate from around the beginning of 1988. The deficit would continue to increase through to the end of 1989. In January 1988 the deficit had been $300 million. By December 1988 it was $1.4 billion and rising.[26]

Exports were performing quite well throughout this period, though not as spectacularly as they had towards the end of 1987. The big change was in imports, which were rising strongly and which would peak towards the end of 1989. Behind the increase in imports was an increase in investment – the long-awaited return of spending on plant and equipment. This increased despite the interest rate increases, partly because profits were now much stronger and partly because capital spending had been allowed to run down.

Towards the end of 1988, plant and equipment spending increased at a truly astonishing rate. In the December quarter of 1988 it was 18 per cent higher (after inflation) than it had been in the September quarter. On a graph it looked like an Everest among its foothills. Investment in building and structures also increased rapidly over this period – but not as rapidly as plant and equipment spending, and it was anyway a smaller item. In the December quarter of 1988, for example, Australian business spent only half as much on new buildings as on new plant and equipment. Australians were also spending a lot on building and renovating homes but, while this spending increased over the period, it was already quite high, and the total was less than a third of spending on plant and equipment. In 1989 Australian business would spend more than $19 billion in current dollars investing in plant and equipment, an increase of 13.5 per cent over the year before. Nor was the investment boom offset by declines elsewhere. Consumer spending, which was two-thirds of all spending, was temporarily checked mid-year and then rose at an even more rapid pace right through to the end of 1989, when everything collapsed. Responding to a sequence of tight budgets, government spending was flat until the second half of 1989, when it rose, but it was the only spending element not humming.

The investment boom was a new and unforeseen element, quite remarkable in the teeth of quite high and sustained interest rates (though the nominal rates were still lower than they had been in 1985 and 1986 during a similar round of tightening to control the growth of demand). Some Treasury analysis suggested that the terms of trade were at fault in increasing domestic income. But a far more plausible candidate was the simple, direct and obvious fact of the investment boom, which might have been partly encouraged by the favourable terms of trade but in no way depended on it.

Through the course of 1988 Keating had conducted what in other circumstances would have been a normal exercise in restraining demand. In earlier years similar exercises had slowed things down. No doubt the interest rate increases would, as Higgins said, slow things down in 1989. But neither Higgins nor Keating nor the forecasters picked the size and force of the upswing in investment spending, which was to change the nature of the policy episode radically. What had begun as a conventional response to increasing demand now became an almost frantic attempt to slow down an investment boom of a size not seen since the end of the previous decade. The great irony is that the new element was the long-awaited and much-hoped-for return of plant and equipment spending – the very type of investment that would most directly support future production, including exports.

The investment boom changed the predicted pattern of economic growth in 1988–89. Growth of gross domestic product was 3.3 per cent, almost as predicted in the 1988 Budget, but its elements were quite different. Spending on home construction rose at twice the Budget forecast. Spending on plant and equipment rose at 19.3 per cent rather than 11.5 per cent. Balancing these, imports rose 25.5 per cent rather than 9.5 per cent and exports by 1 per cent rather than 6 per cent.

Just before Christmas all the major players in Canberra discussed the results of the year of increasing rates and their expectations for the following year. Morgan and Russell first talked together. Morgan told Russell that the November current account deficit was the latest in a rapidly strengthening series of unacceptable monthly outcomes. He had told Russell that at the minimum the Bank 'should move to validate the recent modest creep up in rates'. Russell had agreed with the thrust of that. Bank bills had now moved up 0.25 per cent above the Treasurer's target of 15 per cent, but Keating had indicated (through Russell) that this was 'not a problem.' Russell thought that they needed to drift up a little further, probably to around 15.5 per cent on bank bills. He was worried that they were setting themselves up 'for a bit of a knock in the New Year'. Russell thought it important that the government 'stay ahead of the game on monetary policy', noting that 'we were still looking at a very strong economy' despite tightening since last March–April. Keating was to depart on leave on Friday. Morgan suggested they all have a discussion with Keating when he visited Treasury the following day.

The discussion would have been informed by a JEFG report issued on 14 December.[27] The final report for the year had moved a long way from the Budget projections. John Cosgrove reported that 'the Group clearly saw the pace of economic activity as very strong in 1988–89, feeding into strong import volumes and inflationary pressures'. The current account deficit was now expected to be $12.5b in each of 1988–89 and 1989–90 – still way below its actual result. The CPI would be 6.5 per cent in 1988–89 and 4.25 per cent in 1989–90. He believed that wage breakout was the key risk. JEFG forecast an easing in import volumes from the first half of 1989 in response to easing demand pressures, but if it did not occur the deficit could stall as a percentage of GDP. A downturn in home construction would take the heat off domestic demand. 'It is clear,' Cosgrove wrote a few days before Christmas, 'that the course that has been set for macroeconomic policies needs to be maintained. There is no scope in the near term for any easing of monetary or fiscal policy: on the contrary, some further tightening may well be required.'

Bernie Fraser was unhappy about the apparently inevitable upward creep of interest rates. He wrote to Morgan before the meeting with Keating, 'I still expect improvement in the current account in the first half of 1989' and that 'investment goods have figured prominently in imports (but motor vehicles and consumer goods too).' He believed that 'it is very important to keep this spurt in business investment going for some time yet. Farmers, miners and manufacturers (among others) all appear to be investing strongly in areas which help the current account down the track.' He added, 'It has taken a long time to get businessmen to the investment starting gates and away. Now that we have got them in full flight we do not want to spook them by over-doing interest rate (and exchange rate) rises.'

Monetary policy had been tightened in two major bouts in 1988, the most recent over the last couple of months, since the Budget. Real interest rates were now approaching their highest levels for several years, and he

> would prefer to see some time elapse for the effects of that latest tightening to show up before there was any further substantial tightening. I would not like to see a return to earlier and largely fruitless attempts to deal with wages problems through excessively zealous monetary policies: we jettisoned all that five and a half years ago.

He saw merit in 'the Treasurer and monetary policy both going on holiday during January'.

According to Russell's note of the 21 December meeting,[29] Fraser maintained his position that monetary policy should not be tightened further because it was very important to keep the current investment spurt going. Higgins said there were grounds to be worried but he was prepared to wait and see. The hawks were Ted Evans and David Morgan. Evans said monetary policy could not be considered solely in the light of the balance of payments. The labour market was now tighter than it had been for more than a decade. He would move further on monetary policy now. Morgan agreed with Evans. As a result of the meeting Keating agreed that the Bank rediscount rate should be raised 0.2 per cent — a trivial change.

Morgan recorded a detailed account of Keating's thinking at this critical point in the policy episode. He wrote, 'The Treasurer reiterated his view that the outlays cutting process had run its race — he felt further substantial cuts were ruled out on both moral and practical grounds. The Treasurer was not averse to further monetary tightening; the central issue was whether enough tightening was already in the pipeline.'[30] They all agreed that investment was important, but argued that investment depended on business confidence.

'In the end,' he reported, 'the Treasurer decided that, for the moment, we should seek to keep bank bill rates at around where they were at present (around 15.3 per cent). It was pointed out that this may well need some hike in unofficial cash rates; the Treasurer was relaxed about that.'

The New Year did not bring better news. Even after several rounds of interest rate increases in 1988 and a very tight budget, the January current account deficit, at $1.5 billion, was the highest on record for that month. In February 1989 David Morgan noted few signs of a slow-down despite nearly a year of increasing interest rates. Reviewing the outlook for Keating before a meeting with the bank on 8 February, Morgan conceded that 'the underlying rate of inflation has not declined as expected'.[31]

Despite the 'sizeable shift in economic policy over the past year, it does not appear sufficient to the task in hand given the underlying strength of pressures evident in the economy'. Interest rates were up 5 per cent since the tightening began in April. Ninety-day bank bills were now 16 per cent. But 'apart from some moderation in the very high level of lending for housing, there are few signs as yet that the monetary tightening to date has done much to reduce the demand for credit'.

Morgan and Treasury now seemed to focus more on inflation than on the current account deficit. 'As you wrote into your 1988–89 Budget speech, "while the balance of payments deficit is Australia's number one economic problem, inflation remains Australia's number one economic disease"'.

Morgan had acknowledged that 'economic history is replete with examples of "too much, too late", i.e. tightening policy at or shortly after the peak in activity has already been reached, unwarrantedly intensifying the downturn'. However, Treasury's judgement was that 'the risks of a further modest tightening tipping the economy into recession are not great; they are well outweighed by those involved in relying on the measures already in place to moderate the growth of demand – and particularly checking inflation – sufficiently'. He recommended the bank bill rate be pushed up from 16 to 16.5 per cent. Higgins supported his conclusions.

Only Bernie Fraser had continued to swim against the tide. Writing to Keating in early February on the Budget objectives,[32] he had told him: 'You know my view that there is not a lot of scope left to push interest rates higher.' He proposed a tighter Budget with a $6 billion surplus after the tax cuts. But, as he noted, that would make 1989–90 the fourth consecutive year of no real outlays growth.

Keating had favoured another tightening. The policy rate was taken up another half a per cent in February, to an average of 16.24 per cent in March. Ninety-day bills were now 17.55 per cent.

It had become apparent that the 1988 Budget had indeed mispredicted the economy to a quite remarkable degree. Compared to the Budget-time forecasts, revised forecasts sent to the Treasurer in early March showed dramatic differences. Investment in dwellings was likely to be double the rate of growth predicted in the Budget. Imports would grow at twice the rate. The current account deficit would be much wider. Inflation would be 7.5 per cent compared with 5.5 per cent. GDP growth would not be very different, but that was because the huge growth of imports was not counted in GDP.[33]

Remarkably, Treasury forecasts at this time continued to underpredict the strength of the economy, even while warning that it was strong. In February, for example, a draft submission predicted GDP growth of 3.5 per cent in 1988–89. In fact it grew by nearly five per cent. It expected a current account deficit of $14 billion, well short of the $17.8 billion it would reach.[34]

By March 1989, however, Treasury was coming round to the view that the economy was topping out and would gently decline into a soft landing. For a meeting with the RBA on Friday 10 March it advised that rates should be left where they were. 'At this stage,' it advised, 'we do not favour an immediate further tightening'. Keating was trying to get a better sense of whether the turning point had come. Higgins had reported to him that an intensive review of the state of the cycle had concluded that 'domestic demand has probably peaked,' and 'slowing is likely to occur over the remainder of 1989'.[35] He wrote that 'we presently think a "soft landing" is likely'. Imports would ease, though employment and prices did not yet suggest slowing.

For the meeting with the Bank on Friday 7 April, Treasury again recommended no change, though some tightening had occurred in March. It advised that bank bills rates should be held at 17.5 per cent, with cash rates set accordingly. It noted that ' . . . there are some signs that the pace of economic activity may ease in the months ahead', though 'our judgment is that any slowdown is likely to be moderate . . . '.

On 12 April Keating delivered an Economic Statement announcing tax cuts worth $4.9 billion in return for a commitment to a ceiling of 6.5 per cent in average weekly earnings growth in 1989–90. The reductions would be paid from 1 July. There would be another big budget surplus, he promised, in 1989–90. Keating was widely criticised for adding fuel to demand pressure with tax cuts. By the time the cuts would begin to appear in pay packets, however, the economy was already heading south. The deal had slowed wages growth in the upswing; it would cushion the collapse in the downswing. By chance, the timing was perfect.

Treasury was content to wait and see what would happen with bank bill rates of 17.5 per cent. At the Reserve Bank, Ian Macfarlane, who proved the most prescient of forecasters at this point of the cycle, was warning that a slowdown was on the way, and it would be longer and deeper than Treasury was expecting. Keating and Don Russell had a different view. Within the next twelve months, an election was likely, and they would win it only if interest rates were heading down. Given the continuing strength of the economy, interest rates could only be heading down, they thought, if they had first been pushed up a little more.[36] Towards the end of April, Keating thought rates should probably be raised again. He asked Don Russell to consult Treasury and the Bank, who reported on 24 April.[37] 'The Treasurer felt there may be a need to tighten interest rates a little further. At his suggestion I spoke with a number of people in the Reserve Bank and Treasury about the current stance of monetary policy and whether there was a need for a further tightening.'

John Phillips: 'Markets at the moment are a little messy and there was a strong view around that the exchange rate was now bearing the weight of policy adjustment rather than interest rates. This was a concern as it could spark a major sell of the $A . . . a market view that the economy had topped out . . . he was still hopeful that the economy was slowing but there was concern we may just have plateaued . . . However, he did not believe we should put up interest rates further at this stage . . . Research Dept of the view that a further increase not warranted but may have to move quickly later.'

Bernie Fraser: 'Markets had been easier than expected and the Reserve Bank was doing what it could to keep rates . . . He thought that things would slow a fair bit. He was of the view that holding bills around 17.25 was plenty high enough and that any concern he had was that we might be holding the current level of rates for too long.'

John Cosgrove: 'He was of the view that interest rates should go up a bit more as demand was not slowing sufficiently. He was less convinced than Macfarlane (RB) that we had a slowing on our hands. He felt rates really needed to be around 18 per cent.'

Higgins: 'Stay where we are.'

'I passed this on to the Treasurer and added my view that we should at least wait until JEFG met on Thursday. The Treasurer may then want to speak to the Governor prior to his departure for China.'

By May the key policy-makers were vigorously debating what was happening in the economy. It should have been slowing, and in fact it was slowing down. The numbers would later show that growth was declining fairly evenly from the strong last quarter of 1988 through to the first quarter of recession one year later. But the most politically sensitive of the indicators, the current account deficit, was not declining at all. It was $1.7 billion in February, March and April, then actually rose to just short of $2 billion in May, at the same time as Treasury was telling Keating that the economy was slowing. The current account deficit would continue to increase long after the economy had turned. In August, September and October it would actually exceed $2 billion.

This was the point at which Keating began to be, as he would later remark, hoisted on his own petard. He was appalled by the long string of bad current account deficits, which were now the single most important piece of economic and political news. His colleagues, especially John Dawkins and Peter Walsh, were depressed and bewildered. In 1985 and 1986 they had counted on the J-curve. It had not worked, or at least not in the way they expected. Now the 'twin deficits' theory was apparently not working. A six percentage-point increase in interest rates over fifteen months was apparently not working.

Keating was increasingly sceptical of Treasury advice. In early May Fraser had summed up his thoughts on the current account outlook for Keating.[38] He thought the deficit would be $7 billion greater than the Budget forecast. For the following year JEFG was forecasting a $17.5 billion deficit, with 'a wide error bank about this forecast.' Keating annotated, 'Given the nearly 100 per cent error last year, this is not surprising.' Fraser wrote that a key assumption was that present tight financial conditions would be maintained. Keating annotated, 'of course, we might tighten them'. Fraser wrote that to do more on monetary policy would risk overkill. Keating wrote, 'perhaps much more'. Fraser believed, 'the game is being won, albeit over a longer time horizon than we would all like. We are not facing a disastrous situation.' He wanted monetary policy tight, but no more increases.

Fraser's warning against further increases was disregarded. In Keating's office, Don Russell argued strongly that the government and Keating's reputation could not survive a widening current account deficit. It was the test of policy that must be passed. Now bound to their own view that the government would be judged by the state of the current account deficit, Keating and Russell dismissed objections. Before leaving for Paris and the Soviet Union, Keating and Russell met with Hawke and his economic adviser at the Lodge. With

Russell's strong support, Keating persuaded Hawke to agree to another round of interest rate increases, which would add 1 per cent to the overnight rate. It would peak at 18 per cent in November. It would be, they hoped, the last increase.[39]

12

PLAZA ATHÉNÉE

IN LATE MAY 1989 THE TREASURER was in Paris, staying at the Plaza
Athénée Hotel off the Champs Elysées in the Avenue Montaigne.
He was attending the annual ministerial meeting of the Organisation
for Economic Cooperation and Development, a twenty-four-nation
group of the wealthier market economies, which that year was pondering the remarkable, unexpected – almost unbelievable – fact that
most of its members were enjoying their seventh year of uninterrupted
prosperity.

It was a fact that Ed Visbord, for one, the genial and now relaxed
Australian Ambassador to the OECD, found difficult to accept. A
veteran of the years of bitter struggles over economic policy in Australia in the 1970s and early 1980s, Visbord had been a pessimist so
long he was, as he sometimes said, hoarse. He had worked in Australia's embassy in Washington twenty years before and he had seen
how the United States' trade deficit had caused the collapse of the
Bretton Woods system of fixed exchange rates and, in his opinion,
created the conditions for the high unemployment and high inflation of the 1970s. From his Canberra job as the chief economist
in the Department of Prime Minister and Cabinet he had watched
the US deficit build up again in the 1980s, and he had confidently
expected another US recession, which would become a world recession and engulf Australia. But in that Paris spring of 1989 he was
reluctantly beginning to accept that the world economy was continuing

to expand year after year despite the US budget deficit, despite the US trade deficit, despite these 'imbalances' in the world economy, which were bemoaned in report after report of the OECD.

It was not so much that each consequence predicted had not occurred as that it had and it had made no difference. Economists had warned that the big borrowers of South America would not be able to pay their debts, and it turned out they could not; they had warned that the US budget deficit would explode if taxes were cut and defence spending increased, and the deficit did explode; they had warned that the US trade deficit would become so big that the US itself would become a debtor nation, and it had; they warned that the US dollar was too high and would some day crash, and it did; they warned that share market prices were far too high and would one day plummet, and they were right. They were right in all these things, and the world economy continued to expand.

Visbord had once been certain of things he was not certain of now. Free markets had always been, he would say, almost a religion for him. There were now free markets in foreign exchange, in finance worldwide. But these days, he would also say, no one knew how long the lag was between a policy action and its result. For that matter, no one was sure any more about how the policy instruments of the money supply, interest rates, taxes and spending worked at all. There was even concern at the OECD, which through its staff and its committees brought together the world's best and most powerful policy economists, that they no longer knew quite how the world worked. Within the OECD building on the Rue André Pascal, on the same floor and in practically adjoining offices, two economists could be expecting quite different outcomes from the same set of facts. One well-trained and experienced economist could be predicting (and relishing the prospect of) another crash of the US dollar followed by a swift and savage recession, which would bring a fitting retribution on American politicians for ignoring the budget and trade deficits, while down the corridor another equally well trained and equally experienced economist would be saying, no, the world had changed completely, the pattern of trade surpluses and deficits in the world

was rational, would become usual and be seen as a perfectly acceptable phenomenon in a world where some nations saved more than
others, and where the most profitable investments were not always in
countries that saved the most.

The world economy now puzzled Visbord, as the Australian
economy had puzzled him in the years between the election of the
Labor Government in March 1983, when Visbord was the senior economic policy-maker in the Department of Prime Minister and Cabinet, and his departure for Paris in the middle of 1986. Except for
a blip in 1986, the Australian economy was entering its seventh year
of expansion and prosperity, a record Visbord had certainly not
expected when Labor won office. There had been recessions in Australia in 1974 and 1982, both touched off when monetary policy
was tightened to fight an inflation fuelled by high wage rises. He had
been sceptical of the Accord between the government and the trade
unions when Prime Minister Bob Hawke and Keating had crafted it
in 1983, a scepticism that was at the time shared by the Treasurer
himself. He had expected wages to increase faster than the Accord
allowed, eventually forcing the government to tighten policy as the
last Labor Government had in 1973 and the Fraser Government had
in 1981, decisions that were followed by recessions and the electoral
defeat of the government. He had been pleasantly astonished to see
wages stay within the Accord limits – actually to fall, after inflation,
and employment expand – and later to see the Accord peacefully
renegotiated and wages openly targeted to grow less quickly than
prices.

In the 1980s the world economy and the Australian economy
were both behaving in ways outside his experience. Also new to his
experience was the still relatively young man in Paris who was Labor's
Treasurer but followed policies Visbord had thought no Labor treasurer
would follow; who could be amiable and fun to be around but who
had told the economists of the Department of Prime Minister and
Cabinet that he would cut their heads off if they got in his way. It
was mostly good news, but it was a puzzle.

An important piece of the puzzle was Keating, and Visbord cocked an ear from the fringe of a group of reporters questioning the Treasurer in the thin sunshine on the lawn of the OECD's Château de la Muette. He and his fellow ministers believed the world was running along quite nicely, Keating was saying, though the United States really could do more to close its budget deficit and put less emphasis on monetary policy. No, there were no real disagreements about the policies to be pursued, and all ministers recognised the need to be vigilant about inflation. Australia's problems, which seemed uniquely terrible to Australians in the southern autumn of 1989, were not unlike those being experienced by several other countries in the northern spring, and were problems of prosperity. 'We have a problem of domestic demand running too strongly,' he said. 'We have a very large investment phase on our hands, which is going to take some stopping. The aim of policy is to cut back the call of investment on saving.' He concluded with a dictum distilled from his last seven years as Treasurer, which was also a criterion for judging those years. 'Politics,' he announced offhandedly, 'is all about change. The system runs itself.'

For Keating the high tone of the OECD in Paris was a palliative against two extremely puzzling paradoxes of his career, which had lately become apparent to him. The first paradox was that he had done everything as Treasurer that the experts had told him to do, often with great political fortitude and with reckless determination. Financial markets had been deregulated and the currency floated, wages had been growing below prices, the budget deficit had been turned into a surplus, and now import barriers were coming down. In six years he had initiated or endorsed or certainly accepted a list of measures that the economists said were right and he himself had come to believe were right. They had said that if he wished to deal with inflation, and a trade deficit, and an economy that seemed to be stuck with farm and mineral exports and not much else, he should do such and such, and such and such, and he had. But at the end of six years each of those problems appeared to be very much worse than they had been when he began. Foreign debt was larger, and the trade deficit was high. The current account deficit was running at

about twice the level he had expected only nine months before. Inflation was still stubbornly high. Manufacturing exports had done well,
but were now crimped by a high exchange rate.

That was one paradox of which he had lately become conscious.
Another was that his career was now stalled in the most unexpected
and almost ludicrous way. Six years ago it would have appeared to
him that the most likely path of his career was that Labor would have
one or two terms at most, and then lose. But Labor was now in its
third term and, despite what most political reporters were saying,
Keating thought it had a reasonable chance of winning a fourth term.
A great part of its success was due to him, and this success had, in
his view, the quite ludicrous effect of persuading the Prime Minister that he was a great success and all but indispensable to his party
and to the nation. So Keating was forced to go on year after weary
year as Treasurer, a job in which administration had lately become as
important as politics, and support the vanity of this Prime Minister whom he had always rather patronised. Six months before, Hawke
had agreed to leave after the next election – a solemn pact, witnessed
by Bill Kelty and Peter Abeles. But would Hawke keep his word? He
and Hawke had lately agreed to push up interest rates for what they
hoped and expected would be one last shove, which would stop this
'very large investment phase'. With interest rates already so high, and
people screaming about their mortgages, would there be a fourth
term anyway? And even so he was not sure his achievement in getting
interest rates so high for so long, in cutting spending so markedly
and holding wages so tightly, was as widely applauded in Paris as it
deserved to be. In January he had been offended by an only mildly
favourable draft OECD report on Australia. 'What do these characters want?' he scrawled on the draft. 'A 25 per cent interest rate,
scorched earth, 15 per cent unemployment, 3 per cent inflation? This
is bullshit.'[1]

But for the moment Keating was there in Paris, in spring, staying at
the Plaza Athénée on the last decent trip, though he didn't know it

then, before an election that was still a year away. It was also mid-
way, though he didn't know that either, between the decision to begin
raising interest rates in April 1988 and the decision to begin easing
them in January 1990, two years that would imperil the Labor Government and put his own career in jeopardy. But now he was in Paris,
and if you are tired of Paris, he told reporters at the Château de la
Muette, you are tired of life. By day he could take his allotted place
at the ministerial table between the finance ministers of Austria
and of Germany, and in the evening he could return to the Plaza
Athénée, a hotel so discreet even some Paris taxi drivers hadn't noticed
it nestling unobtrusively amid the jewellery boutiques of the Avenue
Montaigne. It was an old hotel with small wallpapered lifts, where
even modest rooms had good eighteenth-century prints on the bedroom walls, Mumm champagne in the bar fridge, a buzzer to sum-
mon the maid, and a vast bathroom, equipped with Lanvin toiletries,
in which a polite notice requested *les joggers* to come and go by the
service entrance as a courtesy to other guests.

At his favourite Paris hotel Keating could be treated like the
important financial statesman he was. At the OECD he could be
treated with the distinction due to a minister who could report
that his policies were tight as a drum, and the caution due to a politician who, two years before, had so trenchantly attacked the European
ministers over the Community's common agricultural policy that he
had, in the recollection of the US President's international economic
adviser, 'started a riot,' which had led, with American support, to agricultural subsidies becoming part of an international trade negotiation.[2] It might have been the contrast between these gratifying
experiences and the brutal electoral pertinence and economic irrel-
evance of his press conferences with Australian reporters that stirred
his terrible pugnacity. There was one reporter who caught him at the
Plaza Athénée to ask whether he would, as the Opposition demanded,
fly home immediately to deal with Australia's trade deficit and inflation, a query that presented to Keating under the red awning of the
Plaza Athénée the opposite poles around which his life nourishingly
revolved – the most ordinary political savagery, which he would always

wish to meet and beat in kind, and the pleasure and seduction of power, celebrity, and the enjoyment of beautiful things.

Whatever stirred the pugnacity, it was evident. Asked by reporters about a downgrading of Australia's credit rating by Moody's bond rating agency, he snapped that the agency was evidently motivated either by incompetence or malice. The way the Australian newspapers played up the Moody's story, he said,

is part of Australia's cultural cringe. A firm like Moody's . . . some relatively junior executive in Moody's passes a crass comment about Australia, and it makes front page in the Australian media. I mean, say no more! It wouldn't cut a line in a broadsheet anywhere else in the world. It's just part of the cringe the media continues to have.

He mentioned that a deputy secretary of the Treasury, Dr Chris Higgins, had accompanied him to a meeting with the Governor of the Bank of France, formerly managing director of the International Monetary Fund, who had praised Keating's policies. A reporter was not clear about the banker's name.

Reporter: 'Dr Higgins?'
Keating: 'No.'
Reporter: 'Who is this gentleman?'
Keating: 'You might not have heard of him.'
Reporter: 'Probably not.'
Keating: 'Well, you should have. Mr de La Rosière.'

Keating was to fly from Paris to the Soviet Union.

Reporter: 'There has been some criticism of your agenda in the Soviet Union. Is it fairly tight? Are there tourist activities involved?'
Keating: 'It's basically a working visit. I have got a weekend off in Leningrad. This will come as no great shock to you as Australians, where weekends are generally their own unless they see otherwise. A lot of my weekends are not my own because I spend them in the Australian Treasury taking care of the

rest of you. But on this one occasion I am going to be spending one weekend by myself.'

Reporter: 'Is there anything you plan to do while there?'

Keating: 'Whatever it is, you won't be knowing about it.'

In May of 1989, in the midst of a monetary tightening more unpopular than anything he had done as Treasurer, Keating was more likely to intimidate reporters than flatter them. He was more likely to make fun of them to their faces than behind their backs; more likely to scorn their ignorance than explain the facts. These days the people he thought of as his opponents or who had contested his supremacy in economic policy were more likely to be treated with contempt than respect. Ross Garnaut, the former economic adviser to the Prime Minister and a proponent of the float of the Australian dollar in 1983, was really, Keating now believed, a B-grader. John Stone, the Treasury Secretary he had once flattered and treated with wary respect, the official who had been most opposed to the float, was really a B-grader. Now that he had learned his job there were more and more B-graders, and they would potentially include loyal A-graders who ceased to be loyal. The B-graders included the elite of Australian business, the men whom, as he said, paced up and down the cages of the regulated Australian economy roaring like lions and, when the door was opened, crept timidly out like pussycats. It was not all so – one critic, Manning Clark, was astonished to receive an invitation to lunch with Keating, and delighted to find the Treasurer as deeply interested in French history as the venerable historian was himself – but frustration was beginning to tell on Keating.

The truth was that his personality was changing as he grew older and as his upward ascent had been slowed and then arrested in what he believed was a bafflingly ridiculous and paradoxical way. Every success he had within the government and the Australian economy strengthened the Prime Minister, and gradually persuaded Hawke, whom Keating still believed to be a far inferior intellect and politician to himself, of his great success in office and the wisdom of remaining in it.

There had been good times and bad over the last six years, and the last year had been both extremely bad and extremely perplexing. The last nine months had been terrible, beginning with the nearest approach he had yet made to declaring a victory over the almost maliciously perverse Australian economy. He had also made the nearest approach yet to forcing Bob Hawke out of the leadership of the Labor Party. These two goals were necessarily closely connected. In August of 1988, nine months before he came to Paris, he had predicted a falling trade deficit, falling inflation and reasonable growth. But within a few months it become clear that the economy was growing far faster than expected, the trade deficit was on its way to increasing by nearly half instead of falling by a fifth, and inflation was rising to 7 per cent instead of falling to 5 per cent.

As the economy went awry, so did Keating's plan to replace Hawke. So far as the Treasurer was concerned, the real story of the government was the untold and largely untellable story of his relationship with the Prime Minister. He had been contemptuous of Hawke's intellect, and of the emptiness of a series of lectures Hawke had given on national radio as he made his transition from trade union leader to politician. He had later met with Hawke at a Sydney hotel, concluding a deal that Hawke thought ensured him Keating's support; Keating for his part believed the deal committed Hawke to standing aside after some time, preferably short, to accommodate Keating. Keating believed that for the first eighteen months it had been Hawke's government, the second eighteen months had been his, and now they ran it together. But even in those first eighteen months he believed he had grasped the meaning of things better, that he knew what the float meant, for example, better than Hawke. He resented to the point of fury stories alleging that it was Hawke, or at least Hawke's private office and the Department of Prime Minister and Cabinet, who had pushed him and an unremittingly hostile Treasury head, John Stone, towards the float in 1983. He resented to the point of fury stories pointing out that it was Hawke who had mostly chaired the meetings of the Expenditure Review Committee, which was responsible for lowering the size of government. He insisted that Hawke might do a few million here, a few million there and ask his advisers what they should do about this or that, but that in the end it was Keating who put on the performances, who told the spending ministers they had to give something for the government. And it was Hawke who came up later and ineffectually mumbled to Keating that it was perhaps a bit tough, that perhaps they need not cut so deep or so soon. Hawke was a humpty dumpty, he believed, who could only be kept sitting up there if things were arranged to reflect glory on him, even though Keating had done the work. The two men had entirely different viewpoints on what had happened with the Labor Government. To Hawke it was the expected realisation of policies he had decided early, which he brought from a period of long reflection and of economic expertise. To Keating it was all struggle and a succession of difficult victories, in which Hawke was sometimes helpful, and sometimes – particularly in the tax reforms of 1985, when he loudly said that he had to force Hawke to eat a shirt sandwich, he had to force him back into the cart, and nonetheless discovered both that Hawke dumped him at the summit and that Hawke subsequently left for New Guinea hours after he began a Cabinet meeting to consider the final tax package – not helpful at all.

Keating had failed to budge Hawke, and his sixth year as Treasurer had become the seventh and now, delighted as he was to be in Paris, the best he could hope for was another frantic year as Treasurer, then another and another and another before he had a chance to be Prime Minister himself. The seven years had gone by more swiftly than the seven years he had spent on the backbenches before the Whitlam Government was dismissed in 1975, far more swiftly than the next seven years spent on the Opposition front benches waiting, with no great confidence, for the time when Labor would return to government. They had gone with the rapidity of one's middle years and with the now serene belief, as he often said, that whether or not he become Prime Minister, the work he was doing as Treasurer was the most important work he would ever do in his life.

The official who bore most responsibility in May 1989 for telling Keating where the world and the Australian economy were going –

for understanding the puzzle – was also in Paris with the Treasurer for the OECD meeting. Chris Higgins, a deputy secretary of the Treasury about to become Secretary in a reshuffle that would take Bernie Fraser to head the Reserve Bank, had the lean, almost hollowed build of a runner and the pink tinge of someone who needed to be concerned about his heart, a combination that concerned his friends more than it concerned Higgins. He was remarkable for the serenity of his long silences when asked a question, and for the precision of his answers once he had formulated them. He was not an easy person to talk to because little in his conversation was superfluous, and when he had said what he considered necessary and sufficient, he would resume that serene silence until once again prompted to communicate.

Born in Murwillumbah, New South Wales, a year before the Treasurer, he was educated at local schools then earned an honours degree in economics at the Australian National University before working for his doctorate at the University of Pennsylvania, then one of the world's leading centres for econometric research. Returning to join Treasury in 1969, he began work on the first large-scale statistical model of the Australian economy.

At 46, he was younger than Visbord and, unlike most of his predecessors at Treasury, the younger economists whom Treasury could now recruit in a seller's market for economists, Higgins was a very smart academic economist as well as a policy-maker. His doctoral dissertation at the University of Pennsylvania had been directed by the Nobel Prize-winning economist Lawrence Klein, who even years afterward would tell visiting Australians that Chris Higgins was one of the most brilliant students he had ever had.

Though Higgins would disarmingly tell visitors that these days he would have to ask Treasury's younger graduates to help him through the thicket of algebra that is modern economics, his dissertation was the first big mathematical model of the Australian economy, one that was still the basis of the Treasury model. He had also found time, in a career crowded with policy work, to write a model of the Soviet economy.

Higgins walked around the OECD meeting with the elastic sides of his R. M. Williams riding boots barely concealed under grey flannel cuffs, but he was much more familiar with the rue André Pascal than he was with the Australian outback. He had been Director of Forecasting (for the General Economics Branch) on the OECD staff in the early 1980s, a highly regarded economist whom the OECD secretariat had been sorry to lose when he decided, quite early in his secondment, that forecasting at the OECD was fine, and writing about the perils of the world economy was fine, and being paid a high tax-free salary was fine, but they were nothing for him compared to the grandeur and excitement of actually being a policy-maker, a contestant in the great game in a sovereign nation.

The timing of his decisions was not accidental. He had been an assistant secretary of Treasury following monetary policy in the late 1970s when the head of the department, John Stone, had offered him the job as Australian Treasury representative to the OECD. He and Stone had no important disagreements about day-to-day economic policy. They had a difference of style and a difference of philosophy. Higgins was a member of a Labor Party branch in Canberra. Stone was by then a visceral right-winger who had applauded the US intervention in Vietnam, and was now strongly in favour of a smaller government and slowly moving towards the right of Australian politics. Stone was intellectually exciting and formidable, but also domineering. He would later rage against reforms in the public service designed to reduce its permanence and independence of government, but Stone himself behaved much more like a politician than the classical public servant he claimed to be. He held strong views and argued for them vehemently; he insisted on a single Treasury position, which was also his position, and when his advice was refused he would simply await another opportunity to urge it. When Stone suggested Paris, Higgins accepted, and though Stone subsequently offered a promotion to First Assistant Secretary of the Economic Division, Higgins did not return from Paris until Labor was in office and Stone was clearly on a course that would take him out of the Secretary's office. So Higgins had left Paris and the OECD in mid 1984 and come home to the bleak Treasury building among the magpies and pines near the old Parliament House, and he now found himself, six years on, the Secretary-designate of the department.

Like Visbord, Higgins was a veteran of the economic policy battles during the 1970s stagflation. He had been a member of the Labor Party, but he was also one of the proponents of the view that wages had risen so far during the Whitlam Labor Government in the mid 1970s that profits and investment had been squeezed, and unemployment could not now be reduced until the share of profits increased and the share of wages fell. He had shared with his OECD boss and the rest of the OECD staff a horror of the Reagan administration's economic policies, and particularly of the nonchalant disregard for European and particularly French feelings, which was displayed by Beryl Sprinkel, a monetarist who was Assistant Secretary of the US Treasury for Monetary Affairs and later, with the unhappy resignation of Martin Feldstein, the chairman of the President's Council of Economic Advisers. Like Visbord, Higgins would say that if there was one thing everyone agreed on it was that inflation must not be allowed to creep up as it had in the 1970s, because it would have to be controlled some time and the costs of controlling it later were always much higher than the costs of controlling it now. If others in May 1989 were still worried abut the risks of recession from higher interest rates in the United States, Japan, Germany and the UK, Higgins was not. The mood of the OECD meeting, he believed, was to keep up the pressure against inflation. If there was to be any change in policy it should be in the direction of higher rates, not lower. This message was as pertinent to Australia, then one year into a policy of higher and higher rates to counter rising inflation and too rapid growth, as it was for the rest of the developed world. Higgins, who had been in a bruising battle with Bernie Fraser all year over the timing and size of interest rate increases, was a hawk on inflation and would remain so.

But Higgins himself, as the Deputy Secretary who brought together the budget and its forecasts, had made or at least endorsed some of the most egregiously wrong forecasts of the past year and of years before that, despite his brilliance, his training and his experience. He had expected a lot more of the J-curve than it presented, he had expected a serious world downturn in 1985, he had not expected the boom of 1988. He had been wrong nearly as often as he had been right, and this was not just the ordinary difficulty of predicting so complex and undependable a system as the world economy but also because the world economy had changed, even in the few years of the 1980s. It had changed in ways that, despite his silliness and all the gaps between his premises and his conclusions, gave the verdict to Beryl Sprinkel and not to Chris Higgins. He, too, was compelled to recognise that the continued world expansion, despite the US budget and trade deficits and very possibly because of them, meant that the world economy of the 1980s was not like the world economy of the 1970s.

We were now, as Higgins would say using the typology of the OECD, in a type 2 world and we had left the type 1 world behind. In the type 2 world, exchange rates were set by markets and not by governments, capital flowed freely across the borders of the market industrial economies, banks and other financial institutions lent and borrowed freely and decided their own charges. Consumers and businesses might have to pay higher interest on their borrowings, but borrowing couldn't be cut off as it had been when the volume of lending had been controlled by central banks. And countries might have to pay higher interest on their borrowing, and might have to accept a lower value for their currency, but within very wide limits it was evident that they could continue borrowing so long as foreign investors were confident the loan would be repaid. Many of the changes Australia had made since 1983 had been made in other countries so that, just as Australia worked differently, so too the whole world economy worked differently.

There might be some limit, Higgins now believed, to the size of the foreign debt or of the trade deficit for Australia, but it was not easy to say quite what the limit was. He said if there was foreign borrowing, if investment was to be greater than savings, then for a period imports would have to be higher than exports to accommodate it. If a country wanted to borrow, it would have to run a deficit, and so the real issue in policy was how the borrowings were being used, not how big the deficit was. His answer left all kinds of possibilities for the short term, but it was nonetheless a different way of seeing the world from the way Eddie Visbord saw it, though paradoxically Visbord and his department had contributed very much more to the deregulation of the Australian financial system than Higgins or his department.

Six months later Higgins would elaborate it in a speech, which for the first time explicitly registered official acceptance that the world had changed, that the sequence of trade deficits and recession, the constraint of the balance of the payments, which Visbord had identified in the 1960s and 1970s, no longer need occur. There was a view, Higgins cautiously told a public audience in Australia, that might be called the 'consenting adults' approach to capital inflow. If the government was not itself running a deficit and borrowing, then most of the borrowing was done by private corporations, which presumably intended to make money on their borrowing and supply themselves with more funds than necessary to repay them. On this criterion he said 'Australia's current account deficit is relatively benign'. The most recent explosion in the current account deficit corresponded to an explosion in investment, and without the deficit the additional investment would not occur. Higgins presented it as simply a view that some people had, but he offered so few arguments against it and so many in favour of it that it seemed like a very sensible view.

But if the current account deficit was benign, why had the government been fighting it for two years with higher interest rates? And why would Higgins resist interest rate cuts until just before he was killed by a massive heart attack at the end of 1990? The reason was that Higgins thought inflation was important, and there was an opportunity there to bring two decades of Australian inflation to an end. As it had been expressed by the Treasurer himself in the Budget nine months before, 'While the balance of payments deficit is Australia's number 1 economic problem, inflation remains Australia's number 1 economic disease.'

In the type 1 world you couldn't run a big current account deficit; the central bank just ran out of foreign exchange, and it shut down the economy until reserves were up again. You couldn't keep going against a monetary squeeze, because the squeeze took the form of cutting off credit, not just raising its cost. Australia was now in the type 2 world, where the current account deficit could run at double the level Higgins had thought the markets would tolerate, and where higher and higher interest rates did not seem to be having the same effect on household spending and business investment as they had in the 1960s and 1970s or even in the mid 1980s. The loans were continued, increased, even if the cost was higher. There had to come a point when interest rates worked in slowing demand, but where was that point? And when they arrived at it, would there be a gradual slide or a terrific crash? Higgins at least had answers there: high interest rates would have to be maintained for quite some time yet. But there was no reason to expect recession when finally they began to bite.

Certainly the point at which it worked had been a long time coming, and the Treasurer was beginning to get impatient. 'It will all come right, Treasurer,' he would recall Higgins assuring him.[3] The J-curve would eventually work. The twin deficits would eventually work. Eventually, it would all come right.

When Keating returned from Paris he found Fraser more certain that a slowdown of some kind was now under way.[4] Economic indicators were still mixed, with dwelling approvals in April high, car registrations down, employment increasing but vacancies declining. One survey pointed to declining business confidence; another to buoyant investment plans. But as Fraser remarked, 'The indicators can be expected to show a mixed picture for some time yet: economies typically do not swing from boom to bust conditions in a few months.'

Fraser believed:

There are some further signs of a shift in mood during the past couple of weeks. Your own statements immediately prior to your departure recognising a tightening of monetary policy, the Moody's announcement, the end March external debt numbers, and the latest interest rate increases, have forced many people onto the back foot and into a more defensive mode. This will show up in slower domestic demand growth in the months ahead.

The immediate task is to get through to the time when there is unequivocal evidence of slowing in domestic demand – in circumstances where we could chalk up further bad current account numbers – without sparking a major selling off of the $A.

He believed the May current account deficit due on 19 June would be 'particularly nasty' and would have to be countered by Reserve Bank action, including interest rate increases if necessary.

Fraser acknowledged, 'There are others who are disposed to argue for more action immediately.' The International Monetary Fund Mission the previous week, for example, 'indicated that they were less confident than we are of a substantial slowing in domestic demand next year'.[5] The Reserve Bank board, however, decided at its 1 June meeting that things should be kept as tight as they were (bank bills at 18.25 per cent) but further tightening would be best kept to respond to, for example, a bad current account number.

By the middle of 1989 support for Keating's policy of high interest rates and deep spending cuts was vanishing within the Labor caucus. His colleagues knew there would be an election within twelve months. Many were certain they would not survive it. Hawke formally supported his Treasurer, but also listened to his critics. He spoke vaguely about changes that might make it easier for home owners. Among economic commentators and in the business community, the discord in Canberra was interpreted as a sign that Keating was losing control over economic policy.

Keating was convinced he had to make a big speech, reasserting his control and defining policy. He choose an *Australian Financial Review* dinner scheduled for 21 June at a Sydney hotel. An economic adviser, Dr Ken Henry, who had come across from Treasury in September 1986 to work on tax and then microeconomic reform issues, was assigned to write the speech.

The speech drafted, Keating worked on it overnight. By the following morning they had a new draft, and in the late afternoon Keating and Henry left for Sydney. Don Russell thought more work was
needed. Keating suggested changes, which Henry would insert while
flying. Never comfortable in small planes, Henry's stomach heaved
and his head began to spin on the flight as he wrote in the changes.
There was a problem at Sydney's Kingsford Smith Airport, so the
plane had to land at Richmond, at the base of the Blue Mountains
on Sydney's western perimeter. Driving through the suburbs to the
city, Henry sat in the back of the car, discussing changes over the car
phone with Russell, who inserted them into a copy in the office in
Canberra. Even for the Keating office, writing a major speech on the
way to the event was unusual. The complete copy was faxed through
to Keating at the hotel just before he rose to speak.

It asserted that Keating would not be bothered by tricks and
baubles – a reference to the modifications sought by Richardson
and Hawke. He would not be spooked by economic ratbaggery. He
was interested in the fundamentals of getting the current account
right and controlling domestic demand. Inspired by the text, he
embellished the ideas in responses to questions. He wasn't bothered by the nervous nellies of the backbench, he said. He was in
charge, and policy was on track. The papers the next day were lauda-
tory. Once again, Keating had restored public confidence in the
direction of economic policy. It was a turning point in the public
debate.

Treasury forecasters were sure by mid 1989 that there would be a
slowdown, but they weren't sure when. A new JEFG statement at the
end of June reported, ' . . . the timing of the slowdown in domestic
demand during the forecast period is difficult to identify mainly
because of the uncertainties about the point at which the impact of
tight monetary policy begins to outweigh the effects of strong expan-
sionary forces (such as the terms of trade).' Domestic demand was
forecast to grow 8.5 per cent in 1988–89, 2 per cent in 1989–90.

The current account deficit was now estimated at \$17.5b in 1988–89 – a more accurate figure but, since they had all but one of the twelve monthly figures, hardly a forecast. In 1989–90 the current account deficit was forecast to be higher than that for 1988–89 at around \$19.5b reflecting (said the forecasters) the increased foreign debt interest burden and adverse movements in the terms of trade. There was no mention of the risk of financial instability associated with debt and asset deflation, except to remark that 'one area of the economy that is particularly susceptible to sustained tightness in monetary conditions is commercial property development. Perceptions of property values appear to be changing (i.e. being revised downwards).' The report forecast unemployment of 6.5 per cent at the end of forecast period (June 1990), and increasing. It proved to be 6.7 per cent – this was very close.

Higgins' comments on the forecasts drew out some of the salient points. He was by now well aware of the possibility of an asset price collapse, but he believed it was part of the price they must be prepared to pay. He noted that, taken at face value, the JEFG numbers predicted a soft landing, but the economy continued to slow beyond the forecast period. How much further down it would go depended on some factors assessed by JEFG. One was exchange rate fragility, which might hit confidence. Another was the risk of a rapid downward correction of property values. He wrote:

We are all hearing increasing stories of a wave of caution on the part of both borrowers and lenders deriving from expectations that the formerly inexorable upward march in property values has come to an end. Large write-downs could tip some, or even a large number of, balance sheets into real trouble. Some financial institutions could be involved. There is something in this, of course, and as is being demonstrated at this moment for the dwelling sector, it is most important to be aware in advance that there is a price (albeit only partly predictable) we must be prepared to pay for overall slowing in demand and inflation.

The final risk to the forecast was wages and profits. There was little sign of a wages breakout, and provided that endures, it should put a floor under the downturn, both by sustaining employment and moderating the slowing of plant and equipment investment. It is thus possible to envisage a 'correction' in property values (as we saw in 1987 for equity values) which ends up being entirely healthy by not dragging the 'real' economy with it.

Things are different from 1987–88 of course in both the level and duration of high interest rates. Moreover, even in the absence of a wages breakout, if the property and/or financial market correction does give a large jolt to confidence, it could spread to the 'real' economy engendering a downward multiplier process which would produce a hard landing.

He reassured Keating that 'a steady hand on the bridge can steer the requisite narrow course and avoid a hard landing,' providing they hold on to

our present monetary policy settings and be prepared to do so for a considerable period. This may well mean holding short rates for a time above where the markets will be inclined to take us. We will need to endure real rates of interest higher than the rest of the world for some time yet.

He asked Keating to hold to the theme of 'your Sydney AFR speech'.[7]

Keating was disappointed by the forecast of a current account deficit higher next year than the already embarrassing result for 1988–89. (The deficit would actually be $22.2 billion next year, above the forecast of $19.5 billion.) Higgins and Morgan had been two of the most consistent proponents of the twin deficits theory, by which a lower fiscal deficit would result in a lower current account deficit. It was certainly true that if public saving increased, private saving remained the same and investment remained the same, the current account deficit would have to fall. Neither Morgan or Higgins, or for that matter the Treasurer, were yet aware, however, that private saving had fallen by as much as public saving had increased, and that in any case the increase in investment in 1988 and 1989 was so strong it overwhelmed saving.

Keating had now found yet another theory that didn't work, or didn't work in the way predicted or at the time predicted. In his own hand he annotated the JEFG report:

> Noted with thanks. It makes the twin deficits theory look like bullshit. By the end of the year under forecast (1989–90) the govt will have presided over an 8 percentage point shift in the PSBR. It must be a world wide post-war record. 8 percentage points since 1985–86 (6 per cent public and 2 per cent private savings). Yet the current account will, according to these forecasts, be still 5 per cent of GDP. At least I can't be burdened with any more talk about re-weighting the instruments of policy. We now all know what utter crap that is.[8]

The 1989 Budget was once again tight. There was to be a surplus of $9.1 billion, compared with $5.9 billion the year before. Outlays would fall 0.6 per cent in real terms and as a proportion of GDP to the lowest level since the mid 1960s. Statement 2 observed, 'Within Australia, the dominant economic development in 1988–89 was the exceptionally strong growth of private sector spending – the strongest, in fact, since the 1960s.' It argued that monetary policy was too loose in 1986–87. 'With the benefit of hindsight,' Statement 2 claimed, 'it is clear that market sentiment was allowed to drive interest rates below what was desirable in the light of subsequent expansion.' (Other than briefly mentioning the rise in Sydney home prices and an increase in office construction approvals, Statement 2 of the 1989–90 Budget did not mention the asset price boom.)

After the Budget Johnston retired from the Bank, to be replaced by Fraser. The decision had been endorsed by Cabinet in July. Johnston was farewelled on 9 September 1989. He had played an important role in the float, in financial deregulation, and in the ups and downs of economic policy since. Higgins was appointed Secretary of the Treasury.

By September 1989 Treasury was at least thinking about interest rate cuts. Prior to a meeting in early September it advised Keating, 'If, as expected, the slowing in demand gathers momentum and becomes more widespread, some easing of interest rates (which would probably result in a lower $A) would be desirable.' But not now.

Overall [the department believed] there is good reason for the time being to warn against expectations of an early reduction in interest rates . . . It can be difficult to hold financial markets when they get a run on . . . [but] by preventing monetary policy from being eased too far, pressure will be kept on domestic demand – thereby improving the prospects of wages policy achieving a step down in the inflation rate.

They had been fighting now for eighteen months, raising interest rates half a percent, 1 per cent, 2 per cent, 3 per cent – pushing them up and up as month by month the current account deficit got worse and worse and as investment continued not just to do well but actually to boom. 'Don and I did it together,' Paul would later say, to a table of economists in Indonesia and to President Clinton and his advisers over lunch in the White House. The two of them were proud of the way they had withstood the squalls and strains within the party, shouting down Graham Richardson, who was forever running around to see Hawke and telling him housing should be exempted, that it was all too much and Labor was gone for sure. It was a kind of personal contest: Keating and Russell against the economy, against the caucus, against the academic economists; Keating and Russell despiving the Australian economy; Keating and Russell holding out no matter what and indeed going half a point or full point better.

But they didn't expect a recession. Later they would both speak about it the same way – the model in their head was the same. Paul thought monetary policy did not appear to work at all for a long while, and then suddenly it worked all at once. Don would say in a 1991 seminar that he had heard the economy snap, not a slowdown or a steady decline, but an audible snap, something he heard in his office in Canberra not over a period but at a certain moment on a certain day towards the end of 1989. Paul heard it some time towards the end of 1989 too. Bernie Fraser may not have heard it in the Martin Place office of the Reserve Bank, but he certainly came to the conclusion that the slowdown had begun, as had his research chief at the bank, Ian Macfarlane. It would be well into 1990 before the figures confirmed that the economy contracted in the December quarter, but the signs were there.

13

INTO RECESSION

IT WAS AN EPISODE THAT PAUL would replay endlessly in his mind. Years later he was still thinking it through, still pondering how it might have been different, still wondering how a difference of a month here or a per cent there might somehow have prevented that economic earthquake of which he felt the first tremors towards the end of 1989. Years later he was still exploring rationales, still seeking a way of putting it so that it made sense and there was an explanation for it all. Even a month after the March 1993 election, when meeting with his departmental head Michael Keating and deputy secretary Rod Sims in his Canberra office, talking about saving and the current account over the next three years, Paul rapidly came back to what had happened in the last three.

If the current account deficit was the difference between savings and investment, how should we get saving up? One way, said Michael Keating and Sims, was to forget about the tax cuts promised in the election. That would get the projected budget deficit down and be a good start. The big thing, Michael and Rod said, in the rapid dialect we all used after a while, was to use fiscal this time, not monetary. It was unspoken that monetary had been used last time around, and the effect had been so savage that, as we sat in that office nearly two years after the recovery had begun, a million Australians couldn't find a job.

Paul started talking about what had happened to interest rates that last time around. Bernie wanted to knock them off in November of 1989, Paul recalled. He hadn't agreed; he'd wanted to wait until after Christmas. But he did want to get them down, he said, before history revealed itself. So they did start to come down. There was a I per cent cut, then a ½ per cent cut in February, promised during the election campaign, then a 1.5 per cent cut at the beginning of April, and then there was a gap right through to the beginning of August. Bernie had said, 'Let's put monetary policy to bed for a while,' a view that the Bank expressed in a press release; then there was a blue, a big blue with the Bank, the only one Keating ever had, and then there was a long gap from April to August before the cuts resumed. It was that gap that did the damage, Paul now thought — the gap as the board of the Bank, and of course Treasury, resisted. Paul had given Bernie a blast across the table after that press release, a full blast in which he said that the Bank had tried to cut off his options for bringing rates down more quickly. He told the assembled group of Bank officials that they should all go and get jobs somewhere else if they wanted to behave like that. But he had to say for Bernie that mostly he was fighting alone, or alone with just Kelty against the board and Treasury. The department was fighting it so hard that at one point Chris Higgins had actually voted at the board against a recommendation to ease. Bernie was fighting in Sydney while Keating fought on in Canberra and not least against the Department of Prime Minister and Cabinet. The deputy, Rod Sims, conceded immediately that he might have been wrong on that, might have been wrong resisting the cuts, and particularly the October 1990 cut, in which Paul and Don had had to argue before a judicious Prime Minister, concerned, like his department, that the real problem in the economy was not the signs of recession but the likelihood that it might bounce back.

Just as the enormous strength of investment, despite high interest rates, particularly in plant and equipment spending, had been unexpected and for a long while undetected, so too the rapidity and depth of the subsequent recession would be unexpected and for some time undetected. In Australia, as in the UK and the United States and later in Japan, the value of assets like houses and shares had greatly increased during the boom. Share prices had crashed in October 1987, but property values continued to increase. As the economy turned down, so did those asset values, and many corporations found themselves with insufficient security to support their loans and insufficient income to meet the interest payments. Banks and other lenders found themselves with bad debts. The trough in property values and the embarrassment of the major commercial banks contributed to the length of the recession and to the very slow recovery.

Within Treasury the forecasters were aware of the possibility of a debt crisis but did not think it was likely to be serious. As a result Treasury went on predicting a 'soft landing' and supporting continued high interest rates long after the Reserve Bank (now with Bernie Fraser as Governor) began to warn that the coming slowdown would be likely to be a long and deep recession. Keating himself would soon be in advance of both institutions, pressing for rate cuts – though he, too, thought recession would be avoided.

Keating and Fraser were discussing the timing of cuts, continuing and deepening that private line of communication between Treasurer and Reserve Bank Governor that began with Johnston and would now increase in trust, weight and understanding with Fraser. Treasury was pressing views that over the next eighteen months departed further and further from the wishes of the Treasurer to the point where Treasury was barely in the game at all.

At the beginning of December 1989 Treasury was predicting that the quarter would show no growth in domestic demand. At the same time Treasury urged Keating to tell a forecasting conference,

Given the need to keep domestic demand subdued for some time and to reduce inflation significantly, interest rates are likely to be at relatively high levels for the foreseeable future. No one should be expecting a substantial decline . . . the Government will be maintaining a very firm setting of monetary policy until there are clear and unambiguous signs that the slowing in domestic demand is sufficient to ensure downward trends in inflation and the current account . . . That point has not yet been reached.

But there were signs of diminishing demand – a 'clear sign that policy is working'.

When Treasury opposed further cuts in rates it warned that the effect of cuts already agreed was lagged. When it wanted to put them up, it did not look at the effects twelve or eighteen months away – it looked at the economy today. Keating would find as the months went by that both the Treasury and the Bank discounted forecasts and preferred to look at what the advisers called 'history'. They insisted on seeing the numbers rather than the forecast. But the national accounts showed what the economy had been like in the three-month period ending three months before. The current account, or retail sales or car registrations, or housing starts showed what those numbers had been for a month ending a month before. Treasury and the Bank were therefore looking back for guidance on a policy that, they insisted, was designed to change the economy in nine months or a year.

Keating, however, had his own plans. There was an election imminent. Certainly interest rates would have to appear to be reducing before that. He himself felt the economy had turned, and to avoid a recession he would have to begin easing. But by how much, and how quickly? It had been a hard thing to push the rates up against strong opposition. Treasury warned that the economy might bounce back. All the pain of raising rates would have been for nothing.

For Keating there were political considerations to balance. Interest rates should be heading down. But he had committed himself to the current account deficit as a measure of success. His closest adviser, Don Russell, attached much greater important to the current account than did either Treasury or the Reserve Bank. In a November minute on election strategy, he had minuted Keating, 'It is absolutely essential that the current account be declining in the first half of 1990. We must not let the monetary screws off too early.'[1] Russell had apparently shifted from his position of a few years ago, in which high interest rates pulled up the dollar and caused a decline in exports. The note is also symptomatic of a deeper disagreement between Russell and both the Bank and Treasury. In an earlier 1989 note on 'Budget Strategy and the Surplus', he had advised

Keating that 'as to tactics we should set ourselves tests we can pass. The current account is the obvious test – inflation is not'. By the beginning of 1991 the reverse would prove to be true, and Keating would return to lower inflation – his long-standing policy goal – as the test. The successive Accords and tax trade-offs allowed inflation to sink like a stone.

Fraser had wanted to cut the rate by November, but Keating preferred to wait until the New Year. A pre-Christmas cut would be lost, he felt. A cut of 1 per cent was announced on 23 January 1990. At the same time Keating concluded negotiations for another wage–tax trade-off, providing for tax cuts worth \$2.5 billion to be announced during the campaign. The election was announced on 16 February 1990 for 24 March. During the campaign the Bank announced another half a per cent cut. Another 1 per cent was promised during the election campaign.

Treasury resisted doggedly. Even eight days before the election announcement in a meeting on 8 February between the Treasurer and the Reserve Bank, Treasury advised, 'We consider that the current degree of monetary tightness should be maintained for the time being.'[2] Unofficial cash was now 17.25 per cent. Ninety-day bills were 16.25 per cent. The economy was on track for the projected slowdown. The principal task was 'to manage the transition to lower rates without putting hard-won gains at risk'. Markets, it noted, 'are straining at the bit'.

During the campaign Keating formally announced a new agreement with the ACTU. There would be an aggregate wage target of 7 per cent for 1990–91 to be achieved through tax cuts, increases in the social wage, and wage increases. There would be tax cuts from the beginning of 1991. The government would support an ACTU claim for an additional 3 per cent of wages in superannuation over the following three years.

Despite a first-preference vote below 40 per cent, and home mortgage rates which were still above 15 per cent, Labor scraped home, helped along by the preferences of environmentalists. With high interest rates the government at least appeared purposeful, and the rates were now heading down. The recession had not yet hit.

The election won, the battle over interest rate policy continued. Keating upbraided Fraser and Phillips for a press release accompanying the post-election cut, which appeared to postpone further cuts indefinitely. There would not be another cut between April and August. For his part Chris Higgins believed they now had a rare, perhaps unique, opportunity to vanquish inflation. Treasury did not yet see signs that a recession was coming. He warned that if interest rates were lowered too quickly the economy would roar back and inflation would continue.

Towards the end of March, Higgins summed up his thinking for Keating.[3] With the economy slowing and a wage–tax trade-off in place, there was a now a 'good platform' to launch an assault on inflation, the current account, and external debt. The economy had 'clearly entered a period of weak activity'. Treasury now forecast growth in GDP of I per cent in 1990–91. Higgins thought there was some scope for easing monetary policy but,

> It seems to us terribly important to now reach a judgment on a level for official rates that, once reached fairly quickly, should be held for a number of months . . . I think we are all mindful of the lessons from the 1987 and 1988 experience, particularly the dangers of letting the market take interest rates down too far and too fast . . . monetary policy should be avowedly set and conducted in a medium-term context with the objectives of restrained growth in domestic demand and reduced cost and price pressures

and less amplitude in swings.

He also wanted a 'specific objective' for inflation. 'Consistent with achieving less medium-term volatility in the conduct of policy and in changing inflationary expectations, our current judgment is that rates will need to be kept relatively high for some time; we certainly want to avoid a repeat of 1987 when we let markets drag rates down too far.'

Two months later Treasury readily acknowledged the downswing, but it was expecting tax cuts and interest rate cuts to produce 'some recovery in demand and product, primarily in the latter half of 1990–91'.[4] There was even a risk that the economy could bounce back. Unemployment in June 1991 'could be 7.5 per cent.' (A pattern of seriously underpredicting unemployment was beginning. It was 6.5 per cent at the time of the forecast. It reached 7.5 per cent in September, only four moths after. By June 1991 it was 9.4 per cent and rapidly rising.) There were many uncertainties. The downturn could 'turn out to be more severe than expected'. But on the whole

> . . . most of the risks are on the upside, with a distinct possibility of stronger recoveries in private consumption and business investment. A stronger recovery in domestic demand would result in worsening positions for both the current account and inflation.

It did not detect a financial crisis except to note that 'business efforts to strengthen balance sheet positions may still have some constraining effect on their spending', which would offset the danger of strong imports.

Treasury's thinking was conditioned by the experience of the two previous recessions. In a May note stimulated by the 'slight fall in GDP' for the December quarter of 1989,[5] a Treasury officer argued that recession was really a sustained period of job losses, which was now unlikely because – unlike 1974–75 and 1982–83 – there was not a preceding period of rising real wages. Now:

> real wages remain under control, and other fundamentals – terms of trade, profitability, world growth – are also likely to remain positive. For that reason, regardless of whether we experience a technical recession in the US sense, the prospects are for a 'soft landing'.

Rates had been eased in January, February and April, but would not be lowered again until August. The case for a further cut in those months was undermined by statistics, which showed that the economy was still growing. Treasury seized on the mixed evidence. Returning from an overseas visit, Keating found a note from Higgins.[6] Before the Treasurer had left there were 'alarmist' reports about bankruptcies, but data in recent weeks had 'altered the tone' of commentaries. The March quarter GDP increased 1.8 per cent. Employment rose in April and May. Housing loan approvals rose in March. Higgins wrote,

> The impact of these statistics has been to shift private sector views more towards ours, that we remain on a relatively softer landing track, albeit possibly more drawn out. The recession talk, technical or otherwise, is now more muted . . . the economy is proving more resilient than many commentators expected . . . the prospects for a relatively soft landing seem brighter.

He therefore advised that they should 'maintain present monetary policy settings in the period immediately ahead'.

A month later, Ewen Waterman, who had succeeded David Morgan in the Financial Institutions Division, made similar points, claiming that 'the tone of the economic debate has changed somewhat over the past month'. Therefore monetary policy 'should not be eased further in the period immediately ahead'. There was no 'unduly hard landing' in prospect. There had been 3.5 percentage points easing to date, which had not yet shown up. 'Present forecasts have the economy picking up during 1991, with underlying inflation and the current account still at uncomfortably high levels'. It was also noted, however, that long-term bond yields had increased by 1 percentage point since late 1989, while short rates went down 3.5 percentage points.

While Treasury remained opposed to any further easing, Keating and his office wanted to remain flexible. In mid July Treasury supplied a draft of Statement 2 in which it was asserted that 'monetary policy will remain restrained'. It was corrected to read that 'monetary policy will be kept under review'.

Treasury opposed any easing before the Budget. Fraser and Keating, however, wanted a 1 per cent cut in early August. It was agreed by the Reserve Bank board on 31 July. Higgins opposed the cut with Keating, opposed it with Fraser, and opposed it on the board of the Reserve Bank, of which he was a member by virtue of his office as Secretary of the Treasury. It was a serious step for a public servant to act so clearly against the wishes of his minister, and Higgins appeared to be mindful of its significance when he wrote to Keating on 1 August, attempting to delay the cut:[8]

> As discussed yesterday, we are all agreed that there should be some further easing in monetary policy but the timing of that easing is crucial. The CPI outcome is so marginally improved as to warrant careful thought about its timing.
>
> The Board's view at yesterday's meeting was conditioned by the expectation that today's CPI number would be a good one. The number that has been published is not as good as might have been hoped – as also was the case with last Friday's current account – and gives reason to reconsider the timing of the easing . . . The case can also be made for leaving the adjustment until we have the June quarter National Accounts and the Government has detailed its views about prospective developments in the economy in the Budget documents. I have, of course, put that view to the Governor and the Board.
>
> Another reason for thinking very carefully about the timing of this adjustment is that it could be the last move that might be desirable for some time (barring unforeseen developments) and there may be advantages in doing it a little later in the September quarter.[9]

In the reshuffle following the election, Kim Beazley was appointed Minister for Transport and Communications, with a brief to deregulate telecommunications in Australia. By May he had produced his competitive model, one with which Keating strongly disagreed. Beazley wanted to merge Telecom and the overseas telecommunications authority OTC to become a single entity, and to introduce a competitor for telephone services.

Keating believed that the new entrant would be too weak to take on Telecom. He proposed an alternative model in which OTC would be sold to NZ Telecom. The new corporation would be the nucleus of a viable competitor. After the introduction of the new competitor, the Australian market would be fully deregulated or 'fully contestable'. Any other entrant would be welcome. It was strongly opposed by Beazley, who believed that Telecom could be overwhelmed by the unrestrained and largely foreign competition.[10]

The conflict was savage, not least because Keating made it clear he did not think Beazley was clever or forceful enough to handle such a big decision. For his part, Beazley had always regarded himself as a supporter of Keating on economic issues and was offended by this direct encroachment on his turf.

It was a battle Keating could not win, and which Don Russell discouraged him from pursuing. There was a leadership battle looming, and Keating did not need to make an enemy of Beazley. But Keating pressed on, and in the end won a compromise that would alter the whole character of the deregulation. Beazley agreed that the market would be fully open after 1997, which meant that the new competitor had to begin acting with that knowledge from the beginning. On Keating's urging, Cabinet also agreed to open and fair rules to allow the new competitor to connect calls through to Telecom's network.

Discussing another cut in interest rates in October, Fraser sought to trade it for another package with the ACTU to reduce wages growth.[11] Treasury official Ewen Waterman, as acting secretary, insisted that while 'we have always expected economic activity to be weak in the current half year . . . we still expect a recovery to emerge in the course of 1991'. Nonetheless 'we would not argue strongly against a further 0.5 percentage point adjustment now or in the immediate future'. Treasury did not like Fraser's idea of making it conditional upon another wage–tax package. He concluded, 'It is important, especially given the extent of Australia's inflation and external account problems, not to overreact to the present period of economic weakness.'

By this time, however, even Higgins was losing confidence. When he returned in early October from a visit to an IMF meeting in Washington, it was with a ' . . . less optimistic view of the global economy . . . I sensed a greater tendency for a pause in the long expansion [in Europe and US] than I had formerly appreciated'.[12]

Influenced by Higgins' new assessment of worldwide weakness and by further evidence of slowing within Australia, Treasury forecasts were more subdued. In a minute at the beginning of November, Treasury reported, 'The economy is clearly very patchy.'[13] Victoria was bad; Queensland good. Construction was bad; tourism was good. It noted that 'business and consumer confidence is very weak and . . . activity is likely to be weaker in 1990–91 than expected at Budget time'. However, 'we would still expect a gradual recovery in domestic demand during the course of calendar 1991 (although possibly less in the first half of the year than expected at Budget time).' It was important to 'resist the inevitable pressures to pitch policy responses to the lowest common denominator, that is, to relax policy in order to alleviate pressures on the sectors bearing the brunt of the slowdown'. (In fact the economy contracted during the first three quarters of calendar 1991.)

By early November 1990, interest rates had been cut five times. Cash rates were 5 percentage points lower. The exchange rate index was 7 percentage points lower. Higgins fought further cuts. In early November he told the Treasurer, 'At some stage – I think pretty soon – we shall have to dig in . . . and hold a floor under cash rates. Not to do so will store up problems for the recovery and Australia would once again have missed an opportunity to get off the boom–bust activity (and policy) rollercoaster'.[14] The question was where to put the floor. His judgment was that they were already there. ' . . . [T]he recent easing should be the last for some time.' He concluded, 'All in all, we do not see much scope for further relaxation of monetary policy in the short term, barring the eventuality that the economy falls in a real hole which may call for some policy stimulation'.

In early December he reviewed the argument for further monetary easing and concluded that ' . . . we remain of the view that a pickup in spending (and activity) is in prospect through 1991 based on existing policy settings.'[15] Treasury would not object to another half a per cent but it would be better to 'keep your powder dry until late January'.

Looking at the evidence by the end of 1990, Keating was no longer convinced. He wrote on the note from Higgins:

> Chris, I suspect that 16 per cent primes in current circumstances are too high for a proper recovery in 1991. Manufacturing production started falling 18 months ago, inflation now is running at 6 per cent and falling, asset prices are falling and farm incomes have collapsed. GDP has fallen in 3 of the last 4 quarters and in September was lower than a year earlier. All these factors make me think that many businesses will have trouble surviving let alone expand production unless general business rates are lower.
>
> You might therefore examine how the current level of primes lines up with earlier episodes taking account of inflation and asset prices movements and the duration of the current downturn.[16]

Keating did not use the word *recession*, but if GDP was falling and on the latest numbers was lower than it had been a year earlier, the economy was already in trouble. There was no rancour in the note. Keating admired and respected Higgins, valued him as a friend, and shared some of his interests – including music. He accepted that the Secretary offered his advice with sincerity and conviction, and knew that Higgins would not attempt to embarrass him publicly. More often than not, Higgins' advice had been rejected over the past year, but his relationship with Keating had remained cordial.

The Secretary had been told by doctors that he had a serious heart problem, but that he could continue running. Competing in a local race on 6 December, the day after his note went to Keating, he collapsed and almost immediately died. Keating was shocked and deeply upset.

The day after Higgins died, Keating spoke at a Press Gallery annual dinner.[17] He lauded Higgins as a participator in public policy, and went on to speak about the importance of political leadership, the importance of being right rather than popular, and of changing things. Australia's problem, he said, was that it had never had a great leader. America had had Washington, Lincoln and Roosevelt at critical times in its history. We had not had one great leader, not one, though Curtin was a trier. Australia needed a leader who could communicate a vision. Leadership was not tripping over television cables in shopping centres. Keating himself had the confidence of financial markets, the central bank, the unions, and the Treasury. He was the Placido Domingo of Australian politics.

It was not, when you read the words, the assault that Hawke claimed it to be, and there was no doubt an element of Hawke looking for an excuse to repudiate a promise that to him had become more objectionable as its due date came closer. Often, in politics, the actual words do not explain the responses, which depend on the mood of the times and the opportunities taken. But it was a striking and honest speech, a true speech in some important ways, which, because it was not written by his office or department, not pondered about for its political effect, more truly caught Keating at that moment of his life, that time just before the onset of recession, when it was becoming harder and harder to realise the possibilities he had imagined eight years before.

The speech was soon reported, and Hawke was embarrassed by the apparent reference to the quality of his leadership. He spoke at length with Keating, and they agreed to talk again in late January. He asked Keating to come round to his office on 31 January. They talked for three hours. They had not talked so long since 1983, since the first few months of their untried and unbloodied government when Keating would leave his office after dinner and walk to the Prime Minister's office upstairs in the old Parliament House. The two would then talk together about the coming months and years, the Opposition, the characters of union leaders, or their Cabinet colleagues, or their principal public service advisers. The younger man rapidly learnt from the older man as he had from Matt Keating, Jack Lang, Rex Connor and Lionel Bowen; and the older man learnt, too, not least about his Treasurer and the New South Wales Right, which Keating always said he was of but not in, and which had installed Hawke as leader and would keep him there for eight years despite Keating's almost frenzied agitation to succeed him.

They had been friends for a while and their families were friends for a while, but friends are very hard to keep in political life. One reason we have friends is to be unguarded and silly and vulnerable, and you can't be like that in politics. They had fallen out seriously over tax reform in 1985 when Keating believed Hawke should have supported him right through instead of taking a judicious and presidential attitude, as if the Prime Minister himself was just another of the people whom it was Keating's job to convince. They had patched that up, but then had fallen out again in 1986 over the Banana Republic episode. After postponing their problems through the 1987 election year they had been in more or less open warfare through 1988, terminated only by Hawke's promise that he would leave after the next election.

That conversation in 1988 had been almost terse. There had been an election, there had been what Keating regarded as a suitable time, and Hawke seemed to be more attached to the job than ever.

Now there was a sense of final rupture, and with it perhaps the candour of a farewell. They had, after all, worked more closely with each other over the last eight years than either of them ever had with anyone else. Both of them believed the work they had done was the most interesting and important they would ever do, and together they won many battles against opponents both within their own party and on the other side of politics. But now they spoke to each other with brutal directness, the two men sitting alone in the centre of the Prime Minister's room, one of them sometimes standing up and pacing, gesturing. The two of them were watched over a discreet, soundless video monitor by several rapt members of Hawke's staff.

Keating told Hawke it was his turn now, that as long ago as 1980 Hawke had said Keating would get a turn. Now it was the fourth term of the Labor Government with only the very slightest chance of getting a fifth and none of getting a sixth, and still Hawke was there and evidently intending to remain. Keating had been in the engineroom of the government for eight years, he had been sweating and toiling working away at the public service and the Cabinet and the press to get it right and to destroy the Opposition, and it was always Hawke who got the credit. It was always Hawke who was able to play the statesman, as he was now doing as the United Nations struck back at Iraq. But Keating was on a promise – had been since 1988. He wanted to know when Hawke would announce his departure.

Keating's argument swelled and rose but washed over Hawke, secure in his invincible assumption that he alone would win the next election – an election against John Hewson, the most determined of Liberal leaders, who promised to change Australia dramatically. There was that, and there was also his world role. He had been around long enough to know the players. He was trusted and liked. He could solve conflicts overseas, as he solved them at home. Keating might be a good Treasurer but he was not a man of the people. He, Hawke, knew the Australian people, they knew him, and he would win one last victory.

It was not true, Keating replied, probing the vulnerability he detected in the Prime Minister. Hawke knew nothing about ordinary Australians; he was full of vanity and self-delusion. The truth is that Hawke had led a charmed life, a drunk through the 1970s, a man whose career had been helped out at each point by patrons – by Albert Monk who brought him to the ACTU, by Ray Gietzelt who made him President, and then at various stages by Charlie Fitzgibbon, John Ducker and Graham Richardson, and by Keating himself. A long series of patrons had picked him up and pushed him on to the next rung, most of whom if still alive had vanished into obscurity, their hour passed. But he, Keating, was not going to vanish. He did not and would not regard it as the pinnacle of his work and sufficient achievement to have helped Hawke fulfil some grand idea of his destiny. And as for Keating not being a man of the people, I mean, what do you have to do? He was actually born one, not as the son of the manse. He hadn't gone to Oxford. He had left school at 15 and worked as a pay clerk in the SCC, spending his adolescent years not playing cricket but down in the cable tunnels handing out pay envelopes, with cockroaches crawling all over the place eating the lead cables. Hearing about one bloke running off with another bloke's missus, and another up on a petty theft charge – that's what Keating had grown up with.

As to the next election, you only had to look back to the last one. Labor had won but, as a result of Hawke's strategy of seeking minority party support, its primary vote was right down. It might not come back. Labor probably couldn't win. Now was the time for Hawke to get out – as soon as Saddam Hussein was thrown back he could retire in triumph, at the high point of his career, beloved of his party and his nation, undefeated after four elections. Keating would carry on. There was a chance of victory with fresh energy and a fresh approach – but if the government's time was up it was better for Paul to lead the party into defeat, because he could take it. He could go and do something else, because his sense of himself was not so bound up with the job. If Hawke stayed and was defeated, he would come apart.

They talked on and stopped only when exhausted by the talk and the futility of it. Hawke was a statesman now, leading his country in war now just as Curtin had done. Though the war might be distant, and the commitment of a signals squad and a ship might be more symbol than substance, nonetheless it was certainly a war and Hawke was certainly Prime Minister. The Kirribilli deal was off because of Keating's disloyalty and because the party and the country both needed Hawke, and if Keating felt he had to leave, well, he would be greatly missed.

The final collision between Hawke and Keating came at the same time as the economy was slipping into a recession, which would last through most of 1991 and which would be followed by another eighteen months of growth so slow that unemployment continued to rise. To what extent had Keating's decisions caused the recession? An investment boom of the magnitude that Australian experienced in 1988 and 1989 had to end, and would probably have ended with a crash of some kind even if interest rates had not been taken so high for so long. The property price boom, too, had to end with a crash, because it was essentially speculative – property prices moved ahead of the rents that serviced the debt incurred to meet them. The extent and rapidity of the downturn might, however, have been moderated had rates not gone up another notch or so towards the end of 1989, or if rates had continued to come down after March 1990 instead of being held until August. Keating himself thought rates should have come down more rapidly (and should have gone up more rapidly in 1988) but whether it would have made a significant difference is not at all obvious. The differences between the actual policy and a feasible alternative are a matter of a percentage point or two, a month or two – not enough, one would think, to alter the main outlines of the boom and the bust.

It was argued at the time and since that tax increases should have been substituted for some of the interest rate increases of 1988 and 1989. Since the tax increases would have been designed to slow domestic demand to the same extent as an equivalent interest rate increase, their effect on output would have been the same. The Australian dollar would probably be lower, however, which would help exports and slow imports. But again it is highly unlikely that marginal changes of this kind would have changed the size of the investment boom or the depth of the subsequent recession. To the extent that investment spending had to be discouraged, lower interest rates would not have helped.

Keating insisted on the wage–tax trade-offs and consequent tax cuts of the period because he thought tax cuts were essential to obtaining moderate growth in wages during a boom. In all past booms wages had exploded. In the boom of 1988 and 1989 they did not, and as a result inflation plummeted during the downturn. Coming in the second half of 1989 the tax cuts would anyway have moderated the downturn rather than prolonged the boom.

Finally, did the forecasting errors of Treasury make for bad policy?

There is no doubt the forecasts were way off, both on the upswing and the downswing. Going up they failed to identify the magnitude of the increase in demand, and in particular the force of the investment boom. Since the Treasury was consistently pushing for interest rate increases from March 1988, the inaccurate prediction on the way up made little difference. On the way down, Treasury consistently underestimated the downturn, to the point where it was still assuring the Treasurer of a soft landing long after it was apparent that there was a serious recession on the way. Had Treasury forecast correctly (as to some extent the Reserve Bank did), it would have been an argument for earlier and deeper cuts. No doubt both the Bank and Treasury would have continued to argue that the important thing was to crush inflation while the opportunity offered. Since Keating lost confidence in Treasury forecasts from around the end of 1989, they did less damage than they otherwise might.

The important shortcoming of Keating's professional advisers was not the quality of their forecasts but of their analysis. They told a complicated and implausible story about commodity prices, the terms of trade and current account deficits, which reflected the style of thinking before the float of the dollar and provided no sensible guide to policy. They failed to identify the importance of the property price boom until well into 1989 or see its relationship to monetary policy. They did not signal the importance of the 1988 investment boom. If they did not know the pattern, the causes and consequences of what was happening in the Australian economy, their forecasts and advice could be right only by accident.[18, 19]

Having said all that, Keating cannot, as Treasurer, escape responsibility for the quality of analysis or the errors of policy. He himself accepted that monthly current numbers should be the measure of policy success. He had it within his power to announce the tightening of early 1988 more clearly, which might have made some difference. He could have done more to insist on a rate cut between May and August 1990. There were very few important decisions in the period with which he disagreed.

14

THE CHALLENGE

COMING BACK FROM HIS LAST PRESS conference as Treasurer we swung left to the deputy's office while he continued alone down the corridor to visit the Prime Minister. A slim figure wearing a dark double-breasted suit with a red patterned tie and black slip-on shoes, he grinned, nodded back and went on down the long, grey carpeted corridor, past the early Australian engravings decorating the ministerial wing of the new Parliament House, to the glass-fronted booth watching over the entrance to the Prime Minister's suite.

It was then 4.30 p.m. on Thursday 30 May 1991, a grey, drizzly day in Canberra's early autumn. It was the second month of the ninth year of the Hawke Government and two weeks after Keating had passed the record set by Ben Chifley as the longest-serving Labor Treasurer since the Australian colonies federated in 1901. He was now the longest-serving Labor Treasurer and a member of the longest-serving federal Labor government in Australia's history, but as he walked down that corridor he knew that his time as Treasurer was about to end abruptly, and that the government itself would be faced with its gravest crisis since it was elected in March 1983.

He knew Hawke would refuse to resign and allow Keating to take his place; he knew Hawke would win a contest for the leadership of the party; he had even conceded during the tactical discussions in his office that the timing of the challenge rather favoured Hawke. He was going ahead anyway because now he just could not endure remaining in what he called the 'chicken coop' of the ministerial wing office, attending Cabinet and Expenditure Review Committee meetings around the long oval table of the Cabinet Room, beginning again the construction of the Budget from the first cut at reconciling irreconcilable spending plans and revenue forecasts in the Early Expenditure Review Committee meetings in May to the final approval of the Budget documents in early August.

He had them there in his own office, eight consecutive sets of Budget documents, each fatter than the one before, and in each he had gone immediately from weeks of clawing back a million here and a million there from reluctant ministers and cunning public servants in the Expenditure Review Committee to the chaotic drama of writing and editing the text of the Budget statements; week after week of drafting, deleting, inserting and rearranging with three secretaries calling material up on computer screens as Keating and his staff members interpreted and reinterpreted the reality of the previous year and the expectation of the next so that it fitted within an ordered world of sensible plans and expected outcomes, a world contained in the white document of the Budget, a paper world in which the Treasurer was in control, while he and his staff grew groggy from the weeks of working until the early morning hours, with rejected drafts accumulating in piles at the bottom of steel safes with combination locks. 'It can no longer be borne,' he had told me earlier in the week, his head bobbing down emphatically, hands circling. 'It's insufferable. It's too long.'

Between late January and late May in 1991 the economy had slowly subsided. The revised forecasts were ever more sobering, and unemployment crept up inexorably month by month, while Keating stalked Hawke for what he now realised would be a bloody challenge rather than the easy succession he had once thought probable. As Canberra's summer passed into autumn, the Treasurer's office became the command post not only of economic policy but also of a campaign to supplant the Prime Minister. Newly hired as an economic assistant, I watched with fascination as Keating twined politics and policy in preparation for one of the great battles of his career.

Recruited to Keating's office in November 1990, I returned to Canberra to begin work at the end of January 1991. Prior to that, in Washington reporting the crisis between Iraq and the United States over Kuwait for the *Sydney Morning Herald*, I paid little attention to Keating's 'Placido Domingo' speech and its aftermath. By the time I arrived in Canberra, Parliament House television was locked on to CNN, following the fighting as the US and its allies threw Saddam Hussein's armies out of Kuwait. Though Australia's contribution was limited to a signals detachment and a couple of ships out of range of possible action, Hawke's foreign affairs adviser slept at night by his desk and Hawke himself was on television most evenings, brooding in a statesmanlike fashion on events in the Middle East. If there had been a leadership battle brewing, Hawke was now protected by the flag.

The Gulf War was soon over, but by then it was increasingly apparent that the recession would be prolonged and difficult, which at first seemed to pose another obstacle to Keating's ambitions. Hawke was entrenched, but it was also obvious that many ministers and caucus members were now pessimistic about Labor's chances in a contest against Liberal leader John Hewson and quite hostile to the Prime Minister. To many of them any chance was worth taking, even the improbable one of Paul Keating winning the next election. The mood within the party and Cabinet was poisonous. Content to find out about the making of economic policy, I did not ask Keating whether he was planning a challenge, and though it was apparent he was at war with the Prime Minister, he did not volunteer a clear statement. The existence of the Kirribilli agreement was known then to only about half a dozen people. It would be many weeks before I was drawn into the leadership challenge.

Recruited earlier but beginning in the office at the same time as me, political adviser Stephen Smith, formerly the Western Australian state ALP secretary, arrived with a wholly different objective. Paul had called him soon after the 1990 federal election, ostensibly to thank him for the success of the party in Western Australia. Keating had told him that the government was good for another term

or two but not if it was sentimental. Smith said that he was not sentimental. By the time he started working for Keating he knew about
Hawke's promise to resign, he knew Hawke might break it, and either
way he thought Keating should be in the Prime Minister's office.

The battle with Hawke seemed far from Keating's mind in his
Parliament House office at the end of January 1991, when I had my
first long discussion with him for several years – through within a
few days he would again meet Hawke, who would confirm that he
was no longer going to be bound by the Kirribilli House agreement
and would not resign in Keating's favour.

For all Keating's taste, his office was not a very personal room.
It was a room he visited rather than used or dwelt in. There was a
small varnished pendulum clock with Latin numerals, for example,
but it was an electronic Seiko reproduction run by a battery, a gift
from a Japanese corporation. There were two watercolours of Hawkes-
bury River landscapes on one wall. Underneath was a package wrapped
in patterned paper of the kind used in Japan. It leaned against the
wall in a temporary fashion, unopened, for four months and was
finally removed only because everything was removed. He had a small
speaker system and a compact disc player on a shelf behind his desk,
but he did not use it. Behind him were rows of Budgets, May Statements, green-bound House Hansards, Christies catalogues and coffee-
table gift books. The Budgets were heavily annotated, the other books
rarely touched. There was a framed and signed photograph of one
of the four swearing-in ceremonies for a new Cabinet he had attended
in the last eight years. On his desk statistical releases, antiques catalogues, architectural reviews, files and papers were heaped up in
several layers. Every day it was dusted, but in four months it did not
change except for new material put on top. In the drawers he crammed
staplers, paper clips, coloured highlighter pens and a pharmacy of
organic pills, potions and cold tablets. But he could rarely find anything he wanted. On the corner of the desk was a phone bank, with
lines to the Prime Minister's desk and to other ministers.

(His home in Canberra, I would later see, had the same temporary air. His rented house in Beagle Street, Red Hill, was a

straightforward brick veneer home with picture windows mirror-glazed on the outside, wall-to-wall carpets and a pastel colour scheme in which the bits and pieces of his neoclassical collection were startlingly out of place. There were two large paintings in the manner of David on opposite pastel walls, a row of compact discs, a magnificent glass-fronted bookcase stacked with his architecture books, a set of foam-padded chairs, several lovingly restored neoclassical clocks and two superb candelabra with Egyptian slave figures, a polished mahogany cabinet ornamented with carved Pharaonic designs, and a library of video tapes. The combination of middle-class Canberra comfort and treasures crafted in France when Napoleon was invading Egypt was quite startling. In eight years the Keatings had moved three times between rented houses. Not since they had been at 12 Gerard Avenue had the family had a place of their own to arrange as they pleased. Their things followed them around, from garage to garage. Only the Tozer house in Queanbeyan, which Paul was then having renovated and decorated, the stalled renovation in Elizabeth Bay, and later the house the Keatings would buy in Sydney's Woollahra, showed the context he had in mind for his collection.)

He talked a little about my work that first day, but it was mainly, as I was later to see was far more usual, a wide-ranging and rather one-sided conversation. He was wearing a double-breasted light wool suit in a pattern of small black and white checks. He kept his coat on. He drank soda water while he was talking. His voice tired easily – it was a strain to keep it going. He was a little puffy in the face and his holiday tan was rapidly fading. He had been reading Richard Ellmann's *Oscar Wilde*, he said, a wonderful, sad book; also a biography of Wagner, a great man and a great composer who nonetheless, he said, 'sponged off Liszt'. He thought that now I had children I would enjoy a few years in Canberra. Some people needed to visit each other at weekends – Canberra wasn't good for that, because the only people you could visit were people in the same world. But with children it was fine.

By some easy transition he was talking about the arts grants, the Creative Fellowships he had set up in May 1989, because he found

Tozer, a world-class concert pianist, working as a piano teacher at St Edmund's College. He had set up the fellowships apart from the Australian Council because the council, he thought, only gave grants to members of 'the club'. He and dancer Graeme Murphy now had a little project going, he added. One of his favourite pieces of music was Mahler's 8th, the 'Symphony of a Thousand'. He wanted Murphy to produce it for a stage performance in Sydney.

Then he was talking about Iraq. He had agreed to the ships and thought they should go. But he stopped Hawke sending troops and planes. It made no difference to the US, but would make a difference to Australia. He wondered whether it might have been settled by Arab mediation in the first few days. Someone from a US investment bank had told him the US has two kinds of weapons it hadn't used – a threshing bomb for clearing acres of trees, and a gas vapour bomb for removing oxygen from a large area. There would be prolonged difficulties for the US in the Middle East afterward, whatever happened. Hewson would have a big problem with his proposed consumption tax. It cost so much to compensate the losers that there was not enough left to reduce the marginal rate of income tax, which is the only way saving might be influenced. Otherwise it was just an invitation for government to spend more.

Turning finally to the work in his own office, he said that the forthcoming industry statement by the government would be tariff cuts pure and simple, with some sweeteners to make it more palatable. The problem over the next month or so was to stop the silly stuff. A lot of the work there was to stop the silly stuff. And on wages, well, there would be a good system by the mid 1990s, one based on a real devolution and industry bargaining with fewer unions and bigger pay bands. He and Bill had run an incomes policy for eight years – longer than anywhere else in the world. Even now Kelty had to call unions up to get them to reverse wage increases – even in a downturn.

He also talked about the state of economy. He had been to Surfers Paradise, where it was still booming. People couldn't get travel bookings. He still seemed to think that the downturn would be short and mild. He thought the Budget would remain in surplus, for example.

Victoria was the problem – though, of course, he immediately conceded, Victoria is part of Australia.

The despondency of recession was only just beginning to settle over Australia. Its course would become part of the final act of the leadership struggle. In the following four months we would with mounting concern track its dismal path through meetings between Keating and Reserve Bank Governor Bernie Fraser.

Even as late as August 1990, only five months before, Keating had expected the economy to continue to slow down under the impact of high interest rates but not to contract. By November, when the statistics for the three months ended September were published, he knew he had been wrong. The economy had contracted in the June quarter and again in the September quarter. There was clearly a recession, but how long and how deep would it be? Even at the end of January he wanted to believe that the downturn was ending and that growth would soon resume.

During 1990 Treasury forecasters had fought with the Reserve Bank's Assistant Governor Ian Macfarlane over the outlook, with Macfarlane arguing that the contraction underway was much more serious than Treasury expected. By January 1991 Macfarlane thought this recession was different from the past pattern. It had begun with the usual contraction induced by high interest rates, but it had snowballed because this time businesses were loaded up with debt and the prices of assets like property and shares, which were security for the debt, were unsustainably high. A string of financial failures amplified the recession, particularly in Victoria. Treasury had not accepted this view earlier in 1990, partly because to do so implicitly endorsed cuts in interest rates. (Macfarlane did not conclude that rates should be lower – he was interested in crushing inflation while the opportunity offered.) It now appeared that Macfarlane had been right. In January 1991 he was predicting that the contraction could continue for another two quarters, making a full year of deterioration and postponing even the stirrings of recovery until after June 1991.

By the beginning of February 1991 Treasury officials were debating whether the recession was a shallow dip or a serious downturn. The consensus forecast was that output would fall in the year ended 30 June, but by less than 1 per cent, and that it would grow next year. They thought unemployment would rise, but that it would peak around 9 per cent. Inflation would come down, yes, but only to around 5 per cent. And the current account deficit, which so far was consistent with the Budget forecast, would probably rise because of depreciation in October, and it would rise again as the economy expanded next year. The Budget would remain in surplus next year but by only $1.5 billion.

In the bureaucracy that advised Keating, Tony Cole had only just been appointed as the new head of Treasury to succeed Chris Higgins, and it would be some time before he built up his authority. As Governor of the Bank and former Secretary of the Treasury, Bernie Fraser was far and away the most influential of Keating's official advisers. Regular 'debriefing' conferences between Fraser and Keating and their advisers after each Reserve Bank board meeting were the most important occasions on which economic policy was discussed and the state of the economy gauged.

Interest rates had last been cut, by 1 percentage point, on 18 December 1990. After the holiday break the first meeting of 1991 was held on 15 February, when Keating left a lunch with the editors of the *Sydney Morning Herald* at East Sydney's Beppi's Restaurant and drove with Don Russell and Stephen Smith to the barred and guarded side entrance of the Reserve Bank in Phillip Street, near Martin Place. The metal gate was raised as his car turned in, and Keating's driver parked the car on a platform, which spun it around to face the entrance. Escorted by the Bank's green-suited attendants, Keating took the lift to Fraser's office. After a short private discussion between Fraser and Keating the two men joined Bank and Treasury officials in the boardroom for the first major discussion of economic policy in 1991.

Orange rugs were scattered over the marble floor of the conference room. A woven hanging depicting the First Fleet and nearby church of St James, with a surround of red bottlebrush, decorated one wall. On the table were silver-plated water pitchers. A slide screen had been unrolled in one corner of the room.

Seated around the table were Fraser, Deputy Governor John Phillips, Assistant Governor Ian Macfarlane and Assistant Governor Geoff Board, who followed the financial markets. Across from them sat the newly appointed Treasury Secretary Tony Cole, deputy secretaries John Fraser and Ewen Waterman, and the First Assistant Secretary for monetary policy, Neil Hyden. Keating brought Don Russell, Stephen Smith and me.

The recession had not been forecast by any of the members of the official family, but now that it was an indisputable fact, both Treasury and the Reserve Bank wanted to use it to get inflation right down to the level of other developed economies like Japan, the United States and Western Europe. In past months they had both proposed that the government adopt a formal target for inflation, say 3 per cent, as a guide to policy. They had resisted interest rate cuts, arguing that the cuts already made should be allowed time to work. They wanted to make further cuts on 'history', that is, actual recorded deterioration in production or declining inflation, rather than forecasts for deteriorating production or declining inflation.

Fraser opened the meeting by suggesting that Macfarlane might screen 'just a few charts'. Macfarlane said there were no signs of an upswing, and though the feared labour market shakeout had not occurred in January, further falls in employment were to come. Victoria was particularly bad. Inflation was down, though not by much. Inflationary expectations, however, were down for the first time in many years. Credit growth had slowed but not by anything like the extent in the USA. He said the balance of payments forecast in the Budget looked to be OK, though he understood Treasury now thought the forecast was too low.

Geoff Board followed with a briefing on the state of financial markets. The Australian dollar was steady after a major fall in October. Comparing international interest rates, Australia had widened against the US and sharpened against Germany in the last eighteen months. John Phillips said that, compared with Australia, most monetary policies looked extremely loose.

The lights went back on; chairs were pulled back to the table. 'Where does that leave us?' Fraser asked in his distinct whisper, looking around with dark, steady eyes. 'We have to wait for earlier reductions to work through, to bring home the bacon. The board came to the view that notwithstanding the weakness of the economy, having regard to falls in interest rates, we should sit tight for the time being. I think that is about right.'

Treasury had submitted a written brief to Keating arguing that the recession was likely to be extended, with GDP declining further before beginning to recover in mid 1991. 'In our thinking we have come to focus increasingly on the yield curve as one useful guide for policy. If we aim to keep the yield curve about flat, as it now is, this would see nominal short-term rates fall in step with falls in inflation expectations as they impact on bond yields,' Treasury argued. A cut of up to half a per cent as early as the March board meeting could be justified. It was one of the few occasions in which Treasury had actually suggested a cut.[1]

Fraser said there would be two board meetings in March and therefore two more chances to look again at whether another cut was warranted. Keating complained that commercial banks had not passed on to home loans and business loans the cuts to the overnight loan rate already made by the Reserve Bank during 1990. He wanted Fraser to call the banks in and lecture them, but the Governor was non-committal. 'I'd rather sweat on the banks,' said Keating. 'If you give them half a per cent too early they'll just take it. They have to be a bit bloody sensible or they will end up buggering the lot of us.' No cuts were agreed, and the meeting broke up.

Through most of 1988, 1989 and 1990 Keating had committed himself to a lower current account deficit as a goal of policy. Part of his frustration in those years was that the investment boom of late 1988 widened the deficit long after he had publicly signalled his determination to narrow it. Treasury was now forecasting that the deficit would remain quite big. (As it happened, the economy would be weaker and the current account narrower than Treasury forecast.) With two major wage–tax trade-offs and a weakening economy, however, inflation was fading. As Keating would later say, the consumer price index, which had been kept up by import price rises and transitory influences, was 'catching up' with the rapidly falling gross national product deflator, which measured the total price change in all goods and services produced in Australia and which had been influenced earlier by falling wage costs. The possibility that there would not be good news on the current account but good news on inflation, combined with the realisation that the recession was quite deep, induced Keating to accept a significant change in his public line. A week after his first meeting with the Reserve Bank for 1991 he signalled the switch in direction with a speech written for the meeting on 22 February of the Economic Planning Advisory Council in which he argued that Australia was 'snapping the inflationary stick'. It was a phrase he often used to distinguish between a lull in inflation and permanent elimination of it. It was my first speech for him, and it helped to shift the debate over economic policy objectives away from the current account deficit, which I thought misleading, towards an objective that was both attainable and truly important, and to which Keating had in one way or another been striving since 1983.[2]

When he next met Fraser a month later, on 14 March, in the Canberra offices of the Reserve Bank, officials had become gloomier about the recession and more confident that inflation was headed rapidly downward. Fraser reported that the board was concerned about the flat economy but thought there was an opportunity to make gains on inflation. He said the board would look again at its 25 March meeting, and the question then would be whether we do something immediately or wait until there was evidence in the May CPI release for the March quarter that inflation was heading down.

Treasury had advised Keating that the markets had taken

considerable notice of his EPAC speech and assumed that further falls in interest rates would depend on further falls in inflation. Maintaining a flat yield curve was one guide to policy, and on that basis no change was warranted.

Keating said the timing of the CPI release was getting later and later – it was now 15 May, and meanwhile in housing there were skills and resources that might go out of the industry. It was now more than three months since the last cut. 'I think we can go a bit faster,' he said. 'I don't think we can wait until May. I don't think we can wait. It's that bloody late.'

Fraser agreed that there was certainly no chance of the economy running away if rates were cut. It was a question of whether we waited for the CPI or anticipated it.

'The place is subsiding,' Keating insisted.

Cole said he was opposed to a 1 per cent cut. He quoted a small businessman who had told him the worst was behind. His deputy, John Fraser, said the market now did not expect a cut until May, and then only half a per cent. Cole said it would be better to do half a per cent and then wait and see.

'If you are wrong about the economy and we leave the rates up,' Keating said, 'it will give the economy a terrible hiding.' The banks, he added, are 'brigands and cowboys who need flogging.'

'Treasurer,' asked Waterman, 'do you have an open mind on the size of the adjustment?'

'Yes; 1 per cent sends a signal; half a per cent won't be noticed. But I don't mind half on the 27th and half after the CPI.'

Keating looked at Fraser. 'Bernie,' he said, 'you don't have religious fervour about it?'

'I don't have religious fervour about anything,' Fraser said, 'but that method does weaken the nexus between inflation and the reduction of interest rates.'

Keating persisted. He suggested going from the current rate of 12 per cent to 11 per cent and then 'sit it out' for a while.

Macfarlane agreed with Fraser – a cut should be related to inflation, and should therefore wait until the CPI came out.

Keating replied, 'I think that Ian is only partly right. Monetary policy is the short-term swing policy. That's how we have worked it.' (The comment went to the heart of a difference of viewpoint between the Bank and Keating, which at that meeting was not pursued.) 'All you will need,' he added, turning to Fraser, 'is discretion'.

'Yes,' said Fraser, 'we can talk before we do anything and there will be more indicators.'

Driving back to Parliament House, Keating said, 'They go on with all this bullshit because they won't admit it's an art, not a science.' He thought the Reserve Bank had been too slow on the way up and was now being too slow on the way down.

With the economy slipping, Keating continued to press for another substantial cut at the debriefing two weeks later, after the second board meeting in March. Treasury advised Keating for the meeting that the 'economic contraction is slowing', with the housing sector 'close to a turning point.' The salutary lesson from past cycles was 'the danger of easing too far and too long in the slowdown phase', fuelling an unsustainable recovery.[3] However, so long as real interest rates were maintained, nominal rates could be reduced. There was scope therefore to reduce cash rates 'a little'. A half a per cent cut 'would be consistent with flattening the yield curve from its present slightly inverse shape'. The cut should be immediate, with another cut possible at some later time if inflation continued to fall.

'This is like a board meeting,' said Fraser, remarking on the formality as the officials and the Treasurer gathered in the room. 'The real one, not the play one,' replied Keating.

Fraser said he had proposed a 1 per cent cut after the CPI, but the board had preferred only half a per cent, also after the CPI – but they had given him 'latitude'. He added, 'I would prefer to wait and come in with 1 per cent on the CPI.' Keating said he wanted a half now because 'the place might be slipping.' Fraser said things might be bottoming out.

The discussions wandered, with Fraser saying that if there was 'occasion to jump in by a half,' he would do so, but not suggesting a time. Keating wanted a definite time. He suggested the bank cut by 'a half now and then a one on the CPI, and then call it quits'. Treasury had argued for a half a per cent cut. Pulling the discussion back to his proposal for a 1.5 per cent cut in two stages, Keating asked, 'Well, what do you think about this?' Fraser agreed to do a half on Thursday. There would be another meeting to consider the 1 per cent.

A week later, on 4 April, the bank announced that it would reduce cash rates by half a percentage point to 11.5 per cent, bringing the total reduction in cash rates since January 1990 to 6.5 percentage points. The fall in domestic demand, the bank said, 'appears to be flattening out'.

There would be another 1 per cent out in mid May, with the evidence of declining inflation dissolving some of the resistance within the Bank. From February to the beginning of June Keating was able to win consent to a significant fall in the policy rate, but the basis on which these decisions were made appeared to be quite primitive. Discussions at the Reserve Bank, 'debriefings', rarely moved beyond a discussion of the effect of changing the overnight rate on housing mortgage rates and then on the home building industry. Yet the housing industry accounted for only about 4 per cent of GDP. There was not much discussion of the effect of changing mortgage rates on consumer spending (around two-thirds of GDP) or on households generally. Housing loans in fact accounted for only a quarter of the stock of all loans. The total of loans for new dwellings was almost insignificant compared to the stock of debt, yet interest rate changes by the Bank in greater or lesser degree could affect the entire stock, not just loans for new dwellings.

Neither the Bank nor Treasury presented much analysis, nor was there any discussion around the table of the likely effect of short-term rates on long-term rates, or the effect on business lending and investment, the effect of interest rate changes on the exchange rate, or on the price of other assets like stocks and property. There was no discussion or analysis of the balance, for example, between reducing the income of retirees dependent on interest from their savings with reducing the interest cost of home mortgages held by people still in the workforce. There was a widespread practice at the time of maintaining the same level of home mortgage payments, despite falling interest rates – but the extent of this practice and the importance of it was not addressed during meetings or in written analyses. And for all the interest in setting inflation targets, there was no discussion of where rates ought to be in three months or six months or a year, or how alternative wage and budget policy changes might relate to alternative interest rate decisions. Certain relationships, such as that between short-term rates and long-term rates, were held to have great value as guides to policy, but why this should be so or the extent to which it was so was not argued or examined.

Other than a few references in briefing papers to the desirability of maintaining the same real or after-inflation interest rate, there was little discussion of the framework in which monetary policy decisions were made. This was no doubt partly because Keating and Fraser, the only two important participants in these discussions, were so accustomed to each other (and talked frequently other than at these sessions) that their framework or model was now implicit. But it was also that the structure of the interest rate changes did not lend itself to a sensible discussion. There is little point in estimating the effect on investment, consumption, home building or the exchange rate of a half a percent change in the policy rate if the policy rate is 10 or 11 per cent. The effects are too small to measure. Fraser himself murmured during one meeting that maintaining the real rate meant that there would be many reductions to come, since inflation was falling so fast. (This disconcerted Treasury, which was surprised by the rapidity of the fall in inflation.) But this did not introduce an analysis of where nominal rates would be in a year's time and what it would mean. Policy was changed by hints, whispers, murmurs, by unspoken things, more than by written analysis or formal discussions. By all accounts, the board meetings were no more widely or richly informed than the debriefings and often considerably less.

However reached, the cuts were much too late to do anything more than prevent a more serious contraction than the one already underway. Though the December quarter of 1990 had recorded positive growth, the 5 April JEFG believed the March quarter would be negative and perhaps June as well. Treasury now believed that the economy was weakening. Housing approvals and car registrations were both down. As the economy deteriorated, the urgency of the challenge to Hawke increased.

Stopping the silly stuff in Cabinet took most of February. Keating saw himself as the engine of the government, and in the working out of the 12 March statement that is exactly the role he played. It worked well for the government because Hawke was a good chair and Keating was an excellent advocate. It was illustrated vividly during the Cabinet debate on the industry statement – a debate that re-enacted, in its contemporary form, the protection debate, which had been argued in Australia since before the colonies federated.

During 1989 in a deal brokered by Keating's office, the Industry Commission had reported in favour of a 15 per cent tariff for motor vehicles – a higher rate than the IC would normally recommend, but the minimum level likely to be accepted by Cabinet. Keating had successfully fought to prevent John Button's Industry Department entering into negotiations for a new plan for the car industry. Instead he fashioned the debate so that the IC recommendation became the centrepiece for a wider review of tariff policies.

Cabinet and Cabinet subcommittees met frequently during February to winnow out proposals and reach consensus on tariff cuts. With unemployment increasing month by month, and with the ACTU and a large proportion of caucus opposed to any further tariff cuts, the success of the statement depended on the alliance between Hawke, Keating and Button, with support from Howe, Willis and Dawkins.

Throughout February Keating would return from each Cabinet meeting to give his assembled advisers a rundown on what had happened, reading from notes. He took the parts in turn. Bob Hawke was his best – foxy but mute. Keating's Hawke would press his head down, then sideways, screwing up his eyebrows.

On Tuesday 5 February Cabinet looked at a list of dozens of proposals of things that might be included in the statement. But the first item was a discussion on the wool auction system and the Australian Wool Corporation. Auction sales had been suspended because, in supporting an unrealistically high floor price for wool, the AWC had borrowed the entire $3 billion that the Commonwealth was prepared to guarantee. Now Primary Industry Minister John Kerin had come for more. Keating recounted the discussion: 'John wanted another $300–400m in Commonwealth funding to help the AWC pay interest on the debt, and also to help woolgrowers who had sold late in the season and would not do as well as growers who had sold early. If the AWC did not get a subvention, the $3b debt would fall to the government. Hawke complimented Kerin on the fine job he was doing.

'I reminded John that I had wanted a lower auction floor. I opposed extending the Commonwealth loan guarantee to the AWC. I told him the only reason the sales had been suspended was that the AWC had simply run out of guaranteed borrowings. I said it's the woolgrowers' debt; they've had a few good seasons, and they're not going to vote for us, anyway.

'John said that wasn't much of an argument. Bob then asked Kerin to come back with a proposal.'

Cabinet then turned to the list of proposals for the industry statement. A call for ideas had elicited from departments and their ministers many pet ideas that had been discouraged in more rigorous times. Now they came back. One by one Keating knocked them down.

One minister wanted depreciation for earthworks. 'I said you'll have farmers pulling out all the trees.' That was designed to appeal to Environment Minister Ros Kelly and former Environment Minister, now Social Security Minister, Graham Richardson, and succeeded. He added that the potentially massive Very Fast Train project would want to claim depreciation, as would the mining industry, 'but it won't do a thing for manufacturing.' He wondered how earthworks could plausibly be subject to depreciation. Earthworks depreciation was scotched.

Another proposal was to allow a tax deduction on the interest on losses carried forward. This brought forth Keating's most scathing rebuke. 'I told them I've heard some pretty awful proposals in eight years but this one just takes the cake. Not only are we expected to help companies make a profit, we are expected to give money away to losers as well.' Tax deductibility of interest on losses carried forward was scotched.

Someone thought it would be a good idea to allow small businesses to carry over capital gains when their business changed, rather than having to declare them and pay tax. Fine, Keating told Cabinet, for small business. It sounds good for the mum and dad shop, 'but you'll have all the bigger dogs down too, to paw the bone.' That was out, too.

Another minister wanted a 15 per cent limit on superannuation funds invested abroad. 'This wasn't on the paper!' Keating complained to us, in recounting the meeting. 'Think of what this means,' he urged Cabinet. 'Some poor little bugger puts his savings into super and then finds the government is telling him how to invest it.' The minister countered that the superannuation funds now had only 12 per cent abroad, so a 15 per cent limit wouldn't constrain them. Keating was not persuaded. 'I said the ACTU won't wear it. In any case, dividend imputation has slowed them down because they don't get it on overseas shares. There is so much money in these funds, do you want them to simply bid up the price of Westpac shares, to double them?'

These scuffles were merely preliminary to the real contest, which was between Keating, representing the hard edge of economic severity, and Simon Crean, the latest incarnation of government intervention in industry. Crean was the junior minister in Senator John Button's Industry portfolio. Crean proposed that the government, in ways not quite clear, develop 'sectoral policies' by helping to create, for example, an aerospace industry around Avalon. The idea, he said was 'to support our strengths' rather than – in the old and discredited protection policies – support our weaknesses.

'I said to them,' Keating recounted, 'this is exactly what the coalition said in the 1950s and 1960s. You don't think they just said, well, we'll put on tariffs just so we can have higher prices and slack management, do you? They also said they were picking winners.' Keating's strategy for the statement had been to make the key deals privately with John Button, exchanging tariff cuts for tax breaks, and then present to Cabinet an agreed front between the two usually antagonistic departments of Treasury and Industry. But Crean's intervention threatened the strategy. Crean was not part of the deal, and his proposals were not endorsed by Button. The problem, Keating explained to Cabinet, was that 'Simon's not the minister. I mean, we need to have a bit of order. We can't just go dropping in proposals in someone else's portfolio. I'm not opposed to helping industry, like what we did for the North West Shelf project. But to go around nominating industries, which don't now exist, and being nominated by a minister who is not the Minister, well, it takes the cake.'

'It got bit heated, then,' Keating concluded. 'They don't like it getting heated – but it's always like this.'

Three weeks later, on 27 February 1991 Cabinet looked at industry development proposals from Crean. Button and Keating wanted them referred to a subcommittee of the Structural Adjustment Committee of Cabinet. Crean wanted a group of ministers that would include him. Led by Keating, the procedural discussion once again became once of substance, and once again over an issue that lay at the heart of the Australian economic debate. Keating said the idea of Crean's submissions was to pick winners that picked themselves. He produced a letter from former head of the Industry Assistance Commission, now Treasury Secretary, Tony Cole, saying it was unlikely that a group of public servants could pick winners not identified by the private sector.

Keating recounted, 'I told them it was vital that the 12 March statement not be seen as a retreat from opening up the Australian economy.' Some of his colleagues had interjected that other countries did not have a level playing field. 'I said no one but a fuckwit believes there is a level playing field internationally. But it is essential to have a level playing field at home to get resources into the right places. I haven't sweated blood to cut spending to lose it in the hills and gullies of tax scams.' He said to us, 'Once you put your hand up for something you don't believe in, once you go along, you're finished.' He shrugged.

Five days later Button introduced his final submission to cut motor vehicle tariffs to 15 per cent, clothing textile and footwear (CTF) to a range between 15 and 35 per cent, and all other tariffs to 5 per cent by the end of the 1990s. Keating had called him and persuaded him to substitute his original end point of 10 per cent for 5 per cent. The Treasurer offered him tax concessions and 'a place in history'.

Keating recalled, 'Bob asked if anyone had anything to say. I said I wanted to say something. The first thing is that I want to congratulate John for bringing forward a submission that keeps internationalising the place. I mean, thank Christ we have someone here who knows what's to be done around the place. We've had two and half months debate and we end up here with the submissions, and the submissions are for tariff cuts. That's what it comes down to – tariff cuts.'

Gerry Hand said there would be a lot of unemployment. Keating reminded him that the government had been cutting tariffs since 1984. 'The manufacturers won't invest now in anything that's protected.' Hand said CTF reductions would hit certain regions hard. 'I said to him, Gerry, don't give us that bullshit about textiles. Your mates drive away in Mercedes from these little plants. Just one of these little plants with the quotas is a gold mine. The owners are the Saddam Husseins of the textile industry, using those old ducks as shields, these poor old buggers sewing buttons for eight hours a day with their eyes hanging out. It's a stinking spoof on the rest of the community. So Gerry said he supported the workers, not the owners. I said, "Well, Gerry, if you support the workers, why not give them a cheap shirt; why not give them cheap shoes – not three times the world price. You have your heart in the right place, Gerry, but your head is in the wrong bloody place and it's about time you woke up to it."

'Duffy gave an entertaining speech. Duffy is clever but sometimes he talks like a pre-Copernican Luddite-look-alike obscurantist. Gareth was fuming about something being GATT-offensive. I said instead of going over suck-holing the Americans, Gareth, you can go over and argue a case for a change. Bob summed at the end. Made a little speech about lower tariffs and how we are too small to have a protected economy.

'This was one of those meetings where you get no thanks, but I got my way. At the end I said to Button, "Well, we got it." The big thing is that by 1997 no industry in this country can be other than internationally competitive.

'This is not the best Cabinet,' he mused. 'The best was the one in the middle. These things would have got through easily and without trouble in the middle Cabinet. There is not a good mood in there because it is unled. Bob comes in and says nothing. He doesn't set the scene. A lot of them think we will lose next time, and they behave accordingly. The mood is too agnostic, too pessimistic. It's going to the dogs. This show can't go on the way it is going.

'The quality of debate is quite high but there is a begrudging attitude. They think they can't really knock over Keating and Hawke, but they don't really believe in tariff cuts during a downturn. Hawke is always buzzing around politically. Dawkins does, but he wants to help exporters too. Blewett and Gareth want to open, but not too open. Graham supports the open model but left to himself would not. He sees the leadership does. Kerin the same. Cookie does – he's good. Nick wants to do good but is not sure if the gospel is true. Howe was bloody good. He supported the thrust of what was proposed. He said the replacement model is finished. He nodded when I made the points. He is the one with the view closest to mine, funnily enough. The rest of them sing the song, but they don't all really believe it.'

Hawke delivered the statement on Tuesday 12 March. It was, as Keating had predicted in January, all about tariff cuts. Given that it was delivered in the depths of recession, it was extraordinarily courageous.

He said he saw himself as a member of the office, like other members of the office – like another adviser, almost – and somehow his personality and style, and no doubt also the importance attached to the office by outsiders, made it a pleasing, congenial place to work. In the new Parliament House he occupied a suite of rooms across a small courtyard from the Prime Minister's office. We looked out through a trellised wisteria vine, which gradually lost its leaves as summer turned to autumn, to the stone-flagged courtyard. In the centre of the courtyard was a sculpture of copper dragons' teeth. Magpies and currawongs sang on the trellis. On most mornings the gates to the courtyard would be opened and the Prime Minister would drive into the courtyard, the flag flying on the bonnet, followed by an unmarked car carrying two Australian Federal Police bodyguards. 'Look at the flag,' Paul would say, looking across the courtyard to where the Prime Minister's vehicle was now parked, flag furled. 'I mean, a flag on your car!' He was worried about 'him over there'. At any moment, he said, things could go sky high.

Within the office we staff members were all reasonably open with each other, certainly on most policy issues. But we did not talk about the internal workings of the office outside it. Paul and, to a lesser extent, Don Russell were often extremely candid but also highly suspicious and guarded. Paul in particular had an unusual combination of startling candour and discretion along with an unwillingness to trust people he did not know well. He would say of other politicians who confided to the wrong people that they lacked 'tradecraft'. On Paul's instruction Don had arranged with an outside firm to install electronic locks on the office, so that we were outside the Parliament House security system.

There were seven advisers in the office, and about the same number of secretaries. As it happened at the beginning of 1991 the advisers were all men and the secretaries all women. Staff members stayed for years. Three years was normal, but five or longer was not unusual. There were no staff meetings to discuss work flows and office problems, no structure charts to show who did what. These came later, in the Prime Minister's Office. The result was a creative chaos that suited the staff and maximised individual autonomy but appalled Treasury. We each worked individually for Paul and coexisted with each other. He was bewitching. Every parliamentary sitting day 'the boys' would gather in Paul's office to help prepare him for Question Time.

On 15 April Paul sat behind his desk wearing blue smoked bifocals, reading suggested answers to questions we planted with Labor backbenchers, or questions we expected from the Opposition. He marked the text with a yellow highlighter pen. The now-familiar clock ticked back and forth. We sat in a row along a couch, or in chairs around a low table. Don Russell sat in a big chair next to the pot plant.

'Linda,' Paul called to his secretary, Linda Craige. 'Linda – how about some lunch, love?'

Stephen Smith, the political adviser, had a long list. He was not used to Paul and not yet familiar with what mattered and did not matter to him.

'They might ask you about the Westpac survey. Have you got anything on that?'

'It's bullshit,' said Paul.

'It's up and down all the time,' said Don. 'We did it last time.'

'I'll just say this . . . there are lots of different surveys, but the evidence is the economy has bottomed out.'

Paul forked down a steaming plate of stew and rice, which Linda had brought from the cafeteria. He looked at one of our answers. 'This is too much,' he said. 'There's too much here that's unnecessary.'

There was a labor force release showing unemployment at 9.9 per cent.

Stephen said, 'Hewson will ask you about unemployment. You can't just say it was worse in the last recession. You have to say it's terrible.'

'Say it is unacceptable,' said Don.

Paul shrugged. 'I'll say it's unacceptable. Where's a bloody pen? Linda! We can't survive this. What do you think? Not going above 10 per cent. We can't win. What did you think?' He frowned, pushed out his lower lip, let both hands drop to the desk. 'Perhaps we can, if it's heading down.' He raised his eyebrows and forehead, and screwed up his face around his mouth. 'I dunno. I think we're gone. It's nearly two. What else is there?'

So it went, week after week, between the beginning of the Gulf War in Kuwait and the first challenge to the Prime Minister and Paul's resignation at the end of May.

Like monetary policy, wages policy had a political dimension in the looming battle with Hawke. For more than five years the Accord had really been about wage–tax trade-offs made between Keating and Kelty. His connection with the ACTU Secretary through his control over the government end of the Accord was one of his strongest political pillars, because it legitimised Keating's economic policy objectives in the eyes of the labour movement. Moving towards the battle with Hawke, Keating was cultivating Industrial Relations Minister Peter Cook, who supported him against the Prime Minister. Through Kelty's allies Laurie Carmichael and George Campbell of the Metals and Engineering Workers' Union (now the Australian Manufacturing Workers' Union), he cultivated the trade union Left, which might be able to influence the parliamentary Left to withdraw support for Hawke. The basis of the legitimacy was the distribution of tax cuts and the evidence that lower nominal wage growth had allowed much more rapid employment gains (which also meant lower productivity) than in previous expansions. But with unemployment rapidly increasing, the Accord was under strain.

He and Kelty had, as he said, run an incomes policy for eight years, longer than anywhere else in the world. They knew the system of a single six-monthly centrally agreed and determined wage increase could not continue indefinitely, and the more flexible enterprise-related system to replace it had not yet been created. It was a time of transition, as we attempted to devise a new framework. In the office, Keating asked me to assist.

Both he and Kelty believed that the Accord now had to develop towards 'enterprise-related bargaining' to facilitate trade-offs of job rules for higher wages, and to allow wages to differ for different levels of productivity increase and for different degrees of industrial muscle. Because of rapidly falling revenues for several years there would be little room for tax cuts and therefore for the wage–tax trade-offs that had sustained the Accord in past years. A tax trade-off would be difficult, yet it was vital that wages rose no more than was consistent with a much lower rate of inflation than in past years. Over the course of four months this led to increasing emphasis on an employment-based superannuation scheme backed up by government legislation.

He explained his goal to International Monetary Fund official Patrick de Fontenay in a meeting in his office on 7 March 1991. Answering the official's concerns about the Accord, he said that 'to the extent it embodies an agreement on central wage fixation it is outliving its usefulness. The centralised system will count for less; the Accord will deliver less. But informally the leadership of the ACTU recognises that big wage increases are counterproductive. If we did away with the Accord, could we do without some agreement on the wage system? I don't think so. I read that the Bank of England is asking for lower wage claims. Well, that is like peeing into the breeze, as we would say here. In general, any government, not just this one, would do well to have some kind of Accord.

'So, what has it got left for us? It has probably got one more deal in it. It should be the deal that takes us from 5 per cent to 3.5 per cent national wage increases. But there is a problem with the Federal Government surplus. Do we have enough? Over the years the deals have really handed tax indexation back.[4] If we had had indexation, we would have lost the revenue anyway, and the IMF would have patted us on the back. We could risk running back into deficit to get the inflation rate down. Once the inflation rate is down, there is no problem running wages. Even now when we sit down with the ACTU only a short amount of time is spent discussing wages. It's about production, training and so forth; only half an hour is on nominal wages. It would be a pity if a non-Labor government did away with that.'

Paul wanted a wage–tax trade-off, but as the expected surplus dwindled and the inflation numbers improved, there seemed less and less point. It also ran counter to enterprise bargaining, because it substituted to some extent a general and central increase through tax cuts for particular enterprise increases won as productivity bargains. In the second week of March, Keating told Kelty that the wage–tax trade-off would have to be postponed until 1992.

In mid April I was preparing an EPAC speech on productivity themes when the full bench of the Australian Industrial Relations Commission ruled against introducing enterprise bargaining at that stage, remarking in the course of it that the unions and employers were not sufficiently mature for so large a step.

Pre-empting both Hawke and Willis, who wanted to accept the decision, Keating called Cook and urged him to say nothing that sounded like approval of the decision. To me he remarked that the commission was itself quite a feeble tribunal, which succeeded only if the government, the employers and the unions were balancing each other, or if the tribunal's decisions went the same way as the wishes of the three parties. In this case the commission was attempting to act against the wishes of all three parties. During Question Time he rejected the commission's decision, in this instance with the cheerful support of Treasury officials, who strongly pressed for the shift to enterprise bargaining.

On the evening of Thursday 18 April Keating and other ministers gathered with the trade union leadership at a meeting of the Australian Labor Advisory Council. On the government side of the table were Hawke, Cook, Keating and their staff advisers. On the ACTU side were Kelty, Martin Ferguson, Laurie Carmichael, George Campbell, ACTU assistant secretary Iain Ross, and others. As we came in they were discussing strategy in the light of the commission's decision. Kelty was threatening that the ACTU would pursue enterprise agreements, rejecting the commission's decision. There would be a round of direct negotiations. He would release everyone to win industry and enterprise agreements. On the other side of the table Hawke was shaking his head disapprovingly.

Paul intervened as this died down. 'Can we come back to this? Do you want us to abolish the commission? Do you want the commission out of the way? What about we abolish it?' Keating believed the commission had a role in preserving a safety net. His question was designed to focus Kelty. There was a short, horrified silence as the ACTU delegates digested this proposition. Then Kelty said, 'No. It's not right. The commission is a worthy institution but it is run by a few people who are not doing a good job. It should look after the safety net, not try to control outcomes. It is the Accord which gave it its role.'

That night Iain Ross and I reworded Paul's EPAC speech for the following day to reject the commission's decision completely and call for enterprise bargaining. The EPAC meetings were closed, but the text was distributed to the press gallery[5] and marked the first occasion on which the government had formally disputed a major commission decision and called upon it to define its own new role in assisting the parties to reach agreements. Kelty told EPAC that the AIRC decision said the parties were immature. If they were mature they would reject the decision because acceptance of the decision was acceptance of their immaturity. 'We will not be distracted into mediocrity. For the first time the ACTU will be rejecting a National Wage Case decision,' he added. The ACTU held a press conference in Parliament House to announce its rejection of the decision. Treasury officials were delighted. The rejection decision, they said, was 'historic'. Thereafter we were in a new world. The commission would not again be asked to make single decisions for the entire workforce. Its decision repudiated by unions, the government and many employers, the commission would issue a new judgment later in the year, accepting the shift towards enterprise bargaining. When he returned as Prime Minister, Keating would set up the legislative framework to encourage it.

The March 1991 statement and now the shift to enterprise bargaining completed large parts of a reform agenda Keating had progressively adopted over the last eight years. The financial system was deregulated and the dollar floated; tariffs were now on a downward path to insignificance for all but the auto and textiles, clothing and footwear industries; both taxes and government spending had been deeply cut as a proportion of GDP in successive budgets and statements since

1986; the dollar was significantly lower and the country more competitive; the profit share had increased substantially; employment had expanded and now there were the first signs that Australia was making a transition to become a low-inflation economy. Many of the goals had been achieved, but by 1991 Keating was weary from the effort. As he had explained to de Fontenay from the IMF on 8 March, Australia could do well in the 1990s, with lower protection, more competition and better business leadership.

'Now we have all guns blazing away,' he had said, 'but we're running out of ammo. We've been here eight years. In America you are not allowed to stay more than eight years. It will be ten years by the time of the next election. So we are odds-on to lose. It would comfort me if our colleagues opposite knew the problems. After eight years we are battle-weary. There's no joy in cutting spending. There's no joy in monthly current account releases and quarterly inflation numbers. Wear and tear is a big factor. The Opposition doesn't know what toil is – going through it line by line. They will try and get bureaucrats to do it, but bureaucrats don't have the authority to cut spending. We've had the same five people working through programs for seven years. Hawke, Dawkins, Willis, Walsh and me. It has destroyed the health of a lot of us.'

It was a dramatic four months from Hawke's confirmation on 31 January that he would not stand aside for Keating, but its climax could not be postponed for long. It could no longer be borne, Paul told us. The little clock that ticks inside us had signalled that it was time to break. It was the biggest decision of his career, but it had been made deep down many years before, and its execution on Thursday 30 May was simply a matter of walking down the corridor to the Prime Minister's office. The alliance between Hawke and Keating, which had once been the foundation of the government, was now its weakness. 'We used to be the strength of the show, mate, but now the wheels have fallen off,' he would tell Hawke a little later that day, talking softly into the phone by his desk, through which we could hear the raspy croak of Hawke's answering 'mate'. What had once been a source of pleasure and interest and change to both men had become queasy and false, and the consciousness of its deterioration pushed Keating on.

His colleague John Dawkins had earlier stopped by Keating's office to complain of the unbearable atmosphere that, after eight years of shared battles, after four stomach-churning election campaigns, now settled on the Cabinet members in the ministerial wing. Keating had told him then that it wasn't only he, Dawkins, whose mood went up and down without apparent reason. 'So does mine,' he had said. 'He sits on us. You think up something, you want to do something, but at the end of it he is there,' he said, pointing through his windows and across the courtyard to the Prime Minister's suite, 'and he does nothing. It can no longer be borne.'

He knew he would be likely to lose a challenge, but if he were to succeed at all in displacing Hawke, he must first deny the party its preferred option of keeping both men through to the next election. The Gulf War was winding down, but Hawke would soon be leaving for a long overseas visit, and Keating would once again be tied down in preparing the Budget. If he tried now and failed, Hawke would be alone, and caucus members could judge for themselves how good a performer he was without Keating. There would be time enough before the lead-up to the next election for another strike at Hawke if the first failed. Hawke had failed the first time to force out Hayden, as Hayden had failed the first time to force out Whitlam.

In the weeks and then days before the challenge he was pessimistic but cheerful. He had had it stitched up late in 1990, he said, but then it went bad with his press gallery dinner speech and Hawke's chance to dominate TV during the Gulf War. The Cabinet mood had turned frosty. It had once been a welcoming, admiring place but for a while now it had been like walking into a blizzard. Now, he thought, it was perhaps too late — win or lose. There was a political earthquake in Western Australia, he said, and an economic earthquake in Victoria, and either would be enough to defeat the government at the next election. There was still a chance, but the right time had been over two years ago – at the end of 1988 – but both the Right and the Left had told him they would not allow it. And that was when Richo and the rest had wanted to get Brian Burke up as Hawke's successor, a thought encouraged by Hawke. Burke! In all honesty, he said, he didn't know if he could win the next election, but there was a chance. The government had, after all, achieved much. 'What a decade!' he told me as we drove down Mugga Way towards his Red Hill house after a Sunday night wages policy meeting with Hawke at the Lodge. 'And that's the problem with Bob,' he said. 'He hasn't been able to get people to believe we are in a new world.'

He was weary, and his closest staff were weary. They had seen it all so many times. Don Russell had been there since 1985, through the Banana Republic year, the election of 1987, the decision to raise rates in April 1988 and lower them in 1990, the boom and now the recession. Keating's adviser on microeconomic reform, Ken Henry, had fought beside him on innumerable issues, including the 1988 tax cuts, the 1990 telecommunications policy changes, and now the 1991 economic statement. Press secretary Mark Ryan and political adviser Stephen Smith spent all day on the phone or in the corridors. They longed for battle.

Keating knew he wanted to challenge and he knew he wanted to do it soon, but he breathed hot and cold. He was guarded and cautious. He noticed that Laurie Oakes had begun supporting his claims, and agreed to appear on Oakes' program, but declined to confide. 'Oakes knows where the tram is going,' he said, 'and he wants to get off before it hits the buffers.' He invited the *Australian*'s Paul Kelly down for an interview, closing the door on their hour-long discussion. But when Kelly wrote the following day that Keating was no longer prepared to commit himself to go through to the next election as Treasurer, Keating was indignant. It was too naked. It went too far. Kelly was trying to catch up with Oakes.

Far from the well-oiled machine smoothly responding to controls, Keating's campaign for the leadership was cobbled together by devoted staff and by backbenchers hoping for a ministry. Graham Richardson, the supposed kingmaker, was drawn in only reluctantly. Other leaders knew very little until the last moment. Minor figures mattered more. They had less to lose, more to gain. South Australian backbench senator Chris Schacht mattered, and so did Laurie Brereton.

The campaign against Hawke was run without a definite plan, and with a timetable that frequently changed. Even the strategic decisions were taken on the spur of the moment. I was initiated into the details of the conspiracy one night in Sydney two weeks before the challenge, as former Keating staff member Tom Mockridge drove Stephen Smith, Mark Ryan and me back to our hotel after dinner at the Balkan Fish Restaurant in Oxford Street. As we drove, Stephen for the first time asked Tom, 'What do you think of the thermo-nuclear option [the public revelation of a secret pact of which I was only becoming aware]?' Mark mentioned a November 1988 meeting with Peter Abeles, Bill Kelty and Hawke. It was the first I had heard of the Kirribilli House agreement in which Hawke had undertaken to resign some time after the 1990 election. Should it be revealed, and how would the revelation influence caucus? Would it be the necessary peg for the challenge? The object was to justify a challenge to the incumbent leader.

Parked opposite the Southern Cross Hotel, the car windows steaming up, the four of us talked it through. Tom had told me four months ago he thought it was inevitable something would happen, but had warned that Paul would take over a ruined party if he himself was responsible for forcing Hawke out. Tom now said that he had always argued that Hawke would go quietly but had become convinced he would not. There was no alternative to a challenge. They talked over whether Keating would leave Parliament – would 'walk' – if he were defeated, or if he would stay to fight. They talked about whether a challenge could be postponed until after the Budget. They thought Hawke mean and crazy enough to resign if he were defeated and force a by-election in Wills, and how silly it was that Hawke would not resign now, when there was actually someone willing to take the job for him, and how he would risk even losing his own seat if the defeat was as momentous as it now appeared it might be. A drunk knocked on the window of the car, asking for money. I waved him away.

The decision to challenge made, Keating shone. He laughed, told silly jokes, remembered funny stories about his colleagues, acted out entire Cabinet meetings to his staff. He bought a barbell to improve his physical fitness, spent hours directing the renovation of the Tozer house in Queanbeyan and planned the performance of Mahler's Symphony of a Thousand in the Sydney Show Centre. On 16 May he had flown to an executive meeting of the Australian Council of Trade Unions in Melbourne and told the forty or so union officials that while the government might be unpopular now, the coming fight against the Liberals' John Hewson would be dramatic and exciting because it was a fight from behind, and he and all the union officials around the table had gone into elections in which they were four points in front and knew beforehand they couldn't lose and so had merely coasted through. But the fun in this game was to come from behind. What a pleasure it would be to beat Hewson. His manner in the House changed too. When Wilson Tuckey demanded on a point of order that he table a paper from which he was reading, he not only tabled it, he also autographed it with a pleasant line for Tuckey himself. When interrupted, he would speak over the top of his opponents, saying, 'No, no, no one can stop me having my fun, I insist on having my fun.'

In the last week he worked on his indignation, repeating a litany of outrages. He had lost his health working as Treasurer, he told me; he had come in as a young man and now he was a middle-aged man. It had always been a struggle, and the problem was always that bloke over there, in the office across the little courtyard – the office with the limousine parked outside, with the pennant furled on its bonnet. He should have got it in 1988 when he was ready for it; the problem was that, even if they gave it to him now, he was probably beyond doing anything with it. He had had to fight Hawke all the way. He had tried to dissuade Hawke from having an election at the end of 1984 because he believed you get in there for three years – not long enough anyway – and you do what you can in the time, but Bob insisted. He had had to help Hawke through in 1985 when he came apart after his daughter's drug problem became evident, he had buggered up the State of the Nation speech in 1986 – just buggered it up! Keating had had to force him to have an election in 1987 instead of in 1988, when Hawke thought he could win on the back of the Bicentenary and Keating had told him that Australia would have a party on 26 January and wake up with a hangover and that would be that for the Bicentenary. And then finally at the end of 1988 at Kirribilli Bob had promised to step down after the next election but he hadn't, and it was pretty obvious that he wouldn't, and continuing in office was intolerable.

In recent weeks Keating's thoughts had dwelled on his impending resignation, preparing himself for defeat as much as for victory. 'I don't know whether I can turn it around,' he had said to me in a car parked outside his house after a Lodge meeting a few weeks before. 'I don't know whether I can do it in time. But I'll give it my best shot – that's the best I can say.' The sense that the eight years as Treasurer were drawing to an end seemed to make him more reflective than usual. I would hear the side door of his office open with a characteristic hiss of timber against carpet, and he would drop into a chair in my sunny little office overlooking the courtyard and talk. He was reading William Manchester's life of Churchill and had reached the part where he describes the great man's long years on the back bench, warning the appeasers on the front bench of the coming war. 'He was there so long,' he said, 'that a new generation of Tories came in and they laughed at him when he spoke. Laughed at him.' He talked about the Astors and how they hated Churchill because he liked Jews. 'I don't have any heroes,' he said, 'because when you get to my age you realise they all have flaws, but if anything Churchill was a hero. The way he fought against his party for seven years. When he walked into the chamber in the 1930s young Tory members jeered at him. Chamberlain, the foreign secretary – what's 'is name, Halifax, Dawson at *The Times*, the ambassador in Berlin – forgotten his name – they all admired Hitler, were convinced by him. It was a tragedy. Czechoslovakia had a big army. It could have fought, but it didn't.' He was inspired by the idea of being right in defeat, and fighting courageously against the odds. (Waiting for a car one day, he picked a vivid praying mantis off a wall. The insect rotated its head and threateningly swung its legs as he held it. 'Game little buggers,' he said. 'Not frightened of anything.' He said the same about Graham Richardson and Warren Anderson. It was a quality he admired and which Don Russell would later remark was Keating's own strongest quality in leadership — courage.)

Churchill, of course, was a great orator. Paul thought his own voice was thin and poor. If only he had a voice like Barry Jones, he said. He talked abut children. Children closed the circle, he said. Once you had children you couldn't go on believing you had to knock off the other fella — it wasn't what it was about. On the weekend, he recounted, he taken the children to the art gallery for lunch. Then a friend had played him three or four different versions of a Strauss tone poem. One of them was this much better than the other — illustrating with one hand held high, the other low. One could always learn new things. Right now he was helping the Australian National Gallery to buy a couple of eighteenth-century urns. Superb pieces designed by Petitot in 1750, the apex of the rococo, and modelled by Boudard. Curators would never find things as fine as this; they waited until someone came. They hunted in the zoo. They didn't hunt in the jungle, like Paul. He enjoyed books, and of course writing was fine, but painting and music — well, they are something else. They are up here, he said, his hand moving right up in the air.

On the Monday of the week of the challenge he had gone to Manning Clark's funeral in Canberra. He saw the aisles on both sides crowded with friends and admirers of the historian, and he reflected on the uniqueness of the gathering — this particular group assembled at this particular time would never assemble again, because it was the product of the uniqueness of one man's life, a life sufficiently powerful to have touched many lives, many minds. About to leave, he and Annita waited for ten minutes behind the Prime Minister to speak to one of Manning's sons, Andrew. 'Ten minutes,' he recalled. 'With everyone lining up behind. The vanity of the man!'

He had thought about success, too. Flying to Melbourne in a RAAF plane a few weeks before, he had run through the outline of his first statement as Prime Minister while I scribbled notes on the back of a draft agreement between the government and the ACTU. There were the cities – shopping malls were destroying cities. You could see places like Tuggeranong down below, with a huge shopping mall sitting out there waiting for the houses to come. So cities was one theme. Foreign policy? Indonesia – we should have better relations with Indonesia. Trade; investment. Also Malaysia; China. We should concentrate on the Pacific. Another big thing: superannuation.

Minutes before he went down the corridor to see Hawke on Thursday 30 May he had been in a committee room answering questions from the media about the following day's financial talks between the Commonwealth and state governments, about the latest trade and output figures, and forecasts of economic growth, employment and the balance of payments for the coming year, which he had released earlier that afternoon. It was very nearly the hundredth balance of payments release since he had become Treasurer; the numbers ranged all the way from alarming deterioration to deceptive improvement. It was the thirty-fourth issue of the national accounts, the fullest description of the state of the economy as it was two months before, and in his time as Treasurer those thirty-four growth numbers had ranged all the way from rapid increase to swift contraction and now, as the recession ended, neither one nor the other. The forecast at least showed that the recession would end, though it also showed that unemployment would continue to rise, and that even in a year's time it would still be high enough to make the government's re-election unlikely.

It was an unusual thing to present an economic forecast other than in the August Budget. This was an unusual time, however, and he had decided to release it because, whatever grim news the forecast gave about increasing unemployment, it also showed that growth would resume. This therefore narrowed the room for his successor as Treasurer to claim, as Keating and his staff already knew he would, that through diligence and sound judgment he had managed to drag the economy out of Keating's recession. So the night before, while his ally Graham Richardson was visiting the Prime Minister, Treasury's forecasters had been asked to come back in and prepare their forecasts, while statistician Ian Castles had been called at dinner and asked to give Treasury an early release of the national accounts data so that the forecasts would be ready at 3 p.m., and not as Treasury had offered, at 5 p.m., when it would be too late for the timetable Keating had in mind.

A difficult thing, to walk past the plain-clothes police at the entrance to the Prime Minister's suite, to walk past the attendants and secretaries and through the outer office with its pale wood panelling and colourful canvases, to go into that long and simply furnished room with the desk at the far end, to walk across the carpet and up to the desk and tell the man sitting behind it with a welcoming but querying smile – this man Keating now knew as well as he could be known – that their close relationship was terminated and one or the other would have to leave the government and the society that had been their world for the last eight years. All the more difficult because both knew that behind the language one was accustomed to use and the fighting manner one has to adopt there was intelligence, insight and knowingness on both sides. There was the accumulation of endless hours of intimacy and exchange between the two most successful politicians of their day; there was a bond that had to be broken, which was so strong and instinctive that even the following day, when the deed was long done, the two could walk into the Premiers' Conference apparently acting out a cooperative relationship but in fact inescapably captured by it, by the years of routine and habit overwhelming the hours of declared conflict.

A difficult thing to do, and for a while disconcertingly impossible because, when Keating strode past those police, secretaries and attendants, he found Hawke in the deepest discussion with Queensland Premier Wayne Goss and Queensland union leader Bill Ludwig, a man who would within a few hours threaten to 'visit' any Queensland politician who voted for Keating in the leadership ballot. Hawke could not see Keating, so a few moments after we had left him walking down the corridor he was back with us in his own room, slapping the palm of his hand with a ruler as he paced near the telephone on which Hawke would signal that he was free. Under the wall clock stood Laurie Brereton, a short figure with his chest thrust out, hands clasped behind his back, his eyes switching between the clock and Keating as he flatly said, 'If you haven't told him by five, mate, the wheels fall off this thing.' By five, Brereton insisted, because upstairs in the parliamentary press gallery, television reporter Laurie Oakes was preparing film to illustrate a story about the leadership issue. The story was to be broadcast at 6 p.m. but, because there was still at least a formal possibility that Hawke would concede if he saw a challenge was inevitable, Oakes had not yet been told the heart of the story – that at 6 p.m. on 25 November 1988 at the Prime Minister's Sydney residence Hawke had promised Keating in front of two witnesses that he would retire after the next election. The clock was approaching five when Keating picked up the phone and called Hawke, softly saying, 'Mate' into the phone, through which we could hear Hawke's answering croak of 'Mate'. He was still busy and he would call as soon as he was free. 'If he doesn't call you by five, mate,' Brereton repeated, 'you have to just go round there and see him.'

'I spoke to him about it at the Lodge in February 1988, you know,' said Keating, once again working on his indignation. 'I asked him, "Will you go?" He said he wouldn't, so I said, "OK, well, I hope you change your mind but I will stay anyway." It wasn't till he bagged me after the 1988 Budget. I had been up to my arms in blood in that Budget, risking my health, and the day after the Budget he bags me! I went right round to see him. I said, "You envious little bastard! Is that what I get for thirty straight days in the ERC? Well, I tell you right now, mate, I'm not going to be another Charlie Fitzgibbon. I'm not going to be someone else you can walk over! When I decide to come at you, mate, I'll take your head right off!"'

Brereton, who was ignoring this while watching the clock, interrupted to say, 'You've got to just barge in,' but at that very moment Hawke called to say he was now free.

Keating went in and saw Hawke while we waited in his office. In a few minutes the thick door again hissed against the carpet as he came back in and recounted the short exchange. 'I said Graham told me what you said,' telling Hawke that a commitment to think the issue over while away was not enough. 'I always told you I'd let you know when I was going to come at you,' he had said, 'and now it's on.' Hawke told Keating as he had told Keating's emissary, Richardson, the night before that he would think it over and when he got back from Europe he would be quite happy to talk again. But Keating was now familiar with these tactical postponements. Eight and a half years of waiting was too long. 'I have no animosity,' he told Hawke, 'but I either fade away or have a go at your job.' Hawke said he would be quite happy to talk to Keating if his challenge failed, implying perhaps the offer of a job outside parliament. Hawke said he felt no animosity and some affection. Keating said that was how he felt, too.

As he was recounting this conversation, Hawke called. Each minister has a bank of phones, and one line is to the Prime Minister's desk. Paul picked it up and almost whispered, 'Mate'. We could faintly hear Hawke's nasal bark. Hawke wanted the Kirribilli House deal to remain secret. Paul said he had made no undertaking. He said he would have to tell his colleagues. Then the media might get hold of it. 'We have been the strength of the show, but now the wheels have fallen off,' he told Hawke.

He called the staff in. There were about twelve of us. 'We could win,' he said. 'We might lose. If we lose, then the office ends. If we win, we're right and we move around the corner. If not, we'll talk about it.' On the television monitor Peacock was speaking in the House of Representatives. The Opposition was still unaware of the crisis.

The National 9 News was broadcast at 6.30 p.m. in Canberra but at 6 p.m. in Sydney. Don Russell called his mother in Sydney, who put the phone in front of the TV. The broadcast then came through faintly on the speakerphone in Paul's office. 'How is that, Donald?' she asked. 'Fine, mother,' he replied. Oakes' story revealing the Kirribilli House agreement was late in the show, but it was now broadcast.

The challenge had been declared, but the business of government continued. Cabinet was meeting late on the issue of mining at Coronation Hill. Late in the evening Hawke announced a caucus meeting for Friday morning, a tactic designed to settle the challenge before Keating's support could be increased.

Friday's meeting ended without result when Keating refused to move to declare the leader's position vacant, and Hawke refused to resign as Hayden had during the first Hawke challenge in 1982. A motion to declare the leader's position vacant required a show of hands; a ballot for the position was secret. Keating came back to the office highly excited and immediately began drafting a statement insisting that Hawke resign to allow a direct secret ballot between the two of them. Laurie Brereton was there, and Don, Mark, Stephen and me. Graham Richardson arrived soon after.

'Get it out,' Paul instructed Linda excitedly. 'Get it out.'

He called Hawke. 'I'm still your Treasurer,' he said. 'What do you want to do about the Premiers' meeting [which was scheduled for that morning]?' During the short conversation Hawke offered a 10 a.m. caucus meeting with a secret ballot. Richardson mouthed, 'No! No!' while Paul was on the phone, and swung his arm down and towards the door. 'Our people are leaving,' he said in a heavy whisper, making for the door. With Keating's supporters streaming out of Parliament House, Hawke was forced to call the ballot for Monday.

On Saturday afternoon I found them back in the office, on the phone. Paul was calling ministers and backbenchers. 'You're deputy material,' he told Kerin. 'I don't want to hog it,' he told Beazley. 'I only want it for a term, then someone else can have it.' Jimmy Warner brought in curries. Paul, Stephen and Mark agreed that Paul should accept an invitation to appear with Laurie Oakes on the Sunday program. Dawkins wanted Keating to announce support for an inheritance tax and to speak warmly about the ABC. Unless the Left bloc could be broken up, Paul could not win. An inheritance tax is a bad idea in Australian politics – if it is broad enough it terrifies people. If targeted only on the very rich, it yields nothing. Both Keating and Richardson were opposed and it was dropped. Paul called Laurie

Carmichael and other left-wing union officials to see if they could influence their parliamentary colleagues.

He called Queensland members to try to detach them from the AWU faction that controlled the state party. 'You only need to take on these bullies once,' he said, encouragingly.

Stephen took him through a list of colleagues highlighted in green. He gave the names and numbers to Paul.

Keating was often reluctant to phone.

Stephen said, 'He's a chance, mate.'

Paul said, 'He'll never.'

Stephen softly, firmly repeated: 'He's a chance; just touch base. Just say, "I know you think I'm a shit, but Hawke's fucked," mate.' Stephen smiled brightly.

He told his colleagues the leadership needed quality and weight. It needed someone who would forensically take apart the consumption tax as he had taken apart Howard's package in 1987. All the tight detailed stuff came from his operation. 'When this operations stops, it stops.' Hawke's was a Department of Prime Minister and Cabinet government. Politics is people and the glue is integrity — commitments had to be honoured.

Paul was getting hoarse, edgily hilarious.

'In the nuddy, are you, love?' he asked one colleague's wife who stepped out of the shower to pick up the phone. 'Wish I was there.' He told us apologetically, 'She likes a joke. Jesus, she's a sort.'

'He would root a rat with a harelip,' he said of another colleague.

'Mate, all I can say is I'd bring a bit of enthusiasm back, a bit of *esprit*; you'd feel you belong to something,' he said to yet another colleague.

His New South Wales supporters were strong. 'Don't waste your time with me, mate,' one of them told him. 'You've got my vote; call someone else.'

At night he had a single glass of scotch and water. Mark and Stephen drank ginger ale and diet Cokes. Mark's chest was encased in a plastic shell to support his back, which he had recently injured. When he tapped his chest there was a hollow thump.

'We go back a long way,' Keating told an old opponent. 'I would like your vote – it's a quality vote.'

Caucus members complained of the isolation of backbenchers – their poor morale. 'Yes, mate, it's just the same round here [in the ministerial wing],' Paul assured them, 'and if Bob wins, it will be just the same, we would just come back to our little chicken cages like we do now.'

On Monday morning, 3 June, he was still calling, more to build up his vote than in any hope of winning. 'All I can say,' he told one colleague, 'is that I won't win this morning, but I'd like to feel I have the vote of quality people like you.'

As they left, Brereton predicted '45 – no more.' He added, 'it was a good campaign.' We shook hands with Paul and wished him luck.

A short while later he returned. 'We did OK,' he told the assembled staff. The vote was 66 for Hawke and 44 for Keating. We began packing up. Annita picked up the phone. It was the office of the House of Representatives. 'Does Paul want a room wiz a view?' she asked, smiling, her hand over the phone.

Paul held a press conference at 2.05. He then attended Question Time, sitting for the first time in the backbenches.

The ballot was on Monday. We agreed to move out by Friday to allow the new deputy leader, Brian Howe, to move in.

Paul sorted things to go to his new room, things to go into storage, things to be shredded or thrown out. He watched parliament on the TV. He had flu.

'I realise now I was living a lie,' he told me, 'within an old relationship that had changed. I had to do it.'

Watching Question Time, he evaluated performances. 'They're making a mistake going for Hawke,' he said of the Opposition. They should go for the new Treasurer, John Kerin, he thought. They didn't realise how vulnerable he was. 'They have that fly in the web,' he said of Hawke. 'They should leave it there and come back to it later. A new fly has been caught.'

That evening he said, 'We'll be round there,' pointing across the courtyard. 'They did me a favour. I haven't been able to clear my chest in two years.' If he came back it would be because they asked him back. He would be able to get rid of some of the old guard.

By Friday large brown paper bags marked 'Classified Waste' lined the corridors. We arranged for his files to be moved across to the Australian National University. The shredder whirred. Paul shredded documents himself, page by page, reviewing his years in office. He wore loose navy track pants and a navy pullover. He was pale and unwell. He coughed. 'Look at this,' he said. 'From Richo.' On Cabinet Room notepaper Richardson had advised Paul to 'plait shit'. Paul put aside his lists of who voted for whom – 'I keep them for all contests,' he said. 'You must.' He was trying to discover who ratted. On the carpet, standing against the TV, was an autographed photo of a Cabinet swearing in. The battery clock was moved to his new office, Room 101 on the House of Representatives side. Paul left for Port Douglas.

By the time of his defeat and resignation Keating could look back on eight years of substantial achievement in Treasury. Bill Hayden would write that, in the years when Labor achieved most, Bob Hawke was Prime Minister but Paul Keating was the leader.[6] The contribution of politicians is hard to judge because the business is by nature collective. In a Westminster system Cabinet ministers have responsibility for their own portfolios, and it is extremely difficult for any other Cabinet member, including the Prime Minister, to generate a proposal from a department of which they are not the minister. A Cabinet minister cannot succeed without the Prime Minister's support, but a Prime Minister cannot easily cause a particular proposal to come forth from a ministry he does not directly control. True influence, however, is not just in having a name on a Cabinet submission but in creating a climate within government that is receptive to a particular policy line, and in having the imagination, flair and timing to set the government's agenda successfully.

Keating shared with Hawke the credit for the float of the dollar. He had won approval for the removal of many constraints on

Australian banks and for the granting of banking licences to foreign banks. He had participated half-heartedly in the construction of the Accord with the ACTU in early 1983, but in the six years from 1985 to 1991 he was the principal architect of the Accords from the government side. He had pressed for and succeeded in winning Cabinet agreement to tariff cuts in 1988 and again in 1991, though it was the Industry Minister, John Button, who brought the submissions to Cabinet, and the Prime Minister who announced the changes in 1991. In a sequence of budgets he had reduced the size of government back to its level at the beginning of the 1970s and produced surpluses large enough to make a substantial contribution to national saving. He had pressed for and borne the responsibility within government for a compulsory occupational superannuation scheme, which would add to Australian private saving in the long term.

Some of these changes might have happened anyway – but many would not. The frequent revisions of the Accord in deals that traded income tax cuts for lower wages could perhaps only have been won by a politician with his timing, flair, energy and control. Certainly the extent of the swing in the Budget was mainly his contribution.

As he left office both his greatest success and his greatest failure were yet to become apparent. Within two years, a million people would be unemployed as a result of a recession that was perhaps deeper and longer than it would otherwise have been had interest rates been reduced sooner. But it is a 'perhaps'. As we have seen, there were only ever two or three months or one or two percentage points between the feasible alternatives at the times the decisions were made, both as rates went up and as rates came down. The Budget had swung to a record degree. Because of the Accords, wages were not the problem they had been in earlier downturns in 1974 and in 1981. The single most important influence on the character of the upswing and then the downswing was the suddenness and force of an unforeseen and unforeseeable investment spike long after interest rates had begun to tighten. It might be that the magnitude of the recession could have been mitigated if interest rates had been 2 per cent higher three months earlier or 2 per cent lower three months earlier. Most likely it would have made little difference. Not all economic disasters can be foreseen and averted. The politician who claims credit for the upswing inevitably pays the price for the downswing – but it does not mean that he or she could have produced a better outcome.

Keating's policy approach did, however, make a big difference to the nature of the recovery. The Accords held wages through the boom, and the recession wiped the last traces of serious inflation from the Australian economy. Inflation through the late 1980s continued on the momentum of earlier currency depreciation and higher company profits substituting for lower prices. Once competition became fierce and the currency depreciation effects were washed out, inflation crashed.

For seven months from June to December 1991 Paul was a back-bencher. After firing what he told a post-ballot press conference was his 'one shot', he seemed content to allow circumstances to evolve unaided for a while. He relied more than anything else on the steadiness of the contrast he would make with Hawke. 'A politician and a belief in a certain order – that's reasonably deadly,' he told me. These were not circumstances, however, in which Paul could dramatise a new vision for Australia. He had already spent eight years as Treasurer implementing a vision. 'Well, as to vision,' he told me in mid June, 'I have to say that after eight years, I mean, we've *done* the program, haven't we?' The economic battle, he believed, 'has been won'. He thought then and later that the great changes of the 1980s and early 1990s would bear fruit in a transformed Australian economy, and he wanted to be in office to preside over success. He did not have serious policy differences then with Hawke, but he thought of himself as the motive power of the government. He provided its energy and its intellectual force. Once gone, it would become apparent to even the most stubborn caucus antagonist. To his close supporters he repeated a dictum of Lang: 'You may want to lead the party, but you can't lead the party until it wants you to lead it.' He found life out of Cabinet free, refreshing and pleasant. He invested in a proposed pig farm, and negotiated to bring in a Danish producer as a partner. He thought of himself as a clever businessman and wondered why he hadn't got into it earlier; it would be some time before he discovered the pitfalls. He and Annita visited Sydney frequently and began to rebuild old friendships. After a Queensland holiday he returned lighthearted, brown and relaxed. Wearing sunglasses, he slipped in and out of airports in what he imaged was an impenetrable disguise.

He was prepared to offer the party an alternative to Hawke for another six months, perhaps another year, but he eagerly contemplated life after politics. In his office, Room 101 of the House of Representatives, unanswered invitations piled up on tables, his desk and on to chairs, and marched in piles into the annex where Linda Craige managed his disparate appointments. But while he was content to let events take their course, his supporters were not. Those members of his former staff in a position to do so regarded themselves as still working on his behalf to take the leadership. They included Don Russell, political adviser Stephen Smith, press secretary Mark Ryan, and me. We saw him frequently, and assumed that another ballot would be forced. Some backbenchers and ministers were also determined to force another ballot. Laurie Brereton scolded Paul for his lack of interest in the fight. John Dawkins told him that Cabinet was falling apart and Hawke could not continue. Apart from these loyal partisans, many caucus members, gradually mounting towards a majority, watched despondently as the government continued to fall behind in the polls, and the likelihood of an Opposition victory became more and more certain.

Because he lost once, it would take an exceptional opportunity to force another ballot. He knew that from the time he beat Hawke he would need a year to take control of government and produce an impression of activity, direction and optimism sufficient to beat Liberal leader John Hewson. Once past December 1991, with another election due in early 1993, Hawke would be more and more safe from Keating's challenge. In the meantime Hawke had the advantages of incumbency, including paid staff, and the ability to make and announce policy. Paul could not appear to be disloyal to the party. He could not attack the government or overtly do anything that would deepen the appearance of a split and diminish its slim chances of victory. He proceeded with great caution. His first public speech was an uncontroversial argument that Australian municipalities and states should encourage better building design in cities. Wanting to cement his alliance with Bill Kelty, who pressed Keating's claims within the industrial wing of the Labor Party, in his next speech he publicly advocated a legislative mechanism to enforce higher superannuation contributions by employers, bypassing the decisions of the Industrial Relations Commission. Despite both his own and Treasury's objections, Treasurer John Kerin had no alternative but to implement the legislative solution in his August Budget.

By mid August, ten weeks after Keating's resignation, he was no more advanced in his campaign against Hawke than he had been after his defeat in June. But the mood was beginning to shift his way. Unemployment rose each month, despite Kerin's insistence that the worst was over. 'Bad for Hawke, good for me,' Keating told me grimly as unemployment rose. The normal bounce at the beginning of an economic recovery was postponed from one quarter to the next. From mid May until September rates were held steady, then cut by 1 per cent in early September. There would not be another cut until early November. The August Budget was an unconvincing Treasury document, which promised that monetary policy would remain 'sufficiently firm to restrain inflationary expectations'. It alleged that 'too often, governments have delivered a stimulus to the economy at just the wrong time – just as the economy was on the mend'. The implication of a very long economic trough had not dawned in either the Treasury or the Treasurer's office. Many caucus members wondered whether the economy was on the mend at all.

In private and increasingly in public he defined policy differences. He thought the economy needed more of a kick – lower interest rates and a higher deficit. He opposed the drift to grant the states room to impose income taxes, a concession they had long sought and which he had always steadfastly rejected. In this he threw down the gauntlet to both Hawke and the states in a National Press Club speech in

October. Caught out sliding down a path that caucus would never sanction, Hawke rejected the states' bid for direct income tax revenue, and, in doing, so sank the 'new federalism' negotiations, which had been built on the implicit promise of this Commonwealth concession. It was a speech I drafted for Keating with the greatest relish. The central argument of the proponents of state income taxes was that the states themselves should raise the money that the Commonwealth now raises and pays to them as grants. Keating's argument was that, in a country of Australia's relatively small size, it was important that the Commonwealth have the predominant taxing power and therefore enforce national control over fiscal policy. He also believed that the national government *ought* to have a certain degree of influence over the spending levels and priorities of the states. Far from being opportunistic, Keating's beliefs were deeply held and of long standing, as I confirmed when going through his files in preparing the speech.

By mid November he had made a strong case against Hawke, but he was no nearer to forcing a ballot. Hawke's supporters were not broken by anything Keating did but by the extreme force and initial success of Hewson's Fightback! package, which was released on 21 November. His grand plan for a 15 per cent goods and services tax and a 10 per cent cut in government spending, together with funding cuts in income tax and the elimination of payroll tax and petrol excise, appeared to astonish and stun Hawke's Cabinet. The Prime Minister was unprepared to attack it and responded with windy rhetoric. Treasurer John Kerin postponed his attack until a full Treasury analysis was available, by which time he was no longer Treasurer. Their caucus colleagues realised that the hard, economically fluent, sharply analytic weapons of politics had gone with Keating. All that was left was the intelligent policy response of hard-working officials from Treasury and the Department of Prime Minister and Cabinet, who, for all their loyalty, were sympathetic to Hewson's argument.

From the time Fightback! was released until the collapse of his support forced Hawke to call a caucus ballot in late December, Keating did practically nothing. His silence was more eloquent than his speeches. It did not suit him to destroy the Fightback! package systematically. There was nothing he needed to say as the Prime Minister floundered. Hawke sacked Kerin as Treasurer in early December and appointed Ralph Willis, but the government continued to lose support. Worried by the size of the potential loss, and belatedly recognising that Hewson would transform the country in ways quite opposite to their wishes, the Left reconsidered their support for Hawke. When his own inner circle of Cabinet supporters finally told Hawke they would support him but thought he should resign, the Prime Minister recognised that he must either call a ballot himself or face a united party insisting on one.

PART III

PRIME MINISTER

PRIME MINISTER

The 1980s were a time of rapid economic change, during which Keating held the most influential job in the determination of Australian economic policy. The 1990s were to be quite different. The currency had been floated, the financial system deregulated, spending and taxing both reorganised, tariffs cut. The Accord had virtually eliminated industrial disputes for eight years and prevented inflation from rising during the late 1980s boom; by the early 1990s wage–tax trade-offs helped inflation to plummet. The end of the 1980s and the beginning of the 1990s also clouded Keating's record of economic management, because by 1991 the country had entered a long and difficult recession.

By the early 1990s many of the big reforms in economic policy had been accomplished, and in any case Keating would not be Treasurer. After six months as a backbencher in 1991 he would become Prime Minister. He would find that the job of being Prime Minister was quite different from the job of being Treasurer. Like Hawke, Fraser and Whitlam before him, he discovered that having the top job in Cabinet gave him some influence over all his ministers but control over none. He had less influence on economic policy than he had had as Treasurer.

Prime ministers are there to win elections, to organise the membership of Cabinet, to chair it and control its agenda, to give a general tone and direction to government, to assist or to frustrate ministers in the execution of their responsibilities, to defend the government in Parliament and with the media and the public generally, to represent the Australian Government to foreign leaders, and to deal with state premiers.

Although a Prime Minister needs to be informed of everything in his government and be able to defend everything in his government, his actual policy responsibilities are less than those of a good many of his ministers. Keating found himself with major responsibility for women's issues and for Aborigines, largely because his predecessors had located policy responsibility for these areas in the Department of Prime Minister and Cabinet. He found himself responsible for negotiations individually and as a group with the state premiers, although he was hostile to the kind of negotiation on which Hawke had embarked. Only the Prime Minister could discuss arrangements for Australia's head of state, so any move towards a republic would have to come from him. He could and did occasionally use his prestige and influence to initiate major new policies, the execution of which would then be returned to ministers. His industrial relations reforms were an example.

But he would also discover, as had his predecessors, that the most important field of independent action available to a Prime Minister was his monopoly over relationships with leaders in other countries. Effectively, this gave a Prime Minister who chose to use it a way of making foreign policy on a broader scale and at a higher level than would ever be available to a foreign minister or a trade minister. Keating's achievements in foreign policy would be the most important of his period as Prime Minister.

Ultimately, it would be a difficult and perplexing period for Keating. It was the peak of his political career, and for a time it allowed him to play a prominent and useful part on the world stage. It was the richest experience of his political career, but the circumstances of its end, the completeness of his loss, left him puzzled and bereaved. He had, it was said, won the unwinnable election only to lose the unlosable election. He had, it was said, made great advances in Aboriginal affairs, on the republic and in foreign policy but somehow left Labor's constituency unattended. What follows is the story of Keating's four years as Australia's twenty-fourth Prime Minister.

15

THE UNWINNABLE ELECTION

In Room 101 Keating's closest supporters first heard the result of the leadership ballot at 7.20 p.m. on Thursday 19 December 1991 in a radio news flash. Paul had wanted a big win. 'However close, doesn't matter,' said Annita in her clipped, practical way. Paul had been tense and excited, pacing around the office waiting for colleagues to return calls. 'If they haven't called back,' he remarked, 'it means they won't vote for you.'

Returning to Room 101 after the vote, Paul rejected my draft of an opening statement for his first press conference as Prime Minister designate. It had too much economics and too little feeling. Being Prime Minister was different from being Treasurer. It was not that the policy issues changed so much. A Treasurer, after all, is in one way or another involved in most of the important policy issues of federal government. The important change was that Paul was suddenly the nation's leader. A Prime Minister could not, as a Treasurer could, take refuge in technical competence and mastery of jargon. A Prime Minister was judged on personal qualities of leadership. Keating now had to appear contrite over his errors, trustworthy, hopeful and reliable, as well as clever and familiar with policy issues. His audience now had to be the whole nation rather than the press gallery, the official family, his caucus and Cabinet colleagues. He still needed to make the right decisions and know his brief. But he also needed to look caring and humble. He had the advantage that he really did care and that, if he wasn't as humble as he sometimes thought he was, he was certainly without pretension or vanity, a quality that became stronger as he grew older. His disadvantage was that the public mostly saw him fighting. Many discussions in his office turned on the idea that he would do a lot better in the polls if people knew what a charming, modest man he really was. But this would mean he would consciously have to portray this side of his personality, and he loathed falsity of all kinds. It also evaded the fact that his political success had been attained by fighting and personal domination of his opponents. If the Prime Minister wouldn't fight, who in his Cabinet would do it as well? The combination of Hawke and Keating had in some ways been perfect. As Prime Minister, Keating did not have a Keating.

From Sydney, Peter Barron faxed down an alternative statement. It was designed to assure people that Keating was not a trickster and that he would restart government with a fresh approach. A trademark of a Barron statement was a number — nine principles, for example, or in this case three promises. Another characteristic of a Barron statement was its simplicity. If someone was thought to be a trickster, Barron would have them say they weren't a trickster. Barron didn't mind being corny. That was also something we had to learn.

The result declared, the centre of authority in the Australian Government immediately switched from the Prime Minister's Office to Room 101. After six months of Keating's singled-minded but leisurely assaults on Hawke, a multitude of competing and unrelated demands were imposed suddenly and simultaneously on him. Officials and ministers are adept at winning commitments before the new leader has time to talk to others or sort out his priorities. Foreign Minister Gareth Evans was almost immediately on the phone from Jakarta, seeking authority to tell the Indonesian Foreign Minister, Ali Alatas, that Keating would take over Hawke's coming visit to Indonesia. Paul declined, but told Evans that Indonesia would be his first foreign priority and first overseas visit. Officials in the Department of Prime Minister and Cabinet sought immediate authority for Air New Zealand taking over Compass Airlines, an Australian domestic competitor then going broke.

This would have introduced a new and well-funded competitor to the major airlines. The new Prime Minister refused – he would not be rushed on such a fundamental decision.

Time sped up. Following custom, within minutes of the leadership result the Secretary of the Department of Prime Minister and Cabinet, Mike Codd, turned up in Room 101, where he was obliged to sit uneasily in the outer office until Keating could see him. When they met (alone) the Secretary offered to resign, and Paul did not encourage him to stay. But before this could be sorted out Codd proposed a procedure for Hawke's resignation and Keating's appointment, to be effected by letters to the Governor-General. The Department of Prime Minister and Cabinet is a public service department that services whichever Prime Minister is in power at the time.

The Prime Minister's Office comprised his personal advisors, appointed by him. That evening we former staff members testily debated who would do what in the Prime Minister's Office. 'You fuckers,' Laurie Brereton said, catching us arguing. 'Sorting out the plums for yourselves when you are supposed to be sorting out the government!' At some point I called the US chargé d'affaires, Marilyn Meyers, to say that Keating intended no alteration in our relationship with the United States and in particular wanted President Bush to make his planned visit in two weeks; Miss Meyers seemed puzzled by the call and told me she had never doubted either point.

Room 101 was jammed with well-wishers. In the Prime Minister's Office Hawke's principal private secretary, Dennis Richardson, managed a staccato courtesy while we discussed the transfer arrangements. There was a big noisy party in the Cabinet suite opposite, like the party we had held in the Treasurer's office seven months before. We wanted to begin moving into the Prime Minister's Office on Monday. Hawke wanted to use the Lodge through the New Year and then use Kirribilli House for a further period. The details were soon all agreed.

For the next fifteen months Keating would never lose sight of the goal of winning the next election for the House of Representatives. It dwelled in our thoughts. Keating had not defeated Hawke over policy differences, because they were members of the same faction and rarely disagreed.[1] Hawke was defeated because a majority of caucus members was convinced that the government would lose with Hawke as leader and Keating on the backbench. They thought Keating at least had a chance and if Labor lost it would do so in an exciting rather than a boring way. Keating's supporters had argued that only he could reply to the Liberals' policy document, Fightback!, and only he could change policy sufficiently to pull Australia out of recession. Only he could put the Labor Party back in the game. Only he, they argued, could recover the Labor primary vote that had been lost in successive elections since 1983. Now he had to deliver.

Keating and the staff working with him were not at all confident at that point that he would win the election. We thought it was certainly possible to win in favourable circumstances and it would be fun to try. The task, however, was daunting. Labor had won four consecutive elections, and each time its vote had fallen. In the last election its primary vote was below 40 per cent, and its vote after preferences was less than the vote for the Opposition. Since then there had been, as Paul remarked, a political earthquake in Western Australia where corruption had been found in the Burke Government. There had been an economic earthquake in Victoria, which had experienced the recession more severely than New South Wales or Queensland. Labor governments in both states would not survive the coming elections.

The government's morale was low. Many ministers were tired and about done with their political careers, which had already lasted longer than some of them expected or intended. Keating's victory on 19 December ended a leadership struggle that had split the party over the last six months. Hawke was angry and vengeful. His former supporters in Cabinet would not help Keating if he began to fail. The new Prime Minister had been Treasurer when the recession from which Australia was slowly emerging had begun, and his decisions had contributed to its depth. He was well known, but not well liked. Labor had already been in office continuously for nearly nine years when he took office. If he won an election in a year's time the party would have been in office for thirteen years before the following election.

Across Australia 960 000 people were unemployed. Production had contracted in six of the last eight quarters. In most previous downturns production had slowed then fallen for two or three quarters, before bounding back quite strongly. In the recovery of 1984 and 1985, for example, the economy had grown by more than 5 per cent, rapidly creating jobs. This recovery, however, was different. The economy had bumped along on the bottom for a year and a half. We would later learn that it had turned decisively in the December quarter of 1990, the three months in which Hawke's defences had collapsed, but the growth was less than half the rate of past recoveries. It grew by under 1 per cent then, under 1 per cent in the March quarter, by less than 0.2 per cent in June quarter, and by a little over 0.5 per cent in the three months to September before registering just over 1 per cent – still under the usual number in a recovery – in the December quarter.

Month by month Keating and his advisers would wait for signs of the usual burst of activity, the usual happy swing. Hopeful at first that the One Nation statement would bring forward the recovery, our optimism waned month by month. Because growth was so slow, unemployment crept up instead of going down. Going into the election in March 1993 unemployment would be substantially higher than it had been in February 1992. After a year of recovery production would be only a little over 3 per cent higher than it had been when he took office.

It was the same in North America and the United Kingdom, and would later be the same in Japan. From the *International Herald Tribune* I clipped a McNelly cartoon showing George Bush at the controls of a speedboat, looking ahead with boyish excitement. His economic advisers sat behind him shouting, 'Va-Room! Va-Room!' while trying to fix the outboard motor. We had the photocopy taped up in the Prime Minister's Office.

On the other side of Parliament the Opposition now had very

little doubt it would win, whenever the election was called. Many of them thought Hawke was a stronger opponent than Keating and welcomed the leadership change. The Fightback! package still looked good and had comfortably withstood several months' attack by the government. Despite what was said later and widely accepted, Hewson was a very formidable opponent and perceived as such both by the commentators who would later revile him and by the new Prime Minister. He had successfully portrayed himself as an economic reformer by proposing to substitute a goods and services tax for part of income tax, to establish the Reserve Bank as an independent body focusing on inflation, and to encourage individual contracts in employment. As John Howard would later discover, without the GST and individual contracts it was difficult to portray a substantial difference from the economic reform policies of the Labor Government.

It was daunting, but Keating was excited by the battle. For months, he had been discussing what he should do when he took office. Something should be done to boost demand, and he had been saying for some time that Hawke's November statement was nowhere near sufficient. Whatever was done, Melbourne had to be a big part of it because it had been most devastated by recession, and Labor's chances of re-election depended on giving Victorians a sense that things were getting better. And whatever was done had to meet or neutralise John Hewson's promise of big cuts in personal income taxes. Bill Kelty and Victorian Premier Joan Kirner had persuaded Keating to think about Melbourne's interstate rail lines and its port transport links. He was also thinking about an investment allowance for business. But whether there should be one statement or several statements, how much should be spent and how it should be packaged were all undecided.

In Room 101 on Thursday and Friday we had our first serious discussions about strategy for the coming months. I had proposed a major reorganisation of ministries and perhaps departments and a sequence of major statements throughout the year. Keating immediately rejected a major ministerial reshuffle and a departmental reorganisation on the ground that we would lose too much time. John Dawkins proposed that we make a single major statement as soon as possible, and we should have no hesitation in spending some money. 'We have built up a structural surplus we can use,' he said. He proposed that we cut indirect taxes like the wholesale sales tax because that would lower the apparent rate of price increase and eliminate the need for a wage–tax trade-off. He favoured a low exchange rate, targeted with a variable interest withholding tax. Keating was not enthusiastic about the content of Dawkins' proposed statement – but he now liked the idea of one big early statement rather than a series of statements through the year.

We knew broadly that we had to reply to Fightback! with some sort of credible plan for the coming decade – a set of objectives that kept the country moving forward and were also fair and compassionate. We had to accelerate recovery from recession, so jobs would be created sooner. We had to alter Keating's image in the electorate to something more benign. We must, as we said to each other, 'get back in the game'.

Keating recognised that Hewson's income tax cuts were powerful. In several of the last campaigns the Opposition had promised big tax cuts, but this time they had put more effort into showing how they would be funded. In analysing the Hewson tax package some months before, I had been struck by the simplicity and political vulnerability of its arithmetic. Of the revenue raised by his 15 per cent sales tax, around half merely replaced the revenue lost by abolishing the existing wholesale sales tax. All of the remainder went to replace revenue lost through abolishing state payroll taxes, abolishing petrol tax, and compensating some income groups that were made worse off by the new tax. Fightback!'s proposed income tax cuts were actually funded out of a 10 per cent government spending cut and expected increases in income tax revenue itself as the existing tax scales were applied to higher incomes over the next three years. In the argot, they were partly 'funded by drag'. This was a clever idea, one that built on the arithmetic of John Howard's 1987 tax and spending package. It copied Keating's tactic through the 1980s of handing back 'fiscal drag' as tax cuts, and improved upon it by bundling into one package the tax cuts over three years.

Discussing it in Room 101 a day or so after the package had been announced towards the end of November, it was clear that we could do the same. By throwing a tax cut plan forward three years we could capture the same revenue and promise cuts of similar magnitude. We would not copy Hewson's spending cuts so we would be short of his total. On the other hand, we did not need to bring down the top marginal rate as much as he had, because not so many of our voters were affected by it. We could, as Keating immediately pointed out, 'throw it all at the thirty cent rate' at which a skilled tradesman's overtime income was taxed. Not only could we duplicate the most important of the cuts, we would also put them into an Accord package and present them as a trade-off for moderation in wage claims. This was something Hewson could not match and which Keating had already successfully done for eight years.

If we could match the key tax rate for middle-income earners, bring forward the recovery and at the same time offer a competing vision for the coming decade, Keating would have a strong base from which to turn and attack Fightback! The only thing left in the Opposition package, as he pointed out, would be 'the nasties' – the 15 per cent goods and services tax and a 10 per cent cut in government spending. Keating decided that until his own statement was presented he would have little to say about that of his opponent.

The strategy for achieving the goals was clear enough at that point for me to be able to brief officials from Treasury and the Department of Prime Minister and Cabinet at a meeting on Saturday 21 December, less than forty-eight hours after Keating's victory. We were to have a big statement, quite early. We believed a recovery was under way, but it was too slow to prevent unemployment rising. The key objective, then, was not to create a recovery by a huge spending boost and still less to increase public spending permanently by a new set of long-term programs but to bring the recovery forward. This meant that new spending would be reasonably moderate and would be selected so that it automatically fell away as the recovery matured.

If we were to match the tax cuts then the time frame embraced by the statement would have to be at least three years. Run over four years, the economic projections underlying it would embody the usual path of recovery as the economy grows and unemployment falls. Projections of this kind had been used at the summit in 1983.

The Treasury officials at the Saturday meeting immediately objected that such projections were worthless because the economy could not be predicted so far ahead. This was certainly true, but beside the point; projections of this kind were useful as guides that would be continuously updated and changed as new data became available. Forward estimates of government spending and of revenues were made over a three-year time frame, and these estimates depended on estimates for the economy as a whole.[2] The Treasury officials grumbled, but the most telling argument in favour of a long projection period was produced by the official who had arranged the meeting, Rod Sims. An astute senior official running the economic division in the Department of Prime Minister and Cabinet, who had himself been an economic adviser to Hawke, Sims pointed out that we would need a three- or four-year projection scenario 'just to be able to put an 8 in front of unemployment' (that is, get it down to eight point something). The conversation in Sims' office revealed that Treasury and PM&C officials had also come to the conclusion that the economy needed more of a kick than it had been given in the November 1991 statement. Both Treasury Secretary Tony Cole and his deputy John Fraser said they had revised earlier views about the pace of recovery and now were not at all opposed to spending some money and increasing the likely deficit. The recovery would clearly be slow and protracted. They told me a 1 per cent interest rate cut had already been agreed and would be approved when the Reserve Bank board next met; it would be announced at the end of January. They initiated work on the proposed statement that day, with the first material arriving in tabbed folders in our office two days later. The speed of analysis hinted, however, that the material had already been around one or twice in our absence.

On Sunday the new Prime Minister pondered whom to appoint to his ministry. Choosing a ministry is always complicated. There had been seventeen Cabinet places in Hawke's last ministry. Each place varied in prestige or interest or suitability for members of the ministry. In the Labor Party the members of the ministry are chosen by caucus. The Prime Minister gives the jobs and decides whether the jobs are in the Cabinet or outside it. He can also directly appoint parliamentary secretaries, who are not paid extra and have only one additional staff member, but who may use the position to increase their influence within caucus and gain ministerial experience. Though he did not use it on this occasion, the Prime Minister may also define the boundaries between ministers' responsibilities, and he may write letters of appointment, which set out priorities and objectives. (Ministers typically ignore these letters, unless the matters mentioned in them offer them a tactical advantage on an issue.)

Keating had decided to minimise the rewards to his supporters and the penalties on Hawke's supporters, to heal the wounds within the party. Even with all these discretions removed, however, the selection remained difficult. Talents, ambitions and ministerial slots had to be matched.

Both Dawkins and Willis wanted Treasury. Alan Griffiths wanted to be in Cabinet, and there was a case for promoting a younger and energetic Victorian directly into Cabinet – particularly a Victorian who had strongly supported Keating against Hawke. But if Alan Griffiths was to be promoted to Cabinet, then it would only be fair also to promote another younger Keating supporter who was already a minister, Bob Collins. Certainly Bob Collins was of this view. Ideally some of the older ministers like John Button would take this opportunity to stand aside for their younger colleagues. Keating sounded him out, but Button insisted that it would be in the government's best interests for him to remain. It was not possible for all Cabinet ministers to remain and at the same time find places for two more. Keating decided to increase Cabinet by one position to eighteen and to create another by moving Trade Minister John Kerin from Cabinet to the outer ministry.

The most important decision he had to make was the selection of his Treasurer. He thought about doing the job himself as state premiers often had, but quickly conceded it was not possible. It was a difficult, perplexing choice, which Keating knew could make or break his government. Ralph Willis had taken over as Treasurer after John Kerin was sacked. He was intelligent and critical, familiar with the main elements of the job, and well able to explain and defend economic policy decisions publicly. Hayden had replaced him as Shadow Treasurer with Keating just before Hawke took over the leadership in 1983, and Hawke had wanted to bring him back as Treasurer after the victory. Willis had been Keating's most formidable critic in the first six months as the new Treasurer had successfully urged a smaller deficit. Thereafter, however, Willis had more often than not supported Keating. Keating knew the safe and easy option was to keep Willis in the Treasurer's job. He would not be a Kerin and weaken his Prime Minister, but if there needed to be a big change from a current Treasury position, Willis would probably resist it and might not defend it publicly with real conviction. Within the government he was most effective as a sceptic. He was often right, but in eight years he had hardly ever proposed and successfully carried out something new.

John Dawkins, by contrast, had adopted, proposed and carried through many new policies, from public service reform when he was Finance Minister to the formation of the Cairns Group when he was Trade Minister and the Higher Education Contribution Scheme and universities reorganisation when he was Education and Employment Minister. His record in government was second only to Keating's for energy, flair and weight. He had supported Keating's policies more consistently and effectively than any minister other than Hawke. He had also supported Keating's ambitions, to the extent of seeing Hawke in 1988 and asking him to resign. He had been Keating's chief Cabinet supporter in the leadership challenge (at one point proposing that he stand with Keating as deputy, a suggestion Keating delicately rebuffed), and a formidable opponent of Hawke and his Cabinet supporters after Keating went to the backbench. Dawkins wanted to be Treasurer, and rightly believed he had the new Prime Minister's promise.

But Dawkins was not a safe choice. He could adopt both good new ideas and bad new ideas and pursue them with equal vigour.

Surprisingly for a successful career politician, he had a primitive idea of politics and was often attracted by the most obvious kinds of tricks and by advisers and associates of only very moderate ability. He liked gimmicks, some of which were complicated but clever and some of which were merely complicated. 'He likes the glitter, the illusion,' Keating would say, though he also thought he was a very good minister. He liked ideas with leverage – an interest withholding tax that would supposedly solve the current account deficit, a training levy that would supposedly increase industry training – and he placed a high value on what he imagined would be the public reception of an idea. Hampered by an uneasy, suspicious manner, which chilled even his own good cheer and candour, and which perhaps reflected more the circumstances of political life than his intrinsic personality, he was quite unpopular with his caucus colleagues, departmental officials and many of his own staff. He expressed visible contempt for his opponents in argument, and he was gracelessly manipulative in his dealings with people. He liked, admired and tried to imitate Keating's ability to direct the theatre of public debate, but he could not quite get the hang of it. Like Keating, he would go for his opponents' throats, but Keating had a kind of charm, a kind of vulnerability despite his ferocity, which smoothed ruffled feathers. When Dawkins was ferocious he was sometimes just unpleasant.

As far as Keating was concerned, however, his great distinction as a minister was that he had ideas (surprisingly few ministers did) and could get them implemented. It could only have been him, for example, who would take the trouble to switch the timetable so that the Budget was delivered before the financial year had begun rather than after. Only Dawkins would have been so insensitive to the inconvenience to his officials and colleagues. Later Dawkins would do a good deal to move the Budget back towards surplus as unemployment fell.

Dawkins expected to be Treasurer, but Keating was perplexed. He asked his advisers their opinions, and asked it again. Don Russell said Dawkins had imagination and flair and, unlike Willis, would take on Treasury. But he was a risky choice. Keating said he would give Dawkins the job, and then said he wouldn't. Keating understood power, however, and while he knew Willis was the safe and popular choice, it was Dawkins who would quite happily force Treasury to do what he wanted rather than what Treasury wanted. Insisting on his promise, Dawkins told Keating that the Treasurer's job was the only one in which he was interested. Still concerned by any leanings Dawkins might have towards targeting industries for assistance or changing tariff levels, Keating told us he would tell Dawkins he could have the job, but he, Keating, did not believe in that stuff. Dawkins told Keating the following week he had no leadership ambitions, and said he would not remain in politics after Keating left.

'Kerin was Hawke's undoing,' Don Russell remarked the evening of his appointment. 'Will Dawkins be ours?'

Keating had been elected on Thursday 19 December. He then had only five days of work before the country closed down for Christmas. Under a program already agreed, President Bush would be arriving in Sydney on New Year's Eve and going through to Canberra for meetings. This schedule gave the Prime Minister just enough time to get planning going for the economic statement, choose a ministry and move into his new office before turning to his own preparation for the Bush visit. Paul had never had a foreign affairs adviser and now needed one quite quickly. After discussing some other names, which for one reason or another didn't quite work, he decided to try Dr Ashton Calvert, an official of the Department of Foreign Affairs and Trade whom I knew to be first-rate and whom Paul had met during a visit to Japan. Don Russell called him on the Sunday night after the election. Calvert had just returned from a gruelling visit to Cambodia with Gareth Evans. He was asked to come to the Prime Minister's Office first thing in the morning.

Calvert is a short, slight man with spectacles and what at first seems a shy and diffident manner. 'He'll do to get us through the Bush visit,' Stephen Smith told me that first day, 'but we have to find someone else when it's over.' Foreign Minister Gareth Evans was indignant. 'You could have done a lot better,' he said. The new adviser, however, had aspects to his personality not at first apparent. He was one of the most intelligent officers in his department, and his training and experience in foreign affairs were deep. He had a devastatingly sharp sense of humour, but also a certain gentleness and courtesy with people who meant no harm. Unlike many of his departmental colleagues, he was not at all overawed by the fluency or intelligence of the Foreign Minister, Gareth Evans, so that he could and did set about building a separate platform for the Prime Minister in foreign policy. Indeed, Evans' unfavourable response to the appointment perhaps reflected his foreboding. Calvert also understood immediately the political task: to invest the former Treasurer with statesmanlike qualities within six months or so. Within a short while Calvert became one of the most effective members of Keating's inner circle of advisers – in before most of us arrived in the morning, and still there at night, reading the cables, as we left for home.

Preparing for the Bush visit, Keating read and then discarded the customary brief prepared by officials. It was a conventional brief, which assumed Keating would wish to say something about each issue on which Australia and the United States interacted, from nuclear non-proliferation and chemical weapons control to peace moves in the Middle East. Keating preferred to talk about one or two big issues, where leaders could make a real difference. Visits of US presidents to Australia were rare; he did not want Bush to come and go with a game of golf and an exchange of platitudes. Working up his themes, he talked to Australian officials and academics in a series of meetings between Christmas and the New Year. On the 28th, for example, he spoke to Professors Stuart Harris and Ross Garnaut of the Australian National University, to Ken Haydon of the Office of National Assessments, and Peter Field of the Department of Foreign Affairs and Trade. He formed and then rehearsed his message. The US withdrawal from Subic Bay had left a question mark over its strategic engagement in the region. The US needed to look westward to the rapidly growing economies of East Asia. Trade was the key to prosperity. Unlike the US and Europe, which had had the Marshall Plan, NATO and the Common Market, there was no strong institutional structure linking North America and the East Asian economies, despite their increasing dependence upon each other. The Asia–Pacific Economic Cooperation process could and should be a much more important vehicle for cooperation on trade and other economic issues, and the US should help give it more weight and prominence. The way to do this was to have a meeting of APEC leaders. If the Uruguay Round of world trade negotiations succeeded, it would be a bigger, better place for everyone. If they failed, there was a danger of contending trade blocs destroying the global trading system. Either way, APEC was a valuable addition to regional institutions.[3]

Beginning formal discussions with the President at Kirribilli House on the first day of the New Year, Keating told Bush that the public had come to see the government's leadership as tired. It would not have been able to win another election with Hawke, who had not been able to respond to the young Opposition Leader's economic package. He had worked with Hawke on issues involving the United States, and supported Australia's commitment of ships during the Gulf War. But he was worried, he said, about a tripolar trading world being created around the United States, Japan and Europe. US Secretary of State James Baker had spoken of US policy towards the Pacific as a set of bilateral alliances, which terminated in the US, like spokes in a wheel. Keating believed the fabric between the spokes should be strengthened by stronger economic relations between Asia–Pacific countries and between them and the United States. There was a need to develop stronger economic institutions in the Asia–Pacific region. The natural forum was APEC. It was now only a ministerial talk shop, but it had great potential. To strengthen APEC it was worth considering holding occasional meetings at the heads-of-government level. It would be a way for the US President to demonstrate engagement in a regional economic process and give authority to APEC.

He told Bush that it was dangerous for the US to base its relationships in the Pacific on bilateral defence arrangements rather than regional economic leadership. If the US was not fully engaged in

APEC, its model of a market economy and its version of liberal democracy would not be reflected in APEC and the values of Japan's command, managed economy would be. Australia had a very productive relationship with Japan, but it did not want to end up with divided loyalties where its strategic ties were primarily with the United States and its economic ties with Japan. From Australia's point of view it would be much better if Japan and the United States continued to work closely together in a strong economic arrangement.

Talking about the Uruguay Round, both men criticised France, which was opposing agreement to reduce agriculture subsidies. The important thing for French leaders, said Keating, was 'to be able to see flocks of ducks and geese wandering around French villages when they drove through on their holidays.' The United States had to 'crush the bastards'.

Keating seemed little changed by the new job. He did not assume grand ways or even betray, by easy assurance or a lofty manner, any sign that the office fulfilled him. He had, after all, been in high office for nine years. There were, however, differences. He was now always followed by two Federal Police officers. He lived in the Lodge, which made things easier for his family but was in some ways a nuisance. He missed Annita's cooking. Neither he nor Annita enjoyed managing the staff of cooks, cleaners, handymen and so forth, which came with the Lodge and Kirribilli House; they found their domestic lives more complicated rather than less.

His own office, too, had changed. The Treasurer's office was quite big, but the Prime Minister's Office was much bigger. His own room was quite grand, and he also had access to a private sitting room and a small private dining room, all supervised by Guy Nelligan, formally designated the 'Personal Assistant to the Prime Minister' and universally known, to his annoyance, as the Butler. He now had a foreign affairs adviser, a social policy adviser, an environment and Aboriginal affairs adviser, a speechwriter and a substantial press office, as well as the economic advisers and the principal adviser he had had while holding the Treasury portfolio. He would later have an arts adviser and additional speechwriters.

In the old office there were certainly frictions, but everyone at least knew broadly what the others were doing. The whole office celebrated each member's birthday, arrivals and departures. In the big office we tried to keep it up, but there were so many birthdays that it became impossible. Most advisers had less personal contact with Paul than in the old office. For those who knew him this was less of a problem, because they could confidently predict what he would and would not want. For newer advisers, however, it was a real difficulty.

Paul celebrated his 48th birthday with a dinner on Saturday 18 January for his staff at the Lodge, an unexpectedly small two-storey house in vast walled grounds.

At dinner he talked about the architecture of Potsdam, renovating his Elizabeth Bay house, and a Roosevelt biography. He reminisced about the battle against Hawke. 'We had to knock him senseless without leaving any bruises,' he said, recalling the federalism speech. Proposing a birthday toast, Don Russell said, 'You get the staff you deserve,' and that the Prime Minister's great characteristic was his courage. Replying, Paul told us, 'If it was not for all of you, I would have given away' the leadership contest. 'I can make no bigger comment than that.'

Just as he had been when he became Treasurer in 1983, Paul was at first a little nervous, a little diffident about being Prime Minister. As Treasurer he had become familiar with most of the major domestic issues of government. He had watched Hawke working for eight years. He was accustomed to leadership. But he was not so fluent with foreign affairs issues; he was not so comfortable talking about national symbolic issues like the republic. The Prime Minister's portfolio for one reason or another now included Aboriginal issues and women's issues, and it had a big interest in the environment. It took Paul some time to work these issues into his story.

In his well-informed account of Malcolm Fraser as Prime Minister,[4] Patrick Weller describes his subject's busy relationship with his Department of Prime Minister and Cabinet. After arriving in the morning Fraser would pose written queries to the department, seeking written briefs on issues that had arisen in the newspapers or in conversation. A dozen officers of the department could and did brief the Prime Minister directly. He pondered all decisions, arguing them through, sometimes at excruciating length, with his staff and officials. He worked relentlessly and crowded his days with meetings and calls.

As Prime Minister Paul could not have been more different. He had never been a punctual, meticulous person. Some of the requirements of his new job annoyed him. It was important that he be on time for Cabinet, for example, because he chaired it and it couldn't begin without him. But he was often late, and often changed the meeting times. In his mind, he was putting substance before procedure. In the minds of his ministers he was simply disorganised.

A Prime Minister ought to have an open door to his ministers. Some of the ministers, however, were wearisome. Some of them took a long while to learn that Keating wanted to be involved only in circumstances that were truly important or where the minister could not resolve it himself. He loathed it when ministers came around to tell him something merely to have an audience and receive his blessing. He loathed it when ministers would come back again and again seeking a decision they had at first been denied. Sometimes Keating hid in his dressing room and told the staff to say he was out. Often he would defer the appointment day after day. Ministers blamed the staff, particularly Peter Robinson, who guarded the door. A pleasant, intelligent Treasury official, Robinson grew a hard shell. Not even the tirades of Foreign Minister Gareth Evans, who sometimes suspected that Keating was hiding from him in his dressing room, would really trouble Robinson.

Keating guarded his energy by focusing on substance and neglecting procedure. He often ignored aspects of the job unrelated to winning the forthcoming election or coping with the recession. Hawke's days had been filled with an orderly procession of appointments. Keating refused. He would not normally see delegations, ambassadors, public servants, backbenchers, members of the outer ministry, reporters, trade union officials or business people unless there was a particular and pressing piece of business to justify the appointment. Accustomed to visiting Hawke with little notice, for example, the US Ambassador called for an appointment with Keating. Learning that the reason for the visit was of little consequence, Ashton Calvert said he would be happy to see him himself, but the Prime Minister was too busy. When Keating did see people, however, he was frequently generous with his time and dazzling with the force of his charm and interest.

In his approach to government he was not, in substance, unlike Hawke. Except on the issues of pay television and aviation policy, where he was a relentless busybody, he did not often second-guess his ministers. The One Nation statement embraced many areas of government, but after it was delivered responsibility went back to ministers and their departments. As a Cabinet chairman he elicited all views and as Prime Minister rarely attacked other ministers during Cabinet meetings in the way he had as Treasurer. His Department of Prime Minister and Cabinet had a central role in the sequence of economic policy statements in 1992, beginning with One Nation, which increased its policy influence. But Keating did not encourage the department to dictate to other departments, and very few policy initiatives from his department could get far without the cooperation of his personal office advisers.

The most important issues in his first year in office certainly remained economic, but even here he accepted that he could no longer direct events. One Nation apart, he had had more influence over economic policy as Treasurer than he did as Prime Minister. John Dawkins made a point of visiting Keating frequently, sometimes without staff. Keating would often see him alone, or with Don Russell only. The two economic advisers, Ric Simes and myself, were sometimes out of the game. Sometimes the whole office was out of the game. In the second half of the year, for example, the Reserve Bank board gave Fraser authority to raise interest rates if necessary, to counter depreciation of the dollar. Don, Ric and I did not know of this decision until much later, though it would have been very damaging to our election plans if Fraser had used the authority. Keating might well have known about it, but if he did he did not tell us. As an adviser it was possible to propose and press a great deal of policy change. If you knew Keating's general orientation and had a good feel for what would work and would be well received, he would encourage you to take responsibility. But it was very much more difficult to keep informed about things that Keating himself was up to. Often he would tell his advisers only what and when he needed them to know. Sometimes he would forget to tell them at all. Don Russell's freedom of action relied on his having superior information, so he would not keep the advisers informed either.

We advisers jostled among ourselves over who was to do what, but as a group we had more responsibility than I had expected. Certainly we were with a new Prime Minister in the run-up to an election, when political considerations are even more salient than usual and advisers who know their minister's way of thinking are more influential. But it was also true that the battle between advisers and the bureaucracy for day-to-day pre-eminence in policy issues had been fought and won long before Keating became Prime Minister. The influence of office advisers was contested in the Whitlam Government and still resisted in the Fraser Government. By the time Hawke came to office, however, the rising generation of public servants was becoming accustomed to dealing with office advisers and viewed a spell as an office adviser as an important part of their careers. Government had become so complex, ministers so familiar with their portfolios, that it would have been impossible as well as undesirable to recreate the mandarinate of the 1960s and early 1970s. As Treasurer Paul had worked Treasury very hard but taken from it what he wanted and rejected what he and his advisers found useless. As

Prime Minister he probably allowed more policy latitude to his advisers than before, partly because as a coordinating agency the Department of Prime Minister and Cabinet had less advantage in information and expertise over advisers. But the advisers drew on the department for policy work, and rarely intruded into the department's job of coordinating views, managing work committees and executing and overseeing decisions.

Under Hawke the department had built up considerable resources and expertise in preparing possible answers to questions in Parliament. Officers of the department spoke with admiration of Hawke's outstanding peripheral vision, which enabled him to seem fluent, wise and informed on all aspects of government while actually reading out verbatim an answer prepared by the department. Question Time had changed, however, with the Opposition Leader very rarely asking questions requiring knowledge the Prime Minister would not normally possess. The questions were designed to embarrass Keating on issues like unemployment and growth. Whether or not they embarrassed him, however, they would not find him ignorant of the facts. This tendentious style of Question Time suited the office advisers more than the department. Because it addressed questions the Opposition did not ask, the department's brief was not often used.

The Prime Minister himself would rarely read PM&C material, except rapid reviews of a Cabinet submission, briefing books for foreign visits, briefings for Council of Australian Governments (COAG) meetings and so forth. Much less than a tenth of the material ostensibly generated by the department for the Prime Minister was read by the Prime Minister. He saved himself a lot of time and lost very little by this selectivity.

Hawke had left behind an agenda of issues that Keating largely ignored. Large parts of this agenda originated with department officials rather than Cabinet. For example, the Department of Prime Minister and Cabinet in Hawke's time had coordinated a multivolumed report on ecologically sustainable development and planned to devote a big proportion of senior officers' time to its implementation during 1992. For Keating and his advisers, the economy was a far more urgent priority. Hawke had also formalised a program of discussions between the Commonwealth and state governments, in which the states sought less Commonwealth policy control over Commonwealth grants to the states, and more independence in raising and spending revenue. Keating profoundly disagreed with the objectives of this program of discussions, and over time modified them to focus on areas of cooperation in which common problems could be addressed and solved. He was willing to form the COAG, for example, to develop within it agreements on national electricity, gas, rail and water cooperation. He was willing to create a new body, the Australian National Training Authority, to administer Commonwealth (and supposedly state) funding of technical education. He would within a few years use the COAG to advance discussions on the High Court's Mabo judgment and to implement the Hilmer Report recommending competition rules for the professions and state instrumentalities. But he would not allow negotiation of changing the distribution of tax powers, because he strongly believed that the Commonwealth's control over the bulk of revenue was good for the Commonwealth and good for Australia. Treasury, however, continued to press for greater financial independence for the states. Its essential motive was to wind down Commonwealth responsibility for spending in education, health and social welfare.

Keating returned to the economic statement on New Year's Day, as Bush flew on to Japan. The key decisions were how much to spend overall in bringing forward the recovery and what to include. Consultations with business groups were proposed as a means of soliciting suggestions. Their more useful outcome was a business consensus that spending of several billion dollars was required. One issue not yet decided was the form of an Accord renewal. We soon dropped any idea of buying off a particular amount of wage increase, but the Prime Minister was now completely committed to income tax cuts. They were so central to the package that the number of people who knew about them was always very small, and we managed to keep them from the press until the statement was announced.

Meeting his new Cabinet on 7 January, Keating proposed a three-
to five-year 'vision and focus' for the statement, a delivery date of
around 25 February, and a process in which a 'troika' of himself,
Dawkins and Willis and their departments would coordinate the
statement for the whole government.

On Friday 7 February, less than three weeks before the statement
was to be delivered, Keating met with three ACTU leaders at the
Lodge. The meeting was held there rather than his Parliament House
office because the presence of the three officials would probably
become known if they turned up at the ministerial entrance to Parliament House. Keating did not want to encourage enquiry about the
nature of the deal with the ACTU, and the ACTU leaders themselves did not wish the fact of the meeting to be known to their
colleagues.

The ACTU people were secretary Bill Kelty, assistant secretary
Iain Ross, and an ACTU vice-president, metals union leader George
Campbell. They had not invited ACTU president Martin Ferguson,
who was Kelty's rival within the organisation. Kelty made an ally of
George Campbell, who was a leader of the Left and someone who
could prevent Ferguson from rallying the Left against him. Part of
the Prime Minister's job was to help Kelty by making sure that Campbell was on side.

They arrived a little before 10 a.m. and were brought into the
sitting room, which opened on to the paved terrace and the outsized
pergola. For Kelty the sitting room was familiar. Hawke had also held
meetings here, swaying slightly in a chair designed for back muscle
exercise, a bank of telephones (now removed) on a small table at his
elbow. He was also familiar with the collection of Australiana —
the emu eggs on the side table, the clock supported by metal kangaroos, the table lamps with fringed shades — which were collected
and supplied by a diligent committee of prominent citizens.

Keating came into the room as the kangaroo clock struck ten.
It was now four weeks since he had started serious work on the statement, and there were only a couple of weeks left before it would have
to be finalised and printed. There was much to do, but the nature of

the arrangement with the ACTU was vital. It would underwrite a low-inflation recovery, but the philosophical switch to enterprise bargaining and the requirement for a three-year framework were inconsistent with the kind of wage–tax trade-off that had been the basis of recent Accords. We needed a more general understanding, and it was intended to reach one at this meeting.

To the new Prime Minister these were all old friends and acquaintances. He had worked with Kelty now for nearly a decade. Iain Ross had actually been on his staff for four months, to get a feel for how the government worked. He had clashed with George Campbell on many occasions, notably at the 1986 Labor Party conference when the Treasurer had accused him of forcing thousands of metal workers into unemployment with the wage increases of the early 1980s.

Keating sat down in an armchair and immediately started talking about a recording of his friend, the pianist, Geoffrey Tozer, playing music by the Russian romantic composer, Nikolai Medtner. It was a wonderful disc, he said, commending it to Iain Ross, who was introducing himself to classical music via a sequence of CDs suggested by Keating and Laurie Carmichael.

'All the things I told you about at Bill Bradshaw's antiques shop, George, we'll do,' Keating told Campbell, of the forthcoming statement. The railways, the investment incentives, making Melbourne a transport hub – Keating had taken up all these things with an eye both to stimulating recovery with infrastructure spending and to winning support with the Left in the union movement to mitigate the hostility of the Left within the Labor caucus.

'Interest rate cuts alone won't be enough to get the place going,' he said. 'We need the infrastructure spending. Hewson is vulnerable on his goods and services tax, so long as he can be met on income tax cuts.' But he needed some sort of Accord renewal to go with it.

Kelty said the key thing was not now an agreement on a wage number but an agreement on an inflation objective with which wage increases would be kept consistent. The ACTU would defer a wage increase application until after July and would say that it was putting jobs first. Any wage claims would be consistent with the target of an inflation rate no higher than that of our trading partners. The aim would be to meet the target inflation rate, which really meant inflation of less than 4 per cent per annum. If the Industrial Relations Commission rejected or cut the ACTU wage claim, however, the ACTU would expect the government to top up low-paid workers through Family Assistance Supplement payments.

Kelly then discussed what we generally referred to as the choreography – the form in which the public display of reaching agreement would be presented. There would be an ACTU Wages Committee meeting, probably on 17 February. Rather than seeking their agreement at that forum Keating should say that he understood that the ACTU wanted jobs first, that it wanted infrastructure spending, enterprise bargaining and a national wage case. But he knew that the ACTU did not want inflation higher than our trading partners. 'You say, "I understand your position very clearly". You say nothing about tax,' instructed Kelty. The government would then say there should not be a wage claim before 1 July, and that the ACTU should recommit to an inflation objective as agreed during a Lodge meeting with Hawke in 1991. The ACTU executive would convene after the statement and announce its view. One unexpressed reason for not mentioning tax cuts was that an important part of Kelty's constituency, public employees such as teachers, nurses and government workers, actively opposed them. They knew that tax cuts eventually meant spending cuts.

Once One Nation had been devised, presented and explained, Paul sagged. 'It's unravelling,' he said. 'It sank without a trace'. We needed to move on, but we had not planned for the next phase. Ashton Calvert and I thought Paul should travel, not least to dramatise the theme about Asia, Australia's changing orientation, trade and prosperity. He had already indicated in his first challenge to Hawke that improving our relationship with Indonesia was a high priority. At a lunch with the staff on 9 March, one of the few times we met as a group with Keating, he decided to visit Indonesia and Papua New Guinea and to make a major speech on Asia. He said he wanted a Pacific area trade bloc type of speech to reflect his discussion with President Bush. He also wanted discussions with the states about particular reform issues, especially electricity and infrastructure.

The flight to Jakarta was Paul's first journey abroad as Prime Minister. In the cramped office on the plane between the officials' section and the Keatings' beds, Paul planned with Ashton, Don Russell and me what he wanted to tell Suharto: Indonesia and Australia are neighbours forever, they don't want our territory and we don't want theirs, we want to revive a long-term defence relationship. He wanted to tell Suharto that he and Bush had agreed that America and Australia had to be involved in East Asia to counterbalance North Asia. So APEC was the way ahead. It would keep the US engaged in Asia and help to sustain increasing trade across the Pacific. He wanted APEC to be headquartered in Indonesia. Paul had written to Suharto and other key APEC leaders suggesting the idea of a conference of leaders. He did not suggest which year.

Once One Nation had been announced and the foreign policy themes sounded, Keating had established the main lines of his government. He was portraying Australia as entering a low-inflation, high-productivity recovery, assisted by government infrastructure spending. He would strengthen Australia's new export competitiveness. The Accord would be maintained but reshaped towards enterprise bargaining and supported by tax cuts favourable to middle-income employees. He would press ahead with employment-based superannuation and maintain a safety net of social welfare to support those in difficulty. He would build our trading and investment relationship with Asia.

With many of the government's policies now in place, he turned to the long hard task of grinding down John Hewson and the Opposition with daily assaults whenever the House of Representatives was sitting.

Twenty minutes before Question Time on one sitting day, light flooded the little grey courtyard outside the office. Inside, the Prime Minister sat behind his desk. He was eating his lunch on a tray. Despite our good resolutions and his, the desk and benches behind him were now loaded with different piles of paper of uncertain pertinence. Behind him was the biggest pile, his Question Time folders – his ammunition. There were more than four hundred staff in the Department of Prime Minister and Cabinet and another twenty or so in the Prime Minister's Office, but he handled the Question Time file himself. We could add things to it, but we could only take things away by coming in when he was out and surreptitiously removing them. There were now several folders for Question Time. By election time there would be five. Over long years of experience he had evolved this technique of collecting the best numbers, the most compelling arguments, the most damning criticisms, the records of his opponents' inconsistencies, untruths and misstatements in a set of folders, always near at hand. They were the descendants of Lang's dossiers of newspaper clips. They distilled the political discourse of the time. He took the folders to Question Time, and when he went into the election campaign they would go with him.

Four of us sat in chairs in front of the desk, which was again piled high with various sets of folders. Behind him on a shelf were two large red vases, a radio, a water jug and a row of books. Two more assistants sat on the couches in the centre of the office. We were drinking coffee from styrofoam cups. The Prime Minister pushed his tray to one side and read one of our prepared questions with its answer. Under the rules of the House, Opposition and Government members alternated in asking questions. This meant that in practice we could arrange every second question to frame an attack on the Opposition. Traditionally staff would prepare the PM for difficult questions from the Opposition, ones that might test his command of government. But this Opposition rarely asked any questions we could not easily predict and prepare for. Their questions were either rhetorical, such as why the Prime Minister didn't resign now that unemployment was 11 per cent, or they were entirely predictable, such as how could the Prime Minister explain the growing foreign debt revealed in that day's statistical release. This Opposition tactic meant we could spent most of our time preparing our own questions, or 'Dorothies', together with their answers. With rhetorical questions from the Opposition and 'Dorothies' from our own side, Question Time had become boisterous, even by its own generous standards. Paul was occasionally annoyed by the volume of interjections and thought the Speaker should be tougher in 'naming' offending members – that is, warning them that they would be temporarily ejected from the House.

The Prime Minister began rummaging among his piles of paper on the desk, frowning. 'Where is that small stapler?' he moaned. He turned over the papers on his desk, piling them into new heaps. We looked concerned. Ashton turned over some papers near him. He found a green plastic pen, but not a small stapler. 'Where the fuck is it?' Keating demanded of no one in particular. He pressed a button on the bank of phones. 'Linda, get me a small stapler, love.' He picked up the sheets of paper with the questions. 'This is good,' he said. 'I'll say, "the Honourable Member . . .".' He laughed brightly, looked up at our grinning faces, then he frowned. 'Where's the yellow highlighter?' he asked. 'Jesus, what happens to them?' He began moving the piles of paper again. 'Where is it?' We craned forward a little in a display of sympathetic interest, although the novelty of this daily hunt had long worn off. We knew it would not be found. In the stationery room Linda kept a crate of yellow highlighters and another of small staplers. One of us left to get a yellow highlighter.

Guy Nelligan, the butler, brought in Paul's lunch. 'I shouldn't eat this stuff,' he said when Guy left. 'I'm putting on weight. I should have something simple.' He ate hungrily and quickly, reading the next question and answer.

'This is no good, this is hopeless,' he said. 'How can I say that?'

Stephen Smith said, 'Now, mate, we have to change the questions. Leo said he will have to rule it out of order if we don't.'

'Get him on the phone. I'll stiffen him up.'

'Mate, we'll just change the question.'

'Get him on the phone.' Stephen called the Speaker, Leo McCleay, and put Paul on. 'Leo, mate, for twenty-five years . . . Yes, yes, mate.

I know, mate, I know . . . Leo, mate, name them. Just name them . . . OK. Yes, I know. Yes, OK.' The Prime Minister put the phone down. The Speaker was adamant. 'Where are my fucking glasses?' Paul asked.

The policies had been announced, the Opposition had been engaged, but within three months of One Nation it became apparent that the economy was not roaring back. In the last week of May the government touched the first of what would be a series of low points, each more gloomy than the one before. Unemployment remained above 10 per cent and continued to edge upwards. The economy had grown at annual rate of only 3.2 per cent in the first quarter of the year and had now, we later learned, slowed down. Growth and employment were both stuck, and the weeks slipped by.

The foreboding of doom, dispelled for a while by the leadership change and then by One Nation, returned to the government. There were endless meetings about TAFE funding. Paul was threatening to end fiscal equalisation between the states, an idea that had Queensland Premier Wayne Goss mobilising his state's caucus members.

According to the press gallery it had been a dreadful week. In the *Australian Financial Review*, Geoff Kitney's Friday story was headlined, 'Yet another lost week for PM as the rot sets in'. In Melbourne the ACTU leadership was pessimistic and inclined to scold.

Bill Kelty and the Prime Minister talked every now and then, though less frequently than most people imagined. There was no one Keating admired more than Kelty, but Kelty had a different idea of conversation from Keating. Except when expounding at length to people he wanted to win over, Keating spoke in shorthand. Kelty, by contrast, liked to talk things through. He would state a proposition and fall silent, then state it a different way, then repeat it. Presented with an idea, he would lift it up, turn it around, look it over, then put it down again. There was no rushing Kelty. Like others, Kelty had short periods of very frequent contact with Keating when things had to be done, then long periods when they had little contact.

Every three months or so Kelty would press for a meeting of a body known as the Australian Labor Advisory Council, a group that brought together a few Cabinet ministers, the ACTU leadership and the federal secretary of the Labor Party. Its first formal meeting after Keating became Prime Minister was on the evening of Thursday 28 May. As usual it was held in the Cabinet room.

The explicit purpose of the meetings was to give the ACTU an opportunity to raise issues with the Cabinet. An implicit purpose was to give Kelty an opportunity to denounce the government in the presence of his ACTU colleagues. This reassured his colleagues that Kelty was loyal to their interests rather than to those of the government, but not in a way that created a serious split.

The ALAC meeting began at about 5.30. Paul was now quite tired and as the meeting went on he folded himself over the Cabinet table, his hand shielding his eyes. 'Don't you find these lights harsh?' he whispered to me. His face was pale. Iain Ross sat opposite Paul, next to Kelty, and they whispered together happily throughout the whole meeting. Martin Ferguson sat on the other side of Kelty. He had been doing a good job in guiding an industrial dispute in Tasmania. George Campbell was there from the metal workers union. On the government side were Peter Cook, John Dawkins and Bob Collins. The Labor Party's Federal Secretary, Bob Hogg, sat on our side of the Cabinet table.

For the past month an ACTU economist, Grant Belchamber, had been pressing on us a plan to halt the government's announced schedule of tariff reductions. He said the reductions could go ahead when unemployment fell. We knew from past experience, however, that it was very hard to get tariffs down. If the existing schedule was modified it would be very difficult to resume it later, which of course was precisely the intention of those advocating the pause. The tariff cuts were in my view the most difficult and the most important economic reform that Labor had carried out. If we modified the cuts the Labor Government would lose its claim to have transformed the Australian economy for the better.

That evening at the ALAC meeting, it quickly became apparent that the ACTU people wanted to pressure Paul on tariffs. There appeared to have been some earlier agreement with Bob Hogg on this point and perhaps with Stephen Smith. It was the first big shot in what became a serious campaign to get the Prime Minister to halt the announced program of tariff reductions.

George Campbell, federal Secretary of the Metal Workers Union, led off. Tall and lean, with a haircut still suggesting the duck-bill of his youth, Campbell had always been a zealous defender of high tariffs in the metals manufacturing industries. He said he had been trying to stop Bert Evans, the leader of the Metal Trades Industry Association, from launching a national campaign against planned tariff cuts. He said the feeling out there was very hostile and that independents like the new Member for Wills, Phil Cleary, would take Labor seats. He was seconded by Anna Booth, joint national secretary of the Textile, Clothing and Footwear Union of Australia, handsome and well groomed, who spoke in a moderate and persuasive tone. The union leaders said that the economy was in a very sad state, from which the government would probably not recover.

Paul said that things were actually a bit better than they appeared – figures out that day showed a 30 per cent profit rise on the year before, and he expected good national accounts numbers the following week.

Kelty then spoke in his slightly wavering thin tone, softly and sometimes unclearly. His voice fades at the end of phrases, which he then repeats more loudly – sometimes two or three times if he hits on the expression he is looking for. He sat across the Cabinet table directly from Paul and addressed him directly. Kelty only occasionally glances at the people he is talking to. He usually focuses on their collar or tie. 'You have to be *very* careful,' he began, speaking across the table to Paul in that soft voice. 'We have marched a long time behind this banner, a long time, but the banner is slipping down the flagpole. When we look around there is a very small entourage behind us.'

'Always was,' Paul interjected.

'The March 1991 statement was based on the false premise of growth. We lower tariffs when there is growth. They said then it would be all right. That was not our view then and it is not our view now. This is about future tariff reductions. If you lose the next election it will be because of the March 1991 statement. Then you'll have Hewson for a decade. We have set the place up – superannuation, restructuring, low inflation. And he'll come in. We'll have him for a decade. I have never believed in it, but I have accepted it, as you know. Perhaps there is a different way to handle it. A different way. You should reduce tariffs when unemployment is low. It was economists in the March 1991 statement. If we lose, everything we fought for for a decade, we lose to the conservatives – low inflation, super. So why should we reduce tariffs when unemployment is high? The government's strategy was wrong from March 1991. It was shithouse. It was based on the idea that recovery was around the corner. You say you can't change the program. Now, wage agreements with us were never inflexible. Super was never inflexible. You came and told us you couldn't do it, and we changed it. But the tariff is inflexible.'

Paul responded that a pause would not convince investors to invest so long as the end point was still credible. So if the pause was genuinely a pause only, it would not help. But in fact once you stopped you might never get started again. He put the point that these days even protection wouldn't protect – during his visit to Indonesia he had visited places where people were paid $8 a week. No amount of protection would make us competitive with that. If we did impose a pause we would lose the pointy heads and the editorialists. At the morning and afternoon conferences at the papers they would say the government is finished. The judgment would be made. In any case shifts in the exchange rate have a bigger impact than tariffs.

Ferguson said, 'There is a limit to how far we can hold them. My view is that a pause is a plus.'

Keating said, 'We would write ourselves off.'

Kelty then characteristically scrambled the debate by saying, 'I don't support a pause. I just want to look at it in a rational way. The objective is not tariff cuts; the objective is a better country. So we need more industry policy. I don't think a pause is good. I don't know how you get it back.'

Bob Hogg commented vaguely, 'I basically agree with what you are saying. People out there think you don't give a fuck about them.'

During the exchanges I whispered to Paul that the whole discussion was sad. He said, 'You should have heard it in 1987 and 1988 – this is very mild compared to that.' He left soon after to fly to Sydney. The meeting was still going.

The economic news continued to worsen as Canberra's lovely autumn turned to a raw winter. By mid June we were well into preparations for the August Budget and discovering that the ground was dramatically shifting under our feet. The Joint Economic Forecasting Group customarily updates its forecasts after each quarterly set of national accounts, which in turn appears from one to two months after the end of the quarter. The growth forecasts were little changed since May except for one key number. Employment growth for 1992–93 had been cut from 2.25 to 1 per cent. The JEFG now forecast unemployment of around 10.6 per cent in June next year, nearly 1 per cent higher than the prediction we had offered in One Nation. At the same time the employment numbers for May showed an actual decline in employment, with unemployment rising from 10.4 to 10.6 per cent.

Not only was the economy flatter than we hoped but also the budget deficit for the current year and the projection for next year were rapidly increasing. The deficit for the current year was now estimated at around $9.9b compared to $6.8b projected in One Nation, and $13b for 1992–93, compared to the $8b in One Nation and the $10.5b Dawkins had publicly announced after a May review. There was also a $3b deficit in 1995–96 compared to the $2b surplus we had projected in One Nation. A deficit of that size so far into the expansion suggested that the second round of tax cuts announced in One Nation would have to be withdrawn. The deficits numbers were not changing in response to changing economic forecasts. Most of the change arose from re-estimates of tax collections, using similar economic parameters. Cumulatively over five years the

Treasury and Australian Tax Office errors amounted to around $24 billion on the revenue side. They were basically mechanical forecasting errors – quite possibly unavoidable, but in no way related to changed expectations about the economy itself.

Paul became aware of the changes on Tuesday 16 June. We had a short discussion in his office, Don, Ric and I sitting with him in the armchairs in the centre of his room. Outside the Canberra winter was settling in. Paul had been Prime Minister for just under six months. 'This really does us, I think. It really does,' he said. 'Don't you reckon?'

Breezily confident when he had to be, Paul liked to confront the worst case in the privacy of his office. I said the polls were surprisingly good despite continuing high unemployment, and that the economy could look pretty good by March of next year. Paul and Don were gloomily unconvinced by this story, as indeed was I.

Three days later, on Friday 19 June, Paul lunched with Kelty in the Prime Minister's dining room. The curtains and upholstery are grey and pink, and the dining table is made from Tasmanian timbers. Mirrors give a sense of space to what is really a narrow annexe to the Prime Minister's sitting room. One uncurtained window looks out onto the courtyard and across to the Deputy Prime Minister's Office, which Paul had left a year before. Since an unfortunate occasion on which Hawke's staff had unknowingly inscribed their notes into the delicate timbers beneath their papers, Guy had strongly discouraged the use of the room except for formal meals.

We were served smoked salmon, lamb fillet slices and one glass of semillon each. Kelty was once again with George Campbell and Iain Ross. Paul brought along me and Mary-Anne O'Laughlin, a very bright and effective colleague who handled social welfare issues and employment training. Paul wanted the ACTU to allow off-the-job training time to be unpaid. It would be part of the vocational training reform plan. Kelty had a bigger plan, a Grant Belchamber design called the National Employment Strategy, which would slow down the rate of tariff reductions and finance a $2b job creation scheme with a 2 per cent increase in personal income taxes. It was difficult to believe Kelty was serious about the plan, but it was necessary to present it. There was no doubt, however, that he was serious about some kind of plan, which the Prime Minister should announce. Unemployment was still above 10 per cent. Employment was now growing in New South Wales, Queensland and Western Australia, but continuing to fall in South Australia, Victoria and Tasmania.

Kelty wore an open-necked shirt, a pullover with a dark red and green pattern and a checked sportscoat. Keating hated Canberra winters. He was exhausted. He was wearing a pullover under his suit coat. He was coughing.

'You have to make the speech of your life,' Kelty told Keating. 'The speech of your life. It must be like Roosevelt in 1932. You must throw everything you can at jobs. You announce it, you say, "Here is the Keating Plan", then you have a meeting with us. You ask us for tick.'

Kelty spoke at his usual rather high pitch, with slight interrogatives at the end of his sentences. He talked on in a dismal vein about the economy until Keating interrupted. 'Let's talk about how things really are,' he said. He argued that the economy was slow but the fundamentals of inflation and competitiveness were good. The recently announced Westpac $2. 2 billion write-down 'drew the line on the 1980s. They said, "It's over". Now we've moved to a low-inflation country, with a bulge of unemployment sitting in between. That's what's happened. The 1983–92 decade was one of critical change. Phase two is to bring the rest of the population up.'

Campbell said one of his sons was a plumber and couldn't find work. He said his son had said to him the other day, 'Something needs to be done about this fucking country, Dad.'

Kelty added that on its present support Labor would not win a single seat in Victoria.

'Maybe we are done,' Keating said, shrugging.

'No, no; we're not done,' said Kelty, dismayed. 'Well, maybe you are – but losing is not the worst thing in the world. The thing is to go down fighting. Anyway, I don't know that we are done. Hewson is not a quality person. People know that. He's a merchant banker. People think of him as a merchant banker.'

'You could have independents controlling the House of Representatives,' said Campbell morosely, complaining about tariff cuts.

'If you polled people they would be in favour of refining implementation, of making further tariff cuts dependent on reducing unemployment,' Kelty said.

'If you polled people, they would want to increase tariffs,' Keating replied tersely.

They talked about the size of a jobs package. Paul said there was an $11 billion starting point for the deficit in 1992–93. 'I don't know how you go about selling deficits with middle-sized double digits.'

'What about we say we accept an increase in taxation in return for jobs?' suggested Kelty.

'We get wiped out,' Keating replied.

Nelligan interrupted to tell Keating there was a phone call from his mother. 'It will be about money,' Keating said. 'She doesn't like falling interest rates.'

'Tell her to look at the real rates, not the nominals,' Kelty advised.

'You can't bullshit your mother,' Keating replied, leaving the table.

Kelty explained his $2 billion jobs program. Keating said he was prepared to look at regional unemployment and at the other unemployment problems in terms of training. 'The jobs I started with, like clerk in the Sydney County Council,' he said, 'they don't exist any more.'

'You're wrong,' interjected Kelty. 'There are now lots of boring, low-skill, underpaid jobs.'

'Oh, are there? Well, I don't know about that,' said Keating. 'Anyway, the idea of our programs is to make the unskilled more skilled. We come at unemployment that way, through training. If we say RED scheme [a local government jobs creation program], we are really saying to the electorate, "Put us out of our misery in April". Instead we do Jobskills [a job training program].'

'How many jobs do you want?' Kelty asked. 'You can have 40 000 jobs in six months. Give one-third of the dole as a wage subsidy and keep two-thirds for training. We can get 40 000 jobs if you give us an instrument. I'll take six months off. Lindsay Fox is willing to take six months off. We'll do it together. You know me, Paul. You know when I have enthusiasm for things I can do it. I have enthusiasm for these things.'

'I have to keep your enthusiasms on the right track, Bill,' Keating said. 'Two billion is a lot on the deficit but is only 0.5 per cent of GDP, so it's not going to have a big impact. We are going to get 4 to 5 per cent growth anyway, and employment will rise rapidly in the second half of the year.'

'I'm tired of hearing this sort of stuff,' said Kelty. 'Bob told me that in this office one year ago, and a year before that. I didn't agree with it then, either.'

'We'll do something for the kids; that's fine,' said Keating. 'But what about the 30- to 50-year olds? What about Jobskills for them?'

'Great, but it's just words,' Kelty insisted. 'We'll get 100 000. We'll get unemployment below ten. We'll never give in. That's the only thing I will do, Lindsay and I. We'll have committees in every little country town. All you have to do is make the decision you'll go for broke on 100 000 jobs.'

'It's like a rubber band,' said Keating. 'It stretches and stretches, and then it snaps back. That's what happens with employment. You get productivity at first, and then suddenly you get jobs. Employment suddenly catches up.'

'So what are you going to do?' Kelty asked.

'I'm not going to sit like a bunny in the headlights,' Keating replied.

May was poor; June was worse. The unemployment number on Thursday 9 July was 11.1 per cent — a very bad result. (Employment actually rose during the month, which was the only important indicator for the economy. But not much attention was paid to it.) Commentators once again declared the government dead and buried. Just back from the Pacific Forum, Keating was furious with the Canberra press gallery. He said he should apply a flame thrower to the critics. 'I should just go right in there and pick a few — you and you,' he said, pointing to some imaginary reporters. Mark Ryan was scowling at

Keating. Russell was gently chiding him. There was serious discussion in the media of the likelihood of a 'double dip' recession.

The four-year forecasting framework, which had served us well with One Nation, now began to worry us.

On the evening of Monday 13 July we saw for the first time Treasury's Economic and Fiscal Outlook, the basis for the coming Budget. Paul leafed through it in a desultory way. It now calculated the starting point for the 1992–93 deficit at $13.75 billion. Revenue had dropped $5b, and spending had increased $0. 6b relative to amounts predicted in One Nation. The growth forecasts for the coming year had been lowered. There would be unemployment of 10 per cent in June 1993. The budget outcome in 1995–96 had changed from our projected $2b surplus to an $8b deficit.

At a troika meeting on Wednesday 15 July John Dawkins explained why our four- to five-year forecasting framework was causing problems. He wore shirtsleeves and a big fat navy blue tie patterned with large flowers. He looked almost childishly youthful, with a smooth chubby face. He complained it was hard to see across the table now that Paul had had dimmers installed for the overhead lights.

The purpose of the meeting was to work out what to do about the $8b deficit in 1995–96 shown in the Treasury projections. The deficit resulted partly from low growth, but Dawkins said he preferred to understate rather than overstate growth because of slow growth in the world economy. The major problem was that the revenue projected for the coming year, 1992–93, was now $5b less than previously projected. Another reason was the critical response to the growth estimates in One Nation and Treasury's annoyance that these estimates were influenced by the Prime Minister's Office. Dawkins much more faithfully reflected Treasury views in this instance than he imagined. Curiously, however, the One Nation projections turned out to be surprisingly accurate and the Treasury numbers embedded in the 1992–93 Budget quite wrong. Both One Nation and Treasury were too optimistic about 1992–93. In the following years the economy grew as One Nation predicted.

Treasury's numbers showed that tax cuts of the order announced by the Prime Minister in One Nation could not be afforded. The solution, the Treasurer said, was to omit the revenue numbers and the deficit outcome. 'They have never been written in before,' he said in an aggrieved and indignant tone, 'and they're not worth the paper they're written on. We should instead say that as a matter of policy we will maintain revenues at 24 per cent of GDP. It's a kind of revenue trilogy, but in reverse. We say tax won't go lower than 24 per cent. You can then show balance. You can then accommodate the tax cuts.'

The problem with this was that we would have to publish a revenue forecast for 1992–93, and groups like Access Economics would then calculate their own forecasts for revenue in 1995–96. They would see that we could not get to 24 per cent without a tax increase.

As Willis immediately pointed out, the Dawkins tactic 'means we are assuming a tax increase to pay for our tax cut'. Willis had grey wiry curly hair, mottled skin and big hands. Though a pleasant man, he had a whingeing tone and a sour expression, and looked perpetually fretful. What he said, however, was invariably sensible and put calmly. He often expressed things as a joke, at which he alone would laugh. He was a good critic, but quite useless as a politician since his solutions were usually those that would be offered by a mid-level Treasury official. He said we should eliminate the tax cuts and therefore eliminate the deficit.

Dawkins offered another idea. He said we should say that future revenue is too hard to forecast. Paul thought this was possible. He said speculatively, 'We should say it is now impossible to forecast. We will be a bit shy of balance, but it is hard to forecast.'

Dawkins said the Opposition's Fightback! plan had the same problem. They started their calculations in 1991, which meant they too had a $5b hole in 1992–93. Willis pointed out that the Opposition had $15b in asset sales up their sleeve.

'They don't use them,' said Dawkins.

'They will now,' said Willis.

'For Christ's sake, don't let us get hooked up on that One Nation stuff,' Dawkins said huffily.

'John's approach will open us to endless arguments. We should be honest and say these forecasts are the best we have, even though they aren't very good. We will rue the day if we accept John's approach,' Willis insisted.

'Why don't we see where the numbers settle down?' suggested Keating.

With bad economic news, Button and Dawkins were looking for a good political trick. On Thursday 6 August Industry Minister John Button came down ostensibly to discuss the 150 per cent research and development tax deductions for industry, but both he and Dawkins had another subject in mind. He was clearly perturbed by the presence of Don, Ric and me as well as Keating and Dawkins. Paul was uneasy. Button produced a note, handed out copies with the greatest reluctance (and collected them, with one exception, at the end of the meeting), and spoke to it quite nervously. The note was about tariffs. He said it was a purely political issue on which Keating and Dawkins must help him make a decision. He said he wanted Keating to make a public statement that the government would insist on a minimum market share for Australian-made cars. He also wanted Keating to say that tariffs for manufacturing generally would not fall to 5 per cent, as announced, but to 10 per cent. He said that in discussion Dawkins had counter-proposed that the existing timetable for reductions be pushed out two years.

The ministers were sitting in armchairs around the central table, on which sat a bowl of chrysanthemums. Button sat on the chair furthest from the desk, Dawkins on the chair with its back to the main door. Keating walked about, because he had had a back massage earlier. 'Don't mind me,' he said. 'My back's out. I've got to walk around.'

'To be honest with you, John, having fought for this for years I hate giving up on any of it,' Keating said to Button. 'We're now looking at a big deficit and I don't want markets to think the whole model has been thrown out. I mean, I do agree it would cause a lot of trouble in the Liberal Party, but they may turn around and change their policy. It's not as important to them as GST and IR. They may do something slicker, cleverer than us.'

Dawkins was evidently having a change of heart. 'I think stopping at 10 is terrible,' he said. 'But I now think delaying for two years wins nothing for us.'

'Right,' said Keating, enlisting him. 'Now you can say Asia, trade, etcetera, etcetera, and it's uncompromised. It's kept us regarded seriously by the pointy heads, which eventually means we're regarded seriously by the masses. They see our willingness to internationalise as the test.'

Forced on the defensive, Button was more explicit. He said, 'If 10 per cent is our highest tariff, that is quite low. I mean, how can we negotiate with the ASEAN countries if we have nothing to offer? We have eighty people over in DFAT [Department of Foreign Affairs and Trade] doing the Uruguay Round. How many people do we have doing bilaterals?'

Dawkins said a lot of domestic import replacement industry had gone under so there was a risk of high imports as the economy recovered. 'I don't know what we'll do. We'll just have to live through high current account deficits, I guess.'

'The foreign exchange markets will keep supporting us as long as inflation is low and we are internationalising,' Keating replied.

The discussion closed then, to resume the following Wednesday night when Button reappeared and pressed a case to extend the end date for tariff cuts. He then called in his department head, Neville Stevens, a tiny man with a timid appearance, who looked as though he would not say boo to a goose, much less his own minister. Keating asked Stevens what he thought of the option of pushing out the end date. He said, without a moment's hesitation and with utter decisiveness, that there was no point in it whatsoever, and it would certainly be better to do nothing than to do what his minister suggested. Dawkins appeared briefly and said he could now see merit in a delay, but he would support any result. When he left, Keating told Button he was disinclined to alter the schedule. When Button left, Keating told us he was pleased with his decision and the issue would not be revisited.

The ACTU had withheld a national wages claim. In early August Kelty told us he was interested in seeking a minimum wage increase, which would be delivered in a way to give an incentive to enterprise bargaining. Ross and Kelty had believed for some time that a Hewson victory was quite likely, and in any case the Liberals were bound to win sooner or later. When they did, the system of compulsory arbitration, awards and national wage cases would be abolished, as it had been in New Zealand. The union movement had to prepare for this. They believed that if unions struck enterprise bargains they would win membership support and survive the abolition of arbitration. The thing to do was to get the union movement used to it.

On Wednesday 5 August Keating, Dawkins and some staff members flew to Melbourne to discuss Kelty's proposal. Industrial Relations Minister Peter Cook also came to the meeting. Hewson was believed to be using his office in the Treasury Place Commonwealth offices, so we met in the Prime Minister's suite at the Windsor Hotel. Kelty turned up late, with Jennie George, Grant Belchamber and Iain Ross. At 4.50 we seated ourselves around a small polished table under a chandelier. The script for the meeting required that Keating, in the presence of other union officials and other ministers, propose to Kelty an increase that would apply only to people on minimum rates.

'What do we want to talk about?' Paul asked brightly, when everyone was seated.

'You talk,' replied Kelty, attempting to keep Paul to the script. Seeing it would be futile, he went on to propose his idea himself. 'We could do $8 to $10 in a national wage case, with another $10 in the next. That's option one. It's up to you. But we'd have problems. Perhaps with the commission. That's the first option. There's an alternative. We're headed down the enterprise bargaining route. We want to do $10 as a safety net, not as a general increase. So raise the minimum award rate by $10 by an increase in the supplementary payment. That's more attractive. It's cheaper. It makes more sense. It costs less and is more consistent. We could build in a capacity-to-pay provision. More consistent. That's option two. Better. Better. Better.' (An increase in the supplementary payment would apply only to those people on the award minimum. It would otherwise be 'absorbed' into overaward payments. It would not apply to people already in enterprise agreements.)

There was a general discussion. Kelty was writing on a pad, dividing it into two with a single vertical stroke of his ball-point, then putting things into the two columns. Kelty reacted sharply to something and said to Paul, 'You have a predilection for defeat. You said all last year that Hawke must do more, and as soon as you get there you sit around doing nothing.' He then said, 'You've got to do something in terms of a family package.' He mentioned that the minimum rates proposal was one that Ralph Willis had put to him in a meeting at the Lodge when Hawke was Prime Minister. 'Actually Bob was pretty good on national wage cases,' he reflected, philosophically.

Kelty said we needed to put the request for a change to supplementary payments to the ACTU. 'We need to react to you. We will then say we want a bit of a family package. With this approach there will be no national wage case, and there will be no national wage principles.'

Someone asked what would happen if the commission refused to agree. Kelty said, 'The IRC will have to do it, because if the don't, they have no other role. They'll have nothing to do. If they knock it back, we abolish the fucking commission.'

'Option three,' commented Ross.

Keating said, 'We want option two.'

The deal done in the usual way, the ACTU Wages Committee then met with the government on Tuesday 11 August, in a vast yellow-carpeted room on the second floor of Parliament House. The room had very high ceilings with suspended light fittings. The brown bodies of Bogong moths were visible under the white light shades. We were arranged in a square of tables with a hollow centre. The ACTU took three sides, with Bill Kelty, Martin Ferguson, Jennie George and Iain Ross opposite Keating, Dawkins and Cook.

Keating said that we were now in a low-inflation environment. 'Each year we have a discussion with the ACTU about wage settings. We also have enterprise agreements. But we are conscious of the fact that some people cannot bargain increases. We have assured you that the national wage case still has relevance. We would support a CPI-style equivalent adjustment in a national wage case, but the full bench might not award it. Another option is to support an increase in supplementary payments by way of a flat increase. This essentially would be a safety net. We would prefer that path to a national wage case we would not be certain of winning. We would do two adjustments spread over one and a half years. Something between now and the end of the first quarter 1993, and something no earlier than March 1994. There would not be a national wage case. There would be two caveats. The increase would be applied only where there was capacity to pay, and it must be consistent with inflation remaining competitive with our trading partners.'

We moved to a discussion of what was invariably called 'the quantum'. Keating said that two $10 payments would be around 3 per cent. 'That's probably a bit on the high side,' he said. 'Something less would sing a little better.'

Concluding the discussion, Keating asked, '$8 or $10?'

'$10 – got to be,' said Kelty firmly.

'Maybe ten,' Keating conceded, 'but that is the top end of the range.'

'Protection in terms of capacity to pay,' Kelty went on, summarising the agreement. 'Trading partners. You're also asking us to take into account the social wage; is that right?'

'Yes, that's right,' said Keating.

Attempting to catch up with the speed of the settlement, Dawkins intervened. 'I think we need to take into account a discount because of the dollar's depreciation,' he said. 'If we give $10, that's more than 1.4 per cent for a lot of low-paid workers. It would be hard to defend publicly. I would prefer $8.'

'People who get this have had nothing since the last national wage case,' said Kelty in a combative tone.

'I'm just making a point,' Dawkins replied, a little uncertainly.

'Sounds like a quibble to me,' said Kelty, pursuing the retreating Treasurer.

'You'll talk yourself right out of it if you're not careful, John,' Martin Ferguson warned.

'All right, we're offering $10,' Keating said, seeing the beginning of a long fight. 'Let's stop the discussion.'

With three new taxes threatened in the small print, the August Budget was in trouble almost from the announcement. Keating was annoyed with the Budget but fought on. The big break came towards the end of August. He gave a radio interview with an Adelaide station, in which he attacked the Opposition for promising to allow the free import of second-hand cars. He later believed this was the turning point in the fifteen-month struggle against Hewson. Encouraged by this success, he enlarged the attack to include the whole zero tariff policy of the Opposition. In Parliament he also attacked Hewson for promising to tell the Reserve Bank to worry about inflation and nothing else, a policy Hewson himself had opposed some years before. Things were beginning to work our way as the Opposition was forced on the defensive, but the prevailing mood was quite a long way behind. On Thursday 27 August the *Australian Financial Review*'s Geoff Kitney wrote us off yet again with a piece headed, 'Tide Turns for Libs'. It said the government was not now getting a hearing – in other words, people no longer took us seriously.

Outwardly confident, many members of the Prime Minister's Office were privately despondent. They thought Keating was not hearing their advice, which could make all the difference. After another difficult week, Don Russell convened an advisers' meeting in the Cabinet annex on the morning of Friday 28 August. These meetings were irregular and often cathartic. Speechwriter Don Watson and political adviser Mark Ryan would usually attack Don Russell, blaming him for Keating's failure to adopt their many suggestions for his improvement. Watson had an entertaining recriminatory style, though what he had to say was rarely helpful.

'We write speeches about best practice but there is no best practice in this office,' Watson complained. 'This is a sheltered workshop.' He accused Russell of failing to organise the office properly and of controlling access to Keating. He said we were doing very badly and we should not kid ourselves we were doing well.

This released a flood of criticism. Mark Ryan said that in recent months we had talked about the economy and it was now time to talk about something else. He was supported by Watson and Anne Summers, who said Paul should be warmer. Other ministers should do the attacking. Attending his last meeting as an adviser before running for a federal seat, Stephen Smith said Paul was widely disliked in the community. He agreed that he needed to be warmer. Smith said issues like the tariff debate made no difference – they didn't register. He thought that for the electorate the first issue was personality, then the issues, then the future, then Hewson. Various advisers suggested that Paul should get up earlier in the morning, be on time for meetings, smile when he got in and out of cars. There was much amused criticism of Paul's suits. He needed to show his charm in relaxed surroundings. Summers thought there should be a photographer on hand to take pictures of people who met with the PM. They would value them. She said the biggest issue so far as women were concerned was violence against women. Other advisers urged us to say more about health, the environment, child care, the safety net, violence against women, and Aborigines.

As an economic adviser, I disagreed. I said we had not talked nearly enough about the economy, that we had a good story to tell, and that Keating should go after Hewson day after day on economic issues. Our strong issues were tariffs, industrial relations, and the goods and services tax. Don Russell agreed. The election would be determined on these issues, and only Paul himself could lead the attack. As to getting up earlier in the morning, smiling more, or being on time – we had to accept that Keating was Keating, and wouldn't be changing in the next six months.

That afternoon we convened again, this time to discuss the issues with Paul. We arranged ourselves on the couches in his sitting room.

'We've done One Nation and the youth statement and now employment in the Budget,' he said. 'The time for statement-driven activity has now passed. Now is the time to attack the Opposition and sell what we have.

'It's been a very hard year. Before One Nation we were terminal. We were gone. We thought then that we'd catch the recovery, but the truth is we didn't pick the turns. We lived on the presentation at first, and by now we should be living on the growth. But we're not.'

He then ticked off what we should be doing, of which the first was, 'Go for Hewson – unravel him.'

The Budget hadn't worked, he said. There was too much attention to tax. The recovery may be too late. As a result, 'We need to put a little bloc back together – the aged, Aborigines, the arts, the regions. We're assembling the clients. Medicare is another one. I reckon we're now 35 or 36 [the government's opinion poll rating] – we're four points away from last time. Now we must be more publicity-driven, not statement-driven. We've got to get out there. We want a government-sponsored Medicare campaign – we're entitled to defend it. But first we need agreement with the states.'

Described by reporters as completely confident of the outcome of the election, Paul was quite open about the difficulties and the uncertainties in the privacy of his office. There a was a good chance – but no more than that. Part of his distinction as a politician was his capacity to combine the confidence and determination of a leader with the balanced objectivity of an analyst.

Industrial relations was emerging as another issue on which Keating could batter the Opposition. At the end of August he spoke to an industrial relations congress in Sydney, in which he set up the terms of the debate between the government and the Opposition. Offering a charter to employees, Keating said that Labor would preserve a safety net of minimum awards and a 'no disadvantage' test on enterprise agreements.

Flying back in the evening, Keating talked to me as he toyed with a single brandy-and-dry. There had been a high current account deficit that month, reminding him of the problems of the late 1980s. 'The best years in government were 1984 to 1989,' he said. That was when the ministers had energy and big reforms were made in the budget structure. He was also thinking about the future. 'Geoffrey [Tozer] was over last night,' he told us. 'He's won an award for his CD. Now he wants to get back into giving concerts.' Paul recalled how as Treasurer he had driven down from London to set up a deal for him with the head of Chandos Records. Meetings with Tozer always refreshed Paul and reminded him that alternative lives were possible. 'Life is too short,' he said. 'You should arrange your life so you go on and do different things. My theory is that you can keep going, stop getting old, if you can keep moving into something different. That's why I can't forgive Hawke for leaving so late. It's like salmon – they swim upstream against innumerable obstacles, then get stuck in the last waterfall. It's all uphill now because of my age and energy. I'm nearly 50 and Hewson's a young 44.' Hewson was out there campaigning every day. Paul was conserving himself, he said, holding his energy in reserve for the final contest.

With Parliament meeting frequently in the long Budget session, Keating was wearing Hewson down. Concluding a gruelling Question Time on Tuesday 8 September, Keating leaned over to Hewson.

'You're white,' he said. 'Your face is white. You can't take it.'

'I can take care of you,' Hewson said.

'No, you can't,' Keating replied, leaving. 'Your face is white.'

Hewson began whispering to Keating during Question Time. He would whisper, 'You're a loser, Keating.'

The economy wallowed, but the Opposition continued to offer Keating opportunities. Their industrial relations spokesman, John Howard, launched their industrial relations policy in mid October. Under his proposals employers could take employees out of awards without their consent and substitute an individual contract of employment. Characterising the policy as 'take the contract or take the sack,' Paul went on the offensive. With Victoria's Premier Jeff Kennett offering a practical example of what the policy meant, Hewson was in trouble. For the Opposition to win, a majority of the electorate would have to vote in favour of a new 15 per cent consumption tax, in favour of losing the protection of awards, and in favour of facing uncertainty over the future of Medicare.

By the end of October the government was gaining ground. At the beginning of November a poll in the *Sydney Morning Herald* gave the government 40 per cent public support and the Opposition 43 per cent after the undecideds were distributed. It was the best poll for the government since early 1990. Although the government was still behind the Opposition, Keating was ahead of Hewson as preferred Prime Minister.

With Kennett introducing a new industrial relations regime in Victoria and the federal Opposition threatening to do so if it won power, the trade unions were beginning to panic. During an Australian Labor Advisory Council meeting in the Cabinet room on Thursday 29 October, the ACTU threatened to shut down Victoria.

'We can't afford to lie doggo,' Kelty told the meeting. 'We've begged the Victorian Government not to do it. If they refuse, we will then endorse a stoppage. We'll stop power, public transport, warehouses and the waterfront. There'll be absolute industrial buggery between now and Christmas. That's what they don't expect, and that's what we'll deliver.' He suggested that the Federal Government should then intervene to facilitate entry to federal awards for employees currently covered by the state awards and to establish standards for equal pay and job protection.

Such a campaign would have been fatal for our election chances, but ALP Federal Secretary Bob Hogg merely said, 'You have no choice.

I recognise that.' Hogg said it would be very tough election campaign. He asked the unions for $1 million.

'One million is too little,' said Kelty. 'The unions can cough up $3 million. Unions will get destroyed by this lot.'

Jim Maher, of the Shop Distributive and Allied Employees Association, said his union had voted to give half a million to the federal campaign, 'because we see it as the be-all or end-all of our union'. He said they might as well spend it now as wait for it to be taken by the Liberals.

'This is a fight to the death,' said Keating.

'I'll have every union working full time on the campaign for three months, helping you,' promised Kelty.

'I've been warning for years that everything is at stake, but this time it really is,' said Keating, encouraged by their support.

'That's right. It's the real thing,' agreed George Campbell.

During dinner in the Cabinet anteroom, Kelty outlined a strategy for challenging Kennett. The Victorian unions would close down the newly opened Toyota car plant in that state in protest against Kennett's policies. The idea was that the Federal Government would then use this as sufficient cause to invoke the Constitution's trade and commerce power, and override. Keating and his advisors thought it was a lousy idea. The only way to beat Kennett, we said, was for Labor to win the next federal election. Otherwise the unions were gone. Whatever we did between now and then would be undone by Hewson anyway if he became Prime Minister. And all that the ACTU did between now and then by way of shutting down Victoria would lose us votes and make the destruction of unions quite certain.

On 9 November Mark Ryan told us the Newspoll to be announced the next day would put Labor five points ahead — cheerful news. During our discussion prior to Question Time that afternoon a brown and grey moth flitted around the Prime Minister.

'Fucking moth,' said Keating, dodging. 'Keeping on to me'.

'Knows a good suit,' Don Watson remarked.

On Sunday 15 November we flew to Townsville and then to Bundaberg for a tour of the north Queensland sugar seats. During the flight
Paul discussed the election options. He said he did not like the 19
December option – apparently, I later learned, because Bob Hogg
convinced him that the polls showing us in front were wrong. According to Hogg, Labor was 5 per cent behind the 1990 results in two
key seats polled because the Democrats had collapsed and their vote
had gone to the Liberals. This improbable view was contradicted later
that day by a Gallup poll. Mark phoned the key points through to
us in Bundaberg. It showed Labor in front. Keating was undecided.
At the Bundaberg Bougainvillaea Hotel he used his mobile phone to
call around. Outside room 38, Labor MHR Brian Courtice was urging an early election. 'The troops want to go over the top,' he said.
'We want to charge down the Shenandoah Valley and kill all the rebels
we can find.' Courtice was very strongly in favour of an early election; he said that most of caucus was. John Dawkins was also pressing for an early run. Certainly the government's re-election chances
were looking much stronger than they had been at any time over
the past year. Over the last three months Keating had seized on the
Opposition's zero tariff policy, and dramatically announced that a
Labor Opposition in the Senate would not stop a Hewson goods
and services tax. The government had enacted future tax cuts to
increase the credibility of his promise to make them, but he was not
convinced that Labor had a majority yet.

Keating said that he thought the government had only a 40 per cent
chance of winning. The basic decision was that Labor was now doing
quite well but possibly not well enough to win government. This is always
a point of difference between a Prime Minister and his parliamentary
colleagues. From the point of view of caucus members, the key thing
is not to let the peak pass. The government might not win, but fewer of
them would lose their seats. From the point of view of the Prime Minister, however, losing by a little is no different from losing by a lot. As

long as there is a likelihood that Labor would not win a majority now, it makes sense to wait and see whether it improves later. My own view, which I put to Paul when he showed me the research that night, was that at this point the one thing that could lose the election was going early.

The decision made, he thought about other things. Flying from north Queensland to Perth, he talked about music and life after politics. He enjoyed the music of Richard Strauss most at the moment, he said. His friend Ross Gengos had recently played him four different versions of the Strauss tone poems over a single four-hour session. His ear was becoming more discriminating. He looked forward to life after politics. He would get out because it was important to keep moving and developing. If he won he said he might shoot through after a couple of years, and he would choose some style of life that indulged his brain or his eye or his ear. 'Dad had a stroke at 49, a coronary at 50 and died at 60. I don't know if I'm like him, but . . . That's why I'm cranky with Bob; he slowed my schedule.'

He decided against a pre-Christmas election, and on Wednesday 18 November, in a discussion in his office with his assistants, he said the best time would be Saturday 20 February.

Pressed by his colleagues, Hewson changed Fightback! in December to exclude a tax on food and to fund spending programs from the sale of Telecom. Chatting with Paul on Christmas Eve in his office, before we went our separate ways for the holidays, he wondered whether it would have been better to go in December. He might have missed his only chance to win.

By mid January Don Russell was at work on a pre-election statement of the government's achievements and commitments. Meeting with officials from the Department of Prime Minister and Cabinet, we scheduled the statement for the week beginning 8 February. We were careful to avoid all formal reference to election timing. The department would withdraw in the election period, nor could it happily take part in an election statement. But it could help prepare a statement of the government's plans and policies. The timing of an election was not their decision.

Paul was back from holiday soon after, in good time to host a dinner for union leaders on the evening of Thursday 28 January. After the dinner, Kelty, Iain Ross and George Campbell came down to see Keating. Kelty said that Labor was in trouble and that it would lose unless it acted quickly. He felt that Keating should talk to young people and find out what they really wanted. There were terrible problems in Bendigo, Ballarat and other provincial areas. If Labor lost it would be because of the March 1991 statement.

Kelty said that Jeff Kennett had realised union power was just a veneer. He knew he had to go for broke. Paul should do the same. What would emerge from Kennett, and federally if the Libs did the same, was a leaner and meaner union movement. It would be 15 to 20 per cent of the workforce, and would be composed of unions like the Electrical Trades Union.

'Look at the year; look at how much we have done,' Keating told him.

'We won't win,' Kelty insisted, citing slow growth and high unemployment.

'Well, maybe that is why we won't,' Keating said.

The troika of Keating, Dawkins and Willis worked on the content of the pre-election statement. It would promise a cut in company tax and a temporary investment allowance, and more spending on child care programs. Part of the Commonwealth Bank would be sold to fund the higher deficit.

Both Keating and Dawkins also wanted to do something about bank lending, which business people complained was too expensive and too tight. On Thursday 4 February they met in the Prime Minister's room with Reserve Bank Governor Bernie Fraser, Secretary of the Department of Prime Minister and Cabinet Mike Keating, and various assistants.

Fraser was wearing a blue striped shirt with cuff links and a spotted gold and red tie. He was tanned and appeared fit. He had recently returned from an overseas visit. Resisting any proposal for explicit guidance to the banks to lend more for small business, he said we should not turn the clock back on regulation and that the excesses of the 1980s were no reason to do it. We would get accountability through competition. The biggest problem with business lending was lack of demand, although it was true that banks were only lending on projects that had high nominal returns, and were not taking the very low rate of inflation into account. He did not mind encouraging banks to move more rapidly; the question was how to do it.

'The banks have buggered us,' said Paul. 'You hear it perpetually – the banks won't lend. It's like a song. It's three years.'

'There is a problem,' Fraser conceded in his characteristic, even whisper. 'There is sufficient anecdotal material to suggest that some banks are ultra-cautious. But it is better to encourage than to threaten.'

'Banks made errors in the 1980s as they did in the 1890s and the 1920s, for which we are still paying. We need more review power,' Don Russell said.

'We do monitor the banks closely already,' Fraser replied. 'What I'm worried about is a particular sectoral focus – like small business.'

'I am told that banks are still lending on assets, not on cash flow,' said Ric Simes.

'I think banks are lending on cash flow,' said Fraser, 'but we still have reports of them seeking 15 per cent return after tax. They haven't adjusted to low inflation.'

'Put the Rottweilers on them; that's what I reckon,' Keating said sternly.

'Interest rates are still too bloody high. There's no doubt about that,' Fraser suggested.

'I'd take a shotgun to them – bang bang!' Keating continued, aiming an imaginary gun at the ceiling. 'I'll get them if it's the last thing I do. I'll get them when I'm more powerful. At the moment,' he added apologetically, 'the electorate might knock me off.' These strong sentiments were for the benefit of Dawkins, Russell and Simes. Typically, Paul would reassure his more militant hands that he would take savage action later, when he had decided to take none now.

The discussion continued, mostly dwelling on the shortcomings of the commercial banks. Somehow or other, Fraser left the meeting with agreement from the Treasurer and the Prime Minister that the Reserve Bank would pay higher interest rates on commercial bank deposits with the Reserve Bank. He would collect some statistics on commercial bank lending to small businesses and form a small business consultative committee. There would be no directions to the banks to lend more to small business.

By Friday 5 February I was anxious for Paul to approve a major APEC speech scheduled for delivery to the Sydney Institute on Monday. He was preoccupied, moving from room to room within the Prime Minister's Office in deep conversation with John Dawkins, Mark Ryan and Don Russell. Although the pre-election statement was not yet finished, he decided that night to call a Sunday press conference to announce an election on 13 March. Working through Saturday night and into the early hours of Sunday morning around a single big table in the department, advisers and officials cleared the statement by late Sunday morning.

With only one or two exceptions, press gallery reporters predicted an Opposition victory – possibly an overwhelming victory.

On the first morning of the campaign we flew to Sydney to deliver a trade speech to the Sydney Institute. For the first time Keating was in a campaign to win as Prime Minister in his own right. 'This is the start of our own mini-presidential campaign,' he said. He told us how he had driven Annita's red Magna out to Government House. He talked again about the 1980s in the light of the economy depicted in his speech. 'The thing is,' he said, referring to his much-criticised earlier statement on the recession, 'it actually *was* the recession we had to have. Spending was running much too fast. Inflation was too high.

We get no credit now for low inflation, yet it was a great achievement. The key to it was the 1990 Accord deal. It was cheap. All that happened after that was that the CPI caught up with the deflator.'

On Sunday night after a week of campaigning, Keating met with his office advisers, Senator Bob McMullan and Peter Barron at the Lodge. Paul was preparing for a debate with Hewson. We met in the ground floor library. Along two walls were shelves of books reaching to the ceiling. There was a couch, two deep armchairs, and numerous straight-backed armchairs brought in for the occasion. Barron had apparently been there for most of the afternoon, suggesting lines and responding to Paul's suggestions. There were six or so advisers – everyone had something to say, no one wanted to be left out, and no doubt Keating felt all of them should feel involved even though, at this point, they could not really contribute. By now he either knew or did not know the main policy lines, the facts and the arguments. Campaigns are matters of logistics and organisation, of tactics and response. They are best handled by a small number of people.

Barron was smoking. A maid opened the doors onto the terrace to exhaust the smoke, which put Barron in an uncomfortable draught. We were lined up on chairs opposite – Mark Ryan, Don Watson, Don Russell, Greg Turnbull, Ric Simes, Ashton Calvert, Bob McMullan, Anne de Salis, the Prime Minister's administrative and ethnic affairs adviser, Anne Summers and me.

Paul sat making notes on a white legal pad. He used a very fat Mont Blanc pen, although it was more often than not missing. On this occasion he lost the pen almost while writing with it, until we discovered it hiding behind a teacup. A bit later it appeared to run out of ink.

He asked whether he should defend a ten-year record or a one-year record, as well as looking forward. This was a way of asking whether he should present himself as a totally new phenomenon or as the former Treasurer in the Hawke Government who was now Prime Minister.

McMullan said, 'This mustn't be a referendum on the last ten years, or even the last year. It must be a decision on what we will do. You should take the view that the problems are a given – the issue is, how do you solve them?'

Paul went through the lines. Employment was strengthening; there was $130 billion in development allowance applications on the books; the government was locked on to Asia. By contrast, the Opposition was simply proposing a huge new tax on spending, as if this was a cure-all.

As usual, Keating was urged to say he was distressed by unemployment. 'Cheap sentiment,' he said, 'is the villain of public life.'

The negatives for Hewson were GST, contracts, and Medicare. The positives for us were Asia, investment, and caring.

The following Tuesday I visited him in his suite at the Hyatt on Collins in Melbourne. 'The campaign is going down like a turd in a well,' he remarked cheerfully. The first Labor Party advertisements were laughably bad. Mark Ryan and Don Watson were fighting Bob Hogg.

Keating debated with Hewson on Thursday 18 February. The Prime Minister was shrill and venomous, which didn't look good. But he did force Hewson to talk about the GST, which placed it back in the centre of the campaign.

At seven that evening we met Kelty and Ross at Kirribilli House. Kelty had a draft Accord containing some proposals on the form of a national wage increase, which I did not think we could accept. All employees would get the increase unless they had an enterprise agreement. The increase would be given only after attempts to get an enterprise agreement had failed. Paul was changing into a dinner jacket for a function. He came in and out of the discussion in the Kirribilli House sitting room while dressing. We were due to meet the ACTU Wages Committee in Melbourne the following day. Keating wanted it postponed. He was worried about the increases proposed in the new agreement, and about the employment target of 500 000 jobs. But there was now no time to negotiate. 'Bill, I trust you,' Paul remarked hopefully, leaving in a dinner jacket for his next campaign stop.

We met the ACTU in the Cabinet room in Melbourne the following day. There were nearly fifty officials sitting at the table or behind it. Kelty sat in the middle, between Ross and Ferguson. On the opposite side in the middle were Keating and Industrial Relations Minister Peter Cook, with Russell and me behind, and a staff member or two for Cook. In the centre was a large floral arrangement ordered by Guy Nelligan.

The current document now had the 'safety net' going to everyone who did not get an enterprise bargaining increase. There was no commitment to absorb the safety net increase into overaward payments.

Bill spoke first, recalling Keating as Shadow Treasurer walking into the first Accord meeting in Sydney before the 1983 election. Pat Clancy had been there, and Charlie Fitzgibbon. Kelty remembered that Keating had said, 'You can't take this seriously. It's just for the election.'

Kelty summarised the document: 'You have an agreement with the union movement that you are going to put jobs first – at least 500 000 new jobs, also maintain low levels of inflation. We paid for low inflation and we don't want it to go away. Also, we will continue with the devolution of the wages system. There will be access to tribunals to assist the parties and as a catalyst for enterprise bargains.

'There are three steps to get the increases. The union must try to get an enterprise bargain.'

While he was talking I quizzed Iain Ross on the omissions from the agreements. He whispered that Paul should insist on including capacity to pay and absorption.

Paul then responded, asking for both of these. The union secretaries complained bitterly.

Keating said, 'Are you out in the jungle or not? You can't have arbitration and enterprise bargaining too. You are walking back from Accord 6. But you can't walk back – you are in danger from a conservative government. To fall back on arbitrated increases for the higher paid is crazy.'

We then got language that the commission would have regard for 'normal criteria', which meant capacity to pay, and that the arbitrated safety net would apply primarily to lower-paid workers.

Two days before the poll (Thursday 11 March) Paul stopped by my office. I said I thought we were a little behind. 'Yes,' he agreed, 'we are a little behind. But the uncertainty is so great that not even I can say for sure that we will lose.' The campaign had been good, though. We had used the right material at the right times. He himself, he said, was prepared for any outcome, including defeat. 'A year ago when we started out on this, it was a bit of a lark, wasn't it?' he recalled. 'We were behind then, and we're behind now.'

The night before the poll (Friday 12 March) he had dinner with his whole staff at the Imperial Peking Harbourside. When Paul spoke he said that it had been a good campaign, and the outcome was uncertain.

'I know they don't like us,' he said smiling. 'They don't really want to vote for us, but they may. They don't want us, so we had to convince them they would like the other side even less. They don't love us, but we don't want them to love us – we want their votes. They know that too. They know we don't want them to love us. After ten years and a million unemployed, we should not be in the race, but they're finding it very hard to vote for that mean bastard. How good it would be to have three years! The revenge of it!' He talked about multiculturalism, Aboriginals and the arts. If we won we would have a new mandate.

On Saturday night Keating watched the results coming through in a room in the Bankstown Sports Centre. 'It's a tough game,' he said, as Hewson conceded. In the last week or so, he told me, he had thought we would win.

16

IN HIS OWN
RIGHT

Elected with a bigger majority, Paul was exuberant, good humoured, shocked. The win was so much more than any of us had expected. The dismay of our opponents, confident of victory, was irresistibly hilarious. But as the head of the Department of Prime Minister and Cabinet, Mike Keating, warned us at a meeting at 11.30 the following morning in the Ramada Renaissance in Sydney, the re-elected government faced some formidable problems. Chief among these, he believed, was the trajectory of the federal budget deficit. On the calculations of the Department of Prime Minister and Cabinet, with no spending cuts or new revenue sources, the deficit in the financial year beginning 1 July 1993 would be $18 billion. Getting it down to a more reasonable level would mean difficult spending cuts and tax increases. As the economic expansion continued, the deficit would wind down, but by 1996–97 it would not be the surplus we had once projected, or the deficit of around 1 per cent of GDP we had later announced, but a deficit of more than 2 per cent of GDP. 'Within the next few years,' Michael Keating told us, before he drove over to Kirribilli to tell the Prime Minister the same thing, 'we will need to find an extra $10 billion.' Finding means to fill the gap would be the central issue of budget policy with which Keating, John Dawkins and then Ralph Willis would wrestle during the next three years – and their successors thereafter.

Eager to reorganise his ministry and lay down some of the main lines of policy for the new term, Paul postponed a post-election break. He scheduled a meeting with the ACTU executive on the Friday following his victory. During the week I met with officials of the Department of Industrial Relations and advisers to the Minister for Industrial Relations to draw up a list of reforms. A senior official in the Department of Industrial Relations, Lynne Tacy, and adviser to Industrial Relations Minister Peter Cook, Ashley Mason, had already developed the key points.

Over the year we had found industrial relations to be one of our weakest policy areas. We had moved away from central national wage decisions and arbitrated settlements, but we had failed to create the means of reaching enterprise bargains for most of the workforce covered by federal awards. Legislation in 1992 had removed the power of the Australian Industrial Relations Commission to refuse to approve enterprise bargains, except where the agreement disadvantaged employees compared with the award. It was now easier to reach bargains, but employees had to be represented by unions. This veto power allowed some unions to resist the spread of enterprise bargaining. It also limited the making of bargains, since unions covered a minority of employees. We knew that if we wanted to press ahead with a transition to direct bargaining at the enterprise level we would have to amend the legislation to allow employers to deal directly with their employees. Since the ACTU wanted the government to make some other changes to the legislation, we were in a strong position to insist upon this change as well.

Paul was well aware of the problem and wanted changes. Flying to Melbourne on Friday, I discussed possible reforms with him, and during the ACTU executive meeting he outlined the essentials of what would, after much conflict, ultimately be conceded by the ACTU. He told the ACTU that he would remove common law damages actions against striking employees and sign international conventions on equal pay for equal work, minimum wages, and termination and redundancy payments. The watchwords would be a minimum safety net and flexibility. But the government would need to strengthen the penalties against failure to keep agreements. He said the government would have to 'do something about small shops where there is no union' – an inoffensive way of saying we would allow enterprise bargains directly between employers and their employees as a group.

On the same flight to Melbourne, foreign affairs adviser Ashton Calvert won Paul's agreement to a program of foreign visits over the next year or so. Since meeting with President Bush in December 1991, Keating had been pursuing the idea of a meeting of APEC leaders to elevate the importance of the organisation and transfer its agenda from the middle level of the bureaucracy into the Cabinet councils of member governments. To press his views on APEC, and at the same time increase Australia's regional salience, Calvert suggested that Paul visit Korea, China and the United States, and include a visit to New Zealand, which had been postponed during 1992. Paul added Ireland and a brief stop in the United Kingdom.

Strengthened by his victory, and taking advantage of the retirement of a number of his colleagues, Paul was able to freshen his team by appointing new ministers and reshuffling portfolios. Cabinet was increased by one position. Peter Cook became Minister for Trade, Laurie Brereton Minister for Industrial Relations and Minister for Transport, Michael Lee Minister for Tourism and Minister for Communications and Alan Griffiths Minister for Industry, Technology and Regional Development. The new ministry was markedly younger. Of those who first became ministers in 1983 only Dawkins, Willis, Evans, Beazley and Paul himself were now left.

The election victory transformed Paul's political circumstances. When he had first been sworn in as Prime Minister fifteen months before he had never won an election as Prime Minister, and he faced a strong Liberal Party opponent expounding a program of radical change. Economic revival and the defeat of Hewson's challenge were the two overriding priorities of government. Now he was Prime Minister in his own right. His caucus colleagues and the trade unions were delighted and, for a while, grateful. The economy was now growing, and, although growth was now slow, we were confident it would be robust by the time Paul faced another election. Hewson did not resign, but he was clearly finished as Liberal leader. For the foreseeable future, the Liberal Opposition was not a threat.

For all these reasons Paul's position in late March 1993 looked quite strong, but within his office we were also aware that the next election would be quite difficult. As Paul said in his speech to his staff on the eve of victory, he knew the people did not like his government much, but they liked the Opposition less. We knew now that by 1996, when he would face another election, Labor would have been in power for thirteen years and be asking for another three. We knew that Fightback! had been extremely important in turning voters against the Opposition, and it would not make that mistake twice. Although I think we did not understand it well enough at the time, it was also true that the terms of Keating's victory limited his options in ways that would make government difficult. He was committed to a two-stage tax cut, which was now legislated. He could not introduce a uniform wholesale sales tax or a general goods and services tax without being accused of the grossest betrayal.

More important than any of these considerations, however, in determining the character of the next three years was the fact that major elements of the reform agenda to which Paul was committed, and which were within his power to accomplish, had already been enacted. Now Prime Minister in his own right, Keating had achieved the last of the goals he had set himself in his political career. He had told his colleagues and his staff that he wanted only one full term, and there was logic as well as guile in these assurances. The structure of his career was more akin to that of Sir William McMahon and Harold Holt, both of whom had become Prime Minister after a period in the Treasury portfolio. The three prime ministers preceding Keating – Gough Whitlam, Malcolm Fraser and Bob Hawke – had all become Prime Minister directly from Opposition leader. Of the three, only Fraser had had prior ministerial experience, and not in a key economic portfolio.

These three predecessors came to office with an extensive program of change that they attempted to implement. Keating, however, had come to office after eight years as Treasurer, during which he had implemented a program of profound and far-reaching change. Even as Australia pitched into recession, the program of change continued with the 1991 industry statement accelerating tariff reductions. Keating could look back at the float, the deregulation of banking, tariff cuts, the spending cuts and tax reform of the 1980s, the Accords and the sequence of wage–tax trade-offs, which had disciplined government spending while allowing inflation to fall away – all important changes; all achieved. What could he do as Prime Minister to match them? In the mid 1980s he had often said that what he did as Treasurer was more important than anything he could do as Prime Minister. In the opening months of 1994 there seemed to be a good chance he was right. Running against Hewson, he had often said that the worst possible outcome would be if Hewson became Prime Minister in time to take the credit for the transformed economy that Labor had created – a more competitive and resilient economy with low inflation, higher productivity, a stronger trade account. He thought, in other words, that as Prime Minister he could enjoy the fruits of his earlier work.

Certainly, the major tasks of economic reform were changing. The dollar could only be floated once, banks only be deregulated once. Tariffs could be cut more, but at 5 per cent for most manufactures, 15 per cent for motor vehicles and between 15 and 30 per cent for the textiles, clothing and footwear industries, Australia was already a low-tariff country. The industrial relations system needed to be reformed, principally because wage agreements were not made at an enterprise level between employers and employees. He was now proceeding to alter the framework of industrial relations to allow non-union enterprise agreements. But as long as Australia was to have a system of collective bargaining underpinned by minimum awards, rather than the alternative of individual contracts, the reform Keating proposed was as far as he wished to go, needed to go, or would be allowed by his colleagues to go. He was removing the major obstacle to the proliferation of enterprise bargaining. The Opposition would criticise the right of unions to become parties to such agreements, but there was little evidence that this provision made a substantial difference to the attractiveness of enterprise bargaining once the limits of employer and union rights had been clearly established by the commission. The substantial 'reform of the labour market' called for by his opponents really meant the abolition of compulsory awards covering wages and working conditions and their replacement by individual contracts. Keating did not regard this as any sort of economic reform, and hoped the Opposition would be tempted once again to put the issue before the electorate.

Many useful economic reforms were yet to be carried out, but now most of them required the cooperation of the states. The Hilmer competition reforms, for example, required state cooperation, as did reforms in public utilities and ports. They were long, slow reforms with marginal rewards, in which most of the work was done by officials in the federal and state bureaucracies, patching together compromises and leaving to premiers and the Prime Minister those issues on which they could not reach agreement. Keating was good at compromises, partly because of his reputation for truculence. But nothing he could now do in economic reform could approach the significance and value of what he had been able to do in the 1980s.

His political circumstances had changed, and his political style began to change. Exhausted, pondering the ways he should approach this gift of three clear years of government, Paul took a break towards the end of March. By the time he returned he had formed more views about his term of government and his own role. He described these in a staff meeting in the Cabinet Annex on 5 April. He told us that people perceived it as a new government, and they expected value. Over the last year he had had to drive the government from the Prime Minister's Office. That was inevitable in an election year. Now he wanted to encourage ministers to do their own thing – so long as they had reached agreement with him and Cabinet on what 'their own thing' was. He himself wanted to keep a grip on the republic, Aborigines and parliamentary reform. Other areas of government would be handled by the responsible ministers rather than from the Prime Minister's Office. After some discussion at the meeting he agreed to kick off industrial relations reform because his imprimatur would help Brereton. But contrary to the later interpretation of his role, Keating insisted on reverting to the more limited prime ministerial role of Hawke. This ruled out, for example, a cross-government statement like One Nation. By implication it also restricted the role of his staff and of the Department of Prime Minister and Cabinet. Ultimately Keating would find himself compelled to resume the wider role he played during 1992, but it was not his preference or inclination in shaping his job in 1993.

Now that the election was over he also wanted to modify his political style. For a forthcoming speech at an Institute of Directors lunch in Melbourne, his first major policy announcement after the election, he wanted 'a haughty sort of speech'. (Paul uses *haughty* to mean something closer to *lofty* than *proud*, although it contains both senses.) He said the media in Parliament House had been running the agenda too much. The government should not have to meet their demands, he said, and perform tricks in Parliament. He wanted to get ministers and their staffs out of Parliament House offices into department offices, and reduce the Question Time theatre by scheduling less frequent appearances. He wanted Parliament on fewer days, with one minister a day answering questions and perhaps electronic voting. He should be above the ruck – not down in it. 'For want of a better word,' he said, 'I should be Menzian.'

Until the shock of the loss of the seat of Canberra in the by-election in March 1995, Paul would attempt to conduct himself according to the rules he laid down at that staff meeting. He would appear less frequently in Question Time, and subject himself less frequently to interrogation by reporters. But in the 1990s it was not possible to be Menzian or, at all events, not possible for Paul Keating. He did not gain in stature by becoming more distant, and he disarmed himself of two weapons that accounted for a good deal of his success in politics: his ability to dominate his opponents in Parliament, and his ability to shape the way senior reporters in Canberra interpreted the trajectory of political debate. Denying himself these two advantages would cost him more and more as events turned against him. (No member of his staff, so far as I know, suggested this approach to him. I doubt that any of us thought it a good idea. But at the meeting none of us voiced an objection or anticipated the problems that later became apparent. Our failings were of omission.)

At the same time Paul decided on a loftier approach to office; he began to interpret the outcome of the March election not as a rejection of Fightback! but as an endorsement of a philosophy of growth with equity and of engagement with Asia. He also believed that women, people interested in the arts, and Aborigines had been important in his election victory, although the weight of evidence was that Paul had recovered the traditional Labor vote diminished in the last two elections. 'Pig's arse, pig's arse,' he would tell Victorian backbencher Peter Cleeland during a fierce caucus debate in September 1993, after Cleeland said that Labor had not so much won the election as the Liberals had lost it. Keating rightly interpreted the view that he had won by default as an attack on the legitimacy of his government and its ability to act. But as the months went by Paul actually seemed to convince himself of his story, despite the clear evidence of studies of the poll result, and despite the good sense of his own interpretation of the mood in his speech to his staff on the eve of the election.

Whatever it meant originally, the phrase 'true believers', which Paul had used in his election night victory speech, confirmed a sense of exclusivity that had always been a tendency in Keating's inner circle. In the context of an overwhelming election victory, 'true believers' were not the minority who had kept the faith. More than half the electorate were apparently true believers. The phrase came to signify not those who supported him and his policies, but the much smaller group who were always firmly convinced he would win the election. In this sense it should not have included Paul, most of his government, or many of his staff. The phrase and the fuzzy idea behind it encouraged a way of looking at things that would not, in the end, help Keating or the government.

It would take several years and two changes in the Opposition leadership before the consequences of some of these earlier attitudes became apparent. Meanwhile it all seemed to hang together quite well, and rapid economic growth and declining unemployment disguised the difficulties. During the election campaign he had spun together themes about a social safety net as well as a more resilient and competitive economy. He had spoken about bringing forward those falling behind, taking everyone with us, about soft hearts and hard heads. It was drawn from all his experience in Labor politics and clearly expressed in both the 'social wage' aspects of the Accord and in the decisions during the 1980s to redirect welfare towards those most in need. After the election he continued to tie together the themes of economic progress and a social safety net. The theme could be extended to include immigrant communities and Aborigines and to contrast Australia with the United States. Interpreted as a 'new Keating', it was really a new emphasis. As Treasurer, he had talked up Labor's credentials in economic reform. As Prime Minister, he was emphasising his commitment to keeping the country together.

Keating knew during the run-up to the 1993 election that his biggest problem was the widespread conviction that the government had been in office too long. It followed that this sentiment would be even stronger in 1996. He explained this to caucus in a speech soon after the 1993 victory. He also knew that John Hewson and Fightback! would not be there in 1996. It could be a difficult election – perhaps more difficult than 1993. By 1996, however, unemployment would be down and the economy would be strong. And while Hewson would not survive, it was not at all obvious who would replace him, or whether another Liberal leader would do better. As the months went by, with better economic news and a more serious Liberal leadership problem, the balance of probabilities shifted, so that by the beginning of 1994 and for most of that year Keating seemed to have an excellent chance of winning the next election.

National savings, industrial relations reform and parliamentary arrangements were all now on the table as we prepared for the Institute of Directors speech in Melbourne. With the election behind him Keating was for the first time able to give most of his attention to long-term policies. 'The truth is,' he said, flying down to deliver the speech on 21 April, 'in the next five months we can do anything.' The heart of the speech was a public declaration of what Paul had already told the ACTU. He would seek to extend enterprise bargaining to non-union workplaces by allowing employees collectively to make agreements directly with employers. The government would discourage the commission from arbitrating wage settlements. It would instead focus on keeping a minimum set of wages and conditions in awards in good repair. It would also arbitrate general minimum increases, which would apply only to those on the minimum rate in awards. The commission would be asked to simplify awards to the major areas of wages and conditions, so that work arrangements could be agreed between employers and employees in enterprises. These points were broadly agreed between me and the ACTU assistant secretary, Iain Ross, as the speech was written, and were exactly those that we later legislated.

The speech behind us, industrial relations reform passed over to Laurie Brereton until Paul was drawn in at the conclusion of a deal in October. Other ministers brought forward legislation to implement election promises, while John Dawkins began to struggle with the irreconcilable demands to produce a surplus a few years on, while at the same time making the tax cuts we had promised in One Nation. Since One Nation, the estimates of tax revenue three years out had dramatically declined, making the tax cuts harder to deliver while Paul was deepening his commitment to them by putting the new tax scales in legislation.

Paul himself was left with half a dozen issues to deal with. One was the consequences of the High Court's Mabo decision, which overturned the view that at the time of European settlement Aboriginal Australians had no land tenure system that Australian law would need to recognise. The decision on 3 June 1992 instead asserted that common law recognised native title where there was continuous association with the land, and where the title had not been extinguished by a valid act. The Mabo decision had hardly figured in the election campaign, and the advice reaching Keating until after the campaign was that the decision would have only a very restricted impact, if any. It was rapidly becoming apparent, however, that it would change a great deal. It meant that Aboriginal groups could bring legal action to claim land. It seemed to suggest at a minimum that, if they could show that they had had a continuous association with the land, and no valid title to it had been issued after 1788, they could successfully claim ownership. It was possible that the Mabo decision might also be wider than that. While Parliament could override the Mabo decision, it could only do so by discriminating against Aboriginals and repealing its own anti-discrimination legislation. Something would have to be done to clarify the circumstances in which Aboriginal groups could claim land and the procedures they would use. Whatever was done would, however, have to recognise the validity of private titles issued after 1788. For Keating it was, as we immediately recognised, an issue in which he could at best avoid a catastrophic failure. If he failed to find an acceptable solution, the value of mining and pastoral businesses would be decimated by unresolved land claims. If he did successfully find a solution that allowed Aboriginals a clear way to achieve title in even the most limited circumstances, he would not be thanked by an overwhelmingly white and urban electorate. Keating had established a consultative process with the states in October 1992. Mabo would be on the agenda for a COAG meeting in June.

He was also committed to implementing the Hilmer report on national competition policy. It recommended the extension of competition laws to state instrumentalities and unincorporated bodies like law firms. The legislation would require state cooperation. So too would progress on an open national market in gas, a national electricity grid, and a harmonised national injury compensation system. All these issues were handled through the framework of the Council of Australian Governments, which Paul chaired.

The final major issue on the agenda in the early months of the new government was long-term unemployment. Work by Bruce

Chapman and colleagues at the Australian National University demonstrated that the numbers of long-term unemployed would continue
to increase long after the total number of unemployed began to come
down. Mike Keating set up a task force to find solutions.

The diary that Peter Robinson built up on his computer was
already crowded. Somehow he would also have find time for Paul's
trips to New Zealand, China, Korea, the United States, the United
Kingdom and Ireland. It would be a busy year.

Released from the daily weight of the recession and unemployment
that had threatened his career and his record, Keating hoped he could
also leave economic policy to the Treasurer. Growth had been very
slow, and it would not be until July that Paul would confidently predict the economy was 'on the move', but we expected increasing
employment, low inflation, and lower interest rates. It was hard to
reconcile rapidly reducing the budget deficit with election commitments. Paul's commitment to tax cuts was the single biggest obstacle
to producing a budget surplus within a reasonable time. Dawkins'
strategy was to draw him deeper and deeper into the budget process
until Keating himself conceded that altering the tax cuts was the least
unpleasant of the alternatives available.

On 22 April 1993 the troika of Keating, Dawkins and Finance
Minister Ralph Willis, with their assistants, met in the Cabinet Annex.
Like the Cabinet room itself, it is windowless, deeply carpeted and
soundproofed. Its silences are so complete that conversation in the
annex has a peculiar intrusive ring. Spotlights had been replaced by
more diffuse ceiling lights, so Keating no longer wore his blue-tinted
spectacles or had to hold his hand over his eyes. Portraits of the
explorer William Hovell and the writer Henry Lawson hung on the
walls.

The meeting was to look at three Treasury papers that initiated
the budget cycle for the year. They covered the economic outlook,
the fiscal or budget outlook, and budget processes. As Dawkins
promptly explained, the main message of the fiscal outlook paper

was that, even with reasonable economic growth, the deficit would be around $10 billion in 1996–97. We had promised a deficit of around 1 per cent, which would be $5 billion. Dawkins sought revenue increases that built up to $5 billion. 'In this Budget we must take action to build up,' he said, 'even if we don't own up to the magnitude of it.' There would be papers coming forward on revenue options, he said, but not until later. In the meantime, 'we didn't want to know about it.' It was only necessary to know that in his view, 'There are enough options around to get revenues up without a big new tax, and keeping the income tax cuts.'

Finance Minister Ralph Willis had opposed the tax cuts all along. 'Do we really have to regard the income tax cuts as inviolate?' he asked.

'We have up to now,' said Keating. 'Maybe we should wait and see what the revenue options look like.'

'Last year, Ralph, you asked us why we should change the rates so far ahead,' Dawkins commented. 'So now I'm agreeing with you. The issue is maybe pulling the second cut.'

'The tax cuts we were matching no longer exist,' said Willis, sensibly.

'Of course,' said Keating, off on another track, 'the scandalous thing is that they could never have made the tax cuts. Never.' He was annoyed by commentators calling for spending cuts. 'Whatever you do for them,' he said, 'they put it in their pocket and stay on your back. You should never feed them. They line up politically. The lushes of the Opposition were excused. The party of economic attack has to meet exemplary standards.' The meeting ended without decision.

The essential problem in the Budget was that Commonwealth Government spending had been cut from the 29 per cent or so of GDP it had been early in the 1980s to around 24 per cent of GDP, but spending on labour market programs, public debt interest and health services sustained it now at around 26 per cent of GDP. In Keating's experience, spending at around this level was reasonable in the long term, and it would be very difficult to get it down. But while spending was sustained, revenue was falling. Low inflation and low wage increases cut into expected income tax, and the rate of

increase of revenue from taxes on crude oil, petrol, alcohol and tobacco
was falling. As a percentage of GDP, tax was falling to around 22 per
cent of GDP, from more than 26 per cent in the mid 1980s.

In the mid 1980s the budget problem had been to find spending
cuts to make room for the tax cuts that underpinned the Accord. In
the 1990s cuts were much harder to find. Those identified in the 1993
Budget meeting totalled around $1 billion, and caused so much con-
troversy that they had to be modified to win Democrat and Green
support in the Senate. As Dawkins remarked during the 1993 meetings, 'We've been over this stuff so many times in the last ten years,
there is nothing much more in it.' The 'brave days', he said, when they
slashed the budget, had now passed. The only serious option open to
the government was to change the tax cuts promised in One Nation.

Dawkins had been optimistic in April that the government could
afford the first tax cut and still meet its deficit targets with revenue
measures that were not in themselves new taxes. But by July 1994
further Treasury and Finance analysis increased the 1996–97 gap
from $10 billon to $16 billion after various changes to the estimates
of growth and of revenue. The government now needed to find $11b.
Dawkins now believed that the second tax cut would have to be cancelled and didn't really like the first cut. Keating alighted on the option
of bringing forward the first tax cut to the soon-to-be-announced
1993–94 Budget and postponing the next round of tax cuts beyond
1996–97. It would be 'apples on sticks' if it worked out, he told us
with a bright smile. Otherwise we were 'up the flue'. He won Dawkins'
agreement to announcing the first cut and postponing the second,
but there was an important nuance of difference. To Dawkins, postponing the second meant postponing indefinitely. To Keating, it meant
postponing them to a certain date, and then paying them, in full as
promised. The critical words in the speech were fought out between
Don Russell and Dawkins' senior adviser, Alan Evans, and between
Keating and Dawkins. Russell won by slipping words at the last minute
into a speech by Keating at the National Press Club on Thursday
22 July, making it clear that the first round of tax cuts would be paid
'in full'. Dawkins was annoyed.

By the time he brought down the Budget in August, Dawkins had threatened to resign three times in private meetings with Keating. The Budget proposed a deficit of $16b – as a percentage of GDP a lower outcome than the previous peaks of 1975–76 and 1983–84, but nonetheless a big number. With reasonable growth, the government asserted, the deficit would be brought back to around 1 per cent of GDP (nearly $6b) by 1996–97. It would be another year before Keating formally cancelled the second of the tax cuts promised in One Nation. Containing a range of indirect tax increases and spending cuts, the Budget immediately ran into trouble in the Labor caucus and the Senate. It was towards the end of the year before a compromise cleared the Senate, and into 1994 before the caucus and government settled down. Keating would later say that the 1993 Budget had put his re-elected government off on the wrong foot. But tax increases and spending cuts were unquestionably essential to meet immediate and prospective deficit problems, and neither he nor any of us on his staff at the time had cleverer ideas than did the Treasurer and his department. By early 1994, with another Budget being prepared and Dawkins announcing his unexpected resignation, the 1993 Budget was forgotten. Without its severity and John Dawkins' resolution, however, the government's deficit problem several years later would have been far worse.

Within days of becoming Prime Minister in December 1991 Keating had expressed to his advisers and to US President George Bush a well-developed view about APEC. The organisation bonded East Asia, which included Australia's most important economic partners, to the United States, which was our most important security partner. It was built over a thriving economic relationship, which it could sustain and encourage. It reinforced Australia's links with East Asia, which was the most rapidly growing economic region in the world. It gave Australia a seat at the table with major powers like the United States, Japan and China. If the US looked to East Asia for its economic future, then both East Asia and the United States would be better off, and Australia would have its most significant security and cultural partner locked in with its closest neighbours and economic partners.

In several major speeches since becoming Prime Minister he had suggested that APEC vigorously pursue an agenda of liberalising trade by harmonising product standards in the region, and minimising customs delays and documentation. At the beginning of the 1993 election campaign he had set out these ideas in a major speech, and reinforced them in private meetings with APEC leaders over the year.

While wrestling with the deficit he continued to lobby hard for an APEC leaders' meeting. He pressed it in a Canberra meeting with Japanese Prime Minister Miyazawa at the end of April, and with New Zealand's Prime Minister Bolger in May. Keating knew Australia was a small country compared with Japan, China and the United Sates, and it needed to 'use leverage' where it could. Through APEC, it could win 'a seat at the table' with the bigger economies and exercise some influence on them. But if APEC was to be important, leaders must participate.

Visiting Korea and China in the last weeks of June, he continued to talk about the possibilities of APEC. 'The G7 is weak,' he told Chinese Premier Li Peng during a meeting in the Great Hall of the People in Beijing. 'We have slow growth in the US and recession in Europe. We need a political structure to fill the vacuum. APEC offers great opportunities to increase trade and discourage the US from bilateralism.' To see the leaders of APEC meet 'would change the balance in the world'. But China had to weigh in. 'If the APEC plane loses altitude,' he told Zhu Rongji, then responsible for economic policy, 'we won't be on the plane when it crashes. We will be jumping off. So we don't mind pushing it – but we need help.'

With the Chinese and the Koreans Keating was in the company of professional peers. His conversation with Korean President Kim Young Sam was shop. With the Chinese he shared political observations. 'Normally when your growth runs out, your luck runs out with it,' he told one official in conversation. 'But we were able to beat the system by putting across the idea of a country gaining confidence in itself. Complimenting Li Peng on a prolonged discourse, he said that 'everyone in public life has to be a good talker'. At lunch with the President of China, Jiang Zemin, he said, 'politics requires the same skills the world over. It is the universal occupation.' He also warmed to the commercial viewpoint of Chinese officials. Suggesting that China invest more in Australian minerals and energy developments, Keating told Li Peng, 'There is an old saying in commerce – you make your money when you buy.' The Premier nodded assent as this was translated.

At the beginning of July US officials told us that President Clinton had agreed to hold a leaders' meeting at the same time as the scheduled APEC ministers' meeting in Seattle in November. Keating wrote to Clinton congratulating him and confirming his attendance. A few weeks later he wrote to Indonesian President Suharto, whom he identified as the most important of the ASEAN leaders. Now that the first meeting in the US had been accepted, his goal was to reach agreement on having a second meeting in Indonesia the following year. A single meeting in the US could be a media event only. Agreement on a second meeting, which was the main result he sought from Seattle, established a process in which leaders would require imaginative proposals, results and announcements. Indonesia was scheduled to host the 1994 APEC meetings. President Suharto would be the right man in the right position to make a second leaders' meeting a success.

In September Keating visited Clinton in the White House, and two months later the first of the APEC leaders' meetings was held on Blake Island, near Seattle. It was the first time the leaders of the region had ever met as a group. Endorsing APEC's goals of trade liberalisation, the leaders agreed to meet again in Indonesia the following year – Keating's suggestion, and one that confirmed his interest in making the relationship between Indonesia and Australia a pillar of regional cooperation.

The Seattle meetings were the high point of a difficult year. Don Russell had left for the job of Australian Ambassador to the United

States in August, and over the next few years Paul would fail to find a replacement who could replicate Don's peculiar suitability to Keating's style of government and to the balance of intimacy and distance in his nature. He found better administrators and people who had smoother relationships with those around them, but he could not find anyone who possessed Don's intelligence, loyalty, serenity, and fondness for the discreet exercise of power. Don had also held the balance of power within Keating's own office, and when he left it shifted markedly away from cool heads to warm hearts. It had been and remained a cordial office in which the various contending influences respected their opponents' competence and contributions and the need to find a balance between the dry economic viewpoint and large parts of the Labor constituency. Foreign affairs adviser Ashton Calvert also left at the end of the year, and political adviser Mark Ryan and I had left by March 1994.

From his first few months as Prime Minister, Keating had at first tentatively and then with increasing clarity suggested that Australia replace the English monarch with an Australian as its head of state. This required a change to the Constitution that would make Australia a republic. The grounds for the change were, within the Labor Party, so obvious that it required no argument. Equally, the benefits of an entirely ceremonial change of this kind had seemed quite marginal. Like most Labor leaders in the 1980s, Bob Hawke had been in favour of an Australian head of state but had never thought the time was ripe to pursue it. Bill Hayden, though he had no special reverence for the English monarch, had long been concerned that what was apparently a ceremonial change might involve important consequences. In particular he was concerned that an Australian head of state might capture real powers, as Sir John Kerr had already demonstrated were available to the Queen's representative in Australia, and on occasion be driven into conflict with the Prime Minister. In his formal campaign opening speech in February 1993, Paul had inserted the promise to seek a 'Federal Republic of Australia'. On being

re-elected he had appointed Sydney investment banker Malcolm Turnbull to chair a committee to report on proposals for an Australian
republic.

Paul's view, as he worked it out over 1993, was that the change
should be as minimal as possible, and that in particular the Australian
head of state should be appointed or elected in such a way that the
office could not compete for power with a prime minister who had
a majority in the House and whose government was not refused supply by the Senate. His preferred form was for the Prime Minister to
have the right to select the name of the Australian President, with the
requirement that the choice be agreed to by both houses of Parliament. Beyond the marginal changes Paul did not wish to go. In speeches
and press conferences he argued that Australia had reached maturity
as a nation, and its identity ought to be confirmed by a constitutional
change that allowed the appointment of an Australian head of state.
By the beginning of 1995 he and his colleagues had refined these proposals. He proposed a national referendum in the next term of parliament. In a speech to parliament in mid 1995 he set up a timetable
for the move to a republic.

The politics of the change were unusual. There was no urgency
in achieving a republic. In a period in which more substantial political issues were infrequent, young people were attracted by the idea
of a republic. With a good part of its support among ageing conservatives, the Opposition was unable to support a republic and
could perhaps be induced to oppose it, thus casting themselves as
opponents of progress. Within the Labor Party counsels, however,
there were those who properly warned that more votes might be lost
than won by giving high priority to an essentially symbolic issue.
For all these reasons it made sense for Keating to declare himself in
favour of a republic, to deliver a speech on the subject every now
and then, but to move only very slowly towards the goal. In some
ways it was more useful to be in favour of a republic than to have
a republic. Initially caught out by the swing to the republic, Opposition leader John Howard soon came up with his own proposal for
a convention to consider the issue. As an election issue it rapidly

faded. It was not a high-priority concern with any substantial section of the electorate.

By 1994 some of the detailed policy work of 1993 was ready for announcement. There was a green paper on employment and then the Working Nation statement funding training and job creation programs for the long-term unemployed. Spending on these programs would be provided by the sale of Australia's Commonwealth-owned civilian airports. It was followed by the 1994–95 Budget, which took the estimated deficit down to $11.7 billion. Adopting a program of trade liberalisation in APEC, the Prime Minister, the Minister for Foreign Affairs and the Minister for Trade, with their departments and advisers, worked with other APEC governments towards adopting the APEC Eminent Persons Group's goal of free trade in the region, a goal adopted by APEC leaders meeting in Bogor, Indonesia, in November.

In the economy, growth was now quite brisk. Undetected by the Commonwealth Statistician, another investment boom was gathering pace. It would rival in size and strength the capital spending boom of the late 1980s. The current account widened to peak at 6 per cent of GDP during 1995, and the Reserve Bank acted to increase interest rates by a total of three percentage points from the middle to the end of 1994. Unlike the earlier episode, however, the government had not committed itself to a current account goal, and it did not attempt to repeat the protracted tightening of 1988 and 1989.

The economy continued to expand, but with the election of John Howard as Leader of the Opposition the government slipped behind in the opinion polls. Through the middle of 1995 Keating clawed back some of the lead by a vigorous advocacy of a republic, and by the May Budget, which achieved a surplus by selling off the remainder of the Commonwealth Bank. His long-running defence of Health Minister Carmen Lawrence against accusations that she had been aware of the misuse of Family Law Court material in a petition presented to the Western Australian Parliament distracted him from the election battle, however, and by the end of 1995 the government remained well behind the Opposition. The polls suggested a settled conviction in the electorate that Labor had been in office too long. Only if Keating could convince people that Howard was as big a threat as Hewson to Medicare, industrial awards and social security, could he hope to retain office.

After I left his office at the beginning of 1994 I did not see much of Paul. Sometimes, working on APEC issues, I would be one of three or four visiting him in his office in Canberra. Staff members generally have a sceptical and affectionately patronising attitude towards their boss. Seeing Paul now as an infrequent visitor, I once again enjoyed his talent for making the world seem intelligible, exciting and full of new possibilities, at least for half an hour or so. He would recount his conversations with Suharto, for example, quickly sketch the balance of power within ASEAN, and then describe a possible combination, towards which he was working, in which Indonesia, Vietnam and Australia would be politically and economically allied as the three most powerful states in our region. It was not until the middle of December 1995 – as it turned out, four months before the election that would end his political career – that I first returned to talk to him about some matters covered in this book. Even then, though Labor had improved on its worst polls during the year, it was still further behind the Opposition than it had been in December 1993. On the polls it would lose, but the announcement, the day following my interview, of a security pact with Indonesia lifted Labor's spirits and hopes for the election expected in March. The economy was, after all, fine. Paul was disciplining himself to avoid intemperate remarks. In the end, could the voters really prefer John Howard to Paul Keating?

We talked at the Lodge, which by then had changed. There was a warmly welcoming housekeeper I hadn't met, who showed me into the sitting room. It was now the girls' music room, with a cabinet piled high with scores and a piano. The biggest change was in the lounge room or library. Bob Hawke's therapeutic chair had long gone, along with the banks of telephones. Now the emu ashtrays and kangaroo clocks had also vanished, replaced by silver-framed photographs of the children, Paul and Annita. Along one side of the room, which is quite small, Paul had put in two outsize speakers and a cabinet with his amplifier and CD player. There was a table piled with compact discs – on top were Maria Callas, Tom Jones, and Klemperer conducting Richard Strauss. On two of the walls were warm, sensuous paintings by the nineteenth-century Australian artist Rupert Bunny.

Paul himself didn't seem to have changed at all. He was wearing a dark suit with a long silk tie, white shirt and those cufflinks. He had the same way of focusing on you completely, the same energy in explaining and persuading, the same quick intensity, the same ability to slip seamlessly between the small things and great things. Explaining his father's business, he created on a coffee table an imaginary pile of low-slump concrete, describing as it settled its unique characteristics and his father's cleverness in finding a way of mixing and transporting it. He told it with such intensity and concern that I momentarily thought I understood what he was talking about. Somewhere in the house he had a book on concrete mixers, he said, suddenly intent. He might be able to find it. Disappearing for a few minutes, he came back with photocopies of the relevant pages of a book on the concrete mixing industry. He took me through those pages, too. He confirmed his boyhood peritonitis, drawing down his lower eyelid and bringing his face close to mine to show me that he had no eyelashes on his lower eyelids. 'Have to rub them with spit,' he told me again, imitating the action. Talking about his family history, he rushed into his study and emerged a few moments later with a framed photograph of his great-grandfather, a copy of the passenger list of the ship *Mangerton*, which brought John and Mary Keating and their children to Australia, marriage and death certificates, and the pencil box marked 'Matthew Keating 1847'. He then reconstructed the family tree, sitting beside me now on a lounge, running his finger over the dates and names on the documents for me to follow.

'I shouldn't be here!' he laughed, looking around the lounge room of the Lodge and thinking of his grandparents in Annandale.

'I shouldn't be here at all! A lot of it is because of my father. He was really an employer, an owner, but he kept up his interest in the Labor Party. It used to amuse him: he'd be handing out Labor Party voting tickets on the booths during an election and some of his boilermakers from Marlak would come up to him. They'd say, 'No thanks, Matty,' and pick up their ticket from the Liberal booth. '

'When I came into parliament I learned to operate inside caucus and inside Cabinet, but at the same time I had this other stuff that other members did not have – this knowledge of the business world. I knew these people, the people Dad worked with. Then there was the Whitlam Government, and the time I spent as spokesman on minerals and energy. They were important.

'Did you ever find that 1982 Max Walsh piece in the *Bulletin*? I gave an interview and the story broadly was, "Keating goes for growth". You have to remember that economic growth was not in the lexicon from around 1974 to 1980. I said to Hayden, "Use the word, use the word *growth*," and he started to do it.

'Lots of my education was on the job, when I was Treasurer, but I was always genuinely interested in how we could make Australia more competitive. I found other people were interested in the same thing – there was a good conjunction – Bill, Simon Crean in those days was part of it at the ACTU, and Dawkins and others.

'It's like anything else that's really good – it was based on a few simple ideas. The first was to open the place up and make it more competitive. The second was to integrate it with Asia. It was all built on those ideas. You might say enterprise and competition at home, opportunity abroad. But we did it all with attention to income distribution. We used the language of free markets and competition, but we were also socking money away for our constituency. You look at health, social security spending compared to 1983 – they are much bigger now. So it wasn't just tariff cuts.

'As you know, my idea is that our job as politicians is to get the changes in place, because the system runs itself. When the Liberals were in office we had bureaucratic incrementalism. It was run by public servants, and they believed in incrementalism. They had no authority, so they thought of change as a step and then another step. They thought that was good. They could never do something like the float.

'The people were very important during the 1980s. It was done by the little ERC group I had – Dawkins and a few others. We also had Bill Kelty. He could see the sword of Damocles hanging over the head of the union movement, so he was happy with the Accord and tax cuts. The other thing that made a big difference was to have private office staff. And in Treasury it was wonderful period. Even now Bernie says, "I will never see the likes of it again." To have Bernie, Higgins, David Morgan and Ted Evans all at the same time, plus an office – that made a difference.

'There was also the impact of tax cuts in taking our constituency through a period of adjustment. We made an uncompetitive economy competitive, and also gave our people real increases.

'The other thing is that the whole productivity culture has changed so much. Then there was Asia and APEC. Through the leaders' meetings and the trade liberalisation agreements we have contributed to setting up the Asia–Pacific in a way that suits us.'

It was a particularly busy day. We had only just got through his overview of the 1980s and on to the details of his early life when Allan Gyngell was shown into the sitting room, and Paul indicated our interview had to wind up. No longer part of the office, I didn't know that they would discuss the extraordinary, secret negotiations for a defence pact with Indonesia that would be revealed to an astonished press the following day, and the visit to Jakarta that Paul would then make a few days later.

There had been many events in Paul's gradual climb back from the deep hole of the Canberra by-election loss. There was the unexpected surplus in the May Budget produced by the decision to sell the remainder of the Commonwealth Bank, the republic debate, the industrial relations and Commonwealth/state debates and the Innovation statement.

But the biggest thing, I thought, the most characteristic and substantial thing, was that unexpected pact with Indonesia. One of its messages to the Australian electorate was that there might not now be a lot of difference in their policies, but Paul was a leader of substance and John Howard was not. It was one of his best moves — conceived and carried out in secrecy, dependent for its execution on the loyalty and brilliance of staff members like Gyngell and trusted intermediaries like General Peter Gration, cutting through timid and conventional concerns to change the way in which Indonesia and Australia thought about each other — a wonderful production, to be performed the following day to an astonished audience. Of course I didn't know then the outcome of the next election, which we all knew would be within three months or so, but I thought then that Paul would quite likely win, despite Labor remaining 6 per cent behind in the opinion polls.

I saw him next a few days after the New Year. I went over to Kirribilli House in the morning. At a sentry box near the gate there were two police officers who checked me through, and then I sat for a while in the lounge room, where three years before I had sat with Bill Kelty, Iain Ross and Don Russell, bickering about the Accord. There were a few newspapers on a glass-topped table and some old copies of an alternative medicine magazine. When Paul came in we moved to chairs on the verandah, Paul bringing out a straight-backed chair because, he said, his back was bad. He was wearing shorts and a T-shirt. His legs were long, thin and white. It was holiday time. On the verandah there was a surprising din of helicopters and planes overhead, motor boats cruising by the point, and boat loudspeakers describing the Harbour sights for tourists. We talked briefly about the coming election, which I assumed would be called soon after he returned from holiday. I said I thought his chances were now looking better than a few months before. 'Could be,' he said with professional realism, 'but we can lose seven seats in Queensland. We can lose government in Queensland.'

I wanted him to go back over some events of the 1960s and 1970s — the Blaxland pre-selection, his relationship with John Ducker, the leadership struggle between Hayden and Whitlam and then between

Hawke and Hayden. Paul was pleasant and thoughtful throughout the couple of hours of our discussion, but it was obviously difficult for him to drag his mind from the imminent election campaign, which would determine the conditions under which he would end his political career, back to events even before the crowded years as Treasurer. Either way, I thought, he would go — immediately if he lost; in a year or two if he won. But there is all the difference in the world between constructing a new life following a defeat and arranging to commence it at a time of your own choosing, from the prestige of office.

'It's so long ago,' he said, laughing and shaking his head. 'So long ago. It's like I've led four lives.' There was his life growing up in Bankstown, the fourteen years of his life in Federal Parliament before 1983, the eight years as Treasurer, and now four years almost to the day as Prime Minister. Four closely connected lives, one leading into the other, but in unexpected as well as predictable ways.

His biggest concern about his record was that it should seen as something deliberate, planned and voluntary, not as something either accidental or inevitable. 'Don't fall into the trap of seeing it like Paul Kelly does,' he said, as he had several times before.

Labor's poll rating did not rebound in the New Year as its strategists had hoped. Paul went into the campaign well behind, caught up to within four percentage points, then fell behind again. John Howard promised he would make only minimal changes. The only issues were Labor's long stay in office and Paul Keating versus John Howard. The polls consistently showed higher approval for Keating, but Howard was not feared or widely disliked. On election night I went out to the Bankstown Sports Club, a palace of stainless steel and marble veneer. The swing against Labor in New South Wales and Queensland was so big that the election outcome was apparent within a few moments of the first returns. Paul's staff watched glumly as minister after minister lost their seats. At about 9.30 p.m. Paul appeared on the stage of the hall.

He had a few notes. 'We ran a hard campaign,' he said, 'but I think there was always an underlying view that the government had been in office for a long time.' But Labor was leaving behind a proud record.

'We've opened the country up and turned it towards the world as never before, and we've done it in a way that also put a high premium on social equity and social consensus.'

'You can take the boy out of Bankstown but you can't take the Bankstown out of the boy,' shouted one of his supporters. The room applauded.

'That's right,' Paul agreed. The Liberals, he said, had 'not won on the policies they had in the 1980s and the early 1990s. They won on policies in which the Labor Party has created new standards. It takes a lot to lift a country's standards on such big issues. It's not just one term in parliament or even two terms, because the opposing party always thinks they can come and turn it back. But to create new standards and have them explicitly acknowledged by the alternative government is real social advancement and something Labor can be very proud of.

'I think we can also say that in opening Australia up, in peeling the tariff wall away and removing exchange controls and giving the country some real breath and life inside it, we have turned Australia to our neighbourhood, reoriented it to the world. We are now part of this community of nations in East Asia and that's again another legacy of Labor, giving Australia that place in the world.

'I suppose you could say – perhaps in a nutshell – equity and enterprise at home and opportunity abroad has been the thing which has motivated us. And we've left the incoming government a country in good order, with good growth.

'Now can I say that outside of my family I've had two great loves and that's Australia and the Labor Party, and I'm proud to be able to say today that I leave office now as proud of them today as I was when I began twenty-six years ago. I'm exceptionally proud of what Labor has done over thirteen years, and I'm proud of what I was able to do over four, and I've got to say not once did I tackle and take on a second-best option. I never threw a policy fight; I always went for the big ones. And people may say, "Well, that's the big picture", and call it into question. But in the end it's the big picture which changes nations and, whatever our opponents may say, Australia has changed inexorably for the good, for the better.'

After the speech, in which he announced he would not recontest the leadership of the Labor Party, Paul consoled his shocked staff in a small, crowded room off the main floor. He was calm and cheerful. It had been, after all, a decent performance. In four years as Prime Minister he had presided over a good economic recovery that preserved low inflation. He had himself negotiated a compromise solution to the Mabo decision that was acceptable to the Labor Party, to the Aboriginal community, to the Senate minorities, and ultimately to all the states except for Western Australia. He had succeeded in persuading the US to convene APEC leaders' meetings, and already he had attended three. He had successfully pressed for trade liberalisation to be the major goal of APEC, and had seen the organisation adopt an ambitious goal of eliminating trade barriers within a few decades. He had repaired and then very greatly enhanced our relationship with Indonesia, and left our relationship with Japan and the United States on a good footing. He had convinced most Australians that we could not continue with the English monarch as our head of state, and defined the likely replacement as a minimal constitutional change that provided for an Australian head of state. He had overseen legislation that allowed enterprise bargains to proliferate and ended the arbitral role of the Industrial Relations Commission for wage decisions other than for those paid the lowest wages. Because of his government's Working Nation program there were not nearly so many long-term unemployed among the unemployed. With the states he had won endorsement of the competition reforms in the Hilmer Report, and changed for the better the way the Commonwealth and the states ran public housing programs. For his party, he had won a fifth term and in the process killed off, perhaps for many years, the political acceptability of a general goods and services tax and the likelihood that employers would be able to renounce adherence to awards governing minimum wages and working conditions. Instead of losing at the bottom of an economic cycle, which would have left his party torn with recriminations and rival factions, he left it defeated at the top of an economic cycle, with a record his successors could be proud of and defend.

Those were the achievements that outweighed the failures. Because he could not bring the Budget back into surplus more rapidly, the current account deficit was probably higher than it might otherwise have been. Stripped of asset sales and repayments from the states (both of which are treated strangely, but in accordance with OECD accounting standards, as reductions in outlays) the deficit in the last year of Keating's government was $9 billion, or about 2 per cent of GDP. It was higher than Keating had committed himself to in earlier years. It was also higher than predicted in the 1995 Budget, with most of the increase in the deficit coming from slower economic growth than predicted. Largely because of slower growth, revenues were lower and spending higher than expected. The deficit was very high for an economy that had been expanding for three years, but it had fallen very quickly from its peak. Measured on the same basis, the deficit was $17 billion in 1992–93, the year Keating won re-election, and $17 billion the following year. It was not until 1994–95 that it came down to $13 billion. In 1995–96 the deficit was, therefore, about half of its level two years before, and on forward estimates of spending and revenue – 'starting point' terms – it would have continued to fall had the government been re-elected.

While Keating was Prime Minister spending growth had been solid, but not recklessly high. In the 1992–93 Budget spending had grown by nearly 7 per cent in nominal dollars, which was about 4–5 per cent in real terms. Thereafter nominal spending growth fell to 5.1 per cent the following year and 4.6 per cent in 1994–95, before rising to 6.8 per cent in 1995–96. The expansion of the deficit was driven not by spending increases but by very slow growth in revenue. Recession forced revenue down, and the erosion of the tax base in tobacco and alcohol and the income tax cuts of 1993–94 prevented revenues rising as rapidly as they had in past expansions.

The Budget record was poor and Keating's commitment to an income tax cut was one impediment to getting it down.

The great question that hangs over Keating's period as Prime Minister is why he lost, and particularly why he lost on the scale he did.

Following his defeat, both his Liberal opponents and his critics within the Labor Party said that he lost because he interested himself in the 'big issues' of Mabo, the republic and APEC, and did not attend to Labor's middle- to lower-income constituency, which is interested in jobs, incomes and a future for their children. Keating's own explanation is that the basic reason he lost was that the public was tired of Labor after thirteen years, and there had also been various mistakes while he was Prime Minister. The most important mistake, he seems to think, was the 1993 Budget, which, by increasing some taxes and charges, got the government off on the wrong foot.

My own view is that after 13 years the electorate was ready to vote the government out as soon as a plausible alternative appeared. The opinion polls changed decisively when John Howard was elected Leader of the Opposition, and barely altered from then until the election. This supremacy for the Opposition in the polls occurred despite the fact that the economy was recovering and creating jobs quite strongly – though I suspect that the three percentage points increase in interest rates and the economic growth slowdown after the middle of 1994 were much more salient in the big cities than they were in Canberra. Howard was a seasoned performer. He had made mistakes in the past that he did not intend to repeat. He conducted himself with skill and with a good understanding of his opponent. It is evident that there was a presumption by most people that Labor ought to go. Though Keating and Hawke had in the past been able to undo Liberal leaders, including Howard, on this occasion Keating could not. Howard had learned the tricks.

Accused of an obsession with Mabo and the republic, Keating barely mentioned Mabo in the last year of office and referred only fleetingly to the republic once John Howard neutralised the issue by declaring his support for a convention to decide the issue. From about March 1995, a year before the poll, he talked about the economy quite often. It is one thing to talk about the economy, however, and another to get across a message about Australia's bright economic future. Keating did not formulate such a message in novel and newsy terms. After twelve years it is quite difficult to think up a new spin.

The interesting speculation is not why he lost but whether there was anything he could have done to alter the outcome. It was, I think, an indulgent error on Keating's part to defend Carmen Lawrence instead of forcing her removal. His defence of Lawrence stopped the recovery in the polls, which had then begun, and diminished both the republic and the 1995 Budget as issues for the government. Other than the defence of Lawrence, however, Keating was disciplined, attentive and well prepared throughout 1995. I know of no sound policy he could have devised and presented that would have made a difference in 1995 or would have offered him a campaign theme better than those he had. Nor am I aware of any such policy proposed by his critics within the party.

This is not to say that Keating's public personality was helpful. Plainly it was not. But he could no more change that than change his physical appearance, and he had in the past contributed to election victories and won an election himself despite the perception that he was arrogant.

One afternoon a few weeks after the election I visited Paul at the Keatings' rented house in Beagle Street. Annita's parents had stayed there when the family moved to the Lodge. It is a single-storey brick house, with picture windows of mirror-like reflecting glass. Paul was in casual clothes, unshaven. We talked in the lounge room. The silver-framed family photographs I had last seen at the Lodge were now on a side table. Otherwise nothing much had changed from my last visit to Beagle Street at the end of December 1991, just before he became Prime Minister. On the walls were the two Empire portraits I recognised. There were two candlesticks in the form of dark Egyptian maidens and a tall cabinet with a Pharaonic design. Behind Paul was a high bookcase packed with books on art history, decoration, architecture, design and politics. It had been there on my last visit too. While we talked Jimmy Warner called in. He was still driving Paul. The phone rang several times and Paul got up to answer it. Mostly the calls were for the children, and Paul took messages.

Paul had vanished from public view after the election. He had spent the last three weeks moving out of the Lodge and Kirribilli House. The three girls were still at school in Canberra, in the middle of the first term of the year. Until their schooling was sorted out, the family was staying in Canberra. Paul was widely expected to resign his seat before Parliament met at the end of April. Meanwhile, he was tidying up and preparing to take a holiday. Portrayed by rumour as morose and vengeful, Paul was merely fed up – with packing, with moving, with being idle and stuck in a rented house in a Canberra suburb because of the inescapable demands of his children's schooling. He was also exhausted, and feeling the premonition in a lovely Canberra autumn of the chill of another Canberra winter.

He had a backbencher's office in Parliament House and, as a former Prime Minister, would have an office in Sydney, but the whole apparatus of being Prime Minister had vanished. Don Russell and his other advisers were job-hunting, pondering the direction of their lives as Paul was pondering his. The Department of Prime Minister and Cabinet was now serving another master.

It had been a pretty good campaign, he thought, and his only regret now was that 'I was deprived of the right to a close result,' by Ralph Willis's decision to release the fake Kennett letters. These plausible forgeries indicated that the Howard Government would cut funding for the states, and were released by Willis with the concurrence of his senior staff and the national secretarial of the Labor Party a short time after their arrival in the Treasurer's office. Paul thought the gap between him and Howard was closing in that final week. He said he thought the defeat should have been much less, and it was apparent from his conversation that he actually thought it could have been narrowly won. Behind it all, he thought, was simply Australia's reluctance to elect Labor a sixth time in a row and what would by the next election have been sixteen years of office. 'But we were persuading them,' he said, 'we were convincing them that you couldn't just put us aside for three years. The whole set-up of industrial relations and Medicare and social security would be wrecked,' and the thrust to engagement with Asia and trade would be blunted. Then there were the letters, and the moment Paul had heard about the letters – the very moment, driving away from the campaign plane – he knew he now had no chance at all. All Willis and his staff needed to have done was wait an hour or so to discuss it with Keating, to conduct more checks. Nothing would have been lost. 'There are rules in politics,' Paul said, shaking his head, 'and if you break the rules there are consequences.'

These things are unknowable. Certainly the letters shattered Labor in its last few days, but the magnitude of the loss in Queensland and New South Wales was surely beyond redemption by a few final days of trouble-free campaigning. There were things at work there too big for any campaign.

He talked for a while and then he suggested a cup of coffee in Manuka, a shopping centre nearby. Jimmy drove us down and when we arrived Paul called Ross Gengos on his mobile phone. (Paul uses an ear plug and a small microphone with the mobile phone, to mini-mise what he believes to be harmful rays emitted by the telephone.) Gengos came up and we chatted about music. Paul had heard the Canberra Symphony the night before. He recalled how he had first become interested in classical music when he rode a bike to a friend's place, where his friend's father happened to be playing the Warsaw Concerto. They recalled how they had met when Paul had come into the shop in the 1980s. 'The Treasurer bought another version today,' his staff told him, as Keating picked up different recordings of the same concerto, listening to the way conductors and soloists and recording engineers could produce ordinary recordings and, some-times, wonderful recordings. After Paul had been into the shop four or five times, Gengos went out and introduced himself.

The coffee shop owner was a friend. A waitress told Paul he should have won. We walked out and I left them, Paul waving once as he and Gengos went into the back entrance of the music store. Jimmy dropped me off at my hotel where a little over five years before Paul had called me to suggest I join his staff. Jimmy would remain as Paul's driver until he left Canberra, he said, and then go back to the car pool.

APPENDIX
PAUL KEATING'S ACCOUNT OF THE DECISION TO FLOAT

A BIG RUN OF MONEY AGAINST THE currency makes an impression on you. Effectively I had done the depreciation with Bob Johnston in the first week of the government in March 1983 so I had a daily and weekly interest in watching the rate in the weeks and months thereafter. Once you take an exchange rate management system, which defined itself by small discrete movements, and then subject it under pressure to a large adjustment, effectively the market has your form; you have exposed your hand.

Speculators make money from central banks by shifting the rate in small then relatively larger amounts. After a while they are playing you like a trout on a line. In the very open and informal discussions of the kind Hawke and I had in those days (and I might add, for seven odd years thereafter), I told him these things. Even before the speculative runs against us later in 1983, I told him I thought the crawling peg system had seen its best, and even its best was not good enough in terms of competitiveness.

Bob Johnston and I would often talk together before I met Don Sanders and John Phillips ahead of the monthly post-Reserve Bank Board debriefing. He and I found ourselves agreeing with one another that the system had basically had it. Sanders, also a shrewd judge of these things, took the same view as did Phillips. The idea of buying foreign exchange each day, adding it to the money supply and then chasing it out with a long-run cost to the Budget was so absurd that one felt a bunny running such a system. Johnston felt this way and so did I.

By about May of 1993, I said to Johnston that he should prepare a set of measures to employ should we again be under acute pressure which would see the rate set in the market, where we [the Commonwealth and the RBA] remove ourselves from the system. If someone wanted to speculate they would have to find someone else, some other private interest to tango with; anyone but us. Johnston said, 'Treasurer, we'll make a start, we'll put together a War Book, a manual for such a change, which we could rely on when we needed it.' And he did.

At about this time (May 1983), I told Hawke not only did I think that a float was inevitable but it was also desirable for monetary management and for competitiveness reasons. I was completely open with him, frank with him. There was no note or minute; the kind of relationship we had and the quality of our close discussions on something as significant as this was such that any written advice would have seemed very strange to him. The ramifications of such a change were very large indeed. It needed to be broached in the broad before there were any papers flying around.

At any rate, he was pleased by my analysis and the conclusion. We had had a weighty conversation, and he believed he was across the main parameters. As often was the case with him after I had sold him on something, he became an enthusiast for it. I would go in with all the argument, weight, passion and persuasion I could muster, and if I could get him interested or committed he would often subsequently be an enthusiast for it. This was very much the case with the float. He had a broad predilection towards it and, upon hearing cogent argument for it, became committed. But a lot of the ingrained difficulties with it, would remain uppermost in my consciousness, but not his. His enthusiasm sometimes turned to impatience while I actually had the task of making a decision work. But this one, the float, was one which he knew would advance the public welfare and show his government as being prepared to take a very big decision for good reasons. In his terms it had just about everything going for it.

But more than that, for Hawke knew that once the Treasurer (his principal economic minister and adviser) had himself declared his position (however broadly and in principle) there was then very much diminished political risk for him. That's how Hawke thinks. He liked advances; he was even prepared to take chances, but well 'insured' ones. He was never for striking out alone. Once someone of authority in the system was prepared to say 'yeah' to a float, and I had, Hawke had cover and, in a very agreeable sense, cover for something he found himself in broad agreement with. He would then throw the subject around amongst advisers more sagely than otherwise, or more openly than formerly he would have dared to.

But it was these discussions, lounging around Hawke's office, taking part in some loosely structured discussion, a process that made Hawke feel that the due process was being served and Garnaut et al. feel included. It was good therapy, if all too often tedious. But I was always prepared to make the investment for a smooth outcome.

I had indicated my willingness to do it, and Hawke too was for it. The question was rather when to float and how to float and how to bring the system with us. How we would do it with authority and be able to maintain the authority if it went wrong.

The discussion in the ensuing months involved watching how the system was performing and how it might perform in a quantity-based environment.

We were watching, assessing and refining our thoughts. I say 'we', I mean 'me', Johnston, Sanders, Phillips and, by August or so onwards, Tony Cole. This was a big leap for the Reserve Bank. It hadn't done anything like this before. It was convinced but wary.

The markets gave us the time but we needed time. And I think we used it well. Getting their measure, sizing the scene up, learning how we would actually do it.

We were essentially getting ready for the big wave to come as we were convinced it would, having devalued in a big way once before.

By around September the Hawke office, in its general early government exuberance, regarded the decision to float as a foregone conclusion. By September, watching and waiting and looking at questions of execution, it had gone way beyond the limits of its sophistication. A discussion about the future of exchange controls had, I think, barely registered with them.

When the next wave came in October we decided at a meeting we had at the RBA building in Canberra to float the forward rate to get the market focused on setting a rate and to get it thinking and us thinking about how we would manage the spot rate. This meeting was attended by Johnston and some colleagues from the Reserve Bank, Stone and a number of Treasury officials, myself and the relevant people from my office, and Ross Garnaut from Hawke's office. Hawke was not in attendance. In a sense, it was an officials' discussion presided over by me.

At this meeting Stone said the RBA and the bureaucracy were on the whole ill prepared for a wholesale change to a full market-based system. He said the RBA was asking the government to commit to it as an act of faith. He said while the managed system had its limitations, it had insulated Australia from the volatility in currency movements and that, by throwing the system open, we as a small economy would be thrown around like a cork in the ocean. He said he believed the exchange rate would also be appreciated compounding our problems of competitiveness. He said we couldn't be sure that interest rates would be more stable, either. But he said he could agree to free up the exchange market somewhat by the RBA withdrawing from the forward market. This would develop some more depth of experience in the markets in setting the forward rate.

While I did not support Stone's view about insulating us from volatility or the 'cork in the ocean' line, or even the appreciation of the rate, the move to a more open forward market would give us a better handle on the system when we eventually threw it open.

I did not condone Stone's histrionics or some of his more extravagant arguments, but a move to a more open forward rate would give the whole system more experience — including the bank. It would also give us some time. I was not entirely persuaded that the bank had faced up to all the exigencies of what an immediate throw to an open system would entail.

We could have floated entirely about that time but, while Stone's view on the forward rate had emerged as a concession to a float, the intermediate step to a floating forward rate simply meant the throw to an open spot rate was more measured, more certain and less reliant on exclusive RBA management of the change.

The in-principle decision, by then having well and truly been taken, I believed my job – the Treasurer's job – was to see that when we threw the ball we walked away with a Cupie doll.

I told Stone that I saw the float as inevitable and, notwithstanding some of the more weighty arguments he put against it, the next time we faced a run against us, we would float. And we would do it with or without him.

When the big wave came in December, Johnston, Sanders and I discussed the problem all afternoon on the advice we were getting from overseas markets, judging how strong the run might be and whether we felt we should let the rate go.

As the day wore on and the evidence mounted, our view hardened. I discussed this with Hawke in his office through the late afternoon and evening and talked to a few key colleagues about it. Parliament was breaking up that night for the year and, of course, many were not in the mood or of a mind to face such a matter.

By late evening, we had decided to close the exchange on the Friday or otherwise wear a poultice of funds, and I phoned Johnston at home to tell him.

He said, 'You know, Treasurer, with the exchanges being closed we will have to have a large discretionary adjustment or a float.' I said to him, 'Get yourself down here tomorrow morning, Bob, because we will be doing it. We will be floating. You can deal with Stone's arguments.'

The group of us – Hawke, I and our advisers, both office and departmental – met in the Cabinet Room and then later on argued the case to the Economic Committee of Cabinet.

And that was that.

I did the press conference with Bob Johnston, and the new Australian Bank traded the first dollar on Monday morning, and everything went smoothly.

The time we had spent preparing had paid off. The bank was better prepared, we were more confident and the inevitability of it had become more obvious. These factors were all critical to successfully selling it and having it accepted.

NOTES

CHAPTER 1

1. McGregor, Craig, in *National Times*, 27 March 1977
2. Interview with Andrew Denton, Channel 7, 1 November 1995
3. Peters, Merle, *Bankstown's Northern Suburbs*, Bankstown Historical Society, 1977
4. Barton, G. B., *History of New South Wales from the Records*, Sydney, Government Printer, 1889
5. Barton, op. cit.
6. This and subsequent material on Bankstown history relies on Peters' book and on Lea-Scarlett, Errol, *The Faith of Irishtown*, Catholic Weekly.
7. Keating interviews with author, and *The Keating Family*, prepared by the Society of Australian Genealogists, August 1993
8. Keating interview with author
9. Carew, Edna, *Keating*, Allen & Unwin, 1988, p. 11
10. Doug McNally interview with author
11. Keating interview with author
12. Michael Hatton interview with author
13. Michael McCarthy interview with author
14. Mackay, Hugh, *Australian*, 3–4 Feb 1996
15. Gordon, Michael, *A Question of Leadership*, University of Queensland Press, 1993, p. 32
16. Bob Carr interview with author
17. Carew, op. cit., p. 6
18. Baker, Glenn A., *Sydney Morning Herald*, 30 April 1988
19. Keating interview with author
20. Sweet, Richard, *Vocational Education in Upper Secondary Schools: Why? How?* P & C Conference, October 1994
21. Greg Keating interview with author

[22] Gordon, op. cit., p. 33–4
[23] Carew, op. cit., p. 13
[24] Baker, Glenn A., op. cit.
[25] Baker, Glenn A., ibid
[26] Baker, Glenn A., ibid
[27] Carew, op. cit., p. 14
[28] Gordon, op. cit., p. 30
[29] Cumming, Fia, *Mates*, Allen & Unwin, 1991, p. 13

CHAPTER 2

[1] Cumming Fia, *Mates*, Allen & Unwin, 1991, p. 12
[2] Cumming, op. cit., p. 13
[3] Nairn, Bede, *The Big Fella*, Melbourne University Press, 1986
[4] Carew, Edna, *Keating*, Allen & Unwin, p. 20
[5] Carew, ibid, p. 20
[6] Glascott, Joe, *Sydney Morning Herald*, 9 October 1969
[7] Cumming, op. cit., p. 15
[8] ABC 'Four Corners', 18 August 1986. The interviewer was Kerry O'Brien
[9] John Armitage interview with author
[10] Laurie Brereton interview with author
[11] Ron Dyer interview with author
[12] Cumming, op. cit., pp. 10, 11
[13] Cumming, ibid, p. 48
[14] Cumming, ibid, p. 26
[15] Cumming, ibid, p. 40
[16] Bob Carr interview with author
[17] Cumming, op. cit., p. 41
[18] Cumming, ibid, p. 37
[19] Cumming, ibid, p. 32
[20] Cumming, ibid, p. 42
[21] Cumming, ibid, p. 57
[22] Cumming, ibid, p. 58
[23] Cumming, ibid, pp. 59, 70
[24] Blaxland 1969 pre-selection material relies on interviews with Paul Keating and Bill Junor
[25] Bill Junor interviews with author
[26] John Armitage interview with author
[27] John Ducker interview with author
[28] Grattan, Michelle, *Age* date unclear
[29] Interview with Andrew Denton, Seven Network, 1 November 1995
[30] Glascott, Joe, *Sydney Morning Herald*, 9 October 1969
[31] Cumming, op. cit., p. 91

32 Jones, Margaret, *Sydney Morning Herald*, 29 October 1969
33 Carew, op. cit. p. 28
34 Cumming, p. 93

CHAPTER 3

1 Hansard, House of Representatives, 17 March 1970
2 Cumming, Fia, *Mates*, Allen & Unwin, Sydney, 1991, p. 119
3 Clyde Cameron interview with author
4 Cumming, op. cit., p. 120
5 *Sydney Morning Herald*, date unclear
6 Cumming, op. cit., p. 121
7 Cumming, op. cit., p. 121
8 Cumming, op. cit., p. 121
9 *Sydney Morning Herald*, date unclear
10 Cumming, op. cit., p. 119
11 Cumming, ibid, p., 120
12 Cumming, ibid, p., 120
13 Cumming, ibid, p., 120
14 Kerry O'Brien, 'Four Corners', ABC Television, 18 August 1986
15 Hansard, House of Representatives, 16 September 1970
16 Hansard, ibid, 8 April 1970, 28 August 1970
17 Hansard, ibid, 19 October 1970
18 Hansard, ibid, 1 October 1970
19 *Mirror*, 15 June 1971
20 Hansard, op. cit., 29 September 1971

CHAPTER 4

1 Cumming, Fia, *Mates*, Allen & Unwin, 1991, p. 212
2 Uren, Tom, *Straight Left*, Random House, Sydney, 1994, p. 222
3 Lloyd, C. and Reid, G., *Out of the Wilderness*, Cassell, Sydney, 1974, ch. 3
4 Cumming, op. cit., p. 148
5 Barrie Unsworth interview with author
6 Gordon, Michael, *A Question of Leadership*, University of Queensland Press, 1991, p. 51
7 Cumming, op. cit., p. 148
8 Carr, *Bulletin*, 9 October 1979
9 Cumming, op. cit., p. 170
10 Hansard, House of Representatives, 19 May 1975
11 Clyde Cameron interview with author
12 McGregor, *National Times*, 27 March 1977

CHAPTER 5

[1] Clyde Cameron's diary, 23 February 1977. Cameron later published a volume based on his diary. The quotations are from the original.

[2] Caucus minutes

[3] Cameron's diary

[4] Cameron's diary

[5] Caucus minutes

[6] Uren, Tom, *Straight Left*, Random House, Sydney, 1994, p. 298

[7] Edwards, John, *Life Wasn't Meant to be Easy*, Mayhem, Sydney, 1977

[8] Cumming, Fia, *Mates*, Allen & Unwin, 1991, p. 208

[9] This incident is drawn from Kelly, *The Hawke Ascendancy*, Angus & Robertson, 1984, chapter 2.

[10] Kelly, ibid

[11] McGregor, *National Times*, 27 March 1977

[12] Cumming, op. cit., p. 209

[13] Uren, op. cit., p. 298

[14] *Sydney Morning Herald*, 7 December 1981

[15] Carr, *Bulletin*, 9 October 1979

[16] Carr, ibid

[17] Hewett, Jenni, *Sydney Morning Herald*, 21 December 1981

[18] *Australian Financial Review*, 13 October 1981

[19] *Australian Financial Review*, 3 November 1981

[20] *Bulletin*, 2 February 1982

[21] Flynn, Julie, *National Times*, 13 June 1982

[22] Uren, op. cit. p. 323, 336

[23] Summers, Anne, *Australian Financial Review*, 24 January 1983

CHAPTER 6

[1] Author interview with Graham Freudenberg

[2] The deficit on goods and services was 2.7 per cent of GDP in 1981; 2.4 per cent in 1989

[3] The press release disclosing the essence of Stone's memo was issued on Friday 18 March, in the name not of the Treasurer but of the Prime Minister. It asserted, presumably with Treasury advice, that the 'essential outline' of the $9.6 billion deficit projected for 1983–84 had been made available to the former Treasurer, John Howard, on 28 February, though it was not disclosed by him during the election campaign. On a television program on 1 November 1992 Howard claimed, 'I was told the figure over the telephone at a quarter to seven the night before the election.'

[4] Later there would be widely varying accounts of how the $8.5 billion deficit target was selected. It had been chosen by Ted Evans and David Morgan in Treasury and approved by Stone and then by Keating. It was sent to the

Prime Minister. He and his advisers discussed the number while Keating and his advisers waited in the outer office. Hawke then invited the Treasurer in and announced his agreement. Author's interview with David Morgan.

5   They proposed to save $2.1 billion on programs of the previous government, $0.5 billion on tax expenditure savings, and $0.6 billion by cracking down on tax avoidance, leaving $1.7 billion for new expenditure programs, or $1.3 billion after the net cost of Medicare.

CHAPTER 7

1   Hansard, House of Representatives, November 1981, p. 2856
2   Hawke, op. cit. Barry Hughes has since supported Hawke's interpretation, but Hughes himself was not in favour of floating. He was not involved in the discussions between Keating and Johnston and might not have known about them. Nor was he involved in the discussions between Treasury, the Bank and Keating, including the October meeting in Canberra. He was invited by Keating to the final meeting on 9 December, when the float decision was formally ratified. Then and later Keating was reluctant to disclose his real position to those who disagreed with it.
3   Hawke, ibid
4   Author's interview with Tony Cole

CHAPTER 8

1   *Age*, 22 August 1983
2   *Sydney Morning Herald*, 16 December 1983
3   *Australian Financial Review*, 25 July 1984

CHAPTER 9

1   Visbord's note for file, 7 December 1984
2   *Bulletin*, 27 March 1984
3   Discussion with author
4   *Sydney Morning Herald*, 18 June 1985
5   *Australian*, 8 June 1985
6   Keating notes, 6 August 1985
7   Statement 2, 1985–86 Budget papers, p. 62
8   *National Times*, 27 September 1985
9   *Australian*, 18 October 1985

CHAPTER 10

1   *National Times*, 27 September 1985
2   Fraser, 3 February, 1986. 'Noted with thanks', PJK.

[3]   JEFG, 5 February 1986

[4]   Russell, record of meeting 4 May 1986

[5]   Fraser dated 15/06/86, but this date clearly wrong. It is likely to be 15/04/86.

[6]   Submission 4041, 29 June 1986 'The Economic Situation and Policy'

[7]   Treasury had a very literal view of the 'twin deficits' theory, at least when communicating with the minister. For the ERC meeting of 23 February, David Morgan minuted Keating on 'The Magnitude of the Fiscal Adjustment Task in 1987–88'. He wrote that investment needed to increase by 2 per cent of GDP, while the current account deficit needed to fall by about 3 per cent. That meant that savings needed to rise by 5 per cent of GDP. It would be highly desirable to secure some of this by 1988–89. He recommended reducing public sector borrowing in the order of 1.5–2 per cent of GDP in each of next two years, shared equally between the Commonwealth and the States. But 'efforts to substantially reduce the net public sector borrowing requirement over the last two years have been largely unsuccessful, principally because the States have increased their net borrowings.' Commonwealth payments to the States should therefore be cut more. The Commonwealth should aim for a deficit of around $2b, which means they would need to cut $3.8b from the estimate – only marginally less than the $4b cut in 1986–87.

[8]   Interviews with officials and advisers

[9]   *Sydney Morning Herald*, 2 July 1987

[10] *Australian Financial Review*, 29 May 1987

[11] *Sydney Morning Herald*, 13 July 1987

[12] After the election, Treasury also had to digest its part of a major public service reorganisation planned by Hawke and his department head, Mike Codd. Treasury acquired the Industries Assistance Commission, which strengthened its claim to influence over tariff policy. At the same time Hawke created the Department of Foreign Affairs and Trade, the Department of Transport and Communications, the Department of Primary Industry and Energy, and the Department of Employment, Education and Training. Treasury was unhappy with what had been done so far on tariffs. 'Contrary to common impressions,' Fraser reminded the Treasurer after the election, 'little real progress has been made so far in this regard as the effects of decisions to reduce protection lie mainly in the outer years and will be very slow in coming.' The median or most common effective rate of protection for manufacturing actually increased from 11 per cent in 1982–83 to 15 per cent in 1984–85. John Button's steel industry plan, Treasury believed, was no longer serving a useful function. The industry was operating at full capacity, and BHP was actually importing steel.

[13] *Australian Financial Review*, 28 August 1987

14 *Sydney Morning Herald*, 28 August 1987
15 Russell to Treasurer, 24 September 1987, 'Interest Rates and the
    Exchange Rate'
16 Fraser to Treasurer, 22 September 1987, 'Domestic Money and Foreign
    Exchange Markets'
17 *Australian Financial Review*, 28 October 1987
18 Johnston to Treasurer, 6 November 1987
19 Ramsey, Alan, *Sydney Morning Herald*, 26 December 1987

CHAPTER 11

1   Dated 14 January 1988
2   Note dated 22 January 1988 from John Cosgrove, First Assistant
    Secretary, Economic Division
3   *Australian*, 3 February 1988
4   The letter is later referred to, but I was unable to locate a copy
5   2 March 1988, Morgan to Treasurer, 'Meeting with the RBA and
    Treasury: Monetary Conditions and Policy', annotated 'seen by Treasurer
    – DR'
6   30 March 1988, Morgan to Treasurer – 'Monetary Conditions and
    Policy'
7   Interview with Don Russell, Washington, September 1995
8   Discussion with Keating
9   Interview with Russell
10 Interview with Hawke, 1990; discussions with Russell and Keating
11 9 April 1988, Cosgrove to Treasurer. Covering letter 15 April. The terms
    of trade is the ratio of export prices to import prices. They increase
    when Australia's export prices increase, as they did from the end of
    1987. These higher prices are, however, sometimes offset by lower
    volumes, so commodity export incomes do not increase by the increase
    in commodity prices. The Australian dollar was also strengthening,
    which for Australian exporters offset the US dollar commodity price
    rise. For these reasons Treasury's emphasis on changes in the terms of
    trade as an explanation for major changes in Australia's GDP was, by
    1988, misplaced. Nonetheless accounts emphasising the supposed role
    of commodity prices and the terms of trade remain standard for the
    period
12 Later it would be argued that this is precisely what the government
    should have imposed. The record suggests this was never a seriously
    considered option. Treasury's consistent position was that a tax increase
    maintained or increased the size of the government sector, and provided
    the means of expanding spending later. It was therefore opposed on
    those grounds. Keating said that a tax increase would risk the Accord, by
    diminishing after-tax incomes. He also knew that while taxes were hard

to change and required Cabinet approval, interest rates could always be
lowered as well as raised without Cabinet approval. A tax increase was
necessarily something requiring a longer-term view – and neither
Treasury nor the Treasurer at this point would have had reason to think
that the economy would boom, despite the increase in interest rates and
the cuts in spending that they were adopting.

[13]   4 May 1988, Morgan to Treasurer. Minute for the RBA meeting that
        day

[14]   Keating interview

[15]   May Economic Statement, 23 May 1988

[16]   Morgan to Treasurer, Meeting with RBA and Treasury, 9 June. Dated
        '08/05' but must be 8 June 1988. Noted with thanks by Keating in his
        writing.

[17]   Morgan to Treasurer 12 July 1988 concerning 12 July meeting with
        RBA. Noted with thanks by Keating in his writing.

[18]   1988–89 Budget, 23 August 1988, Statement 2

[19]   Discussions with Keating

[20]   Discussions with Keating

[21]   Morgan to Treasurer 7 September 1988 regarding meeting with RBA
        Thursday 8 September

[22]   In Parliament three years later (Hansard, 11 March 1991), Keating
        would insist that ' . . . the Treasury never advised me to tighten monetary
        policy early in 1988 because it shared a view with the Reserve Bank of
        Australia at the time – a view shared by the Bank of International
        Settlements – that monetary conditions after the stock market crash
        should be left accommodating . . . it was not a view I agreed with. I
        actually argued against the Treasury and the Reserve Bank to increase
        interest rates in January 1988 and again formally in March 1988.' He
        pointed out that his recommendation for an increase had occurred before
        the NSW state elections, in which Premier Barrie Unsworth was fighting
        for his political life.

[23]   Morgan to Treasurer, 15 September 1988, 'for the record'

[24]   Higgins to Treasurer, 19 October 1988

[25]   Advising the Treasurer prior to the meeting on 4 November 1988 with
        the RBA Morgan noted (3 November) that domestic demand was still
        very buoyant, although 'the market' had pushed 90-day bills from 13.5
        per cent in August to 14.25 in November. Treasury's judgment was that
        that domestic demand would remain strong well into 1989. He
        reiterated the point that they were all 'very conscious of the importance
        of the economy not being overheated in 1989 if the wage–tax cut trade-
        off is to be successful'. He reported that both Treasury and the bank
        believed 'that overall objectives would be served by taking out a bit more
        insurance against too much demand in 1989–90. The recent tightening

in monetary policy has been an important step, but we recommend unofficial cash rates be moved up around another ½ per cent to ensure that there is a quick increase in all prime lending rates to around 16 per cent and bank housing rates to around 15 per cent, with pressures for at least some banks to move beyond those rates.' (Noted with thanks PJK, but not in his writing.)

The bank was also using the forthcoming wage–tax trade-off to justify higher rates. In a background note for the Treasurer, 'Financial Conditions and Policy, 3 November 1988' the RBA informed him that the Board met on 1 November and noted (in this order) continued strong growth in economy, apparent stickiness of the CPI around 7 per cent, and strength in import volumes.

'Given also the shortening of the time before the tax–wage negotiations foreshadowed for the first quarter of 1989, the Board was of the view that monetary policy should be held firm enough to produce some modest further tightening in domestic demand conditions. It decided that the Bank should:
- in its domestic operations, aim for financial conditions a little firmer than at end October;
- in its foreign exchange operations, seek to ensure that movements in the exchange rate are well based.'

[26]   Seasonally adjusted, nominal dollars

[27]   Morgan summary for Bernie Fraser of a 20 December discussion with Russell

[28]   22 December 1988, Cosgrove to Treasurer, reporting on meeting of JEFG, 14 December

[29]   Russell, 23 December 1988, note for file

[30]   Morgan to Waterman, 22 December 1988

[31]   Morgan to Treasurer (dated 8 February 1988 but must be 1989) re monetary policy meeting with RBA later that day

[32]   Fraser to Treasurer, 10 February 1989, budget objectives

[33]   Cosgrove, 1 March 1989. Table comparing Budget time forecasts with current forecasts.

[34]   Cosgrove to Treasurer, 27 February 1989. Draft Cabinet submission on economic situation and outlook

[35]   Higgins to Treasurer, 22 March 1989

[36]   Interview with Russell

[37]   Russell, 24 April 1989, monetary policy note for file

[38]   Fraser to Treasurer, 9 May 1989

[39]   Russell interview, 1995, Washington, and other off-the-record interviews. According to Russell's later account, this last increase was designed to pop the ballooning expectations of the asset price boom. The argument was that the government would have to go into the next

election with interest rates coming down but, to permit that, they would first have to go up. Before interest rates could credibly be lowered, domestic demand would have to come down to the level of output growth, which really meant that import demand would have to be rapidly and dramatically curtailed. To the extent that slowing asset price increases was the motive, it succeeded. Mortgage rates rose to 17 per cent. House prices in Sydney and Melbourne reached a plateau around this time. But equities prices had flattened out long before the interest rate increases began, and the property price boom was not the cause of either the current account deficit or of increasing investment spending. The boom in investment took off most spiritedly months after the interest rate rate increases began in April 1988, and it would continue to increase well into the middle of 1989. There is a long lag between investment decisions and the appearance of investment spending in the statistics. The increases of April and May 1989 may have slowed it, but there is no strong reason to think an additional 1 per cent increase would markedly affect investment spending. Russell placed a great deal of stress on stopping asset price increases. Since asset purchases were funded by debt, the purchaser focused not on interest rates but on expected asset price increases. The object of the last hit was to persuade people that asset prices could not continue to increase indefinitely. Asset price inflation, however, had not been important in policy-making up to that point and only became really important in subsequent analyses of what had happened in the late 1980s. As Treasurer, Keating would later blame bank lending for the boom and the crash.

CHAPTER 12

[1]   OECD Draft Report, 10 January 1989
[2]   W. Alan Wallis, Under-Secretary of State Economic Affairs
[3]   Discussion with Keating
[4]   Fraser to Treasurer, 9 June 1989, 'Some Live Issues'
[5]   The IMF mission was predicting a current account deficit of $20 billion in 1988–89 (the actual was $22b, compared with Treasury's forecast of $17b). In a note Morgan said the IMF wanted further tightening including interest rate increases but preferably fiscal tightening – no doubt meaning a postponement of promised tax cuts. Morgan contrasted this with the current government view that enough tightening was already 'in the pipeline'. The IMF also wanted interest rates to be held high to combat inflation – not brought down at the first sign of weakness.
[6]   29 June 1989, JEFG June 1989 Round, final draft
[7]   Higgins to Treasurer, 3 July 1989, commenting on enclosed June 1989 JEFG report

8   PJK, 11 July 1989, hand-written. Keating habitually added the private savings provided by compulsory superannuation to those generated by budget cuts and tax increases and described the result as a shift to saving. He ignored substitutions and shifts. Because of lower corporate saving during the boom, however, private saving overall had fallen, at the same time as investment spending was rapidly increasing.

CHAPTER 13

1   Russell to Treasurer, 7 November 1989
2   Waterman to Treasurer, 7 February 1990: Monetary Policy, for meeting with RBA on 8 February and RBA Board on 6 February. Ewan Waterman had succeeded Morgan.
3   Higgins to Treasurer, 28 March 1990, 'The Economy and Policy: An Overview'. Marked 'Not dealt with'.
4   Draft Cabinet submission on the economic situation and outlook, 2 May 1990. Intended for meeting of the Expenditure Review Committee on 7 May.
5   8 May 1990 note on what defines a recession
6   Higgins to Treasurer, 5 June 1990. On-return Briefing Notes
7   Waterman to Treasurer, Monetary Policy
8   Higgins to Treasurer, 1 August 1990. Monetary Policy
9   Higgins' reference to the disappointing Consumer Price Index and to the forthcoming National Accounts, both of them measuring periods earlier in the year, demonstrates the Treasury tactic of waiting for 'history' on the downward leg of monetary policy episodes.
10   Keating was *not* advocating the privatisation of Telstra, a charge that emerged during the 1996 election campaign. He might not have had any objection in theory, but in practice in the Labor Cabinet and caucus of 1990 it would not have been considered a remotely serious policy proposition.
11   Waterman (acting secretary) to Treasurer, 3 October 1990. Monetary Policy
12   Higgins to Treasurer, 10 October 1990. Visit to Washington for International Monetary Fund
13   David Borthwick, First Assistant Secretary, Economic Division, to Treasurer, 2 November 1990. Short-term Economic Prospects.
14   Higgins to Treasurer, 2 November 1990. Monetary Policy
15   Higgins to Treasurer (with annotation from Treasurer on back), 4 December 1990, Monetary Policy
16   Handprinted annotation under PJK initial dated 5 December 1990
17   Kelly, Paul, *The End of Certainty: the story of the 1980s*, Allen & Unwin, Sydney, 1992, p. 621
18   It was later said that the boom and the bust were both consequences of

reckless borrowing by business and lending by banks. Certainly total borrowing did increase over the period, though Australia was not among the economies that increased gearing most dramatically. Nor was rapid lending growth unique to 1989. Measuring lending to the private sector by all financial intermediaries, lending increased 17.5 per cent in 1981, 16 per cent in 1982, 12 per cent in 1983, 12 per cent in 1984, 17.8 per cent in 1985, 19.9 per cent in 1986, 15 per cent in 1987, 18 per cent in 1988, 22 per cent in 1989, 14 per cent in 1990, 3 per cent in 1991, and zero in 1992. It is interesting that lending growth was nearly as high in 1981 and 1986 as in 1988 and 1989. The distinctive characteristic of the later boom was that lending growth fell away dramatically in 1991 and 1992, compared with 1983 and 1984. These numbers suggest that financial deregulation was *not* the cause of increased lending in the late 1980s (though increased lending by banks as one component of lending was caused by deregulation) and that, while increased lending did not account for the boom, rapidly shrinking lending might have had something to do with the length of the subsequent recession. Conversely, it might also have been caused by it.

[19] Following the crash it was widely said that the investment spending of 1988 and 1989 had been wasted in speculative asset price rises (e.g. Kelly p. 498). But speculative asset sales waste nothing – they merely transfer assets around, and the last one holding the asset when the boom ends bears the loss. This is as true for newspaper corporations and television stations as for paintings by old masters. Wealth is transferred between holders. 'Investment' spending, which is the value of investment goods produced, is only wasted if it fails to yield a return. During the 1988–89 boom non-dwelling construction, which includes factories, shops and hotels as well as offices, accounted for no more than a third of investment spending. Office construction was a fifth of the total of investment spending. By industry category, 40 per cent of the investment of the period was in manufacturing. Investment overall was mainly in new plant and equipment. This was not only twice the size of spending on new buildings and structures but also the one that changed most dramatically over the period. For what the distinction is worth, a Reserve Bank study concluded that there had been a modest rise in the proportion of manufacturing investment that went into the tradable goods sector during the boom. But over the period the range of tradable goods in Australia, i.e. the range of goods that were internationally traded, grew markedly. It certainly included, for example, hotel accommodation. There is very little evidence that capital spending in 1988–89 was 'wasted'. Typically, capital investment in Australia comes in big lumps, as it had in 1980–81 and would again in 1994–95.

CHAPTER 14

1   Treasury's fondness for the yield curve was mysterious. The yield curve is a graph showing how short-term interest rates compare to long-term interest rates. All things being equal, long-term rates should be higher than short-term rates because a premium should be required to persuade lenders to accept a longer and therefore more uncertain contract, and borrowers should be willing to pay more for it. If long-term rates are in fact the same as short-term rates (a flat curve) or lower than short-term rates (an inverse curve), this might indicate that lenders expect inflation to fall, and interest rates with it. This is how Treasury interpreted the curve. But lenders would also, from experience, expect short-term interest rates to continue to be reduced in a downswing, which is another reason for long-term rates to be lower than short-term rates in a recession and higher in a boom. If this second cause of the shape of the yield curve is important then Treasury advice on the yield curve amounts to adopting a policy because the market expects the policy-makers to adopt that policy. If the first cause is important, it amounts to assuming that the market forecast of inflation is cleverer than the policy-makers' forecast of inflation.

2   The idea for the speech at that time arose in conversation with Ian Macfarlane, whose understanding of where the economy was going proved quite remarkably correct. My views were influenced by economic training in the US, where economists had had more time to get used to floating exchange rates from the 1970s and dramatically altering current account balances in the 1980s. In Australia the argument for disregarding the current account as an objective of policy had been put with great courage and good sense in a series of papers by Professor John Pitchford at the ANU, but it was a more widely respected view in the US than among Pitchford's colleagues in Australia. Though some of his colleagues considered them quite eccentric, Pitchford's views were firmly based on standard economics. His argument was simply that the current account is the gap between domestic saving and domestic investment. Both investment and saving can vary for reasons that might or might not require a policy response. If politicians are for one reason or another worried about the deficit, then it would be better to increase saving (for example, by increasing a government surplus) than to cut private investment. Treasury papers reveal that this view is a common one in Treasury. John Stone had argued in the late 1970s and early 1980s that higher goods and services imports were the necessary counterpart of capital imports. Bob Whitelaw, who was First Assistant Secretary directing the international area of Treasury through the mid 1980s, warned in memos in the early 1980s about adopting the current account as a goal of policy. Chris Higgins had similar views, which turned up in

various issues of Statement 2 of the Budget. In using the current account
deficit and the depreciation of the dollar (for example, during the 1986
Budget crisis) to win tighter fiscal discipline, Keating solved one problem
by creating another. Trade Minister John Dawkins, Finance Minister
Peter Walsh, Industry Minister John Button and many members of
caucus began to see the current account as almost their only measure of
economic success. Walsh seemed to believe that the late 1980s were an
economic disaster for Australia simply because the current account
deficit widened. In Keating's office, Don Russell acted upon the premise
that the current account was the measure of economic success and
therefore political success. As Keating later reflected (see Chapter 12), he
was hoist with his own petard. By contrast it made sense as a policy goal
to cut inflation, which favoured speculative assets against income-
producing assets, which continuously distorted the tax system and
appreciated the currency, and which, through wage catchup and through
nominal depreciations, threatened always to accelerate and require a
tougher policy response.

[3] Instances from which this salutary lesson was drawn were rarely specified.
I doubt this lesson could be drawn from the experience of the 1981–82
recession and the subsequent recovery in 1983. Nor did it prove true of
the recovery from 1992 onward. Just as the thinking of some Treasury
officials took a while to adjust to floating exchange rates and the
elimination of capital controls and their impact on, for example, the
terms of trade and the balance of payments, so too the style of some
Treasury advice took a while to adjust to the dropping of monetary
targets in 1985. Having a consistent monetary policy in the 'medium
term' when monetary targets were in place meant attempting to keep to
the target, which meant interest rates would move in whatever direction
with whatever amplitude at whatever time was necessary to keep the
monthly or quarterly money growth targets on track. It was, in fact, a
policy that could justify frequent interest rate changes. When targets
were dropped some Treasury officials retained the 'medium term'
language, now taken to mean that interest rate levels ought to be stable.
While the term remained, the conceptual underpinnings for it vanished.

[4] Progressive income tax scales take a higher proportion of income as
income increases. Thus tax revenue will increase by more than any
particular percentage increase in wages. Tax 'indexation' usually means
that tax scales are periodically adjusted so that while the tax take from a
given set of employees increases as a percentage by the increase in average
weekly earnings, it does not increase by more than this increase.
Sometimes the term is used to mean that the tax take may increase by
more than the wage increase, but only to the amount attributable to the
real as opposed to nominal increase in wages.

5   EPAC speech texts were not designed to be read to the Council members sitting around the Cabinet table. Keating summarised the main points in an informal presentation, but the fiction that the speech was given allowed us to provide much longer texts for the press, with supporting arguments, than if Keating had actually spoken the speech.

6   Reported in the *Australian*, Monday 1 April 1996

CHAPTER 15

1   On policy matters there were very few differences in eight years. One was over petroleum resources rent tax, and there was a dispute in the last days over Coronation Hill.

2   Officials sometimes drew a distinction between 'forecasts', which describe the economy as it might be expected to be, and 'projections', which could be quite arbitrary and merely offered an explicit platform from which to assess the magnitude of deviations. In practice, however, a three-year projection has to be plausible and is no different from a long-range forecast. It will not be accurate, but forecasts are not accurate either.

3   Keating had listed relations with Indonesia and the importance of APEC (also, surprisingly, relations with New Zealand) as his foreign policy priorities in a conversation with me in May 1991. He developed rather than acquired these themes as Prime Minister. The idea for an APEC leaders' meeting, which was one of the most fruitful suggestions in Keating's period as Prime Minister, came through Ashton Calvert from Alan Gyngell, who was then head of the international division in the Department of Prime Minister and Cabinet. It had been floating around for some time, but had been rejected as premature for APEC. When Keating came to office we discovered Australia's interest in APEC was managed by middle-level officials of the Department of Foreign Affairs and Trade, with very little involvement by senior officials. It was the same in respect to our APEC partners. APEC issues did not come to Cabinet. There was an established routine of fruitless APEC meetings on issues such as product standardisation. By proposing leaders' meetings, which would automatically elevate APEC issues to the top political level, Keating hoped to breathe life into the organisation. Two other powerful forces were emerging at about the same time. One was a US State Department official, Sandra Kristoff, who over three years took APEC issues from the middle of the State Department to the President's desk. Another was agreement on the appointment of an APEC Eminent Persons' Group, which would be chaired by US economist Fred Bergsten. Later, President Suharto of Indonesia would play a key role. Weller, Patrick, *Malcolm Fraser PM: a study in prime ministerial power in Australia*, Penguin, Melbourne, 1989

ABBREVIATIONS

ACTU	Australian Council of Trade Unions
AIRC	Australian Industrial Relations Commission
ALAC	Australian Labor Advisory Council
ANTA	Australian National Training Authority
APEC	Asia Pacific Economic Cooperation
COAG	Council of Australian Governments
CPI	Consumer Price Index
EPAC	Economic Planning Advisory Council
ERC	Expenditure Review Committee
ERMC	Exchange Rate Management Committee
GDP	gross domestic product
IMF	International Monetary Fund
JEFG	Joint Economic Forecasting Group
NIFC	National Income Forecasting Committee
OECD	Organization for Economic Co-operation and Development
TWI	trade weighted index

INDEX